Freedom of Religion

and Belief

This study, the first of its kind, reports on freedom of religion and secular thought in over fifty countries throughout the world. The individual's right to hold beliefs and to conduct themself according to such beliefs is a core human right. The World Report offers a detailed and impartial account of how this neglected freedom is understood, protected or denied in all regions of the world.

The report consists of short edited entries based on drafts commissioned from experts, where possible living in the countries surveyed. The entries, divided by region and introduced by a regional overview, cover themes including: the relationships between belief groups and the state; freedom to manifest belief in law and practice; religion and schools; religious minorities, new religious movements; the impact of beliefs on the status of women; and the extent to which conscientious objection to military service is recognised by governments. The countries included in the report reflect in each region the diversity of religious traditions and their influence on the state and society.

Beginning with an extensive introduction that analyses the United Nations standards on freedom of belief, the World Report sets out starkly the degree to which religious intolerance, conflict and discrimination are a continuing global reality. However, the report draws on examples of accommodation and co-operation between different religions and beliefs and identifies the main challenges to be overcome if the diversity of human conviction is to be established in an increasingly interdependent world.

Kevin Boyle is a Professor of Law and the Director of the Human Rights Centre, University of Essex. He is a Barrister at Law in Northern Ireland, the Republic of Ireland and England with considerable experience of international human rights litigation under the European Convention of Human Rights. **Juliet Sheen** is a Fellow of the Human Rights Centre, University of Essex. In 1994 she established an independent consultancy in human rights, specialising in the area of freedom of religion and belief.

0415159784

Freedom of Religion and Belief

A World Report

Edited by

Kevin Boyle
and
Juliet Sheen

London and New York

First published 1997
by Routledge
11 New Fetter Lane, London EC4P 4EE

Simultaneously published in the USA and Canada
by Routledge
29 West 35th Street, New York, NY 10001

Typeset in Sabon by
Ponting–Green Publishing Services, Chesham, Buckinghamshire

Printed and bound in Great Britain by
TJ International (Padstow) Ltd, Padstow, Cornwall

British Library Cataloguing in Publication Data
A catalogue record for this book is available from the British Library

Library of Congress Cataloguing in Publication Data
A catalogue record for this book has been requested

ISBN   0–415–15977–6 (hbk)
ISBN   0–415–15978–4 (pbk)

Everyone has the right to freedom of thought, conscience and religion; this right includes freedom to change his religion or belief, and freedom, either alone or in community with others and in public or private, to manifest his religion or belief in teaching, practice, worship and observance.

(Universal Declaration of Human Rights, Article 18)

The World Report project was made possible by a grant from the Pew Charitable Trusts of Philadelphia, USA

Contents

Editorial

The Human Rights Centre at the University of Essex. The Centre was founded in 1989 by members of the departments of Law, Government, Philosophy, Sociology and Economics. The interdisciplinary centre is an expansion of the Centre for International Human Rights Law which was established in 1983. The Centre aims to give a focus in Britain for research, publication and teaching in the interdisciplinary study of Human Rights in their global, regional and local contexts. It is distinctive in the emphasis it gives in its work to the integration of human right theory and practice.

Professor Kevin Boyle (Editor) is Director of the Human Rights Centre, University of Essex. He was the first Director of Article XIX – the International Centre Against Censorship, where he edited a world report on freedom of expression.

Alison Jolly was the Research Officer for the World Report. She completed her MA in the Theory and Practice of Human Rights at the Human Rights Centre, University of Essex, in 1993.

Dr Juliet Sheen (Editor) has worked on law reform and policy development in discrimination and human rights. *Discrimination and Religious Conviction*, the research report she wrote for the New South Wales Anti-Discrimination Board, was circulated to all delegates by the UN Human Rights Centre at its 1984 Geneva seminar, where she represented Australia. Since then she has been involved in international moves to implement the 1981 Declaration.

The Editorial Board consisted of Kevin Boyle, Geoff Gilbert, Françoise Hampson, Alison Jolly and Juliet Sheen.

Susan Rhodes was the financial manager for the project.

Preface

Any examination of freedom of religion or belief today needs to address the massive religious revival which is characterising the end of the century. Should we anticipate in the wake of this revival an increase in tolerance, enlightenment and freedom, or are we to be faced with greater intolerance and discrimination, condemned to a further period of extremism, darkness and inquisition?

If considerable progress has been made in the legal status of the right to freedom of religion and belief over the past few decades, reality can still fall short of acknowledged standards. Certainly, the incidence of violations has not shown such a rapid improvement.

Religious freedom does not seem to have won over the minds of people everywhere. Each religion has a tendency to consider that it is the sole guardian of truth and is duty bound to behave accordingly, an attitude which is not always conducive to inter-religious tolerance. What is more, each religion may be tempted to fight against whatever it defines as deviant either within its own faith or at its boundaries, which is equally unlikely to encourage internal religious tolerance. Moreover, crimes committed under the mantle of religious freedom – especially those perpetrated by or ascribed to groups bedecked with religiosity – inevitably provoke extreme reactions, resulting in greater intolerance and discrimination towards anything which does not belong to the established order.

Intolerance persists in the world and sometimes assumes dramatic proportions. Religious extremism persists and appears to threaten entire regions. The interweaving of the religious and political, whether explicit or concealed, continues to underlie attitudes and behaviour, and to fuel and entrench conflicts.

In short, no religion is safe from violation. Intolerance is not the monopoly of any particular state or religion; discrimination based on another's religion or belief continues to be an everyday phenomenon.

There can be no overstating the truth that all forms of intolerance and discrimination are born in the human mind, and it is there that change is needed if tolerance is to be built and discrimination eliminated. The contribution to be made by education and culture is crucial. It is with this in mind that the World Report on Freedom of Religion and Belief was conceived. The Report is a clearly structured examination of the subject offering very useful information and commentary on some 58 countries. It constitutes a very important addition to our knowledge of freedom of religion and belief around the world, to the strengthening of freedom in general and of tolerance in particular. This book is destined to become essential reading not only for the initiated but for the general reader too.

Abdelfattah Amor
Special Rapporteur on Religious Intolerance of the United Nations Commission on Human Rights
Dean, Faculty of Law, University of Tunis
President, International Academy of Constitutional Law

United Nations Declaration

on the Elimination of All Forms of Intolerance and of Discrimination Based on Religion or Belief (1981) proclaimed by the General Assembly of the United Nations on 25 November 1981 (Resolution 36/55)

THE GENERAL ASSEMBLY

Considering that one of the basic principles of the Charter of the United Nations is that of the dignity and equality inherent in all human beings, and that all Member States have pledged themselves to take joint and separate action in co-operation with the Organization to promote and encourage universal respect for and observance of human rights and fundamental freedoms for all, without distinction as to race, sex, language or religion,

Considering that the Universal Declaration of Human Rights and the International Covenants on Human Rights proclaim the principles of non-discrimination and equality before the law and the right to freedom of thought, conscience, religion and belief,

Considering that the disregard and infringement of human rights and fundamental freedoms, in particular of the right to freedom of thought, conscience, religion or whatever belief, have brought, directly or indirectly, wars and great suffering to humankind, especially where they serve as a means of foreign interference in the internal affairs of other States and amount to kindling hatred between peoples and nations,

Considering that religion or belief, for anyone who professes either, is one of the fundamental elements in his conception of life and that freedom of religion or belief should be fully respected and guaranteed,

Considering that it is essential to promote understanding, tolerance and respect in matters relating to freedom of religion and belief and to ensure that the use of religion or belief for ends inconsistent with the Charter of the United Nations, other relevant instruments of the United Nations and the purposes and principles of the present Declaration is inadmissible,

Convinced that freedom of religion and belief should also contribute to the attainment of the goals of world peace, social justice and friendship among peoples and to the elimination of ideologies or practices of colonialism and racial discrimination,

Noting with satisfaction the adoption of several, and the coming into force of some conventions, under the aegis of the United Nations and of the specialized agencies, for the elimination of various forms of discrimination,

Concerned by manifestations of intolerance and by the existence of discrimination in matters of religion or belief still in evidence in some areas of the world,

Resolved to adopt all necessary measures for the speedy elimination of such intolerance in all its forms and manifestations and to prevent and combat discrimination on the grounds of religion or belief,

Proclaims this Declaration on the Elimination of All Forms of Intolerance and of Discrimination Based on Religion or Belief:

Article 1

1 Everyone shall have the right to freedom of thought, conscience and religion. This right shall include freedom to have a religion or whatever belief of his choice, and freedom, either individually or in community with others and in public or private, to manifest his religion or belief in worship, observance, practice and teaching.
2 No-one shall be subject to coercion which would impair his freedom to have a religion or belief of his choice.
3 Freedom to manifest one's religion or beliefs may be subject only to such limitations as are prescribed by law and are necessary to protect public safety, order, health or morals or the fundamental rights and freedoms of others.

Article 2

1 No-one shall be subject to discrimination by any State, institution, group of persons or person on the grounds of religion or other beliefs.
2 For the purposes of the present Declaration, the expression 'intolerance and discrimination based on religion or belief' means any distinction, exclusion, restriction or preference based on religion or belief and having as its purpose or as its effect nullification or impairment of the recognition, enjoyment or exercise of human rights and fundamental freedoms on an equal basis.

Article 3

Discrimination between human beings on grounds of religion or belief constitutes an affront to human dignity and a disavowal of the principles of the Charter of the United Nations, and shall be condemned as a violation of the human rights and fundamental freedoms proclaimed in the Universal Declaration of Human Rights and enunciated in detail in the International Covenants on Human Rights, and as an obstacle to friendly and peaceful relations between nations.

Article 4

1 All States shall take effective measures to prevent and eliminate discrimination on the grounds of religion or belief in the recognition, exercise and enjoyment of human

rights and fundamental freedoms in all fields of civil, economic, political, social and cultural life.

2 All States shall make all efforts to enact or rescind legislation where necessary to prohibit any such discrimination, and to take all appropriate measures to combat intolerance on the grounds of religion or other beliefs in this matter.

Article 5

1 The parents or, as the case may be, the legal guardians of the child have the right to organize the life within the family in accordance with their religion or belief and bearing in mind the moral education in which they believe the child should be brought up.
2 Every child shall enjoy the right to have access to education in the matter of religion or belief in accordance with the wishes of his parents or, as the case may be, legal guardians, and shall not be compelled to receive teaching on religion or belief against the wishes of his parents or legal guardians; the best interests of the child being the guiding principle.
3 The child shall be protected from any form of discrimination on the grounds of religion or belief. He shall be brought up in a spirit of understanding, tolerance, friendship among peoples, peace and universal brotherhood, respect for freedom of religion or belief of others and in full consciousness that his energy and talents should be devoted to the service of his fellow men.
4 In the case of a child who is not under the care either of his parents or of legal guardians, due account shall be taken of their expressed wishes or of any other proof of their wishes in the matter of religion or belief, the best interests of the child being the guiding principle.
5 Practices of a religion or beliefs in which a child is brought up must not be injurious to his physical or mental health or to his full development, taking into account Article 1, paragraph 3, of the present Declaration.

Article 6

In accordance with Article 1 of the present Declaration, and subject to the provisions of Article 1, paragraph 3, the right to freedom of thought, conscience, religion or belief shall include, *inter alia*, the following freedoms:
(a) To worship or assemble in connection with a religion or belief, and to establish and maintain places for these purposes;
(b) To establish and maintain appropriate charitable or humanitarian institutions;
(c) To make, acquire and use to an adequate extent the necessary articles and materials related to the rites and customs of a religion or belief;
(d) To write, issue and disseminate relevant publications in these areas;
(e) To teach a religion or belief in places suitable for these purposes;
(f) To solicit and receive voluntary financial and other contributions from individuals and institutions;
(g) To train, appoint, elect or designate by succession appropriate leaders called for by the requirements and standards of any religion or belief;
(h) To observe days of rest and to celebrate holidays and ceremonies in accordance with the precepts of one's religion or belief;
(i) To establish and maintain communications with individuals and communities in matters of religion and belief at the national and international levels.

Article 7

The rights and freedoms set forth in the present Declaration shall be accorded in national legislation in such a manner that everyone shall be able to avail himself of such rights and freedoms in practice.

Article 8

Nothing in the present Declaration shall be construed as restricting or derogating from any right defined in the Universal Declaration of Human Rights and the International Covenants on Human Rights.

INTERNATIONAL COVENANT ON CIVIL AND POLITICAL RIGHTS

Adopted and opened for signature, ratification and accession by [United Nations] General Assembly resolution 2200 A (XXI) of 16 December 1966. Entered into force on 23 March 1976.

Article 18

1 Everyone shall have the right to freedom of thought, conscience and religion. This right shall include freedom to have or to adopt a religion or belief of his choice, and freedom, either individually or in community with others and in public or private, to manifest his religion or belief in worship, observance, practice and teaching.
2 No one shall be subject to coercion which would impair his freedom to have or to adopt a religion or belief of his choice.
3 Freedom to manifest one's religion or beliefs may be subject only to such limitations as are prescribed by law and are necessary to protect public safety, order, health, or morals or the fundamental rights and freedoms of others.
4 The States parties to the present Covenant undertake to have respect for the liberty of parents and, when applicable, legal guardians to ensure the religious and moral education of their children in conformity with their own convictions.

GENERAL COMMENT NO. 22 [ICCPR ARTICLE 18] HUMAN RIGHTS COMMITTEE, FORTY-EIGHTH SESSION, 20 JULY 1993

1 The right to freedom of thought, conscience and religion (which includes the freedom to hold beliefs) in article 18 (1) is far-reaching and profound; it encompasses freedom of thoughts on all matters, personal conviction and the commitment to religion or belief, whether manifested individually or in community with others. The Committee draws the attention of States parties to the fact that the freedom of thought and the freedom of conscience are protected equally with the freedom of religion and belief. The fundamental character of these freedoms is also reflected in the fact that this provision cannot be derogated from, even in time of public emergency, as stated in article 4 (2) of the Covenant.
2 Article 18 protects theistic, non-theistic and atheistic beliefs, as well as the right not to profess any religion or belief. The terms belief and religion are to be broadly construed. Article 18 is not limited in its application to traditional religions or to religions and beliefs with institutional characteristics or practices analogous to those

of traditional religions. The Committee therefore views with concern any tendency to discriminate against any religion or belief for any reasons, including the fact that they are newly established, or represent religious minorities that may be the subject of hostility by a predominant religious community.

3 Article 18 distinguishes the freedom of thought, conscience, religion or belief from the freedom to manifest religion or belief. It does not permit any limitations whatsoever on the freedom of thought and conscience or on the freedom to have or adopt a religion or belief of one's choice. These freedoms are protected unconditionally, as is the right of everyone to hold opinions without interference in article 19 (1). In accordance with articles 18 (2) and 17, no one can be compelled to reveal his thoughts or adherence to a religion or belief.

4 The freedom to manifest religion or belief may be exercised 'either individually or in community with others and in public or private'. The freedom to manifest religion or belief in worship, observance, practice and teaching encompasses a broad range of acts. The concept of worship extends to ritual and ceremonial acts giving direct expression to belief, as well as various practices integral to such acts, including the building of places of worship, the use of ritual formulae and objects, the display of symbols, and the observance of holidays and days of rest. The observance and practice of religion or belief may include not only ceremonial acts but also such customs as the observance of dietary regulations, the wearing of distinctive clothing or headcoverings, participation in rituals associated with certain stages of life, and the use of a particular language customarily spoken by a group. In addition, the practice and teaching of religion or belief includes acts integral to the conduct by religious groups of their basic affairs, such as, *inter alia*, the freedom to choose their religious leaders, priests and teachers, the freedom to establish seminaries or religious schools and the freedom to prepare and distribute religious texts or publications.

5 The Committee observes that the freedom to 'have or to adopt' a religion or belief necessarily entails the freedom to choose a religion or belief, including, *inter alia*, the right to replace one's current religion or belief with another or to adopt atheistic views, as well as the right to retain one's religion or belief. Article 18 (2) bars coercions that would impair the right to have or adopt a religion or belief, including the use of threat of physical force or penal sanctions to compel believers or non-believers to adhere to their religious beliefs and congregations, to recant their religion or belief or to convert. Policies or practices having the same intention or effect, such as for example those restricting access to education, medical care, employment or the rights guaranteed by article 25 and other provisions of the Covenant are similarly inconsistent with article 18 (2). The same protection is enjoyed by holders of all beliefs of a non-religious nature.

6 The Committee is of the view that article 18 (4) permits public school instruction in subjects such as the general history of religions and ethics if it is given in a neutral and objective way. The liberty of parents or legal guardians to ensure that their children receive a religious and moral education in conformity with their own convictions, set forth in article 18 (4), is related to the guarantees of the freedom to teach a religion or belief stated in article 18 (1). The Committee notes that public education that includes instruction in a particular religion or belief is inconsistent with article 18 (4) unless provision is made for non-discriminatory exemptions or alternatives that would accommodate the wishes of parents or guardians.

7 According to article 20, no manifestation of religions or beliefs may amount to propaganda for war or advocacy of national, racial or religious hatred that constitutes incitement to discrimination, hostility or violence. As stated by the Committee in its General Comment 11 [19], States parties are under the obligation to enact laws to prohibit such acts.

8 Article 18 (3) permits restrictions on the freedom to manifest religion or belief only if limitations are prescribed by law and are necessary to protect public safety, order, health or morals, or the fundamental rights and freedoms of others. The freedom from coercion to have or to adopt a religion or belief and the liberty of the parents and guardians to ensure religious and moral education cannot be restricted. In interpreting the scope of permissible limitation clauses, States parties should proceed from the need to protect the rights guaranteed under the Covenant, including the right to equality and non-discrimination on all grounds specified in articles 2, 3 and 26. Limitations imposed must be established by law and must not be applied in a manner that would vitiate the rights guaranteed in article 18. The Committee observes that paragraph 3 of article 18 is to be strictly interpreted: restrictions are not allowed on grounds not specified there, even if they would be allowed as restrictions to other rights protected in the Covenant, such as national security. Limitations may be applied only for those purposes for which they were prescribed and must be directly related proportionate to the specific need on which they are predicated. Restrictions may not be imposed for discriminatory purposes or applied in a discriminatory manner. The Committee observes that the concept of morals derives from many social, philosophical and religious traditions; consequently, limitations on the freedom to manifest a religion or belief for the purpose of protecting morals must be based on principles not deriving exclusively from a single tradition. Persons already subject to certain legitimate constraints, such as prisoners, continue to enjoy their rights to manifest their religion or belief to the fullest extent compatible with the specific nature of the constraint. States parties' reports should provide information on the full scope and effects of limitations under article 18 (3), both as a matter of law and of their application in specific circumstances.

9 The fact that a religion is recognized as a State religion or that it is established as official or traditional or that its followers comprise the majority of the population, shall not result in any impairment of the enjoyment of any of the rights under the Covenant, including articles 18 and 27, nor in any discrimination against adherents of other religions or non-believers. In particular, certain measures discriminating against the latter, such as measures restricting eligibility for government service to members of the predominant religion or giving economic privileges to them or imposing special restrictions on the practice of other faiths, are not in accordance with the prohibition of discrimination based on religion or belief and the guarantee of equal protection under article 26. The measures contemplated by article 20, paragraph 2, of the Covenant constitute important safeguards against infringements of the rights of religious minorities and of other religious groups to exercise the rights guaranteed by articles 18 and 27, and against acts of violence or persecution directed towards those groups. The Committee wishes to be informed of measures taken by States parties concerned to protect the practices of all religions or beliefs from infringement and to protect their followers from discrimination. Similarly, information as to respect for the rights of religious minorities under article 27 is necessary for the Committee to assess the extent to which the freedom of thought, conscience, religion and belief has been implemented by States parties. States parties concerned should also include in their reports information relating to practices considered by their laws and jurisprudence to be punishable as blasphemous.

10 If a set of beliefs is treated as official ideology in constitutions, statutes, proclamations of the ruling parties, etc., or in actual practice, this shall not result in any impairment of the freedoms under article 18 or any other rights recognized under the Covenant nor in any discrimination against persons who do not accept the official ideology or who oppose it.

11 Many individuals have claimed the right to refuse to perform military service (conscientious objection) on the basis that such right derives from their freedoms under article 18. In response to such claims, a growing number of States have in their laws exempted from compulsory military service citizens who genuinely hold religious or other beliefs that forbid the performance of military service and replaced it with alternative national service. The Covenant does not explicitly refer to a right of conscientious objection, but the Committee believes that such a right can be derived from article 18, inasmuch as the obligation to use lethal force may seriously conflict with the freedom of conscience and the right to manifest one's religion or belief. When this right is recognized by law or practice, there shall be no differentiation among conscientious objectors on the basis of the nature of their particular beliefs; likewise there shall be no discrimination against conscientious objectors because they have failed to perform military service. The Committee invites States parties to report on the conditions under which persons can be exempted from military service on the basis of their rights under article 18 and on the nature and length of alternative national service.

THE SPECIAL RAPPORTEUR ON RELIGIOUS INTOLERANCE

The Special Rapporteur on the Implementation of the Declaration on the Elimination of All Forms of Intolerance and of Discrimination Based on Religion or Belief – the Special Rapporteur on Religious Intolerance. The first Special Rapporteur on Religious Intolerance was appointed in accordance with resolution 1986/20 of 10 March 1986, by the United Nations Commission on Human Rights. The mandate has been extended each year since that date, and the current Special Rapporteur, Abdelfattah Amor of Tunisia, works in accordance with Commission of Human Rights Resolution 1994/18.

The Special Rapporteur transmits to governments summaries of allegations forwarded to him which appear, *prima facie*, to indicate violations of the right to freedom of thought, conscience and religion. In some cases, the Special Rapporteur seeks information from governments on specific aspects of allegations, and governments are encouraged by resolution 1994/18 to invite the Special Rapporteur to visit their countries in order that he may carry out his mandate more effectively. In the case of serious allegations, the Special Rapporteur may resort to the use of the urgent appeal procedure.

In accordance with his mandate, the Special Rapporteur may make appropriate recommendations in accordance with the United Nation's advisory programme in human rights. The purpose of these visits is to establish dialogue and enhance understanding.

In his work, the Special Rapporteur makes full use of credible and reliably attested information received from a broad range of governmental and non-governmental sources. Individuals or organisations wishing to send information to the Special Rapporteur may write to:

> Professor Abdelfattah Amor
> Special Rapporteur on Religious Intolerance
> Center for Human Rights
> United Nations
> Geneva
> Switzerland

Acknowledgements

The editors wish to thank the following people and organisations without whose contributions the project could not have been accomplished.

Writers and researchers

Patricia Abozaglo, Edward Phillip Antonio, Fateh Azzam, Kevin Bampton, Maria Ines Barnechea, Greg Barton, Roberto J. Blancarte, Marc Carillo, Julia Christanopolous, Roberta Clarke, Felix Corley, Milagros Isabel A. Cristobal, Ray Dabrowski, Amel Daddah, Vojin Dimitrijevic, Shirley Eber, Djohan Effendi, Said Essoulami, Tamas Földesi, Tom Gallagher, Felipe Gonzalez, Jeremy Gunn, Bahey El-Din Hassan, Martin Heckel, Rhoda Howard, Larry Hufford, Gan Kong Hwee, Ian Iacos, Michael Jansen, George Joffe, Ousmane Kane, Douwe Korff, Marnia Lazreg, Cayetano De Lella, Gerrie Lubbe, Creuza Rosa Maciel, Muhammad Mahmoud, Alivastros Manitakis, Roy H. May, Cecilia Medina, Chris Moffatt, Adebayo Okunade, Andrei P. Osadchuk, Gerald Parsons, Joanne Perkins, Borislav Petranov, Louis Edmond Pettiti, James Phillips, Andy Pollak, Mohammad Ali Saif, H.L. Seneviratna, Juliet Sheen, Barbara Stapleton, Alice Erh-Soon Tay, Hazhir Teimourian, Robert Tielman, Chris Tremewan, Vo Van Ai, Einar Vetvik, Abdulrahim Vijapur, Francis Loh Kok Wah, Philip Walters, Koichi Yokota, Andrzej Ziolkowski.

Additional research and comment

Simeon Beckett, Pierre Bosset, Gary Bouma, Michelle Brandt, Vicky Bui, Rajeev Dhavan, Brian Fegan, David Forfar, Tom Hadden, Helen Hartnell, Fatima Houda-Pepin, Jeff Kaplan, Natan Lerner, Salman Mehzoud, Siobhan Mulally, Kinhide Mushakoji, Ian Neary, Angela Otaluka, Jayan Patel, Martin Prozesky, Anika Rahman, Bertram Ramcharan, James T. Richardson, Saba Risaluddin, Hugh Roberts, Adel Omar Sherif, Soli Sorabjee, Ethan Taubes, Kenzo Tomonaga, Richard Wilson, Andy Youngman.

Consultants

Elizabeth Isichei, Lene Johannessen, Todd Landmann, Gary MacEoin, Penny Magee, Sue Nichols, John Taylor.

International Advisory Board

Abdullahi An Na'im, Emory University, USA; Margaret Bedggood, University of Waikato, New Zealand; Theo van Boven, University of Limburg, Netherlands; Rachel Brett, Quaker Peace and Service, Geneva; Francis Broglio, University of Florence; Cole

Durham, Brigham Young University, USA; Eve Fesl, Griffith University, Queensland; Jeremy Gunn, Attorney, Washington; Chatsumarn Kabilsingh, Faculty of Liberal Arts, Thammasat University, Bangkok; Farrukh Khan, London School of Economics; Joke Kniesmeyer, Generale Diakonale Raad, Netherlands; Gregory Kroupnikov, University of Riga, Latvia; Enda McDonagh, Maynooth College, Ireland; Gary MacEoin, San Antonio; Mutambo Mulami, All Africa Conference of Churches; Kinhide Mushakoji, Secretary-General, International Movement Against Discrimination and Racism; Sue Nichols, Chair, United Nations, New York: Non-Governmental Organizations Committee on Freedom of Religion or Belief; Bhikhu Parekh, Department of Political Theory, University of Hull; Aviezer Ravitsky, Department of Jewish Thought, Hebrew University of Jersulam; Martin Scheinin, Institute of Public Law, University of Helsinki; Soli Sorabjee, Former Attorney General, India; John Taylor, Conference of European Churches, Geneva; Robert Tielman, Co-Chair, International Humanist and Ethical Union; Salih Tug, Dean of the Faculty of Theology, Marmara University; Einar Vetvik, Norwegian Institute of Human Rights; Wenzao Han, General Secretary, Amity Foundation, Nanjing, China; James E. Wood, jnr, Director, J.M. Dawson Institute of Church–State Studies, University of Baylor, USA.

NGOs CONTRIBUTING RESEARCH MATERIALS

All Africa Conference of Churches, Amnesty International, Arab Institute for Human Rights, Article XIX, Asia-Pacific Human Rights Information Center, Calamus Foundation, Churches Human Rights Forum, Droits de l'Homme Sans Frontières, European Council of Churches, Federation International des Droits de l'Homme, Human Rights Watch, INDEX on Censorship, Information Network Focus on Religious Movements, Initiative for Peace and Co-operation in the Middle East, International Association for Religious Freedom, International Humanist and Ethical Union, International Movement Against Discrimination and Racism, Justice and Peace, Keston Institute, Minority Rights Group, Parliamentary Human Rights Foundation, Public Affairs Committee for Shi'a Muslims, Soka Gakkai, United States Institute for Peace, World Conference on Religion and Peace.

The World Report project was sponsored and funded by the Pew Charitable Trusts, Philadelphia, USA.

NGO CONSULTANT

The Tandem Project, Director: Michael Roan, Chair: Barbara Forster

NGO ASSISTANCE

United Nations, New York: NGO Committee on Freedom of Religion or Belief, Chair: Sue Nichols
United Nations, Geneva: NGO Committee on Freedom of Religion or Belief, Chair: Adrien-Claude Zoller

Note from the editors

Entries for this report were drafted largely during 1994–5 and have been updated where possible, to the beginning of 1997.

The transliteration of non-English words varied significantly among the writers of the draft entries, depending on their first languages and those of the regions they wrote about. The vicissitudes of conversion between different word-processing programs have also occasionally caused minor problems, especially with diacritical signs. The editors have endeavoured to enhance uniformity within entries and in the book as a whole for the most commonly used terms while maintaining some individual differences, depending on context. The editorial difficulties of dealing with material in different languages and from the many regions of the world have been manifold and the editors, while being responsible for the text, none the less apologise for any inadvertent discourtesies or inconsistencies on this score.

Abbreviations

BCE   before the Christian era
NGO(s)   non-governmental organisation(s)

UNITED NATIONS DECLARATIONS AND INSTRUMENTS

1981 Declaration   Declaration on the Elimination of All Forms of Intolerance and of Discrimination Based on Religion or Belief

CEDAW   Convention on the Elimination of All Forms of Discrimination Against Women

CERD   International Convention on the Elimination of All Forms of Racial Discrimination

CRC   Convention on the Rights of the Child

ICCPR   International Covenant on Civil and Political Rights

ICESCR   International Covenant on Economic, Social and Cultural Rights

UDHR   Universal Declaration of Human Rights

EUROPEAN INSTRUMENTS

ECHR   European Convention on Human Rights
OSCE   Organisation for Security and Cooperation in Europe

Key to statistics

Unless otherwise indicated, figures in the box beginning each country entry are taken from the *Country Human Development Indicators* (1995), United Nations Development Programme, Human Development Report Office, Geneva. Other sources are listed below. All statistics were compiled by Sue Nichols.

[a] United Nations Development Programme (1994) *Country Human Development Indicators* Geneva: UN Human Development Report Office.

[b] John W. Wright (ed.), *The Universal Almanac* (1996) Kansas City, USA: Andrews and McMeel.

[c] *The Europa World Yearbook* (1994) London: Europa Publishers.

[d] *Philip's Geographical Digest* (1994–1995) Oxford: Heinemann Educational Books.

[e] *World Fact Book* (1995) Central Intelligence Agency, Washington, DC: Office of Public and Agency Information.

[f] Information on Northern Ireland supplied by United Kingdom Information Service, New York.

[g] Information on the Occupied Palestinian Territories supplied by the UNRWA Liaison Office, New York, USA.

[h] Statistics on Serbia do not include Montenegro, unless so indicated.

KEY TO CONVENTIONS

State ratifications of international and regional human rights conventions are indicated as follows:

1 International Covenant on Economic, Social and Cultural Rights; 16 December 1966; entry into force: 3 January 1976.

2 International Covenant on Civil and Political Rights; 16 December 1966; entry into force: 23 March 1976.

2(a) Declaration regarding Article 41 of the International Covenant on civil and Political Rights (competence of the Human Rights Committee to receive communications by a State Party against another State Party); entry into force: 28 March 1978

2(b) Option Protocol to the International Covenant on Civil and Political Rights; (competence of the Human Rights Committee to receive communications from individuals claiming to be victims of violations of any of the rights in the Covenant); entry into force: 23 March 1976.

3 International Convention on the Elimination of All Forms of Racial Discrimination; 21 December 1965; entry into force: 4 January 1969.

4   Convention on the Elimination of All Forms of Discrimination against Women; 18 December 1979; entry into force: 3 September 1981.

REGIONAL CONVENTIONS

Af   African Charter on Human and People's Rights; 26 June 1981; entry into force: 21 October 1986.

Am   American Convention on Human Rights; 22 November 1969; entry into force: 18 July 1978.

E   European Convention on Human Rights; 4 November 1950; entry into force: 3 September 1953.

Introduction

WHAT THIS BOOK IS ABOUT

This report presents the results of a project designed to explore the state of freedom of conscience, religion and belief in the world.[1] The work grew out of a perception that too little is known about the experience both of enjoyment and of violation of this freedom today. It is a human rights report, that is, its terms of reference are the international standards which recognise, define and defend this freedom. Its underlying principles are those of international law, which upholds the right of all human beings to equal respect for their particular beliefs and for their right to live by them, alone or in community with others, while observing a strict neutrality as between the merits of different religions and other belief systems. Neutrality, however, does not mean indifference nor is it a synonym for hostility.

The study includes nearly sixty country entries broadly representative of the geo-political regions of the world. The reader is only given an initial exploration of how freedom of conscience, religion and belief as internationally espoused freedoms are understood in theory and practice within these diverse states. A study of this nature has not been attempted before. The extent to which freedom of belief is enjoyed in the contemporary world and how different cultures and legal systems respond to diversity of religious and secular beliefs in their midst, is a neglected topic in human rights research. The process of reaching consensus on the norms governing freedom of conscience, religion and belief has been protracted and is far from complete. Questions of religion, ideology or belief are among the most sensitive matters in international relations and in international human rights exchanges within the United Nations and regional bodies. Diplomatic discourse has preferred to confine itself largely to abstract reference to situations of 'intolerance' or 'religious extremism', for example, rather than identify specific violations. The general wariness towards, if not lack of interest in, the subject by many governments, has resulted in a studied neglect. Yet for the bulk of humankind, belief is the most significant of all aspects of life and the freedoms to maintain, to manifest and to transmit their beliefs to their children, are among the most important claims made by citizens everywhere on their governments.

Freedom of thought, conscience, religion and belief is far from being universally enjoyed. Discrimination and intolerance in matters of religion or belief are a serious dimension of the catalogue of violation of human rights in the world including situations of gross violation. Religious persecution of minority faiths, forcible conversion, desecration of religious sites, the proscribing of beliefs and pervasive discrimination, killings and torture, are daily occurrences at the end of the twentieth century. Even in a world which has emerged from the paralysis of the Cold War, little it appears can be done for the victims. In 1995 the United Nations could not even afford to publish their complaints.[2]

None the less there have been landmark studies initiated by the United Nations which have gathered and analysed information supplied by governments.[3] There also have been impressive strides in recent years in the scholarly analysis of the existing international standards from both religious and neutral perspectives.[4] This scholarship has included the recent two volume study undertaken at Emory University (in the United States) on religious rights, a major initiative which, like the present study, has been encouraged and funded by the Pew Charitable Trusts.[5]

The World Report can be thought of as complementing such work by offering a more concrete, empirical and contextual interpretation of how freedom of religion and belief fares in different regions and states. The common framework for each country study in the World Report consists of key factors identified in the literature and the international standards, the relationship between belief groups and the state and the inter-relationships among belief groups within a particular society. The study also seeks to take the subject and the debate beyond the issues of state, law and religion, by looking at men and women in relation to religion, at education and at conscientious objection among other themes.

Furthermore, the World Report draws on the work of the United Nations Human Rights Commission which for the last decade has appointed a Special Rapporteur to undertake the tasks of monitoring religious intolerance and interceding with governments on behalf of victims of discrimination and persecution.[6] The annual reports submitted by the Special Rapporteur to the Human Rights Commission confirm a depressing reality reflected in this study, that a considerable number of situations and incidents of intolerance towards those who differ in religious conviction are attributable to the extremes within religious communities themselves. A distinguishing characteristic of the freedom of religion and belief is, therefore, that it is not only capable of being violated by the state but by the people who make up the state. Indeed, religious minorities who may be the target of discrimination can also be the source of intolerance to others as well.

Difference among human beings in matters of fundamental belief ideally might be thought of as a matter of celebration but in practice it is rarely so. Most conflicts past and present involve rejection of difference coupled with assertions of superiority of belief or exclusivity of truth, which in turn are reflected in patterns of discrimination, intolerance, persecution, and even genocide. This study does not disguise the reality of religious conflict whether or not it is entwined, as it usually is, with ethno-nationalism or competition over resources or territory. However, it has also sought (where it could find the evidence) to report examples of cooperation and accommodation between different religions and beliefs.

The Report does not seek to rank countries in terms of a scale of intolerance. Even if indicators could be devised to establish such a scale, the truth is that there is little to pick and choose between the countries or regions of the world. Intolerance towards others, be they individuals or minority communities and whether based on negative attitudes towards their beliefs or on other perceived differences, is a universal problem. It is the scale of the problem and differences in the consequences of intolerance which distinguish one situation from the other. There is no difference in essence.

The task of building tolerance, therefore, presents a universal educational challenge. In this study we define the ideal of tolerance as requiring popular understanding of the extraordinary diversity of fundamental beliefs held by human communities and an acceptance by all of the right of each individual and each community of believers to equal respect for their fundamental beliefs. The United Nations Charter enjoins the nations of the world 'to practise tolerance and to live together as good neighbours'. Fifty years later the injunction remains the supreme requirement of an international order based on human rights, democracy and peace. We hope that this study can contribute to that imperative goal.

HOW THE REPORT WAS PREPARED

The World Report consists of short edited entries, initial drafts of which were prepared by experts, where possible living in the countries surveyed. Writers were given guidelines to ensure comparability of responses but entries have not been standardised. As a result, while broadly covering similar themes, they reflect also issues of concern for these freedoms that are specific to different countries or regions, among others, indigenous beliefs in Latin America, Muslim schools in Western Europe, registration of religions in Eastern Europe, and freedom of religious expression in South East and East Asia. The book is organised into world regions with a short introductory overview on regional themes.[7]

A country-based approach allows the distinctive nature of the manifestations of freedom of religion and belief to emerge and provides insight into both the obstacles and opportunities for securing its enhanced protection. Each country included could be the subject of a monograph-length study and, indeed, some draft entries were. However, having a wide range of countries with a common focus of issues will stimulate more extensive study of specific countries. At the same time, to have attempted to include every country in the world would have resulted in entries of excessive brevity. Subject to ensuring representativeness and the obvious significance of major states, the choice of a country for inclusion in the Report was solely a matter of the availability to us of information and expertise on any country.

Preparing this study has been very much a collective enterprise and we have built on the work of others. The United Nations sources already mentioned and other reports have been drawn upon to supplement the draft entries prepared by country experts, including reports prepared by human rights NGOs, by different religious groups, by inter-faith bodies and humanist organisations. The opportunity was taken through interviews with the permanent representatives of states at the United Nations in New York to explain the project and to seek information. Governments were not, however, shown entries in draft. Those who have contributed to the study are acknowledged. The UN New York and Geneva NGO Committees on Freedom of Religion or Belief have been central to the guidance and preparation of the Report. The Tandem Project has also been associated with the work in a special way.[8] The initial proposal was developed in conjunction with the Tandem Project which has had a key role in disseminating information about the Report's progress. However, the editorial responsibility has been that of the Human Rights Centre. The International Advisory Board has been a valuable resource for identifying writers and for editorial advice. We have also had special assistance from scholars with regional expertise and in the field of women and religion. The book owes a special debt to the many non-governmental organisations, religious and secular, which are active in the defence of freedom of religion and belief as well as the promotion of tolerance and understanding between all religions and beliefs.[9]

INTERNATIONAL STANDARDS ON FREEDOM OF RELIGION AND BELIEF

The key to using the Report is contained in the elements of these freedoms as they have become recognised and defined in international law since Franklin D. Roosevelt first included freedom of religion in his famous 1941 Four Freedoms speech.[10] (The reader is referred for more extensive treatment to the studies cited above and to the bibliography at the end of the book.) The international human rights movement was born in response to the racist ideology of National Socialism, discussed in the entry on Germany. From the Holocaust, the ultimate outworking of centuries of European intolerance against Jews, came a new idea, that of individual human rights, to be internationally defined and guaranteed to all persons everywhere in virtue of their humanity, without distinction as to race, sex, language or religion. To maintain that vision undimmed and to have taken even modest steps towards delivering it, have been perhaps the most important achievements of the world community in the last half of this century. The core standards agreed on by states on freedom of thought, conscience, religion and belief, are set out in the International Bill of Human Rights.[11] The foundation was laid when the General Assembly proclaimed the Universal Declaration of Human Rights in 1948. Article 18 of the Universal Declaration provides:

> Everyone has the right to freedom of thought, conscience and religion; this right includes freedom to change his religion or belief, and freedom, either alone or in community with others and in public or private, to manifest his religion or belief in teaching, practice, worship and observance.

In many respects the meaning of this article has been a paradigm of the debates over the nature of human rights which have continued at all levels, diplomatic, political, scholarly and popular since 1948. Thus Article 18 raises the issue of the universality and indivisibility of rights, of the primacy of international law over national law and religious codes, of individual, minority and collective rights and of the relationship between rights, duties and community. Each of these subjects comes up in the discussion of human rights in general, but has historically given rise to and continues to give rise to particular complex problems in the theory and practice of implementing freedom of conscience, religion and belief, as will be clear from the country entries.

Ideas of religious toleration and respect for conscience did not emerge spontaneously after the foundation of the United Nations. These ideas including freedom of thought can be traced to many world cultures but most influentially to European thought and experience. The concepts in Article 18 represent a millennium of struggle in Europe for individual freedom of thought and religious freedom against the power of church and state.[12]

But if the emergence of freedom of thought and freedom of religion and belief are linked to European civilisation, how stands the claims that human rights are universal? There is a considerable literature on the subject which cannot be gone into here.[13] All answers seem to converge on the distinction between the origin of ideas and their dissemination and conscious adoption. That these freedoms were first codified from European experience does not mean that the thoughts and values behind them are not reflected in other civilisations and cultures. The entries in this Report clearly confirm that religious belief, which gives a transcendental meaning to life, is universal. The injunction to practise tolerance towards those of different beliefs is in fact more a characteristic of the teaching of faiths other than historical European Christianity. Further, the majority of states in the United Nations, representing diverse cultures, have accepted in binding international agreements the present norms. The universality and indivisibility of all human rights were formally affirmed by the member states of the United Nations in the World Conference on Human Rights in 1993.[14]

However, a more complex challenge to universality arises when the international norms of freedom of religion or belief are scrutinised more closely in terms of their meaning within actual belief systems and living cultures. There are fundamental differences in perception between religions as to the relationship between the individual, the community and any transcendental norm. Many reflections of these differences emerge from these entries, but three in particular may be noted here, that of the freedom of the individual to choose a religion different from the religious group of which he or she is a member, the relationship between state authority and religious belief and the claims of some religions to exclusive and final truth. From a particular religion's position on the first flow ascriptions of apostasy, heresy and the question of proselytism. From the second arise implications for freedom of minority faiths in countries where the majority claims a privileged relationship with the state or nation or even fusion of nation, state and religion. The third issue relates to the relationships among different religions and beliefs. It is a characteristic of religion, and often of secular ideologies, to claim exclusive truth for their tenets or doctrines. How doctrines of superiority and exclusivity in matters of religion or belief can be reconciled with the essentially pluralist and neutral principles of the international human rights standards, or with the duty on states to ensure that these standards are implemented in their respective countries, remains without an adequate answer.

It is the task of the international human rights movement to try to achieve consensus on prescriptions for such questions. One milestone in standard setting was the adoption of the 1981 UN Declaration on the Elimination of All Forms of Intolerance and of Discrimination Based on Religion or Belief.[15] This Declaration, building on the provisions of the International Bill of Human Rights, gives more detailed content to the right of individuals and groups to hold and manifest beliefs and more specific guidance for all states on steps they must take to promote tolerance and eliminate discrimination. The almost twenty years it took states to agree its terms reflected the genuine difficulties and sensitivities of the subject for governments as well as the tensions of the Cold War.[16] In 1993 the international standards governing freedom of religion and belief were given a considerable boost with the adoption of authoritative guidelines under the ICCPR by the (UN) Human Rights Committee.[17] Considerable agreement, therefore, has been reached on the content of these freedoms in international law, even if there remain areas of genuine disagreement. Such remaining disputes, mainly over the interpretation of the requirements of international standards, must be clearly separated from the more serious reality, reflected also in this Report – the open repudiation in practice of what are already agreed international norms on freedom of conscience and which are binding on the states that violate them.

SCOPE

In international law, freedom of thought, conscience, religion and belief are highly inter-related freedoms and all must be protected. Protection is not limited to religion, but extends to non-theistic and atheistic beliefs as well as the right not to profess any belief. It encompasses 'freedom of thought on all matters, personal convictions and the commitment to religion or belief whether manifested individually or in community with others'.[18] Freedom of religion, therefore, is not to be interpreted narrowly by states for example, to mean traditional world religions only. New religions or religious minorities are entitled to equal protection. This principle is of particular importance in the light of the evidence reflected in the country entries that new religious movements are a recurring target for discrimination or repression.

Non-discrimination

The duty not to discriminate against any religion or belief is the clearest of all of the international requirements. The 1981 Declaration proposes that discrimination is prohibited not only at the level of state bodies but also at every level of society. This means that religious communities are themselves under a duty to treat those of different and even unpopular beliefs fairly and with tolerance. The state is required to take concrete measures to ensure equality of treatment in matters of religion or belief through the rescinding of laws that enforce any unjustified distinctions on grounds of religion or belief. It has equally a duty to provide remedies or redress for those who are victims of any discrimination or intolerance because of their faith or secular beliefs. Prohibition of discrimination is directed in these standards not only at acts which affect beliefs directly, for example, a refusal to give planning permission for a temple or religious meeting place, but extends to the treatment of believers in all spheres including employment and promotion, housing, education and social benefits.

Family, upbringing and education

Parents have the right to decide how to bring their children up in the home according to their conscience and moral principles.[19] This is intended to recognise that parents may hand down their beliefs, practise their religion and worship in the home without interference from the state. The child in turn has the right to receive education in matters of religion or belief that are in accordance with the wishes of the parent. The child cannot be subjected to religious education to which parents object, a contentious issue in many countries where public education requires religious education and instruction in the tenets of one faith. In such cases non-discriminatory alternatives must be provided. However, the state is not obliged to provide education or schools which meet the wishes of the parents in matters of religion or belief. It is obliged, however, to respect the liberty of parents to establish schools which do provide education in conformity with their religious convictions or beliefs. The emphasis on parental rights is balanced by a requirement that religious practices or beliefs must not be injurious to the child. The child must also have access to education which protects it from racism and intolerance and must be taught to respect the beliefs of others. The United Nations Convention on the Rights of the Child requires, in turn, respect for the child's right to freedom of thought, conscience and religion, in the light of its evolving capacities.[20]

Manifesting religion or belief

Article 18 freedoms make a fundamental distinction between the right to have convictions – a right which is protected unconditionally – and the freedom to manifest those beliefs either alone or in community with others 'in worship, observance, practice and teaching' which may be subject to limitations. That freedom of manifestation can embrace a range of activities and essentially concerns the guarantee of other freedoms to believers, including freedom of expression, assembly and association. The Human Rights Committee has sketched the main features as follows:

> The concept of worship extends to ritual and ceremonial acts giving direct expression to belief, as well as various practices integral to such acts, including the building of places of worship, the use of ritual formulae, and objects, the display of symbols, and the observance of holidays and days of rest. The observance and practice of religion or belief may include not only ceremonial acts but also such customs as the observance of dietary regulations, the wearing

of distinctive clothing or headcoverings, participation in rituals associated with certain stages of life, and the use of a particular language customarily spoken by a group. In addition, the practice and teaching of religion or belief includes acts integral to the conduct by religious groups of their basic affairs, such as, *inter alia*, the freedom to choose their religious leaders, priests and teachers, the freedom to establish seminaries or religious schools and the freedom to prepare and distribute religious texts or publications.[21]

This listing of what constitutes the practice of a faith or belief was not intended to be exhaustive. The 1981 UN Declaration adds the right to establish and maintain communication nationally and internationally with fellow believers. But it does indicate core rights which adhere to religions, congregations, divisions and branches of religious and secular belief as autonomous groups and entities. It is in this sphere of collective activities that religions in particular are likely to have to relate to the law and government administration; this is where many complaints arise over bureaucratic obstruction or failings of the state.

Restrictions on the right to manifest

The conditions under which the right to practise religion or belief can be legitimately limited under international standards are that any such restriction based on law is proportionate and is necessary 'to protect public safety, order, health or morals or the fundamental rights and freedoms of others'. According to the Human Rights Committee, states have a duty to interpret restrictions narrowly so as to allow the maximum freedom and only for the purposes specified. Thus a state may not infringe on religious practices, while claiming national security as a justification. In its interpretation of the ground of restriction on public morals, the Human Rights Committee considered that any such limitation on freedom of religion or belief should not be based on principles derived from a single tradition.[22] Nor should any restriction constitute discrimination. Finally, the Committee included as legitimate restriction measures intended to prevent manifestations of belief which amount to propaganda for war or advocacy of national, racial or religious hatred that constitutes incitement to discrimination, hostility or violence.[23]

The duty to secure the freedoms in law and practice

As in the case of all international human rights established under treaties and agreements, there are specific duties placed on states to ensure that the protection of freedom of conscience, religion and belief is secured through law. The country entries, therefore, include the sources of national protection as reflected in constitutions as well as legislation. It is of course a commonplace, amply demonstrated in this Report, that law is easier to proclaim than to enforce. Nevertheless, the existence of positive legal obligation to eliminate discrimination and to protect religious freedom as well as freedom of thought is an essential foundation. Equally fundamental is the existence of accessible and effective remedies for victims of discrimination. Freedom of conscience, religion and belief in these respects is no different to other rights in its dependence on the rule of law and a democratic society.

CONTENTIOUS ISSUES

If the core of the freedom is clear, there are aspects which remain in contention or are uncertain, as follows.

Religious or national law versus international law

How may interpretations of religious law become harmonised with international human rights standards? There is a clear challenge of explanation in arguing that the core of tolerance is to accept the reality of diversity of religions and belief in the world, while rejecting the thesis that the substance of this freedom may be different in different cultures. Thus some interpretations of *shariah* law pit Islam against the principle of the primacy of international law, and practices in other countries based on national law directly ignore the requirements of the right to freedom of conscience, religion and belief. The case of China comes to mind. All claims to universality of rights have a credibility problem when we contemplate the denial of full religious freedoms and other rights to the one fifth, or one quarter of the world's population who are Chinese. Nevertheless, the priority accorded to the core international law standards with respect to human rights cannot be answered as a matter of international law by claims of national sovereignty or the requirements of religious law or custom.[24]

Claims of superiority or inferiority of religions and beliefs

Freedom of religion includes the right to believe that one has exclusive truth and that what another believes is lacking in truth. Nevertheless, there is a concern with the implications of beliefs that are regarded by their adherence as superior or inferior. Under the international standards you may not treat anyone less favourably by reason of their not sharing your beliefs and there can be no discrimination based on differences of belief. Yet that is precisely what happens in many parts of the world. Discrimination and intolerance are justified by reference to the inferiority or the untruth of the opposing beliefs, whether religious or non-religious. More thought needs to be given as to how to establish the regime of equality that international law requires where different religions and non-religious ideologies within different countries define opposing beliefs as inferior, false or heretical. Perhaps the answer lies as much in the past as in the future. In the third century BCE, the Rock Edicts of King Asoka, who established a Buddhist kingdom in India, proclaimed that if you give others' beliefs no respect, you will damage the status of everybody's beliefs, including your own.

Choosing and changing religious commitment

The best known and most discussed aspect of freedom of religion is whether it can ever be legitimate to place restraints on the individual acting to abandon altogether a religion to which he or she was committed and to replace it with either another religion or with other beliefs, for example, secular beliefs. The straightforward answer would appear to be 'no'. The individual has the right to exercise freedom of conscience with regard to questions of faith. It is not permissible to sanction a person who converts to another faith or who abandons all belief in religion. If that is the case, does it mean that the concept of apostasy is incompatible with the international consensus on the meaning of freedom of religion? This is a sensitive issue but it seems likely that attitudes of intolerance (and actions prompted by it) accompany allegations of blasphemy or apostasy, just as it may be questioned whether such matters may ever be objectively assessed. The international standards make it clear that there may be no coercion in matters of religion; this is also a central tenet in Islam. However, certain interpretations of Islam do not accept the right of a person to abandon that religion or to convert to another. The language in certain of the international texts speaks of a right to 'have or adopt' a religion, language which is somewhat unclear. However, the Human Rights Committee has interpreted that language boldly to mean that the individual has the right to 'replace one's current religion or belief with another or to adopt atheistic views, as well as the right to retain one's religion or belief'.[25] But there is no Islamic state that will formally accept that position. A serious question arises where the Islamic *shariah* is enforced, leading to the violation of other rights, for example by the use of the death penalty for apostasy or blasphemy.[26] The conclusion for now is that many Islamic countries stand outside the international consensus on this question.

Proselytism

A linked issue is the question of the right to encourage persons to convert from one religion to another: the issue of proselytism. Forced conversion is clearly a stark violation of human rights but is it permissible, as occurs in some countries, to effectively prohibit proselytism? Is it permissible to impose any restrictions on the freedom to promote or teach the truth as the believer sees it and thereby to persuade another to adopt those beliefs? In Malaysia the former British colonial government introduced in the constitution a provision, still enforced, that no Christian missionary work could be undertaken in predominantly Muslim regions. This was justified on grounds of communal peace and stability. Can it also be defended in human rights terms? The international standards are less than clear. The one international decision by a human rights body on proselytism is a very cautious decision indeed. In the case of *Kokkinakis* v. *Greece*, the European Court of Human Rights, in considering the Greek law which had led to the imprisonment of a Jehovah's Witness for seeking to convert an Orthodox believer, referred without further explanation to proper and improper proselytism.[27] But what is improper proselytism? When the US Equal Employment Opportunity Commission circulated a draft set of guidelines on the issue of religion at work as a part of the matter of unlawful discrimination, there was an outcry which led to the draft being withdrawn. The reaction was allied to the prayer in school issue and the EEOC was accused of trying to drive expressions of religion out of the workplace, that is to ban the display of crosses, prayers put upon the walls or the wearing of religious emblems.[28]

A new context in which such controversies arise today is in the new democracies in Eastern Europe and Russia involving religious competition between the predominantly Orthodox churches and Christian evangelicals who have flocked to these countries after the collapse of communism. In Africa the well-financed advances of Islam have brought protest from Christian churches. Another context is the competition between evangelical Protestants and Catholics in Latin America. The resolution of these questions lies in the human rights' concept of balance. The right of a religion to teach what it considers to be the truth, to promote itself and to gain new members, has to be balanced against the entitlement of everyone to respect for their existing beliefs or lack of them. No-one may be required to reveal his or her beliefs nor be coerced into abandoning them. The key concept is the rights and freedoms of others. New, more detailed international standards are clearly required on proselytism and religions that seek to recruit and convert should be involved in any discussion of such standards.

Religion and state

Discussion of the sphere of religion leads inevitably to the issue of the state, religion and politics. It cannot be said that the international standards require the separation of church or religion and state. Some countries have broken such a formal relationship as in the case of Turkey or France and a country such as the United States was established on the principle of strict separation. However, as this world survey demonstrates, a large number of countries (if not the majority) do posit a relationship between the political community, that is the state, its institutions and administration and a current or historically predominant religion (or religions) of its citizens. The nature of these relationships, including those in Islamic countries, is quite diverse and reflects constant adaptation. The sole international requirement is that any variant of such a relationship should not result in discrimination against those who are not of the official religion or of the recognised faiths. The Human Rights Committee has added that the same principle applies where the state adopts an official ideology.[29]

Is it possible to establish a system of equality as regards all faiths while privileging one? Norway believes so, while in contrast, Sweden has set the year 2000 as the date to end the link between the Lutheran Church as the state religion and the Lutheran Church has voted in favour of this decision. In the United Kingdom there is some debate over disestablishment of the Church of England, in fact now a minority religion in terms of membership in the country. There are surviving privileges accorded to that Church, for example in membership of the non-elected chamber of Parliament, the House of Lords. But as the entry reveals, it could not be concluded that the survival of such remnants of the former Anglican ascendancy leads to significant and ostensible disadvantage or discrimination for other faiths.

Other examples of the situation of religious minorities, brought out in the Report, include the Copts in Egypt or the Protestant minority in Costa Rica, and do raise questions about the practical difficulties in securing equality between religions where the state endorses and supports one faith and implicitly or explicitly pronounces it as the true religion. Nowhere has this issue been more debated than in Israel. Is it the state of the Jewish people, and what about its non-Jewish citizens? Israel defines itself more usually as a Jewish and democratic state. Of course the statement that Israel is a Jewish state is not to say it is a theocratic state. There is religious freedom in Israel for all the religions of its people. But where religion is considered to be constitutive of national identity, as in this case, or in the case of Greece or Russia, how can one address the requirement that there should be no inequalities in the treatment of different faiths? It is sometimes said that majorities have rights as well as minorities and even if there is as, for example, in the case of the United States, a wall of separation between religion and the state, the impact of dominant trends in the religion of the majority on governmental affairs of the whole community cannot be held back by such a constitutional defence. The palpable influence of conservative Christian movements in the United States over the last decade illustrates that point.

It might be argued that the direction of the international norms is towards the position that religions should occupy the terrain of civil society.[30] Religions or churches should not be part of the state, or the state part of them. That is not to prescribe any particular model of relationship between state and religion; in particular it does not require that vision of secular society which banishes religion from public affairs. There is clearly a growing rejection in a country like the United States of the privatisation of religion. Secularists are accused of wishing religion to be invisible and not to interfere. The idea that religion belongs only to the private sphere is meaningless to the vast bulk of believers of all religions in the world. The proposition that religion or similar beliefs nevertheless should be autonomous from the state can be said to flow from the requirements of a democratic society which respects human rights including the requirement that each citizen should count equally with all other citizens. But there are still many unresolved questions. For example, is it legitimate to prohibit confessional or religious political parties, as occurs in some countries?[31]

Conscientious objection to military service

Although the 1981 Declaration is silent on this topic, the Human Rights Committee has stated in its General Comment on Article 18 of the ICCPR that it considers that such a right can be inferred from that article, 'inasmuch as the obligation to use lethal force may seriously conflict with the freedom of conscience and the right to manifest one's religion or belief'.[32] The Committee also noted that there is a trend among countries to acknowledge such a right. On the other hand, in some countries, and Greece is a clear example within the European Union, people are sent to prison because they refuse military service, particularly Jehovah's Witnesses, who object to military service everywhere in the world. Such prisoners are prisoners of conscience, recognised and campaigned for by Amnesty International on that basis.[33] Is there a need for the right to refuse to kill to be explicitly recognised in the international standards on conscience? The Human Rights Committee has called for no distinctions to be drawn between conscientious objectors on the basis of their beliefs. It would constitute discrimination if only certain, i.e. religion-based, objections were recognised. Similarly, complaints have been raised in some countries that alternative public service offered to conscientious objectors can be punitive in intent, for example, where such civilian service is longer than the term of military service. It is clear from this study that more work needs to be done at the policy level to secure this freedom.[34] It remains little understood or accepted, particularly where the law provides for conscription. It is notable that progress (France is an example) has come about only when compulsory military service is being phased out. The scope of conscientious objection beyond compulsory military service is even more uncertain. Such issues as a doctor's right to refuse to undertake certain medical procedures including abortions is not acknowledged in the international standards although it may be in different countries.

GENERAL OBSERVATIONS

While the value of this work is not the conclusions that the editors draw but the country entries themselves, nevertheless we may offer some brief general comments, recommendations and suggestions for the future. However, we should emphasise that the exploration of freedom of conscience represented by this study is intended to open the subject for debate, not to pronounce that it is closed by making unqualified assertions or predictions.

The universality of belief

The capacity for belief is a defining feature of the human personality. It is an attribute which finds its social expression in movements, religions, and ideologies throughout human history. It is instructive to note that no society has been identified in this Report whose members profess no beliefs. There is equally no society in which recognition of religious belief is absent, although there were enormous efforts in this century to create such under communism, Albania being the extreme example.

The universality of the claim to freedom of religion and belief is therefore not in doubt. There is no country studied which does not acknowledge the freedom even if it is qualified in principle or practice. All states have policies which address the reality of belief. The central issue, and the purpose of this Report, is to inquire whether or not such state policies are based on contemporary international human rights standards. One answer is that many are not. But another is that few states are uninfluenced by these human rights standards or can hope to prevent such influence over the longer term. Another is whether the cause of freedom of thought and religious freedom is advancing or regressing in the world. It is possible to answer that question in the light of what is covered in this Report and from the reports of the Special Rapporteur on Religious Intolerance, in pessimistic terms. It is, however, also possible, if a longer-term perspective is held, to conclude that progress is and can be made in reducing intolerance. A key indicator must be the increasing acceptance by states of international human rights standards through ratification of the main human rights treaties. Almost three-quarters of the world's states have ratified the International Covenants of the United Nations and a similar percentage of the countries here have ratified these treaties. All members of the United Nations are bound by its Charter which in Article 1 specifically identifies the elimination of discrimination including religious discrimination as a common purpose of the United Nations. In addition, the world community has at the level of formal consensus accepted the indivisibility of human rights, civil, political, economic, social and cultural. The relationship between all human rights, democracy and development is equally part of that consensus.

The task ahead is to deepen the global consensus on the values of human rights, development and democracy as a whole. In other words, the elimination of intolerance and discrimination fuelled by religious or ideological prejudice cannot be separated from the general human rights challenge facing the world.[35]

Religion as a source of conflict

Common concerns in each country are religion and belief as sources of friction or dispute. These concerns parallel or are reflected at the international level, for instance, in the ambiguities of the standards or what are felt to be gaps in the standards, such as proselytising. Fomenting religious hatred is prohibited in international law and states are obliged to enact laws to counter such acts.[36] This Report does not pronounce on the link between religion and conflict, although clearly reflection on that is to be found in many entries, for example, in Algeria, India, Mexico, Northern Ireland and Yugoslavia. Nor is the Report directly concerned with ethnicity and religion or national identity and beliefs, issues of central concern to our contemporary world, although inevitably such themes emerge in various entries. These are the themes of a parallel research project being undertaken by the United States Institute of Peace.[37]

The international standards identify and protect freedom of thought as the core freedom through which human beings search and find their beliefs, whether religious or of another kind. Throughout the history of religions and secular ideologies there has been tension between the exploration or criticism of given beliefs and the fear that the authority of beliefs is undermined by the search for new paths to truth. This inevitable tension is the true site of religious conflict and persecution in history. Heresy and heretics are not only an image from the past. This Report shows that rejection, persecution and discrimination towards those who have taken a different path remain a major cause of intolerance. The Ahmadis in Pakistan and the Bahai's in Egypt, Iran, and Malaysia are some examples as are the Jehovah's Witnesses in several countries of Eastern Europe, in Greece and Singapore.

These are examples of active tension and hostility over religious differences. But there are also examples of the historical legacy of such conflicts to be found everywhere in the world. The divisions in the Christian Church and within Islam have shaped the modern world. Levels of consciousness about differences in Catholic and Protestant faiths vary but remain a potent source of intolerance in parts of Latin America, in Mexico and in

Northern Ireland. The divisions between the Shia and Sunni branches of Islam provide an equally relevant context for the prospect of building tolerance in the Middle East.

Today new religious ideas, expressed through new religious movements and bodies, face a perception that the beliefs expressed are wrong or do not qualify as religious.[38] Although the objection to new religious movements is often expressed in criticism of their methods, it is at bottom a rejection of their freedom of thought which stimulates hostility and restrictions on their organisations and activities. The challenge remains considerable to establish an ethic of tolerance towards those who differ on religious grounds.

The legacy of oppression

The effect of long oppression of belief such as happened in current and former communist states has had a strong impact on religious practice, distorting it and forcing it into limited forms of expression even though the spark remains. In particular, oppression constrains the capacity of a family to preserve its practice of belief and hand it down the generations. Where fear rules that a child may say a word out of turn, or, for whatever reason, reveal an identity which draws the wrath of authorities or, indeed, the neighbours, then the freedoms are eroded. There is an expression which has become a leitmotif of the efforts to produce lasting peace in Ireland, the concept of equality of esteem. The concern to secure equality of esteem between the two ethnically and religiously divided cultures in Northern Ireland has significance, if in varying degrees, for just about every country studied in this project. Ireland also brings out perhaps the most striking feature of these country studies. The inheritance of history, especially the occupation and colonisation of the South by the North, is not a legacy that is long since forgotten. Particularly in matters of thought and beliefs that define the very identity of the human being, it is not surprising that the hurt and the effects of colonisation and imperialism emerge so strikingly from the entries in Asia, Africa, the Middle East and Latin America as well as from the entries on the Eastern European countries occupied by the former Soviet Union. That colonialism was the carrier of Western religion, is an uncomfortable thought to come to terms with. The treatment of indigenous peoples and their beliefs by Christian and Islamic expansion is still part of the burden all the world shares. However, the continuing role of the state in religious intolerance in some countries should not be ignored. China, Viet Nam, Sudan are examples. In Germany, democracy is used as an ideology to impose conformity. It has been dismaying to discover that the state, and some of its politicians and people, are using what are known from the past to be well-worn paths of discrimination and intolerance and of inciting intolerance towards a new religious minority, the Scientologists. Perhaps the fear of a renascent millenarianism, a feature of Nazi Aryan ideology underlies this response, however inappropriate it may be to some new religions.

Women

The themes of women in religion, and women and religion, have a definite dimension in this Report, which were hitherto neglected aspects of the freedoms. It is not an exaggeration to say that, as in so many aspects of life, women, half the human race, have been invisible within churches and religions which have been dominated by men. Women's modes of practice and organisation may be, as with other minorities, invisible and ignored. An important result of women's campaigns over their human rights was the UN General Assembly Resolution of December 1993 on The Elimination of all Forms of Violence Against Women.[39] The resolution rejects the private–public distinction in making clear that states have a duty to prevent and to punish all violence against women.

13

It also declares that no cultural or religious justification can be invoked to justify such violence and calls for the elimination of the harmful effects of 'traditional or customary practices, cultural prejudices and religious extremism' of which women are victims. The entries bring out a range of issues of equity, equality and non-discrimination and the matter of representation and participation in the full life of belief. The ideal might be inclusiveness so that all feel ownership of the religion. However, this creates challenges for the reconciling of authority with acknowledgement of the different modes of belief. Does it raise issues of human rights concern if women have to worship separately from men or are relegated to the back of the congregation during services? These are not easy issues to resolve but they emerge in different countries in this study. One perspective might be to see the question of women in religion as part of a larger debate about democracy within religious communities, movements and churches. Another might be to see the issues as raising queries about the development and direction of religious leadership around the world. Several entries also touch on the matter of homosexuality and the place of lesbians and gay men in religious groups and organisations.

Secular thought

Religion is perennial yet the tendency has been widespread in some secular societies and in materialist world views to see religions as being a prop to support the human being, a comfort, a childish toy to be grown out of. This view evolved in the course of the last two centuries and has a complex history within views of human progress, inevitable improvement, evolution and scientific knowledge. The tradition of secular thought that dismissed religion needs to come to terms with the perennial nature of religions and beliefs, rather than regretting that somehow (despite all odds) it still exists. The labelling of Islam as medieval reflects this thought process somewhat; it also does some considerable injustice to historical realities and complexities of belief systems in centuries before our own.

Just as there is a need for inter-religious dialogue, so there is also a need for the secular and the religious to meet on common ground and learn to articulate a respect for each other. Frequently secular groups have fashioned themselves through the rejection of religion and this constitutes an obstacle to dialogue which needs to be overcome without threatening the underlying nature of secular belief. In the countries of the world where religious nominalism is the norm or where ever larger groups of people are abandoning formal adherence to religion, there is a need to encourage such people to examine the nature of their own secular beliefs, and to articulate them in positive terms, not just as a rejection of the beliefs of others. Self-respect is the first step. Respect for the concept of belief itself is a prerequisite for acceptance of a plural society in which all beliefs are held to be inherently worthy of respect. Then the rejection of other, different versions of the truth need not seem as a licence or a warrant for intolerant attitudes and behaviour.

The role of law

A democratic order which aims to foster tolerance and respect for the freedoms under review cannot function without law. The sampled countries mostly have formal legal protection of these rights. This, however, is only the beginning in terms of seeking an answer to how freedom is protected. Law is generally not seen as a relevant mechanism to most believers for issues affecting them, and, indeed, in some countries it might be seen as an instrument of oppression and government interest rather than a means to gain individual or group rights. In some countries, because of expense or distance, the legal system is out of reach for the majority of people. One possible future could be to envisage greater use of the courts to promote and defend freedom of thought, conscience, religion or belief. However, this must proceed on the basis of a greater general understanding of the nature of these freedoms as well as, for most countries, the need to strengthen the role of national legal institutions in the protection of human rights in general.

The future

There is no difficulty in identifying concrete steps at the international level to enhance the cause of freedom of thought, religion and belief in the world. The priority agreed by all religious and human rights NGOs and observers should be to enhance the mechanism of the Special Rapporteur on Religious Intolerance. The key to a more pro-active role on behalf of those thousands of victims who appeal to him yearly is a proper budget; the current Special Rapporteur has described his present one as derisory. But that is not likely to be achieved in isolation from a greater financial commitment by all states to the current modest UN expenditure on human rights work.

There is a consensus among those concerned that freedom of thought, conscience, religion and belief should be the subject of a new international human rights convention. The disagreement is over what priority should be given to this goal. We adopt the position of the Special Rapporteur that it cannot be an immediate objective. The priority work at the level of international standards should be to make the 1981 UN Declaration better known and to develop education for tolerance. Human rights NGOs and all religious organisations have a major role to play in these tasks. States have already the clearest duties in international law to counter violence and discrimination in matters of belief. NGOs, religious and secular organisations have an equally clear role to highlight violation by states and others, to defend the persecuted and to promote tolerance.

The Special Rapporteur has identified education for tolerance as his key goal and we would agree with this. The role of legal mechanisms in restraining sectarian tension and conflict, for example, is secondary to the role of education and to positive policies supported by the state and faith communities whose policies should be the elimination of discrimination and the promotion of tolerance through dialogue with those who differ. Greater experience of the practice of tolerance can be consolidated by new internationally binding standards.

Intolerance in all its forms of practice – ethnic, racial, national, sexual, cultural, religious – has at its root beliefs about the superiority of the prejudiced and the inferiority of the victim or target of intolerance. Often prejudices and acts of discrimination and intolerance will draw on justifications which merge beliefs as to inferiority or superiority concerning ethnicity, nationality, colour, or religion. In many countries – the former Yugoslavia comes to mind, if not the whole of Europe – it is difficult to isolate what is religious prejudice from intolerance inspired by racism, ethnic or nationalistic feelings and ideologies. Tolerance is indivisible and policies to be pursued to discourage intolerance, hatred and discrimination should begin with that truth. The common core of any such policy has to be education that leads to the acceptance of human equality and diversity with respect to beliefs. In the apt slogan of the European Youth Campaign against Racism, Xenophobia, Anti-Semitism and Intolerance, which marked the Council of Europe's contribution to the 1995 UN Year for Tolerance, the goal is 'All Different All Equal'.

NOTES

1 Although all four freedoms are interconnected there is little separate discussion in this Report of freedom of thought. Freedom of thought has been considered as a separate freedom in work on academic freedom. See the World University Service (WUS) (1993) *Academic Freedom 2: A Human Rights Report*, London: Zed Books.

2 See the complaint of the Special Rapporteur on Religious Intolerance to the Human Rights Commission, E/CN.4/1996/95, 15 December 1995.

3 The most influential was A. Krishnaswami (1960) *The Study of Discrimination in the Matter of Religious Rights and Practices*, for the Sub-Commission on Prevention of Discrimination and Protection of Minorities, New York, E/CN.4/Sub.2/200/Rev.1. See also T. van Boven (1989) *Elimination of All Forms of Intolerance and of Discrimination Based on Religion or Belief*, E/CN.4/Sub.2/1989/32; E. Odio Benito (1986) *Study of the Current Dimensions of the Problems of Intolerance and of Discrimination on Grounds of Religion or Belief*, E/CN.4/Sub.2/1987/26.

4 T. van Boven (1991) 'Advances and Obstacles in Building Understanding and Respect between People of Diverse Religions and Beliefs', *Human Rights Quarterly* vol. 13, p. 437; T. van Boven (1989) 'Religious Freedom in International Perspective: Existing and Future Standards', in *Des Menschen Recht Zwischen Freiheit Und Verantwortung*, Berlin: Ducker and Humbolt; B. Dickson (1995) 'The United Nations and Freedom of Religion', *International and Comparative Law Quarterly* vol. 44, 327; B. G. Tahzib (1996) *Freedom of Religion or Belief: Ensuring Effective International Protection*, The Netherlands: Kluwer.

5 J. D. Van Der Vyver and J. Witte Jnr (eds) (1996) *Religious Human Rights in Global Perspective*, 2 vols, The Hague, Martinus Nijhoff.

6 The first Special Rapporteur appointed in 1986 was Mr Angelo Vidal d'Almeida Ribeiro (Portugal). The post is held at present by Professor Abdelfattah Amor (Tunisia). See p. xxiii.

7 Two regional workshops were held, one on Asia–Pacific in Osaka in conjunction with The International Movement Against Discrimination and Racism (IMADR), and one on the Middle East in London. An international conference to mark the 1995 UN Year For Tolerance was held on Freedom of Religion and Belief, in London, September 1995.

8 The Tandem Project, Minneapolis, USA, was founded in 1985 to promote the 1981 Declaration on the Elimination of All Forms of Intolerance and of Discrimination Based on Religion and Belief.

9 It had originally been planned to include a listing of all religious and human rights groups active in the promotion of these freedoms and in combating intolerance. However, the sheer volume of such groups, national and international, has meant that the idea had to be abandoned for reasons of space.

10 L. B. Sohn (1995) *The Human Rights Movement: From Roosevelt's Four Freedoms to the Interdependence of Peace Development and Human Rights*, Cambridge, MA: Harvard Law School Human Rights Program.

11 The International Bill of Human Rights consists of the Universal Declaration, the International Covenant on Economic, Social and Cultural Rights, and the International Covenant on Civil and Political Rights with its Protocols. For the texts of these instruments on freedom of conscience, see p. v and p. xx, pp. xvii–xxiii.

12 S. C. Neff (1977) 'An Evolving International Legal Norm of Religious Freedom: Problems and Prospect', *California West International Law Journal*, vol. 7, pp. 543–86.

13 See A. J. Milne (1986) *Human Rights and Human Diversity – An Essay in the Philosophy of Human Rights*, London: Macmillan; A. Cassese (1990) *Human Rights in a Changing World*, Oxford: Polity Press; M. Freeman (1996) 'Human Rights, Democracy and Asian Values', *Pacific Review* vol. 9 pp. 309–23; Rhoda Howard (1993) 'Cultural Absolutism and the Nostalgia for Community', *Human Rights Quarterly*, vol. 15, pp. 315–38.

14 Vienna Declaration and Programme for Action Adopted by the World Conference on Human Rights, 25 June 1993, UN Doc. A/Conf.157/23. K. Boyle (1995) 'Stock-Taking on Human Rights: The Vienna World Conference on Human Rights, Vienna 1993' *Political Studies*, vol. 43, pp. 79–95.

15 Adopted by the United Nations General Assembly, Resolution 36/55 of 25 November 1981. For text see pp. xvii–xx.

16 H. A. Jack (1982) 'How the UN Religious Declaration Was Unanimously Adopted', New York, World Conference on Religion and Peace; J. A. Walkate (1989) 'The UN Declaration on the Elimination of All Forms of Intolerance and Discrimination Based on Religion or Belief (1981): An Historical Overview', *Conscience and Liberty*, vol. 2, Winter 1989.

17 General Comment on Article 18 of the Covenant adopted by the Human Rights Committee under Article 40, ICCPR, CRP.2/Rev.1. 20 July 1993, hereafter General Comment.

18 General Comment, para. 4.

19 See also Article 13, International Covenant on Economic, Social and Cultural Rights.

20 Article 14 and see for a thorough international and comparative account of the subject, C. Hamilton (1995) *Family Law and Religion*, London: Sweet and Maxwell.

21 General Comment, para. 4.
22 Ibid., para. 8.
23 Ibid. and see also Article 20, ICCPR.
24 Controversy over the claim by Sudan of precedence for its internal law based on *shariah* over international standards, was rejected in a 1994 resolution of the Human Rights Commission calling on that country to bring its national law into line with the international human rights standards to which it was a party. The vote was thirty-five for with nine against and nine abstentions. China voted against.
25 General Comment, para. 5.
26 The Special Rapporteur on Religious Intolerance has called attention to the abuse of blasphemy laws and proposed a study of the subject from the human rights' standpoint, 1995 Report of the Special Rapporteur, E/CN.4/1995/91, para. 269. See also the discussion in the entries on Pakistan and Great Britain.
27 *Kokkinakis* v. *Greece*, judgment of the European Court of Human Rights, Series A, 1993. The Court stated: 'A distinction had to be drawn between bearing Christian witness and improper proselytism. The former corresponds to true evangelism; the latter represented a corruption or deformation of it which was not compatible with respect for the freedom of thought, conscience and religion of others,' para. 42. See General Comment, para. 8.
28 See entry on the United States.
29 General Comment, para. 9.
30 We are grateful to David Beetham for these thoughts drawn from an unpublished paper. See also D. Beetham and K. Boyle (1995) *Introducing Democracy: Eighty Questions and Answers*, Oxford: Polity Press and UNESCO.
31 The Special Rapporteur drew attention to a trend in prohibiting such political parties, without taking a position on the issue: see his 1995 Report; E/CN.4/1996/95 para. 63.
32 General Comment, para. 11.
33 Amnesty International (1993) *Greece 5,000 Years of Prison: Conscientious Objectors in Greece*, London: Amnesty International Publications.
34 See A. Eide and Mubanga-Chipoya (1983) *Question of Conscientious Objection to Military Service*, UN Commission on Human Rights, E/CN.4/Sub.2/1983/30; see also, Conference of European Churches (1966) *OSCE Human Dimension Seminar, Aspects of Freedom of Religion*, Warsaw, 16–19 April 1966, Hanover.
35 This is also the clear message of Professor Amor, the Special Rapporteur, in his annual reports on religious intolerance to the United Nations Human Rights Commission.
36 K. Boyle (1992) 'Religious Intolerance and Incitement to Religious Hatred', in S. Coliver (ed.) *Striking a Balance: Freedom of Expression, Hate Speech and Non-Discrimination*, London: Article XIX, and University of Essex; J. Symonides (1995) 'Prohibition of Advocacy of Hatred, Prejudice and Intolerance in the United Nations Instruments', in *Democracy and Tolerance: Proceedings of the International Conference, Seoul, Republic of Korea*, Paris: UNESCO, pp. 79–100.
37 United States Institute for Peace is an independent, non-partisan, federally funded research institute. Its Working Group on Religion, Ideology and Peace, director David Little, is publishing a six-part study of how and why certain religions and similar beliefs create or contribute to hostility and conflict as well as why they are frequently a cause of discrimination and persecution. The editors acknowledge here their indebtedness to the reports published on Ukraine and Sri Lanka in this series.
38 E. Barker (1989) *New Religious Movements: A Practical Introduction*, 4th edn, London: HMSO, see pp. 144–48.
39 Resolution 48/104. A Special Rapporteur on Violence Against Women has been appointed by the UN Human Rights Commission.

Africa

REGIONAL INTRODUCTION

Religion is only one source of conflict in contemporary Africa, where many troubles are caused by other factors such as forms of neo-colonialism, the ambitions of war lords, or by a kind of ethnic consciousness ('tribalism'), which is really a modern invention. In pre-colonial Africa, ethno-linguistic groups were not identical with political units. Colonial governments used 'tribes' as building blocks to understand and govern the complex societies which surrounded them. The post-colonial inheritance of manipulation can be seen in the genocide of a million people in Rwanda.

Many of the conflicts in contemporary Africa are rooted in social and economic difficulties, a struggle for a small and ever diminishing cake, a struggle in which underdevelopment is perpetuated through cycles of poverty and violence. Tribe and religion have often been used as rallying cries by politicians or war lords. This is not only true of Christianity and Islam. Mobutu's programme of authenticity in Zaire was a transparently cynical attempt to utilise pride in an attachment to traditional culture to bolster a corrupt and unpopular government.

The polarisation of Christians and Muslims in sub-Saharan Africa was an unintended consequence of colonial rule. Colonial administrators tended to respect Islamic culture. They admired its tradition of literacy and centralised states because they feared that offending Muslim susceptibilities would lead to revolution and even to some kind of pan-Islamic movement and they therefore tended to exclude Christian missionaries from Muslim areas. However, the much greater opportunities available in the early years of independence were open only to the Western-educated pupils who had been through mission schools.

Over the last fifteen years or so the religious map of Africa has been transformed by the rise of fundamentalism and revivalism, both Christian and Muslim. Where these are found in geographic proximity to each other the results can be explosive. The vast expansion of Christian fundamentalism over the last fifteen years is often associated with what has been called the Gospel of Prosperity, which has obvious appeal in situations of increasing poverty and disorder. There is often a belief that the Endtime is near, which tends to discourage development projects, as does a proliferation of supernatural explanations. The rise of Islamic revivalism, itself part of a much wider movement beyond Africa, raises some of the sharpest issues concerning religious freedom on the continent. Sometimes fundamentalist and revivalist movements reflect despair at poverty and unemployment; sometimes their proponents do not so much inflict as suffer terror or repression.

The now defunct apartheid regime in South Africa justified itself in religious terms; its members perceived themselves as Christian. However, one of the most significant sources of unflagging and effective opposition against apartheid came from within a wide range of religions, including Christian, Muslim, Hindu and Jewish, now working together in the new South Africa. In several parts of Africa, the state has persecuted religious movements, including some independent churches. Most states are members of the Organisation of African Unity and are parties to the African Convention on Human and Peoples' Rights. However, the implementing system of the Convention, the African Commission on Human Rights, has yet to make a major impact on human rights consciousness on the continent.

A subtle but prevalent form of the violation of human rights in terms of their cultural rights and of their identity as peoples has been the contempt commonly shown by 'world religions' such as Christianity and Islam for indigenous African cultural and spiritual traditions and world views. Statistics which purport to count traditionalists are completely unreliable. Traditional religion is no longer the individual's primary religious identification although many of its concepts still flourish, for instance, in the fear of witchcraft and the consultation of diviners in time of crisis. This kind of accommodation has always been typical of African Islam. Nor should one overlook the increasing phenomenon of African acculturation in both established and independent Christian churches throughout the continent.

ALGERIA

Algeria	
GDP (US$bn)	36
Population	26,100,000
Annual population growth (%)	2.8
Urban population (%)	53
Working population (%)	24
Literacy (%)	57.4
Ratifications	1; 2, 2(a), 2(b); 3; Af

Algeria, a colony of France from 1830–1962, has endured one of the longest and most difficult colonisation periods of any Arab country. The beginning and the end of the colonial period were marked by a curious symmetry. For example, France's invasion of Algeria resulted in a massive uprooting of tribal populations whose land was seized. Similarly, during the war of decolonisation, the French government uprooted entire villages in order to fight nationalists more effectively. This, along with a protracted guerrilla warfare which lasted nearly eight years (1954–62), contributed to the erosion of the social fabric and traditional values.

Women have been the symbolic centre of the struggle between coloniser and colonised. There has been strong resistance to the education of women for various reasons, including the association of the home with a language which was not foreign and with customs presided over by women as the keepers of a threatened ancient Islamic culture. The veiling of women has also become a cultural strategy expressing resistance to colonial power, but side by side with this ideology, women – unveiled – were used in the armed struggle for liberation. After independence, the perceived need for re-inculturation forced women back into domestic roles in spite of promises to respect the equality established during the time of crisis. In 1966, the new president Colonel Houari Boumédienne declared: 'our society is Islamic . . . we are in favour of the evolution and the progress of women . . . but this evolution must not be the cause of the corruption of our society'.

A sense of displacement thus pervades Algerians' conception of themselves and has, in the past five years, taken on the characteristics of an identity crisis in which religion plays a significant role.

Ethnic and cultural factors

Algeria's 26.1 million people form an ethnically mixed population where Arabs and Berbers (the original inhabitants) have mingled together over the past twelve centuries. Berber-speakers constitute 25 per cent of the Algerian population. Although it is not always evident who is a Berber or who is an Arab, people in the Kabylie region generally believe that they are 'pure' Berbers. Berber-speaking people are also found in the Aures mountains, in the southern region of the M'zab and throughout the Sahara desert, home of the Tuareg. People of Berber–Kabyl origin tend to be heavily represented in government and in the professions.

In the wake of an ill-formulated linguistic policy adopted by the state to make Arabic the official language, an opposition movement formed in the Grande Kabylie and at Algiers University in the mid-1970s to demand that the Berber dialect from the Kabylie be adopted as a second national language. This movement has become known as the Mouvement Culturel Berbere (MCB) which finds its political expression in the Rassemblement pour la Culture et la Democracie. However, most Kabylie people prefer to support the more established and inclusive Front of Socialist Forces led by Ait Ahmed, one of seven historic leaders of the Algerian Revolution.

Media portrayal of the Berber inhabitants of the Kabylie as 'secular' and anti-Islamists ignores the complex ways in which Islamist ideology has intersected with social class and ethnicity. For instance, one of the artisans of an 'anti-Western' campaign (which began in 1970) and an advocate of the cleansing of Algerian culture of its corrupt 'Western' influence was the Berber Mouloud Kasim Anit Belkacem, Minister of Religious Education and Religious Affairs from 1970–77. Mr Kasim was also a strong advocate of 'arabisation' or making Arabic the national language.

Algeria is a predominantly Sunni Muslim society. Islam came to Algeria in the eighth century in its sweep from the Middle East across North Africa and towards the Iberian peninsula. Before Islam was established, the native Berber population practised customary beliefs although the elites tended to be Christian; St Augustine was a native of Algeria, then a province of the Roman Empire. During the colonial era, the French used the White Fathers to attempt to convert Algerians to Catholicism. Some converted willingly, but most were children who had lost their parents in the war of conquest and in the famines of the 1860s; Msgr Lavigerie raised them as Christians to break their links with their Muslim relatives. In contrast, a century later, during the war of independence, the late cardinal Archbishop of Algiers became an impartial advocate for reciprocal understanding and from 1971 was influential in Rome's inter-religious dialogue.

French and Jewish minorities left in large numbers upon Algeria's independence from France in 1962. French and other European nationals in Algeria today are generally associated with embassies, businesses and corporations. French people who chose to remain in Algeria after independence are now being pushed out by the violence of the last three years directed at 'foreigners' by a radical faction of the Islamist movement, the Armed Islamic Group. In 1994–95, several French and Spanish nuns and priests were killed and twelve Croatian and Bosnian workers of the Catholic faith were murdered in 1993. Those who convert to Christianity do so secretly and worship in private as conversion is unacceptable in the general community. Despite the minute size of the Jewish community today, anti-Semitism still features in public discourse and the media, according to Jewish organisations.

Political and economic background

After independence and up to 1990, Algeria had a one-party political system; although the wartime Front of National Liberation became the governing party, the president and his associates formulated policy. The army kept a close watch on government matters. A National People's Assembly was – and still is – Algeria's legislative body; the judiciary was not independent of the government; the press was state-controlled and opposition was not allowed.

The new state first established a socialist economy inspired by the former Yugoslavia but in 1965, after a *coup d'état* brought Colonel Boumédienne to power, socialism took an indigenous turn, labelled as 'Islamic socialism'. The economy continued to be state-controlled and private enterprise was tightly regulated. Although the state was determined to avoid dependence on the West, it still remained dependent on oil and natural gas revenues.

In 1978, after Colonel Boumédienne's death, President Chadli Bendjedid began to slowly liberalise the economy while at the same time affirming Algeria's commitment to socialism. But by the mid-1980s, mismanagement and corruption became a matter of public concern as the international oil crisis reduced Algeria's income and revealed the weaknesses of the economy. Foreign debt of $26 billion shocked a nation accustomed to thinking that Algeria's socialist economy, while restrictive, was sound. Austerity measures seemed to have enriched a small class of people – the 'Hezb Franca', tied to the state apparatus – and to have impoverished the majority. An International Monetary Fund-negotiated programme of structural adjustment resulted in a dramatic rise in commodities prices which took heavy toll of the middle class and the poor. Before this economic crisis, Algerians had enjoyed free education and medicine, reasonably priced medical drugs and inexpensive transportation. Such services compensated for relatively low salaries and kept social unrest at bay.

Increased unemployment, extremely rapid population growth and a lack of political participation led to youth riots in 1988 which called for the democratisation of Algerian society. Furthermore, there had been an unsuccessful, localised Islamist armed uprising in 1987, directed by Mustafa Boyali who had created the Mouvement Islamique Algérien in an attempt to unify and coordinate the many loose *jama'at* or Islamist groups that began to appear after Boumédienne's death. These two significant events paved the way for the 1989 constitution which guaranteed, among other things, freedom of association and speech. Within months, over fifty parties were formed and scores of newspapers in French and Arabic appeared across the nation. The Front of Socialist Forces, banned in the early 1960s, re-emerged. The most noteworthy new party that emerged was the Islamic Salvation Front (FIS), aimed at establishing a new form of government based on Islamic or *shariah* law.

Constitutional protection of human rights

Algeria's legal system is essentially modelled on the French. There is no legal prohibition in the 1989 constitution against the exercise of one's religion. However, as Article 2 states that 'Islam is the state religion', this implies that proselytising by other religions is prohibited, as is apostasy. Article 28 makes all citizens equal before the law regardless of birth, race, sex, opinion or 'any other condition, personal, or social circumstance'. Article 39 guarantees 'freedom of speech, association, and assembly' and Article 40 guarantees freedom to create 'associations of a political nature', thereby opening the way for a multi-party system. Article 35 guarantees freedom of conscience and of opinion. Insulting or inciting hatred of one or more people belonging to an ethnic or philosophical group or to a particular religion is punishable under the Penal Code.

There is no provision in the constitution for Islamic law or *shariah* tribunals. This has been a source of concern to Islamists who argue that a state cannot have Islam as its religion without also implementing the *shariah*. Family law, based on the *shariah*, is administered by family courts. However, the family law may violate the constitutional guarantee of equality before the law regardless of factors such as sex. The 1984 Family Code prevents women from contracting marriage without a guardian, limits their right to divorce and condones polygamy, among other things.

The Ministry of Religious Affairs protects places of worship of the Christian and Jewish communities. The Ministry also appoints *imam*s to state and privately funded mosques. The government noted, in its response in 1993 to the Special Rapporteur on Religious Intolerance, that places of worship had been used by religious figures both for incitement to hatred for people of science and learning, and for preaching tolerance and rejecting extremist political ideologies. The government has removed *imam*s for preaching that rejects the government's approach and security forces reportedly monitor Friday sermons at the larger mosques. Some of the pro-government *imam*s have been assassinated.

Ideological spectrum

Algeria is marked by competing ideologies: some religion-based, others secular (communist/Trotskyist or liberal), still others secular but ethnic group-based. Religious groups and associations – such as the Ennahda (Renaissance) of Abdallah Djaballah and Hamas (Fervour) of Mahfoud Nahnah – exist which, although intent upon the application of the *shariah* have not resorted to violence or advocated the overthrow of the government. However, the most important ideology is the one put forth by the Islamic Salvation Front (FIS).

The Islamist movement in Algeria is a response to two things. First, there is a perception that Algerian culture has been dislocated by an industrial–modernist state which hid behind the hollow and contradictory ideology of 'Islamic socialism'. This state created two generations of people, one feeling uncomfortable in French, the other uncomfortable in Arabic as a functioning language. That Algerian culture seemed to have been devalued was reinforced by messages emanating from television broadcasts which reached even poor neighbourhoods via satellite. The second was the state's history of disastrous economic management and evidence of corruption at the highest levels of government which compounded the sense of deprivation as well as betrayal that individuals experienced.

FIS's ideology is a mixture of the ideology of the Ulama Movement of the 1930s with its conservative social code and its advocacy of a return to religion as a guide for daily action, as well as ideas emanating from the Pakistan Islamist Maududi and the Egyptian Muslim Brotherhood. These external sources explain both the FIS's and the Armed Islamic Group's insistence on declaring the Algerian state to be in a condition of heresy (*takfir*) which requires concerned Muslims to engage in a struggle (*jihad*) against it. In addition, these sources allow the Islamist movement to declare the larger society to be in a state of ignorance (*jahiliya*) reminiscent of the ante-Islamic era. To save society from reverting to this condition, re-Islamisation is in order. This explains the advocacy of the veil for women and the enforcement of rules of proper conduct for a 'good Muslim'.

The political and economic programme of the FIS lacks specificity. It is, however, predicated on a conception of man – both generic and real man as it excludes women – that extols virtue in accordance with the *shariah*. Thus, in the future Islamic republic, there will be no need for the police because the God-fearing individual does not need to be policed. The political system will be composed of a 'parliament' (*majlis shura*) composed of men chosen for their personal qualities. The head of government is the 'emir' who must also display qualities that befit his position as a leader of a Muslim community. Private ownership will be respected and upheld. National sovereignty over natural resources will be upheld although there is no indication that nationalisation will be decreed. Women's role in the future Islamic republic would be to stay at home and rear children even if this meant paying women to do so. Covering the head is emphasised; FIS members have offered free veils to young women in poor neighbourhoods in Algiers.

Elections and the Islamic Salvation Front

In 1990 the Islamic Salvation Front (FIS) won municipal elections and in 1992 it won 25 per cent of the National People's Assembly seats. A second round of national elections which would have given it the majority of seats was cancelled and the military stepped in. The success of the FIS was due to a combination of factors including citizens' discontent with the ruling party, high abstention rate, coercion of rural voters, and a general scepticism by the public towards a large number of previously unknown parties.

A state of emergency was declared in 1992. The leaders of FIS, Ali Benhadj and Abassi Madani, were arrested and the party was banned. The FIS responded by ordering its Army of Islamic Salvation to carry out assassinations of members of the government, the police and the military as well as their relatives. At first slow, the government's reaction gradually intensified as its troops and security services began using torture and speedy executions to hunt down members of the Front. In addition to government response and repression, a vigilante group calling itself the Organisation of Free Algerians targeted and killed relatives of individuals known or suspected to be members of the Front.

A radical faction of the FIS also emerged in 1993 – the Armed Islamic Group – with the aim of bringing the government down by terrorising the civilian population. The Armed Islamic Group has targeted foreigners working in Algeria, journalists, members of the government, women and educational institutions. More than 700 schools have been destroyed within three years on grounds that their teaching is not religious. Acts of sabotage against power stations, bridges, telephone wires and government warehouses have become a common occurrence throughout the country.

New multi-party, presidential elections in 1995 were intended to help the government gain legitimacy in the eyes of the world community, particularly of the West. The FIS joined in an opposition front with other groups, and called for the election to be boycotted. There were also calls for the closing of prison camps, the liberation of political prisoners and an amnesty for some political crimes.

However, 75 per cent of the electorate voted, according to official figures. As the FIS is banned, most its voters were said to have supported the moderate Islamist party Hamas, which received 25 per cent of the votes. Thus the current president of the military government, Zeroual, was returned with a greater percentage of the vote than the FIS had won at the 1992 elections. The secular Kabylie leader received 10 per cent. While the people do not condone state violence, the government is seen as the only institution that can restore order. In November 1996, a constitutional referendum on banning political parties founded on religion returned official figures of 85 per cent in favour.

Restrictions on free expression and manifestation of beliefs

The military-dominated government imposed considerable restrictions on the media. In 1994, for instance, a decree was issued prohibiting publication of information about political violence and security-related issues from any source other than the official one. Government raids on Arabic and French language newspapers were also reported.

As well as these restrictions, the many people who sustain Algeria's press, its diverse publications and vigorous intellectual and artistic life have been seriously depleted by the assassinations of journalists, editors, writers, artists and musicians, intellectuals, academics, teachers, health professionals – in short, anyone whose writings and activities indicate (or are held to indicate) that they do not conform to the strictures of extremism.

The atmosphere of fear and intimidation as well as the experience of harassment and violence from both religious extremists and the government have created conditions in which non-conformist convictions may be concealed and customary activities curtailed. The current socio-political unrest has made it difficult for individuals to practise their religion as they see fit. Both the Islamic Salvation Front and the Armed Islamic Group have attempted to enforce a strict code of conduct. Women feel the pressure to wear a style of clothing that does not necessarily reflect their religious convictions but may help them to avoid harassment or even death. Conspicuous worship has also created invidious comparisons between Muslims who prefer to pray at home after working hours and those who interrupt their work to fulfil their religious duty.

Women as targets of religiously motivated violence

Certain types of crimes that used to be rare have become frequent: killing and raping women. While men are killed because of their functions or their political affiliation, women are assassinated as women. The Observatoire National des Droits de l'Homme, a human rights group, has identified over 400 women who were killed or wounded in 1993–94; this figure is deemed conservative. The number of women who have been raped is difficult to ascertain as many women do not report a condition that evokes strong feelings of shame for themselves and their relatives. Women have been killed for not wearing the veil, refusing to engage in temporary marriage (*mut'a*, an Iranian custom unfamiliar to Algerians), being married to foreign men, working, and living alone. Victims have been as young as 9 although old women have also been raped and killed. Often women are tortured and killed. Recovered bodies of female victims frequently display signs of mutilation.

The FIS spokesmen abroad often deny ordering the death of women and claim that the government has deliberately accused them of these crimes in order to embarrass them. However, women who have escaped from camps where they were imprisoned by Islamist men have told otherwise. The leaders of the FIS, before their arrest, had made statements about women and their place in the future Islamic republic that have contributed to the climate of intolerance, if not misogyny. Two professional women in Algiers have reported that their names were called and distributed in an Islamist mosque as enemies of the people; both later received death threats.

EGYPT

Egypt	
GDP (US$bn)	34
Population	59,000,000
Annual population growth (%)	2.4
Urban population (%)	44
Working population (%)	29
Literacy (%)	49.1
Ratifications	1; 2; 3; 4; Af

Egypt, at 59 million people the largest Arab state, has a mixed economy and has been undergoing structural adjustment from state-controlled economic structures to a market economy. Per capita income has been declining since 1988, widening the gap between rich and poor. Education levels are lower for women than for men, and up to 90 per cent of rural women are illiterate. There are few cultural and linguistic differences among Egyptians generally, such as Berber-speakers to the west.

Religious and belief composition

The large majority of Egyptians are Sunni Muslims, Shias being estimated at only 5,000. Jews number only a few hundreds, but there are 6 million Egyptian Christians, according to official statistics, or 5 per cent of the population, a conservative estimate according to the Christian denominations who consider the figure is closer to 10 million. Catholic (including Eastern Rite churches) and Protestant denominations could account for around a million people. Adherents of the Egyptian Coptic Orthodox Church are the largest Christian community in the Arab world, dating from the beginnings of Christianity before the introduction of Islam. Egypt is a singular case of a society growing in democracy but where little progress has been made in stemming official and unofficial intolerance and discrimination – actively promoted by Islamic thinkers and extra-legal Islamist militant groups – against a religious minority and against dissenters from Islam.

The political system

Egypt's partial independence from British colonial rule began in 1922 and full independence finally came in 1953. In the mid-1970s, Egypt became a presidential republic, its political system based on restricted pluralism. In 1993, President Hosni Mubarak was elected for a third six-year term. The ruling National Democratic Party (NDP) dominates the People's Assembly and the Shura (consultative) Council, maintains control over the major media and state economic establishments, organises general elections and controls the committee which approves the establishment of any new political parties. The capacity of the twelve legal opposition parties to voice their opinions is extremely limited as their winnable seats are restricted to less than a third of the total. Many boycotted the elections in 1990. The NDP therefore controls all legislation, amendment of the constitution and the re-election of the president. Political parties based on religion – among other characteristics – are prohibited by law. Consequently, one of Egypt's main opposition groups, the Muslim Brotherhood, cannot establish a legitimate political party.

Freedoms of association and peaceful assembly have been affected by the long period of emergency rule since 1981. Since 1993, security forces have cracked down alike on militant Muslim extremists – principally the al-Gama'a al-Islamiya or Islamic Group – and on non-violent Islamist groups to counter episodes of urban terrorism and political assassination. Islamists have been tried before military courts, administratively detained, tortured and some have died in custody, according to the Egyptian Organisation for Human Rights.

The Muslim Brotherhood has worked for an Islamic state through democratic means and has apparently been allowed to operate openly and even participate in elections although it is not a lawful political party. However, the government reportedly saw it as becoming tied to the extremist cause. In the months preceding the elections in late November 1995, security forces rounded up 200 Muslim Brotherhood activists and just before the elections, fifty-four Brotherhood members were sentenced to imprisonment for 'holding secret meetings and preparing anti-government meetings' associated with observing the polls. The government was returned to power, its credibility damaged by condemnation of vote rigging. The Egyptian Organisation for Human Rights has called on the president to allow Islamists to carry out peaceful political activities without harassment.

Constitutional and legal system

Egypt's constitution, whose proclamation affirmed human freedom and dignity, states that the official religion is Islam and that the principles of the Islamic *shariah* are the primary source of law. Other sources such as the Napoleonic Code are also a basis for Egyptian law. The *shariah* is the source of family, inheritance and personal status law, applying only to Muslims. Egypt ratified the international covenants in 1982. Egypt's constitution makes such international treaties part of internal law and it has also become a party to the African Charter of Human and Peoples' Rights. Egypt's ratification of the ICCPR and CEDAW was made on the assumption that they are compatible with the *shariah*.

Article 40 of the constitution guarantees equality among citizens, allowing no discrimination on the basis of race, origin, language, religion or belief. Government policy allows all citizens without distinction by race, religion or colour to attend education, associate in clubs and societies and access state facilities and services, among other things. Article 46 also guarantees freedom of belief and freedom of religious observance, while Article 19 states that religious education is a basic component of public educational curricula. Article 47 guarantees freedom of opinion.

Although certain legislative measures could be contrary to Egypt's own constitution and human rights agreements ratified by the government, some law reform has taken place and the Supreme Constitutional Court – Egypt has an independent judiciary – has ruled in several cases that some legislative provisions are unconstitutional under Article 40.

In October 1994, President Mubarak annulled the 1978 'Law for Protecting Social Peace and the Internal Front'. This law, which has been considered inconsistent with freedom of thought and belief, had been used to outlaw political and ideological groups. Activists were banned from political activity or appointment to the top state posts, especially those influential in forming public opinion. Opponents had also been banned from office in trade unions and membership of political parties.

The president has also amended other laws contrary to freedom of conscience including the 1980 'Law for Protecting Values from Debasement' or Shame Law. This statute had committed each citizen to the 'duty of protecting religious values' and outlawed such acts as 'denying divinely revealed laws and contradicting their teachings'. Those who carried out such acts could be prosecuted in the Court of Values and, if convicted, banned from holding public posts and from political activity.

Discrimination and questions of minority status

The presence in Egypt of armed terrorist groups aiming to overthrow the government to create an Islamic state has had unfortunate repercussions on all Egyptian civilians, notably on any whose beliefs, practices and expression do not conform to a conservative Muslim norm. Measures used or introduced by the state to control community strife and terrorism have allegedly been exploited by officials and by civilians as vehicles for intolerance against Christians – notably the Copts – as well as against adherents of non-conforming beliefs, including those with secular beliefs and atheists. These people have become the targets for religious discrimination and violence born of religious intolerance. Questions have been raised by the (UN) Human Rights Committee about the adequacy of protection afforded by the state to ensure the cultural life and even the survival of such minority groups as mandated by Article 27 of the ICCPR, so long as the government continues to deny that such minorities exist.

Egyptian government policy supports the concepts of national unity and equal rights for all citizens. All its citizens have the right to Egyptian nationality and all may claim their rights under law. The concept of a religious minority is highly controversial as it is considered to endow the status of second-class citizen, with lesser rights. Members of numerical minorities such as the Copts are thus reported to regard the term with at least ambivalence. The Egyptian government cites the Coptic Pope Shenouda III as remarking that the terms 'majority' and 'minority' are used to imply discrimination, separation and differentiation 'unbecoming to the sons of Egypt, homeland of all'.

While Nubians, to the south, had been acknowledged as an ethnic minority in Egypt's first report under the ICCPR in 1984, the government definition of a minority – 'an ethnic, linguistic, social, cultural or geographical distinct entity' – does not include religion, unlike the ICCPR Article 27 statement of the rights of ethnic, religious and linguistic minorities.

Penal legislation affecting freedom of belief

There are several laws dating from the 1940s which were introduced to combat political ideologies such as communism. Article 98B of the Penal Code outlaws the spread or instigation by any means of ideas calling for changing the political principles of the constitution, the social order or advocating that one social class should control other social classes.

Article 98F of the code penalises the exploitation of religion to promote or advocate extremist ideologies to stir up sedition, to disparage or belittle any divinely revealed religion or its adherents, or to prejudice national unity or social harmony. Similar provisions apply to the spreading of ideas against the basic principles of the state's socialist ruling system.

Baha'i adherents considered to be heretics and others regarded as (if not actually) atheists have been convicted and imprisoned under Article 98 for opposing the basic principles of the ruling system of the country and promoting extremist ideas which disparage or belittle divinely revealed religions. The government considers that certain legislation – such as Article 98, Article 160 (disrupting religious observance and damaging religious premises or artefacts), Article 161 (open attacks on religions with public rites by publishing distorted versions of their scriptures or ridicule by publicly mimicking their celebrations) and Article 176 (public incitement to hold a religious community in hatred or contempt) – contains restrictions necessary to combat communal tension. The state regards them as legitimated by CERD Article 4 which requires incitement to racial hatred to be prohibited by law.

Freedom of thought, conscience and belief

Farag Fouda – author of a paper on minorities and human rights in Egypt and later assassinated by political Islamists – wrote that freedom of belief, according to international human rights standards, is an ultimate one which includes human beings' right to believe in whatever they want or to change their religion as they wish, at any time. This concept has not been acknowledged in the different Egyptian constitutions or, indeed, among Egyptians generally, including intellectuals. The common understanding in Egypt of the meaning of freedom of belief is that of the right to choose among the different accepted religions. The Supreme Constitutional Court confirmed this interpretation in a ruling issued in 1975 which limited the religions protected by the constitution to the three 'divinely revealed religions' only: Islam, Christianity and Judaism.

Discrimination against Baha'i adherents

The most prominent example which signifies the discrimination against members of non-accepted religions and beliefs is that of the Baha'i religious group who number up to 10,000 people. The Baha'i beliefs are not recognised as a religion in Egypt, and members are prosecuted by the official religious establishment, Al-Azhar, which considers them infidels and apostates from Islam. The Baha'i community has long experienced discrimination and intolerance. A presidential decree in 1960 ordered that all Baha'i communities should be dissolved, and banned the practice of their religious rituals and the circulation of literature promoting their beliefs. Their assets were confiscated and given to another association teaching the Qur'an.

In 1993, the (UN) Human Rights Committee enquired about the right to choose a religion in Egypt and the right not only to hold a belief but also to manifest it. The Committee drew attention to the rights of Buddhists and other members of non-revealed religions. Noting particularly that the Supreme Court had apparently declared the Baha'i faith to be a deviation or apostasy from Islam and that therefore its followers could be deprived of protection to which they were entitled, it was pointed out by a member of the Committee that this was incompatible with ICCPR Article 18. The limitations allowed by Article 18 (3) were said not to extend to the Baha'is as they did not present an objective threat to public order; they did not engage in violent activities nor did they organise large and disorderly gatherings and they did not advocate violence. It was considered particularly dangerous for a state to affirm that an individual disagreeing with the authorities constituted a threat to public order and that their rights could therefore be restricted. Concern was also expressed that Baha'is, being thought heretics, might be accused of distorting scripture and thus liable to imprisonment under Article 161 of the Penal Code.

Baha'is cannot marry Muslim women and if a Muslim man decides to convert to Baha'ism, he has to divorce his Muslim wife (the same restrictions apply to Christians). The question of the status of children born to such unrecognised marriages has been raised by the Human Rights Committee, as the Juveniles Act did not permit distinctions or discrimination among juveniles on religious grounds. Egypt was one of the first nations to sign the Convention on the Rights of the Child. However, Egyptian courts have apparently upheld the practice of not allowing Muslims to change their identity document to record their conversion to another religion. Consequently, they are obliged to register their children as Muslims and once so registered the children must receive Islamic instruction in school, however contrary to their parents' wishes.

Discrimination against secular beliefs

Intellectuals suspected of holding atheist views have also been prosecuted by the religious and judicial authorities. In 1990 the Islamic Research Institute of Al-Azhar presented a petition calling for the confiscation of a novel by Alaa Hamed, entitled *A Distance in a Man's Mind*. The Azhar petition claimed that the novel included atheist and pagan ideas denying religions, and that thus the novel could be considered a call to revolt against the basic social structure.

Al-Azhar called for Hamed to be tried under Article 98F of the Penal Code. After precautionary detention for several months, the novelist was tried by the State Security Court which sentenced him in December 1991, together with the publisher and the owner of the print shop, to an eight-year imprisonment and fine. The court justified its sentence by saying that the novel represented a threat to national unity and social peace. However, the sentence was not served as it was not ratified by the Prime Minister. A further prison sentence was given in 1992 for Hamed's allegedly blasphemous novel, *The Mattress*, because a love scene took place upon a prayer rug; this was regarded as showing contempt for Islam. This conviction also resulted in the author losing his job.

Discrimination against the Coptic Christians

There have been particular historical episodes when Copts faced oppression and discrimination which usually coincided with eras of economic crisis and general political oppression in which, though these difficulties left their effects on all Egyptians, they impinged more severely on the Copts. Copts in the rural south are often the target of violence in towns and villages where extremists advocate the creation of an Islamic state.

In the current political climate, there is worrying evidence of a trend which may lead to the Copts being treated as a separate, discriminated-against minority, not just as Egyptians who practise a different faith from the Muslim majority. Episodes of discrimination and intolerance towards Coptic Christians which go unchecked, however, reinforce the concept of their community as a group with lesser rights.

Laws, administrative orders and common practices which legitimise discrimination against the Copts and other Christians are reported to include the following:

1 The lack of equality in relation to the right to build and maintain places for worship. All Christian churches in Egypt are subject to an 1856 law, sole legal remnant of the Ottoman era, known as the 'Hamaiouni Line'. This law sets various restrictions against the building of new churches or restoration, renewal or even maintenance of existing ones without what is now a presidential decree. Although building regulations also apply to mosques, the application procedure for Christians is cumbersome and marked by lengthy delays. While Egyptian jurists have pressed for an equitable modern law, the government continues to state that the old law is necessary for the security of churches. However, it has notably failed to protect the Copts from attacks and destruction of churches and church property by Islamist extremists.
2 Muslim judges rule in civil cases related to Christians, taking notice only of Islamic religious law. In the case of a civil marriage between a Muslim and Christian couple,

the courts' ruling is said to be usually in favour of the Muslim partner, granting the right to keep the children allegedly because Islam is 'the best religion', and because other religions 'develop pagan practices'.

3 Although Copts have been the educated elite and participate at all levels of Egyptian society – and one is the former Secretary-General of the United Nations – they are proportionally unrepresented in the most senior posts in Egypt's public life. According to one study, there are fourteen Coptic deputy ministers among 600, ten heads of public sector companies among 360, two ambassadors among 127. There is not a single Coptic governor, head of university or even a dean of faculty.

4 Some Coptic endowments or property have been taken over by the Ministry of Endowments. Their returns are spent for non-Coptic purposes.

5 The publicly-funded Al-Azhar University is open to Muslim students alone, although other branches of knowledge than Islamic religion are taught there. Coptic educational institutes receive no public funding. Copts have fewer opportunities to join teacher training institutes, to be nominated for official scholarships abroad or to be accepted in military academies. Egyptian universities lack courses related to the Coptic era in Egypt and Coptic language, literature, archaeology or art.

6 According to human rights monitors, the authorities offer incentives for those who convert to Islam, while those who convert to Christianity, or follow Christian missionaries, may be subject to arbitrary detention under emergency laws. In several cases, those who converted from Islam to Christianity have allegedly been tortured by state security officials. Such officials have also allegedly harassed, intimidated and threatened Christians who are in contact with their Muslim peers. Contention about conversion has also brought into being people from both sides who are willing to use force to 'rescue' or reclaim those who are considered their adherents. A human rights monitoring group has also claimed that rape has been used to bring Christian girls within the Muslim fold, because that makes it almost impossible for them to return to their families without harm because of loss of family honour.

Promotion of sectarian intolerance and violence

Sectarian violence has grown in Egypt since 1972, when Islamist groups formed their own military wings against the state, escalating in the past twenty years into massacres and assassinations for sectarian reasons. In 1992 more than thirty-seven attacks took place against Christians in eleven Egyptian provinces. These attacks involved killings, injuries, forcing Christians to pay 'tribute' (*jizya*), burning or destroying houses, shops and churches, death threats, banning Copts from practising their religious rituals, not allowing them to celebrate weddings or to mourn, and limiting their trade and businesses.

Political Islamist groups have grown in strength over the past ten years. They have influenced school curricula, the education process and the media, encouraging the development of religious extremism and sectarianism in educational, religious and media bodies. It has become very common to find articles in newspapers or cassettes on sale which disparage the Christian religion and the Coptic Church, or which declare that the Bible is not the word of God. Some official television religious programmes directly criticise the Christian faith, allegedly referring to Copts as pagans.

Islamists have targeted political opponents among thinkers, politicians, writers and novelists, stigmatising them as apostates or infidels who offend Islam in the interest of Western 'crusaders'. They have also sued intellectuals over charges of violating Islamic belief, cases which are reported by Islamist-oriented newspapers in a sensational way, thus reducing the impact of such thinkers on public opinion. Writers have been attacked, intimidated and forced to withdraw from or avoid open debate, as standing firm may lead to assassination. The fate of Farag Fouda and the Algerian intellectuals are etched on the mind of every writer, a recollection which encourages self-censorship.

In contrast, the many Islamist groups publish their views through articles in newspapers, issue cheap books and cassette tapes, distribute leaflets and make speeches in mosques. As a place of worship may not be used for anti-government speeches, the Ministry of Religious Affairs is said to propose themes and monitor sermons but its attempt to combat extremism may have little effect in practice on unauthorised mosques.

Political Islamists have also mobilised the Al-Azhar University to use its legal authority to censor a large number of books and art. However, though President Mubarak has given public support to Al-Azhar's censorship role, its authority has been resisted by the government and the courts in some instances. When a delegation of Al-Azhar scholars confiscated books at the 1992 Cairo International Book Fair, President Mubarak cancelled their orders and the books went back on display. On another occasion, a court rejected Al-Azhar's order to confiscate a book, ruling that the Islamic research establishment's reasons were not related to religion, but were more of a political and ideological nature.

Legal pronouncements of eminent scholars have, on occasion, been associated with violent events demonstrating intolerance. An *ad hoc* committee of Al-Azhar scholars issued a statement only a few days before the killing of the secular intellectual Farag Fouda accusing him of being non-religious and strongly against anything Islamic. Following Fouda's assassination, a spokesman for the Islamist group, Al-Gama'a Al-Islamiya, said in a BBC radio interview that his group had 'carried out the legal [Islamic] punishment for the accusations announced by Al-Azhar scholars against Fouda a few days before his assassination'. Sheikh Gazzali also issued a religious ruling (*fatwa*) when called as a witness by the defence at the trial of those accused of killing Fouda. He declared that anyone who objected to the implementation of the *shariah* was excommunicate and an apostate from Islam, and that anyone who killed such a person should be tried with leniency because they would only be carrying out the legitimate *hudud* punishment. The local Arabic press reported the *fatwa*.

In universities, followers of the political Islamist groups apply intense pressure to limit the academic freedom of those with secular philosophies. In Cairo University, an academic committee would not promote Professor Nassar Hamed Abu Zeid because his writings on the origin of the Qur'an 'contained atheist ideas', revealed 'lack of belief' and were seen as 'an insult to religion'. His following of a liberal school of Islamic thought had also reportedly brought him to think that Qur'anic verses about women, for example, should be considered in the context of the pre-Islamic period where women were treated as nothing at all.

Meanwhile, a group of Islamist lawyers sued Abu Zeid and a civil affairs court ordered him in 1995 to divorce his wife because he was an atheist and an apostate from Islam who had published research allegedly 'attacking Islam and inciting disrespect for Islam's rulings on tradition'. According to Islamic laws, such people cannot be married to Muslim women. Abu Zeid's life was in danger, especially following Sheikh Gazzali's *fatwa*. The Cairo Appeal Court confirmed the ruling of apostasy and the armed Islamic Jihad group thereupon issued a statement condemning Abu Zeid to death and describing as an 'infidel' anyone who objected to the ruling of apostasy on the grounds of freedom of expression or opinion. Although Cairo University has reversed its decision and appointed Abu Zeid a professor, he cannot teach because of the threats to his life and has left Egypt. In August 1996, the Court of Cassation rejected his appeal against the lower court ruling; the Egyptian Organisation for Human Rights appealed to the President to intervene.

Education

Basic education is free and compulsory, the aim of the curricula being to teach Egyptians to believe in God and hold charity, truth and humanity in high esteem and to provide them with the fundamental requirements to affirm their human dignity, as the government has stated. Private schools must follow the same syllabuses and curricula as state schools, according to the 1981 Education Act. Compulsory religious instruction takes place for two hours a week. Christians are obliged to memorise Qur'anic verses as part of Arabic studies. Sectarian ideas have all the more easily spread among school children as the curriculum does not reflect the religious and cultural diversity of Egyptian society. Belatedly, the government has realised the dangers of the growing influence of religious extremism on the educational process. Some measures have been taken, such as the removal of passages in school texts which encouraged intolerance and religious fanaticism, but it remains too early to assess their effect.

In 1995 the Special Rapporteur on Religious Intolerance, Mr Abdelfattah Amor, published reports that although the Ministry of Education has directed to the contrary, religious extremism is manifest in schools, in some of which Muslim and Christian children are segregated while, in other schools, Christian students have experienced victimisation and harassment. One attempt by a school to discipline students who had played an anti-Christian cassette in class was greeted by communal rioting and the petrol-bombing of the local church which injured over fifty Christians.

Conservative teachers and school personnel – as well as students and their families – apply pressure to extend the observance of religious practices by promoting the wearing of Islamic dress by girls. The government first banned outright the wearing of the *niqaab*, a black veil covering the whole of a girl's body, and subsequently tried to ban the wearing of a *hijab*, a veil which covers only the hair and neck, unless it was done with parental approval. In May 1996, the Constitutional Court upheld a ministerial decree banning the *niqaab*, declaring that school uniform was already modest and compatible with religious values.

Women's status, personal law and religion

Egypt has entered reservations to its ratification of CEDAW. Personal law is governed by the *shariah* and particularly affects the status of women. Other laws give women lesser rights than men in matters such as working outside the home, renewing passports and in matters of inheritance.

The increasing presence of women in universities and in the professions and the development of women's rights organisations have been matched by the growing Islamist women's movement which rejects 'Western' influences. Veils and traditional clothing are more in evidence today than in Egypt's more secular and cosmopolitan past, as up to four-fifths of women wear some kind of veil, often as a symbol of cultural pride. Feminists and women's activist groups differ in their interpretation of the veil. Many view this and other restrictions of women's freedom as increasingly oppressive, symptoms of the fragility of cultural identity in times of radical change, and of the wish of increasing numbers of well-educated young men to claim more than their fair share of limited employment opportunities.

The growing conservatism of Egypt is felt by women's rights organisations. The Arab Women's Solidarity Association and its publication have been closed down under the law concerning associations; its assets have reportedly been handed over to an Islamist women's organisation. The Association for the Development and Enhancement of Women, which makes loans to small businesses run by women in urban slums has been challenged before the Fatwa Office of the Ministry of Religious Affairs for using interest payments, as a violation of Islamic law.

Personal status law was first codified in 1929. In 1985, the Supreme Court struck down the reformed code promulgated by former President Sadat in 1979 because his decree was an excessive use of presidential power. Its place was taken by the more restrictive Law No. 100 which passed through the People's Assembly after much lobbying by women's groups of all persuasions. However, current reform proposals may soon address such matters as model marriage contracts consistent with Islamic law and a bill to strengthen woman's rights to divorce and a fair share of her husband's property.

Egypt's reservations to CEDAW concern Articles 2 (eradication of discrimination), 9 (equal citizenship rights) and 16 (eradication of discrimination in the marriage and the family). The Egyptian government representative has stated that Islamic law already liberates women from discrimination. Compliance with the most basic of CEDAW provisions, Article 2, was made conditional on that compliance not running counter to the *shariah*, so broad a reservation that it has been questioned whether the state intends to undertake reforms consistent with its international obligations. Egypt's Article 16 reservations were made 'out of respect for the sanctity deriving from firm religious beliefs' that governed marital relationships, in view of the complementarity of spouses 'which guarantees true equality'. Woman's lack of financial obligation as well as her right to own her own property is held to be balanced against men's superior rights to divorce without judicial approval. It has been noted that the cumulative effect on women of such differences in rights is very large, particularly when they are poor.

Female genital mutilation

A form of female genital mutilation is widely practised in Egypt as in other African cultures from ancient times; its source is unconnected with Islam or any other specific religious tradition although it was adopted into some early Christian and Islamic cultures. It could be described accurately as a tragically discriminatory ideological practice based on masculinist ideals of women's sexual purity. It has been reported that in Cairo, 73 per cent and in rural areas 95 per cent of young girls were affected. The more severe form, infibulation, is practised in some parts of Upper Egypt. The practice affects women's health in many ways and death may result.

The government has attempted to eradicate the practice since 1959, but its decree allowing only physicians to perform it did not control other practitioners from doing so. Because of the persistence of the custom in back-street shops and 'clinics', the government has now made the practice allowable if performed in a public hospital. However, many procedures continue to be performed privately.

In 1995, the Sheikh of Al-Azhar issued a religious decree (*fatwa*) reportedly announcing the procedure as a 'laudable practice that does honour to women' and stating that it was a religious duty as important as praying to Allah. The practice is referred to as *sunna*, a preference of the Prophet. The Egyptian Mufti, however, like most of the world's Muslim religious leaders, points out that the practice is not Islamic as it is not mentioned in the Qur'an; there is no evidence that the Prophet required it for his daughters. A year earlier, the Mufti reportedly said he would support a ban if medical specialists recommended it, stating that a young girl's modesty did not depend upon the practice but rather on a good religious and moral education. The Minister for Population stated at the time that the ban would be insufficient in itself to eradicate the practice as education campaigns were greatly needed. Women's groups have long recommended this course of action, but also acknowledge the difficulty of abolishing a cultural ritual which carries so much symbolic weight especially in areas of extreme poverty and lack of access for girls to quality education.

Conscientious objection

Military service from one to three years is compulsory in Egypt. There is the possibility of exemption but conscientious objection is not recognised.

MALAWI

Malawi	
GDP (US$bn)	2
Population	10,200,000
Annual population growth (%)	3.4
Urban population (%)	12
Working population (%)	43
Literacy (%)	53.9
Ratifications	1; 2; 4; Af

Malawi is one of the world's poorest and least developed countries, with a per capita GNP of just over $200, a life expectancy of only forty-five years and a high infant mortality rate. Most of its 10.2 million population are dependent on rural subsistence agriculture which is drought-affected and insufficient to provide staple foods. Foreign exchange earned by Malawian tobacco exports goes to service foreign debt. Malawi is critically dependent on aid for food, health, water and economic stability.

Literacy rates are low – twice as low for women than men – owing to an absence of free compulsory primary education and to the fact that almost half the children between the ages of 6 and 15 are not in education. Christian aid assistance is a significant feature of health and education delivery and, in a country with limited communications infrastructure, much information dissemination is through the churches.

Malawi achieved independence from British rule in 1964. From 1966, life President Hastings Banda and the Malawi Congress Party ruled over a one-party state in which free expression and public debate, among other human rights, were ruthlessly repressed. Detention without trial, disappearances and assassination enforced Banda's rule. He impoverished the country for his own aggrandisement without establishing the hospitals, schools and universities its people badly needed, relying instead on shrinking amounts of foreign aid to provide the basic necessities of Malawians' lives.

In 1992, after violent riots and donors' freezing of foreign aid, Banda was forced to agree to a referendum in 1993 which supported multi-party elections and the country began its progress to democracy, to the practice of human rights and the rule of law. In 1994, the United Democratic Front was elected and Mr Bakili-Muluzi became president; the following year brought former President Banda and others to trial for conspiracy to murder political opponents.

The status of religion and belief

Reliable figures about Malawians' religious affiliations are elusive; estimates of adherents to Christian denominations range from 40 per cent to 65 per cent of the population, with more Protestants than Roman Catholics. Around 20 per cent of the population are Muslim. Newer beliefs, ranging from the Jehovah's Witnesses to other evangelical groups are firmly established and – within the restraints of the former regime – have rapidly expanded. American-based evangelical groups have embarked recently on a large church-building campaign, mirroring the mosque-building initiatives of the early 1980s.

The Muslim community in Malawi live mostly in the south, among the ethnic groups around Blantyre, Zomba and Mangoche which were most exposed to Arabic slave traders. A substantial number of Asian Muslims enlarges the African Muslim community. Together with the smaller grouping of Hindus they experience racial discrimination because of their status as Asians. With restricted citizenship, they have been economically and geographically restricted as a result of a long-standing perception of Asians as being economically threatening.

The state has, in general, tolerated rather than encouraged Islamic practices. Some tension has grown since the late 1970s between the Muslim and other religious groups when scaremongering about the growth of fundamentalism and allegiances to external Islamic powers was fuelled by the financing of a large mosque-building programme. Similar concerns were raised during the election campaign as the United Democratic Front was headed by the only Muslim to gain political advancement under Banda, Bakili-Muluzi. The Aford and MCP press during the election drew strong identifications between UDF and Islam, alleging large payments of campaign finance by an Islamic state.

There is no official state religion in Malawi and most people have some degree of traditional belief, although in some areas animistic beliefs are the most significant element of local patterns of faith. However, the former President Banda's membership and one-time status as elder of the Church of Scotland, together with the tradition of Protestant participation in government within Malawi has resulted in the projection of Malawi as a Christian country. This has marked legislative and political policy to the extent that most Malawians state that it is a Christian country and often themselves will claim some adherence to a Christian faith. Indications of the level of importance that Christian ethics and religious practices have had in forming national policy can be garnered from the rigid censorship of 'anti-Christian' and 'immoral' literature, as well as the outlawing of blood transfusions and contraception up until the mid-1970s.

However, following the transition to democracy and the 1994 election with its ecumenical presidential investiture, the new President Bakili-Muluzi – a Muslim – has made a conscious effort to be seen to rise above any religious divisions. Muluzi's stated policy for Malawi is that 'there should be freedom of worship in this country' and 'the government will encourage the Church to be the conscience of the nation and speak out against any form of injustice'. He has been assiduous in cultivating the support of Christian groups in Malawi.

There was some discussion over making a formal allusion to 'God' in the introductory section of the constitution, but this was rejected as being potentially alienating for those who had no religious beliefs. The country is thus avowedly one committed to tolerance of religion and other belief.

Much of the education infrastructure of Malawi depends on the churches, through their support of mission schools and cooperation with secular ones. There is no separate provision for Islamic education. The only Islamic and free school was closed in 1989 on the pretext of the need to integrate children into mainstream cultural values.

The political and legal context

Human rights protections guaranteeing the right to free conscience had been included in the constitution of 1964, but were removed within three years of its coming into effect.

Malawi under Banda saw little systematic denial of freedom of conscience, except with regard to some traditional practices that the state deemed to amount to 'witchcraft' and the persecution or exclusion of some religious minorities, most notably the Jehovah's Witnesses. Atheism, especially when linked with socialist beliefs was strongly discouraged, while Hindus suffered more as a function of discrimination against non-citizen Asians whom the state had branded as being economically threatening and had restricted in their places of business and residence. An informal presidential decree blocked the establishment of religions that were not registered with the government.

The period 1993–94 saw the reintroduction of guarantees of religious freedom within the constitution, first as an interim reform of the existing constitution and then in the new 1994 constitution. This had followed on from unprecedented conflict between the churches – particularly the Roman Catholic Church – and the state which led to religious leaders forming the representative basis of political opposition to the excesses of the Banda regime.

Aside from the constitutional limitations, there was little in the way of formal regulation of religion. It was the direct and non-legal approaches to rule, generally employed by Banda – directives to the Malawi Young Pioneers and the Youth League – which effected most of the policy of religious intolerance.

Malawi became a signatory to both of the International Covenants in March 1994 and it became justiciable in domestic courts under the new constitution. The new constitution also includes specific provision for human rights, including the protection of freedom of conscience and religion and the prohibition of discrimination on the grounds of religion or belief.

Section 33 of the new constitution guarantees that '[e]very person shall have the right to freedom of conscience, religion, belief and thought, and to academic freedom'. These rights are non-derogable and may not be subject to restrictions or limitations. Section 42 guarantees '[e]very person who is detained, including every sentenced prisoner . . . the right to be given the means and opportunity to communicate with, and to be visited by his or her . . . religious counsellor'.

The Senate (yet to be confirmed) is intended to contain representatives of 'religion, who shall include representatives of the major religious faiths in Malawi'. No specific provision guarantees the right to propagate religious faiths, although Section 34 guarantees that '[e]very person shall have the right to freedom of opinion, including the right to hold opinions without interference and the right to hold, receive and impart opinions'.

During the debate on the new constitution, the issue of a right to establish religiously selective schools was debated but was rejected on the basis that this amounted to discrimination in access to a national resource.

The role of religious groups in the political transition

Banda cultivated an image of Malawi as a Christian, and more specifically a Calvinist country, being proud himself of being an Elder of the Church of Scotland. The churches, who had been active – especially the Presbyterian Church missionary representatives on the Legislative Council – in the promotion of the original native political organisations and independence for Malawi, had enjoyed a certain amount of benefit from being in a privileged situation. They took an active role in such bodies as the Censorship Board, which restricted a number of secular and anti-Christian publications on the grounds of protecting public morals or protecting against religious insults. During this period some individual churchmen from Catholic and Protestant denominations took part in direct or indirect opposition to the Banda regime, frequently resulting in their deportation.

The churches continued, in the words of one Church of Scotland official, with 'this unsatisfactory collusion' until Easter of 1992 when a pastoral letter issued by the Roman Catholic bishops unambiguously exclaimed the importance of political and social justice in support of the growing public unrest and opposition to the government. The role of religious organisations at all levels of Malawian life, ranging from education through to health, meant that the removal of this institutional support posed the most serious threat to the government's authority. The Malawi Congress Party Conference went further than the government press condemnation of 'meddling bishops', by debating the murder or execution of the bishops. A tape of this discussion, broadcast on the Chichewa service of the South African broadcasting corporation, polarised the churches and the state. Religious leaders figured heavily in the opposition committee set up in October 1992 to discuss political liberalisation in Malawi. The cross-section of faiths included reflected the strong ecumenical tradition in Malawi. Among the actions by outside church groups in solidarity with the Malawian faiths was the expulsion of Banda from the Church of Scotland and the intercession by a Papal emissary on behalf of the Catholic bishops.

The churches organised mechanisms for education and monitoring during both the referendum in 1993 and the 1994 elections. Several religious leaders contested seats, representing opposition parties, participated in the constitutional debate and took up active roles in new human rights groups. Religious services and broadcasting were extensively used as a means of encouraging peaceful political activity and civic education.

Discrimination against minority groups

Under the Banda regime, the Jehovah's Witnesses (established in Malawi in the 1920s) were subject to extensive restrictions, arising from their conscientious objections. Their refusal to buy Party cards and boycotting of elections started in 1964 and they were subject to violent attacks by the youth organisations of the Malawi Congress Party. Former President Banda refused to accept that these were anything but provoked attacks and in 1967 the MCP annual conference voted to ban the sect on the basis that they were perpetrating 'a vicious propaganda against [the person of the President] and the Government in general' and that they were 'inimical to the progress' of Malawi. They were declared an unlawful society under a Penal Code ministerial order. By 1972, after reports of many thousands of Witnesses leaving Malawi, the president stated that although allegations of this outflux were untrue, the Witnesses had no right to police protection since they provoked others. Employers were ordered to dismiss members under pain of revocation of business licence, while the public was exhorted to chase them out of the villages. Their property was confiscated and members of the sect were murdered or imprisoned on a wide scale. There is no accurate figure as to how many Witnesses were subjected to confiscation or imprisonment. Tens of thousands of Witnesses were forcibly repatriated in the early 1970s, many of whom were imprisoned for periods of up to three years for membership of an illegal society. Many were released by 1977, although human rights organisations around the world continued to report torture, forced repatriation, killing and imprisonment. In 1992 in the only recent reliable official survey of the prison population, thirteen Jehovah's Witness women were reported as being detained without trial. The restriction on the group was removed in September 1993 and remaining prisoners seem to have been released. The Jehovah's Witnesses membership has since grown considerably. However, although they are no longer targeted for persecution, their conscientious objection to participation in political processes is still greeted with hostility and social exclusion. The electoral authorities expressed concern that they were campaigning during the 1994 elections against voting, registration and political participation.

Animistic and traditional beliefs remain very strong in Malawi where they have long been either curbed or exploited for political ends. To the extent that traditional beliefs could be used to threaten the state or the person of former President Banda, they were subject to direct repression. The Witchcraft Act, still extant from the days of the British Protectorate, effectively restricts the practice of certain traditional activities. Until the 1970s convictions for witchcraft continued, with criminal sanctions. The common and customary law of Malawi also recognises that crimes may be procured by means of witchcraft.

In contrast, the Malawi Congress Party also took advantage of traditional superstitions to influence the population. During the 1993 referendum and the 1994 election traditional witchcraft was deployed to deter people from voting for opposition parties. Most notably this involved the exploitation of the Nyau secret society, predominantly to be found in the central region. At all-male Nyau cult meetings certain individuals – Gule wa Mkulu – through the wearing of masks, take on the spirit of an animal and are given the power to bless, curse and powers of prophesy. Morally and – until recently – legally, this prevents the individual concerned from being responsible for his actions while giving him a position of significant authority in tradition. Nyau were procured to attend political meetings and instruct people to vote for MCP. This led in some instances to clashes and the arrest and prosecution of Nyau dancers in contravention of taboo. The government, in a reply to the NGO Article xix expressed concern on the issue, stated that Nyau was a tradition that did not pose a threat to the transition. The Joint International Observer Group considered this during the elections and the matter was resolved, in so far as it could be, through pressure on the relevant political and local authorities. However, Nyau meetings continued in the central region even after the elections and continued to be a basis of directing the local people's political behaviour.

Women

As well as being victimised by those in power, women have been implicated in political persecution and were an important support base for President Banda. Arrest and imprisonment of women were common, two prominent prisoners being Margaret Banda, a prominent lay member of the Anglican Church and the lawyer and university lecturer Vera Chirwa. Women's organisations such as the Women's League had been used to enforce the obligatory purchase of Congress Party cards and strict dress codes applied to women (as well as men).

MAURITANIA

Mauritania	
GDP (US$bn)	1
Population	2,100,000
Annual population growth (%)	2.4
Urban population (%)	50
Working population (%)	33[a]
Literacy (%)	36.2
Ratifications	3; Af

Located at the western end of the African Sahelian belt, Mauritania has an impoverished economy characterised by scarce national resources, heavy dependence on fish exports and global market prices, huge reliance on foreign aid, a negative balance of payments and the weight of debt servicing. Three-quarters of the population were nomadic herders until the time of the great Sahelian droughts of the 1970s and early 1980s, since when settlement has gradually taken place. Mauritania remains handicapped by poor human development and slavery has only recently been officially abolished, not for the first time.

Population and culture

The 2.1 million Mauritanians are distributed among five major ethnic groups. The political volatility of ethnicity makes reliable data difficult to obtain. The Arabo-Berber group, composed of 'white Moors' (Beidan) and 'black Moors' (Haratine, i.e. 'one who has been freed') – a distinction not based on skin colour – constitutes over 80 per cent of the population, according to official 1983 statistics, and lives in the north. The four black African Mauritanian tribal groups – Halpulaar (Fulbe), Soninké, Wolof and Bambara – under 20 per cent of the population, were traditionally cultivators and herders living in the south along the Senegal River.

Religion is an important factor of cultural *rapprochement* among Mauritanians as the population is virtually all Muslim, specifically Malakite Sunni Muslims. Islam, since the eleventh-century Almoravid movement, has become a key element in national identity. Other religions have little impact as they are confined to the tiny number of foreign residents. Shia adherents are confined to the small Lebanese community which is allowed to practise privately.

Internal faith divisions and relations are therefore an important feature of Mauritanian life. Most people are traditionally attached to a brotherhood. Brotherhood founders or leaders are divided among three main paths or ways, the Qadiriyya, the Tijaniyya and the now marginal Shadiliyya. The Qadiriyya dates back to the sixteenth century, has more scholarly leaders and more social prestige than the later Tijaniyya which has simpler rituals and does not pursue Islamic learning to the same extent but which, as a missionary movement, has spread and made gains at the expense of the Qadiriyya. A branch of the Tijaniyya, the Hamalliyya, played a significant role in resistance to French colonial administration during the 1930s and 1940s; it aims to purify ritual and return to the original teachings of the founder. Although brotherhood membership cuts across ethnic and tribal or regional lines, thereby reinforcing Islam's unifying role in Mauritania, there is still ethnic and tribal or regional predominance within each brotherhood.

Legal and political structure

Independence from the French colonial administration came in 1960. The first con-stitution, adopted in 1959, allowed the formation of opposition parties but was modified in 1964, beginning a one-party regime which lasted until 1978 when a military coup replaced the constitution with a Military Chart. Between 1978 and 1991, Mauritanians experienced five military coups. The security forces are dominated by Arabic-speaking Moors.

President Maawiya Ould Sid'Ahmed Taya announced in 1991 that multi-party rule would return. He promulgated the country's third constitution, modelled on the French Fifth Republic's and presenting the regime as a democratic Islamic Republic. This duality has introduced an element of ambiguity into the legal system.

On the one hand, rights and freedoms typically attached to a democratic system are formally acknowledged. The constitution guarantees the citizen the right to equality and respect for basic freedoms and rights as a human being, including freedom of opinion and expression. Mauritania has ratified the CERO and the 1981 African Charter of Human and Peoples' Rights. On the other hand, these commitments to human rights are to be contained within the limits inscribed in the people's attachment to Islam. The preamble begins thus: 'Confident in the all-mightiness of Allah, the Mauritanian people . . .'. Mauritania is a member of the Islamic Conference Organisation.

No matter how political power has been organised, national political processes have remained centred around tribal, regional and ethnic identities. The attribution of government seats is carefully regulated by the state, 'good representation' consisting of forming a government composed of one-third Black-Mauritanian to two-thirds Arabo-Berber ministers. The state's patronage networks are dominated by Moors, reflecting the cultural identity of the group currently in power.

The Black-Mauritanians' protest against such representation – and other cultural policies – is yet another stable dimension of national political dynamics. However, their protests and state responses have gradually been escalating from student riots in the 1960s and 1970s about the Arabisation of the education system to more open and violent confrontation by the extremist Black-Mauritanian liberation movement FLAM and its military branches FURAM and the FRUIDEM in the early 1990s.

Islam has been used by the state ever since independence as a potent source of legitimacy. In 1980, the *shariah* was for the first time fully applied in the country, a measure which damped down anger with the state in traditional Beidan (white Moor) circles over the official abolition of slavery.

Religion, belief and state

Mauritania was established as an Islamic republic from independence in 1960 and the new constitution confirms that Islam is the religion of the people and the state. Accordingly, the president must be a Muslim and Islam the sole source of law, although the preamble states that the country is 'open to the demands of the modern world'.

Since 1966, a government department has been responsible for 'Islamic affairs' or 'Islamic orientation'. It manages mosques – attributing mosque plots, nominating and paying an allowance to mosque leaders (*imams*) – and traditional Islamic schools. The 1991 constitution also created an Islamic High Council whose five members are designated by the president. Though it has yet to be called upon formally, its role is to express views on issues when it is consulted by the president.

The application of the *shariah* has not been straightforward. From independence to the early 1980s, 'modern' French-inspired law was used to settle disputes involving the administration, questions relating to modern techniques and technology, and commercial dealings. There followed a period when the application of Islamic law was extended and important portions of the law were adapted to the *shariah*. For a brief period in the early 1980s, the *hudud* (physical sentences prescribed by the *shariah*) was strictly enforced – in the aftermath of Black-Mauritanian student protests and the official abolition of slavery – though it is no longer applied, a 'hypocrisy' that Islamists have not failed to denounce.

Today, while the *shariah* prescriptions on 'Islamic morals' are unambiguously formulated in the Penal Code, other parts of the law suffer from lack of clear codification and judges are required to ensure that the older legal texts applied are 'in full conformity with the spirit of the *shariah*'. Mauritanian jurists have attempted to clarify the confusion but this has met some resistance from the state. In the absence of a sustained effort by the state itself to better integrate secular and religious sources of law, justice has proceeded by case by case interpretation.

Despite the constitution's rejection of religion–state separation, the state tries to keep religion at a reasonable distance from the centres of power while leaning on it as a potent source of legitimacy. The state has never repressed an Islamist political organisation even though the constitution prohibits religiously grounded political parties. Thus the Oumma Party's political activities were not hindered: propagandist preaching, mosque debates, distribution of audio tapes and also overt alliances with legal opposition parties during elections. The state now seems caught between its reluctance to restrict Islamist movements and its apprehension over the growing resonance of Islamist discourse within civil society.

Discrimination

The social context of Mauritania influences the relations between various groups and within Islam. Mauritania is a highly hierarchical society through every ethnic group; social practices and perceptions remain caught up in the rigidity of inherited statuses. Though the existence of castes is clearly incompatible with the spirit of the constitution, caste members are not only submitted to a social 'quarantine' but are also structurally unable – without positive state intervention – to extract themselves from their traditional socio-economic status. This is the situation faced by the Haratine (black Moors). Even though slavery has been officially abolished three times, ex-slaves of Moor descent are still a striking example of a large communal group – over a quarter of the population – which forms a distinct social class.

Another key axis of discrimination is ethnicity. Latent ethnic tension is a stable parameter of Mauritanian political dynamics. Following the 1989 border crisis with Senegal and horrific popular pogroms in the two capitals, the Mauritanian state reacted with violence against Black-Mauritanians. In the early 1990s, systematic purges were made within the armed forces, the administration and in the rural population settled in the Senegal River valley. Therefore there have been great changes from the French colonial period when Black-Mauritanians dominated the economy and civil service. After independence, they and the black Moors are significantly under-represented in senior positions of authority, those being held predominantly by Arabic-speaking white Moors.

Internal faith relations

Relations among branches of Islam are affected by the relative tolerance and pacific character of Sunni Islam. Though the brotherhoods played a significant role in organising and mobilising the resistance movement before independence, they did not evolve into competing modern political parties. In contrast, the urban-based Islamist movements which first emerged in the 1970s are overtly political and seem to appeal to urban Moorish youth and disadvantaged groups including those Haratine living in the shanty-towns of the capital, Nouakchott. These two groups are particularly active in regular mosque meetings; they volunteer for public preaching on Nouakchott streets and go on missions to rural locations.

Modern Islamism, however, has had little impact on Black-Mauritanians, who remain faithful to their traditional brotherhoods. Brotherhood leaders regard the Islamist movements with latent – not open – hostility because they represent the strongest threat to their traditional ascendancy.

All groups approve of the state's integration of Islamic moral prescriptions into the Penal Code, explicitly prohibiting homosexuality, adultery, consumption of alcohol and the conduct of games of chance.

Promotion of religion or belief and proselytism

There is no legal restriction on the call to Islam (*dawa*), the act of preaching in public places. Although the state most likely has eyes and ears in mosques where Islamists preach and debate, these activities are not restricted.

Acknowledged by Islam, the two other religions of the book – Christianity and Judaism – are theoretically free to organise their practice in places dedicated to their observances. However, they have no right at all to disseminate those beliefs outside those grounds. Any activity related to other religious systems – including polytheist religions – remains prohibited. Mauritanians may not enter non-Muslim houses of worship nor may they possess their sacred texts. Article 245 of the Penal Code prohibits beliefs involving the practice of magic.

The Roman Catholic Church is the sole non-Muslim faith which is officially recognised. Its six churches are operated by fewer than ten priests addressed to a congregation of fewer than 5,000 people, mostly Europeans and western and central Africans.

The public administration is cautionary in its dealings with the Catholic Church. The Archbishop has been repeatedly reminded – in all kindness and by friendly *imams* – that if he were to convert a Mauritanian, that would ensure that the convert would be beheaded. The church has been sporadically subjected to overt acts of intolerance and its activities are targets for criticism. In September 1993, two priests were seriously wounded by an Islamist on the church grounds in Nouakchott. In the aftermath of the 1989 crisis with Senegal and also during the Gulf War in 1991, priests and sisters were openly threatened in Atar and in Nouadhibou. During ethnic tension in 1987, a catechist from Guinee Bissau was arrested for hanging holy pictures in his rented room.

Christian churches have been subjected to negative press campaigns by independent newspapers known to be sympathetic to the state. *Le Point* carried a headline 'Beware of the Catholic network!' in August 1993, referring to a Catholic priest's work with the capital's street children, in association with CARITAS, an NGO working closely with the health and welfare administration. Similarly, the Minister for Information recently condemned the Lutheran World Federation's rural radio seminar on the Guinea worm.

This distrust of Christian churches is diffused throughout society. Parents keep watch on clerical interest in their children. For instance, in Kaedi, a Catholic priest was politely asked not to initiate discussion about religion and faith with their children. Similarly, when in September 1993 the rumour circulated that Mauritanians had been converted to Christianity, the Catholic Church was swiftly accused of abusing Mauritanians' hospitality.

Conscientious objection

The right to conscientious objection is not protected as such, other than through the formal freedoms of opinion, thought and expression within the 1991 constitution. Given that Islam is the only religion allowed to Mauritanian citizens, religiously grounded objection is hardly likely to be recognised. Indeed, Article 306 of the Penal Code states as follows:

> Any Muslim guilty of the crime of apostasy, either in words or in acts, in an apparent or evident manner, shall be offered three days to repent. If he/she has not repented during that period, he/she shall be sentenced to death as an apostate, and his/her wealth shall be confiscated by the State.

Education and the family

The constitutional preamble proclaims the state's respect for rights attached to the family, foundation of the Islamic society. However, these rights are limited by religious and language constraints imposed by the state.

Religious – that is, Islamic – education is mandatory. The Moral, Civic and Religious Instruction syllabus consists of the teachings of the Qur'an, the life of the Prophet, the *Hadith* (words of the Prophet) and the history of Islam; it is taught throughout primary and secondary schooling. In a society entirely devoted to Islam, this is not generally perceived to be a serious hindrance to citizens' freedoms and rights. It precludes such things as sexual education which might have been instrumental in preventing the spread of AIDS and other sexually transmitted diseases among the young.

Parental antagonism has instead been aroused by the language constraints within the structure of the education system. In particular, in 1979 the Ministry of National Education made it compulsory for the children of a Moor mother to be placed in the Arabic language option, while Black-Mauritanian parents have a choice of whether to place their children in any of the three Arabic, 'bilingual' (in fact, French-dominated) or 'national languages' (Pulaar, Soninké or Wolof) options. Black-Mauritanians have overwhelmingly opted to have their children educated in French.

Although there is no public funding for private schools, parents are not necessarily entirely free to organise private schools according to their own value or belief systems. Such schools are subject to the same language and religious education constraints as the public schools, as all pupils are required to sit the same examinations at the end of primary and secondary schooling. As the amount of Arabic has gradually increased in the education system, so the ethnic divide has widened until today the linguistic division has reached university level. Analysis of the names of students registered at the University of Nouakchott reveals that more than three-quarters of the Black-Mauritanian students are placed in 'bilingual' sections while almost all students of Moor descent are in the Arabic sections. Unsurprisingly, education remains a point of conflict in Mauritania.

The media

While the 1991 ordinance states that the press, printing work and book selling are unrestricted, fourteen newspaper issues were seized by the public administration – eleven between May and August 1994 – and one newspaper was closed down for a month. In only two of these cases were newspapers informed of the reason; both concerned alleged blasphemous content. In the first, a Mauritanian intellectual had affirmed in a French edition that a person could renounce their faith and, in the second, a cynical tone was used in an Arabic edition to note how the anniversary of the ruling party was more instrumental in raising mosque-renovation funds than the Prophet's birthday. Analyses of the human rights situation were the more likely cause of seizure of newspaper issues.

Religious publications (newspapers, magazines, sacred and religious books) can be produced and distributed freely, at least in theory. Among Nouakchott's largest bookstores is an Islamist bookstore selling Arabic Islamic literature at modest prices. Books of Muslim theology are also published, appealing to more traditional and orthodox intellectuals.

Several video clubs were closed by the police in September 1994 to have their tapes reviewed for any insult to Islamic or 'human morals'. Potential curbs on parabolic antennas have also been discussed.

State-owned broadcasting, the media most adapted to the predominantly oral character of Pulaar, Soninké and Wolof cultures, offers them a disproportionately low amount of airtime.

Personal law and women's status

Though women have legal rights to property, divorce and child custody, women's status in Mauritania cannot be dissociated from the status of women as defined by Islam. In this, they are clearly distinguished from and essentially unequal to men. Islam further recognises men's right to take up to four wives. Polygamy is practised by Black-Mauritanians, the Moor community having adopted the practice of multiple divorces. The state has not interfered with the practice of female genital mutilation except by allowing health workers to educate midwives about associated health dangers and about the fact that the practice is not required by Islam.

The difficult task of harmonising Islamist views on women with human rights standards of freedom and equality is not perceived as a priority by the state. It superficially promotes ideals of women's emancipation and active participation in government and in the development process. Although the constitution guarantees equality before the law and full political participation for women, it was not until 1971 that two women were elected to the National Assembly and not until 1987 that a number of women were appointed to cabinet-level positions.

However, the status of women has gradually improved and the National Women's Movement has been intermittently successful in demanding registration of marriages and divorces, discouragement of polygyny, limiting the size of dowries and establishing a women's rights code. In the past, girls were educated only at home or briefly in religious schools. Many young girls were betrothed or married by the age of 8 or 10 and unmarried teenage girls were socially unacceptable. In the last decade, many more female children have attended primary and secondary school and have gone on to university and, increasingly, the professions.

Women are still struggling for their rights and Mauritanian delegates were among those who formed the Court of Women who gave testimonies on violence against women in the Arab world in Beirut in June 1995.

Women in religion

Muslim tradition discourages the notion of female religious leadership, and, indeed, their leadership in general, although Mauritanian women have occupied political office. Women are allowed to attend public worship at the mosque where they are segregated from men, but they are discouraged from attending; most pray at home. In the predominantly Sufi Muslim brotherhoods, there are a few female religious scholars with some guidance and leadership role, but they are the exception. The Tijaniyya brotherhood encourages women to attend mosques and participate in mosque debates but they must sit behind the men and children. Women's participation in modern Islamist movements remains subordinate.

MOROCCO

Morocco	
GDP (US$bn)	28
Population	25,400,000
Annual population growth (%)	2.5
Urban population (%)	47
Working population (%)	33[a]
Literacy (%)	40.6
Ratifications	1; 2; 3; 4

Politics and society are powerfully intertwined in Morocco, part of a historical continuum stretching back before the French colonial period (1912–56). Morocco is unique in North Africa in that its monarchy claims its origin from the Idrissids in the tenth century and descends from the Alawite dynasty in the seventeenth century. King Hassan II has ruled for over thirty years. The Moroccan government is in the process of nation-building to ensure the country's stability and modernisation in transforming Moroccan society.

Morocco's 25.4 million people are almost equally split between urban and rural populations. Primary school attendance in urban areas is double that of rural areas. Girls have a lower rate of literacy than boys. About 65 per cent of Moroccans speak Arabic while Berber-speakers make up the balance together with just over half a million people from other ethno-linguistic minorities.

Religious composition

Over 98 per cent of the population are Muslims, almost all Sunni Muslims of the Maliki rite. There is also a tiny Baha'i community. The remainder are comprised of a small Jewish community (around 7,000) and a Christian community (69,000). The Christians, mainly temporary European residents, are mostly Roman Catholic, although there is a small Anglican community in Tangier and about a thousand Protestants in Casablanca.

The Jewish community has been established in Morocco for over 2,000 years. Under the French protectorate they were given equal rights as citizens and, though they have experienced discrimination and attacks associated with the establishment of Israel and the Six Day War, the community now maintains good relations with the government and Jews are well represented at senior political, legal and government levels. There have been some anti-Semitic utterances by Muslim clerics, primarily comments on Israel. Progress on the Middle East peace process is thus important to the future of Jews in Morocco especially if Islamist movements grow stronger.

Ethnic and language composition

Most of the population is ethnically Berber; there is no religious or ethnic divide associated with the difference between Arabic-speakers and Berber-speakers. Berbers today form a major element in cities such as Casablanca and Marakesh as well as among the 800,000 Moroccans who work in Europe. They also dominate at least two political parties. Modern literary Arabic is an official language alongside French. As part of a programme to preserve historic components of Moroccan identity, in 1994 the king announced that Berber would be taught in schools as well as Arabic.

Economic factors

Morocco is in the process of economic reconstruction, the costs of which have been felt in static or declining living standards leading to social discontent expressed in country-wide riots in 1984 and 1990. The most important factor remains the harvest which affects rural subsistence economy. Women do most of the hard rural labour. Political solutions are likely to be sought if living standards worsen; in the North African context, this could involve a move towards political Islam. Although in Morocco the nature of the monarchy does much to lessen this prospect, there remains a serious possibility of consequent social unrest.

The political system and non-government movements

The Moroccan political system is democratic in form – a single Chamber of Deputies elected both directly and indirectly. Although the government is chosen from the largest political party, the cabinet must be approved by the king. Both the cabinet and the king may institute legislation. However, no legislation may alter the status of the monarchy or the position of Islam.

The constitution and the legal system forbid attacks on Islam and on the monarchy. Attempts to alter the political system are penalised, including the constitutional prohibition on a single party state. Opposition parties include the original nationalist movement, the socialist party and the long-established communist party.

The monarchy retains power because its authority stands outside the law; the king is Commander of the Faithful, a traditional title given to caliphs. His power is based on the fact that the accession of a monarch to the throne has to be approved by the Moroccan Islamic community through the ceremony of the 'handshake', a document declaring loyalty in return for guarantees to preserve Islamic order. This is only a formality today, the constitution establishing monarchical rights through primogeniture. In practice the Moroccan king is far more the 'shadow of God upon the earth' to whom, as ruler, 'obedience is due' (a further attribute of caliphs) than a consensual leader of an egalitarian Islamic community.

The limits of free expression are widely understood since royal patronage is the key to the process of integration and advancement. The formal democratic system is thus limited by the informal system which encourages conformity because of the implications of the exercise of royal power.

The major clandestine opposition is now formed from the many branches of the Islamist movement. This, however, is relatively weak in the Moroccan context, not just because of the efficiency of the security services but also because a large part of the legitimate political Islamic field is occupied by the monarchy in its capacity as caliph and Commander of the Faithful. The most widely supported movement has been al-Adal wa'l-Ihsan (Justice and Charity) whose founder is now under house arrest. Some extremist Islamist groups are derived from the Ikhwan al-Muslimin (Muslim Brotherhood). The teachings of a 1960s' Ikhwan leader executed in Egypt have inspired the founding of the Ash-Shabiba al-Islamiyya (Islamic Youth) movement, a group violently opposed to Morocco's government and monarchy and now based in Europe.

Moroccan society is undergoing widespread and profound changes towards a recognisably modern type of society as found in European democracies, accelerated by policy decisions by government and palace to adhere to the European Community despite the growth of Islamist movements in the Middle East and North Africa.

The beginnings of a genuine civil society in Morocco can be discerned in non-governmental organisations such as human rights monitoring groups, that have appeared in recent years. The government, which was elected to the UN Commission on Human Rights in 1988, allowed all human rights groups to register as legal entities in 1989.

The legal system

Although the legal system is said formally to be in accord with the *shariah*, in practice it is grounded in the Napoleonic legal principles derived from French law; this is particularly true of the criminal code which covers political offences.

The constitution states that the judiciary is independent but judicial appointments are made by a council presided over by the king, himself the ultimate judicial authority given his responsibilities both as caliph and *imam*. Judicial process and legal review are controlled by the Supreme Court based in Rabat.

Morocco has ratified the major human rights instruments. However, there have been constant complaints from Amnesty International and other monitoring organisations that the international conventions have not been observed. This is particularly true of past repression of persons accused of what are, in essence, political offences. Though a Deputy Ministry for Human Rights was established in 1993, Morocco continues to be condemned for its treatment of political prisoners and for arbitrary arrest, torture and disappearances.

Personal status law

Religious law, practised in special *shariah* or *qadi* courts, is confined to personal status law, such as divorce and inheritance. Women have now been given equal status with men in divorce and maintenance and the law on polygamy has been amended. Jewish personal affairs are conducted under Jewish religious law administered by rabbi judges and notaries. Christians also have a separate personal affairs code.

Personal status laws which particularly restrict women have been commented upon by the (UN) Human Rights Committee, a member of which expressed concern that it appeared that they did not ensure the right of individuals freely to found a family. Muslim women cannot marry Jewish or Christian men unless the men convert to Islam, whereas wives of Muslim men may retain their different faiths. The existence of three different personal law codes affects such women's inheritance rights if they do not convert.

Government progress in bringing its legislation in line with the ICCPR has been noted by the (UN) Human Rights Committee which particularly drew attention in 1994 to traditions and customs which were an obstacle to implementing the ICCPR, especially with regard to equality between women and men.

Freedom of religion

Islam is the official religion of the state with the king as guarantor in his capacity as Amir al-Munimin and *imam*. Freedom of religion is guaranteed by the constitution within the appropriate Islamic context. Although the legal system does not discriminate against practitioners of other religions – traditionally they would have been accorded inferior status as *dhimmis* – certain constraints apply, such as the prohibition against proselytising to convert Muslims to another religion. A Muslim who abandons his or her religion is legally prohibited from doing so and becomes an apostate. The practice of Christian evangelism is affected by this. The (UN) Human Rights Committee has expressed concern that it is illegal for a person to change religion.

Similarly, the religious freedom guaranteed by the constitution applies in the public sphere only to Judaism and Christianity, not the other major religions, though there is no evidence of interference with private worship. Should religious activities contravene laws dealing with public or private morality, such private religious practice would not be allowed. Public promotion of atheism, though not specifically prohibited, would be contrary to Islamic precept.

As well as mosques, there are numerous Qur'anic schools – curriculum monitored by the government – where children learn the Qur'an and Arabic to prepare for more senior schooling, ultimately leading for some to tertiary education at the ancient university in Fez.

Free religious expression is limited to a certain extent. For example, the Ministry of Religious Affairs ensures that all *imam*s adhere to an officially approved text as far as the Friday *khutba* (sermon) is concerned, so that political criticism does not form part of religious discourse; mosques must close after the service.

Baha'is' religious freedom has been formally restricted since 1983. In 1962, three Baha'is accused of proselytising were condemned to death, sentences later commuted on appeal. In 1983 sixteen women and men were detained, apparently because they were identified during a census of associations and professional bodies. Sentenced to prison, three abjured and in 1984, the women were released and the men were given much shorter sentences.

Despite the small size of the Baha'i community (under 200 people), the government has continued to support its prohibition of public meetings and activities associated with Baha'i beliefs – private worship is allowed – by stating that the beliefs are regarded as heretical and likely to foment anarchy. The (UN) Human Rights Committee, however, has regretted that no progress had been made by Morocco in its statements about Baha'i freedom of belief, and reminded the government that freedom to manifest beliefs is required by Article 18 of the ICCPR as all beliefs of individuals have to be accorded equal respect.

The issue of proselytism has also affected the Protestant Christian community. In 1984, evangelists abroad (Marseilles and Malaga) sent unsolicited material through the post to

Moroccans, an action which was considered to be proselytism. As a result, a hundred members of the Protestant community were questioned by the authorities and the visits of Protestant pastors to Morocco were restricted. Some Muslims attend bible meetings run by evangelical missionaries. In 1993, a Muslim was imprisoned for corresponding with a Christian radio programme in France and his bible teacher, a Brazilian missionary, was fired from his teaching position.

No declaration about religion is required for any public post or to take part in public activities.

Women and religion

After independence, the new state carried out a mass education programme which, in rural areas, was limited to males only, but which resulted in a new class of educated urban men and women. The age at marriage is much later and an increasing number of highly educated women are entering the professions and civil service. In response there has been a conservative movement against such Muslim women.

Traditional arrangements of space segregation of the sexes are dissolving and Islamic concepts of the state's relation to women and women's relation to knowledge have been challenged, often by female Muslim scholars in Morocco. The 'Third World' stereotype of the deprived, marginalised and excluded Muslim woman is not characteristic, although there are still disabilities which affect women's lives.

NIGERIA

Nigeria	
GDP (US$bn)	30
Population	102,100,000
Annual population growth (%)	2.8
Urban population (%)	37
Working population (%)	31
Literacy (%)	52.5
Ratifications	1; 2; 3; 4; Af

With 102.1 million people, Nigeria has the largest population in sub-Saharan Africa. A former British colony, it celebrated its independence in 1960, with a federal constitution. This divided Nigeria into eastern and western regions and a much larger northern region, dominated respectively by the Igbo, the Yoruba and the Hausa. These large ethnic groups and the division of Nigeria into 'north' and 'south' were the products of colonial rule. In pre-colonial times, Yoruba-speakers, for example, did not form one large state and did not act together in a unified way. The north–south division has some religious dimension but is more important as a core symbol of identity.

In 1966 the First Republic was overthrown in a military coup where Igbo soldiers played a leading role. Their aim was to establish a unitary rather than a federal government and to eliminate corruption, but inevitably the event was seen as an Igbo takeover and this led to massacres of Igbos in the north later in 1966, and then to a civil war between Nigeria and Biafra which ended with Nigerian victory in January 1970.

One of the problems of the three (later four) regions was that smaller ethnic groups – some of them larger than many modern nations – were invisible in terms of political structure. In 1967 Nigeria was divided into twelve states, a number twice increased. The disadvantage of this was that government became ever more expensive. After a long period of military rule, elections were held and the Second Republic was inaugurated in 1979. It was overthrown in an almost bloodless coup in 1983.

Since independence, both civil and military rulers have often been accused of bribery, corruption and intimidation. These accusations became much more serious in the 1980s as Nigeria, despite its great resources of oil, was plunged into an ever-deepening economic crisis and galloping inflation pauperised salaried workers. In 1993 elections were held in which it is widely accepted that Moshood Abiola was elected president, but they were immediately abrogated and military rule continued.

In November 1993 General Sani Abacha seized power and has since acted as head of state and commander-in-chief of the armed forces. Moshood Abiola remains detained, as does former ruler General Obasanjo; both Yoruba, they oppose the domination of Nigerian politics by northern Muslims. Although General Abacha announced a three-year transition to democracy in October 1995, this has already been disrupted as special tribunals including military representatives continue to try and sentence people accused of treason. Playwright and human rights activist Ken Saro-Wiwa and eight others were executed on 10 November 1995 despite international protest. Nigeria has been temporarily suspended from Commonwealth membership and sanctions were proposed.

Legal system

The 1979 constitution is still in force although the 1989 constitution has been suspended. However, rule by military decree prevents the emergence of an independent judiciary capable of performing its traditional role. The military's operational and administrative strategies, showing no respect for law courts and flagrantly flouting court orders, are incompatible with the rule of law. Arbitrary arrest, detention, disappearances and other alleged human rights abuses have been reported. Nigeria ratified the ICCPR and the ICESCR in July 1993 as well as the African Charter on Human and Peoples' Rights under which it has submitted only an initial general report.

Nigeria's legal system is based on English common law. The Customary Courts, for civil matters of customary law in the southern Nigerian states, are an exclusive jurisdiction. The Shariah Court of Appeal has jurisdiction over Islamic personal law matters but is not an exclusive jurisdiction because non-Muslims may apply to it and the *shariah* may be applied to non-Muslims, especially if they live in the midst of Muslims. In 1977, a debate on whether judges in the Shariah Court of Appeal should be Muslims or simply versed in Islamic law polarised the country.

Religious and belief composition

Nigeria has numerous religious and secular belief systems and bodies; new ones are claimed by the Christian Association of Nigeria to number up to 5,000. Though these proportions have been contested, nearly half the Nigerians are said to be Muslim, Christians about a third (Protestant–Catholic proportions being two to one), and African indigenous and traditional beliefs are held by over a quarter of Nigerian people. Christianity and Islam are officially recognised religions despite the professed secularity of the Nigerian state. Each includes some extremist splinter groups.

Christianity consists of the Protestant, Roman Catholic and Spiritual–Evangelical–Pentecostal churches which flourish all over Nigeria. The Protestant denomination includes the Anglican, Baptist, Methodist and Christ Apostolic churches, the Jehovah's Witnesses, Seventh-Day Adventists, the Presbyterians, the Unitarian Brotherhood Church and the Salvation Army. The urban Spiritual–Evangelical churches include breakaway movements from Protestant Churches and other indigenous Nigerian churches and movements. Islam consists of a wide variety of groups and movements, such as the Qadiriyya, Tijaniyya, Jama'atu Nasril Islam and Maitatsine movements; the head of Islam in Nigeria is the Sultan of Sokoto. There are also some urban-based new religious movements: the Grail Message Lodge, Krishna Consciousness, Guru Maharaji and Rosicrucian groups.

Christianity and Islam have coordinating bodies: the Christian Association of Nigeria and the Supreme Council for Islamic Affairs. Central coordinating bodies exist for each of the Christian denominations; most have official publications.

The African traditional religion and belief system – closely associated with local culture and communities – consists of the African indigenous or traditional beliefs and some secret societies. Adherents believe that inanimate and natural phenomena have souls and some great men or women are believed to have divine status. Christianity or Islam may be followed together with traditional practices by the same person or community. In western Nigeria in 1974, 92 per cent of surveyed Catholic secondary schoolboys (88 per cent of girls) said they believed in witchcraft and 10 per cent of Catholic parishes surveyed declared themselves to have been victims of witchcraft in the previous year.

Traditional religion has had to survive the period in which it was condemned by Western religion as pagan and fetishistic. The lesser status of traditional beliefs, together with a non-exclusive approach, has led to the assumption that all traditional believers are nominal Christians or Muslims. In the last two decades, Catholic seminarians have been bringing the understanding of their African identities to develop their Christian theology. The fact that Christians and Muslims are generally better off than traditional believers has contributed to their conversion and the expansion of Pentecostal 'holiness' and 'prosperity' churches, among others.

Atheism and free thought were first taught publicly in the late nineteenth century by Herbert Jumbo in Bonny. Educator Tai Solarin, who died in 1994, was a publicly declared, confirmed non-deist in the twentieth century. He separated religion from education and occupied himself solely with secular goals.

Conversion

Because the two dominant religions evolved out of Christian missionary evangelism and the religious militancy of Islam through *jihad*, they have dwarfed other religions and beliefs, especially African traditional beliefs. Few minority believers are exclusively so. In most cases, adherents of non-dominant religions are also members of the dominant ones. Because of this and because they are relatively few in number, they enjoy a considerable level of tolerance while experiencing far more discrimination at official levels. Regarded as 'unbelievers', they come under pressure to change their religious identities, beliefs and practices. Religious organisers of retreats or camping offer very poor people free transportation and meals. In some circumstances, the voluntariness of subsequent conversions has been questioned.

Children's evolving capacity to make their own religious decisions was questioned in a case involving a 16-year-old Christian girl in Kaduna in 1990. The Muslim who had allegedly converted her made a claim of custody over her. A lawyer handling the case stated that the child's change of faith did not divest the father of his paternity rights to custody while the child was a minor. However, the Muslims in the case were said to claim that they had to appoint a guardian for the child because the father was no longer in the position to cater for the interests of the new faith once the child had embraced it.

Regulation of associations

Although secret societies were an accepted part of pre-colonial life, regulation of their activities was first suggested in the 1940s and later incorporated in the 1979 and suspended 1989 constitutions. Some secret societies are religious and some may primarily have rituals, their status as religions being open to question. In the late 1980s various military decrees were promulgated which, temporarily or otherwise, prohibited religious or secret societies. The formation, name, membership, motto and symbol of a political party should not be associated with any religion or cult or have any religious connotation.

Military governments have from time to time banned religious activities in public, in the mass media or in schools and universities, such as the ban on religious activities in Oyo state schools in March 1994. The Maitatsine movement was by a federal order declared an 'unlawful society'. The movement's claim to profess the Islamic faith was disputed by authoritative Muslim opinion that regarded the group's actions as 'criminal and un-Islamic'. Although there have been wide press restrictions, news media and religious institutions are, however, allowed to express religious views.

The activities of secret societies, found mostly on university campuses, have been intimidating and provoked hostile reactions in the community. Violent clashes between secret society members and groups or individuals in the community led to over seventy deaths in Nigerian universities between 1993 and 1994.

Religion–state issues in Nigeria's suspended constitution

The protection of freedom of thought, conscience and religion contained in Nigeria's 1979 and the suspended 1989 constitutions may be summarised thus:

(a) prohibition of a state religion, that is, a particular religion should not be taken as an official religion in the country;
(b) everyone has the freedom to practise their religion according to their conviction; and
(c) while teaching of religion is allowed in schools, there should be no compulsion in matters of religious education.

The secular formulation of the religion–state relationship has been the subject of some dispute between Christians and Muslims. While Christians have interpreted the constitution to mean that Nigeria is a secular state and consider this appropriate given the country's heterogeneity, the Grand Khadi of Abuja, seeing church–state separation as Judaeo-Christian Western doctrine, declared in 1994 that in Islam it is not acceptable to separate state from religion and that one provision in the constitution does not make Nigeria a secular state. Muslims refer to the preamble to the constitution which invokes the guiding image of a harmonious state 'under God'. They point to Christian manifestations in the nation's public life and institutions as evidence that 'Islamic civilisation' has been subjugated by substantially Christian 'Western civilisation'. The common law is seen as laden with Christian ideals and doctrines, Sunday is a work-free day of rest in contrast to Muslim Friday prayer day, the cross is used as a symbol of medical and health services – not the Islamic crescent – and other matters to do with the establishment of calendars and the association of Christian festivals and holiday periods. The fact that this pervasiveness is a legacy of British colonial imposition is also noted.

Christians, in their turn, accuse the government of propping up the political and economic power of the Muslims. Former President Babangida went so far as to declare in 1986 that Nigeria should join the Organisation of the Islamic Conference (OIC), but this decision led to tension between the two religions and between Christians – who considered it a ploy to make Nigeria an Islamic state – and the government. The government neither confirms nor denies that it made moves to join the OIC. In response, it set up a committee to consider the issue, with half Muslim, half Christian representation, which ended in a stalemate. Eventually renamed as an Advisory Council on Religious Affairs, to advise on religious harmony, it could not decide upon its own chairman because the two religions voted as blocs.

Others see no contradictions in the constitution's preamble. For instance, Christians, Muslims and the Godians in Abbia State in 1992 joined in an open-air inter-faith service to dedicate the newly civilian state as God's Own State.

State support and privileges

Islam and Christianity not only play prominent roles in the nation's political, social, cultural and economic life, but they also receive recognition and assistance from the state. The new federal capital, Abuja, contains a 'cultural zone' for religious buildings. Only Christians and Muslims were allocated land and funds to build a National Mosque and National Cathedral. This decision was criticised by radicals and progressives as well as minority religious groups. Most Government Houses – especially in the southern states – have churches and mosques built at government expense.

Only recently have traditional religious believers started fighting for recognition at state and national levels. This delay is partly a reflection in part of the illiteracy of most traditional believers – in contrast to the higher education levels of adherents of the two major religions – a factor which contributes to their general lack of knowledge of their rights and of how to lobby government to act in their interests. However, associations of traditional believers are protesting against the degradation of their lands in the oil-rich south-west while easterners are striving for recognition of their traditional medicines.

The government has adopted an even-handed policy towards the two main religions in the matter of public holidays and facilitating pilgrimages. Public holidays are observed during both Christian and Muslim festivals. While Sunday is a work-free day, government offices and institutions are allowed either to observe the Jumat service or to work half-day on Fridays. Even in universities, the time for Jumat prayers is free of lectures. In addition, the government plays an important role in organising pilgrims and the welfare of pilgrimages of both Christians and Muslims. As well as establishing Pilgrims Welfare Boards, the state grants pilgrims concessional fares and foreign exchange rates when they travel to Jerusalem or Mecca.

The proliferation of religious groups has civil and legal consequences, such as conflict over their names. The Celestial Church of Christ unsuccessfully requested the federal High Court to prevent the Corporate Affairs Commission from registering another sect – Celestial Evangelical Church of Christ World Wide – because of its similar name. Not all, however, regard the rapid growth of religious groups negatively, preferring to see this as proof that Christianity is alive and growing.

Education

Denominational schools developed out of nineteenth-century Christian mission schooling. All schools were taken over in the mid-1970s by the government. Christianity and Islam are the only religions in school curricula and devotional services are mainly conducted in either. Religion is a consideration in decisions taken about where to post teachers. In 1961, the Jamaatu Nasril Islam society established the first Muslim secondary school in northern Nigeria.

Government takeover did not really change existing practices in schools which had been confessionally based. Children from a religion or denomination other than that of the former proprietor or the religion of their teachers, especially the principal, have little option other than to accept the instruction offered even if it is contrary to the wishes of their parents. Parents' constitutional and educational right to withdraw their children from unwanted religious instruction or observance is unlikely to be exercised for fear of sanction. Difficulty in organising instruction by other religious beliefs is a contributing factor; some may not be organised to be imparted in this way. The Lutheran Church also claims that even where Christians are the majority, Muslim leaders produce more Islamic teachers than Christian teachers to give religious instruction. Applications by other religious groups have also been refused by the Ministry of Education.

Relations within and between belief groups

The emergence of radical evangelism in Christianity and Islam, aimed at sustaining the membership or winning new recruits, has generated some problems within and between religion or belief groups. Although the call of radical Muslim and Christian preachers and denominations finds a ready reception in the larger society, including the universities, more orthodox Muslims and Christians are concerned at this development.

A number of positive inter-faith initiatives have taken place at the local level. In 1993, for instance, the Lutheran Church and other supporting religious organisations held an International Conference on Christian–Muslim relations in Plateau State. The conference issued a communiqué of observations about discrimination and conflict in Nigeria and made recommendations for building common ground, leadership, removal of discrimination and promotion of inter-faith dialogue.

Manifestations of intolerance and their consequences

Intolerance of religion and belief in Nigeria has manifested itself through sporadic civil unrest and some internal armed conflict. In places where Christian and Muslim religious revivalisms are in geographic proximity, the results can be explosive. Between 8,000–10,000 Nigerians died in religious violence between 1980 and 1987, and over 3,000 people have reportedly been killed since. Similar incidents have not happened to Muslims in the south partly because there the communities and even families are religiously heterogeneous.

Crises of civil unrest and armed conflict which include manifestations of religious intolerance have political, economic, social and ethnic undertones. The two dominant religions have attacked each other and experienced internal rivalries. Muslims in the north have objected to attempts by Christians to build new churches near mosques, to witness in public or to hold religious crusades in the town centres of northern cities where to do so might incite Muslims to violence.

Some Muslim outbursts were occasioned by Christians. The 'Kafanchan crisis' began at a College of Education in central Nigeria. The Muslim Students' Society objected to a banner erected by the Fellowship of Christian Students that read 'Welcome to Mission '87 in Jesus Campus'. The banner was removed but a talk during the mission by a northern Christian was felt to misinterpret the Qur'an. Subsequently, Christians in Kafanchan attacked Muslims, with swift reprisals following in a number of northern cities.

The Kano riots in 1990, in which hundreds died, were sparked off by a mission from Reinhard Bonnke. In 1991, a Muslim group which claimed that two of its prophets had been blasphemed in a Christian publication attacked the *Daily Times* office in Katsina and burned copies of the offending publication.

Christians have responded to provocation by Muslims incited to religious extremism. One Muslim preacher allegedly stated that Christians would have nothing to fear as they would have to convert to Islam; this extremism is not without its critics among Muslims. The preaching of Muslim revivalist leaders led to riots in Katsina (1991) and Zangon-Kataf in Kaduna State (1992). Hearings before the Civil Disturbances Special Tribunal – criticised for being dominated by Muslims – revealed rioters' claims that they were under orders from some Hausa Muslim elders to attack Christian Katafs. On this basis they had only allowed to pass those people who could correctly recite *shahada*, an affirmation that one is a Muslim. In such conflicts, all believers have suffered; at least 1,833 were killed and hundreds injured. Some 5,000 women from Christian women's groups marched in protest. About 845 houses were reportedly looted and burned, at least 192 vehicles destroyed, with nineteen churches and eleven mosques burned down; a claim for compensation has been made. Six Christians were later sentenced to death for their role in the riots.

In a further incident in 1993, the central government had reportedly promised that the Christian Sayawa community would be represented by its own leaders but the plan was blocked by the Muslim-dominated Bauchi State administration. Fighting broke out between Muslims and Christians when the Sayawa were forced to entertain a Hausa-Fulani state minister. In the ensuing melee, hundreds of people were killed, thirty-eight villages were destroyed, 1,500 homes wrecked and churches and mosques burned. In February 1996, sixty members of the Christian community in the Muslim-dominated state were sent to trial before a special quasi-military tribunal; none of the Muslims involved has been charged.

In December 1994, the head of an Igbo Christian, Gideon Akaluka, was brought before the emir of Kano. Accused of blasphemy, Akaluka had been in prison when he was killed. The government remained silent about this, although the Sultan of Sokoto – the spiritual leader of Nigerian Muslims – denounced violence in the name of religion.

Internal religious intolerance has also occurred, largely attributable to extremism, petty jealousies, power struggles and personal or doctrinal conflict. The Ahmadis' belief, structured in the modern way around missionaries, western-style schools and publishing houses, was denounced as heresy by the World Muslim League in the early 1970s and many Nigerian Muslims left it then. The Maitatsine Movement (with an estimated 10,000 followers) which had a leader who claimed to be the prophet for African Muslims in place of Prophet Mohammed was responsible for riots and disturbances mostly in northern Nigeria; these were aimed at more orthodox Muslims.

Among Christians, evangelical crusades can lead to expressions of intolerance. Several breakaway factions have produced a proliferation of Pentecostal movements. Old as well as new denominations have had bitter leadership squabbles, some of which, in the Anglican Communion and the Celestial Church of Christ, eventually needed judicial resolution. The seven-year tussle in the Celestial Church over the successor to its spiritual head has yet to be decided by the Court of Appeal. In the Christ Apostolic Church, some members and churches have been declared 'outcast'. Orthodox Baptists object to their congregation being members of 'secret societies'; this has led to the emergence of Gospel Baptist churches. Recently, an Archdeacon moved out of the Church of Nigeria (Anglican Communion) to form the Episcopal Church Mission. As a radical evangelist, he had expressed scepticism over some traditions of the church.

Women in religion

In all the major religions, there are more women than men and there are more women, young adults and youths in the spiritual–evangelical groups than in mainstream religious groups. Although most cultural religious groups and societies are dominated by older men – women are excluded from the secret knowledge of masquerade – women dominate witchcraft, both a life force and a source of dread.

In the Christian churches and in Islam, women participate but have limited involvement at the leadership level. Generally, Muslim women are relegated to the background in religious and non-religious roles; they cannot lead prayers. Some Muslims contend that it is 'un-Islamic to make a woman a leader of any society'.

In many mainstream Christian churches, women are not allowed to lead or preach. However, the ordination of three women was carried out unilaterally by the Anglican Bishop of Kwara Diocese in December 1993; it was voided by the Church of Nigeria (Anglican Communion) in January 1994. The controversial issue of women's ordination therefore remains unresolved. The situation is different in spiritual and evangelical churches where women found and lead their churches.

The recent history of post-colonial politics, in which both Christianity and Islam have been used for establishing oppositional power groups, has intruded on women's lives in serious ways. Under Hausa custom, purdah demands that women remain in seclusion when they marry and are heavily veiled when outside the home. Women in Kano are married very young – as young as 9 years old – and polygamy is common. Seclusion at an early age leads to illiteracy among most Hausa Muslim women. Women not in seclusion – unmarried, widowed and unescorted – are liable to be attacked by vigilantes.

Women still suffer subjugation and discrimination through the use of religion to set the conditions under which they live their lives. In Muslim Nigeria and in African traditional religions, a woman's consent is not required for a valid marriage to be performed. Child marriages are encouraged. Islamic law gives a widow one-quarter of her deceased husband's property and female children have half the share of their brothers. African indigenous cultures consider that women are the property of their husbands, have no inheritance rights of their own and may themselves be inherited by their deceased husband's next of kin. Christian converts may also still be affected by the custom of their original community.

African Christianity is still evolving distinctive forms for African communities and many cultural customs disadvantageous to women interact with both masculinist and liberatory aspects of Christianity with very uncertain results for women. For instance, menstruating women must often withdraw from many domestic and public activities, but women may also develop distinctive forms of healing ministries and evangelical leadership not easily available in other Christian cultures.

SENEGAL

Senegal	
GDP (US$bn)	6
Population	7,700,000
Annual population growth (%)	2.8
Urban population (%)	41
Working population (%)	34
Literacy (%)	30.5
Ratifications	1; 2, 2(a), 2(b); 3; 4; Af

Senegal is a country where human rights including freedom of conscience are protected and promoted. On the whole, the various religions cohabit in peace; some Islamist groups do not support freedom of conscience but they are a very small minority. Fighting against the separatist movement in the Casamance region in the south does not seem to be related to the issue of freedom of religion and belief.

In spite of the short rainy season and the dry climate, the economy of Senegal on the extreme west of Africa is based on agriculture, chiefly peanut farming; there is a move towards diversification and self-sufficiency. A high proportion – 62 per cent of Senegal's 7.7 million population – are illiterate and three-quarters of them are women who in rural areas are often prevented from going to school or drop out early because of household commitments. None the less efforts are made by the public authorities and non-governmental organisations to increase literacy. Schools are encouraged to teach in French, the official language.

Ethnic composition

Four predominant ethnic groups make up Senegal and six language groups are distributed around the country. The Wolofs, representing 42.7 per cent of the total population, are greatest in number and constitute most of the 61 per cent rural population. The preponderance of the Wolof people in the main centres of the country has resulted in the Wolof language being used as the language of communication in most of the country, thus reinforcing the domination of the Wolofs, who are strong Muslims.

The Halpulaar (Fulbe) are the second largest ethnic group, representing 23.7 per cent of the population of Senegal; their language is spoken throughout the African sudano-sahelian belt. The Senegalese Halpulaar, farmers and pastoralists, were traditionally based in northern Senegal but desertification has caused them to spread through the country. Their ancestors led various religious revolutions during the eighteenth and nineteenth centuries in western Africa and they are deeply Islamised.

Unlike the Wolof and the Halpulaar, 90 per cent of whom are Muslims, the Sereer (14.9 per cent of the total population) are mainly Muslims but also include large communities of Catholics, particularly in the regions of Fatick and Thiès.

The Joola – 5.3 per cent of the population – are mainly based in the southern regions of Ziguinchor and Kolda; they include a mix of Muslims, Christians and followers of traditional religions. A further group are the Mandingues (2.2 per cent of the population) based mainly in the regions of Kolda and Tambacounda.

Religious composition

Senegal is strongly dominated by monotheistic religions. According to the 1988 census – which does not indicate the extent of religious practice or nominalism – 93.8 per cent of religious followers are Muslim and 4.3 per cent are Christian; 1.6 per cent are members of indigenous ancestral cultures, mostly based in the region of Ziguinchor.

Senegalese Islam is strongly influenced by Sufi religious brotherhoods. The largest brotherhood is the Tijane (Tijaniyya) – nearly half the population – which includes more than ten independent sub-divisions. The Wolofs and the Halpulaar are the main followers of this brotherhood which came from Algeria. The Mouride brotherhood is the second largest (over a third of the population), founded by Senegal's Ahmadu Bamba. The Mourides in the region of Diourbel are farmers, traders and enjoy substantial economic power as well as political power, due to their unity. Other brotherhoods are the Qadiriyya (10 per cent of the population) and the Layènes.

These brotherhoods are influenced by Sufism, a movement within Islam that has accommodated the local religious culture and the All Saints cult. However, Senegal also has adherents of a kind of Islamic faith which is more rigorous and restrictive: the Jama'at 'Ibad al-Rahman and Falah movements based in Thiès and Dakar. These movements, very active in urban areas, include many paid workers and Arabic-speaking Muslims who work at spreading Islam within society, but revivalist Islam remains in the minority, representing less than 5 per cent of the population.

Christianity is the second religion in Senegal. Christians are fairly numerous within foreign communities. They are predominantly Catholics, except for a small number of Protestants of various denominations.

The largest religious groupings have a great deal of influence in public life. The religious brotherhoods of the Mourides and the Tijanes have often given their support to the ruling Socialist Party in exchange for favours, such as building roads on land owned by the brotherhoods or appointing brotherhood members to important public posts. Catholics form an important pressure group mainly through the eminence of Catholics in public life, such as President Senghor – president for twenty years – and Madame Elisabeth Diouf, wife of the current President, Abdou Diouf, elected in 1981.

Constitutional system

Senegal gained independence from France in 1960 and had a one-party system from 1964–74. The country is now governed by the Constitution of 1963, revised several times, which decrees that Senegal is a secular, democratic and social republic whose institutional bases are first the President of the Republic and the Government, then the National Assembly and, finally, the Constitutional Committee, the State Committee and the Supreme Court of Appeal. Although these institutions establish the principle of the separation of powers, the Socialist Party controls the executive as it has a comfortable parliamentary majority and the President of the Republic nominates the magistrates who preside over the State Committee, the Court of Appeal and the Constitutional Committee, and thus has influence on the power of the judiciary.

There has therefore been much debate as to whether Senegal is best classified as presidentialist or parliamentarian. However, political power in Senegal does not unduly favour any of the ethnic, linguistic or religious groups and, in turn, relations between the main religions and government have been (with few exceptions) positive. Muslims, who are by far the largest religious group in the population, did not contest the power of

President Senghor, a Catholic and a Sereer, nor did the two largest ethnic groups, the Wolofs or the Halpulaar. In the 1970s, separatist pressures came only from the Joola people in southern Senegal.

State and religion or belief

There is no official religion in Senegal. All religions are free to form their own associations. Similarly, nothing prevents Senegalese from creating organisations which would aim at promoting atheism or humanism.

The state prohibits the identification of political parties with any particular religion or sect – out of concern about inciting conflict and division in Senegal – under Article 3 of the constitution which states that 'Political parties . . . have the duty to respect the Constitution and the principles of national sovereignty and democracy.' They are not allowed to identify themselves with any particular race, ethnic group, sex, religion, sect, language or region.

Violation of the right to freely exercise religion is an offence under Articles 230–230(b) of the criminal code. A law of 1965, amended in 1981, relates to seditious associations and prohibits any associations whose activities are intended to practise racial, ethnic or religious discrimination or incitement. Incitement to racial hatred, and publishing whatever may incite racial, ethnic or religious hatred, are some of the criminal offences framed to combat any manifestations of such tension. It is a punishable offence for state officials to unlawfully deny a right to any citizen on the grounds of racial, ethnic or religious discrimination.

Constitutional standards

The preamble to the constitution declares that Senegal:

> proclaims her independence and her commitment to the fundamental rights which are defined in the 'Declaration des Droits de l'Homme et du Citoyen' of 1789 and to the 'Declaration des Droits de l'Homme' of 1948.

Article 19 of the constitution provides:

> The State guarantees that everyone shall have freedom of conscience, shall be free to teach and practise the religion of his choice. Religious institutions and communities have the right to develop freely with no interference from the State. They have the autonomy to regulate and administer their own affairs as they see fit.

Other guarantees of freedom of opinion and expression are also contained in the constitution. Senegal has ratified the African Charter of Human and People's Rights and the main international human rights instruments.

Religion and media

On the whole, Senegal's religious groups enjoy the freedom to propagate their beliefs. They publish reviews and films, and broadcast television and radio programmes on the official channels. The Jama'at 'Ibad al-Rahman, the Muslim Student Association of the University of Dakar and the Islamic Study Centre issue publications. The Catholic dioceses of Dakar and Saint-Louis publish their own reviews. Protestants have no publications at the moment but the Protestant Church broadcasts a short weekly radio programme.

The state radio and television channels ensure that religious programmes are adequately covered. Senegalese television broadcasts a weekly religious programme organised by the various current brotherhoods. In addition to these religious manifestations, dominated by sufism and the All Saints cult, there is also a weekly programme which concentrates on the doctrinal aspects of Islam. Catholic Mass is televised on Sundays. During the period of fasting, television time is granted to Muslims in Ramadan and Christians during Carême.

Because of its militant tendency in favour of a politico-legal system which would favour Islam and therefore dispute secularity, the 'Ibad al-Rahman Muslim Movement seems to suffer from discrimination. The movement has complained that it is denied the right to broadcast on official channels.

Family and religious education

Article 15 of the constitution stipulates that: 'Parents have the natural right and duty to bring up their children. In this task they have the support of the State and of the Public Authorities.' In Senegal, everyone has the right to bring up their children in the religion of their choice. The leaders of the various religious groupings unanimously favour the introduction of religious education in state schools. The state, however, has always been opposed to it in the name of secularity. To promote education, the state grants funding to all schools recognised by the Ministry of National Education, including private denominational schools which may be freely established.

To children born in Muslim families, religious education consists of learning all or part of the Qur'an and of practising their religious obligations. There are Qur'anic schools in the smallest street in the smallest village in Senegal, teaching only religion. Through flexible time arrangements, many Muslims are able to attend both a state and a private school at once. The Mouride brotherhood has an Islamic university in Touba.

Protestant churches have at their disposal libraries and centres where their followers can be taught Protestant education. There are many private Catholic schools which have catechism classes and welcome children of all denominations. Many Muslims send their children to Christian schools; they do not have to learn Christian doctrine. These schools illustrate the generally pacific co-existence between Muslim and Christian communities.

The Christian Centre project in Tivaouane

Muslim–Christian co-existence was most seriously endangered in 1986, when the Senegal Catholic Church built a huge religious centre in the town of Tivaouane, seat of the Tijane members of Al-Hajj Malick Sy. It was built to house, amongst other things, a chapel to allow 300 parishioners from the towns of Tivaouane, Mboro and Taïba to worship. According to the Bishop of Saint-Louis, it was the Tijanes' religious leader in Tivaouane who firmly opposed the inauguration of this chapel. Allegedly, threats to destroy the chapel and physically harm parishioners were made which led Senegal authorities to take over the centre. The chapel was converted into a non-religious social centre which is now administered by the Senegal Ministry for Social Development.

This event, however, has not persisted in people's memories and has thus not prevented Muslims and Christians from living together in relative harmony. To that extent, celebrations which originally were Christian celebrations and Easter are celebrated by both Muslims and Christians, even though Muslims do not attend the religious service. Similarly, at the end of the Ramadan or of the Feast of the Sacrifice, it is not unusual for adherents of other religions to join in the festivities.

Shariah followers and non-Muslims

Within the Muslim community of Senegal, followers of the *shariah* are least inclined to a system which guarantees freedom of conscience, because of the orientation of their particular system of faith. They regard themselves as the heirs of classical Islam and are strongly opposed to those who advocate secularity as a method of government, and they regularly criticise public authorities in their publications. The emergence of strict Islamic teaching in Senegal reflects the influence of the Iranian Revolution and the financial support of Gulf States for Islamic revival.

The religious movement called Da'irat al-Mustarshidin wa al-Mustarshidat, founded by Moustapha Sy, was dissolved by the Interior Ministry following serious public violence which led to the death of six police officers and later to human rights abuses of those detained.

The Islamist movements are learning how to live in a multi-denominational country and have in recent years been less aggressive than they were at the beginning of the 1980s.

Conscientious objection

Military service is not obligatory in Senegal and no question of objection of conscience has arisen.

Personal law and women's status

Article 1 of the Constitution of Senegal guarantees 'equality before the Law between all citizens without any distinction of origin, race, sex, religion'. In Senegal, there are women who play an important role in Islamic education and there are very active women within the Muslim community who lead their community and religious education.

However, Senegal's second CEDAW report acknowledged that the lower status of women arose from a belief in their inferiority which had various sources. The revealed religions asserted the powers of the husband in relegating women to a position of subservience while also assigning a role to women in accordance with Islamic rules on inheritance. Indigenous customs were also said to have instilled a concept of inferiority by regarding women as a production tool, to be bought by men through the bride price charged as compensation for women leaving the parental home. Forced labour under colonial rule also reduced women to the status of merchandise used as a pledge for honouring debts.

Women's rights were first recognised after the Second World War when they gained French citizenship and the right to vote and as they joined men in the socio-political movements which led to independence. After 1960, the rights of women were re-established in the application of customary law as the customary courts had previously only applied those of the husband in family disputes. The Family Code of 1972 established equality in a consensual marriage, required recording of marriages at civil registry offices, regulated personal and marital property, ended the capacity of men unilaterally to repudiate their wives and instituted consensual divorce. The law has since been amended to specify women's equality in rights and responsibilities or to remove provisions held to be discriminatory and contrary to women's dignity as human beings.

In 1981, for instance, the law was amended to eliminate the concept that a married woman could not leave the conjugal home without her husband's permission; this had also previously been a punishable offence, and a new provision reaffirms women's full civil capacity under Senegalese law, the law no longer recognising a husband's objection to a wife's working outside the home.

However, the state has acknowledged that an obstacle to the full development of women is polygamy as the law still permits a man to have two to four wives simultaneously. The Islamic law on succession, assigning to the daughter one half the inheritance made over to the son, has been made part of the Family Code. Senegalese women have sharply criticised these provisions – rooted in socio-cultural, traditional, economic and religious traditions and strongest in rural areas – as perpetuating inequality. They are said to prevent women from more effectively ensuring and safeguarding the interests of their children.

SOUTH AFRICA

South Africa	
GDP (US$bn)	104
Population	38,800,000
Annual population growth (%)	2.5
Urban population (%)	50
Working population (%)	38
Literacy (%)	80.6
Ratifications	4

South Africa's state and society are in a period of transition from totalitarian rule based on the racial ideology of apartheid to a fully participative democracy. In April 1994 the first democratic elections took place and in May, President Nelson Mandela, leader of the African National Congress, was inaugurated as the first black president of South Africa.

Religion and belief have played a crucial role both in creating and maintaining the system of apartheid as well as resisting it, influencing the process of change and the protection of human rights. The observation of traditional religious beliefs always formed an integral part of indigenous African cultures. While religious diversity is, and always has been, a fact of South African society, this fact has not largely been accepted and acknowledged by its dominant religious group.

Religious intolerance arising from the dynamics of the counter-reformation in Europe was a formative force in the colonial society from its earliest days. In 1652 Christian settlers arrived, followed by Muslim slaves and political exiles from the Indonesian archipelago. Calvinism was the first type of Christianity to take root in South Africa during the seventeenth century and this tradition was so strongly protected by the occupying Dutch East Indian Company that it was not until 1780 that even Lutherans were given freedom of worship. Bias against other traditions within Christianity was compounded by the Statutes of India in force in the Cape as part of the wider Company domain. These laws forbade Muslims to practise their religion in public or to propagate Islam, transgressions punishable by death. Jews were forbidden to settle in the Cape.

Religious freedom was granted in 1804 under the reforms of Jansens and de Mist. Catholics achieved the right to worship freely only after the end of the Company period in 1806 when the British assumed control. Hindus and Muslims were brought to South

Africa as indentured labourers in the second half of the nineteenth century and Eastern European Jews came at the end of the century.

The Cape territory was taken over by Britain which later also took control of the area today known as KwaZulu-Natal. Colonists of Dutch origin moved into the interior, establishing the provinces of Orange Free State and the Transvaal later in the century. In the struggle between the British and the Dutch, indigenous landowners became subjugated. Several wars were waged against black tribes while the British and Dutch descendants also fought each other. Non-Protestants were disenfranchised in Transvaal until 1902. The 1930 Quota Act ended Jewish immigration from Europe because of fears of Bolshevism; in 1937 the German Aliens Act curtailed German Jewish immigration. Anti-Semitic feeling is associated with the far-right wing of Afrikaner nationalism. South Africa left the Commonwealth and became a republic in 1961.

Ethnic and religious diversity

The population of the Republic of South Africa is estimated to be 38.8 million people of whom 77.5 per cent are black (African), 12.5 per cent white, 7.5 per cent coloured and 2.5 per cent Asian. Of the numerous languages spoken, eleven are recognised as official languages.

South Africa is a country of religious plurality. The best available data – 1980 – show that 77 per cent of the population claimed affiliation with some form of Christianity: 20 per cent of the population (over 30 per cent of the black population) belonged to the African Independent (or indigenous) Churches organised into over 4,000 denominations; the Dutch Reformed Churches (Nederduitse Gereformeerde Kerk) accounted for 14 per cent, the other mainstream Protestant Churches (Anglican, Methodist, Presbyterian, United Congregationalist, Lutheran and Baptist) for 23 per cent, the Roman Catholic Church for 9.5 per cent and the Pentecostal Churches for 1.5 per cent of the total population. Smaller Christian groups such as the Salvation Army, Seventh-Day Adventists and Jehovah's Witnesses were also present. Religions other than Christianity accounted for 4.5 per cent of the total population: 519,380 Hindus, 328,440 Muslims, 125,000 Jews and 10,780 Buddhists as well as smaller groups such as Baha'is, Zoroastrians, Sikhs and Jains. A large bloc, the remaining 19 per cent, would include people who have no religion, those with secular beliefs, those who object to stating their religion, and those whose belief is not classified, such as African traditional religions.

Non-Christian affiliation aligns with race and ethnic background to a considerable degree. With the exception of the relatively small number of Jews, white Muslims and white Buddhists, all the adherents of religions other than Christianity are black: African, coloured or Indian. These adherents, together with black Christians, found themselves on the receiving end of the ideology of apartheid. Black South Africans felt that for as long as they were not free politically, they were not free religiously; they felt tolerated but not free. Every situation of prejudice was therefore seen not only as racial but also as religious prejudice.

Apartheid as policy and theology

Slavery was the basis on which white colonial power was built in southern Africa. Blacks were excluded from all decision-making processes in the country and the economic and social foundations of apartheid were laid in which blacks' right to their own land was denied and white capitalist enterprise – and the exploitation of the country's vast mineral wealth – rested on conveniently available and poorly paid black labour.

Theories making absolute the differences between peoples and particularly between races arose in the eighteenth century partly to legitimise the slave trade and use of slaves. Some argued – in the course of the discovery of the laws of nature – that observed differences in wealth, class and race were part of the natural (that is, created) order, hence intended by God. In the Dutch Reformed Church, biblical support was found in 'the curse of Ham' (Genesis). Blacks were seen as descendants of Ham and therefore, as subjects of this curse, destined to be hewers of wood and drawers of water.

In the 1950s and 1960s, there was much international controversy as other parts of the World Alliance of Reformed Churches pressured the Dutch Reformed Church to change its ways; the South African church contained white, coloured and black branches. Some branches of the Dutch Reformed Church in South Africa, more conservative than others, arrived at a revisionist exegesis of 'the curse of Ham', a clear case of self-legitimating theology. As the criticism increased, the theology was held with greater fervour and sources of current anti-government protest are still to be found among conservative Calvinists.

Systemic and structural racism

In 1948 the National Party came to power and officially implemented the apartheid policy on a population where policy had not yet overridden a more fluid situation in which, though racial discrimination was endemic, black, white and coloured South Africans interacted to a considerable degree. The theory and practice of apartheid were useful to those in power as it ensured that the country was kept divided in order to frustrate the development of a national identity and culture.

Apartheid sought to enforce total racial separation in virtually every area of life and its organisation, through a tissue of laws, regulations, structures, institutions, policies and practices which affected a person's experience and expectations from the moment of birth, the conditions under which their life was lived and beyond the grave. The Population Registration Act 1950 classified people at birth into one of four categories: white, mixed race or coloured, Indian or African. These records still exist for people born before 1991.

Racially and ethnic-based schooling and ethnic-based universities were created and only English and Afrikaans were permitted as the medium of instruction in schools after the first four years of schooling. Private education which did not fit the authorities' scheme was suppressed, though in Catholic schools in the late 1970s and 1980s, significant moves to desegregate were made. Between 1948 and 1990, a plethora of ethnic-based ministries administered and reinforced the inequalities in educational resources and quality. Even taking into account the improvements since the abandonment of apartheid, the per capita expenditure on white children is still four times that spent on black children.

Only Christianity was recognised in public television and radio broadcasting; prayers at state functions were solely Christian. Religious education in schools formed part of an educational strategy to promote 'Christian nationalism' and apartheid theology and education.

Freedom of religion

The preamble of the 1961 and 1983 constitutions acknowledged the sovereignty of Almighty God and although the tri-cameral system brought Hindus and Muslims – as Coloureds – into parliament for the first time, the 1983 constitution declared that one of the national objectives would be 'to maintain Christian values and civilised norms and protect freedom of worship'.

However, freedom of religion and belief during the apartheid era was outward freedom only. Although religions were free to worship, erect places of worship and propagate their beliefs, the apartheid laws – in particular the Group Areas Act – placed restrictions on where people might live. Buildings such as mosques and Hindu temples could only be erected in areas set aside for Coloureds or Asians. The mosques left behind when large numbers of Muslims living in District Six of Cape Town were forcibly removed under the Group Areas Act were not demolished but were left empty and uncared for because all Muslims left the area. All religious work was under government control; schools, hospitals and welfare programmes had to comply with apartheid regulations, catering for each racial group separately.

Religions in resistance

In 1982, the Anglican synod had rejected the Prohibition of Mixed Marriages Act and Section 16 of the Immorality Act. Clergy were advised to ignore government instructions and give sacramental marriage to people they were unable to marry under law. The white Dutch Reformed Church insisted at the time that the legislation should be retained.

Thousands of young whites refused to fulfil military service duties in black townships and in the repression of the African majority. The 1983 Defence Amendment Act divided conscientious objectors into 'religious' and 'political' categories. Political objectors were imprisoned for six years and religious objectors were given lengthy and repressive forms of alternative service. Church leaders – apart from the white Dutch Reformed Church – called for an end to conscription, considering that the existing provision for Christian pacifists to be allowed alternative forms of service did not go far enough as it did not include moral or ethical objectors.

The discrimination and deprivation which apartheid caused led to resistance in various ways from the black population. Violence and armed conflict erupted as the regime attempted to crush those supporting the renewed African National Congress's Freedom Charter: the United Democratic Front, the Congress of South African Trade Unions and the ANC itself. People and organisations supporting religious, secular and atheistic views were united by the goal of human rights.

Building on a tradition of struggle against racism in South Africa, religious leaders and a contextual or liberation theology were prominent in the resistance, the leaders often entering protest organisations quite independently of their religion's structures. Progressive re-interpretative Islamic thought also moved hand in hand with progressive political thought, contributing to support in the coloured community for the liberation movement.

In 1985, church leaders all over South Africa led protest marches in a show of civil disobedience. The Kairos Document was published. Those who wrote it – from the wide range of Christian traditions – challenged the legitimacy of the state and opened up communication between the prophetic church and the liberation movement, particularly the ANC. The World Council of Churches facilitated the strengthening of these relationships.

Early in 1989, President F. W. de Klerk took office and the possibility of discussions became real, especially as the international community, by means of economic sanctions and sports and cultural boycotts, had isolated South Africa and the economy was stagnating. In 1990, with the removal of prohibitions on liberation movements and the release of political leaders from prison, notably Nelson Mandela after twenty-seven years there, the end of apartheid was in sight.

Although the economy is improving – the industrial sector is strong – there is still great poverty; unemployment in the formal sector is 40 per cent while half of the black South Africans available for work are unemployed or work in the informal sector. Many migrate or commute to work from the 'homelands'. In 1992, 1.7 million black children were not in school. There are vast numbers of landless people – 8 million in squatter camps – and the conflict between possession and dispossession is likely to continue. Horrendous levels of violence were produced by apartheid and by those defending it in the name of an ideology of national security and anti-communism (the military, the security forces and the police), as well as by those resisting apartheid and by warring factions and vigilantes. Political violence has been aimed at disrupting a peaceful transition to democratic rule. Human rights abuses have been massive. Thousands were killed or injured and over 12,000 children were held in adult prisons in 1992 alone.

From 1990, the South African Council of Churches and others have helped to nurture the process of negotiation and tried to check the growth of a culture of violence. Four ecumenical task forces deal with violence, political justice, education for democracy and economic justice. Initiatives in educational reform, affirmative action and schemes for land redistribution are discussed. However, most Christian congregations remain apathetic rather than inspired to prophetic witness; the white Dutch Reformed Church is still engaged with the Broederbond and resists merging into common communion in a non-ethnic unified church. Hope may instead reside in changes within the churches: in the strength of Christian women, in African Independent Churches, in the growth of small Christian communities, and in national and in Pan-African church cooperation.

Representatives of various faith communities took part in offering prayers at President Mandela's inauguration and the openings of national and provincial parliaments. Many faiths are now represented through national television. Archbishop Desmond Tutu, who retired in 1996, heads the Truth and Reconciliation Commission, set up by the government to hear evidence of crimes under apartheid and to reconcile victims with perpetrators.

Women and gender equality

Women inside and outside religious organisations have struggled to put sexism on an agenda which has hitherto had racism as the priority for action. Much of the strength of women's consciousness today derives from the large and powerfully resistant women's church groups formed in response to the dominant theology.

Constitutional guarantees of gender equality have been demanded by women from a government also besieged by communities seeking validation of their systems of personal law, Muslim or African. Avenues which women can now explore in order to gain redress for marital injustices could disappear if codified personal law leads to greater uniformity of approach among religious or customary authorities. While progressive religious organisations prefer to use consultations to work through potential conflicts, conservative leaders prefer to lobby for political alliances on specific issues. Among Muslims, progressive leaders place their hope for the future in women's assertiveness, strong progressive mosque communities, the liberating experience of the 1980s, growing interest in Islam in tertiary education and in continued good relations with non-Muslims.

Freedom of religion and belief in a new South Africa

In his historic speech in parliament on 2 February 1990, former President F. W. de Klerk, among other things, envisaged a Bill of Human Rights which would include a clause on religious freedom. The Transitional Constitution contains provisions which protect freedom of religion, belief and opinion, allow non-compulsory religious observances in state and state-funded institutions on an equitable basis, and allow for legislation validating religious personal status law.

Responding to the prospect of a Bill of Rights, the South African Chapter of the World Conference on Religion and Peace (WCRP–SA) initiated a process of consultation within all the religious communities in South Africa, resulting in the adoption of a Declaration on Religious Rights and Responsibilities. While not enjoying any legal status, the importance of this document for the future lies in the fact that it was the product of multi-faith negotiations and deliberations and that it has subsequently been endorsed by most religious bodies and organisations in the country. WCRP–SA was strongly criticised by various religious groups in June 1992 when it suggested that there should be a 'formal link between religions and the state' in the form of an 'independent inter-faith advisory body'. Its view was that such an authority need not challenge a separation of church and state, but rather encourage better understanding between faith communities and assist their contribution to building a just society.

The WCRP Declaration acknowledged three important principles: the reality of religious diversity in South Africa, separation between religion and state, and equal opportunities for all religions in societal life. The document called on the state not to identify with or favour any particular religious tradition. This point generated quite a controversy. Many hoped that the 1996 constitution would stipulate that the conduct of state affairs would be free from identification with or bias towards any specific religious tradition. In particular they criticised not only the substantive content of the 1993 Provisional Constitution but its preamble which, in calling for a new order of national unity in South Africa, formulated the declaration of the people of South Africa in terms of a 'humble submission to Almighty God'. In the support for a secular state which is neutral between different religious persuasions and also between atheism and theism, appeal was made to the aim of the constitution to define and protect the rights and freedoms of all citizens, protecting minorities as much as the majority.

The preamble in the text ultimately certified by the South African Constitutional Court in early December 1996 does not include those words. Instead, the preamble now ends 'May God protect our people', followed by the opening line of one of South Africa's two national anthems in each of its official languages. In English, it is 'God bless Africa'.

Education and the new South Africa

Desegregation has started in almost every white school – though this change is uneven throughout the country – by ending any form of discrimination on admission to schools. For instance, in Gauteng Province, schools which had never previously admitted a black pupil opened their doors in 1995 to 300–400 African children and legislation has since been passed to prohibit any kind of discrimination in school admission. Attention has also been given to ensuring that pupils are encouraged to learn, whatever their language background, and that no pupil will be punished for expressing themselves in a language which is not the school's language of learning.

Christianity is no longer the sole faith taught through religious education in schools. Schools' governing bodies, according to Gauteng State's new legislation, are to work out the best way of accommodating the religious needs of students ('learners'). The Gauteng School Education Act 1995 sets out the framework for the religious policy of a public school in that province. This framework aims to develop a national, democratic culture of respect for the country's diverse cultural and religious traditions, and the principles of freedom of conscience and of religion.

This framework of principles governs policy, practice and behaviour in schools. No public school employee is allowed to indoctrinate students in a particular belief or religion; no public or private school employee is allowed to denigrate any religion. Students at public schools or subsidised private schools have the right not to attend religious education classes and religious practices at their school. Parents have the right to provide direction to their children on these matters, consistent with the child's evolving capacity (this takes up provisions of the Convention on the Rights of the Child), though this right is limited in situations involving subsidised private schools where it is necessary to preserve the religious character of the school. No school employee may discourage any student from exercising their right to conscientious objection, nor is any such employee obliged to participate in religious education classes and practices at a public school.

However, for many, these improvements are still far away. The racial geography of the old South Africa has left a legacy of townships and rural areas where the majority of African children go to school and where it would be rare indeed for a white or Indian child to attend such a school. Historically white schools, too, have taken an assimilationist attitude and marginalised African languages, based on unquestioned assumptions about the inevitability of using the dominant language, English, as the medium of instruction for the future. A non-racist or anti-racist curriculum is needed in all schools. In Afrikaans-medium schools which are accommodating African children, real understanding of religious pluralism has been slow to develop. The future of Afrikaans-medium schools was one of the issues on which Deputy President de Klerk and the National Party pulled out of the government of national unity when the new constitution was adopted by the multi-racial parliament in May 1996.

Peace with justice in the new South Africa will entail work to remove the structural bases for discrimination and the acknowledging of multiple bases for forming identity and challenging stereotypes. The role of education will be crucial in the future. Powerful and popular symbols of unity and reconciliation are needed, as well as a commitment to confront the past, if a viable non-racial society is to be constructed where all South Africans are treated equally in dignity.

SUDAN

Sudan is the largest country in Africa, bordering nine other countries and the Red Sea. Its 25.9 million people live mostly around the Nile and its tributaries; 75 per cent of the Sudanese live in the north. About 70 per cent of the population live in rural areas, 20 per cent in urban areas and 10 per cent still follow a nomadic life. Agriculture, the mainstay of the economy, provides about 90 per cent of export earnings and employs about 70 per cent of the workforce. The country's economy, adversely affected by drought, which peaked in the 1980s, and a continuous process of desertification, is caught in a cycle of war and famine.

Over the forty years of Sudan's independence, it has been ruled by the military for three-quarters of the time. Fresh elections were held in 1996 but were boycotted by opposition

Sudan	
GDP (US$bn)	21.5[b]
Population	25,900,000
Annual population growth (%)	2.7
Urban population (%)	23
Working population (%)	35[a]
Literacy (%)	42.7
Ratifications	1; 2; 3; Af

groups. A year earlier, President al-Bashir had urged people to vote for deputies who would fight on behalf of Islam and were 'prepared to sacrifice their lives and property for the sake of the Shariah.' One goal which has united military and democratic governments of the Sudan has been a commitment to establishing an Islamic society. What has divided them has been the question of an Islamic state and the pace of implementing the *shariah*.

The response to Islamisation policies on the part of religious minorities of the south, as well as unequal economic development, have fuelled the civil war which has brought chaos to Sudan since 1955. Perhaps 1 million people have died as a result during the past forty years and 2 million have been displaced within Sudan and as refugees to neighbouring states since the 1980s.

The UN Special Rapporteur on human rights in Sudan concluded in early 1994 that grave and widespread violations had taken place, including arbitrary detention and torture and killings as well as abduction, rape and slavery of women and children and the use of children in both the government's and rebels' militia. Displaced people live in sub-human conditions in camps, engage in marginal economic activities and are constantly harassed by the authorities.

Ethnic and religious composition

Sudan is characterised by the ethnic and religious diversity of its nearly 600 indigenous groups speaking some 400 languages. Between 30 per cent and 40 per cent of the country's population identify themselves culturally as Arabs. Arab groups have enjoyed a dominant position in the country for many centuries. In the north, Islam gradually supplanted Coptic Christianity and the indigenous religions.

Other major groups such as the Nubians, the Beja, the Nuba, the Fur and the Zaghawa have converted to Islam. Although they have retained their languages, more Arabic is spoken as communities move to urban centres. The Nuba of southern Kordofan have on the whole retained their languages and religions though their way of life is changing and they have come under the influence of Islamisation. Together with the ethnic groups of south Sudan, these comprise the indigenous population of Sudan; they are located towards the borders and the coast of the country in such a way that they encircle the minority of Arab origin.

About 73 per cent of the Sudanese are Sunni Muslims who follow the Malikite rite, 16.7 per cent adhere to indigenous religions and 9.1 per cent are Christians, including Coptic Christians. Muslims are predominantly organised in Sufi *tariqas* (brotherhoods), the largest of which is the Khatmiyya brotherhood whose followers mostly live in the north and east of Sudan, whereas the Ansar brotherhood's following is largely in the west.

The adherents of indigenous religions live mainly in the south, the Nuba Mountains and the Ingassana region. Many black African Sudanese are Christians in churches which include the Roman Catholic, Anglican and other Protestant Churches, the Africa Inland Mission, and a number of Pentecostal and indigenous churches. Catholic missionaries arrived in the south in the late nineteenth century, followed by Presbyterians from the United States and Anglicans from Great Britain, establishing English as the lingua franca of the southern educated elite.

Civil war and the political system

British–Egyptian colonial rule from 1899 to Sudan's independence in 1956 accelerated the socio-economic development of the north while the Closed Districts Ordinance 1936 restricted contact between northern and southern Sudan and the Nuba Mountains. The south, with its indigenous societies, was protected from modernisation and was never fully integrated into Sudan's nation state. The boundary between south and north was considered by the British to be a division between 'Arab' and 'African' cultures. Christian missionaries were channelled to the south and Islamic proselytising was prohibited there. The Sudan government has now redrawn it to bring the Nuba Mountains and the Ingessana mountains into the administration of the north.

The single most devastating impact on Sudanese people and the economy came from the civil war between south and north which re-erupted in 1983. The war largely took place in the south and on the north–south boundary. The first civil war of 1955–72 had come about because the people of the less developed south were at a disadvantage in a united country. When Nimeiri signed an agreement giving regional autonomy to the south, the fighting stopped, but in 1983 he revoked the south's autonomy – dividing it into three areas – at the same time as proclaiming the rule of the *shariah* (Islamic law). In 1985, the scholar Mahmoud Mohammed Taha was executed. Taha was the chief representative in Sudan of the trend in Islamic thought which recognises the *shariah* as a historical interpretation of the Qur'an and the Sunna, and allows that norms may vary according to changing circumstance.

After the June 1989 military *coup d'état* which toppled the elected government of Prime Minister Sadiq al-Mahdi (leader of the Umma Party) and installed Lt-Gen. Umar Hasan Ahmad al-Bashir as head of state, the government's policy towards the south became more intransigent and it steadily mobilised all the country's resources to achieve a military victory over Sudan People's Liberation Army (SPLA). The new government was (and still is) dominated by the National Islamic Front (NIF) of Dr Hasan Abd Allah al-Turabi which advocated the implementation of the *shariah* and the Islamisation of the entire country.

The government's commitment to a military solution has overstretched the country's resources and led to severe economic hardships. Since 1993 a programme of economic liberalisation and structural adjustment has been undertaken. The regime's regional and international isolation – and defaulting on its debt payments – has made Sudan ineligible for the resources of the International Monetary Fund.

The Revolutionary Command Council for the National Salvation Revolution (RCC) dissolved itself in October 1993 and appointed Lt-Gen. al-Bashir as President. NIF supporters reportedly hold key posts in public office and senior appointments in Sudan. In January 1992, the 300-seat Transitional National Assembly was appointed which may propose and pass legislation, ratify treaties and veto government decisions. The Assembly has issued a document which sets out a number of freedoms and fundamental rights for

Sudanese people including a statement of respect for all 'heavenly revealed religions and sacred beliefs' which the state is to protect from abuse; the state also is to prohibit religious persecution and intolerance.

In February 1994, the government re-divided the country into twenty-six states, appointing some northern ministers to assist governors of southern states, and vice versa; in practice, the states are firmly under the executive and legislative powers of the centre.

Opposition to the NIF comes from two sources: the Sudan People's Liberation Army (SPLA) which controls most of the south and the National Democratic Alliance (NDA), the political coalition which embraces the northern parties and of which the SPLA is also a member. The SPLA has been waging a war since 1983 calling for a 'New Sudan' of even development, equitable distribution of wealth and power and free of cultural hegemony. In 1991, the SPLA split into a mainstream calling for self-determination and a splinter SPLA-United calling for outright separation for the south. The NDA includes the banned Umma Party, the Democratic Unionist Party, the Sudanese Communist Party and other forces. It is committed to the return of a multi-party democracy but is still divided over the issues of secularism and the south.

The war has brought a climate of repressiveness, informing, surveillance, investigation and documented severe human rights abuses by government and rebels alike, not to speak of exploitation of food aid and the internal displacement of several million people. Freedom of expression effectively does not exist. The media are controlled by a code which restricts coverage of many matters including subjects that might raise religious or racial tension.

In 1994, the government had been engaged in negotiations with the rebels – self-determination and the relationship between religion and the state being the major items of disagreement – but the war continued. Experience of living in an environment of random and arbitrary violence, coupled with the deaths of several generations of family members, have entrenched a climate of resistance in the south. In 1977 rebels in both north and south joined forces to make their first combined offensive.

Ideology and cultural diversity

The coming of the present government to power has accelerated and intensified a process whereby the ethnic, the cultural and the ideological have come into violent collision. The regime holds to an ideology based on its interpretation of Islam and views itself as a missionary regime entrusted with the message of spreading Islam in Sudan, the rest of Africa and beyond.

The authorities' assurances of their respect for the country's religious and cultural diversity is at odds with their policies and conduct which have indicated a firm commitment to Islamisation. Where such a policy might lead is demonstrated by what has been taking place in the Nuba mountains since 1989. As inhabitants of a marginalised region, some Nuba people were attracted by the SPLA's call for a 'new Sudan' and joined in its armed rebellion. In this region government planes are alleged to have bombed civilian and refugee camps. In 1993, important shrines and mosques of the Khatmiyya and Ansar orders which support the rebels were put under the control of the security forces. It is claimed that the Nuba people have been forcibly relocated *en masse* to sites run by the Islamic Call organisation (Dawa Islamiyya), a semi-official body involved in relief and proselytisation work under the state assimilationist policy.

The legal system and implementation of the *shariah*

The most significant development since the 1989 coup has been the commitment to the implementation of *shariah* as a basis of the country's legal system. The Sudanese legal system was a composite one made up of the customary laws of different regional groups, *shariah* law and the religious laws of various confessional groups and English common law. For about three decades, the statute law determined the recognition and scope of application of customary and religious laws. However, in 1983 former President Ja'far Nimeiri decreed that *shariah* should be the country's national law. *Hudud* punishments were immediately introduced, as was a provision on free interpretation allowing a judge to convict for non-statutory offences allegedly prohibited by the Qur'an and the Hadith. There were no immediate changes to civil law. After the overthrow of President Nimeiri and between April 1985 and July 1989, the Shariah Penal Code remained in force though the implementation of sentences handed down by the courts remained frozen.

Although, after the 1989 coup, President al-Bashir had publicly pledged to put the issue of *shariah* to a referendum, in March 1991 the *shariah* was reactivated in the north. Though the non-Muslim south has been exempted from *shariah*, non-Muslim southerners who live in the north may still be subject to its provisions, as the following case shows. Michael Gassim, an 18-year-old Christian from the south, along with three accomplices, was caught in connection with the break-in of a shop in Port Sudan and put on trial. Only Gassim was sentenced to cross amputation (the cutting off of the right hand and the left foot) while his accomplices, all Muslim northerners, were given various terms of imprisonment. Michael Gassim's brutal punishment was seen by southerners as a clear case of religious and racial discrimination.

Since 1989 the head of state has been responsible for the supervision of the judiciary and judicial appointments. Judges suspected of being opposed to the regime or being anti-*shariah* were replaced. Sudan is distinctive in the proportion of the judiciary who are women.

Sudan has ratified the main international human rights instruments but its adoption of *shariah* precipitated new challenges for the country's commitment to human rights standards, notably with respect to the freedoms of thought, conscience and religion or belief. These have been the subject of scrutiny and comment by international committees monitoring the implementation of human rights covenants as well as by the Special Rapporteur on Sudan.

The *shariah* does not recognise religious freedom as an open quest. Whereas it recognises the right of non-Muslims to adopt Islam, it does not recognise the right of Muslims to recant Islam. The rights of non-Muslims to manifest their religions or teaching and to propagate them are curtailed.

Although the September 1983 *shariah* laws did not provide for apostasy, Mahmoud Mohammed Taha, the revered 76-year-old leader of a modernist Islamist group, was none the less convicted of apostasy and executed in January 1985. Taha's case was seen by many within Sudan and outside as a blatant misuse of the law as he did not reject Islam but merely held views that were not acceptable to those in power. Article 126 of the 1991 Penal Code now criminalises apostasy and makes it a capital offence should the offender persist in it after a certain period of grace granted by the court. The provision has been condemned by the Special Rapporteur on Sudan as a direct contradiction of international law, as it can be used not only against members of religious minorities who convert – especially those who do so under compulsion – and then change their minds, but also against any Muslims who dissent from the official position on religious matters.

Islamisation and conversion

Sudanese non-Muslims who believe in revealed religions are not treated as *dhimmis*, with fewer rights as citizens, but are included in the secular concept of a common citizenship based on belonging to a nation-state. But for the substantial minority who follow indigenous religions and are regarded as polytheists, the regime has actively engaged in Islamic proselytisation. Public and private funds have been poured into building mosques which are seen as an important tool of Islamisation.

According to the 1994 report of the UN Special Rapporteur on Religious Intolerance, the Sudanese government claimed that Muslims in the south were 18 per cent of the population, outnumbering Christians at about 17 per cent, an estimation which is politically motivated as the government sought to justify its appointment of southern Muslim individuals to top political positions in the south without them having a political constituency in a community overwhelmingly comprised of Christian Sudanese.

Indigenous religions have so far shown a remarkable degree of resilience, recent reports indicating a shift back to traditional religions – though Dinka people are rapidly converting to Christianity – in the face of the government's programme of Islamisation. Indigenous religions are felt to be part of a southern identity as distinct from a northern identity. However, in the Ingessana mountains on the north–south boundary, forced assimilation to Islam has been reported, under the guise of cultural assimilation.

Recent converts to Christianity have been persecuted. In 1990, a Muslim *imam* was baptised, calling himself Sylvador Ali Ahmed. He was tried and sentenced to six months in prison as well as being dismissed from his work, forbidden the custody of his children and dispossessed of his property. The authorities, however, released him after he had served his sentence, possibly because of international reactions to his case owing to close monitoring by Christian organisations.

Although an *en masse* conversion to Christianity took place in the early 1970s in the village of Nafia in the eastern Nuba Mountains, in August 1993 the village reportedly was put under siege by security forces to make it reconvert to Islam. Two men were detained, subjected to torture in a secret detention centre and were afterwards taken to a mosque and forced to recite the *shahada*, thus identifying themselves as Muslims. Besides force, the government has apparently tried to induce the village people back to Islam by distributing gifts, including food aid, according to Roman Catholic bishops. In Wau, Torit and Kapoeta, Christians who convert to Islam have been renamed and even circumcised, but they continue to go to church in the hope of more aid relief.

The impact of the churches' advocacy of human rights

Whereas indigenous religions operate under the constraints of limited resources and a lack of an international voice, by contrast Christianity, with its organised international presence, can forcefully bring its plight to public notice, for instance, through the visits of the Pope in 1993 to Khartoum and the Archbishop of Canterbury to the south in 1994, visits which highlighted within the country and overseas the issue of restrictions on freedom of religious belief and practice in Sudan.

Churches and church-run centres have come under increasing pressure and harassment, including restrictions on religious activities and the movement of religious personnel and the detention of the editor-in-chief of Radio Juba in May 1992 for having announced the beatification of the Sudanese Sister Bakhita. No churches have been able to be built or repaired in Khartoum since 1969. In May 1992 the Roman Catholic Church centre of al-Nuhud, which supported 500 displaced Catholics, in the western region, was closed down and three priests and several nuns were expelled from the city. In September 1992, all the remaining foreign missionaries in the southern capital of Juba were deported. The city was at the time besieged and the government justified its act as protecting the missionaries.

The New Sudan Council of Churches (NSCC) was established in the SPLA-controlled areas in the south, as an independent humanitarian relief and aid organisation for the civilians in these areas. However, the government has seen it as proof of the churches' entanglement with the SPLA. The NSCC distanced itself from the SPLA when in 1992 it called upon the United Nations and the international community to intervene to save the civilian population and to investigate the government's and the rebels' human rights abuses. In 1991, some members of the Sudan Catholic Bishops' Conference signed a pastoral letter stressing the importance of non-violent resistance in the face of the regime's discrimination against Christians. The security forces ordered the signatories in January 1992 to withdraw the letter on the grounds that it threatened national security and was likely to provoke civil strife.

An incident that was seen as part of the government's concerted effort to humiliate and intimidate the church was the public flogging in September 1993 of Bishop Peter al-Birish, the Anglican Bishop of Khartoum, for alleged adultery. The court had sentenced him without following the formal *shariah* procedures to substantiate the charge.

Sudanese and non-Sudanese church activists made an active effort to involve the international community. In late 1993, Pax Christi International, a Catholic human rights group, paid a visit to Sudan and produced a report highly critical of the regime's human rights record. In a letter to UN Secretary General in August 1992, the bishops of Sudan and six other African states condemned the persecution to which Christians were subjected in Sudan. In October 1992, the Pope met with Sudanese bishops and expressed his concern at what he described as the regime's drive to impose on the country a single religion and a single culture. In March 1993, Bishop Macram Max Gassis, the Bishop of El-Obeid, addressed the UN Commission on Human Rights, giving an account of human rights violations and religious discrimination and calling upon the international community to take a more active role and work towards putting an end to the regime's violations.

Following the meeting between Pope John Paul II and the President of Sudan, some positive measures were introduced, such as the abrogation of the law on missionary societies and the assignment of land to Christians for building churches. A new government-sponsored body, the Society for Religious Dialogue was established in 1995 as was a Human Rights Council. Human rights commissions, charged with disseminating information, are planned for each state.

Coptic Orthodox Christians

Since 1989 the Copts – up to 200,000 followers of the Egyptian Coptic Orthodox Church – have also been persecuted. Their ancestors had been forced to convert to Islam under the Mahdist state (1881–98). Though present-day Copts have not been formally forced to convert to Islam, they have been discriminated against and forced to endure (or flee from) such things as closure of their churches, mass dismissals from official posts and judicial institutions, and imposition of Islamic dress on Coptic women. Alarmed by the momentum of Islamism and by the fact that the September 1983 *shariah* laws remained intact, the Copts have formed the Christian Alliance, a pressure group that publicises the discriminations against non-Muslims and calls for equality. The position of Sudanese Copts is made all the more vulnerable by the rise of Islamist revivalism in Egypt and the attacks on Copts and their property there.

Suppression of difference within Islam

Islam has been exploited by various groups and political parties in Sudan to safeguard and promote their respective interests. The 1989 coup led to the concentration of power in the hands of the National Islamic Front and the exclusion of other political and religious forces. The two major Muslim brotherhoods – the Khatmiyya and the Ansar – which constitute the mass bases of the Democratic Unionist Party and the Umma Party respectively, were suppressed. Both are committed to multi-party democracy within which to pursue potential Islamisation programmes.

Within the intellectual space created by the current regime, different or competing interpretations of Islam are not allowed. The mass media and the national curriculum are the most potent means to disseminate the official conception of Islam and exclude other conceptions, thus manipulating the feelings and beliefs of Sudanese Muslims. The media is used for 'demonising' Christians, Jews and the Western world generally for problems that are primarily economic, political or military. However, Christian religious services are broadcast on the television on Sundays. In July 1993, a Ministry of Social Planning was established as part of the Islamisation programme. It absorbed the former Ministry of Religious Affairs and Endowments, whose dissolution underlines the regime's conviction that the secular and the religious should not be separated.

Atheists

The status of atheists in Sudan is addressed by Article 126 of the 1991 Penal Code. In its reference to apostasy the article covers converting from Islam to another religion, giving up organised religion altogether or professing agnosticism or atheism. The article presupposes a Muslim background and hence protects only Islam. Some northerners from Muslim families have become agnostic.

The Sudanese Communist Party (SCP), though guided by Marxism–Leninism, has never espoused atheism. On the contrary, many Muslims joined the party and it expressed favourable views about Islam. However, Islamists insisted that, as an 'atheistic' party, the SCP had no place in a Muslim Sudan. In 1965, they successfully campaigned to have the SCP outlawed. When the SCP re-emerged between 1985 and 1989, its legitimacy went unchallenged but since then it has been banned and its members subjected to harassment, repression, detention and torture.

Education

Secular education was introduced at the end of the nineteenth century, before which period only formal Qur'anic education was available. In 1986–88, 39 per cent of Sudanese men were literate and 10 per cent of women. Northern children are more likely to attend school and reach higher levels of schooling than those in the south where war damage to schools and displacement, and in the west famine, have disrupted schooling.

Language is an emotional and political issue in the south where the people prefer English as a medium of instruction rather than their indigenous languages. The independence of church-run schools has been seen by several Sudanese governments to need restriction.

For instance, in 1962, the Abbud government enacted the Christian Churches Missionary Act and then expelled all foreign missionaries; Arabic language use and Islamic instruction were imposed on southern schools.

In 1992, the General Education Regulation Act stipulated that Islamic instruction and the use of Arabic language were compulsory at all levels of education. In November 1991, the government had announced the switch from English to Arabic; a pass in Arabic became a prerequisite for access to tertiary education, placing southern students at a disadvantage to their northern counterparts. The Minister of Education also appeared on television announcing that students were required to conform to the Islamic way of life and stated that the Assembly had confirmed regulations making students comply with an Islamic dress code.

The Roman Catholic Comboni schools operating in the north also came under concerted government pressure to Islamise them. Even though Catholic, the Comboni schools have always offered a secular curriculum and opened their doors to Muslims. The authorities' first move was against the schools the churches had set up for displaced children who camped outside Khartoum. An Islamic curriculum was imposed on the schools and the children were required to recite the Qur'an with no enquiry into their religious background. In August 1993, the Comboni schools received a directive to conform to the government education policy. The schools closed during 1992 and 1993 as a consequence. The Catholic Church and the authorities eventually reached a compromise whereby there is official representation in the schools' administration and Muslim female students must put on the official veil while non-Muslim female students have to put on 'decent dress'. In all state schools Islamic religious instruction is given but Christian children may exempt themselves. They may receive their own religious instruction after school hours often in the school buildings.

Universities, once autonomous and independent, have been similarly affected by the state Islamisation policies and the NIF dominance of staff and student associations.

Conscientious objection

There is no recognition of conscientious objection to military conscription in Sudan. Only those males between the ages of 20 and 45 who are students or in 'essential' employment may be excepted from orders to register for military training or, reportedly, from random sweeps. Military training includes Islamic instruction and prayer regardless of the belief of the conscripts.

University staff and school teachers, among others, have been called up to train in the militia camps of the Popular Defence Force where life is apparently harsh for those who do not support the NIF. In 1990–91, eight lecturers were dismissed from Gezira University for conscientiously objecting to such training; several lecturers at the Sudan University of Science and Technology have also objected.

Women and religion

President al-Bashir said in 1990 that an exemplary Sudanese woman was one who devoted herself to domestic duties, looked after her husband and children, took care of herself and her reputation and applied herself to be a good Muslim. The regime's commitment to particular interpretations of the *shariah* places women under several legal disabilities which violate their rights as envisaged by international human rights instruments.

However, rigidly interpreted Islamic personal law, which does not give equality to women in marriage, divorce and inheritance, applied to Muslims long before the enactment of the *shariah* in Sudan in 1983. Last century, many restrictions were placed on women, segregating them from men, restricting where they could work and keeping them out of public view, and diminishing or nullifying the value of their evidence in court. Education is open to both sexes but tradition gives women fewer opportunities than men.

Practices in application of Islamic personal law have varied in the past but are now systematised in the restrictions codified in the Personal Law for Muslims Act 1991. A woman cannot contract her own marriage; it must be concluded by a male guardian. However, her consent to marriage is required and urban women have not been slow to use the courts to get marriages annulled to which they did not consent. *Talaq* divorce is allowed only to men.

In 1991, the government also enforced its Islamic dress code on government offices (employees and client visitors), and on female students and teachers. Women are required to cover the whole body and the head, with the exception of the face and the hands, in loose garments. Those who do not conform are subjected to harassment by official and semi-official bodies and may end up going to court and being flogged, as did several young women who were charged with wearing immodest dress and consuming alcohol on New Year's Eve 1993.

As only men may interpret Qur'anic verses and the Sunna, women cannot contribute to any potential development of progressive interpretation. Customary law also discriminates against women because it regards them as property. Little has been done about this by a state whose primary goal regarding indigenous societies is to assimilate them through Islamisation.

Conclusion

The issues pertaining to the freedom of thought, conscience and religion or belief in Sudan have become inextricably linked with the question of secularisation, the *shariah*, identity and the civil war. The current regime's version of politicised Islam faces the challenges of secularism and pluralism. Many people in the opposition would like to separate religion from the state and politics. Recognition of the country's diversity would be the starting-point for any serious attempt to tackle its problems.

Human rights activists consider that the *shariah* does not provide an appropriate legal philosophy or framework to address the country's problems. The regime insists on what it describes as its 'Islamic choice', also insisting that this is the choice of the 'Muslim majority'. It argues that the human rights enshrined in international instruments and conventions are relative values that should be judged against the precepts of Islam and the dictates of *shariah*. Those who oppose the regime, however, insist on the universality of human rights and would like to see international and human rights instruments and conventions integrated into the country's laws.

TUNISIA

The tradition of a one-party state still lingers in Tunisia despite legislative elections in 1994 which introduced opposition parties to the National Assembly for the first time since independence in 1956. Tunisia has attracted criticism over human rights for restrictive policies towards democratisation practised by the Ben Ali government.

Tunisia	
GDP (US$bn)	14
Population	8,400,000
Annual population growth (%)	2.2
Urban population (%)	56
Working population (%)	30
Literacy (%)	62.8
Ratifications	1; 2, 2(a); 3; 4; Af

Tunisia's population in 1992 was nearly 8.5 million, over half living in an urban setting. Young people predominate. In 1990, 37.3 per cent were under the age of 15 and 28.6 per cent were aged between 15 and 29 years old.

Tunisia's economy is currently going through major restructuring and is growing. The unemployment rate is 14.4 per cent, widely considered to be the result of free market liberalism. As 75,000 new workers enter the job market each year, the government has been trying to create employment, seeking foreign investment and boosting tourism.

Religion, language and ethnic background

Ethnic background is closely allied with religious affiliation. Arabic-speaking people form 98.2 per cent of the population and practise Sunni Islam in both the Maliki and Hanafi rites, the latter being introduced by former Ottoman rule. The small Berber-speaking population of 1.2 per cent, living to the south and on the island of Djerba, practise Ibadi Kharijism, which dates back to the period of the original split between Sunni and Shia Islam and is strongly egalitarian, considering that the caliphate should be purely elective, in the hands of the community.

The small European community – 40,000 people, mostly French and Italian Christians – are Roman Catholics, Greek Orthodox adherents and Protestants. The Jewish community of 20,000 lives mainly on the island of Djerba. Religious freedom is fully enjoyed by these minorities.

The major class or caste distinction within the relatively homogeneous Tunisian population results from the Ottoman occupation. People born of marriages between the native Tunisians and Ottoman Turks formed an urban caste closely connected with the government and still distinct today, though their political significance has long since disappeared. Indeed, the urban populations of Tunisia, particularly along the coast, are traditionally of very heterogeneous origins. As a result of the *corso* – piracy legitimated as religious warfare under Ottoman rule – large numbers of Christian slaves were held, some of whom eventually married into the local population.

The dominant language is Arabic, with French as the main commercial language. Although, as a minority, Berber-speakers are vulnerable to the pressures of centralisation and literacy in the dominant languages, they face no direct discrimination. The use of French does, however, form a kind of indirect cultural discrimination as it is necessary for commercial, professional and administrative activities. Tunisians who lack fluency in French are thus excluded from the mainstream. As Islamist sentiments have come to play a major role in the political scene, so a deliberate rejection of French in favour of Arabic in professional and public communication has become an increasingly common mode of political protest.

The political system and non-government movements

The constitution provides for a National Assembly elected by universal suffrage, renewable every five years, as is the presidency. The Assembly has legislative power but is subject to presidential control. The president is head of state, head of the executive branch of government and commander-in-chief, thus making all official appointments, civil and military.

The marginalisation of the Assembly has been intensified by the party political system. Until 1994, Tunisia was effectively a single party state. The Rassemblement Constitutionnel Démocratique (RCD) was the direct successor of the national liberation movement of the French colonial period which ended in 1956; it was led until 1987 by its founder and president-for-life, Habib Bourguiba. The major Islamist movement al-Nahda (Islamic Renaissance) party was banned in 1981, along with two other Islamist and Arab nationalist movements.

The current president and party leader, Zine al-Abidine Ben Ali, altered the constitution to remove the lifelong basis of the presidency and multi-party democracy was established in Tunisia. However, the RCD and allied parties occupied all the Assembly seats. In the 1989 elections, al-Nahda movement candidates therefore stood as independents because their party had been refused registration; they amassed informally 16 per cent of the vote. Electoral law was modified in 1994, allowing a specific percentage of Assembly seats for opposition parties.

There is no doubt that a significant minority supports the al-Nahda movement. One powerful reason for this is the level of unemployment which has grown since the late 1960s, especially in the south and in the cities, to which poorer people from the country have been migrating. Hardest hit by unemployment have been high school and university graduates. From these populations come the cadres of well-educated, frustrated young men among whom may be found the more extreme elements of Islamist opposition; they were occasionally involved in terrorism through the 1980s, including a rebellion against the former regime.

Tunisia's principal Islamist movements stem from the long tradition of Salafiyyism which runs through North African independence movements and from the activist traditions of the Ikhwan al-Muslimin (Muslim Brotherhood). The 15/21 Movement, for instance, is a progressive movement which claimed a Marxist–Islamist heritage and endorsed democratic pluralism.

The popular legitimacy of the Islamist movements has also been increased by the Algerian crisis, which has polarised the Tunisian people, leading to an even firmer resolve by the government to exclude the al-Nahda movement from any formal and legal political role. As well as human rights violations by the police against men that have been arrested, Amnesty International has drawn attention to allegations of torture and sexual harassment of women relatives and associates of al-Nahda movement members and communists.

The legal system

Tunisia's constitution states that Islam is the religion of the state. Its legal system is derived from two sources. On the one hand, Islamic *shariah* law covers much of personal status law while civil, commercial and criminal law is derived from the French legal tradition as is the structure of legal institutions. The (UN) Human Rights Committee has called for greater independence of the judiciary from the executive branch of government.

Tunisia has ratified the major human rights instruments. In 1991, the government formed an official body to monitor human rights in Tunisia, the Higher Committee of Human Rights and Fundamental Freedoms, a move welcomed by the (UN) Human Rights Committee in 1994. In 1996, Amnesty International and the International Commission of Jurists lodged protests about the jailing for eleven years of the head of Tunisia's main legal opposition party, alleging fabrication of charges against him. Reportedly, other human rights organisations have also been harassed.

Freedom of religion or belief

Freedom of religious expression is guaranteed. People are free to adopt whatever convictions they wish as part of their private lives. The National Charter of 1988 states as follows:

> the protection of the fundamental freedoms of human beings calls for the strengthening of the values of tolerance, the banishing of extremism and violence in all their forms and non-interference in the convictions and behaviour of others, with the exception of leniency and pardon, in order for religion to involve no constraints whatsoever.

A Ministry of Religions oversees the enforcement of laws on religion under the Penal Code. These laws include the 1958 regulations for the exercise of the Jewish religion which authorises Jewish cultural associations, subsidised by the communities in Tunis and Djerba, which administer Jewish affairs, manage teaching establishments, maintain synagogues, and provide for kosher slaughtering and food products with the help of rabbis. The Chief Rabbi, paid a salary by the state and appointed by presidential decree (after consultation) is invited to attend national festivities and events. There was wide media coverage of the 1993 pilgrimage to Djerba, where North African Jewry pay homage to a Talmudic sage. President Ben Ali has publicly expressed his determination to ensure that the community will be able to live undisturbed by anti-Semitism. A 1964 international agreement between the Holy See and Tunisia guarantees free practice of the Roman Catholic faith; the prelate of Tunis is appointed by the Vatican and accredited by the government.

The practice of non-Muslim religions is, however, limited by legal prohibitions against proselytising: conversion of Muslims is a criminal offence. There are legal impediments preventing non-Muslims standing for public office.

The government has rarely interfered with religious practice unless it has had significant political implications. A law was passed in 1988 to prevent mosques being exploited for political and partisan purposes. The Ministry for Islamic Affairs administers mosques, appoints *imam*s and ensures that all *imam*s avoid politically contentious material in their Friday sermons (*khutba*). A regulation from the Bourguiba era was revived in order to forbid women's wearing of headcoverings as a sign of support for religious revivalism; this has encouraged discrimination. Women who wear the headcovering have reportedly been refused government employment, access to visit imprisoned relatives and even medical treatment.

Although the constitution formally guarantees freedom of expression and the right of reply, the media is state-controlled. Since 1993, the Press Code definition of libel has included expressions based on religious and racial extremism. Amnesty International noted hundreds of convictions in that year under laws restricting freedom of assembly, expression and association.

In 1995, Tunisia hosted an international conference at Carthage on Education for Tolerance in the Mediterranean Basin at which it encouraged wide-ranging efforts to promote tolerance in order to change attitudes and establish new ways to behave. In particular, Tunisia sought support for a Carthage Pact for Tolerance in the Mediterranean, to disseminate and consolidate the values of tolerance.

Women and personal status law

In the 1930s, Tunisia's reform movement proposed the emancipation of women, Tahar Haddad propounding that the programme for life was to be found in the interaction between modernising and the general principles of Islam. At its independence, therefore, Tunisia adopted a pro-active approach to ensure rights and equality for women. Among Muslim-dominated countries facing the challenge of modernisation, Tunisia is a leader in the progressive adaptation of Islamic law to the complexities of modern life. Women were accorded full citizen rights under the constitution. Women are generally accorded equal status before the law and are also represented in public life; two women, for example, are government ministers and 45 per cent of the judges are women.

The government has described its civil code as being of Islamic inspiration, choosing the provisions of the doctrine of different Islamic traditions while taking into consideration the need to reconcile respect for the Islamic religion with the imperatives of modern life. Adoption, for instance, is included, a matter not recognised in the *shariah*.

Among other measures in the personal status code, polygamy was banned in 1957, as was *talaq* divorce, both women and men having the right to divorce, amended in 1992 to require a magistrate to attempt to reconcile couples. Women are allowed control over reproduction, including abortion, as not being contrary to Islamic principles. Laws on women's entitlement to maintenance after divorce have been amended. Although a woman still inherits only half of her brother's entitlement, the law of inheritance has been reformed to allow greater equality between the generations and between men and women; difference of religion has no effect on succession.

Other reforms in the personal status code now strengthen the protection of women against violence and emphasise the mutual duty between husband and wife – being more in line with the practice of the Prophet himself – thus removing a previous requirement for a wife to be obedient, which had been used to justify beating.

A 1981 survey found that only 51 per cent of Tunisian women were aware of the progressive family code. Illiteracy is primarily a female phenomenon. An active education programme supported by the government has made school attendance compulsory to the age of 16, boosting the participation of girls. Whereas the government has hoped through its education programmes to temper the force of Islamist extremism, the personal status code is not supported by the al-Nahda movement, which regards it not as a reform but as a departure from the *shariah*. There are considerable numbers of women in the movement.

Despite its progressive track record in women's rights and its reform of personal status laws, Tunisia continues to maintain its reservations to various CEDAW articles, as well as making a general declaration that it will not enact domestic legislation to implement CEDAW requirements where they conflict with Chapter I of the constitution – presumably a reference to the state religion which is Islam. However, Tunisia envisages gradual progress in integrating CEDAW norms into the national legislation.

ZIMBABWE

Zimbabwe	
GDP (US$bn)	5
Population	10,500,000
Annual population growth (%)	3.2
Urban population (%)	30
Working population (%)	41[a]
Literacy (%)	83.4
Ratifications	1; 2, 2(a); 3; 4; Af

In 1965 Ian Smith, then Prime Minister of Rhodesia, declared unilateral independence from Britain, precipitating racial conflict and the imposition of sanctions which were undermined by the Rhodesia–South Africa link. The war of independence resulted in the establishment of the nation of Zimbabwe in 1980. The ensuing 1982–87 civil war between the Shona and the Ndebele – the ZANU and ZAPU factions of the independence war's Patriotic Front – was eventually resolved politically through the Unity Accord of 1987 in which Joshua Nkomo took the post of senior minister in President Mgabe's office.

Zimbabwe is a republic. The head of state and government is a president who is also commander-in-chief of the defence force. The president is elected by voters on a common roll for a period of six years. The legislative body of the country is the Parliament in the form of the House of Assembly. The ZANU-PF government was for some time effectively a single-party government with a Marxist–Leninist orientation with some links to North Korea. The new democratic spirit has been felt by Zimbabwe though until recently the future of multi-party democracy in Zimbabwe was uncertain. A number of opposition political parties now exist, none linked to any religion.

Zimbabwe today is a multi-ethnic and multi-religious society of 10.5 million people. The ethnic composition of Zimbabwe is as follows: 66 per cent Shona; 16 per cent Ndebele; 11.7 per cent other African ethnic groups; 4.5 per cent British; 1.1 per cent Afrikaner; 0.3 per cent coloured; 0.2 per cent Asian (mainly Indian). Before independence there were 250,000 white people, but today there are only 80,000, an ageing population. Racism – including the colour divide – remains a major social issue. Whites, coloureds and Asian groups may receive different treatment because they are excluded from the concept of 'indigenous' which is used to refer to black Zimbabweans. Furthermore, the distribution of wealth remains structured in racial terms because the end of British colonialism in 1980 left the bulk of the economy in the hands of a small white minority. Redistribution to black farmers of land belonging to the white community has been delayed.

Religious organisations

Traditional religions are practised by over 40 per cent of Zimbabweans. There are over 120 indigenous churches whose membership is inter-ethnic. There are no institutions which represent non-religious or secular beliefs. Christian churches make up the largest religious community: Catholics (674,000), the Zimbabwe Assemblies of God Africa (500,000) and Anglican and Methodist Churches with smaller congregations. Mainstream churches include the Catholic, Anglican, Methodist, Lutheran, Brethren in Christ, Baptists and many other churches from colonial times. Most of these churches (with the exception of the Catholics) belong to the Zimbabwe Council of Churches.

The breakaway Independent Churches include various types of the Vapostori (Apostles) and ma Zion (Zionists). They are the fastest growing churches in Zimbabwe, differing from mainstream churches in their leadership – black and indigenous – as well as in structure and doctrine. The second fastest growing group of churches – popular with the young – are the Pentecostal Zimbabwe Assemblies of God (Africa). Many have links overseas, especially with conservative American religious organisations. Other minority religions and new religious movements include the Christian Scientists and Jehovah's Witnesses, and the Unification Church.

Islam is practised among African Muslims from neighbouring countries such as Mozambique and Malawi, also among Asians and a few coloured people. Baha'i is practised by both Africans and Asians. There is a Jewish community, as well as Hindus and Buddhists.

Religion–state relations

Church–state relations have changed over the past fifteen years. At independence, mainstream Christian churches were at first concerned that they would be identified with the former colonial government. They placated the incoming government by supporting its policies of inculturation and self-reliance under a socialist agenda for development and restored their hierarchies unhindered. Local grass-roots Christian churches which had grown up during the war for independence declined.

During the civil war, however, the churches became more articulate and critical. Given the social teaching which came out of Vatican II, the Catholic Church was more able to deal with ZANU-PF's Marxist–Leninism than other mainstream churches which were struggling to re-establish and financially support themselves, having lost many missionaries and priests at independence. The Catholic Bishops Council publicly protested against violent repression of dissidents and their communities which resulted in massive human rights abuses; members of the Catholic Commission for Justice and Peace were arrested in 1986.

After the Unity Accord in 1987, it became possible for the first time to air criticism without being labelled for or against ZANU or ZAPU. A social movement demanding democratisation emerged, in which the church – Catholic, Protestant and evangelical – was in the forefront of demands for public accountability for massacres in the civil war period as well as for the consequences of economic restructuring. The mainstream churches joined with the legal community in launching Zimrights.

Relations between religious groups and the state are generally good. Zimbabwe is home to many religious groups which operate freely without any interference from the government. Former President Banana's call for the rewriting of the Bible to suit African culture is not held in high regard by local scholars and theologians.

Economic structure

Like many Third World countries, Zimbabwe is at present adjusting to the requirements of the World Bank and International Monetary Fund. During the decade following independence in 1980, the new government at first deployed a socialist strategy to reshape a century-old colonial economy stifled by sanctions. Deregulation, however, came at a cost. Structural adjustment, introduced in the early 1990s, has brought retrenchments and unemployment. Market forces have pushed the prices of basic commodities to levels beyond the reach of most people, and primary school education and basic health care are also no longer free. In 1992 Zimbabwe experienced the worst drought on record.

Government economic policy has been heavily criticised by the churches, concerned about the relationship between religious and economic well-being, and especially by the Catholic Commission for Justice and Peace which seeks long-term development with priority for alleviation of poverty and provision of basic needs.

The legal system and constitution

The legal system operates under a mixture of Roman–Dutch law, English common law and customary law. The Customary Law and Local Courts Act 1990 created a unitary court system from headman's courts right through to the Supreme Court, allowing customary law matters to be heard at any level. The judiciary is independent.

Formal separation of powers with freedom of conscience and religion are guaranteed under the post-independence constitution. There is no established church or religion. The constitution's Declaration of Rights guarantees various rights and freedoms, including prohibition of racial discrimination. Basic provisions on freedom of conscience are included:

1 Every person in Zimbabwe is entitled to freedom of thought, religion or belief.
2 No person may coerce another person to receive religious instruction other than his or her own.
3 Every religious community has the right to offer instruction to its members in the course of providing education for them whether or not the community is in receipt of financial assistance from the state.
4 No-one may be coerced to take an oath if the latter is contrary to his or her religion.

A sub-section provides for the exceptions under which sections 1 or 3 may be set aside. The law can act to limit freedom of conscience under three conditions:

(a) in the interests of defence, public safety, public order, public morality or public health;
(b) to protect the rights and freedoms of other persons, and
(c) in requiring that any place offering education must meet certain standards or qualifications.

Some conscientious objections have been overridden by government policy, limiting manifestations of belief on the ground that the rights of others have priority. For instance, the Vapostori (Apostles) Church of Marange refuses, on religious grounds, to use modern medicine. Members of the church will not send their children for immunisation as they believe that prayer will address their physical needs. The government has intervened in order to immunise the children of the Vapostori. Some Vapostori groups also do not believe in Western education and therefore refuse to send their children to school. Theologically, they believe that Western education is of this world, ungodly and therefore spiritually unsuitable. Politically, some Vapostori consider it to be a purveyor of European values, at variance with African cultural values of self-reliance, community and hard work. The Education Amendment Act 1991 makes primary school education compulsory to enable a child's fundamental right to education, a fact of which they were reminded by Senior Minister Nkomo in 1991.

The va Pusa wa Pusa sect has been banned on the basis that it practised ritual sex with minors.

Religious education

The Education Act makes provision for parental choice as to the form and content of religious instruction to be given to children. When Zimbabwe became independent in

1980, the government 'emphasised the need for there to be firm moral principles on which to build the nation'. It wished to create an atmosphere in which its professed ideology of socialism would co-exist with religious and moral principles. In 1991, President Mugabe asked the mission churches to reassume responsibility for primary education not only because of the difficulties of economic restructuring but 'to renew the moral fibre of the nation'.

The Ministry of Education administers the Religious and Moral Education Curriculum in schools starting from early primary grades through to secondary school. The syllabus for Grades 1 and 2 specifies six basic aims for religious and moral education:

1 To help the pupils develop an awareness of the Supreme Being.
2 To understand their own religions and traditions and through creative dialogue with those traditions develop their own belief system.
3 To develop an acquaintance with those religions they are likely to encounter in Zimbabwe in order to come to an appreciation of both the differences and similarities of their and other people's religious traditions.
4 To inculcate a spirit of tolerance and cooperation in the pupils by encouraging respect for differences.
5 To enable perception of a closer relationship between religion and morals.
6 To enable the pupils to draw out the implications of their belief systems for moral behaviour and to live out, through positive action, their religious and moral principles.

In higher grades, the emphasis progressively rests on religious education in general and Christianity in particular. Commitment to a multi-faith approach has been frustrated by lack of adequately religiously trained teachers in a position to provide instruction in the tenets of Islam, Hinduism, Judaism and other religions that children are likely to encounter in Zimbabwe.

Both the Education Act and the constitution allow for the establishment of private or community schools along ethnic or religious lines. Community schools which provide religious instruction include the Jewish, Greek and Islamic schools or pre-schools in Harare.

In the early 1990s the government attempted to introduce a course on political economy in the schools, to enhance understanding of social realities. However, because the churches and other religious groups objected strongly – they feared that political economy was a euphemism for atheism and that the course was intended to gradually replace the teaching of religion in schools – the programme did not proceed.

Intra- and inter-religious relations

The tensions of the wider society have been echoed in the ZANU–ZAPU split within the Lutheran Church's council, which caused the government informally to intervene in 1990, without objections from the members. However, the relationship of the religions in Zimbabwe is very largely one of quiet co-existence rather than active ecumenical dialogue or cooperation. In at least one instance some of the mainstream Christian churches have expressed opposition to Islam, discussing the possibility of developing an anti-Islamicisation programme.

The mainstream churches of the Zimbabwe Council of Churches have criticised the Pentecostal groups, particularly those with links to the new religious–political right, for aligning themselves with ideological movements which promote a religious message in favour of the rich and powerful classes of society. However, condemnation of Christian fundamentalism is not universally shared among the religions. The synagogue in Harare has been used by some of these religious groups, just as it has been made available to other Christian groups.

The Pentecostal church movement is large, well-organised, self-sustaining and operates at grass-roots level. Its reliance on the American packaging of the gospel is offset by local references to deliverance from witches and demonic spirits, destruction of charms and magical substances. The former colonial government had passed a Suppression of Witchcraft Act and autonomous Pentecostal churches have been dealing with witchcraft accusations and cleansing, acting as movements for witchcraft eradication. They are also movements for post-war healing, cleansing those who committed acts of violence and reconciling others with the dead. Women and young people are helped to restructure social relations traditionally dominated by male elders and behaviour which helps to develop responsible citizenship is emphasised.

Broadcasting and the media

The Zimbabwe Broadcasting Corporation is controlled by the government. Christianity was the 'established' religion of the colonial structure within which modern institutions were developed in Zimbabwe and most religious representatives who participate in religious broadcasts are drawn from Christian churches. The practice of favouring Christian churches has not been openly challenged by the other religions who scarcely participate. The ZBC regularly screens a programme – *The 700 Club* – produced by a United States new religious–political right group, without objection from the churches.

The state controls major newspapers but the independent free press is slowly growing. Religious groups own or operate magazines, newsletters and publishing concerns. The Membo Press is run by the Catholic Church. Some churches import material from overseas for distribution in Zimbabwe.

Women

Since independence, progress has been made in matters affecting women's equality. Some eight women were ministers in government in 1993. Late in 1996 the first woman was installed as a tribal chief, a position with the power to hear and decide disputes on family and other matters. A white paper on the draft inheritance law has been issued which will clarify women's inheritance rights in particular. The government has acted to prosecute and educate to eradicate certain traditional practices such as refusal to bury a woman unless *lobola* (bride price) has been paid by the widower. In training sessions, the Chief Magistrate has warned that the custom of forcing a widow to marry her late husband's brother is illegal. Also unacceptable is the practice of paying compensation and slaughtering a cow to appease the spirits in cases of incest.

The Americas

REGIONAL INTRODUCTION

The colonial experience had a lasting impact on all nations of the region. Indigenous communities were subdued, natural resources were plundered, and 'enclave' communities were established for the economic benefit of the colonial masters. The dominant British colonial expansion in North America left a Protestant-based liberalism that became enshrined in the constitutions of both Canada and the United States. The Iberian colonial experience left a much different mark on Latin America. There too, the indigenous communities were subordinated and 'enclave' communities were set up, but the Spanish and Portuguese brought with them Catholicism, which profoundly changed the region's political, social, and cultural trajectory. The region's nations were all independent by the 1840s (with the exception of Belize and many other Caribbean nations); however, after 1823 the United States began to assert its hegemony in the region under the auspices of the Monroe Doctrine.

There have been different historical and regional trends in exemplifying tolerance in North and South America. The USA and Canada had the challenge of integrating immigrant populations into religious belief systems different from those of the original colonial regimes and 'settlers'. Both countries have had to deal with the issue of indigenous peoples, where there continues to be great intolerance, both formally and informally, of indigenous belief systems and practices. And both countries exhibit intolerance for the more extreme religious groups and often reveal a misunderstanding of them.

There are three factors, however, which differentiate the USA and Canada. First, Canada has a strong separatist movement which may increase intolerance in the future. Second, although it has not manifested itself into a strong separatist movement (with the possible exception of the Nation of Islam), the legacy of slavery and the struggle for civil rights in the USA have had an obvious impact on tolerance and belief. Third, the USA suffers from the following historical irony: it was established as liberal (and therefore secular) and yet exhibits a high degree of civil religion.

Latin America is a predominantly Roman Catholic region and has an historic tradition of an alliance between church and state. Since independence in Latin America (1820s–1840s), the Catholic Church has been challenged by both external and internal factors. Externally, it has been challenged by liberals in the nineteenth century, various authoritarian regimes in the twentieth, new Protestant and Pentecostal movements from North America, and syncretic religious movements that combine Catholicism and indigenous or African belief systems. Internally, it has been challenged by radical priests and bishops who were influenced by Vatican II (1962–65) and by the development of liberation theology.

By 1995, there are no military regimes in power in the Americas, and most countries are striving to deepen and enrich their democracies. The freedom of thought, conscience, and belief as a whole is more protected now than it ever has been in the history of the region, but there are still reasons for us to remain cautious in making observations that appear too sanguine. In general, there still appears to be a gap between those rights guaranteed in principle and those enjoyed in practice.

ARGENTINA

Argentina	
GDP (US$bn)	229
Population	33,400,000
Annual population growth (%)	1.5
Urban population (%)	87
Working population (%)	38
Literacy (%)	95.9
Ratifications	1; 2, 2(a), 2(b); 3; 4; Am

Argentina, a country of substantial resources, has a mixed economy traditionally based on agricultural exports, to which was added between 1930 and 1960 a state-led expansion of industry and the service sector. More recent change to respond to market forces has resulted in concentration of income, high unemployment (over 11 per cent in 1994) and under-employment, together with a regressive tax system. However, Argentina has had strong economic growth lately and has a good record in social welfare. Half of the Argentine population of 33.4 million live in the Province of Buenos Aires, where major business is located.

Argentina is today a federal republic and a multi-party democracy. Parties and other political groups are not restricted. The Justicialista Party, now in power, was originally the Peronista Party. Its ideology was then close to the social doctrine of the Roman Catholic Church, but it now advocates neo-liberal policies. The new constitution includes a broad range of social and individual rights guarantees, including the right to resist dictatorships, and also establishes equality of opportunities for men and women. Freedom of expression, thought and teaching are also guaranteed. The major human rights instruments have been incorporated in the constitution. Discrimination on ideological, political, racial or religious grounds is prohibited and racist propaganda is a criminal offence. Although the constitution recognises the ethnic and cultural pre-existence of indigenous people, and entitles them to receive bilingual education and to communal ownership of the land they have customarily occupied, these rights have not been effectively enforced.

From dictatorship to democracy

For more than seven years (1976–83) Argentina suffered the most crushing dictatorship of its history, alongside an unprecedented socio-economic crisis. In the period of the 'dirty war', individual rights were suppressed, the constitution was replaced by edicts of the governing military junta, political activism was banned and rigorous censorship imposed. Thousands of political prisoners were kept in sub-human conditions. Approximately

30,000 people 'disappeared' and more than a million fled into exile. Among those oppressed for ideological reasons, many Jews were particularly targeted as 'reds'. Argentine production capability was devastated and its society was pervaded by terror. A huge external debt was accumulated.

Engagement in the Malvinas War brought the end of the military dictatorship. Argentina's defeat enabled unions and other groups of the civil society to reorganise themselves and push for democracy, achieved with the election of Raúl Alfonsín as president in December 1983. He sought to restore human rights. However, the military refused to take responsibility for its actions, ultimately succeeding in making the government invalidate judicial convictions of high-ranking officials for human rights violations. As recently as November 1994, President Menem publicly defended the actions of the army during the clandestine repression experienced by the country under military rule. In a country where terror is still pervasive, his speech was felt to be ominous. In 1995, public statements of officers willing to break the military code of silence led to a national soul-searching about collective guilt.

The accusation continues to be made that the Catholic Church colluded in the 'dirty war'. The Argentine hierarchy had long been the most reactionary in all Latin America, with all but four or five of its sixty bishops supporting the military dictatorship since it seized power in 1976. Archbishop Antonio Quarracino (now a cardinal and president of the Bishops' Conference) stated in public in 1983 that the 'disappeared' were all in gilded exile in Paris and other capitals. The bishops consistently refused to protest against the disappearances. When Bishop Adolfo Pérez Esquivel, who had been held in abominable conditions and tortured for fourteen months in an Argentine jail, received the Nobel Peace Prize in 1980, the Bishops' Conference publicly dissociated itself from him and also rejected the international movement for non-violent action he founded, the Peace and Justice Service (SERPAJ). Former prisoners have testified that priests were attached to interrogation centres and prayed for those being tortured.

In April 1996, after protests against a weaker statement, the Catholic Church issued a document asking forgiveness 'for the misdeeds that could be attributed to it' during the period. However, the document has been criticised for showing no assumption of responsibility by the institutional church; it reportedly stresses the fact that Catholic activists took part in security as well as guerrilla forces.

Progress made in the area of freedom of thought and expression is undeniable when compared with what happened during the 'dirty war' when intellectual enquiry and ideological debate were suppressed. However, academic and press freedom remain contentious issues and television and radio remain state-controlled.

Ethnic and religious composition

Argentina's population is the result of nineteenth- and early twentieth-century immigration, primarily from Mediterranean Europe but also from other European countries. In the past twenty years, a million indigenous and *mestizo* people have come into Argentina from bordering states Bolivia, Paraguay, Uruguay, Chile and Peru, and more continue to do so. Traditionally a country of refuge for Europeans, Argentina received fleeing Nazis as well as Jewish survivors of the Holocaust after the Second World War. Immigrants have also come from Arab countries, particularly Syria and Lebanon, and in recent years from other South American countries and south-east Asia.

Both Spanish conquest and Argentine military expeditions in the last century vastly reduced the indigenous population and deprived them of their lands. Their lives are marked by poverty and ill health, unemployment, lack of government services and education. Their different ethnic groups live mainly in four northern provinces and in Patagonia to the south. Very different ethnic groups and cultures therefore co-exist in Argentina. According to the 'melting pot' theory, public education and compulsory military service are intended to blur cultural differences and create a new cultural identity.

Roman Catholics are predominant in Argentine society followed by significant Muslim, Jewish and Protestant minorities, new and established; the national census does not collect information about religion or belief. Protestant groups are increasing. The fact that the Argentine population is 87 per cent urban and highly secularised explains why important sectors do not practise or profess any religion.

Religion–state relations

While there has been some recent weakening of the historical bond between the Argentine state and the Roman Catholic Church, its status *vis-à-vis* other religious organisations still continues in the *patronato regio* tradition. The federal government still finances and supports the church. Other religious groups consider that this policy discriminates against them by earmarking for just one church benefits from taxes paid for by all citizens whatever their beliefs. However, a constitutional amendment in 1994 removed the requirement that the president and vice-president had to be Catholics. This change was acceptable to many Argentines, though not to the Catholic hierarchy.

Privileging of the Catholic Church also occurs in the appointment of chaplains in state services. Protestant ministers, Jewish rabbis and Muslim *imam*s have to receive authorisation from a Catholic priest to act as hospital chaplains. However, although only Catholic chaplains are appointed in the army, there has been recent parliamentary debate about changing this policy.

Religious affairs are regulated nationally. The Secretariat of Worship in the External Affairs Ministry has the authority to permit (or deny) religious groups to function throughout Argentina by registering them in a national register of religions. A proposal to replace and update the existing regulations is being debated in the parliament. Ultra-conservative Catholic Church elements have supported government proposals for limitations on the activities of so-called 'sects'; however, Protestant churches have been involved in the consultations. In the opinion of the Human Rights Ecumenical Movement (MEDH), the new bill for the regulation of religions is restrictive rather than comprehensive because it contains criminal provisions. MEDH also argues that the bill runs counter to the principles of separation of powers that characterise republican regimes.

Education

In 1988, the Argentine government reported that there were 1,300 private schools of various religious denominations. In both private and public schools, religious instruction may be provided outside school hours. However, through a constitutional amendment in the Province of Buenos Aires, Christian education has been mandated in Buenos Aires' public schools, a development which has been protested against by the teachers' union and religious groups' representatives. Article 199 of the Buenos Aires provincial constitution now states that:

> The purpose of education is to form individuals with a transcendental dimension, in an integrated manner and respectful towards human rights and human freedom. Children's character is to be formed to worship national institutions and their symbols and according to Christian moral principles, while respecting freedom of thought.

Catholicism excludes women from ministry, but feminist theology has been taught at the ISEDET ecumenical seminary in Buenos Aires by visiting American scholars and students there have now organised their own courses. The Centro de Estudios Cristianos sponsors a feminist theology network which meets regularly and has mounted major conferences.

Discrimination and intolerance

In general terms, tolerance, individual freedoms and political rights are respected in Argentina. However, there are remnants of authoritarianism, discrimination and intolerance which are related directly or indirectly to the freedoms of expression, religion and belief.

Women's groups have worked for removal of sanctions against contraception, abortion and remarriage after legal separation under varied and dangerous political conditions. Child-rearing is well supported with generous paid maternity leave and other special allowances but economic difficulties, including catastrophic inflation rates, have affected women's lives in particular. Economic circumstances have interacted with pressure from the Vatican to downgrade political action in the church's base communities, previously a source of support for women.

The general ideologies of both the Catholic Church and rapidly growing forms of evangelical Protestantism are reflected in state policy, especially in relation to sexuality. When the Minister denied the Buenos Aires Metropolitan Community Church's request for authorisation to function as a church, MEDH claimed that the Secretariat had exceeded its mandate – to register beliefs – by its action of assessing beliefs. The Metropolitan Community Church has a basic ministry for lesbians and homosexuals. Even though the church has branches in Europe, Africa, the Pacific and North America, the Minister disapproved of the sexual choices of its congregation and argued that the church's creed harmed public morality.

Discrimination against homosexual people is prevalent although there have been some moves to make such discrimination unlawful. Among instances of religion-based intolerance can be numbered recent pronouncements of Cardinal Antonio Quarracino, who provoked public concern when, on the state media, he suggested that homosexuals and lesbians should be segregated from heterosexual society by being confined to a 'special zone' where they could live in accordance with their values, under their own separate laws and constitution.

Although the state denies that there is any official discrimination on the grounds of religion or belief governing entry to military officer ranks, the judiciary or the external affairs service, there are, however, informal mechanisms and a culture of exclusiveness which have the effect of impeding non-Catholics from entering and rising within these professions. Officers in the army have always been Catholic. This did not, however, stop such officers during the period of the 'dirty war' from persecuting fellow Catholics who were committed to the defence of human rights; all who were committed to such ends were persecuted then. The fact that Protestant, Mormon and Jewish soldiers are mistreated in the army today proves that, in spite of progress, there is still religious intolerance within the institution. MEDH argues that the injuries that caused the death of soldier Omar Carrasco in 1994 could have been motivated by intolerance towards his Pentecostal Church membership.

In other cases in 1994, a civil servant demanded that a Jewish rabbi take off his kippah before his business could be attended to. The official was subject to administrative discipline proceedings only. The second, more serious, incident involved Alberto Pierri, the President of the Chamber of Deputies, who called a Jewish-Argentine journalist a 'lousy Jew'. He is still in office.

Thus, despite an active Jewish community of 300,000 mostly supported by other Argentines, anti-Semitism is still an issue in Argentina. Terrorist bomb attacks have taken place against the Israeli Embassy in Buenos Aires (1992) and the Israeli Mutual Society of Buenos Aires (July 1994), in which over 120 people died. These attacks have caused the Jewish community increased concern, given the state's record of ineffectiveness in protecting the community and upholding convictions for human rights violations. In 1996, the state extradited former Nazi SS-officer Erich Priebke to Italy to face charges associated with the Ardeatine Caves massacre of Italians (including Jews) outside Rome in 1944. As with war criminals Mengele and Eichmann, Priebke had lived for many years undisturbed in Argentina.

Among other instances of discrimination, the MEDH has also commented on irregularities observed in the judicial procedures under which members of the Christian group, The Family, were arrested. Nobel Prize winner, Bishop Adolfo Pérez Esquivel, has also shown concern for the detention of Yoga School attendants in Buenos Aires. In both cases it is claimed that the authorities resorted to irregular procedures such as unlawful entry during the night. Some twenty-one adults from The Family were jailed in June 1993 on charges including child abuse, slavery and illegal association, and 130 of their children were taken into state custody; they were released in December 1993, but the prosecution appealed. The Supreme Court confirmed in June 1995 that they should remain released, the Argentine Attorney-General having stated that the allegations against them were groundless. Action for compensation is being taken.

Conclusion

Selective intolerance thus affects the lives of specific groups who demand to be recognised in their religious, sexual, moral or ideological choices and practices, even when they differ from the majority. Whereas the cultural ideology of *lo argentino* (the Argentine) assumes that different identities can be fused into one dominant culture, selective intolerance demonstrates that, speaking in general terms, the majority have yet to accept the concept of a 'mosaic' in which different parts constitute the whole. Under the concept of unity in plurality, no-one should feel obliged to renounce their beliefs, ethnic and cultural identities, religion or life choices as some do now.

BRAZIL

Brazil is a federal republic consisting of twenty-six states and a federal district around the capital Brasilia. In the last decade Brazil returned to democracy after twenty years of military rule (1964–85). The 1980s will be remembered as a decade when corruption, poverty and inflation rocketed out of control, as did the police. Violence and assassinations occurred throughout the country.

Although the military dictatorship established in 1964 formally ended with the return to constitutional government in 1983, the legacy of its gross violations of human rights continues to hang heavily on the country. In 1968, trades unions, student organisations and all other civic groups were formally banned, leaving no intermediate bodies to protect the citizen from the state. The only protest voices that survived in civil society were segments of the Catholic and Protestant Churches. They played a primary role in

Brazil	
GDP (US$bn)	360.4
Population	153,800,000
Annual population growth (%)	2.4
Urban population (%)	76
Working population (%)	44
Literacy (%)	81.9
Ratifications	1; 2; 3; 4; Am

recording the tortures, killings and disappearances under the military regime. Today, although the military are back in barracks, they have never acknowledged their human rights violations. There has been no Truth Commission to set the historical record clear as a prelude to the restoration of the memory of the victims.

Socio-economic background

Archaic social structures and dramatic social and economic inequalities characterise Brazil. Of its nearly 154 million people, 42 million live well below the poverty line and a further 16 million live in extreme poverty. Disparity in income distribution is among the widest in the world. Only 2.1 per cent of the national income goes to the 20 per cent of the population at the bottom of the social pyramid, while 51 per cent goes to the top 10 per cent. Professional politicians govern in alliance with the rich. Thus, despite its vast resources, growing economy and recent fall in inflation, Brazil's economy is gravely skewed.

Growing structural unemployment has been a major factor in rapid urbanisation. At least 76 per cent of Brazilians now live in cities, most of them in shacks that form vast shanty-towns on the edge of the city proper. There are up to 3 million street children, prey for death squads, a third of whose jailed members in 1991 turned out to be military policemen. Land reform is an urgent issue. In 1995, the 15-year-old Landless Worker Movement increased its activism, occupying land and gaining political muscle; President Cardoso has promised to award land to 280,000 families by 1998.

The degree to which violence and assassination can be carried out with impunity is still a matter for great concern since extra-judicial killings by police and vigilante groups, by landowners and their agents and by invaders of indigenous lands reportedly continue to occur. Many of the victims are poor and black. Although slavery was formally abolished by imperial decree in 1888, before the establishment of the republic, in 1995 the President denounced the continuing debt-enslavement of thousands of Brazilians, mostly Guarani people in the Amazon region, held under death threats in forced labour on plantations.

Ethnic composition

Brazilian people have come from many different ethnic origins, mainly indigenous, but also African and European, including Portuguese. The Jewish community is very long established and today there are also substantial Arab and Japanese populations.

The slave trade, which brought Africans from the Guinea coast, Angola and the Mozambique coast to work on Brazil's plantations, operated from the sixteenth century to the nineteenth century. Nearly half of Brazilians have some African ancestry. Racism is an issue in Brazil, where census statistics have been collected under skin colour categories. In 1989, for instance, 55.78 per cent of the population were said to be 'white', 5.05 per cent 'black', 38.63 per cent 'brown' and 0.54 per cent 'yellow and undefined' according to an official sample survey (PNAD). Only in 1976 did African-Brazilians gain permission to attend school without having a police registration.

According to the Missionary Council for Native People (CIMI), the indigenous population is increasing in Brazil. The Council estimates that there are 250,000–300,000 indigenous people, representing around 200 different peoples who speak 170 languages and live in some 10.52 per cent of Brazil. The government controls access to their officially designated areas.

Religious composition

The Roman Catholic Church has been the uncontested majority religion from the Portuguese colonial period. Catholicism was a mechanism of domination and power. A Catholic culture was created in the country from the first days of conquest, suppressing the beliefs and traditions of the indigenous people and also the African slaves.

Later, Protestant missionaries, although no threat to Catholic power, suffered intimidation and persecution; the Catholic Church saw Catholicism as the only truth without which there was no salvation. Protestants hid their faiths as the African-Brazilians had done, to avoid ideological persecution. Such pressures lessened after the Second World War, although Pentecostals continued to be the victims of violence.

The situation changed in the 1950s, with the Catholic Church devoting more of its attention to social issues, and the Pentecostal churches competing more openly in the devotional area. In the period of the military dictatorship, the Catholic Church suffered severe setbacks with the suppression of its rural trades unions and arrest of the leaders of the Basic Education Movement (MEB), and of other priests and lay people who were involved with Catholic Action.

The expansion of the Pentecostal Church after 1950 encouraged the growth of other evangelical churches. Today there are around 4,000 Pentecostal churches in Greater Rio. The fastest growing of these is the Universal Church of the Kingdom of God, a now huge religious enterprise founded in 1977, which has 850 temples in Rio de Janeiro alone, an estimated 3 million followers, and forty-five temples in other countries. The way the church has proceeded in spreading its prosperity theology has recently come under scrutiny by the federal police as a result of allegations by one preacher who left to found a rival ministry, who also leaked videotapes of church officials' conduct during their money-raising activities.

Protestant clergy have over forty institutions for religious training and there are fifty-four missionary organisations. Protestant churches run many orphanages, creches, houses for elderly and hospitals. On the national level, a form of ecumenical forum (the VINDE) brings together many of the Protestant groups.

While the national census identifies about four-fifths of Brazilians as Catholic, the pattern of church attendance shows that many Catholics attend church far less often than Protestants, members of Spiritist Centres or of such African-based beliefs and practices as Kardexism, Umbanda and Candomble. African-based Christian religions, especially Candomble, and evangelical Protestant groups are the most rapidly growing in Brazil. Women are leaders and powerful as healers in Candomble and Umbanda.

Constitutional guarantees

The 1988 constitution enshrines the separation of powers. A federal judiciary oversees the constitution's human rights guarantees. Brazil has ratified the American Convention and the main international human rights treaties. The constitution provides that freedom of conscience must not be violated. There is no state religion and freedom of religious worship and places of worship is guaranteed. Chaplaincies for public and military organisations are legally provided for. Religious or political beliefs may not be invoked to avoid legal obligations.

While religious leaders confirm that, at the level of governmental action, there is no longer interference with freedom of religion and belief in today's Brazil, there was considerable persecution during the period of military rule. Many religious people were arrested, tortured and killed.

Ecumenical approaches and inter-faith activities

The Catholic Church, finally accepting that it is just one of Brazil's religions, has found fresh ways to fulfil its mission in the new environment. Brazilian bishops have laid new emphasis on the Bible, influenced by the Protestants and the Christian base communities. There has been more open examination of questions of faith and of issues such as abortion, homosexuality and AIDS. The clergy has been redistributed so that now 80 per cent of them are to be found working with the poor. The new approach is evident in dealings with other churches; the hierarchy has changed its attitude to dialogue and cooperation.

Examples of inter-faith activities include the following:

1 An ecumenical version of the Universal Declaration of Human Rights was widely distributed to all dioceses and parishes.
2 A major ecumenical organisation (CESE) brought together the Catholic, Episcopal, Anglican, Methodist, Orthodox, United Presbyterian and Independent Presbyterian Churches and the Evangelic Church of Lutheran Confession.
3 The Catholic Church participates in the National Council of the Christian Churches of Brazil.
4 A Presbyterian pastor was officially seconded to work as assessor of the Cardinal-Archbishop of São Paulo's diocese.
5 The group Union and Black Conscience was established in 1981, under the patronage of the National Conference of the Bishops of Brazil.
6 Elements of African rituals were incorporated in the liturgy of the group of black pastoral workers and priests.

There are many different groups and humanitarian organisations created and run by churches, such as the Centre for the Defence of Human Rights and the recently established Inter-Religious Fund for Life Against Hunger. The declaration of the principles of the Fund was signed by more than twenty religious groups and believers, such as Buddhists, Spiritists, Protestants, Hare Krishna members, Jewish people, Catholics and adherents of African-based beliefs. The Fund will help people who are excluded from a society of privilege and who belong to no church. The Inter-Religious Movement uses the organisation to raise the question of tolerance and to facilitate dialogue. Subsidies, donations and resources are also shared. Today, other events are celebrated ecumenically, such as Christmas.

Intolerance between churches

There have been a number of occasions, however, when the churches have competed with and confronted each other. During a visit by the Pope to Brazil, the Protestant churches called out gatherings of their faithful which outnumbered those of the Catholics. On Holy Days such as Easter Sunday, the public gatherings of Catholics may be upstaged by a parallel event for which greater numbers of Protestants are mobilised. In September 1995, there was an outcry when a member of the Universal Church of God, on television, reportedly desecrated an emblem of the country's patron saint, claiming that it did not work.

The presence of Protestants is changing political and cultural life previously dominated by Catholicism and which previously linked Catholic celebrations to political authority. Since 1990, up to eighty Protestants have been elected to political office; some Congressional and Senate members have formed a Protestant branch.

Protestant churches and African-based traditions compete for converts among the same population, the poor and the nominal Catholics, and are expanding at similar rates. Although Protestant churches use African rhythms to sing to God, the old racism – a reminder of the slavery period – persists throughout Brazil.

Churches and indigenous religions

The 1988 constitution guarantees to the indigenous people their social organisation, languages, beliefs and traditions, and the right to keep their traditionally occupied lands. However, Congress has not yet finished demarcating lands and issuing legal titles. Indigenous Brazilians are among the poorest Brazilians and are politically marginalised. Some have been killed by gold-miners and others in the Amazon region.

Despite the fact that the government guarantees indigenous people's rights, the churches often ignore their traditions. Evangelisation did not restrain the extermination that extinguished most indigenous peoples during the first century of colonisation. Today, despite population increases, indigenous peoples represent only 0.2 per cent of the Brazilian population; diseases like malaria and measles continue to reduce their numbers. Although many missionaries have been criticised by those with spiritual power in their communities for not understanding the basis of indigenous religious beliefs ('We believe directly in God'), the Missionary Council for Native People (CIMI), which coordinates 300 missionaries, attempts to educate and change the attitudes of priests, sisters and lay people, so that they respect the indigenous culture. This education also is extended to Lutheran, Methodist and Presbyterian missionaries. Only the missionaries of Novas Tribos do Brasil are said still to follow the old line of imposing baptism and the catechism on indigenous peoples.

Anti-Semitism

Distorted religious training is said to be responsible for most of the anti-Semitism which exists in Brazil; Jews may prefer not to inform even close friends that they are Jewish. There is also active anti-Semitism promoted by neo-Nazi and anti-Zionist supporters, some of whom have attempted to form a political party. Open expressions of Nazism were nurtured in southern Brazil among German immigrants after the Second World War, many of whom had Nazi ties or anti-Semitic prejudices. Although racist manifestations are contrary to Brazil's constitution, revisionist books on the Holocaust and *The Protocols of the Elders of Zion* continue to circulate.

The media

The 1988 constitution abolished censorship and provides for freedom of expression and a free press. In Rio de Janeiro there are currently over a hundred religious publications and media bodies. There is, however, competition between churches over the media in which evangelical Protestants have proved particularly successful. For example, the Universal Church of the Kingdom of God operates fourteen television stations (including Jovem Pan Television in São Paulo), forty radio stations and several newspapers. Despite its traditionally privileged position, the Catholic Church does not yet own a television station.

Education

The 1988 constitution states that religion must be taught as part of the basic school curriculum. The Federal Council of Education decreed in 1993 that religion should be taught in Brazilian schools and colleges. Each school may choose its teaching staff. Several states in Brazil have ecumenical commissions in order to guide and carry out religious education in the schools.

Private schools are not obliged to offer religious education but are free to educate children according to their beliefs. There are thirty Jewish day schools, although only about half of the 20,000 school-age Jewish children attend them.

In the universities, courses on religions, celebrations, beliefs and current philosophies can be found. University extension courses are run on African-based religions, as, for example, how to prepare the offering to *orixas*, dance and celebrations.

Women

Women in Brazil have long struggled against powerful sectors of the Catholic Church and the state for basic rights, especially in matters of sexuality and reproduction. Divisions in the church between progressives opting for the poor and social reform, and those who reject such approaches in favour of traditional spirituality, have affected women's campaigns for decriminalisation of abortion and for recognition of the injustice of 'honour' killing of women for sexual transgressions. Theologies of liberation tend not to draw attention to the position of women in Catholicism, although nuns are the strength of Christian base communities and the majority of participants are women. The syncretic Catholic Mary–African Goddess is a powerful symbol of liberated women.

A 1987 study sponsored by the National Conference of Brazilian Catholic Bishops found that 4 million illegal abortions were carried out annually and were responsible for an annual death-rate of women of 400,000. However, the retirement in 1989 of the famous human rights supporter Cardinal Dom Helder Camara, the subsequent repression of liberation theology, and the reluctance of the state to implement suitable measures, have meant a slowing down of progress in relation to women's reproductive health, as well as of agrarian reforms which directly affect women's well-being. Non-implementation and avoidance of laws in the new constitution which do strengthen the legal status of women are the main concerns of women's groups.

CANADA

Canada	
GDP (US$bn)	494
Population	28,500,000
Annual population growth (%)	1.5
Urban population (%)	77
Working population (%)	50[a]
Literacy (%)	99
Ratifications	1; 2, 2(a), 2(b); 3; 4

Canada is a wealthy country of 28.5 million people, with a mixed, market economy. For the most part, freedom of religion is well established in this predominantly secular country in which religion is considered a private matter, not subject to the purview of the state, and tolerance is highly regarded as an aspect of democratic and egalitarian society. Children are increasingly likely to be taught that all religions are equally valuable paths to the truth. Fresh issues of religious freedom and equality arise as new minorities enter the country and as the principles of human rights – increasingly referred to by all sectors of the population – become more precisely defined in the interpretation of Canada's Charter of Rights and Freedoms.

As a whole, Canadians easily accept the idea that a diversity of religious beliefs can co-exist inside a nation which is secular not only in law but also to a considerable extent in culture. The press reports with outrage acts of religious intolerance. Inter-faith dialogues are common. Canada's official policy of multi-culturalism encourages a diversity of religions as part of the diversity of cultures.

Political structure

The nation of Canada was formed in 1867 under the British North America Act, now the Constitution Act 1982. The last province to join the federation was Newfoundland in 1949. Canada is a parliamentary democracy with a federal system of government: ten provincial governments and two northern territories. In 1999 the North West Territories will be divided into two areas, the eastern part to be renamed Nunavut; the indigenous Inuit people will take a more active part in its government.

There is a strong secessionist movement in Quebec, a province originally settled by French immigrants and conquered by the British in 1759. In 1993, the Liberals in the Canadian parliament took power from the Conservatives, who were replaced by an opposition split between the Bloc Québécois, which advocates separation for Quebec, and Reform, a western-based party. Before the 'quiet revolution' that occurred in Quebec about 1960, the powerful provincial Union Nationale party and the Roman Catholic Church had been strongly linked, but no such linkage can currently be made between the church and any particular political party in Quebec. Canadian political conflicts tend to be between regions; the movement for secession in Quebec identifies itself in regional and linguistic, rather than in religious, terms.

In November 1995, voters in Quebec rejected a proposal for a separate entity. Most French-speakers voted to separate but were marginally outweighed by those supporting Canadian unity: primarily Anglo-Canadians, immigrant communities and indigenous peoples. About 80,000 Aboriginal people live in Quebec; their English-speaking is a product of missionary education. The Northern Cree and Inuit peoples have advocated a right to separate from Quebec and form a province attached to Canada, stating that they have never ceded sovereignty to Canadian or provincial governments.

Legal structure

Canada has had a written Charter of Rights and Freedoms (the Charter) since 1982. The rule of law and separation of powers are fully protected in Canada; the government is subject to the judgements of the courts and obeys their rulings. There are separate federal and provincial jurisdictions. There is no officially established religion in Canada; nevertheless, the presence of religion is invoked by the preamble to the Constitution Act which begins with the clause, 'Whereas Canada is founded upon principles that recognise the supremacy of God and the rule of law . . .'; however, this has never been interpreted to mean that there is any one particular established religion. On the other hand, there is no clause prohibiting the establishment of any one religion, or of religion as such.

Article 2(a) of the Charter protects the fundamental freedom of 'conscience and religion', while Article 2(b) protects 'freedom of thought, belief, opinion and expression'. These guarantees of freedom of religion are supplemented by Article 15(1) which states that every individual 'has the right to the equal protections and equal benefit of the law without discrimination . . . based on [*inter alia*] . . . religion'. Article 27 states that the Charter 'shall be interpreted in a manner consistent with the preservation and enhancement of the multicultural heritage of Canadians', thus adding to the protections that cover Canadians of diverse origins.

Canada's commitment to religious as well as other forms of diversity is enhanced by its commitment to multi-culturalism. The Multiculturalism Act 1988 proclaims that 'multi-culturalism is a fundamental characteristic of the Canadian heritage and identity'. Much effort is devoted by government agencies and the public school system to promote the ideals of multi-culturalism. The ideal of multi-culturalism has supported the freedom religious minorities have to express their beliefs through practices different from the mainstream. Section 1 of the Charter 'guarantees the rights and freedoms set out in it subject only to such reasonable limits prescribed by law as can be demonstrably justified in a free and democratic society'.

Many Canadians, both those recently arrived from non-European immigrant groups and those from European ethnic groups other than English and French, warmly embrace the ideal of multi-culturalism. Beyond mere tolerance for minority cultures, the principle promoted is one of honouring the diverse origins and customs of Canadians. Religion is often viewed primarily as an aspect of culture; thus, religious freedom is viewed as part of the principle of cultural celebration. To have a compulsory day of rest on the Christian Sabbath was held to be inconsistent 'with the preservation and enhancement of the multi-cultural heritage of Canadians', according to Supreme Court Chief Justice Dickson.

The Canadian Human Rights Act (1985) and all provincial human rights codes explicitly prohibit discrimination on the basis of religion. The various types of religious discrimination that are proscribed in federal and provincial codes include public display of signs and symbols intended for religious discrimination; publishing or advertising hate literature; denial of access to public facilities or to private lodging on the basis of religion; religious discrimination in employment, employment agencies or advertisements for employment (except for organisations whose purpose is to promote a particular religion); religious discrimination in the purchase of property; and religious discrimination within trade unions. Although the number of formal complaints about religious discrimination received by the Canadian Human Rights Commission is very small, provincial commissions handle greater numbers, mainly in the area of employment.

The Criminal Code of Canada contains laws protecting religious worship from disruption (Section 176). The code also prohibits 'blasphemous libel' (Section 296); this is not confined to Christianity but pertains to any religion. However, the law clarifies that

> No person shall be convicted of an offence under this section for expressing in good faith and in decent language, or attempting to establish by argument used in good faith and conveyed in decent language, an opinion upon a religious subject.

Religious groups, like any other private group, are free to establish themselves or to disband as they wish; no registration with the state authorities is required.

Ethnic and religious composition

Many Canadians have multiple ethnic origins. In the 1991 census, 20.5 per cent of the population said they were of British ancestry only, 22.5 per cent of French ancestry only, 18.5 per cent of other European descent and a further 22.3 per cent is of mixed French and British descent, or of mixed French, British and other descent. This means that over 80 per cent of the population are of mainly European descent, chiefly British and/or French.

A further 7.5 per cent of the population gave Asia, Africa, Central and South America and the Caribbean as an indication of their descent; this percentage includes those identifying themselves as 'black' Canadians. Some 2.8 per cent identified themselves as 'Canadian' only. A maximum of 1.6 million, or 5.9 per cent, is estimated to be of Aboriginal descent. By the year 2006, the government estimates that 13–18 per cent of the population will belong to the category 'visible minorities', a term used to refer to people who might experience discrimination by reason of their skin colour. Aboriginal Canadian peoples are not considered to be an 'ethnic group' but rather to have their ethnic origin among First Nations who have a special relationship with the state based on unique entitlements.

According to the 1991 census data on religious adherence in Canada, 83.3 per cent of the population declared themselves to be Christian, 45.2 per cent Roman Catholic and 36.2 per cent Protestant. Taken together, all non-Christian religions accounted for only 4 per cent of the population, but numbers of Buddhists, Muslims, Hindus and Sikhs have well over doubled – even tripled in the case of Buddhists – in number since 1981, primarily as a result not only of migration but of refugee settlement. No religious affiliation at all was reported by 12.5 per cent of Canadians, a 90 per cent increase on 1981. New religious movements may be difficult to identify in census data; however, the Church of Scientology had 1,220 members in 1991, for instance.

All religions other than the religions of Canada's indigenous peoples were introduced into Canada via immigration. There is no absolute correlation between a particular faith group and descent. British-Canadians of Irish origin tend to be Roman Catholic, while some people identifying themselves as French may be Muslims or Jews. Many of the latest non-European immigrants to Canada who have arrived since non-racial immigration criteria were introduced in the 1960s are Christian, for example, immigrants from Hong Kong, Korea and India. Notable also is the growth of Chinese influence in Canadian Protestantism.

Thus the non-Christian proportion of the population is considerably less than the non-European proportion. Moreover, the rate of conversion from minority religions to

Christianity is high; about 20 per cent of the children of Jews, Hindus and Muslims in Canada in 1990 had converted. Among Canada's indigenous peoples, many are Christians, frequently incorporating into Christianity elements of their traditional religion.

The one-eighth of the Canadians who identified themselves in 1991 as having no religious affiliation reflects the general decline in religious practice in Canada in comparison with the past. It also includes those who have secular philosophies, such as the organised, but very small, group of humanists. Most people who reported in the 1991 census that they had no religion probably do not consider themselves to be atheists or even agnostics; they are not a significant organised force either on the religious or the political scene in Canada.

Most Canadians still identify with a particular religious group and turn to that group for life-cycle ceremonies connected with birth, marriage and death. Nominal adherence is usually found in the more established churches as the proportion which weekly attends their religious services has declined: 23 per cent of Canadians in comparison with 53 per cent in 1957. Roman Catholics are more likely to attend than others. However, in contrast to this decline, the smaller conservative Christian denominations number over a million and Protestant evangelicals as a whole may have up to 2.7 million adherents and considerable influence. On any given Sunday, there are likely to be more people in services of, for instance, Pentecostal Assemblies in Canada than there are in the Anglican Church. This trend is expected to continue.

Structural and systemic discrimination and tolerances

There have been a number of cases in the courts that have tested the extent of tolerance and discrimination within Canadian institutions and structures formed historically according to mainstream Christian norms. Canada has traditionally had laws that designate Sunday as a day of rest when commercial establishments should be closed. Courts have overturned some Sunday laws when they found that their primary purpose was to establish the Christian Sabbath. Laws have been permitted to stand when it was established that their purpose was secular, for example, to establish a common pause day for parents and children.

As all religions are equally protected in Canada, employers are expected to make reasonable accommodation for all workers' religious holidays, even though the Christian festivals of Easter and Christmas are national holidays. Although trade union membership is compulsory once a work unit has been unionised, the courts have permitted exemptions from membership on the basis of individuals' religious beliefs.

In dealing with claims by religious minorities for their community religious practice to be respected, courts have recognised some claims while rejecting others, depending on the circumstances of each case. The Hutterites, a pacifist agricultural group living communally on collectively owned farms, lost their claim in 1969 that restrictions on the acquisition of communal properties in Alberta constituted religious discrimination. In 1957 the British Columbia courts ruled that the Doukhobors – descendants of nineteenth-century Russian dissenters from the Orthodox Church – had neither the right to state-supported separate schools nor the right to withdraw their children from public schools whose teachings opposed some of their religious tenets.

Court cases concerning the Jehovah's Witnesses have been of great importance in establishing the principles of freedom of speech and religion. In Quebec, Witnesses were quite severely persecuted during Union Nationale rule (1930s–50s). Eventually, their right not only to worship freely but to proselytise and to make statements highly critical of the Roman Catholic Church was protected, although during the Second World War they were banned ostensibly because they were a threat to national security. Attempts made to expel Witness children from schools because they refused to salute the flag and sing the then national anthem, 'God Save the King', were overruled.

In the last ten years, there have been at least 700 disputes in which one parent's religion, as a Witness, was at issue, primarily in child custody and access matters. Although the courts have been guided by the 'best interests of the child', court rulings have varied, in some cases allowing children exposure to both parents' religious beliefs and practices, while in others preventing non-custodial parents from exposing their children to their religious beliefs and practices. In some cases, rulings have conveyed a judicial attitude that it is not the child's best interest to be raised as a Witness, which entails long hours at church – unusual from the point of view of less devout Canadians – and the obligation that baptised minors, like adults, take part in proselytising activities.

Cases concerning the legal capacity of parents to deny their sick children medical treatment have come before the courts. The Witnesses' religious objections to blood transfusions have been held not to prevent state intervention necessary to save a child's life or to protect it from serious impairment, matters judged to be pressing and substantial state concerns which may legitimately limit Charter rights and freedoms. Some Christian Scientist parents, who also reject standard scientific medical treatment, have been convicted for following only spiritual health care for sick children.

Canadian Jews suffered very strong legal, institutional and social discrimination in the past. Before and during the Second World War, Canada's policy on Jewish refugees was best summed up by the phrase 'none is too many'; during the Holocaust the government went so far as to deny Jewish citizens of Canada the right to sponsor their spouses and relatives into the country. Afterwards, all legal and institutional discrimination against Jews was gradually removed.

Muslims, a more recently arrived group, have also been subject to some acts of institutional insensitivity. In October 1994, because the Ottawa public school system had opened later than usual to accommodate the Jewish High Holidays, the Islamic Schools Federation of Ontario filed suit, demanding that the Ottawa School Board 'cancel classes on at least one of two Muslim holy days in schools where there are a substantial number of Muslim students', as a similar act of accommodating religious practice.

In 1994, a Montreal Catholic school principal expelled a Muslim girl for wearing the traditional *hijab* (head-scarf). This incident created a major public furore. The Quebec Human Rights Commission raised issues of human rights and responsibilities by contributing to the debate on religious pluralism in Quebec as a social and ethical challenge. It considered that a process of public reflection was needed on questions related to the organisation of the exercise of individual rights.

Interpreting the protection of multi-culturalism in Canadian law as protection of their religion against insult, some Muslims called on the Canadian government to prohibit importation of Salman Rushdie's novel, *The Satanic Verses*. In another matter, in 1994, the Canadian Society of Muslims recommended that the Ontario government should allow private arbitration within the Muslim community for some marital matters normally referred to the courts, or alternatively to introduce Muslim *shariah* law to regulate personal and family affairs among Muslims. Not all Canadian Muslims would agree with this proposal.

Among the other more recently arrived religious minorities, Sikhs have brought court challenges against school regulations prohibiting students from wearing *kirpans*, or small daggers; initiated Sikh males are required to wear the *kirpan* as an object of religious significance. The courts have ruled in these cases that denial of the right to carry a *kirpan* is a reasonable limit on freedom of religion, under Section 1 of the Charter.

Perhaps the worst incidents in the Canadian history of religious discrimination have occurred as part of the government's treatment of indigenous Canadian peoples. Canada was originally a settler colony; European settlers forced indigenous peoples off their land, often imposing inequitable 'treaties' upon them. Indigenous customs, some of deep religious significance, were banned, such as the potlatch ceremony of the Kwawkewlths people of British Columbia in which goods were distributed in ritual gift-giving, a ceremony which was banned from 1884 to 1951. Sacred lands and cemeteries were also expropriated.

Until the 1970s, Aboriginal children were forced or pressured (for instance, by threatened withdrawal of welfare payments from their parents if they refused to comply) to attend residential boarding schools run by Roman Catholic and Protestant missionaries. The Christian beliefs and customs which were part of the life of these schools were imposed upon indigenous people; they were denied the right to speak their own languages or practise their own religions. Entire communities are now trying to cope with the severe after-effects of violence and sexual abuse which – in more than a few instances – accompanied such drastic changes in life, belief and community.

Today, there are still disputes over sacred lands and cemeteries, most notably the armed stand-off between Mohawks and the Quebec police in 1990 in a dispute over ownership of a burial ground. Indigenous peoples have also claimed that restrictions on the hunting of fresh game in Canada violate their freedom of religion, as fresh game is part of their religious ritual. Freedom of religion for Aboriginal prisoners is still not fully guaranteed. Although prison officials have made attempts to facilitate Aboriginal rituals, such as sweet-grass ceremonies, elders in charge of these rituals still find their status in the prisons not as secure as that of, for example, Christian chaplains. This is an issue of no small significance, as Aboriginal peoples constitute a disproportionately high percentage of prisoners in Canada. A Royal Commission of Aboriginal People has been examining issues ranging from self-government to social, economic, cultural and educational matters.

Concerning new religious movements, the Church of Scientology has been recognised as a religion through several administrative decisions on matters such as tax exemption and authorisation to perform marriages.

There is minimal, if any, formal discrimination against non-believers in Canada. In 1986 a Manitoba secondary school student who was an atheist was expelled from his school for refusing to stand during the daily recitation of the Lord's Prayer; the Manitoba Human Rights Commission ordered him reinstated. Provision is made in the courts so that non-religious people are not required to take oaths on any Holy Book.

Social discrimination, prejudice and intolerance

A poll conducted in 1993 by the Canadian Council of Christians and Jews found that seven out of ten Canadians thought that tolerance of diversity was 'one of the best things about Canada' while at the same time they wanted to see greater integration of Canada's ethnic minorities within a broader Canadian culture. This slight unease about difference is explored further by polls which regularly show that a minority – about 12–14 per cent of Canadians – hold highly intolerant racial views, which are usually applied to Jews as well as to other racial and ethnic minorities. In a 1991 survey on attitudes to multi-culturalism and citizenship, about 12 per cent of respondents strongly believed that multi-culturalism would 'destroy the Canadian way of life'; on the whole, the pollsters reported, Canadians felt 'less comfortable with people whose origins are Indo-Pakistani, Sikh, West Indian Blacks, Arab or Moslem than they do with persons with other origins'. About a quarter of Canadians in a 1993 poll felt that 'the fabric of Canadian society is being threatened by non-white minorities'; these prejudices affect religious as well as racial minorities.

In 1993 the League for Human Rights of B'nai B'rith Canada recorded 256 incidents of anti-Semitism, including such incidents as defacing synagogues and Jewish cemeteries as well as harassment of Jewish individuals. Muslims also suffer such incidents; for instance, their mosques are sometimes defaced. The social image of Muslims is connected to prejudice against dictatorial Arab regimes in the Middle East, and there is little understanding among the Canadian population at large of the diversity of origins and beliefs among Muslims. Popular beliefs erroneously connecting female genital mutilation with Islam, and assuming that women have no rights whatsoever in Islamic law, also contribute to prejudice against Muslims.

Sikhs, with their distinctive turbans, also face discrimination and harassment. Strong public opinion was aroused in the 1980s against permitting Sikh recruits to the Royal Canadian Mounted Police to wear their turban, although many police forces and the Canadian army already provided uniform turbans for Sikh recruits. In Hamilton, Ontario, teenagers in August 1994 were harassing Sikhs on the streets. The national convention of the Royal Canadian Legion (an organisation of war veterans) has upheld a ban on admitting Sikhs, including Sikh veterans, to their premises unless they remove their headgear. Some RCL branches, however, have rejected this policy after a show of strong public support for the Sikhs. These incidents send a message to members of minority religions that they are still not fully accepted as members of Canadian society.

Continuing social discrimination against some minority religions has resulted in a recent attempt to curb public discussion and eliminate language that might be considered offensive by religious and other minorities. In keeping with the ideology of multi-culturalism and the belief that no speech upsetting to minorities (religious and otherwise) should be permitted, the Province of Ontario in 1993 issued guidelines to its colleges and universities asking for internal codes of conduct that would prohibit, *inter alia*, speech 'offensive' to minorities.

Such a policy may introduce a greater curb on freedom of expression than the law itself does. Canada has had in its Criminal Code provisions prohibiting spreading false news and promoting race hatred. Two famous cases tried under these laws, those of Ernst Zundel and James Keegstra, have invalidated or cast doubt on these provisions. Zundel, a West German immigrant, published and disseminated literature denying that the Holocaust had occurred. He was acquitted when the Supreme Court of Canada ruled unconstitutional the prohibition against spreading false news as being contrary to freedom of expression. Some members of the UN CERD Committee have expressed concern about this outcome as it seemed to exonerate an advocate of 'revisionist' theory. Keegstra, an Alberta high school teacher, viewed the Jews as a conspiratorial group and instructed his history students accordingly for many years. The Supreme Court of Canada ruled the hate law constitutional – it prohibited the dissemination of hate against an identifiable group – but in September 1994 Keegstra himself was acquitted by the Alberta Court of Appeal. Thus although religious minorities are still protected against the spread of hatred in Canada, legislative curbs on free speech are now narrower.

Promotion of religious belief and proselytising

Although there are no legal restrictions in Canada preventing individuals from changing their religions, there may be some restrictions at the provincial level. For instance, the Manitoba Human Rights Code permits employers to discipline workers for '[i]mproperly using . . . employment or occupation' as a forum for promoting their religious beliefs, among other things.

The various religious groups have their own rules about conversion with which the state does not interfere. Roman Catholic teachers in state-supported Roman Catholic schools may run the risk of losing their jobs, for instance, should they abandon Catholicism. Minority religious groups have been concerned about losing their adherents, frequently through intermarriage; the state does not interfere either to promote or to limit such conversions.

The 1953 Saumur case in Quebec set the precedent for freedom of religion and the right to proselytise; Jehovah's Witnesses were granted the freedom to distribute their literature. However, the activity of public proselytising, such as going door-to-door seeking converts, is practised by very few groups, such as the Witnesses and the Mormons (Latter Day Saints). Public opinion seems to regard such proselytising as an invasion of personal privacy. For this and other reasons, for example, Witnesses have been abused or even physically attacked; between 1991 and October 1994, there were forty-five 'preaching assault' cases against Witnesses in the province of Quebec alone.

The various religious groups are free to speak publicly on issues of concern to all Canadians, occasionally even advising congregants on how to vote in elections. The Catholic Church has spoken forcefully against abortion, a decision which is seen in Canada as a matter of concern solely for a woman and her physicians. Secular Canadians sometimes feel that religious groups have too much say in national social policy decisions, and that their forthrightness is a form of interference in the separation of church and state; on the other hand, many religious Canadians believe that secularism has taken over the state as an ideology.

Ecumenical and inter-faith activities

The largest Protestant churches in Canada are the United Church and the Anglican Church. The United Church, the result of an early inter-faith move in 1925, united Methodists, Congregationalists and two-thirds of the Presbyterians in Canada into the one religious body.

The Canadian Council of Churches was established in 1944, and by 1989 had fifteen full members, including five Orthodox churches. The Conference of Canadian Catholic Bishops has been an associate member of the Canadian Council of Churches since 1986. There are several ecumenical training establishments, an ecumenical Student Christian Movement, and other ecumenical organisations such as the Women's Inter-Church Council.

The recently formed Evangelical Fellowship of Canada (founded in 1964) unites up to 1.7 million people in the more conservative Protestant denominations. The Inter-varsity Christian Fellowship, a coalition of evangelical student groups, now seems to be, if not the largest of the student Christian organisations, at least as large as the Newman Centres (Catholic) and larger than the Student Christian Movement.

The Canadian Council of Christians and Jews, formed in 1947, has been a very active part of the religious community. In 1977, the Canadian Christian–Jewish Consultation was established to liaise between the Jewish and Christian communities, including the Canadian Jewish Congress, the Canadian Conference of Catholic Bishops, and the representatives of the Canadian Council of Churches. Working groups promote dialogue between Christians and people of other faiths, such as Hindus, Muslims, and Buddhists.

Although they lack formal links, Jewish and Muslim organisations cooperate in combating racism and religious prejudice. Muslim, Jewish and Christian groups have had joint consultations on issues to do with the Middle East and, more recently, the Bosnian war. One example of joint action on the provincial level is the Ontario Multi-Faith Council, representing most major world faiths, which, by agreement with the government, determines how religious and spiritual care is to be provided through chaplaincy services in Ontario's correctional facilities, hospitals and community programmes.

Education

Until quite recently public schools in Canada were Protestant schools. In Ontario, from 1944, one hour of Protestant instruction per week was mandated by law; children were obliged to say the Lord's Prayer at assemblies every morning, although in recent years individual children could be exempted from such requirements if their parents so requested. In legal challenges since 1982 the teaching of religion in the schools has been increasingly circumscribed. The 1990 Zylberberg case prohibited prayer in public schools in Ontario, noting that even though exemptions were permitted, there was pressure on children from minority religions to conform. For some time after, however, some school boards defied the law and one multi-religious group has appealed against current restrictions on religious teaching and expression.

The official policy in public schools throughout Canada is increasingly to teach about the equality of all religions or to avoid discussion of religion altogether. Many parents claim that, in effect, this policy imposes an ideology of secularism on children. On the other hand, non-Christian parents have objected to extended celebrations of and school projects about Christmas, for instance. These celebrations and projects are particularly common in the primary grades.

Although Canada has no established religion, Roman Catholic schools are supported by public funds for historical reasons. At the time of the Union of Canada in 1867, Section 93 of the British North America Act gave the provinces exclusive powers over education laws and also continued the privileged status of 'denominational, separate or dissentient' schools. This privilege is carried over into Section 29 of the 1982 Charter. Thus public funding of Roman Catholic schools cannot be challenged as discriminatory under Section 15 of the Charter.

In the event, only five provinces support Roman Catholic schools with public funds as four provinces did not possess separate (religious) schools at the various times they entered the Canadian Union and so were under no obligation to provide funding later. Manitoba abolished Roman Catholic schools in 1890 and, despite legal judgements that it should not have done so, was not forced to reinstitute them. In Ontario, Roman Catholic schools have been supported by public funds up to Grade 10, extended to Grade 13 in 1985, since when – on the grounds that they are now completely state-funded – Roman Catholic schools are obliged to admit non-Roman Catholic children. Roman Catholic children may, if their parents prefer, attend the public (non-religious) schools. The Supreme Court ruled in 1996 that state funding was neither required nor proscribed.

However, Roman Catholic school boards are still permitted to discriminate against non-Roman Catholic teachers in their employment. Such schools are also still permitted, in

Ontario and elsewhere, to demand conformity to church doctrine in teachers' private lives; for example, Roman Catholic school boards may deprive of their employment teachers who divorce or who marry outside the Roman Catholic faith. Teachers have challenged these practices.

In Newfoundland, no provision is made for a purely secular school system, there being only the Roman Catholic, the Pentecostal, the Seventh-Day Adventist and the integrated systems. The latter, the largest system, consists of the Anglican, United Church and Salvation Army schools which united in 1968. In Alberta, there is a publicly funded Roman Catholic school system but the provincial government also pays part of the costs of other religious schools. In Saskatchewan, the provincial government initially funded Roman Catholic schools only at the elementary level, extended to the secondary level in 1964.

The situation in Quebec is extremely complex, since a significant English-language minority lives in that province and is entitled to schools in the English language. There are Roman Catholic and Protestant school systems but no secular schools. Both Protestant and Catholic schools must accept eligible students, no matter what their denomination, as they are 'common' schools. Attempts in Quebec to secularise the school system by dividing it along language rather than religious lines have been thwarted by the fact that religious education is enshrined in the Constitution Act. Into this complex context, issues of parental, children's, teachers' and school rights and responsibilities have been raised by questions surrounding the wearing of the Islamic head-scarf by students or staff. One Muslim school had demanded that a non-Muslim female teacher comply with the same dress code as the pupils.

In some provinces, the tax system obliges citizens to identify their religious affiliation. In Alberta and Saskatchewan, Roman Catholics must direct their school taxes to Roman Catholic schools and if they wish to send their children to non-Catholic state schools, they may be required to pay tuition fees. In Ontario, Roman Catholics may direct their taxes to Roman Catholic schools if they wish.

Parents are free in Canada to establish private religious schools. In some provinces, the government pays part of the costs of such private schools while in others the parents pay the entire cost, as well as paying their regular school taxes. In Ontario, the Ontario Alliance for Christian Schools, together with the Canadian Jewish Congress, have been campaigning for state funding for non-Catholic private religious schools, on the grounds that to fund Roman Catholic schools and not fund the schools of other religions is a form of discrimination. The Ontario government has opposed these claims on the grounds that one purpose of public schooling is to socialise all children to be Canadian citizens, and that a further fracturing of the school system along religious lines would undermine this essential task.

Many of Canada's universities were originally established by Christian denominations. Until the end of the Second World War, many universities had formal or informal rules regarding the maximum number of Jewish students they were willing to accept. Most universities are now part of a state system, however, and none discriminates against faculty, staff or students on the grounds of religion. The number of private universities and colleges is increasing, usually through the efforts of conservative Protestants; several require faculty to subscribe to the religious beliefs of the institution.

Conscientious objection

There is no conscription and no compulsory national service in Canada; thus the issue of conscientious objection to such service does not arise at present. During conscription in the world wars, conscientious objectors were permitted to perform alternative service, but those, such as the Jehovah's Witnesses, who claimed that even alternative service was against their religious beliefs were jailed. Any new occasion for conscription would require the issues to be reconsidered under Charter principles.

Internal religious affairs

The policies of the different religions or beliefs concerning gender and sexuality are not considered a matter for state concern or intervention. Several instances of inequality between male and female adherents occur in the various faiths in Canada. The Roman Catholic Church does not permit women to be priests and in other ways restricts their status. Orthodox Judaism and some branches of Islam also restrict the roles that women can play within their religions. Anti-discrimination legislation does not affect a religion's ability to include or exclude women as part of its doctrine. Religious personal law, such as affects divorce rights of Jewish and Muslim women, is not recognised in Canada where all women enjoy equal legal rights with men, regardless of the customs of the religious group to which they adhere.

General 'equality' statements reflecting the norms of the dominant culture do not, however, take sufficient account of difference. A history of discrimination and destruction has affected indigenous women, such as the long-standing problem of 'native status' in which an Aboriginal woman who marries a non-Aboriginal man loses her birthright as an Aboriginal and her right to live on a reserve. Other gender and religion–race matters of discrimination are similarly the concern of immigrant women.

As human rights for homosexuals enjoy protection under Canadian law, various religious organisations are battling with the question of what rights, if any, homosexuals should enjoy within their religious communities. Some Protestant churches now have a policy that open homosexuals may be ordained as ministers; others will ordain homosexuals as long as they are not sexually active.

In other internal matters, the courts occasionally intervene to ensure rules of fairness. In a 1992 case, for example, the courts intervened in a dispute among Hutterites on the grounds that the expulsion of some members from a Hutterite colony had violated rules of natural justice. The courts have also sometimes intervened in disputes about dismissals of ministers or priests from their jobs. Court decisions steer clear of doctrinal matters and focus on the rules of fair play that are expected to guide administrative justice within any Canadian institution.

CHILE

Chile, a long strip of country lying between the western Andes and the Pacific Ocean, today has a thriving market economy; it is a major copper exporter, other export income being earned from fruit and fish meal.

Ethnic and religious composition

Most of Chile's 13.6 million people are of mixed European–indigenous descent and most live in urban areas. In 1992, over 10 per cent of Chileans 14 years or older declared that they considered themselves part of the Mapuches (the largest indigenous group), the Aymaras and the Rapanuis (Easter Islanders).

Roman Catholicism, the most widespread religion in Chile, was introduced by the Spanish in the sixteenth century. In the nineteenth century, small groups of Protestants

Chile	
GDP (US$bn)	41
Population	13,600,000
Annual population growth (%)	1.8
Urban population (%)	84
Working population (%)	39
Literacy (%)	94.5
Ratifications	1; 2, 2(a), 2(b); 3; 4; Am

and Anglicans and, in the twentieth century, small Jewish communities settled in Chile. There has also been some immigration from Arab countries, many converting to Catholicism. The 300,000 Palestinian immigrants form the largest such community outside the Middle East. Over the last few decades, some Protestant denominations of United States origin have obtained adherents, such as the Church of the Latter Day Saints (Mormons), the Jehovah's Witnesses and Pentecostal churches.

In Chile today there are estimated to be about 5,000 different religious organisations or new religious movements. Of nearly 10 million Chileans aged 14 and over in 1992, 77 per cent were Catholics, 13 per cent were Protestants and 4 per cent belonged to other religions. The Jewish community, for instance, numbers 15,000. The small Muslim community is growing and building its mosques. People who have no religion or are atheists constituted nearly 6 per cent.

Political and legal structure

According to its constitution, Chile is a democratic republic, organised in a presidential system, similar to that of the United States. Its judiciary is formally independent and the legal system follows the Napoleonic code. The 1980 constitution provides for some checks and balances, although the predominance of the presidency is evident as the constitution was designed to enable former dictator General Pinochet to continue as head of state and government. The military regime (1973–90) also left a legacy of other restraints that conspire against effective representative democracy. For instance, members of the Constitutional Tribunal, which has the capacity to play a crucial legal and political role, were appointed during the Pinochet regime; the Council of National Security also has a civilian–military character and has some constitutional powers. The current government has proposed constitutional reforms, but it is uncertain whether they will be passed.

Freedom of religion or belief

Freedom of conscience, religion and belief is recognised in Article 19.6 of the constitution:

> The Constitution ensures freedom of conscience, manifestation of all beliefs and the free exercise of all religions not opposed to morals, good customs or public order.

> The religious confessions may build and keep churches and their dependencies under conditions of hygiene and security determined by laws and ordinances.

> The churches, the religious confessions and the religious institutions of any religion will have, in regard to their goods, the rights conferred and recognized by the legislation currently in force. The churches and their dependencies, devoted ex-

clusively to the service of a religion, will be exempt of all kinds of territorial taxes.

Article 19.2 sets forth as a fundamental right equality before the law and prohibits discrimination. From 1989, human rights provisions in treaties including the International Covenant on Civil and Political Rights, its Optional Protocol and the American Convention on Human Rights have had constitutional status in Chile. However, Chile has made reservations to these treaties to the effect that they do not cover any alleged violations of human rights which 'began to occur before 11 March, 1990'. These reservations are intended to prevent international scrutiny of 'disappearances' during the era of the military regime.

The criminal code establishes sanctions for those who infringe the free exercise of a religion. Infringement may consist in disturbing, preventing, interrupting or delaying the exercise of a religion (Articles 138 and 139). Another legal remedy is the *recurso de protección*, which was introduced for the protection of freedom of conscience and of religion as well as for many other constitutional rights in 1980 but has yet to be invoked for the guarantee of this specific liberty.

In 1993, Congress passed constitutional reforms aimed at ensuring respect for indigenous people by protecting or exempting their customs. The law acknowledged their unique cultures and recognised them as part of the heritage of the Chilean nation. It also established the right of indigenous communities to community activities in sacred sites, cemeteries and *nguillatun* courts (Mapuche ceremonial sites), and to have access to their ancestral lands and waters. The development of bilingual education in some schools is also included.

Religion–state relations

The current constitutional provisions on freedom of conscience and religion are the result of two centuries of evolution in Chile. Under the 1833 constitution, which was in force for nearly a century, the state was united with the Catholic Church: 'The religion of the Republic of Chile is the Catholic, Apostolic and Roman, with exclusion of public exercise of any other.' However, although public exercise was prohibited, as immigration from Protestant countries increased (especially from England and Germany), an interpretative law allowed non-Catholics private exercise of their religions and the establishment of their own schools and cemeteries. During the last decades of the nineteenth century, a series of legal reforms established civil marriages and civil cemeteries.

The constitution of 1925 separated the state from the Catholic Church. It guaranteed freedom of conscience and religion in similar terms to the current constitution. None the less, the Catholic Church was perceived to have retained a privileged status under the 1925 constitution and a public legal personality such as other churches did not have, because the state was constitutionally obliged to pay substantial sums of money to the Catholic Church for a five-year period, and because the president was empowered to conclude concordats with the Vatican, which further strengthened the position of the Catholic Church in Chile. These provisions implied a formal constitutional recognition of the Catholic Church by the state. Other churches, in contrast, had to seek legal recognition of their juridical personality from the government in order to enjoy their rights; furthermore, they were subject to the same legal accountability as any private corporation.

The commission in charge of drafting the latest Chilean constitution considered that all churches and religious confessions have public legal personality because, in its view, any discrimination in this respect would represent a violation of the principle of equality before the law. Nevertheless, the formal difference in legal status between Catholicism and other religions remains.

Recent legislative proposals

Prompted by a request from the Protestant churches and other religious groups, a bill was introduced in Congress in October 1993 to end any discriminatory treatment of religions in Chile; it had not been approved by 1996. The legislative proposal states that it is not acceptable for religious institutions to depend upon an executive decree in order to have legal personality, because that infringes the principle of the separation between church and state and is more an act of religious toleration than one of recognition of religious freedom. The bill proposes that churches and other religious institutions – other than the Catholic Church, the current legal status of which would remain unchanged – should have automatic right to legal personality, following publication in the *Official Gazette* of a certificate issued by the Ministry of Justice. Nevertheless, under the bill, the Ministry has the power to object to the recognition of legal personality, after gazetting. The Ministry of Education has general portfolio responsibility for religious affairs in Chile and there is also a civil servant in charge of religious affairs, attached to the Ministry of the Interior.

Article 18 of the bill proposes that religious ceremonies and general meetings and assemblies shall always be public, as opposed to secret, in order to prevent activities that are considered to be contrary to morals or from which injury to persons might result. This clause may conflict with the interpretation given by the Human Rights Committee to Article 18 of the ICCPR.

The bill is limited in its application. Legal differences between the Catholic Church and other religions or beliefs will continue, and associations of a humanist or atheist nature will still have to apply for formal recognition of their legal personality.

Religious practice in the armed forces, the police and the prisons

In 1910, military chaplaincies were established in all branches of the armed forces, with priests and bishops paid by the state and integrated with the military echelon. The main official ceremonies of the armed forces continue to include the celebration of Catholic rites. Difficulties between the military and the Catholic Church during the seventeen years of the military regime helped the Protestant Church to gain converts in those institutions. Protestants have now established missions in the armed forces, but they do not have the kind of institutional support available to Catholicism. In response to the demand that has arisen for the accommodation of religious practices other than Catholicism, Article 19 of the new bill concerning religions proposes that religious practice by members of the armed forces and the police as well as by prison staff shall be reasonably accommodated in those institutions. Their superiors would previously have had to have authorised participation in activities associated with the various faiths of service members. The bill recommends that the institutions facilitate, as far as can be done, the places and means to carry out religious activities.

Influence of the Catholic Church on politics and public policy

Until 1966, the Conservative Party expressed adherence to Catholicism and was perceived to be 'the Catholic Party'. The Christian Democrat Party is not confessionally affiliated, though Catholics are prominent in it. Unlike other Latin American countries with a traditional confessional basis, Chilean legislation has never required those who hold high public office to be Catholic. In the last fifty years, five presidents have been Masons and one a Marxist.

Since Chile became independent nearly two centuries ago, regular controversies have arisen between church and state over civil marriages and civil cemeteries, on education and over the abolition of an established church. The influence of the Catholic Church is still evident in the areas of legislation, the media and education. The current controversial issue is the possible introduction of legislation to permit divorce. Chile is among the few countries in Latin America which do not have civil divorce proceedings. The Catholic Church has opposed reform and placed pressure on public opinion against change. Catholic bishops have openly criticised Christian Democratic members of Congress who · are Catholic and favour reform.

The Catholic Church and inter-faith relations

As the dominant religion in the country, the Catholic Church has traditionally looked on other churches with suspicion. After Vatican II, however, relations between the Catholic and other faiths improved, especially with established Protestant traditions. An ecumenic Te Deum is now celebrated on Independence Day. Links between the Catholic Church and the Jewish community have become stronger. On the other hand, as the number of newer Protestant religious groups have increased, the Catholic Church defined their growth as a menace because they are highly oriented towards proselytism, and many people have converted from Catholicism to these denominations.

Instances of religious intolerance and discrimination

During the era of the military regime (1973–90) some attacks against Catholic churches occurred, almost always against churches whose priests were known to be critical of the government. These attacks ceased after Chile's return to democracy.

The Church of the Latter Day Saints (Mormons) started in Chile in 1956; by 1976 it had 25,000 members, by 1983, 160,000 members and today, 400,000 members. In the last few years many attacks have taken place against its churches; thirty churches were destroyed in 1986 and, in 1990, sixty-six were damaged. The Mormons have apparently been seen as an arm of the United States government or, at least, as representing a strong American influence. Although criminal investigations into these incidents were opened, no charges have yet been laid. Chilean public opinion seems noticeably less harsh in reacting to such attacks than when reacting to attacks on Catholic churches.

Another type of discrimination has been suffered by the Jehovah's Witnesses, some of whose beliefs are not fully respected, especially when they come into conflict with the law. For instance, in a recent decision, notwithstanding the wishes of a Witness patient suffering from a brain haemorrhage and his relatives, a court ordered the required medical treatment to be carried out.

Education

Parents are generally free to bring up their children according to their own convictions. There are private schools run by different religious denominations. In the public education system, Catholic religious education is not mandatory. Primary and secondary students may choose alternative religious education. Churches are required to submit a detailed programme to the Ministry of Education for approval. To date, the following religions have obtained approval: Adventist, Anglican, Baha'i, Baptist, Catholic, Jewish, Lutheran, Methodist and Orthodox. In practice, most schools teach Catholicism. The very few children who are not Catholic are placed in an awkward position that inclines them to resist any attempt on the part of their parents to exempt them from Catholic courses. The result is a strong social pressure to adhere to Catholicism.

The university system includes several Catholic universities, some state-funded and very prominent, in particular, the Pontifical Catholic University of Chile. At this university, the university authorities have enforced conservative Catholic values. For instance, a performance of the Maya-Quiche legend 'Popol-Vuh', was supposed to take place in a tent on campus. As the play included some nudes (as in the original version), the authorities decided to move the play off campus, despite protests. When the play was later staged on campus there were no nudes.

Professors who oppose conservative Catholic ideas, or hold views on issues controversial in conservative Catholicism, may not feel free to express them. This is considered to affect academic freedom, especially as the Pontifical Catholic University of Chile receives state funding.

The media

After Chile's return to democracy in 1983, censorship of books ended. Various religious denominations own several publications and radio stations; there is a predominance of Catholic-owned media. For several decades, only state-owned and university-owned television channels were allowed to transmit programmes. Several channels were owned by Catholic universities. Chile now has privately owned channels but the influence of the religion-owned channels is still very significant. For example, in Santiago, the capital, two out of six regular channels are religion-owned and in the provinces this percentage is even higher.

Conscientious objection

There is no recognition of conscientious objection in the law, either on religious grounds or for any other purpose. Chilean state officials feel generally free to ask citizens about their religious affiliation and practice. The military informally asks people preselected for the draft to say if they are not Catholic, reportedly in order to identify and exempt Jehovah's Witnesses from military duties because of their beliefs. Those who are in the process of becoming Catholic priests are also excluded from the draft. There has been a recent debate about the need for a system of alternative service to the military draft but no change seems likely at the moment.

The police ask people they detain for information about their religious affiliation. Though this power is not explicitly conferred by any law, it has been approved by the Supreme Court, to assist in identifying people summarily detained for street offences.

Women and religion

The world-wide problem of discrimination against women in various forms can also be found in the pattern of women's participation in Chilean religious groups. The Catholic Church and class distinction in Chile combine to reinforce domestic–motherhood roles for women and this has been reflected in written statements and government policies over the last two decades. Proportionately fewer Chilean women than in surrounding countries work outside the home or enjoy access to tertiary education.

Although many of the numerous grassroots women's groups, especially Communal Kitchens and Health Groups were originally formed with the support of the Catholic Church, in the years before the restoration of democracy in 1989 the church withdrew its support from groups which became more broadly politicised. While the women's movement's rallying cry is 'Democracy in the country and in the home', the latter has proved difficult to achieve. The Catholic Church has put obstacles in the way of provision of rights to divorce and rights over decisions concerning reproduction.

COSTA RICA

Costa Rica	
GDP (US$bn)	7
Population	3,200,000
Annual population growth (%)	3
Urban population (%)	48
Working population (%)	38
Literacy (%)	94.3
Ratifications	1; 2, 2(b); 3; 4; Am

Costa Rica's image of tolerance and peacefulness is based on a fifty-year history of uninterrupted democratic government, progressive social legislation, and a constitution that prohibits a standing army and enshrines individual liberties as well as social and economic rights. That same constitution, however, also establishes the Roman Catholic Church as the official church in this small Central American state. This constitutional provision raises issues of religious liberty and is a source of conflict between the Roman Catholic majority and Protestant and other Christian minorities over the rights and privileges their respective institutions enjoy within the nation's legal structures. Costa Rica is the seat of the regional human rights system, the Inter-American Commission and Court of Human Rights.

Socio-economic background

Costa Rica's population of over 3 million people is mostly of European-American origin or mixed European-American and indigenous American origin, but with a significant population of African-Americans (6–8 per cent), primarily in the Caribbean coastal region and smaller groups of indigenous Americans (1–2 per cent) located mainly in the south, bordering Panama. The Euro-American and mixed descent population tends to dominate all aspects of economic and political life; hence Costa Rica is sometimes described as a 'white enclave' in Central America. Although there are no forms of legal discrimination, many African-Americans privately complain of social marginalisation due to race; the areas where they predominate are the poorest in the country. African-Americans, however, are represented in business, the various professions, in the universities and in the government. The 24,000 indigenous peoples are largely un-recognised socially and culturally, as well as being economically and politically marginalised from national life, some having been denied national identity cards (and thus citizenship) until the early 1990s.

Costa Rica still maintains living standards superior to other Central American countries. Overall, the people enjoy a high standard of living; redistribution of land, and almost universally available health and educational services date from the 1940s. The economy is based on agriculture: 65 per cent of foreign exchange is generated through the export of agricultural products, mainly bananas and coffee. About 40 per cent of the population is rural.

These conditions and a very high education and literacy rate for women have, however, not ensured equality of participation for them. Despite the Family Code of 1974 and its progressive 1988 amendments as well as the 1990 promulgation of the Law on the Promotion of the Social Equality of Women, only 28 per cent of women are economically active. Costa Rican women tend to marry and have their children while young and often head their households (one-third of all households had female heads in 1990). Culturally, the majority of women are excluded from major decision-making and experience strong social pressure to confine their interests to home and children, a model reinforced by Catholic values; class difference results in discrimination against poorer women, especially visible over the past decade of economic stress. The Women's Movement of the PLN political party confines its activities to issues such as housing, single mothers and provision of day nurseries although increasing numbers of women are entering politics and the bureaucracy.

Political structure

The government is a functioning, liberal democracy. The 1949 constitution guarantees individual rights and social rights. Political tolerance is perceived as a fundamental characteristic of Costa Rican life. The constitution guarantees that 'No-one can be disturbed or persecuted for manifesting opinions nor for any act that does not infringe the law' (Article 28). This is coupled with the right to free association and to meet for political and other purposes (Articles 25–26) and with the right of freedom of movement. Costa Rica grants political asylum to all who seek it and has a history of competing political parties of different political ideologies and persuasions, including several professing Christian socialism.

Religion and belief

Religiously, 80 to 85 per cent of the population is Roman Catholic; about 12 per cent Protestant or Pentecostal; the remaining 3–8 per cent are Adventists, Mormons, Jehovah's Witnesses and similar groups. The entire Protestant community is composed of sixty-five denominations or independent groups, with some 2,500 churches. In the past thirty years, the numbers of Protestants, and especially Pentecostals, have grown extremely rapidly. There are also very small groups of self-styled 'gnostics' and 'esoterics', a Hare Krishna commune, a retreat centre of the Ching Hai International Meditation Association and a humanist organisation. Many indigenous Costa Ricans practise their own traditional religions, often combined with Roman Catholicism. There also is a strong 3,000-member Jewish community whose religious life revolves around a large Orthodox Synagogue and school, and a smaller Reformed Synagogue.

Church and state

Confessionally, Costa Rica is officially a Roman Catholic country. Article 75 of the constitution declares:

> The Roman, Apostolic, Catholic Religion is the religion of the State, which contributes to [the church's] maintenance, without impeding the free exercise in the

Republic of other religions (*cultos*) that do not oppose universal morality nor good customs.

Roman Catholicism and the state were long intertwined before independence from Spanish rule in 1821. Unlike the situation in other Latin American countries, Costa Rica's Roman Catholic clergy did not oppose independence and the Roman Catholic Church was declared the official religion in the country's first constitution. Although the Liberal movement in the mid-to-late nineteenth century stripped the church of many of its privileges and expelled the religious orders, these privileges were restored in 1942 and the church was granted an influential role in education and social welfare. Following the 1948 revolution that marked the beginning of modern Costa Rica, the Roman Catholic Church was again accorded official status and after 1970 it began receiving a series of benefits and privileges not available to other groups.

Although the Ministry of Foreign Relations has 'and Religion' attached to its name, no government agency or ministry has responsibility for religious organisations and there is no law regulating religious groups.

The privileged status of Roman Catholicism

The official status of the Roman Catholic Church conveys several immediate privileges: the government pays the salaries of clergy, subsidises buildings and other programmes and activities and exempts the church from paying property and import taxes.

Except for the Roman Catholic Church, no other religious organisation can be legally established as a religious organisation but can be incorporated legally only as civil associations. They are thus not eligible for the privileges accorded Roman Catholicism. This not only affects them economically in terms of taxation, but also in terms of religious beliefs and practices. For example, Roman Catholic clergy are by law civil servants for the purposes of performing marriage ceremonies; no Protestant pastor can perform a legally binding marriage, for which civil ceremonies are required.

Religious education

Religious education – that is Roman Catholic Christianity – is required by law. Non-Roman Catholic parents can exempt their children from the religious education curriculum by petitioning school authorities. The Constitutional Chamber of the Supreme Court ruled in 1993, however, that schools do not have to provide religious instruction to an exempted child in her or his own creed. The religious liberty and constitutional questions concern who has the authority to determine the content of the religious curriculum and who is deemed a qualified religion teacher.

Article 75 of the constitution is interpreted as meaning that the Roman Catholic Episcopal Conference is the 'rector' of all public religious education and the bishops are responsible for determining curriculum content. A Roman Catholic priest is employed in the Ministry of Public Education to oversee the religious education programme. The Archbishop considers that this exclusive authority is necessary to ensure that 'the faith of the Church and not a snake in place of bread' is taught in the schools. He argues that Costa Ricans 'freely decided' for Roman Catholicism and, therefore, that the majority religion should have exclusive responsibility for the curriculum.

According to the Civil Service Code Regulations on Career Teachers, only those authorised by the Episcopal Conference may teach religion in schools. Furthermore, 'The Missio Canonica is granted only to those who have concluded the formation process in the Superior Normal School of the Institute of the Pedagogy of Religion.' Not only does this automatically exclude all Protestants, it also excludes graduates of the Ecumenical School of Religious Sciences of the National University, an academic department staffed primarily by Roman Catholic priests.

The Archbishop argues that the bishops must give their permission in order to ensure that a 'person is prepared, not just academically but spiritually in order to teach the authentic faith of the Church'. This is because 'the most fundamental level of religious education is the personal testimony of the educator'. Thus the Episcopal Conference requires 'moral acceptability' of its religion teachers, such as being married to another Catholic in a Catholic marriage ceremony and not being divorced.

In a recent case, the president of the Association of Religion Teachers was dismissed for publicly questioning these subjective criteria and the Costa Rican Human Rights Commission, a non-governmental human rights agency, has challenged the constitutionality of the *missio canonica* before the Supreme Court. The suit alleges that government policy is based on an erroneous interpretation of Article 75, and that the *missio canonica* provision violates articles of the constitution, including Article 56 guaranteeing the right to work. After four years, the Court still has not given judgment.

In 1994 the Human Rights Committee of the United Nations expressed concern 'for the pre-eminent position given to the Roman Catholic Church' and called on the government of Costa Rica 'to adopt measures assuring that there is no discrimination in the exercise of the right to religious education'. It stated that, 'The actual practice of submitting the selection of religion instructors to the authorization of the National Episcopal Conference does not conform to the [ICCPR].'

Church influence on the government

The Roman Catholic Church exerts considerable informal influence; it cannot be openly confronted by the government and the church has veto power in areas especially important to it. The government, however, does not necessarily do 'what the church wants'. Indeed, the church has been a consistent critic of the economic policies of several recent governments with little notable impact. Furthermore, the Ministry of Health makes artificial contraception devices readily available and condoms are promoted as a defence against AIDS, practices to which the church objects.

Two recent cases, however, illustrate the kind of power the church can have. Over several years, the Ministry of Public Education prepared a sex education curriculum for use in the public schools, involving different sectors of society, including the Roman Catholic Church, in preparing the textbooks. In 1991, however, after consulting with the bishops, the president postponed the sex education programme. Two years later, before the textbooks could be distributed, the Archbishop pronounced them unacceptable and called for new ones, saying that they did not adequately conform to church teaching on sexuality. The textbooks were not released and the sex education programme was postponed again.

The Roman Catholic Church also has been successful in censoring material it deemed detrimental to the church. In 1989 it opposed the exhibition of the film, *The Last Temptation of Christ* as a 'severe offence' to Christ. The film was then prohibited even for private viewing or for discussion in critical forums. The Censorship Board based its decision primarily on the religious reasons that the film pictured an 'incorrect interpretation of Christ' and was 'disrespectful and defamed Christianity'.

Freedom of worship and belief

Clearly no-one in Costa Rica need be fearful of government reprisals for having a particular religious belief or for worshipping as they choose. Thousands of Christians go to their respective non-Roman Catholic churches every Sunday and during the week without encountering danger or opposition. The Jewish community maintains an active religious life with no overt evidence of anti-Semitism; indeed, the government recently publicly criticised a local magazine for what was perceived as an anti-Semitic report on the local Jewish community. The Hare Krishna and Ching Hai Meditation Association invite visitors to their ceremonies and activities every Sunday. Religious organisations are readily granted legal status as civil associations.

Still, there are discretionary actions by public officials and government offices that Protestants perceive as infringements on their right to worship. These actions are primarily directed towards places of Protestant worship. For example, by invoking laws regulating 'places of public meetings' – which refer not to churches, but to bars, night clubs, and theatres – municipalities have refused building permits for non-Roman Catholic churches. Overcrowding of public areas, lack of parking space, scandalous and noisy meetings, all have been alleged as reasons for denying permits. In one case, although the city government alleged that the neighbourhood did not want a Protestant church in the area, a legal challenge resulted in the issuing of a permit.

More often, the Ministry of Health has closed churches for allegedly not meeting health codes such as adequate sanitary facilities or, especially, acceptable noise levels. Reasons given for closing buildings have been in general terms, 'the well-being of the neighbourhood' or 'general security', and based on laws regulating 'public spectacles', or, if specific, are given in arbitrary fashion leaving little room for correcting the problems. Thirty-seven different churches were closed in 1992 but were allowed to re-open later.

Noise is a major source of contention. Some churches, especially Pentecostal ones, broadcast extremely loudly to the neighbourhood, to a degree that exceeds the number of allowable decibels established by the Ministry of Health. However, Protestants point to the arbitrary and selective nature of the enforcement of these health codes, suggesting that the real reasons for their enforcement relate more to religious beliefs than to the requirements of the codes.

Other regulations also are perceived by non-Roman Catholic Christians as discriminatory and as infringements on their right to worship. Their pastors are not allowed to visit the sick in public hospitals nor those incarcerated in jails with the same liberty as Catholic priests. From the mid-1980s to the early 1990s, foreigners seeking permanent residency were refused if they stated their profession as 'missionary'. No reasons were stated for the regulation.

In 1990 legislation proposed in the National Parliament sought to severely curtail non-Roman Catholic worship activities. Ostensibly oriented to Catholic and non-Catholic alike, the proposed law regulating 'cultural activity' would have made it very difficult for non-Roman Catholic churches, especially loosely organised Pentecostal and other 'free' churches, to obtain legal status as associations. Furthermore, a national registry of 'religious organisations' requiring public filing of complete doctrinal positions, would have been established. The law also would have limited the hours that worship services could be conducted, limited the use of musical instruments and would have required the approval of 'the neighbours' before a building permit could be issued for a church. According to the nation's leading newspaper, the purpose of the proposed law was 'to exercise control over basic aspects of the creeds in our country'. Although this law has not been enacted, it suggests that in the absence of effective constitutional guarantees of religious equality, such a law is always a latent possibility.

Still, religious adherents who are not Catholics are vigorously present in Costa Rica: in business, in professions, in universities as students and professors and in the government. Their worship services are held throughout the week. They publish a newspaper, have radio stations and television channels, sell religious books from their own bookstores, proselytise from door-to-door and conduct massive 'evangelistic campaigns' in the national stadium. They have private schools and universities – where religion from their perspective is taught – that are fully accredited by the Ministry of Public Education; one is the Jewish day school. They own institutions offering a variety of social services, from health care to youth camps to pastoral counselling. The government has contracted a Protestant agency to conduct government-related alcoholic rehabilitation services. The country also is the headquarters and language training centre for numerous non-Costa Rican (mostly North American) Protestant mission organisations that work throughout the region.

Conclusion

The constitution, rather than guaranteeing religious liberty, provides for religious tolerance in which no obstacles are put in the way of the exercise of other religions. However, religious liberty implies equality while mere tolerance does not. Equality of religions does not have a basis in Costa Rican law; hence the various forms of legal discrimination favouring a single Christian denomination. However, the Roman Catholic Church has repeatedly recognised the right of Costa Ricans to choose and practise their own religions, including access to religious instruction for their children, although not in the public schools.

Discrimination on the basis of religion or belief is thus in Costa Rica more of a structural kind, a matter which may encourage some government officials to discriminate in particular instances. There is, however, little evidence of intolerance. No-one worships in fear in Costa Rica and people of religious persuasions other than Roman Catholic participate freely in national society.

CUBA

Cuba	
GDP (US$bn)	13.7[b]
Population	10,800,000
Annual population growth (%)	1.4
Urban population (%)	75
Working population (%)	44
Literacy (%)	94.9
Ratifications	3; 4

Two overriding concerns have shaped the history of freedom of religion, thought and conscience in Cuba since the revolution of 1959. The first of these is the enshrinement and defence of the revolutionary process moving Cuban society towards communism; freedoms are defined within and delimited by this process. The second is the perceived need to defend the nation against hostile intervention and subversion. The history of the past three decades has provided considerable reason for such concern. It has also created a permanent state-of-war mentality in which the exercise of certain freedoms is carefully conditioned. This is mirrored outside the country where the very mention of Cuba often evokes a passionate and polarised response.

Demographic and social background

The national territory of Cuba is formed by thousands of islands and keys; the largest is the island of Cuba. With its capital, Havana, less than 200 kilometres from the United States, Cuba's location has contributed to a close, complex and difficult relationship with the United States, a relationship which has strengthened some of the concerns shaping religious and other freedoms in Cuba.

Cuba's current population of 10.8 million is difficult to analyse precisely in ethnic and racial terms because of centuries of mixing of people of Hispanic and African descent and because race discrimination policy prohibits such data collection. In comparison with pre-revolutionary Cuba, life expectancy and access to health care have improved for its people; adult literacy is 94.9 per cent and school enrolment is comparable. The collapse of international communism, however, and the economic, commercial and financial embargo by the United States have had a serious impact on the Cuban economy.

Since 1959, the nation's resources have been controlled by the state, which also directs economic and financial planning. Private property and family inheritance rights exist, with restrictions, but private ownership of major productive resources is generally not allowed. Churches, institutions and religious denominations may own property which is needed for the exercise of their legitimate religious functions. Some congregations and churches own and operate cooperative farms, small factories and other enterprises which employ church members and are in keeping with socialist norms and state economic policies.

Political and constitutional structures

Cuba's constitution of 1976, revised by the National Assembly in 1992, defines Cuba as:

> a socialist state of workers . . . organised with all and for the benefit of all as a united and democratic republic, for the enjoyment of political liberty, social justice, individual and collective well-being, and human solidarity.

Article 3 states that supreme political power resides with the people and is exercised directly or through Assemblies of Popular Power at local, provincial and national levels. The Council of State – comprised of the President of the Republic (Fidel Castro), six vice-presidents, and twenty delegates of the National Assembly – is, in practice, the chief legislative and executive body. The Council is also a supreme court of appeal for political and criminal cases in the judicial system. Cuba has not ratified the ICCPR and CESCR though it is a party to CERD and CEDAW.

The judicial system, headed by the Supreme Popular Tribunal, uses both professional and lay judges, all elected by the corresponding popular assembly. Judges and courts act with a degree of independence from political authorities; more than half are estimated not to be members of the Communist Party of Cuba (PCC).

The PCC is given a major constitutional role in the Cuban state. It is constitutionally defined by principles of Marxism–Leninism and the thought of José Martí. At its 1991 party congress, the PCC supported constitutional change which would permit direct, secret, popular election of candidates to the provincial assemblies and the National Assembly, a change incorporated in the 1992 revised constitution but not yet implemented. The PCC also agreed to admit professed religious believers to the party.

In actual practice, all political power is said by some observers to be in the hands of a small group of individuals, perhaps as few as twenty, who are said to exercise multiple roles in the political structure to form an interlocking directorate. While the PCC membership has been criticised as a new privileged class in Cuban society, others deny this, saying that they are expected to be models of selfless dedication to society. Nevertheless the major influence of the PCC and, to a lesser extent the armed forces, in the life of the country is undeniable. State and party are integrated.

Dominant and opposition forces and groups

In Cuba today, political life is not divided by conflicting racial or ethnic allegiances or identities. Sincere efforts have been made over the past few decades to ensure the participation of all racial and ethnic groups, and of women, in all levels of political life, although there is still much room for improvement.

About fifty political opposition groups exist in Cuba. In 1992 many of these small groups were loosely organised under two umbrella organisations: the Cuban Democratic Convergence and the Cuban Democratic Coalition. Statements, actions and personal associations of members of these groups are at times denounced as counter-revolutionary by government or PCC officials. Some are under surveillance, have been detained and harassed by security forces or have been threatened and attacked in their homes by government-promoted 'popular rapid response brigades' reportedly set up in 1991 as 'an organisation for ideological and political combat'.

The possible connections between internal opposition groups and external forces – in particular sectors of the Cuban exile community based in Miami and agencies of the United States government, notably the Central Intelligence Agency – are seen as hostile and threatening to the existence of the revolutionary state. Given the history of numerous attempts by such external forces to invade Cuba, most dramatically in the Bay of Pigs incident in April 1961, the government attempts to monitor and control internal opposition and dissent groups.

Religion and religious beliefs

About 45 per cent of the Cuban population professes active affiliation or identity with some religious belief. This includes Roman Catholicism (32 per cent), Protestant faiths (10 per cent), African or Afro-Caribbean beliefs and practices (1.6 per cent) and others (1.4 per cent), including 1,200 Jews. An additional 49 per cent are identified as agnostic and 6 per cent as atheist. In a 1994 survey of 1,002 adults in almost all areas of Cuba, 20 per cent of the respondents said they took part in a religious service within the month preceding the survey, and 12 per cent said they took part in Santeria, an Afro-Caribbean religious movement. Some Protestant churches, like the African spirit groups, empower women in leadership. Over the past thirty years, estimates of Sunday church attendance in Cuba have varied between 10 and 30 per cent.

The spectrum of religious beliefs and groups in contemporary Cuba is a product of history. Roman Catholicism was introduced by Spanish colonial conquerors at the beginning of the sixteenth century, in a process which also precipitated the elimination of the island's indigenous people and, at least ostensibly, their religion. Beliefs and practices based on African tribal religions were introduced by slaves brought to Cuba from that continent during the Spanish colonial period, and were later modified and sometimes mixed with evangelical Christian beliefs and practices to become the basis of belief systems such as Santeria.

The Roman Catholic Church enjoyed a privileged position in Cuba under Spanish rule. When Spanish dominance declined and control of the United States over Cuban affairs increased after 1900, Protestant churches, many begun and supported by parent denominations in the United States, flourished. Small Jewish communities – primarily Sephardic Jews who had fled the Inquisition in the seventeenth century and European anti-Semitism in the nineteenth century – and other groups completed the picture.

Despite (or perhaps because of) Roman Catholicism's close relation to colonial Cuba's ruling elites, Catholicism remained largely confined to the cities and the upper and middle classes in the years before the 1959 revolution. The large majority of Cuba's poor and rural population, including Fidel Castro's parents, had little contact with priests or other representatives of official Catholicism. In addition, Cuban Catholicism's identification with Spain and Spanish colonial rule alienated Cuban patriots and independence proponents throughout the nineteenth century, and many of these espoused anti-clerical, if not specifically anti-religious sentiments. Later, and to a far lesser degree, the close and often dependent connections of many Protestant groups to the United States – perceived by many nationalist Cubans as the new imperial power – increased the sense of alienation between organised religion and independent patriotism.

Thus, the revolution of 1959 was not the first or only event to precipitate a sense of crisis between religious belief and patriotic duty, for such tension was an already established feature of Cuban society.

Legislation on freedom of thought, conscience, religion and belief

The 1992 revision of the constitution removed references to 'scientific materialism' as the basis for the Cuban state. The revised constitution contains various statements of rights relating to thought, conscience and religion. Regarding religious freedom, Article 8's wording is pro-active, not merely tolerant: 'The State recognises, respects, and guarantees religious freedom.' The principle of separation of church and state is declared. Article 8 also states that 'different beliefs and religions enjoy equal consideration'.

The right to freedom from discrimination specifically includes religious belief. This places the full weight of the constitution behind freedom from discrimination on the basis of religious belief, especially in those areas where discrimination against religious believers had been most criticised: government and military office and university admission.

Article 55 of the constitution adds a specific guarantee of freedom of conscience as well as of religion. It also recognises and guarantees the right to change religious belief or to have no religious belief.

Article 39 deals with education and specifically bases the educational system (controlled by the state) upon 'scientific and technical advances' and the ideals of Marxism and of José Martí. It also guarantees freedom of artistic expression which is not contrary to the revolution. Article 53 states that freedom of the press and of speech are guaranteed, but must conform to the purposes of a socialist society. The media are controlled by the state 'for the interest of society'. Article 54 guarantees freedom of assembly and organisation to social and popular organisations, and again guarantees freedom of speech and opinion which is 'based on the unrestricted right to initiative and criticism'.

However, it has been pointed out that the centrality of Marxism–Leninism as the official ideology of the state, and the specific normative leadership role accorded the PCC, exclude any sort of ideological pluralism in areas such as politics or education. Moreover, Article 62 stipulates that none of the liberties recognised in the constitution can be exercised in ways contrary to the constitution or other laws, or in ways which conflict with the existence and purposes of the socialist state or the decision of the Cuban people to build socialism and communism. Amnesty International has concluded that 'such an approach has seriously limited in practice the exercise of freedom of expression, association, and assembly, in particular'.

The practice of freedom of religion

Although religious persecution does not seem to be systematic or widespread in Cuba, the experience of particular minority religious groups differs from that of most Cubans; Baptists, Jehovah's Witnesses and Seventh-Day Adventists have been monitored, harassed and detained. Religious organisation and expression are regulated considerably by the state.

Religious groups are required to register with the provincial registry of associations of the City of Havana; the Ministry of Justice, consulting with the Interior Ministry, has the power to decide whether to recognise organisations. Religious groups may only carry out their practices in designated places and religious holidays and processions have been banned since 1961. The construction of new churches is forbidden and many congregations violate the law by meeting privately in people's homes, a practice which is prohibited by law as unauthorised assembly of more than three persons, and punishable by up to three months in prison and a fine. Members of the armed forces are still prohibited from allowing anyone in their household to observe religious practices; elderly relatives are exempted only if their beliefs do not influence other family members and are not 'damaging to the revolution'.

Religions may not have access to the mass media. The media remain under the ownership or control of the government. In the past few years, some specifically religious radio and television programmes have been permitted, and some churches have negotiated for their own printing facilities, although this is not always achieved.

Religious believers may and do occupy public office and senior public appointments. The presiding judge of Cuba's Supreme Court from 1961 until his retirement in 1980, Enrique Hart Ramirez, was a practising Catholic. At least three delegates in the current National Assembly are Protestant ministers, one of whom is pastor of a congregation which has developed its own cooperative farm and small factory, and which carries on a vigorous worship and religious education programme. Religious views and practices seen as supportive of the broad humanitarian goals of the revolution are encouraged. Religious charitable organisations function, including Caritas, an international development agency associated with the Catholic Church. On various occasions, Fidel Castro has singled out the Catholic nuns who administer hospitals, convalescent homes, orphanages and other social institutions as models of selflessness and dedication to which all revolutionaries should aspire.

Propagation and continuance of religious belief

There are restrictions upon the propagation of religious ideas in Cuba. Attitudes which consider religious belief to be counter-revolutionary, whether arising from rigid ideological conviction or as a judgment upon past experience, continue to interfere with some expressions of religious belief. The state-controlled educational system generally precludes private church schools, but seminaries and other specialised educational institutions operate. In 1989, approximately forty Catholic seminarians were training for the priesthood in two seminaries in Cuba, and over one hundred have been ordained in Cuba since 1970. Sunday school religious instruction and Bible study also continue, especially within the context of worship services, but also occasionally in private homes, although these may be monitored by party or government officials or security forces. At home, some parents educate their children in religious beliefs, while others express concerns that to do so would be to risk denunciation for counter-revolutionary activity.

Conscientious objection

The use of religion for political purposes which are perceived to undermine the state or the revolution is prohibited. Jehovah's Witnesses and some Seventh-Day Adventists have been monitored and harassed by the Committee for the Defense of the Revolution because they are considered to be 'enemies of the revolution' as they will not accept military service or take part in state organisations. They have been accused of forming illegal associations, of clandestine printing and of contributing to juvenile delinquency because they refuse to honour the symbols of the Cuban state.

Developments in church–state relations

Despite signs of 'peaceful co-existence', the history of church–state relations in Cuba since 1959 has been stormy as the churches – in particular the Roman Catholic Church – and the revolutionary leadership have undergone major changes and tensions in their relationship with each other.

The triumph of the revolution in 1959 found the Roman Catholic Church in Cuba theologically and institutionally unprepared to deal with a changing social and political situation. Theologically, the Catholic Church maintained a rigid exclusion of socialism, and especially communism, as inherently atheistic and antithetical to faith, a position curiously reflected by that of orthodox Marxism–Leninism and its strict adherents among the Cuban revolutionaries who regarded religion as inherently counter-revolutionary. The theological and pastoral opening to the world afforded by the Second Vatican Council was still unavailable to the Cuban Church. Institutionally, the Catholic Church was bound to the interests of those social classes from which it drew its financial support, the wealthy and the middle class, and to the culture and politics of the source of a majority of its clergy, Franco's Spain. These represented the very interests most repudiated by the revolution of 1959.

Thus, the support which Catholic Church leaders gave the initial triumph of the revolution quickly dissipated as the revolutionary government began to carry out its promises of major change in Cuban society. Laws and policies changing the ownership of property and the educational system were especially threatening to the interests of the Catholic Church. Property reform undermined or eliminated the financial basis of the classes which supported it. Nationalisation of the educational system brought the Catholic Church's major institutional enterprise under state control. Many foreign priests felt that they had lost their reason for being in Cuba (in 1959, two-thirds of all the Catholic priests in Cuba were teachers in the Catholic schools). By 1960, Catholic bishops were denouncing the communism of the revolution and confronting government policies. In 1961, some priests had become more militant and the government expelled more than 130 of them. For the next five years or more, remaining Catholic clergy encouraged the faithful to leave Cuba and the government regarded the church as being alienated from the revolution, or as actively supporting its enemies. The number of priests and laity dropped drastically. Catholics who supported the revolution became alienated from the institutional church and some left it.

By the early 1970s, conditions changed. A gradual opening of the relationship between the Catholic Church and the revolutionary government became possible, increasing by the mid-1980s. One such condition was the gradually felt impact of the second Vatican Council and especially of the Medellin process in which the Catholic Church in Latin America increasingly adopted a 'preferential option for the poor'. Together with this came the example of Christian socialism in Allende's Chile and the role of religious faith in the Nicaraguan revolution of 1979, both of which had an impact upon the Cuban Church and perhaps more significantly upon the Cuban revolutionary leadership, especially Fidel Castro. The Cuban Church increasingly became a polarised church in which some remained alienated from the revolution while others sought accommodation between faith and revolutionary life, stressing the common humanistic goals of each. Both the government and the Catholic Church hierarchy have made conciliatory gestures towards each other over the past decade and have usually responded positively to each other's overtures.

Throughout most of this difficult history, the Protestant churches have generally fared better than the Catholic in relation to the revolution and the state, partly because they had smaller numbers and influence within the socio-political scene at the start of the revolution and partly because of the relatively working-class, more rural orientation of most Protestant churches. Protestant churches were less of a target of revolutionary censure and more able to identify with the social purposes of the revolution. Difficulties have arisen primarily when Protestant denominations have been perceived as dependent upon the United States for ideological and financial support and direction.

Current attitudes and prospects

The complexity of the current situation of religious freedom results in part from divisions within both church and state regarding the proper relationship between religious belief and revolutionary practice. Many in the revolutionary government and the PCC continue to regard religious belief as antithetical to official ideology. Typically, this attitude translates into a policy of pro-active neglect: leave alone the actual practice of religion and it will wither away through education and example. But the bitter legacy of the history outlined above leaves many in the government and the PCC wary of religion – especially the Catholic Church – as a potential enemy presence within the country. In this situation, pro-active neglect can easily slip into reactive repression.

Pointing out that rigid ideological attitudes towards religion are increasingly outdated and unscientific, President Fidel Castro and some of the leadership have periodically tried to educate their own government and party members to the need to admit that religion and revolution can be, and in some places have already shown themselves to be, mutually supportive if not integral. From the government perspective, this explains the openness towards official dialogue with the churches in Cuba during the past decade, the progressive constitutional reform and changes in party membership policy.

The spectrum of attitudes in government and party is matched by that within the churches. While many remain alienated – some see in the church a refuge from the revolutionary society based on atheistic ideology or even a base for their political opposition – others have embraced the revolution as a practical way to live their religious faith in the current historical situation. Still others seek greater recognition of specifically religious values and expression and call for dialogue and a reconciliation between church and state which would end governmental and party discrimination.

At the personal level of everyday life, some Cubans experience the complexity of the problem of religious freedom in Cuba today as a double hiding. When they are with Christians, they keep their work with the revolution hidden; when they are with revolutionaries, they keep their identity as Christians hidden. Others who are more open, attending church, known to be religious and working in state-supported professions, have done so with no ill consequences. The Jewish community, for instance, has grown, largely as the result of regular visits from a rabbi based in Mexico and also because of the response from within a community so long bereft of spiritual sustenance.

Women

Although the constitution stipulates equal rights for women in all spheres of life, discrimination on the basis of sex is punishable by fines and imprisonment and many aspects of women's lives have improved enormously, women still have difficulty in ensuring full implementation of the policy. Instead of major executive positions being given to women in response to their part in the Marxist revolution, women have experienced political persecution for querying some of the consequences of particular Marxist policies, and the manipulation of family planning and abortion policies in favour of the state rather than the welfare of women.

GUATEMALA

Guatemala	
GDP (US$bn)	10
Population	9,700,000
Annual population growth (%)	2.9
Urban population (%)	40
Working population (%)	34
Literacy (%)	54.2
Ratifications	1; 2; 3; 4; Am

Guatemala has been a repressive and violent nation, especially in the rural indigenous regions. In 1954 a CIA-sponsored coup overthrew the democratically elected Arbenz government, bringing back oligarchic and military control which quickly melded the ideologies of anti-communism and national security. Thirty years of brutal dictatorships, from 1954–84, have destroyed the rural community.

From 1978–83 – a period known as *la violencia* – Guatemala first suffered under the rule of General Lucas Garcia, a regime so corrupt and so violent that, even in the context of Cold War politics, the Reagan administration withdrew its support. In 1982 a coup brought to power General Rios Montt, an evangelical preacher and elder of the Church of the Word, whose brother is a Catholic bishop. General Rios Montt allowed the military to be brutal in their attempt to drain the highlands of support for the combined guerrilla forces, the Unidad Revolucionaria Nacional Guatemalteca (URNG) and he also continued earlier policies of 'cleansing' urban Guatemala of all popular activist opposition to the military dictatorships.

In 1983 the military replaced Rios Montt with General Mejia Victores who began the process of carefully guiding Guatemala back to a form of elected civilian government which would enable Guatemala to appear democratic. In 1985 a new constitution brought to office a democratically elected civilian president and congress. However, the military retained the real power. The Mejia Victores government enacted a variety of laws protecting the army's position of control in the highlands, its independence from parliamentary interference and impunity from prosecution for human rights abuses.

Of the following regimes, the Cerezo government proved inept and corrupt and in spring 1993 former President Serrano dissolved Congress and the judiciary, suspending all civil rights. Massive opposition from representative civil sectors, combined with rapid international isolation and immediate suspension of economic aid, quickly undermined military support for Serrano who fled the country. Backed by the popular sector, Congress selected then Human Rights Ombudsman Ramiro de Leon Carpio as Guatemala's new president to serve the remainder of Serrano's term, to January 1996.

For the first time since the decade 1944–54, the popular movement in Guatemala has formed a political party, the New Guatemala Democratic Front (FDNG) whose executive includes academics, human rights activists, trade unionists and women's rights activists but contains limited representation of indigenous Mayan groups.

Guatemala's human rights record remains the worst in Central America with killings and forced disappearances, as well as other violations, not only continuing but increasing between 1994 and 1995, according to the Guatemalan Human Rights Ombudsman. The sources of human rights abuses in recent Guatemalan history are these: death squads linked to the military; counter-insurgency warfare waged by the military; the creation of Civil Defence Patrols (PACs); impunity for military officers who commit human rights abuses; and the URNG. International human rights organisations generally agree that 10 per cent of human rights abuses originate with the URNG, while 90 per cent are military-related. The internal armed conflict had driven thousands of indigenous people into Mexico as refugees – some were repatriated in 1992 – and into the jungle. The military forcibly settled those it found in camps as a counter-insurgency measure, while other displaced people formed communities in resistance (CPR) within the jungle. The Civil Defence Patrols (PACs) drew all male residents into the military structure in order to dominate the indigenous population. Strategic hamlets were established from which to patrol the countryside and keep watch on each village and community, setting one person against another and increasing the violence.

Popular hopes that President de Leon would be an outspoken advocate of human rights faded before the power of Guatemala's military. Although he started to deal with corruption by reforming the legislature and the Supreme Court, the prospects for improvement in the situation facing indigenous people in particular – long the target of military and security force campaigns – remained very uncertain. The PACs have been renamed 'Committees for Peace and Development' and the military commissioners who run them have been 'demilitarised', but the reality of army control and the non-voluntary nature of the PACs remain.

In 1996, Alvaro Arzú Irigoyen was elected president, promising to further democracy. The government and the rebels declared an open-ended truce to help end the long insurgency. By the end of the year a Peace Treaty had been signed.

Constitutional provisions

The Guatemalan constitution contains an impressive catalogue of human rights, including these:

Article 36. Freedom of Religion. The exercise of all religions is free. Any individual has the right to practice his religion or belief, both in public and in private, through education, worship, and observance, without other limits than the public order and the respect due to the dignity of the hierarchy and the faithful and other beliefs.

Article 58. Cultural Identity. The right of individuals and communities to their cultural identity in keeping with their values, languages, and customs is recognised.

Article 66. Protection of Ethnic Groups. Guatemala is made up of various ethnic groups among which are native groups of Mayan descent. The State recognises, respects, and promotes their form of life, customs, traditions, forms of social organisation, the wearing of Indian dress by men and women, their languages, and dialects.

[Other rights guaranteed include the rights to education, health and work.]

However, a decade of civilian governments has proved that a new constitution cannot, in and of itself, overcome a historical reality steeped in structural and institutional violence and racism. The nation will remain undemocratic until there is civilian control of the military, a truly independent judicial system and a political decision-making process that offers the popular sector and indigenous peoples meaningful opportunities of influence.

Social and religious composition

With a rapidly expanding population of 9.7 million people, Guatemala is the most populous country in Central America. Over half the people of Guatemala are indigenous Mayans, in twenty-one language groupings. Up to 50 per cent of indigenous people speak Spanish, which is also the language of the remainder of the population who are *ladinos*, people of mixed descent who identify with the dominant Hispanic culture.

Over 86 per cent of the total population lives in poverty; 75 per cent of the rural population has no access to health care and 82 per cent of the rural population has no access to safe drinking water, the worst figures in Central America. Indigenous people's life expectancy is 44 years, their illiteracy rate is 77 per cent and higher in areas where they predominate.

While being the richest Central American nation in terms of natural resources, Guatemala has the most unequal structure of land ownership and income distribution in all Latin America. The large and small estate system dates back to Spanish colonial times (1542–1821); 61 per cent of the total population lives in rural areas where 2 per cent of landowners own 65 per cent of the arable land. As the system spreads and disparity of land distribution becomes greater, parcels of land become smaller and smaller and the indigenous *campesinos* descend into even greater poverty. They are forced to farm the sides of mountains for survival and so the land suffers from deforestation, soil degradation, watershed deterioration, pesticide abuse, contaminated water and the disappearance of wildlife. There has been massive migration to urban areas.

The major religions are Catholicism, 65 per cent of the population, and Protestantism, 35 per cent. However, many indigenous peoples practise a syncretic Christianity, combining Catholicism with Mayan spiritual beliefs. There is a community of about 1,000 Jews.

The interplay of traditional and Christian beliefs has been and remains very complex and strongly linked to the history of human rights in Guatemala. During the sixteenth century, indigenous peoples were often relocated from the jungle to villages, to be Christianised. However, traditional beliefs persisted. For instance, among the Q'eqchi'-speaking Mayas in the province of Alta Verapaz, traditional identity is grounded in the community and in the mountain beliefs and practices that anchor each community firmly to a specific place and its 'owner'. The mountain spirits – *tzuulta'qa*, at once the physical features of the sacred landscape and the male–female spiritual beings themselves – play a vital role in agricultural production and human reproduction through fertility and healing rituals.

During the 1970s, the Q'eqchi' were re-evangelised by both Catholic priests and lay teachers of religion and by evangelical Protestants, replacing the powers of traditional elders and religious brotherhoods. While collective and sacrificial rituals were curtailed, healing and pregnancy practices which were more individual and related to the female domain continued. The lay teachers of religion, committed to liberation theology with its preferential option for the poor, established Christian base communities, facilitating a class-based insurrection against Guatemala's economic elite and the military.

The massive dislocation of population caused by the internal armed conflict naturally had an adverse effect on traditional religious practices so tied to particular places; the impact was less on Christian practice needing only a Bible and the memory of songs and prayers. The military manipulated Q'eqchi' concepts associating sickness with guilt, saying that they would be redeemed if they repented of their ways. In many camps only evangelist Protestant groups were allowed to proselytise; the military identified Catholic teachers of religion as the cause of violence while they also suppressed traditional gatherings and activities. The military then reconstituted the refugees from the camps into armed hamlets guarded by civil patrols (PACs), where they brought together people from different areas, languages and customs.

Today, led by the Catholic lay teachers of religion, an ethnic revivalist movement is growing among the indigenous peoples, resurrecting earth beliefs and practices to create a new pan-Q'eqchi' ethnic identity expressed through reworked versions of old symbols and traditions.

Church and state

The interests of the state, the property-owning class and the institutional church have coincided in Guatemala. Before 1979, the hierarchy of the Catholic Church in Guatemala spoke out against anyone, including priests, nuns and lay Catholics who opted to actively pursue an ideal of social and economic justice for the poor and indigenous people. Shortly after the CIA-sponsored coup of 1954, the Archbishop of Guatemala City had forged an alliance with the Guatemalan economic oligarchy and military high command. The Catholic hierarchy at this time was also joined in an 'ecumenical politics' by conservative evangelical Protestant denominations.

Protestantism in Guatemala has a history unique in Central America. In 1871, General Justo Rufino Barrios, an advocate of an economic theory rooted in international trade, was opposed by the landed aristocracy and its defender, the Catholic Church hierarchy. Up till then it had been illegal to practise any form of Christianity other than Catholicism, but in 1873 Barrios issued a Freedom of Conscience Act, resulting in a surge of Protestant investors, especially Germans, who invested in coffee production.

In 1882 Barrios was persuaded by the wife of the US Consul, a Presbyterian, to recruit Protestant missionaries. As a result, Reverend John Clark Hill arrived in Guatemala City and was given land near the National Palace to build a Presbyterian church. Rev. Hill emphasised secular education, science, technology and free trade, forging a long-standing alliance between Liberal Party dictators and the Presbyterian Church.

Today, 35 per cent of Guatemala's population is Protestant or Pentecostal. While Protestantism is stronger in Guatemala than in any other country in Central America, there is no history of socially liberal Protestant theology because the goal is eternal salvation for the individual. While the Protestant Church thus presents the image of being apolitical, this image has never matched the reality of significant political alliances and influences, right to the present day.

In the 1970s, President Lucas Garcia worked closely with conservative evangelical groups based in Florida to send missionaries to rural Guatemala to preach a message of individual salvation to come in the next world while emphasising strict allegiance to existing social and political institutions. Ex-President Serrano and ex-dictator and current President of the Congress Rios Montt have continued this political and spiritual alliance between conservative evangelical Protestantism and right-wing politics in Guatemala.

In contrast, an alternative synthesis of theology and politics emerged among Catholics in Guatemala in conjunction with the Second Vatican Council in 1962, followed by the Latin American Bishops' Conference in Medellin, Colombia, in 1968 which recognised the rights of the poor to seek a better life in this world and called for a cessation to all oppression of the poor. Priests, nuns, and lay Catholic leaders began a social analysis process that examined the structural and institutional roots of poverty and violence. In rural Guatemala, this led to organising credit unions, cooperatives, *campesino* networks and groups demanding agrarian reform. Christian base communities were formed.

This organisational effort of rural indigenous *campesinos*, urban poor, students, university faculty and unions was seen as subversive. The modern era of repression against Catholic advocates of a theology of liberation began with the assassinations of two priests in 1976 and 1978. The number of assassinations of priests and teachers of religion grew in following years. In 1980 and 1981, ninety-one priests and brothers, and sixty-four nuns fled Guatemala after receiving death threats. Some seven Catholic radio stations were bombed while another was burned; twelve religious formation houses and several parochial schools were closed. All Christian base communities were considered subversive and lay teachers of religion were primary targets of threats, disappearance, torture and assassination.

In 1980 a joint statement on human rights was issued by the fifty-two Jesuits of Guatemala and their Superior for Central America, calling for a more just distribution of land and wealth. It documented human rights abuses and implied that a root cause of the violence was structural and institutional. Officially, the government responded that the Jesuits were 'agents of a network of enemies that operate to feed Marxist subversion'. Unofficially, the Secret Anti-Communist Army (ESA) released a simple statement: 'Kill all the Jesuits in the country.'

While most of the violence against religions in 1980 and 1981 was directed against the Catholic popular church, Protestants were not immune. During the years 1980 and 1981 forty Protestant religious leaders in rural indigenous villages were assassinated. In 1981, fifteen development agencies, including Church World Service, OXFAM and Mennonite Missions, received letters from death squads threatening personnel with death if they did not leave the country immediately. One Mennonite missionary, Rev. Troyer, was assassinated in front of his spouse and five children. He had worked in an area in which over 1,500 indigenous people had been murdered by death squads and regular army units.

132

This experience led a small number of Protestants to move towards social activism, asserting that the salvation offered by Christ is integral, that is, it affects not only the soul but the whole person and society as well. In 1988, a group of Protestant theologians gathered in Medellin, acknowledging that Protestants had largely failed to address social ills; they called for greater commitment to social issues. From this point it has no longer been possible to stereotype all Guatemalan Protestants as politically right-wing.

The response of the Catholic Church to the violence has also changed. In the last decade the Guatemalan Archbishop Prospero Penados de Barrio began to move the Catholic hierarchy away from its traditional conservatism. In 1988 and 1989 the institutional church released pastoral letters, 'The Cry for Land' and 'Declaration of Coban'. The Catholic Church has become, over the past five years, one of the main threats to the Guatemalan army's relatively unchallenged reign. The archbishop stated in 1993 that, 'The enemy of the church is violence; you can never achieve anything by force. And for this reason, [the government] misconstrue[s] the work of the church.' The Catholic Church remained a target of attacks in 1994, through assassinations, death threats and intimidation.

Thus those who practise and live a Christianity rooted in pre-Vatican II Catholicism or historic Guatemalan Protestantism are 'free' to worship as they please and to proselytise. However, those Christians, Catholic and Protestant, who practise and live a theology of liberation were victims of intimidation, threats, attacks, disappearances and assassinations. Teaching the story of Exodus has been a subversive act in Guatemala.

Liberation theology, however, is continually criticised by women because patriarchal oppression is not recognised by it. Women have played a major part in active resistance to violence and repression. Majority female human rights groups such as the Guatemalan Widows' National Coordinating Group and the Mutual Support Group for the Families of the Disappeared originated in and are maintained by Christian communities, although now separate from the Catholic Church because of its perceived cautiousness.

Investigation and education for human rights

During the peace negotiations, the government, military and URNG agreed to the creation of a Truth Commission to investigate human rights abuses in recent Guatemalan history. However, the military convinced the other parties to accept a Truth Commission with no power or authority to name those responsible for human rights abuses.

In this vacuum, Archbishop Penados announced that the Documentation Center of the Archbishop's Office of Human Rights would, in 1995, begin a two-year research project aimed at 'historical recovery', to study and analyse mechanisms of violence used against the people of Guatemala over the past thirty-five years of war and repression. Archbishop Penados has stated that, 'reconciliation must be the foundation for a just peace; that reconciliation must be based upon trust; and, that trust can only be established through an honest search for truth'. The historical recovery project is an inter-diocese project, national in scope and naming violators of human rights.

As human rights abuses by both government and guerrillas against indigenous people increased in 1994, and again in 1995, speaking out in the cause of human rights has been fraught with danger. Human rights abuses against journalists have caused a self-imposed censorship throughout the national media. According to the directors of the archbishop's Human Rights Office, education on human rights is difficult and dangerous in rural Guatemala. A major problem in indigenous regions is that the peoples have never, in five centuries of colonisation, felt that a written constitution or laws could be used to protect and promote indigenous rights. The goal of the archbishop's human rights education project is to enable the indigenous peoples to overcome their fear, based on past experience, that those who talk of human rights will become targets for violence, and instead to 'assume ownership' of the Guatemalan Constitution and international human rights documents. The Guatemalan bishops' pastoral of July 1995 drew attention to the huge gap in wealth between the top fifth and bottom fifth of the population. In their view, true peace cannot be gained until Guatemala's three main problems are resolved: corruption, impunity and unjust distribution of wealth. Although the journey will be a long one, the growth in strength of Mayan organisations and the contribution of the civil society and the Catholic Church to the peace process are developments which give some hope for lasting peace.

MEXICO

Mexico	
GDP (US$bn)	329
Population	88,200,000
Annual population growth (%)	2.8
Urban population (%)	74
Working population (%)	39
Literacy (%)	88.6
Ratifications	1; 2; 3; 4; Am

In the 1990s Mexico experienced a number of major changes to its long entrenched political, social and cultural systems, which have impacted positively and negatively on questions of tolerance and freedom of conscience. However, despite economic reforms, Mexico remains a country characterised by a high level of foreign debt, unequal distribution of wealth, substantial poverty, endemic violence and political upheaval.

The election of President Salinas de Gortari in 1988 heralded a concerted effort to modernise the economy and society culminating in the North Atlantic Free Trade Agreement (NAFTA) in January 1994. Assassinations of important politicians from the ruling Institutional Revolutionary Party (PRI), in control for sixty-five years, now the world's longest-governing political party and, in March 1994, the uprising of the Zapatistas among the indigenous peoples of Chiapas have brought to the fore how much resistance there was to the reform policies from traditional sources of power. Nevertheless in the adoption of a new constitution in 1992, Mexico made decisive steps towards the full recognition of human rights. The long history of forced exclusion from public life of the Roman Catholic Church, the faith of the majority of Mexicans, ended with constitutional change granting the church a legal entity. President Ernesto Zedillo took office at the end of 1994; some degree of political pluralism is in the wind as opposition parties now control 4,000 of the 19,000 municipal elected offices.

Mexico's population – over 88 million – is predominantly Catholic. In the 1990 census of Mexican people over the age of 5, 89.7 per cent stated they were Catholic, 4.9 per cent were Protestants (such as Presbyterians, Baptists, Adventists, Pentecostalists and Jehovah's Witnesses), 1.5 per cent were of other religions and 3.2 per cent had no religion. There are 50,000 Mexican Jews. Along with two or three other similarly impoverished states, Chiapas – the southernmost – had more Protestants and people who declared they had no religion than most Mexican states. A humanist organisation is being formed.

Intolerance of belief manifests itself in three different ways. First, the remnants of the old anti-clerical laws continue to impinge on religious groups and individual believers, despite the 1992 reforms. Second, intolerance is displayed by denominational groups towards different ways of thinking, as a rule secular ones, especially those related to a more liberal morality and public health programmes. Finally, intolerance has emerged in the form of inter-religious disputes, particularly in the small indigenous communities.

Religion, belief and the 1917 constitution

After the Mexican Revolution took place in 1910, the legal framework for belief and public worship was laid down in the world's first socialist constitution in 1917. This constitution was replaced in 1992. Mexico's long struggle for independence and the internal struggle between the Roman Catholic Church and popular aspirations were reflected in the 1917 constitutional provisions which sought to break down the church's institutional power base.

Article 3 of that constitution declared that education would be free and secular. All religious communities or pastors were prohibited from establishing or running primary schools or educational centres for farm labourers and peasants; Article 5 forbade the setting up of monastic orders; Article 24 limited public worship to within churches; Article 27 decreed that religious associations could not have legal capacity to acquire, own or administer real estate or the resulting capital. All church property was declared forfeited to the state. Finally, Article 130 created the most far-reaching restrictions on political activities undertaken by religions and clergy. In particular, denominations were denied any legal personality. Furthermore the various states were allowed to regulate the number of ministers of religion in each part of the federation. Clerics were prohibited from publishing on national political issues and from criticising national institutions. They were denied the right to vote as well as their right to associate for political purposes. Educational qualifications obtained in religious institutions would have no official recognition. Any political groupings with a title using a word connected to or hinting at any religious denomination were outlawed as were meetings of a political nature in places of worship.

Even though these radical restrictions often remained unused, none the less this was the legal framework around which religious bodies worked until 1992. In 1988, the former president announced that he would modernise the relationship between the state and the church, with three aims in mind: a separation of state and church, secular education in state schools and freedom of belief.

The 1992 constitution and the law on religious bodies

After three years of informal public debate, the movement to reform the constitution culminated in January 1992 in substantial changes to the above-mentioned articles followed by a new law on religious associations and public worship in July 1992.

The reform of Article 3 removed the prohibition on religious bodies from involvement in education. This eased the position for many denominational schools – generally Catholic – that had been working on the margins of the law.

Another provision rescinded and left to regulation by laws the ban on ownership of real estate by the church. However, ownership was to be limited to what was necessary only, though what constitutes 'goods necessary to the objective of ecclesiastic activities' is difficult to define. The discretion given in the new law to the Secretary of State to control church ownership has been much criticised as limiting its independence and freedom of action.

Reform of Article 130 gave the church and other religious groups legal personality; it conceded the right to vote to priests and lifted the limitations on freedom of expression imposed on preaching and religious publications. However, at the same time, the amended article left some restrictions on religious groups and their leaders. Article 130 still prohibits the use of places of worship for meetings of a political nature and churches may not own or administer any broadcasting media.

Nevertheless, the reform of the articles in the constitution represents a considerable step forward by recognising, in some areas, the right to religious freedom as required of the state of Mexico by its international human rights commitments.

Critics point, however, to what remains to be done, such as lifting the ban preventing ministers of religion from offending patriotic symbols in any manner. The state still has power to prevent or permit acts of public worship, as places of worship are registered at the Religious Affairs Branch of the Department of Internal Affairs. The clergy lack complete rights as citizens, to be elected and hold public office; the bans on religious association for political purposes and the prohibition on ownership of mass means of communication have also been criticised. Finally critics point to the need to lift the ban on religious education in state schools.

Education

The UN Committee on the Rights of the Child has expressed its concern about a large percentage of children living in difficult circumstances, especially children belonging to minorities or indigenous communities, who have not completed their primary education. The Mexican government has created indigenous education centres for children aged from 6 to 14. The literacy rate has increased in the past twenty years to 88.6 per cent.

Privately maintained schools constitute 12 per cent of Mexican schools, with the state supporting the rest. Access to non-state schools is unrestricted; such schools operate within the provisions of the federal Education Act. Some opposition to the state curriculum has been voiced because it is completely secular. Article 3 (i) and (ii) of the 1992 constitution are as follows:

i   Freedom of belief being guaranteed by Article 24, education shall be secular and as such maintained completely separate from any religious doctrine;
ii The guiding principle for education shall be based on the results of scientific progress. It shall combat ignorance and the effects thereof: servitude, fanaticism and prejudice.

Some private schools provide religious education. Most Jewish youths, for instance, attend one of the nine Jewish schools in Mexico.

Conscientious objection

One major limitation on freedom of thought and belief is the refusal to accept conscientious objection. The state concedes it has no legislation covering such matters, stating that military service is considered a social duty in Mexico. However, membership of the Mennonites is included among grounds for total or partial exemption.

Article 1 of the new law on religious associations sets down that 'religious convictions in no way free [anyone] from the requirements of the law of the land. Nobody can use religious motives to justify avoiding responsibilities and obligations prescribed in law.' The amended Article 130 expressly indicates that 'ministers of worship cannot . . . offend in any way national symbols . . . nor in any way encourage their rejection'. This measure is implicitly directed against groups like the Jehovah's Witnesses, who openly refuse to pay homage to the flag or sing the national anthem. Jehovah's Witness children have been expelled from school or penalised in many ways; the National Commission on Human Rights (CNDH) received 118 complaints in 1991–92. The Commission concluded that a legal and constitutional basis existed to punish children who refused to salute and honour the national flag and to sing the national anthem including expulsion. Taking into account the right of the child to education, the Commission recommended that:

> expulsion be the last resort for cases of disrespectful attitude towards symbols of national importance [and] if when refusing to honour the symbols a child remains respectful, an alternative disciplinary measure be used, as expulsion is dispropor-tionate and contrary to the right to education; the disciplinary measure should consist of time spent on some subject related to good citizenship.

Although state commissions on human rights have promoted this course of action, expulsions and discrimination against Jehovah's Witness students have continued, for instance in schools in the state of Baja California where the State Director of Public Education recommended suspension for up to eight days, to be maintained through the school cycle. Staff who similarly objected to saluting the flag or singing the national anthem were to be disciplined and suspended for 'lack of integrity'.

The attitude of the education authorities in the state of Baja California is symptomatic of a general intolerance towards this religious group. Owing to the intervention of national and state human rights bodies some expulsions have been avoided.

Religious groups limiting the freedom of conscience of others

Attacks and restrictions on freedom of thought and action are also to be found among religious groups, directed at people with different beliefs and with secular beliefs. Strong feminist groups have long campaigned against violence against women and religious denial of equal rights for women; the feminist journals *Mujer* (1920) and *Fem* (1976) were both founded in Mexico. Conservative forces within religious groups are ranged against free-thinkers, artists, feminists, homosexuals or any person or social group that openly challenges Christian morality as they perceive it. Governmental public health institutions are also targeted with the objective of stopping contraceptive and family planning campaigns or the fight against AIDS.

In July 1992, for example, in the state of Guanajuato, the governor cancelled a conference on abortion owing to the intervention of the Bishop of Leon. A month before, the governor of the state of San Luis Potosi, at the instigation of various Catholic organisations, banned the activities of Mexfam, a civil association dedicated to sexual education and the dissemination of information on family planning.

Some conservative religious groups have been unscrupulous in their tactics. Thus the Catholic organisation Provida (pro-life) recently accused the Ministry of Health in the state of Tamaulipas of carrying out a secret campaign of sterilisation behind a smokescreen of anti-tetanus injections. The Minister of Health in this region sued the organisation for libel. This type of incident undermines the government's ability to run appropriate sexual education campaigns, particularly aimed at the poor.

Anti-clericalism and anti-Semitism

There has been a revival of anti-clericalism and anti-Semitism, reflecting conservative social reactions to political change. Anti-clericalism has a long history in Mexico, due to the old struggle between civil and religious power; it has not totally disappeared. Anti-clericalism has grown along with the increased involvement by Catholic and Protestant clergy in social and political issues. Recently, hostility has become quite common towards priests and nuns who are accused of being preachers of liberation theology or simply guerrilla–priests. One of the most vilified groups has been the Jesuits, because of their work in very deprived areas and their involvement in the struggle to demand rights for indigenous peoples and farm labourers.

When the conflict flared up in Chiapas, one of those first accused of having instigated the uprising was Bishop Samuel Ruiz, the Bishop of San Cristobal de las Casas. His participation as the key mediator between the government and the rebels, as well as the sermons on peace preached in the cathedral of this region in the interests of a church open to social demands rather than closed to them, have provoked suspicion and criticism by conservative groups and local leaders. Although these elements called on the Vatican to depose Bishop Ruiz on the grounds that he was out of line with the majority of the Mexican bishops who reject liberation theology and consequently threatened the unity of the church, the Vatican daily newspaper *Osservatore Romano* in February 1995 rebuked them. It accused large landowners and economic power brokers in the region of sabotaging dialogue and promoting violence and bloodshed.

As regards anti-Semitism, the Jewish community has reportedly become concerned about the ideology of 'neo-mexicanism' whose adherents promote an idealised image of Mexico's indigenous past and scorn Europe's role in forging the national identity. The Jews are singled out as the cause of problems which haunt the Mexican and Latin American nations. The Party of the Mexican Eagles has painted the external walls of Mexico City's Cathedral with anti-Jewish graffiti on several occasions, claiming that Mexican Jews control the state's politics and finances and are responsible for the conflict in the state of Chiapas. However, to the Jewish community, Mexico's general pluralism and tolerance are said to make these manifestations seem anachronistic and insignificant.

Indigenous communities and inter-religious conflicts

Since 1992 there have been belated but important steps to recognise indigenous cultures and to review the legal framework that affects indigenous peoples. Article 4 of the constitution was updated to recognise the multi-cultural and multi-ethnic composition of Mexico. Indigenous peoples' organisations have come to speak of five centuries of marginalisation, pillage, violence and injustice and also of native resistance to this oppression. There were estimated to be still 5,400 prisoners of indigenous origin in Mexican jails in 1995, even though the National Indigenous Institute has been able to get 8,000 released in the last five years.

The issue of indigenous rights has been combined in the last few years with political demands that came out of the increasingly difficult economic and social situation, including the government's economic model which has badly affected the disadvantaged classes in society, particularly in indigenous areas. The agrarian reform mandated in Article 27 of the 1992 constitution has often been implemented to the detriment of indigenous peoples and more equitable land distribution is needed. This political movement, taking place within the slow and difficult process of modernisation, politicised many religious matters and led to many political questions acquiring a religious aspect.

Owing to their identical ethnic composition, the two states of Oaxaca and Chiapas experienced major problems of this type. In both cases an explosive social situation combined with the appearance of religious movements other than Catholicism and led to the questioning of the traditional power structure. Therefore, religion for many people appeared to be a direct cause of conflicts whereas it was rather a catalyst of social tension, stemming from political developments.

Oaxaca: tradition and intolerance

In a study carried out in Oaxaca between 1975 and 1992, at least 352 cases of the violation of human rights due to religious motives were noted, primarily in areas with many indigenous people. Conflict happened when the honour of local customs and tradition was questioned; fifty-three of the incidents occurred when Protestants among the community did not contribute to the fiesta of the patron saint.

Another important cause of conflict is the refusal to participate in the *tequio* and the cooperative work around the Catholic Church. The *tequio* is an ancient system that pre-dates the Spanish Conquistadors, which was co-opted in the colonial period, and through which all the members of the community are responsible for the carrying out of certain work for the good of the community. When such a task concerns renovating or simply maintaining the Catholic Church, members from other religions have refused to cooperate. The problem is further complicated as, in addition to this ancient custom, which establishes a customary right, the *tequio* was recently given constitutional status in the state of Oaxaca. This enables legal penalties to be imposed for failure to fulfil *tequio* obligations. Religious minorities are also persecuted for not observing traditional religious obligations and for failing to participate in the town's feast-day and civic functions.

Violations of freedom of religion or belief in these cases may be extreme; they range from unjustified imprisonment to death, and include the threat of expulsion from school, denial of services, evictions, fines, insults, beatings, and the refusal to provide services such as education or even burial of the dead. In the cases that occurred in Oaxaca, the main means of repression was illegal imprisonment, closely followed by threats and evictions.

In September 1994, various Protestant churches asked the state office to stop the harassment, threats and repression of preachers and parishioners of denominations other than Catholicism. Protestants cited the case of Preacher Eliseo Justo Miguel who was detained on 31 August in the town of San Pablo Yaganiza, in the Sierra Villa Alta, with the consent of the mayor of the town, for not wishing to participate economically or in person in the festivities celebrating the local saint. This was, according to the complainants, the fifth occasion that this town council had violated the religious rights of Protestants. On the other four occasions other Protestants had been imprisoned on similar charges.

A month later, the harassment of Protestants continued unabated in this community. Of the more than forty families who belong to the Missionary Church of Agreement, twenty had agreed to comply with the community service required but the others refused; their electricity and water supplies were cut off by the local authorities. The state government in Oaxaca denied that religious freedom had been violated, as the problem did not consist of preventing adherence to evangelism 'but rather concerned fulfilling one's responsibilities to the community'. Breaches of freedom of conscience or religion were thus converted into a problem of community traditions, for which respect was claimed to be as important as freedom of religion or belief. Similar incidents have occurred in other states.

Evictions in Chiapas

The phenomenon of evictions supposedly on religious grounds began in Chiapas in the municipality of San Juan Chamula, later spreading to other areas. From 1974 to 1995, 15–20,000 people have been evicted, the larger part of whom sought refuge in the suburban area of San Cristobal de las Casas and formed large communities there. These evictions were carried out with the apparent complicity or lack of interest of the state authorities. However, the explosive political atmosphere of the last few years, in addition to the attention paid by numerous human rights defence organisations as well as the potential offered by the new legal framework for religion under the 1992 constitution, have drawn renewed attention to the situation.

Nearly 30 per cent of Chiapas's population are indigenous Mayans (900,000 people). In mid-1993, according to the UN Special Rapporteur's 1995 report, at least 454 indigenous people – Protestants and Catholics – were evicted from the municipal area of San Juan Chamula because they had converted to a Christianity unacceptable to the Chamula 'bosses' (*caciques*). Anyone found reading the Bible has allegedly been threatened with expulsion from Chamula lands and Christians who do not take part in traditional festivals are marginalised and risk stirring up popular resentment.

The real reason for these evictions was to perpetuate the traditional control exercised by the Chamula 'bosses', who did not themselves hesitate in 'converting' to the orthodox Catholic Church in order to maintain control of those who were questioning it, be they Catholic priests or Protestant ministers. The implicit alliance between these local landowners and the state authorities, both linked to the official political party, led to human rights abuses and evictions being carried out with impunity.

The indigenous armed uprising of 1 January 1994 polarised the positions of the traditionalists and dissidents and caused more tension, abuse of religious rights and violence born out of desperation. Chiapas had become practically ungovernable, with groups of peasants squatting on the estates of big landowners, occupying mayoral offices and blocking roads, at the same time as clashes between peasants and cattlemen became more common, and powerful anti-clerical groups denounced priests who were committed to social causes. The presence of the Zapatista National Liberation Army (EZLN), though it gave no direct armed help to these indigenous communities, stimulated the old demands and acted as a major moral support for all dissidents, whether social, political or religious.

The rebellion in Chiapas shook the traditional structures of power. Changes which followed included the return to San Juan Chamula of a Catholic priest from the diocese of Tuxtla Gutierrez, the region's capital. The permanent threat of civil war also made the interim governor of Chiapas wish to resolve the issue of evictions. The National Commission of Human Rights (CNDH) circulated a recommendation asking the Chiapas Government and Congress to guarantee the right of those evicted to return to their communities, to guarantee peaceful co-existence and the right to belong to the religious belief of one's preference, and even the taking of pertinent measures against the municipal authorities of San Juan Chamula.

Meetings were convened in July 1994 between the traditionalist Chamula leaders and the evicted Protestants. The Second Meeting for the Reconciliation agreed on these points:

- To maintain the voluntary nature of traditional *cargos* (obligations and duties). On their return the Chamulas will have the freedom to accept or reject the *cargos* offered to them.
- On their return there shall be no distinction among them for the collection and the economic cooperation needed for celebrating the traditional festivals.

- Freedom will continue as regards consumption of alcoholic beverages, the use of tobacco and the buying of candles. Those who perform a *cargo* or who assist at celebrations or in any other circumstance will not be obligated to consume them.
- The figure of San Juan [the town's patron saint] will be respected, acknowledged as the community's representative and not be criticised.
- Respect for traditions. Both sides agree to treat each other with respect and not criticise the other's religious beliefs. They will tolerate religious worship at home and avoid aggressive proselytising.
- The plan of return by mutual agreement. Neither side will resort to violence nor use aggression as a way to resolve differences but rather will at all time turn to dialogue, agreements and the law.

However, these agreed principles could not be put into practice because the traditional religious authorities in San Juan Chamula would not accept them. Furthermore, unilaterally, 584 Chamula Presbyterians decided to return home even without the agreement of the state and local authorities. This return then led to a wave of similar actions by other evicted Protestants, so that 900 indigenous Protestants from Zinacantán returned home despite warnings of danger from their own national directorship.

In September 1994, the Protestants who had returned unilaterally complained of a new wave of threats. Although the municipal president received a recommendation to make use of his office and maintain order, the CNDH warned that there was insufficient security in the area to guarantee the physical integrity and property of those 584 Protestants. The following months were to bear these fears out, as the numbers of returning Protestants grew, and pressure on returnees to leave and incidents of intolerance and extreme violence against those who stayed continued. Calls to reconvene around the negotiating table were ignored. The Protestants started an international campaign to pressure the Mexican government to stop the religiously motivated evictions in Chiapas and have the human rights of the Protestant community respected. The changing political conditions eventually did allow at least a few hundred of those evicted to return home and the pressures on state government made it offer some minimum guarantees of safety to them.

In the last two years, the government has attempted to overcome the security forces' 'culture of impunity' by reforming the Office of the Attorney-General, supporting the CNDH and establishing human rights commissions at state level. The vast majority of the 1,484 public servants condemned by the CNDH in 1994 were members of the security forces; 60 per cent of the 850 Chiapas State police officers were dismissed for crimes while in uniform or when working as police without proper registration. President Zedillo has also introduced a number of law enforcement and judicial reforms.

PERU

Three-quarters of the 22.4 million people who live in Peru live in poverty and many live in extreme poverty, especially in the mountainous regions. Even though infant and child mortality are very high, Peruvians are a young population; 43 per cent are children. Some 70 per cent of the people live in and around cities.

Legal and political system

The 1980s was a very violent period for the Peruvians. Armed violence resulting in 27,000 deaths and millions of dollars' worth of material damage was caused by the Shining Path (Sendero Luminoso) and the Tupac Amaru Revolutionary Movement, together with the

Peru	
GDP (US$bn)	22
Population	22,400,000
Annual population growth (%)	2.6
Urban population (%)	71
Working population (%)	40
Literacy (%)	87.3
Ratifications	1; 2, 2(b); 3; 4; Am

repressive activities of the state armed forces. The anti-terrorist strategy of the present government has been successful to the extent that most of the leaders of the Shining Path have been captured. In addition, the state armed forces have been and continue to be involved in serious violations of human rights.

Campaigning against Peru's corrupt and privileged power structure brought Alberto Fujimori the presidency in 1990. However, in April 1992, he seized extra-constitutional powers, closed the Congress and called new elections to elect a new unicameral Constituent Congress with legislative functions. Although the 1993 constitution called for an independent body composed of lawyers and judges to recommend new judges, this procedure has not yet been put into practice. After the coup, President Fujimori dismissed the Attorney-General, thirteen Supreme Court Judges and 130 other judges. The provisional judges he named to replace them still continue in office.

According to the 1993 constitution, Peru is a social republic, democratic, independent and sovereign. The Peruvian legal system contains a number of mechanisms to protect human rights under the constitution and other legal processes. Peru has ratified the major international human rights instruments, but, under the 1993 constitution, they are not binding on the courts. Appeal may be made to the InterAmerican Commission for Human Rights and the (UN) Human Rights Committee.

Ethnic, linguistic and cultural composition

In 1993, over four-fifths of Peruvians spoke Spanish and nearly 20 per cent, living mostly in rural areas, spoke indigenous languages. In 1976, there were fifty-six ethno-linguistic groups settled in the Amazon region. Quechua and Aymara are the main indigenous languages. There are other small ethnic minorities, such as Asians and black Peruvians of African descent.

Spanish colonisation produced a mixed race in which the indigenous population of Peru constitutes by far the greatest element. The wealthier classes, however, regard themselves as being radically different from peasant and indigenous people. Racial discrimination – direct, indirect and systemic – continues. For example, indigenous languages are not recognised in the school system; there is racial discrimination in employment; and indigenous groups in the jungle areas do not have their land rights protected by the law. Only since the Velasco government's (1968–76) land reforms have indigenous people begun to form organisations to affirm their ethnic identity.

Religions and beliefs

Although 92 per cent of Peruvians have been baptised in the Catholic Church, census figures show a fall between 1981 and 1993 in the number who identify themselves as

Catholics from 95 per cent to 89 per cent. In addition, Catholicism has different meanings for different people. 'Popular Catholicism', a fundamental aspect of Peruvian national identity, combines elements of Christianity with those of pre-Hispanic religious cultures. Particularly in the south and central Andean region, the principal divinities of Catholicism have been transformed to fulfil symbolic functions within the cultures of the various language groups. For example, the rituals rendered to 'mother earth' and the 'Apus', spirits of the mountains and particular gods of the community, are widely observed in rural Peru.

Because of the privileged position of the Catholic Church, it is only in the past forty years that Protestant churches have appeared in any number in Peru. Their members are mainly converted from Catholicism. Between the 1981 and the 1993 censuses, the proportion of Peruvians with Protestant beliefs doubled to 7 per cent.

There are some fifty-five Protestant groups. Two types of churches are distinguishable: Protestants which are grouped in the Concilio Nacional Evangelico del Peru (CONEP) and eschatological churches which emphasise the end of the world in their preaching. Almost all Protestants come from the poorest sectors of Peruvian society who feel marginalised and unprotected. In cities, one factor that influences the migrant indigenous *campesinos* to join the Protestant churches is that, in so doing, they are able to better themselves and have their religious needs cared for after the rupture with their background culture on migrating.

Only 0.3 per cent of Peruvians belong to religious groups which are not Christian. There is a Jewish community of 3,000 which is widely accepted. The traditional beliefs of small groups of indigenous people in the Amazon jungle have also continued undisturbed by evangelising or migration.

In 1988 there were fifty-two groups mainly connected to eastern cultural traditions, esoteric and gnostic traditions. New religious movements have appeared in Peru only in the past fifteen years; groups based on eastern religions are not marked by religious exclusiveness. Their members come from the poorer Peruvians.

Between the 1981 and the 1993 censuses, the proportion of Peruvians declaring that they had no religion rose from 0.2 per cent to 1.4 per cent.

Church–state relations

From the conquest of Peru by the Spaniards in the sixteenth century, the Catholic Church retained a close bond with the state. After independence from Spain in 1821, at first all religious practice except Catholicism was forbidden under the republican constitution. This was followed by a period of *de facto* tolerance and a third period in the twentieth century, in which reformers urged parliamentarians to pay heed to the petition of Protestants for religious freedom. Amendment of Article 4 of the 1860 constitution then removed the previous prohibition and substituted the words, 'The Nation professes the Catholic Apostolic and Roman religion and the State protects it.' Peru is distinctive in Hispanic America in that its constituent Assemblies have historically equated Peruvian identity with Catholicism.

From the colonial period, relations between the state and the Catholic Church were regulated by the *patronato regio*. In 1874, Pope Pius IX's Papal Bull gave the President of the Republic of Peru the same right of patronage that Spain had previously enjoyed. The 1933 constitution maintained the church–state union, the *patronato regio* and the election of the bishops by Congress. It protected the Catholic religion though it did not profess it.

Change came with the 1979 constitution. Article 86 states:

> Within an independent and autonomous regimen the state recognises the Catholic Church as an important element in the historical, cultural and moral formation of Peru. It gives it its collaboration. The state may also establish forms of collaboration with other confessions.

The patronage was thus eliminated and, following an agreement with the Holy See in 1980, the independence and autonomy of the Catholic Church of Peru were established. The 1993 constitution confirms this arrangement.

Growth in freedom of religious practice

While Protestant churches had previously functioned more or less in secrecy but without interference from the authorities, from 1915 it became legal to build Protestant churches without having to hide their real identity. Around this time, the Methodist Church took part in the struggle for rights such as civil marriage, as Catholic marriage provided the only legal form in Peru.

However, a Supreme Decree of 1945 still allowed only the Catholic Church to practise its rituals in public. All other religions were confined to their places of religious observance and violations were punishable under the Penal Code. This decree was frequently invoked in the provinces to prohibit Protestant meetings in private houses, and even in public buildings, rented for religious worship.

The present Peruvian constitution stipulates in Article 2 that freedom of conscience and religion is recognised in both its individual and collective forms and protected as long as they do not offend morality or disrupt public order. The extent of change in modern Peru is shown by the fact that in 1994 Ephraim Rosenberg was sworn in as prime minister, not – as used to be customary – by bowing before a crucifix but by swearing on a Jewish Bible.

Religious groups in politics

While the institutional church was not involved directly in politics, Catholics see themselves as playing an important role in politics and in society in general. Two members of Opus Dei, a very conservative movement within the Catholic Church, are members of parliament. In the 1960s, the Social Christian Movement and Christian Democracy were political parties that followed the social doctrine of the Catholic Church.

Protestants have been a political presence throughout the history of Peru, pressing for constitutional guarantees of freedom of thought and religion. They see themselves as assisting in the process of democracy in modern Peru. In 1990 Protestants formed a political party which won seventeen parliamentary seats.

When the Protestants supported Alberto Fujimori in the 1990 presidential elections, in some Catholic parishes fliers were distributed and priests talked at Mass about the dangers for the Catholic community if he were elected. Ironically, after Fujimori seized greater powers in April 1992, the Protestants withdrew their support while Catholic members of Opus Dei became his close allies in Congress.

Not all Catholics or Protestant groups have the same attitude towards political involvement. One group of the Pentecostals is against it for theological reasons. Another, the Israelite Mission of the Universal Pact, has won two congressional seats.

Religious groups in grassroots organisations

The participation of the members of the churches in their grassroots organisations and communities is increasing. In the Catholic Church, in urban and especially in rural areas, many members of the Christian base communities and Christian animators are also leaders of Campesino Federations, of local development committees, health promoters and community Defence Groups. The Catholic and Protestant movements have been forerunners in the defence of human rights and in the past ten years the Protestants have been more active in community affairs, especially in rural areas.

Since 1980 the Shining Path group, driven by Maoist ideology, waged a civil war which has cost the lives of over 25,000 people. Rural areas have suffered most and, in these areas, members of the Protestant churches and pastoral agents of the Catholic Church. While at first Shining Path did not attack the Christian Church directly, ultimately priests, organisers and members of Christian base communities were killed, along with *campesinos* in their thousands. As well as Shining Path, armed forces, police and military groups have also been responsible for the killings of Catholics and Protestants.

The ideology of the Protestant churches, focused on God, has been seen as a competitor by the Shining Path, whose ideology had a secular focus on revolution through a peasants' war. The Protestants have, in turn, identified the Shining Path as the Anti-Christ; the war of the last days against this spiritual enemy would ensure the salvation of their souls. Thus, both secular and religious ideologies have competed for the support of the same impoverished, displaced population from the mountains.

In one instance, in the Valley of the Apurimac River, where Shining Path had disbanded the Campesino Federation, Protestants became the strongest supporters in the struggle against Shining Path. Shining Path retaliated by burning churches filled with Protestant worshippers. This confrontation, which began in 1984, was eventually won by the Protestant churches; Shining Path were expelled and Civil Defence Committees were consolidated.

Inter-faith relations

An ecumenical attitude is becoming more common within certain sectors of the Protestant community. However, the eschatological churches are less ecumenical than those which came from the European Protestant tradition. Minority religious groups win followers by proselytising, 'hitting the streets' and going from house to house. In the heavily populated lower middle-class to poor area of Lima, their message is spread through personal contacts, massive preaching events and through radio. Adventists rely on periodical campaigns in strategic areas of the city to attract followers, while the Mormons and the Jehovah's Witnesses go from house to house every Sunday.

Cooperative relations between Catholics and Protestant churches that come from the European tradition are made easier because they have the same Christian roots. Protestant movements in the shanty-towns are seen to have something in common with the progressive sectors of the Catholic Church, 'a new way in living religion'. Both Catholic and Protestant organisations have cooperated in human rights campaigns.

In contrast with the first generations of Protestants who experienced the hatred of Catholics towards Protestants and vice versa, the new generations live in a different context. They are more disposed to dialogue and critical of sectarian attitudes in their own ranks. Ecumenism is seen as necessary to allow a pluralistic society to function without intolerance. However, there is still a certain degree of conflict. While some

Protestants consider it absurd to talk of religious war in a society that practises religious plurality, for others ecumenicism is synonymous with communism and trying to unite the Catholic Church with the Protestant. In 1993, when Protestant pastors were asked how much hostility they experienced from other churches, three-quarters said there was none, while 5 per cent strongly disagreed with them.

Some sectors of the Catholic Church have also felt uncomfortable with the presence of new religious movements, leading to conflict and competition. The Catholic Church has found ways to minimise internal conflicts (such as over liberation theology) in order to unite forces against other groups. It emphasises the use of the Bible and adopts Protestant techniques, using song and appealing to the emotions.

One instance of inter-religious conflict arose in the case of the Virgin of the Tree, in Chincha. For Catholics it was a divine miracle but, for the Protestants, it represented satanism. The Catholics strove to preserve the tree but finally the Pentecostals burned it down. Similar incidents have occurred elsewhere. For example, in the shanty-town called El Agustino in Lima, the Church of the Assembly of God had a building opposite a Catholic chapel. On Sundays, the Pentecostals of the Assembly of God shouted over loudspeakers, making it impossible for the Catholic worshippers to hear Mass.

The newer churches have a greater tendency to consider themselves the only true church of Jesus Christ than the older ones from the European Protestant tradition do. Although sectarian attitudes are instilled in their followers by many such churches, often the faithful themselves are pragmatic and attend more than one church whether by invitation or out of curiosity.

The media

Though Protestant churches distribute a weekly bulletin to the press, it is only published if it relates to the media agenda of politics, education, human rights or the economy. The purely religious element is not regarded as newsworthy. The same applies to the Catholic Church, with the exception of the newspaper *El Comercio* which has the highest circulation nationally. However, religious celebrations such as the Procession of the 'Lord of the Miracles' and some important regional feasts, part of popular tradition, attract ample coverage.

Television and radio carry a wide range of religious broadcasting. Printed material is imported from around the world. The Catholic Church and the Protestant churches own two radio stations each and transmit programmes on other stations as well.

Education

The Catholic Church has always played a very important role in education in Peru. The curriculum for the religion courses in state schools today is drawn up by the National Office of the Peruvian Episcopal Conference for Catholic Education. Students can be excused from attending these courses. Article 14 of the constitution states that 'Religious education is taught respecting freedom of conscience'.

There are 820 Catholic schools at all levels, as well as teacher training institutes. Of these centres, 221 are fully financed by the state and 445 in part, while 154 are self-financed. They provide education for over half a million students. One large-scale Jesuit educational initiative, started in 1966, promotes education and works in a common project with the participation of teachers, parents, students and community. Conservative Catholic movements, Sodalitium and Opus Dei, also run schools, universities and educational programmes directed towards the middle and wealthy classes of Peruvian society. The union of Catholic educational institutions has campaigned to have the government allow each school to establish its own curriculum within certain parameters set by the Department of Education.

The Protestant churches were involved in the establishment of public education in Peru. Today the Protestant Center for Pedagogy Support groups together sixteen of the 130 Protestant schools. They train teachers and produce materials for religion courses, for teachers and students. Protestant teaching materials are also sought by teachers from state schools. Though three state school religious curricula have been approved by the Ministry of Education (Catholic, Protestant and a third without the religion course), there is no Protestant teacher who teaches such a course in a state school. Likewise, the state, which finances and supports a large number of Catholic educational centres, has not yet supported any Protestant school. Protestants are planning to establish a university.

There is one Jewish day school attended by about 80 per cent of Peru's Jewish children.

Women in religion

According to Peruvian Catholic women, they – who are the majority in the Catholic Church – have always been present but, until recently, only in an anonymous, almost invisible manner. In 1985, Talitha Cumi, an organisation of Catholic women was founded, but there is still no sign of change with respect to women holding hierarchical positions in the Catholic Church and it maintains an ambiguous stance towards religious feminist activists. Liberal theologians are discouraged from espousing any form of feminist theology or acknowledging the feminisation of poverty.

In recent years, however, women have become active in pastoral work, in prayer groups, catechetics and everything to do with the family. Women's role is seen as needing to be fortified and developed yet not in competition with men. Women put their distinctive stamp of consistency, dynamism and vitality in organisations concerning health, survival and human rights, though many activists lost their lives due to Shining Path terrorism.

Within Protestant churches, women do not take on ministerial roles. The Methodist Church is the exception as five of its thirty pastors are women. A woman heads the seminary where eighteen young future pastors (half of them women) from different Protestant churches are trained. Traditionally Methodist women dedicated themselves to education in their schools while the men busied themselves in pastoral work. However, now the hierarchy of the Methodist Church openly supports women as leaders.

In the Protestant churches, it is generally considered that women should be restricted to the level of teaching positions only, reserving ministerial positions for men. A significant number of Protestant women also provide services to feed the poor and undernourished Peruvians. However, they have been criticised by their church and families for participating in their local communities. They are accused of neglecting the Lord's Work in favour of social work or getting involved in politics, while at home they are criticised for neglecting household chores.

None the less, some Protestant women gathered in March 1994 and issued a declaration that denounced the marginalisation of women in the Protestant Church and in society. They said that being put in second place hindered the development of their gifts and ministries; they wanted their right to serve the Lord to be recognised and also to be channels of his grace in his different ministries. They said they should be allowed to participate in decision-making and in undertaking responsibilities to serve the community as leaders and pastors.

Conclusion

Though relatively little religious conflict occurs in Peru, there is no knowledge of the 1981 UN Declaration. State schools still effectively impart only the Catholic religion. There is a considerable need to educate Peruvians about the concept of tolerance and what constitutes intolerance in order that they can exercise fully their rights as citizens.

TRINIDAD AND TOBAGO

Trinidad and Tobago	
GDP (US$bn)	5
Population	1,300,000
Annual population growth (%)	1.3
Urban population (%)	70
Working population (%)	41
Literacy (%)	97.4
Ratifications	1; 2, 2(b); 3; 4; Am

Trinidad and Tobago is a Caribbean island state which was under Spanish rule until the nineteenth century and British rule until independence in 1962. Trinidadian society is marked by ethnic and religious diversity. In the past, peoples of different racial and cultural origins were brought together through the experience of African slavery and Indian indentured labour. The inter-relationships in plantation society were characterised by racism, class and colour discrimination and cultural hierarchy, making internal divisiveness a fundamental condition of society. Notwithstanding these foundations, the process of creolisation has facilitated accommodation and social tolerance for socio-cultural differences, though ethnic and identity politics remains a strong dynamic within the country.

Social pluralism is expressed primarily in the practice of different religions. Race and religious affiliation correlate as do, to a lesser extent, social class and religious affiliation. Roman Catholicism is practised by most African and European descendants. The Protestant faiths, with the exception of Presbyterianism, are practised mostly by the African population. Hinduism is practised almost exclusively by East Indians. Islam is practised by both East Indians and Africans, with the former dominating as leaders. African-derived religions such as the Orisha movement and the Spiritual Baptists (the Shouters, an African-based Christian movement) are exclusively practised by African descendants.

In the past, the eradication of primary vestiges of African heritage and culture was a deliberate policy of the planter class and the colonial government, although the only collective religious practice outlawed by legislation was the Afrocentric Shouter movement. In 1917 the Shouter Prohibition Ordinance (repealed in 1951) gave police wide powers to enter 'shouter houses' without warrant. African-based religious practice among the African population was driven underground if it survived at all. Many Spiritual Baptists joined Roman Catholic churches to give themselves the affiliation they needed to enter schools and gain jobs. The Summary Offence Ordinance also prohibited drumming, obeah and other cultural practices associated with African-based religious movements. These prohibitions, though not enforced, are still on the statute book.

As a consequence of these colonial policies, most of the African population in Trinidad and Tobago practise some form of Christianity, largely Roman Catholicism, though there has been a shift towards Pentecostalism in recent times. African religion survives in the Shouter and Orisha movements. While East Indians who migrated to Trinidad have been transformed by the plantation experience and social interactions with the African population, these experiences did not result in the formation of a 'new homogenised or Europeanised Indian'. Some 24 per cent of all East Indians are Hindus while 6 per cent are Muslim.

In a total population of about 1.3 million, the main religious groups are Roman Catholic (33 per cent), Hindu (25 per cent), Anglican (15 per cent), Muslim (6 per cent), Presbyterian and other Christian denominations (14 per cent); the number of Jews is minute. These religious movements have co-existed peacefully and there is a growing ecumenical or inter-faith movement. In 1983, the Inter-Religious Organisation of Trinidad and Tobago was formed comprising all the major religious organisations. The major objective of the organisation is 'to foster collaboration of all religious organisations with a view to bringing about the spiritual, intellectual and economic advancement of the people of Trinidad and Tobago'. The leadership is rotated annually and representatives of the organisation sit on a number of Ministerial-appointed committees addressing ecclesiastical affairs.

Non-governmental organisations with developmental and humanist agendas have long been active and free from political interference.

Economic and political background

Trinidad and Tobago is a primary oil producer; its GNP per capita is among the highest in the Caribbean region. Successive governments since 1980 have implemented programmes of economic stabilisation and structural adjustment. However, as this has been accompanied by withdrawal of state-provided social services, the programmes, which are directed by international financial institutions, have adversely affected most people's quality of life by increasing disparities in income distribution.

Trinidad and Tobago is a parliamentary democracy. From independence in 1962, electoral politics in Trinidad and Tobago have been based on a two-party system which mirrors and helps to reproduce the political divisions between the African and East Indian communities which each constitute roughly 40 per cent of the population. The traditional division between the two was bridged only briefly in 1986 when a coalition of parties came together to fight the elections successfully against the party which had been in power for some thirty years. However, the coalition split along ethnic lines a year later. There was also a short-lived attempted coup in 1990 by a small group of Muslims.

Constitutional guarantees

Under the constitution which enshrines fundamental rights and freedoms, the courts are given power to review enactments of parliament. Anyone who alleges that their rights and freedoms have been, are being, or are likely to be contravened may apply to the High Court for redress. Trinidad has ratified the main international human rights treaties.

The right to freedom of conscience and religious belief and observance without discrimination by reason of race, origin, colour, religion or sex is recognised expressly in the constitution. The formulation used guarantees the principle of equity and non-discrimination between faiths and religions. In addition, the constitution guarantees freedom of thought and expression and freedom of association and assembly, both without discrimination by reason of religion. Religious or belief organisations are free to worship and assemble, to establish charitable and humanitarian institutions, to teach religion, and to write and disseminate their publications.

The right of the individual to equality of treatment from any public authority in the exercise of any function is also guaranteed. Thus not only is the right to religious belief and observance protected but so too is the right not to adhere to religious belief or practice. However, apart from these constitutional provisions, there is no legislation which prohibits discrimination on the basis of religion, race or sex as a result of private (non-state) action and therefore it is possible for private individuals to discriminate in, for example, employment-related matters or in wholly private educational institutions. Specific anti-discrimination legislation prohibiting discrimination between non-state agents would assist civil society in combating intolerance.

Religion and state

While the preamble to the constitution affirms that the nation of Trinidad and Tobago is founded on principles that acknowledge the supremacy of God, there is no official religion and no connection between any particular religion and the state. However, while there is little direct or formal discrimination on the basis of religion in Trinidad and Tobago, the perception that the Christian religions, particularly Roman Catholicism, are privileged by the state is widespread among the non-Christian communities. The question of the state's commitment to genuine multi-culturalism and equality of treatment of all major religions has arisen in Trinidad and Tobago in a number of ways in recent times.

Despite state neutrality towards religion, the Office of the Prime Minister has responsibility for 'Ecclesiastical Affairs'. Through this portfolio, financial and land grants are made to religious organisations. In 1992, in response to representations from religious organisations, a Special Committee was appointed to study the basis upon which financial grants were made to religious bodies. The Committee recommended an increase in ecclesiastical grants by the state. The size of the grants is determined according to a specified formula which takes account of the size of the membership of religious organisations and the same criteria apply to all qualifying religious organisations. In 1994, twelve Christian and Hindu organisations received funding, to qualify for which they must be incorporated by statute.

The Office of the Prime Minister also may grant state lands to religious organisations so that they can erect buildings on them. Such an organisation must have over 300 members and be incorporated by statute. Should any organisation allege religious discrimination by such a public authority, redress may be sought under constitutional guarantees to equality of treatment.

All buildings occupied as the places of public worship of any religious denomination are exempt from government rates and taxes and their owners exempt from liability for repairing private streets.

Holy days, festivities and public holidays

Although there is no law recognising the general right to freedom to observe days of rest and to celebrate holidays and ceremonies in accordance with the precepts of one's religion or belief, the constitution prohibits compulsory school attendance by children on any day specially set apart for religious observance by the religious body to which their parents belong.

The issue of the distribution of public holidays is a bone of contention in Trinidad and Tobago, given its symbolism in connection to the state's stated commitment to equal treatment and recognition of all religions. Before 1995, there were thirteen public holidays of which seven were religion-based. Of these, five related to Christian, one to Hindu (Divali) and one to Muslim (Eid) commemorations. A Joint Select Committee of Parliament in 1994, in its majority report, found the number of Christian holidays to be disproportionate and recommended – successfully – that one should be replaced by the 'Indian Arrival Day' advocated by the East Indian community. However, its recommendations – in response to the requests of adherents to the African-based Orisha movement – for a public holiday commemorating the birth of the deity, Lord Shango, as well as another holiday commemorating the lifting of the prohibition on the Shouter movement, were not adopted by government.

The National Council of Orisha Elders considers that to exclude the Orisha faith from these symbols of national recognition reinforces the psychological oppression of 'the worshippers and devalues the religion in the eye of the general public'. Others also consider that the Orisha tradition has not been given the same respect and recognition as other religions such as Christianity, Hinduism and Islam.

Education

The constitution guarantees the right of parents or guardians to provide a school of their choice for the education of their children or wards. Under the Education Act, nobody can be refused admission to any public school on account of their religious persuasion, race, social status or language or that of their parents. Despite the state's neutrality with regard to religion, religious instruction is a mandatory part of public school curriculum, except that any pupil may be withdrawn by their parents from religious instruction or observance without forfeiting any educational benefits.

There are 471 public primary schools in Trinidad and Tobago of which 123, 26 per cent, are government-run. The rest are managed by denominational school boards: 122 Catholic, 151 Protestant, 52 Hindu, 15 Muslim and a few other schools.

Some state-assisted secondary schools are denominational. Under a 1960 agreement known as 'the Concordat', denominational schools were allowed to retain their rights of ownership over their schools despite receiving substantial state funding. Denominational school boards are permitted to veto curricula and to recruit up to 20 per cent of their students on a basis other than the results of the Common Entrance Examination.

The Concordat preserving the denominational character of the state-assisted schools is the subject of continuing national debate, since it is perceived as privileging the Roman Catholic religion. Although the level of state support to Roman Catholic schools is perceived as being disproportionate, it relates to the long history of church involvement in the educational system.

There have been several court cases alleging discrimination in denominational schools. In Sumayyah Mohammed's case – 'the *hijab* case' – a girl was denied entry (though not admission) into a Roman Catholic secondary 'assisted school' because she would not comply with its dress code. The Muslim girl had asked the school for permission to wear the *hijab* as was her religious practice. While the High Court found that there had been no breach of the girl's constitutional rights, none the less it stated that to withhold permission to wear the *hijab* was irrational. The school could provide no evidence that conforming to the *hijab* would negatively impact on the school or its traditions.

151

In Maharaj's case, an East Indian woman was overlooked by the Teaching Service Commission for appointment as principal of the state-assisted Presbyterian School. The Presbyterian School Board advised against her appointment since she was not a 'regular church goer'. In her appeal, the High Court held that the Teaching Service Commission, whose mandate and composition are provided for in the constitution, acted irrationally and unfairly to the applicant given that she was the most qualified applicant for the post.

The family

In recognition of the diversity of marriage customs among the dominant ethnic groups and of the need to redress problems caused by colonial non-recognition of the cultural practices of a sizeable proportion of society, the laws of Trinidad and Tobago allow the registration of three different types of marriage: marriages of Hindus and of Muslims and also under the Marriage Act, which is open to anyone regardless of religion. Marriage officers may be appointed from among the membership of the appropriate communities; Hindu and Muslim marriages may be performed only where both people belong to the same religion.

The minimum legal ages for marriage indicate that there may be some inequality of treatment on the basis of sex. The Muslim Marriage and Divorce Act provides that a girl need only be 12 years old although the boy must be over 16 years. Under the Hindu Marriage Act, girls must be 14 and boys at least 18 years. The general statute is silent on the question of minimum age so that English common law applies, allowing boys to marry at 14 and girls at 12 years.

The media

There is no official state policy on broadcasting with respect to religion. The state-owned radio station, however, allows fifteen minutes air time daily for religious broadcasting. The Inter-Religious Organisation determines how this time is allocated. Any other religious programming on the state-owned media is then subject to normal commercial considerations.

In a case in which the Orisha movement claimed that a film had portrayed its religion in an offensive light, the High Court held that the state-owned television, as an autonomous body, was not amenable to constitutional litigation. Furthermore, the expression of views on a religious practice of an organisation did not contravene the right to freedom of conscience and religious belief.

Women and religion

The issue of discrimination against women in religions has focused in Trinidad and Tobago, as elsewhere, on the prohibition against women as ministers of religion. In the Roman Catholic Church, the ordination of women as priests is prohibited, although women run the university chaplaincy, lead worship in the absence of priests and provide the church's extensive social services.

The 1992 decision by the General Synod of the Church of England to ordain women as priests was welcomed by members of the Anglican Church and the Trinidad and Tobago diocese has stated that it will now ordain women. Women have been ordained as ministers in both the Presbyterian and Moravian denominations. Women do not only act as ministers in the African-based religions of the Spiritual Baptists and Orisha movements, but they also are leaders.

Among those who practise Hinduism, there is no central authority but, rather, a number of discrete organisations. In 1993 the Arya Pratinidhi Sabha inducted its first woman as a *pandit*, a qualification necessary for the granting of a licence as marriage officer under the Hindu Marriage Act. This induction was controversial within the Hindu community and the country's largest Hindu organisation, the Sanatan Dharma Maha Sabha, condemned it. Pandita Rampersad acknowledged at her induction that the pioneering role she had undertaken would be a challenging one given the patriarchal power relations within the Hindu religion.

Likewise, the matter of women giving the sermons in the mosque has been an issue for Muslims in Trinidad and Tobago. In July 1995, a female doctor, Anesa Ahamad, read the sermon for the first time at a weekly prayer meeting at a mosque run by the Ahmadiyya movement, a group seen by those in the Islamic movement as holding 'revolutionary views on Islamic teachings'. This act of reading the sermon by a woman was variously condemned by them as 'sacrilegious', 'anti-Islamic' and 'against the teachings of the Holy Founder of Islam'.

The general problem of identification of the national interest with a particular model of the ideal woman can be seen in Caribbean cultures. Women in Trinidad and Tobago continue to face considerable hurdles in asserting gender equality. These hurdles are more complex for women who want to affirm their cultural identity while rejecting unequal power relationships between men and women. It was to this dilemma that Anesa Ahamad alluded when she asserted her right to 'fulfil [herself] as a woman and as a Muslim and as a Trinidadian without these things cancelling each other out'.

Conscientious objection

No-one is obliged to take a religious oath in a court. People with no religious belief or for whom taking an oath is against their religious belief are allowed to make an affirmation instead of taking an oath. Military service is not compulsory in Trinidad and Tobago.

UNITED STATES OF AMERICA

USA	
GDP (US$bn)	5,920
Population	255,200,000
Annual population growth (%)	1.1
Urban population (%)	76
Working population (%)	50[a]
Literacy (%)	99
Ratifications	2, 2(a); 3

In the United States of America – today, a nation of over 255 million people – 'official' history describes a nation that was founded by God-fearing Europeans who immigrated to a primitive wilderness in order to escape religious persecution in their native lands. These Europeans founded a country where all citizens would be free to worship God according to their own consciences. The new Americans subsequently fought a revolutionary war (1776–83) to free themselves from the British monarchy, its unrepresentative parliament and its established church. Through their elected representatives, the former revolutionaries drafted a constitution in 1787 and a bill of rights in 1789 that guaranteed rights to freedom of speech, freedom of the press and freedom of religion.

Like all 'official' histories, this both reveals and conceals the truth. In particular it pays scant attention to attacks on indigenous American peoples, to the institution of the slavery of African-Americans, or the intolerance that many founders displayed against minority faiths. But it reveals an important aspect of American culture: the image of itself as having been founded on principles of freedom, tolerance, and liberty, including religious liberty. This self-image has proved to be a powerful weapon in the hands of minorities who seek to show the disparity between the self-image of tolerance and the reality of intolerance.

In reality, the first European settlers set foot in the seventeenth century on land populated by indigenous American peoples (referred to earlier as 'Red Indians', now usually as Native Americans). The vast majority of these immigrants were European Protestants. Although there tended to be greater religious freedom in the colonies than there had been in England and France, Massachusetts, for example, was notoriously intolerant towards dissenters and executed some Quakers who made the mistake of preaching their beliefs.

Some of the newly arriving Europeans demonstrated a remarkable tolerance and concern for the original inhabitants but such concerns were not widely shared. Historically, the United States government has shown little respect for indigenous American rights, customs and beliefs and repeatedly violated treaties with indigenous American peoples. Federal troops attacked and killed them and settlers drove them off their ancestral lands.

Christian missionaries, hired as government Indian agents, for over a hundred years assisted in implementing the federal Indian policy, to convert 'savage' Indians into Christian citizens and separate them from their traditional way of life. Reservations and Indian Nations were placed under denominational administrative control and missionary groups had Indian lands conveyed to them. In the 1890s, the Ghost Dance religion was put down by the military, the Sun Dance religion was outlawed and other ceremonies were made Indian offences to be punished by withholding rations or by imprisonment. Regulations forbidding traditional ceremonies continued until 1934.

The Atlantic slave trade which brought the major ethnic minority to America also brought their strong African religious traditions into their exile and enslavement. Because they were forbidden to practise these, especially dance in any form, they subtly and ingeniously blended important concepts into their Christian practice, particularly in vocabulary and musical forms. Distinctive forms of Christian ritual evolved in segregated congregations and the result has been continued segregation in large parts of mainstream Christian denominations up to the present day. The music and body movement of these forms have been very influential in modern American music, especially women's powerful vocal genius, and crucial in the civil rights movement.

Although immigration from England continued during the nineteenth century, the most dramatic change came with the arrival of Irish, French, and Italian Catholics who tended to congregate in the larger cities of the east coast. With increasing Catholic political power in urban areas, Protestants became much more vehement in their manifestations of intolerance. Some political parties and movements during the nineteenth and early twentieth centuries were based upon abhorrence of Catholicism.

Anti-Semitism similarly increased along with the mounting Jewish immigration from Europe in the late nineteenth and early twentieth centuries. Even as late as the 1950s, residential areas, clubs, universities, and businesses actively discriminated against Jews.

There has, however, been a significant improvement in religious tolerance and attitudes towards diversity during the past fifty years. Even fifty years ago politicians, public entertainers, and other public figures felt little public pressure against making racist, anti-Semitic, or other remarks that denigrated ethnicity and minority religions. Today, the number uttering such statements is small; any political figure would face immediate public censure for speaking intolerantly about minority religions or races.

Tolerance of diversity

According to the 1990 census, African-Americans constituted 12.1 per cent, Hispanic-Americans 9 per cent, Asian and Pacific Islander Americans 2.9 per cent and Native Americans 0.8 per cent of the population. The rest of the population consists of people of largely European descent. However, although the United States is a country that often prides itself on being a melting pot for different nationalities and cultures, only relatively recently has significant attention been paid to the positive values that minorities bring to the larger culture.

Within the last forty years there have been several events that have helped move the public towards greater tolerance for others. After the Supreme Court decided in 1954 that school districts could not segregate students on the basis of race – as such schools were inherently unequal – the following twenty years was a time of intense political strife but the era of lawful racial segregation was at an end. However, the legacy of the past remains and the deeper wounds of racism cannot be cured by the order of a judge.

John F. Kennedy, in 1960, was the first Roman Catholic to be elected President of the United States, though most Protestants voted against him. Kennedy's victory largely destroyed the issue of 'Catholic versus Protestant' in subsequent elections. The mass civil rights movement began during Kennedy's presidency. The Civil Rights Act of 1964 became sweeping legislation that, as amended during subsequent years, has formed the basis for the law prohibiting discrimination on the basis of race, religion, or national origin in the fields of education, housing and employment. The movement also brought several African-American religious leaders into the national spotlight, such as the Rev. Martin Luther King, Jr, and Rev. Jesse Jackson.

Religious composition

Religion flourishes in the United States today. It has a most openly and professedly religious culture, church attendance is high, financial contributions to churches are high and the number of people identifying as atheists is very low. There are very many different churches.

Nevertheless, many conservatives assert that the country has wandered from its religious path and that irreligion dominates public discourse. Arguments that secularism dominates the government, academia and the private world as well are difficult to sustain in the context of pervasive 'civil religion'. Few elected public officials would be willing to express any doubts as to the existence of God. Public ceremonies frequently begin with an invocation for divine protection. Presidents, whether Republican or Democrat, invoke the name of God in policy speeches. Atheism, as a legacy of the vigorous post-war suppression of communism, communists and assumed communists, is not popularly accepted.

A salient characteristic of the religious landscape of the United States is the sheer number of active denominations: more than a hundred major churches and thousands of smaller independent churches. Thus no denomination has ever constituted a majority in the

United States as a whole. In this sense all denominations are minorities in the United States. Although statistics on religion vary widely, an overwhelming number of Americans identify themselves as Christians and a clear majority of those are Protestants. Jews constitute between 1–2 per cent of the population and there are smaller numbers of Muslims, Buddhists and Hindus. There are several black Muslim movements, whose members are African-American.

Ethnic background does not necessarily correlate with religion. One commentator has noted that of the approximately 1.5 million Americans of Arab descent, only half a million profess to be Muslim. Similarly, only 47,000 profess to belong to an indigenous American religious faith. Approximately 46 per cent of Native Americans are Protestants and 21 per cent are Roman Catholics. Evangelicalism and fundamentalism often cut across simple denominational lines. Evangelicals comprise approximately 25 per cent of the total population.

African-Americans have many black churches, the major ones being Baptist congregations and the African Methodist Episcopal Church. Although the Southern Baptist Convention was founded 150 years ago partly to defend slavery, the Convention in 1995 issued a resolution to 'repudiate historic acts of evil such as slavery'.

The First Amendment of the Constitution

The United States is officially, constitutionally and historically, a secular state. As a result of the American governmental structure, laws affecting religion and belief originate at the national, state, and local levels. The principal legal text governing the relationship between religion and the state is the First Amendment to the federal constitution:

> Congress shall make no law respecting an establishment of religion, or prohibiting the free exercise thereof; or abridging the freedom of speech, or of the press; or the right of the people peaceably to assemble, and to petition the Government for a redress of grievances.

These few words form the universally accepted framework governing the legal relationship between government, religion, and politics in the United States.

The Supreme Court has been relatively strict in holding that, under the establishment clause, the federal, state and local governments may not, directly or indirectly, demonstrate any preference for any church or any religious belief. The expression that has entered deeply into Americans' consciousness about religion and politics is that there should be a 'wall of separation between church and state'. This means that the government should not act as an arbiter of religious disputes nor establish any religious tests, nor propose or favour any religious doctrines. Conversely, religion should have no control over public offices or public acts.

There is a vigorous debate in the United States about the relationship between religion, tolerance, politics, and law. This debate sometimes generates fierce controversy over such issues as abortion and the role of religion in state schools. The Supreme Court typically decides two or three well-publicised cases per year on the scope of religious freedom in the country. The debate also rages in the political arena among candidates for the presidency as well as at the community level where parents, teachers, and school boards throughout the country argue about the appropriateness of prayers in school, Bible reading and moral education.

During the last thirty years, religious leaders have figured prominently in controversial political issues affecting the country. The Rev. Martin Luther King Jr, one of the principal architects of the civil rights movement, overtly appealed to religion as a basis for striking down segregation and many of his opponents overtly appealed to religion to oppose him. During the Vietnam War, many religious leaders throughout the country opposed American military action in South-East Asia because they believed it violated religious precepts. During the past twenty years religious revivalists have become increasingly more active politically, most typically, although not exclusively, supporting candidates of the right; their political leaders have included the Rev. Pat Robertson and the Rev. Jerry Falwell. More recently, prominent candidates for national office have openly and vigorously called for support from religious groups.

Under Article VI of the constitution, neither the federal government nor the states can require an office holder to belong to or adhere to any particular religious faith. In 1961 the Supreme Court struck down a Maryland law that had required notaries public to swear a belief in God. Neither the federal government nor the states impose any religious requirement on political office holders, electors, or public employees and no office holder is required to take a religious oath.

Both federal and state governments, as well as most private employers, are prohibited from making employment decisions based upon the religion of the applicant. Title VII of the Civil Rights Act of 1964 (as amended) also prohibits religious discrimination in housing and education and requires employers to make 'reasonable attempts' to accommodate employee 'religious beliefs and practices' unless such an accommodation imposes an 'undue hardship on the conduct of the employers' business'. The Equal Employment Opportunity Commission's guidelines on religious harassment – implementing the current law against religious discrimination – have received objections from religious groups that the guidelines would prevent religious practices such as evangelising in the workplace. However, complaints have been received about the pressure of proselytising on people whose beliefs are different and find the approach unwelcome or who do not wish to discuss religion at work. The EEOC received 319 such harassment claims in 1993.

The federal tax code provides two significant tax benefits to religious, educational and cultural organisations. Duly qualified organisations may be exempted from federal income taxes as long as they are non-profit and not engaged in partisan political activities. Tax deductions may be claimed by people who contribute to such corporations. A very wide range of religious and other non-profit organisations is exempted. For the most part, the tax laws do not discriminate between religion and non-religion nor among religions. The Church of Scientology, long engaged in lawsuits with the Internal Revenue Service, was finally granted tax exempt status in 1993.

Religious Freedom Restoration Act 1993

Prior to 1990, the Supreme Court had interpreted the free exercise clause of the First Amendment to mean that government could not interfere with religious practices unless it were able to show a 'compelling' need to do so. In 1990, adherents of the Native American Church argued in the Supreme Court that their religious freedom had been impermissibly abridged by the state of Oregon; two men had smoked peyote as part of a religious ceremony, despite the fact that the drug was illegal in the state. Their employment was terminated once it was found that they had smoked peyote and they subsequently were denied unemployment benefits. Although the Supreme Court could have decided that the state had a compelling interest in restricting drug use, in denying the appeal, the Court held instead that the state needed only to have a reasonable basis for restricting religious practices, thus changing the standard (the Smith decision).

The state of religious tolerance in the United States today was revealed when groups from across the entire political spectrum were outraged by the Court's decision, believing that the Supreme Court's decision would severely undercut religious freedom for all citizens. A coalition of more than fifty religious and civil rights groups developed a strategy to present Congress with draft legislation that would, to the extent possible, reverse the Smith decision. Although members of the coalition differed about many things in church and state relations, they all agreed that the 'compelling interest' test should be restored. In response to their petition to enact such a statute, the United States Congress voted the Religious Freedom Restoration Act into law. The statute requires governments to have a 'compelling interest' before forcing individuals to engage in activities that are inconsistent with their beliefs. It is likely to become the single most important piece of legislation to allow religious persons exemptions from laws that would otherwise – even if inadvertently – interfere with the practice of their religion.

Struggling with tolerance and intolerance

In February 1995, the Jewish Committee published a statement in the *New York Times*, supported by 250 eminent Americans, to repudiate the 'message of hate' conveyed in statements made by leaders of the separatist black Muslim group, the Nation of Islam, which allegedly attacked 'whites, women, Jews, Catholics, Arabs, gays and African Americans who criticise their persistently divisive message'. The Committee and its supporters considered that a better approach lay in joining their voices together 'in a message of faith in each other, of shared devotion to America's highest ideals of freedom and equality'.

None the less, one of the major events of 1995 was the Million Man March which Louis Farrakhan and the Nation of Islam led through Washington's streets. Farrakhan preaches a message of black self-reliance to African-Americans for whom race discrimination and disadvantage are still an issue of great heat. There remains a flavour of condescension combined with patronising liberalism in the relationship between black and white Christianities. Political power lies with white Christianity and it has developed in recent years into forms such as the Christian Coalition and other large groups which represent white interests and, in many sub-groups, discriminate against black, Jewish and Muslim populations.

Some state and local governments have prohibited speech that is demeaning and degrading to certain classes of people. Although 'hate-speech' laws typically target activities that are offensive on the basis of race or sex, they would be applicable to speech targeting religious groups. However, courts have struck down the laws for being inconsistent with constitutional free speech provisions. As a result, the discussion raised by such laws has had more impact than the laws themselves.

Since 1991, the US Department of Justice annually has compiled and published 'Hate Crime Statistics'; the crimes range from capital offences to intimidation. Of the more than 7,600 hate crimes committed in the United States, racial and ethnic bias accounts for 70 per cent and religious bias for 18 per cent. By far the largest portion of the 1,189 religious-bias crimes are committed against Jews (88 per cent) while only 2.5 per cent are committed against Catholics, the second highest religious group suffering overt acts of discrimination.

From 1995 to mid-1996, around forty black churches were burned down in the southern states; some white churches, synagogues and a mosque also suffered arson attacks. That racism has contributed to the arson attacks is not much in doubt. Those whose churches have been destroyed have described the impact of the burnings as striking at the heart of the black community. A bipartisan Bill was introduced into Congress in May 1996, increasing federal jurisdiction to prosecute arson at houses of worship. President Clinton has conferred with state officials, congregations, and Congress members to discuss prosecutions, rebuilding of churches and prevention of arson. Meanwhile the National Council of Churches as well as religious groups nationwide are helping to rebuild the destroyed black churches. In August 1996, two members of the Ku Klux Klan were charged with the burning of several black churches.

Despite lingering intolerance of Protestants towards Catholics, one of the major improvements in religious tolerance in the United States has been the progressive incorporation of Catholics into mainstream politics, entertainment, law and business.

Minorities whose practices do not fit standard work arrangements are those most likely to encounter situations in which their employment may be at risk. The most common plaintiffs in religious civil rights litigation are people whose religions require them to worship on Saturday and whose employers do not provide sufficient accommodation, which they are required to do unless that would constitute undue hardship. When a Sikh argued that his employer, the New York Transit Authority, had violated his religious freedom by requiring him to wear a helmet instead of his turban, the employer countered that this was a reasonable job requirement for a subway car inspector who had to crawl under cars and work with heavy equipment.

Although there remains a great deal of room for improvement, some businesses are progressively making positive accommodations of manifestations of belief, thus demonstrating that flexibility in work arrangements is practicable. At a coalmine on Navaho Nation land, the proprietor's collective bargaining agreement with the local labour organisation includes a special medicine man insurance benefits package in the company health scheme. Many Navahos still seek traditional tribal healing ceremonies for various ailments. Although more time and money were involved in this manner of healing than in attending a suburban surgery, the company considered that it was important for the company to be sensitive to the traditions of so many of its employees; 480 such consultations were made in 1993.

Education

For more than fifty years the Supreme Court has acknowledged that private, religious schools have the constitutional right to operate and to educate children, just as children have a constitutional right to attend these alternative schools, provided that the schools satisfy neutral and objective state educational standards.

A famous Supreme Court decision in 1972 (*Wisconsin* v. *Yoder*) held that Amish children could be exempted from state compulsory education laws on the basis of the free exercise clause. The Court decided that compulsory education, after a certain age, would interfere with the religious lifestyle of the Amish people. In many ways, this decision was the high point in Supreme Court jurisprudence on the rights of religious believers.

The manner in which religion is treated in state schools is probably the most contentious and divisive issue in the United States pertaining to freedom of thought. Since the 1960s, the Supreme Court has remained reasonably consistent in holding that state schools cannot advocate or promote religious teachings, particularly confessional teachings. Neither teachers nor students can lead classes in organised prayers nor can they use the Bible or the Ten Commandments for devotional teaching. These decisions of the Court were designed to promote tolerance for all beliefs. They have been strongly criticised by the political Right for not allowing talk about God while permitting discussion of other contentious subjects.

Currently, there is a movement to amend the constitution in such a way as to allow devotional, though non-sectarian, prayers to be given at state schools. But even the supporters of this constitutional amendment – the first change that would be made in the constitutional relationship between church and state in over 200 years – argue that if the First Amendment were interpreted correctly, then there would be no need for any change. In the face of a Congress which could support the proposed amendment, President Clinton has urged schools to allow all students to exercise their rights to religious expression, including private and voluntary prayer at school.

Conscientious objection

The United States terminated compulsory military conscription in 1973. The Supreme Court has resolutely refused to hold that the First Amendment provides a basis for exemption from compulsory military service. However, major cases have decided issues relating to conscience and belief which have been influential in subsequent litigation, notably that a conscientious objector need not have a personal God but the objection could be based on religious training and belief even though the person might not consider themselves religious. That the objection was sincerely and deeply held was crucial.

Although conscription was suspended, from 1980 all 18-year-old males have had to register with the Selective Service System in case Congress should decide to reinstate compulsory military service. Some people have raised religious objections to registering with the Selective Service. Others become conscientious objectors while serving in the military but are rarely granted exemption from duty.

The Old Order Amish group objects to paying (and receiving) social security taxes as part of their belief in self-sufficiency and in taking care of their own sick and elderly people as a religious obligation. In 1988 Congress agreed to exempt only the self-employed among the Amish and any other religious group with theological objections to social security.

Jewish and other religious groups see dissection as desecration of the body and therefore object to autopsy procedures. A Laotian American family, part of the Hmong community, objected to the dissection of and removal of organs from the body of their son which had occurred without their being consulted. The court ruling in subsequent litigation – holding that reasonable state requirements had precedence over religious objections – occurred under the influence of the Supreme Court's decision in Smith's case and before the Religious Freedom Restoration Act was passed restoring First Amendment rights.

Intolerance towards particular forms of belief

There have been incidents of intolerance towards religious minorities and adherents of secular beliefs. On Sunday morning, 28 February 1993, a hundred officers affiliated to the Federal Bureau of Alcohol, Tobacco, and Firearms, which alleged that the Branch Davidians had stashed assault weapons and ammunition, raided their centre near Waco, Texas. Four officers and six Davidians were killed in this initial assault. During the following fifty-one days, armed federal officials surrounded the compound, while newspapers and television covered the standoff that elicited international media atten-tion. Some portrayed the Davidians as wild-eyed fanatics who stocked a small arsenal of weapons. Others painted the Davidians as an insular group that was being unfairly harassed by federal officials. Federal officials from the beginning sought to portray the

Branch Davidians as fanatics and referred to them increasingly as a 'cult'. Although reputable academic advice about the messianic adventist group was available, officials reportedly turned instead for their information to the Cult Awareness Network, a group which the National Council of Churches regards as deeply intolerant of religious liberty. On 19 April federal officials stormed the compound with the ensuing loss of life of eighty-six people, including seventeen children. In February 1994, eleven Branch Davidians were acquitted of murder and conspiracy charges, though some were convicted on lesser charges, for actions in the first assault by the federal agency on their centre.

Of the major religions in the United States, Islam is subject to the most consistent manifestations of intolerance. Muslims consider that they face widespread discrimination in the workplace and by society at large. The American-Arab Anti-Discrimination Committee has documented scores of instances where Muslims have been verbally and physically harassed. Mosques, Muslim-owned stores, and homes have been vandalised. The number and frequency of attacks often can be correlated to the international political situation, the worst period for American Muslims occurring during the Gulf War.

Many Americans share negative stereotypes about Islam. To a question about whether Islam condones terrorism, 41 per cent of the respondents in a survey answered 'yes' and almost half believed that Muslims are 'anti-American'. Although editorial cartoonists have long since ceased drawing caricatures of Jews, Muslims continue to be caricatured in mainstream American newspapers. The stereotyping of Muslims is attributable, in part, to ignorance of the diversity of the Muslim world. Many Americans assume that 'Muslim' and 'Arab' are synonymous.

The media has bombarded Americans with images of Islamist terrorists. The most damaging event for Americans' perception of Islam was the Iranian revolutionaries' taking of American diplomats as hostages in Tehran during the administration of President Carter. Americans repeatedly observe instances of Islamist extremism in the form of terrorist killings in the Middle East and North Africa and, most recently, New York City's World Trade Center bombing. Americans generally are appalled by the death threats issued against Salman Rushdie. Most recently, Muslims were first to have the blame attributed to them by the media for perpetrating the Oklahoma bomb blast, though members of right-wing militia have since been indicted. Muslim Americans immediately experienced increased discrimination and harassment. Muslim women who adopt covering styles of dress (including the head-scarf) are particularly susceptible to discrimination.

Although concerned people feel that Americans ought to differentiate between religion and terrorism, they have failed to do so and, as a result, there is considerably less public censure or opprobrium attached to people who make biased anti-Muslim statements than there is to any other major religion. This is a serious problem that could be remedied by concerted actions of Muslims, Christians and Jews. Although there are some very modest signs of improvement, such as the appointment of the first Muslim chaplain in the army in late 1993, there is much work left to be done.

The legacy of lack of acceptance and equality for indigenous American traditional beliefs persists despite the enactment of the American Indian Religious Freedom Act of 1978. Practitioners of indigenous American religions are among the most vocal people arguing that the government and the law interfere with their rights to believe and to practise their religion, asserting that the statute has 'no teeth' and has been flouted by federal agencies. Legislation such as that protecting wild animals and prohibiting the use of drugs has been used to impede indigenous American traditional practices such as possession of sacred eagle feathers, religious use of peyote and access to sacred sites for the performance of rituals.

Supreme Court decisions have been particularly damaging to indigenous American religion. In Lyng's case, in 1988, three indigenous American groups had attempted to stop the federal government from building a logging road on their most sacred 'high country' land, the unique source of their religious power. Although the Court acknowledged that the government did not have a compelling need to build the road – alternatives were available – and although the building of the road would have a devastating impact on their religious practices, the First Amendment did not provide the relief sought. Consequently there are no enforceable safeguards for indigenous American worship at sacred sites. In Smith's case, when the Court refused to find any constitutional guarantee for Native Americans to use peyote in their religious ceremonies, critics of its opinion have argued that the members of the Court were insensitive to the needs of the Native Americans because their beliefs are formed and expressed in a different way from the didaco-Christian tradition. Indigenous Americans have seen a need for law to be developed to protect sacred sites in America adequately.

Atheists, while constituting only a small minority of Americans, maintain a visible and active presence. While no laws in the United States directly impose any civil disabilities on persons who do not believe in God, some occasionally impose indirect burdens, such as oaths of office which include the word 'God', even though the Supreme Court in 1961 declared that such oaths were unconstitutional.

Atheists and free-thinkers also complain that they are frequently forced to observe or participate in the religious conduct of others. These government-sponsored manifestations range from the printing of 'In God We Trust' on American currency, the phrase 'one nation under God' in the Pledge of Allegiance to the Flag, and the erection of religious symbols (such as nativity scenes and crosses) on public property.

Issues of freedom of association, in which private freedom of expression may not have to accommodate dissenting opinion, have been raised in the USA Supreme Court's recent ruling in favour of the Hibernian Society which did not wish to include gays in the St Patrick's Day Parade in Boston. They have also arisen in relation to the fairness or otherwise of the administration of scouting in America. A committee of the Free Thought Society of Greater Philadelphia, together with other rationalist and freedom of religion organisations, have worked for some years to persuade the Boy Scouts of America (BSA) to allow children to join the scouting movement without having to sign an oath to God. Children and their parents are often not made aware of this requirement until the point at which a boy is rejected as ineligible for the scouting movement because of his belief and feels humiliated. While the Girl Scouts have changed their policy to allow anyone who objects to saying 'God' to put the object of their beliefs in that place, the BSA has made no such accommodation to the pluralist world.

The BSA also has the practice of making charter agreements with community organisations which want to sponsor a scouting programme in their area. One Protestant church sponsoring the programme refused to appoint as the cub master a Muslim voluntary leader, on the basis that he was not of the right religion; the BSA stated that it allowed each sponsor of the programme to select the leaders. In 1996, the Pennsylvania Human Relations Commission found that a woman and her son (both atheists) had been discriminated against unlawfully by the BSA and the Chester County Council because of religious creed. The Commission made orders for redress and compensation and its decision is now under appeal.

It is not unusual for Hindus and devotees of Krishna Consciousness to face difficulties when moving into communities. The most typical obstacle they face is local zoning laws that are used to block the building or furnishing of a temple. The Indian community is thus sometimes faced with difficult legal problems in addition to the ordinary cost of erecting a house of worship. More serious are the gangs of young vandals in some communities who have attacked Hindu women who wear the 'bindi', the red circle on the forehead that signifies marital fidelity. Calling themselves the 'Dotbusters', these youths have terrorised some communities and have led to some notorious, if isolated, murders.

Promotion of tolerance

There has been a significant improvement in tolerance among religious believers during the past fifty years. Protestants, Catholics and Jews are now all reasonably well accepted into the mainstream of American life. Moreover, many once-marginal faiths also have been accepted, including the Jehovah's Witnesses, Mormons (the Church of Jesus Christ of Latter Day Saints), Christian Scientists, Seventh-Day Adventists and Assemblies of God. 'Eastern religions', especially Buddhism and Hinduism, have become extremely popular with a growing segment of the population.

Many communities respond to acts of intolerance by holding public manifestations of support for the victims. For example, after the fire-bombing of a synagogue in California early in 1991, the local community held a rally where several hundred Christians marched in front of the Yeshiva Aish HaTorah Institute holding signs stating 'Christians support our Jewish neighbors' and 'Hate will not be tolerated'. The marching was joined by sixty sympathetic motorcyclists wearing full leather and chain regalia. In 1993, when vandals painted swastikas on phone booths and newspaper boxes throughout Washington, DC, the *Jewish Monthly* reported that fifty people spent a day removing the markings.

Several organisations in the United States engage in training programmes to teach about peaceful methods of responding to violence and respect for different religious communities. The Anti-Defamation League's programme, 'A World of Difference', gained support from hundreds of large corporate contributors. The programme provides training to school teachers, police departments, colleges and universities and to communities.

The Governor of New Jersey responded to the 'Dotbusters' (described above) by instituting a state-wide programme in 1990 that established Human Relations Commissions at the rural level. Community leaders, all of whom are unpaid volunteers, develop programmes of education and training at the local level to respond not only to the anti-Hindu vandalism, but to all forms of intolerance. This approach attempts to supplement the enforcement of anti-hate crimes by promoting good alternative programmes.

The city of Billings, Montana, witnessed an outbreak of anti-Semitic vandalism. White skinheads who had vilified and intimidated African-American and Jewish religious communities – among others – then attacked the homes of the Jewish residents who had placed menorahs in their windows during Hanukkah. Public-spirited activists in the community, including some in the police department, were appalled by what they saw happening in their town. They took an innovative approach to the problem by distributing hundreds of menorahs throughout the community. Christians in the community placed the menorahs in their windows in a spirit of solidarity with their besieged fellow residents. The widespread placement of menorahs in windows not only removed the isolation that the few Jews felt, but it brought the community together in showing that they rejected the message of anti-Semitism. No vandalism has occurred since and race-hate communications have diminished.

Internal religious affairs

Indigenous American women have long enjoyed a variety of forms of empowerment in their religions, especially in shamanic healing practices, group decision-making and, in some areas, as warriors. Indigenous American religions have both myth and ritual reflecting women's importance. In the last three decades, there has been a revival of religious practice with prominent women leaders.

In the nineteenth and early twentieth centuries, many Christian women found themselves called to preach both as itinerants and locally, and as exhorters and leaders of prayer. Women's call to preach was particularly recognised in evangelical, pentecostal and holiness groups. Today, many religious groups and churches have women in positions of spiritual authority. Some 10 per cent of the students in Protestant seminaries in 1972 were women and in 1986 this had increased to 26 per cent. Most of them were considered likely to be the first female pastors for their congregations. The number of women clergy nearly doubled between 1977 and 1986. Whereas almost all male clergy were married, a survey in 1983 established that 45 per cent of female clergy were unmarried and 32 per cent had only ever been single. At the beginning of the 1980s, the first female rabbi was appointed in Reform Judaism.

While there has been progress for women in the Mormon Church, the role of women has been restricted by the Southern Baptist Church. American Catholic women have long been among the most vocal in the world in trying to change the attitude of their church, seeking a greater role for women in liturgical life in general and in particular, ordination. Some Catholic women activists have lost their teaching positions (for example, Dr Carmel McEnroy, RSM, a seminary lecturer, in April 1995), or have been expelled by their religious orders for espousing feminist causes condemned by the Vatican.

In the Episcopal Church, after Bishop Righter ordained an openly gay Anglican priest in 1989, ten bishops unsuccessfully filed charges of heresy against him and now are to ask the Episcopal Church to adopt a law making clergy abstain from sexual relations outside marriage. The Metropolitan Community Church, however, ministering to the homosexual community, was first formed in the United States so that gay and lesbian people could express their spirituality openly without the risk of discrimination and harassment. The question of ministering to the large number of people living with AIDS, and those bereaved, has increased the pressure long felt among American homosexuals for greater recognition of their presence in congregations and the role they should openly play in pastoral care.

Major differences among women have occurred in relation to religious attitudes towards abortion and the part played by fundamentalist Christianity and sections of the Catholic Church in influencing the judiciary and politicians against decriminalisation of abortion. Medical staff and women attending clinics have suffered serious harassment and violence from both clergy and lay people involved in 'right-to-life' campaigns. Also, the failure of women's organisations and others to achieve the successful passage of the Equal Rights Amendment in recent years is partially attributed to the influence of Christian fundamentalist groups.

Asia–Pacific

REGIONAL INTRODUCTION

For the purposes of this report, the Asia–Pacific region includes countries of South Asia, East Asia, South-East Asia and the Pacific, excluding the Eastern rim. While its diverse ethnic, linguistic and religious mixture makes the region a natural place for clash and confrontation, it has also provided the location for developing experience over many centuries of how to encounter and accommodate differences.

The region is marked by the struggles of peoples for independence from colonial powers or for a change of political system. The pressures of modernisation and rapidly accelerating economic growth, particularly among those nations whose population is mostly extremely poor, have had an enormous impact on culture, class and religion, showing, for example, in gender issues through which women's human rights are primarily mediated. The anxieties associated with rapid transformation have led to a rise in communalism, a clinging to a particular vision of the past to sustain community by promoting hatred of others.

Although strategic and economic interests involve the nations of the region in the various alliances of power politics, at the moment they are at peace with each other. Since the Second World War, there has been a move from inter-state conflict to intra-state conflict – involving state military, police and paramilitary forces and extra-legal militia – with a concomitant rise in intolerance before, during and after conflicts. Indigenous peoples throughout the region have to struggle against the competing claims and larger powers of economic development, exploitation and environmental destruction which lead to dispossession, the breaking up of their communities and the breaking down of their ways of life and their culture.

Many states in the Asian region are not only in the post-Cold War era but also in their post-Bandung era in which they are disillusioned about their independence stage and have come to conceive of themselves as having a special mission primarily to promote economic conditions and industrialisation and to resist outside forces as Western imperialism.

The argument that 'Asian values' – recalling family-based, patriarchal traditions, virtues of hard work and obedience – are different from 'Western values' was originally used as an anti-imperialist argument, but has now been co-opted to support the authoritarian state. Although the argument implies a fundamental difference between the East Asian states and the capitalist Western ones, these states have in the twentieth century readily absorbed Western concepts of capitalism, communism and even fascism. Their interests and economic involvements, however, largely coincide.

Democratic realities are coloured by culture, history, religion and economic conditions. The proportional relationship among differing kinds of rights differs within each state, sub-region and regionally. As Asia is moving increasingly towards democratic forms of the state, there is a real prospect of merging respect for human rights with Asia's own strong community traditions. The religions of the region set precedents for the proper treatment of people and for proper relationships with the natural world. These can be drawn upon in seeking to develop a local and regional discourse on human rights and finding a way to reconcile all generations to rights which may develop further the Western understanding of rights.

In the 1990s, that Third World states are major abusers of human rights has come more into focus since the end of communism. The lack of a regional governmental organisation and a regional court of human rights in the Asia–Pacific region limits the capacity of non-government organisations to address intolerance and conflict regionally. However, promotion of national mechanisms for human rights and prospects for sub-regional cooperation are being explored.

AUSTRALIA

Australia	
GDP (US$bn)	295
Population	17,400,000
Annual population growth (%)	1.7
Urban population (%)	85
Working population (%)	49
Literacy (%)	99
Ratifications	1; 2, 2(a), 2(b); 3; 4

Australia is generally regarded as a tolerant country. Pride in a viable multi-cultural, multi-religious society supports initiatives to make its institutions more responsive to the needs of the wide range of Australians.

Indigenous peoples have lived in Australia for over 40,000 years while in the 200 years since the British invaded in 1788, the continent has been settled by wave after wave of immigrants from all parts of the globe. For this reason, public discussion is dominated, on the one hand, by the implications of immigration and the government policy of multi-culturalism and, on the other, by Aboriginal land rights and reconciliation with Aboriginal peoples, redressing past injustice and current inequality. Women's rights are still on the human rights agenda for this still deeply sex-segmented society.

Ethnicity, race and religion

Over the centuries, Australian Aborigines evolved a complex system to sustain the largely arid land and its peoples by spiritual and ritual means. However, after invasion, their values were trivialised by a majority culture little able to recognise the validity of one so different from its own; Christian missions played a complex role in this process. Between 1788 and 1970, Aboriginal communities were systematically broken down to the extent that Aboriginal and Torres Straits Islanders now constitute only 1.5 per cent of Australia's over 17.4 million people. None the less, Aboriginal culture did not die out but has been proudly reasserted in recent years. Aboriginal people still retain and develop their relationship to land and kin in a religious framework, most fully in several remote areas in the central and northern regions, and more indirectly if influenced by or practising Christianity.

The beliefs of the population of Australia today are related to a diversity of immigration sources, in contrast to immigration patterns of fifty years ago when over 95 per cent of the population was born in English-speaking countries with mainstream Christian cultures. Overseas-born people have constituted around 20 per cent of the total Australian population since 1971, with the proportion of Asian-born rising steadily.

Australia's culture is secular. The number of Australians reporting a religious affiliation (to an optional census question) continues to fall. Nearly three-quarters are Christians. In 1991, Catholics were 27.3 per cent of the population and Anglicans 24 per cent. Mainstream Christian congregations are shrinking while charismatic and pentecostal churches are growing. The proportion of people declaring they have no religion has risen to 12 per cent. There are multifarious minority groups including new – and decades-old – religious, philosophical and secular, humanist movements.

In 1991, 2.6 per cent of the Australian people were Jews, Muslims or Buddhists or other non-Christians. This proportion is growing quickly because of recent immigrants and refugees. In the census, 4,330 people stated that they practised traditional Aboriginal religion. The urban indigenous population are more likely to be Christians but are renewing contact with their traditional history and metaphysics.

Ethos, political and legal structure

Australians frequently assert the existence of shared values in their cultural diversity, those of liberal democratic traditions and the concept of all human beings as equally worthy of freedom and respect, summed up in the phrase 'a fair go for all'. Australian public affairs are conducted with vigour and minorities as well as mainstream institutions may lobby effectively for their interests. The fact that Australians have poor knowledge about the legal basis and political functioning of their own country has recently become a matter for concern.

The Commonwealth of Australia is a parliamentary democracy composed of federated states and territories. Its head of state is the Queen of England, head of an established Protestant Church. The question of whether Australia should become a republic is a live topic of public discussion as the country is secular, multi-cultural and committed to equality. However, the Labour Party, on whose agenda republicanism ranked highly, lost power in 1996, after thirteen years, to the Liberal–Country Party coalition for whom it is only a minor issue.

Australia became a federal body with the adoption of the Australian constitution of 1901. Human rights protection at the constitutional level is very weak. Section 116 contains a limited guarantee of freedom of religion only. It prohibits the federal government from passing laws to establish any religion, to impose any religious observance, to prohibit free exercise of religion or to require a religious test for public office. This guarantee does not apply to the states and their laws. Action promoting constitutional reform and bills of rights at state and federal levels has had a chequered history.

Multi-cultural policy

Government multi-culturalism policies aim to bring all Australians to fully participate in society and development. Australian institutions are expected to acknowledge, reflect and respond to its culturally diverse communities. In 1992, the Australian Law Reform Commission recommended that the law should become more sensitive to cultural and linguistic differences in Australian society. Included among its recommendations were some addressed to customs and religious laws governing marriage. There is now only one family law regime in Australia. In July 1992, Australian family law was extended to cover all residents, including territories in the Indian Ocean which had had personal law for Muslims, a legacy of former Singaporean administration.

Aboriginal reconciliation and self-determination

It was only in 1992 that an Australian prime minister first publicly acknowledged how non-indigenous Australians had dispossessed the Aboriginal peoples. A statutory Council for Aboriginal Reconciliation has been established but deeper changes in employment, housing, education and health status of indigenous Australians – and in the attitudes of the media and other Australians – will take many years to accomplish.

Although Aboriginal people had never surrendered and handed over their land, they were regarded by the colonists as incapable of entering into treaties. Under the doctrine of *terra nullius* (the assumption that the land belonged to nobody and could therefore be taken without treaty or compensation), Aboriginal customary title to land was not recognised. In 1992, the doctrine was at last overturned by a High Court decision, *Mabo* v. *the State of Queensland*. A watershed in Australian history, its implications will take many years to work through law, politics, government policy, economic development and many other areas of Australian life.

The former federal Labour government responded to the decision in Mabo by enacting the Native Title Act 1993 to recognise remaining areas of native title. Further incorporation of customary laws into general law has been met with resistance. The change of federal government in 1996 has revealed a considerably more conservative approach to indigenous issues. When the High Court subsequently ruled that pastoral leases and Aboriginal land rights could co-exist, the government talked of amending native title legislation and even the Racial Discrimination Act.

Protection of sacred and significant sites

Aboriginal peoples alone have the right to determine how central to their spiritual traditions certain land may be. However, this right is hotly contested in a country where economic exploitation of natural resources is common. The issue is whether other Australians can respect indigenous beliefs, knowing they are genuinely held. Aboriginal sacred and significant sites are poorly protected by inconsistent state-based laws. A safety net exists – though infrequently used – in the form of the federal government's capacity to order the protection of such sites.

One such project – building a bridge to Hindmarsh Island in South Australia, over the mouth of an estuary – became the focus of political and legal contention involving state and federal governments and political parties. Approval had been given to the developers by the South Australian government without properly consulting Aboriginal people over heritage sites. The then federal minister was asked to intervene and in 1994, he granted a twenty-five-year protection order over the site.

The land in question is claimed to have supreme spiritual and cultural significance for the local Ngarrindjeri people. Ngarrindjeri women tended and passed on the knowledge concerned with the life force which was associated with the spot. The 'women's business' was secret, only to be revealed – painfully, reluctantly and to women only – under the threat of imminent destruction of its locale. The then federal Minister sent a female legal expert to consult with the women.

The developers challenged the order with the support of the South Australian government; it was overturned by the full Federal Court because the male Minister had refused to read the secret and women-only information. Extraordinary political manoeuvring followed, leading to a royal commission of inquiry by the South Australian government into the veracity of the women's beliefs. The royal commission's conclusion that the beliefs were fabricated was met with condemnation by both Aboriginal people and the former federal government. A further federal inquiry experienced obstacles through the unwillingness both of the Aboriginal women to provide information again to support the application and of the new government to appoint a female Minister to make a decision. The inquiry was successfully challenged in the courts and the bridge has received the current government's support. Jurist Elizabeth Evatt has received the legislation.

Politicisation of the issue and media simplification fed community prejudices that Aboriginal beliefs must satisfy higher standards of uniformity and veracity than Judaeo-Christian beliefs. Little attention was given in the dispute to the effect of past government policies of dispossession and dispersal on Aboriginal beliefs.

Religion and state

Religion and state are interwoven to a significant degree. Australian social and political structures evolved from a monocultural framework dominated by the established Church of England in particular and mainstream Protestantism in general. In the nineteenth century, no denomination had any greater rights than any other, but the blessing of God is relied upon in the preamble to Australia's constitution of 1901. Requests to take the affirmation or an oath on a sacred text other than the Bible are now rarely questioned in court. The NSW Court of Appeal in 1992 declared that religious groups govern themselves by consensual compact as voluntary bodies and civil courts have no role in their internal governance and discipline, only in disputes over property.

Australian law privileges religious activities in indirect ways. Together with government funding, rates concessions and exemptions, tax-deductibility of donations and tax exemptions are much valued by all not-for-profit organisations, including religious bodies. Nearly half of the fifty largest community social welfare organisations in Australia are affiliated to religious organisations; smaller ones are multifarious in this important sector of Australian life.

Recent government proposals have been made for greater accountability by non-profit bodies. Some religious groups refuse to apply for government funding on the basis that this might compromise church–state separation. Officials handling applications for funding or exemptions from unfamiliar or unpopular minorities may not consider these applications strictly on their merits, according to the experience of some minorities.

Intolerance, discrimination, law and conflict resolution

Secular in popular ethos, Australians are most familiar with the practices and structures of mainstream Christianity. Anti-Semitism persists, as does anti-Muslim feeling, while some new religious movements have also experienced active persecution. Because intense belief of any kind causes the average Australian some discomfort – religion being regarded as of peripheral importance in life – even committed Christians may experience discrimination or intolerance in situations where they are in the minority.

The federal Human Rights Commissioner may investigate and attempt to settle any complaints about discrimination guided by the UN Declaration on the Elimination of All Forms of Intolerance and of Discrimination Based on Religion or Belief. Federal ILO 111 powers also allow investigation of related employment complaints. However, there is no appeal to a court process to determine federal cases of religious discrimination. Religion is a ground for complaint about unlawful discrimination in only three of the Australian states and two of its territories, where cases decided by tribunals may be appealed to higher courts.

Claims of failure to accommodate religious practice constitute most of the complaints about discrimination on the basis of religion or belief, such as refusing to employ Muslim women in jobs such as check-out operators in supermarkets because they would not remove their headcoverings. However, there have been some positive developments. In 1993, the Waverley Municipal Council in Sydney developed a policy which allowed all its staff, whatever their religious, ethnic or cultural background, leave to meet their special religious and ceremonial obligations. In New South Wales, Sikh bus and train drivers now wear turbans made of cloth the same colour as the rest of their uniforms. In the prison system, chaplains usually represent mainstream Christian faiths but there are now more minority prisoners; in New South Wales, funding for an Orthodox chaplain was negotiated.

However, a number of minority religions have had their settlement in a new land impeded by racial and religious hostility at the local level. Applications for religious developments such as schools, temples and mosques must be approved by local government councils before building can start. In 1990 the NSW Ethnic Affairs Commission, after consultation, put together a strategy to overcome obstacles to religious establishments by providing accurate information; a similar strategy was developed in Victoria. As part of its multi-cultural policy, the Springvale Council in Melbourne established a forum for all local faith leaders, entering into a covenant of good neighbourliness which is renewed at an annual inter-faith service.

Intolerance based on belief is rarely acknowledged to be a domestic issue. None the less, there have been sporadic occurrences of extreme intolerance towards religious minorities in Australia in which the full weight of the bureaucracy and the law has been proved to be excessive and compensation has eventually been granted. Notable cases have involved the Ananda Margiis and the Seventh-Day Adventists.

In 1992, The Family of Love, formerly the Children of God, experienced the latest episode. After intense surveillance, the police – accompanied by television media – broke down doors of private houses allowing welfare authorities to take into protective custody more than 120 children in six communities in Sydney and Melbourne. This was done on the basis of allegations by former members and anti-cult organisations of sexual abuse and brainwashing of children. No attempt had been made to consult directly with The Family or with any arms-length source of information. No item of evidence of the practice of sexual abuse involving any of the adults or children could be produced in court. The matters were resolved by high-level mediation; claims of damages against government bodies have been made.

Racial hatred and vilification laws

The federal Racial Discrimination Act 1975 contained no provisions curbing incitement to racial hatred until the Racial Hatred Act was passed in 1995 after twenty years of debate about the issues; it instituted both criminal offences and a civil complaints mechanism. The definition of race and ethnic origin was broad enough to cover Sikhs, Jews and Muslims.

Recommendations had been made by the Royal Commission into Aboriginal Deaths in Custody, the National Inquiry into Racist Violence and the Australian Law Reform Commission, among others. Several Jewish synagogues have been fire-bombed by arsonists in the last few years. Vandalising, burglaries and attempted arson of mosques and Islamic centres have also occurred. Muslim women have been threatened and frightened; some have had their *hijab*s pulled off in the street. These incidents took place in the period of the Gulf War in 1991, when there was a distinct rise in incidents of racial and religious intolerance.

Especially in rural districts, a culture of intolerance may be nurtured by extreme right-wing ideologies containing concepts of racial purity. Following acts of racist violence and other crimes, members of small neo-Nazi groups have been imprisoned in recent years.

In Queensland it is an offence to incite racial or religious hatred; other states have made racial vilification unlawful as part of their discrimination laws. Under the NSW Anti-Discrimination Act 1977, one complaint about anti-Semitic material published in 1993 by a local newspaper was successfully conciliated with a retraction by the publisher. Various exceptions to the racial vilification provisions allow public acts done reasonably and in good faith, usually for purposes in the public interest; there is no exception for religious instruction. However, religious instruction and discussion are excepted from provisions dealing with homosexual and HIV/AIDS vilification, respectively.

In a multi-religious country with no established church, blasphemy laws (in the statute or in common law) are considered anachronistic. Some states abolished the offence while others are reviewing it. Damage to personal and religious susceptibilities may be better remedied by laws on vilification or offensive material. The Islamic Council of NSW and the Church of Scientology continue to campaign for religious vilification to be specifically prohibited.

Conscientious objection

Under the National Service Act 1951, not currently invoked, Section 29A allows those with conscientious beliefs exemption from military service or combatant duties. A belief may or may not be religious in character and may or may not be part of the doctrines of a religion as long as it is sincerely held. As a result of the Vietnam War, conscientious believers who cannot participate in a particular war may be exempted.

There have been cases of conscientious objection in employment. In 1988, Marett, a member of the Christian Revival Crusade, refused to pay a levy in support of striking union workers because he already donated a tenth of his income to the church. The management of Petroleum Refineries Australia gave in to union pressure and banished Marett to a small hut (except for scheduled work-breaks) and gave him no work to do, although they paid him. After six months, he was dismissed and took action for discrimination. The Victorian Equal Opportunity Board ordered his employer to pay him damages.

Although adults may legally refuse medical treatment, child welfare legislation overrides parental objection regarding a child under 16 and the objection of a child aged 16 or 17. Although medical and dental practitioners can act without parent or child consent to save a child's life and Supreme Court orders may otherwise be obtained, none the less

Jehovah's Witness couples, considered suitable to adopt a child, are obliged to sign an agreement to allow medical treatment, including a blood transfusion, on the child.

Health professionals may object to participating in legal terminations of pregnancy in public hospitals. Although the law and professional ethics demand that they provide medical treatment regardless of their own opinions, in practice hospital administrators accommodate their objections. Professional codes of conduct state that conscientious objection should be respected.

Conscientious and cultural objections as defences

In a case in which the owners justified their refusal to rent a property to an unmarried couple by reference to their Christian principles, the NSW Equal Opportunity Tribunal found that unbiased access to available housing was the socio-economic right which took precedence over the conscientious belief of an individual landlord.

The Law Reform Commission's report on multi-culturalism has addressed the question of whether cultural defences should be allowed for criminal offences and whether there should be exemptions from the criminal law on the basis of moral or religious objections. There are a number of such exemptions from criminal liability in specific instances, for example, exemption from meat industry laws for religious slaughter of animals for human consumption.

Requests for recognition of conscientious beliefs include the Sikh community's wish for exemption from laws prohibiting possession of weapons in public, to carry ceremonial *kirpans* and exemption from requirements to wear crash helmets which interfere with religious headdress. Shivite Hindus want exemption from drug laws to allow them to smoke cannabis on Shiva's birthday.

The commission concluded that no general or partial cultural defence was desirable but that parliament, when creating statutory offences, should consider the implications for people from particular cultures and faiths. Some practices, though based in genuine beliefs and customs, might not be exempted.

Cases of female genital mutilation are rare in Australia and hard to prove. While calls for legislation to ban the practice have primarily been based on genuine human rights concerns, some have been tinged with anti-Muslim prejudice. Muslim organisations in Australia want the ancient practice made a criminal offence; several states have since done so. As recommended by the federal Family Law Council in 1994, a national programme of education to eradicate the practice, conducted by and among the affected communities, has been instituted.

The media

Mainstream Christian religions have generally established good media relations. Religious minorities, particularly those which are not Christian, have pointed out the influence of the media in shaping issues affecting them. Jewish commentators have noted the tendency of media with left-wing affiliations to cloak anti-Semitism in the guise of anti-Zionism. Muslims have a bad press in Australia which has contributed to prejudices, discrimination and violence against Muslim Australians.

Minority religious groups and new religious movements have difficulty correcting media stereotyping, bias and incorrect information in the tabloid press, sensationalist television and talk-back radio. They are frequently last to be consulted by the media and first to be lumped into a single 'harmful cult'. In 1996 the Australian Broadcasting Authority held that broadcasting standards were breached when a radio programme taking a sceptical approach to religion aired a discussion in which the Church of Scientology was 'gratuitously vilified'.

Proselytising and the new religious movements

No religion or belief and no specific proselytising practice is proscribed as such in Australia today, although this has not been true in the past for the Jehovah's Witnesses in wartime and the Scientologists in peacetime. As has been the pattern in the past, there were calls in 1993–94 for official investigations into various groups and their activities, ranging from new religious movements to personal development groups. Attempts to form a NSW parliamentary select committee of inquiry into means of combating so-called 'cult' activities have not proceeded.

The question of individual freedom to join and leave religious groups often focuses on whether coercion has been involved to any degree. Deprogramming is an issue for some movements, such as the Church of Scientology. While voluntary but organised persuasion, so-called 'exit counselling', is publicly advocated by CultAware, Scientologists claim that some families have used force to get their members to leave. Police are allegedly reluctant to get involved with a failed deprogramming, seeing the dispute as a family affair. One case taken to court to gain an apprehended violence order against an alleged de-programmer of a Scientologist was dismissed and one earlier committal hearing for kidnapping a Unification Church member, though recommended for trial, did not go ahead.

Education

Since the 1880s, state schools in Australia have generally had a legislative commitment to secular education as well as a statutory obligation to allow religious organisations access to children of adherents to give them instruction in their own religion, if parents wish this or unless they object. The National Children's and Youth Law Centre considers that parents' needs should be counterbalanced by an equal respect for the freedom of competent children to make their own choice in religious matters in state schools.

Some parents, students and teacher organisations have been concerned that con-fessionally based religious education in government schools may undermine parts of the departmental curriculum, especially in personal relationships, social sciences and science teaching. Pressure to give creationist proponents 'equal time' in government school curricula has been strong in Queensland. The subject does not form part of the nationally accredited science curriculum and questions on evolution are optional in the Higher School Certificate science examinations. In 1994, the Anglican Archbishop of Brisbane publicly criticised the influence of creationism, saying that authorities which publicly funded schools had a right to have views on what was taught and that this did not conflict with freedom of religion.

Catholic schools won a long fight for state aid in 1963. Funding to such schools was challenged, unsuccessfully, by secularist groups who championed the cause of free public education for all in 1981 when the High Court ruled that funding the Catholic school system was not tantamount to establishing religion. The granting of state aid has increased the number and variety of private schools, such as small Christian community schools run by Protestant groups. Anglican systemic schools are being established. The New Schools Policy is now being revised in a way which should make it easier to establish private schools.

A high proportion of Jewish children go to Jewish schools: 75 per cent of their primary school children and 55 per cent of their secondary children. Some Muslim primary schools and one secondary school have been established; more are planned. They have encountered community opposition in the past when finding sites.

Exemptions for religious educational institutions are found in federal and state discrimination laws. Concerns have been voiced in national public inquiries into equal opportunities for women and into equality before the law, about the rights of women to freedom from discrimination in employment in religious schools. In 1993, nearly two-thirds of private school teachers were women.

Unfair dismissal cases have been heard where a teacher's private life is the matter at issue. Cases include dismissal for having been married in the church of another Christian faith and dismissal of unmarried pregnant teachers living in *de facto* relationships. Pregnancy is visible; male teachers living in such relationships have not been dismissed.

The Law Reform Commission has stated that religious freedom and the right to enjoy culture and religion must be balanced with the right to equality and with the principle of non-discrimination. The Commission considers that there can be no religious basis for discrimination on the basis of sex and pregnancy.

Inter-faith initiatives

It is fifty years since Catholics and Protestants last hurled insults at each other in the schoolyard, the legacy of past antagonisms between Australians of Irish and English backgrounds. Mainstream Christian churches are together involved in social justice issues; relations between them function smoothly and notable progress has been made in ecumenical links.

In 1994, the National Council of Churches in Australia (NCCA) was formed, adding the Roman Catholic Church to the former Australian Council of Churches. The new body has thus been considerably strengthened in its authority to speak on behalf of the largest segment of Australian Christians. Church organisations which take a strong evangelical line, such as the NSW Council of Churches, continue to resist the wider religious pluralism.

Inter-religious activity significantly expanded in the 1990s to include major non-Christian faiths. There is an increasing interest at the local level in the belief and practices of others. In one Melbourne suburb where the number of Muslims had dramatically increased, the local ministers fraternal in 1993 organised a study series on understanding Islam which examined how Christians might respond to the local Muslim community.

An Australian Council for Christians and Jews has been formed. After an incident where a prominent Jewish leader visiting a church school became concerned at the seemingly anti-Jewish nature of passages in Christian scripture being taught there, prominent Jewish and Christian academics met to set guidelines on the treatment of such texts in the context of religious instruction.

The Uniting Church now has relations with both Muslim and Jewish communities. The World Conference on Religion and Peace – much of whose work in Australia focuses on ethnic minority faiths – has expanded nationally. The NCCA also has a Commission for Dialogue with Living Faiths and Community Relations, which connects with the Action Group for Religious Liberty whose membership includes the new religious movements, among others.

Internal religious affairs

With a few exceptions, such as the Salvation Army and the Religious Society of Friends where gender equality was a founding principle, Australia's churches have not kept pace with the change in community perception about women's right to equality. Despite a history of female ministry in its component churches over the past fifty years, even in the Uniting Church women comprise only fifty-five of its 383 ordained ministers. At the same time as external pressure for change has increased, so too has internal pressure through the activities of women's lobby groups within the churches, such as the Movement for the Ordination of Women, Ordination of Catholic Women, WomenChurch, Feminist Uniting Network, and a number of Christian women's spirituality groups.

Views on the legitimacy of women's claim to ordination in the Anglican Church of Australia have been polarised, some dioceses (notably the Sydney Anglican Diocese) relying on the doctrine of 'headship' to resist change. After the Anglican Church of Australia eventually determined that there was no theological barrier to women's ordination, some bishops claimed their right as bishops to ordain women without waiting for the church canon to change. At the end of 1994 there were 120 women priests in the Anglican Church of Australia. However, the number attending the Sydney Anglican Synod in 1994 was only three out of 250 clergy.

One church has rescinded its former policy; the Continuing Presbyterian Church now interprets biblical references to 'man' and 'men' literally. Two of its five remaining women ministers unsuccessfully challenged in the civil courts the church's decision to ban female ministry because their authority was now brought into question. A male theologian was declared heretical for defending female ministry on the ground of merit and for questioning the validity of male-only ministry, the first heresy charge since 1934.

Catholic women at all levels joined together in 1993 to form the organisation, Ordination of Catholic Women (OCW). When Pope John Paul II declared in May 1994 that the Catholic Church had no authority to confer priestly ordination on women and that this view must be held definitively by all Catholics, there was an outcry from Australian Catholics of both sexes and strong protest from OCW and other women's groups.

Recent cases of sexual and child abuse by Christian clergy and religious figures have prompted urgent discussion of the use of the sacred power bestowed with ordination, the quality of selection, education and supervision of priests and others and the churches' protection of those who criminally assault women and children in their pastoral care. Mainstream churches have publicly apologised for past abuses; most have brought in policies to prevent future occurrences.

Compulsory celibacy for Roman Catholic priests has also been made an issue, in terms of its limiting the concept and practice of priesthood. Because of this limitation, some Catholic parishes are without resident ordained personnel.

Muslim women are precluded from leadership of mosque communities, but they have received the firm support of their *mufti* to gather into women's organisations to extend women's knowledge of Islam and to encourage them to live Islamically. The mosque-based Muslim Women's Association was formed in 1983. Wearing the *hijab* (in a number of cultural forms) is regarded by some but not all Australian Muslims as a mark of religious commitment and the freedom to enter the public world of education and employment. The articulate presence of Muslim women in the media and in government counters the stereotype of Muslim women as silent and powerless.

Australia has a long history of Chinese migration, but until recently there were few temples or Chinese orders of religious. Several major Buddhist temple complexes have now been completed and these reflect the Buddhism of Taiwan, in which there is an increased number of ordained women renunciants (*bhikksunis*). In the Chinese Buddhist Temple in Parramatta (Sydney), the entire *sangha* is female and women chiefly administer the building of a large Buddhist complex near Wollongong. Two Korean Buddhist temples and some Vietnamese temples also have some *bhikkhsunis*. Theravada Buddhists from Thailand and Sri Lanka have established small temples and monasteries. Thai monasteries in Australia have some *maejis* who are renunciant but not ordained, because the women's ordination lineage of Theravada Buddhism has died out and would need to be reintroduced through the lineage of Mahayana Buddhism, a controversial move supported by western Buddhist renunciants and some groups in Asian countries.

Sex role complementarity expressed in religious ritual is central to Aboriginal life and Aboriginal women have been discriminated against both in relation to the dominant culture's interpretation of their ritual life, by the law and by both the secular and Christian feminist ideologies. The experience of some aspects of Christian mission and the government's forced and secret removal of young children (often to 'Christian' homes and institutions) from Aboriginal groups between the 1950s and 1970s resulted in appalling damage to women and kinship–land religious ties.

Within mainstream religions, Aboriginal experience is varied. In some forms of evangelical Christianity, women can become pastors and, in liturgies, some form of accommodation to Aboriginal religious practice is often made. In some areas, Aboriginal liturgy groups and social centres, some coordinated by women, have been sponsored by the Catholic Church. A recent request to ritually install an important Aboriginal icon in St Patrick's Cathedral in Melbourne was, however, refused and, in general, Aboriginal theologians and others report on-going discrimination in mainstream religions.

The existence of homosexual co-religionists is known but not usually acknowledged publicly as legitimate within a variety of Christian institutions, many of which supported homosexual law reform as a human rights issue. Some Anglican men and women have been dismissed from church employment and excommunicated for openly declaring they were gay or lived in gay relationships under a Sydney Anglican synod policy adopted in 1985. However, one Anglican in the Perth archdiocese, openly gay, was ordained in 1992. There has been resistance to requests for ordination from gay candidates in the Uniting Church of Australia.

Whereas homosexuality is roundly denounced by the *mufti* of Australian Muslims, Buddhists in Australia do not have a declared policy. Many Christian denominations and also some Buddhist centres have gay and lesbian spirituality groups. It is significant that some of the better-known counselling and care centres for HIV/AIDS, together with celebration of special ritual for those with this illness, are associated with some Catholic institutions and parishes and several Anglican and other Protestant parishes.

CHINA

China has the largest population in the world: nearly 1.2 billion people. Its strong centralising government has often attempted to impose uniformity on a country marked by immense diversity of culture, ethnic origin, language and nationality. China has always been a country of many religions. Some major religions remain intricately intertwined with each other, in their development, practices and rites, how they perceive the role of deities and gods, and how they see their role relating to social and political life as well as religion and belief. After the demise of the Cultural Revolution, the diversity of Chinese

China	
GDP (US$bn)	506
Population	1,183,600,000
Annual population growth (%)	1.9
Urban population (%)	28
Working population (%)	59[a]
Literacy (%)	79.3
Ratifications	3; 4

beliefs and practices has in recent years become more evident and vigorous. With economic changes, internal migration flows, demands for and exercise of autonomy at the local level – and greater commerce with the West – China's centralised communist government is today facing an era of increasing uncertainty.

Ethnic and religious composition

In China fifty-six national minorities are officially recognised. Han peoples, comprising over 90 per cent of the population, are themselves marked by diversity: eight separate languages are spoken. In sensitive border areas of Xinjiang, Tibet, Inner Mongolia and Yunnan, over 90 per cent of the population is comprised of minorities. Minority groups such as the Hui and the Manchu are scattered throughout China.

In 1956, Zhou Enlai announced that there were about 100 million religious believers in China, the same number as the Department of Religious Affairs of the State Council estimates today. Disparity in the origin and collection of statistics makes actual numbers hard to assess. For instance, as much as 80 per cent of China's population may be termed 'religious' if customary beliefs and practices in the countryside are included. However, Buddhists form the largest body of believers and official figures state that there are 3 million Catholics, 3 million Protestants and 10 million Muslims, although religious sources give higher estimates.

There is religious variety among ethnic minority groups. Besides Islam – distributed over the north-west areas of China and the Hui, Tunhsiang, Paoan, Salar, Uighur, Kazakh, Uzbek, Tadjik, Tatar and Kirghiz national minorities – there is Theravada Buddhism, practised by the Dai, Pulang, Penglung, Achang and Va minorities in the south-west of Yunnan province. Eastern Orthodoxy is practised by the Russian and Ewenki minorities. Mahayana Buddhism is practised in Tibet.

Religion and ideology

Marxist–Leninist ideology has been the basis of the People's Republic of China since it was established in 1949. Marxist materialism is not the belief that only matter exists. The belief in God exists too, as a belief held by human beings; but the object of that belief, God, is an illusion constructed out of empirical material by human fantasy and as a reaction to the empirical 'material' world and the human being's position in it. The communist regime in China perceived religion as a tool by which it directed a set of 'state religions' to serve state needs and goals.

Confucianism was the state-fostered religion of the Han period from the second century before the common era. Political commands were almost given the status of commands of the gods, through the concept of the Mandate of Heaven. Confucian idealism stressed the cultivation of moral character, appreciation of the dominance of the family and of the state, loyalty, filial piety, benevolence and human understanding. Confucianism rejected any concept of the individual and state interests overrode individuals' interests and rights.

The emergence of Taoism and the entry of Buddhism in the second century marked the introduction to China of organised systems of voluntary religion. They paved the way for Christianity which came to China at the beginning of the seventh century, at the same time as Islam, a religion of migration. With voluntary religion came the possibility of individualism and dissension. There is still tension between the Confucian ideology of the self subsumed in community and ideologies which concentrate on self-enlightenment, self-fulfilment and community well-being as a function of personal spiritual satisfaction.

With voluntarism in religion also came the concept of a division between religious and secular power. Religion came to pose a threat to the political leadership; hence the rebellions organised by the religious groups down the centuries to the modern era. Chinese Marxists found in religion both a threat and an ally, a competitor for collective allegiance, spiritual inspiration and practical loyalty and a basis for transference of that loyalty.

To a socialistic regime, the sense of individual spiritual freedom which religion gave to believers represented the old conflict between the well-being of the self and that of society at large. In this, communism found an unexpected ally in Confucianism where rights have no independent, absolute value. No general words for right or duty existed at the end of the nineteenth century. When compounded words were invented, except for those which contained common Confucian ideas and values, none sounded either natural or familiar and all failed to take deep root for many years.

Constitutional and legal situation concerning human rights

All four Chinese constitutions – of 1954, 1975, 1978 and 1982 – provided for a general freedom of religious belief, though none have provided for freedom of conscience or belief in general. In the 1982 constitution, principles are enunciated that have direct or indirect implications for freedom of thought, conscience and belief. The 'Four Principles' provision in the preamble commits the nation to 'adhere to the people's democratic dictatorship and follow the socialist road' 'under the leadership of the Communist Party of China and the guidance of Marxism–Leninism and Mao Zedong Thought'. Article 24 of the constitution says that 'the State strengthens the building of socialist spiritual civilisation'.

Although there are no specific sanctions against those who resist 'construction', several campaigns against spiritual pollution and the introduction of Western ideas of liberalism were launched when Deng Xiaoping came to power. Disapproved-of activities linked with political belief or conscience can be brought within the criminal law through provisions against counter-revolutionary activities and under administrative rules.

The Chinese government has not become a party to the International Covenant on Civil and Political Rights, claiming that its constitution sufficiently secures such rights. The rights mentioned in the constitution are freedom of speech, of assembly, of association, of procession and demonstration, and appeal against the conduct of state functionaries. However, these are granted to citizens as good citizens, not human beings *per se*. Hence, 'enemies of the state' are seen as putting themselves outside the protection of the constitution.

Various criminal laws contain provisions which can be used to punish people by trial and imprisonment for the peaceful exercise of fundamental human rights such as freedom of opinion, association and dissemination of information. Counter-revolutionary and rebellious acts are punishable by death. 'Rehabilitation through labour' led to the establishment of many special labour camps designed for people considered to have 'anti-socialist' views or who were 'hooligans', who could be detained there without trial. However, in March 1996 the National People's Congress approved legal proposals including the presumption of innocence and right of access to legal representatives.

Resistance and repression of freedom of thought

Despite such repressive powers, Chinese students and intellectuals have been working for the last decade and a half towards the expansion of the civil rights of freedom of speech, press and assembly which are formally guaranteed under the 1982 constitution. They also seek the political right to influence the choice of leaders and the direction of policy. Their success, however, has been chequered.

After a brief period of liberalisation in 1978–79, dissident writers and human rights advocates were arrested, beaten, imprisoned and sent to be 're-educated'. In 1987, the 'anti-bourgeois liberalisation campaign' attempted to neutralise the effects of what was seen as official endorsement of China's exposure to foreign culture in the early 1980s. Intellectuals were expelled from party membership and removed from official and employment positions. Criticism by citizens on subjects such as leadership, corruption or non-economic policy directions was not tolerated.

In the 1980s, the media also came under tight control. In 1989, for instance, the Communist Party threatened to dismiss the editor of China's only almost independent newspaper, the *World Economic Herald*, for publishing an anti-Marxist address by political theorist Su Shaozhi. Some thirty newspaper editors and reporters were reported to be in prison in 1990. Foreign reports of world and local events are all carefully controlled, selected and directed to a limited readership. Other methods of speech are also suppressed. The medium of wall posters as a mode of free expression is now illegal and violators are subject to at least brief detention. The party does not admit to the existence of political prisoners of conscience because they are 'counter-revolutionaries'. Under Deng Xiaoping, political dissenters were harassed, arbitrarily arrested and harshly punished without fair trial.

Among the estimated 2–5 million prison or labour camp population, a small percentage falls under the category of 'counter-revolutionary' offenders. The use of torture and degrading treatment of prisoners has been documented. In 1994 an estimate of 1,400 executions per year was reported. Large posters appear in the cities with the names of prisoners to be executed; those who have already been executed have large red ticks next to their names. The threat implicit in these posters is itself a form of thought control, coupled with policy which deliberately keeps the population ignorant of the facts of repression.

The policy of withholding information about suppression of thought and conscience was at its strongest during the events of May–June 1989 after about 300 students started demonstrating in Tiananmen Square for democratic reform in China. By 17 May, protesters numbered over 1 million people, holding banners demanding the resignation of Deng Xiaoping, but at no time calling for the overthrow of the Communist Party. On 20 May, the State Council decreed martial law in parts of Beijing and on 4 June troops dispersed the crowds leaving between 700 and 7,000 dead.

Communist policy on religion

The official Chinese view of religion at the start of communist rule was not directly hostile. Mao Zedong declared: 'We cannot abolish religion . . . In settling matters of an ideological nature . . . we can only use democratic methods of discussion, of criticism, of persuasion and education.' The First Plenary Session of the Chinese People's Political Consultative Conference in 1949 declared there was freedom of religion.

Though the Chinese communists believed that theistic religion would ultimately disappear, pragmatic considerations encouraged an approach of monitoring and regulating all religions, placing them under central control, and cutting them off from any kind of foreign aid or influence, especially Catholic ties to the Vatican. Freedom of religion became freedom of religious belief and freedom of religious activities became freedom of 'normal' religious practices.

There have been four stages in the evolution of Chinese communist policy. From 1949–56 the religious policy of the Chinese Communist Party divided believers into two groups. The first were the 'imperialist religious forces', foreign missionaries and believers who were unsympathetic to the party's policy; they were deported or arrested. The second were those who supported the party's religious reform policy and lived in peace with it on the condition that they reorganised themselves into new religious bodies controlled by the party under the 'three selves' principle: self-mission, self-funding and self-administering. This was a period of vitality and success for the Communist Party of China. Atheism was extensively disseminated among the people. Some believers were converted to atheism during the political movement of 'remoulding ideology'.

The second period, from 1956–65, saw the party implementing a policy of intensified fighting against 'rightists' which laid heavy stress on class struggle in the ideological sphere. Religion as 'spiritual opium', a 'narcotic', was subject to severe criticism. Religious believers were labelled 'backward elements' and severely discriminated against. In the hunt for bourgeois elements and 'counter-revolutionaries' of all colours, people with objectionable social and political backgrounds and thoughts, religious belief and political standpoints were all targeted. With 'left deviationism' strengthening and then on the rampage, the 'Four Clean-ups' became the excuse for mobilising believers to criticise themselves, exposing the reactionary, swindling nature of religion, forcing monks, nuns and priests to speak against religion and advise the masses not to believe in any religion by using their own experience as an example, coercing monks, nuns and priests to self-betrayal, wrecking religious premises, destroying religious books and damaging relics, and so on.

The third period, from 1966–76, when Mao Zedong died, was the ten years of the Cultural Revolution. The party's Gang of Four held up religion in all its forms as an alien, reactionary force. Monks, nuns, priests and ordinary believers were criticised, accused and denounced at meetings as 'monsters and demons', suffering as severely as did 'capitalist roaders'. Believers suffered every kind of discrimination. Temples and churches were closed, destroyed, damaged or converted to secular and even sacrilegious uses. The property of religious bodies was stolen or confiscated, religious books and religious cultural relics were deliberately destroyed by burning or other ways.

The fourth period began in 1977 and continues to the present. Since the Third Plenary Session of the Eleventh Central Committee of the party, the party put forth the ideological line of 'emancipating the mind and seeking truth from facts'. It summed up its experience of the past, especially examining and affirming the mistakes it made in the area of religion. The policy was promulgated in 1982 in 'On the [Party's] Fundamental Point of View and

Basic Policy on the Question of Religion in the Socialist Period of Our Country' (No. 19 Document). Under the guidance of this document, a new phase began in which religion is more or less tolerated provided it conforms to state-approved principles and organisation. Religious believers are being made to understand that they are not now inferior to other people. Yet the scars and memories of past persecution and suffering can hardly be said to have healed or faded; many believers still keep a low profile.

Religion and state

Article 36 of the 1982 constitution guarantees only freedom of religious belief, not free exercise of religion or belief:

> Citizens of the People's Republic of China enjoy freedom of religious belief.

> No state organ, public organisation or individual may compel citizens to believe in, or not to believe in, any religion; nor may they discriminate against citizens who believe in, or do not believe in, any religion.

> The state protects normal religious activities. No-one may make use of religion to engage in activities that disrupt public order, impair the health of citizens or interfere with the state educational system.

> Religious bodies and religious affairs are not subject to any foreign domination.

The state protects under the constitution only 'normal religious activities'; state organs determine what is normal and lawful. Thus, when belief compels action that is disapproved of, individuals come into conflict with the state, no matter how legitimate (in terms of internationally recognised rights) and non-violent their actions may be.

The Religious Affairs Bureau, founded to achieve the organisational fusion of state and religion, governs the affairs of religions in China. Officials of the Bureau, which defines what is 'normal' religious activity, are non-believers themselves, ostensibly to prevent bias towards any particular religion. However, their decisions on this subject are often arbitrary and uninformed, resulting in inconsistent application of policy. The eight national patriotic religious associations which are accountable to government religious institutions and the Bureau have some autonomy but the strong presence of party members ensures that directives are followed in such matters as recruitment of candidates, temple finances and printing of religious material. Religious activities are restricted solely to officially designated and registered places of worship. Any religious activity outside of the control of the religious associations is illegitimate.

There have been problems in implementing the religious policy. The government has recognised that although 'underground religious organisations' are prohibited, this has not had the effect of eradicating them. Generally, local authorities try to merge them with the patriotic associations or they turn a blind eye to their existence. In provinces such as Shandong and Fujian, Christian household meetings seem now wholly open. It has been recognised that many such organisations are not against the government but meeting because there is no church near, or because of differences about doctrine rather than politics. They are not 'matters of contradiction between the people and the enemy'. But where underground religions are organised by hostile elements using religion to carry out illegal activities or commit crimes, in the authorities' view, or 'have dense superstitious colours and utilise superstition to defraud people', their religious doctrines and purposes are seen as secondary to criminal ones. Thus, underground Catholics who take orders from the Vatican are representatives of imperialist power and hence to be placed under surveillance.

'Penetration' by a foreign power is a term used to indicate a religion carrying out political penetration with the intention of subverting the government and socialist system through controlling Chinese religions. However, 'normal' contacts with 'pure' foreign religions, such as developing relations between Buddhists in non-Marxist Taiwan and those in China, the source of Taiwanese Buddhism, are now permitted. More and more compatriots in Taiwan return to the mainland to 'look for their foundations', to 'pay homage to their ancestors', and many other activities associated with ancestor temples. Most of these activities have been acknowledged to be friendly intercourse among people.

Early in 1994, two separate sets of regulations on religious activities were issued by the State Council – Regulations on the Management of Places of Religious Activities in the PRC and Regulations on the Management of Foreign Persons' Religious Activities in the PRC. Publicity proclaimed them to be the first step towards national legal regulation of religion. Despite their all-China character, both sets of regulations provide nothing substantively new. In clearly placing the powers of control in the hands of local administrative organs, questions of religious freedom and its scope are removed from possible legal and judicial supervision.

There remain physical and psychological impediments to the implementation of the party's religious policy. The response of believers has been tentative partly because of reluctance to display their faith for fear of exposing themselves to future discrimination and persecution. Not all property of religious organisations has been restored, some sites lying idle or used only for tourism. Lack of financial resources and of official recognition of titles to leadership contributes to lack of confidence in the beneficial effects of the current policy. Conversion of a minute number of party members has also been interpreted in some quarters as entering into rivalry with the party.

Confucian practitioners

Immediately after 1949, Confucianism was subject to much oppression, while during the Cultural Revolution, anything that gave Confucianism a manifest religious quality was vandalised or destroyed. Confucius's tomb was desecrated, an ultimate expression of contempt in Chinese eyes.

Since that time, however, there has been a revival of Confucianism and its ceremonies and rites in China. The 'Anti-Confucius Campaign' was officially discredited under Deng Xiaoping, and during the last decade, Qufu (where Confucius lived) has been restored. Even though restoration is undoubtedly directed at attracting tourism, large numbers of Chinese tourists are also visiting the town and taking part in elaborate memorial services.

Taoists

Taoism – which has a political tradition characterised by rebellion – was condemned in the Cultural Revolution as a 'magical' and 'superstitious' cult. Today, religious Taoism, in one form or another, is practised by millions of people distributed over south-central China, south-east China and the Tuchia, Chuang, Paonan, Puyi, Mulam, Ching, She, Miao and Korean national minorities. Many of the old beliefs and practices still exist in China and temples have been reopened, including the huge White Cloud Temple in south-west Beijing, with twenty priests and 5,000 volumes of Taoist literature.

However, Taoists are deprived of a sense of community, having few overseas connections and their lineal Heavenly Master living in Taiwan. An official religious association has been established and one of the Heavenly Master's family (not a direct descendant) is being trained as a priest with the support of the government. There were reports in the 1980s of some Taoists being imprisoned and executed for attacking the prevailing political order.

Chinese Mahayana Buddhists

During the Cultural Revolution, Buddhist temples were closed or destroyed, monks were imprisoned or frightened into secular life, and other forms of persecution were carried out. Today, China's tens of millions of Mahayana Buddhists live mainly in central-south China, south-east China and Tibet. Restoration of temples and monasteries has been undertaken; there are now over 2,200 temples and academies in use, many also used for tourism. There is also considerable publishing activity and an extensive Buddhist library.

Any man or woman over 18 years wishing to become a Buddhist monk or nun must have parental permission and must be accepted by an 'approved' institution. Monks and nuns are required to wear normal attire when in the streets and are urged to participate in 'productive labour'. The amount of freedom Buddhists enjoy varies according to local authorities and disparity in Chinese Buddhist Association (CBA) supervision.

However, there are still restrictions on Buddhists. They must be members of the 'patriotic' church (CBA), which is pledged to cooperate with the government's religious policy and support 'socialist modernisation'. Buddhism does have international links but the CBA has been used by the government to promote political goals abroad.

Muslims

Islam in China has always been intricately linked with issues of nationalities and territoriality. Constituting between 40–60 million people, Muslim national minorities are a power group in China – one-fifth of its minorities – and have a history of defending their own culture.

From 1949–64, Muslims were severely persecuted for their religion, their cultural practices were attacked and whole villages were annihilated. During the Cultural Revolution, there was further insurrection, persecution and destruction of mosques. Even after the Cultural Revolution, open repression did not stop immediately. In 1977, 1,200 Hui people were killed in an uprising against religious persecution. Because ill-treatment of Muslims during the Cultural Revolution brought strong criticism from Muslim states, the Chinese government has been less harsh on them than it has been on other religious groups. Chinese Muslims have over the years made important contacts with the global Pan-Islamic movement, especially in the Arab world. Likewise, Muslim populations are concentrated in strategic border areas and resource-rich areas of economic importance.

Of China's over 50,000 houses of worship, most are mosques in active use. Since 1978, mosques in rural areas have been allowed to handle their own religious activities. Travel to Mecca is allowed, with more than 1,000 Chinese going each year for the last seven years. Islamic texts are printed in China and young men engage in Islamic studies. Muslims are allowed separate cemeteries and holidays during major religious festivals. There are 240 Muslim restaurants in Beijing alone. Muslim groups may use their own spoken and written language, may develop their own culture and education system and have developed their own media and publications. Muslim populations have also been given more political autonomy in recent years.

Not all religious repression of Muslims has ceased. In Xinjiang, Qinghai and Ningxia for example, laws which forbade the religious education of youths under 18 and restricted the building of mosques were enacted in 1988. The Sufi movement has also been curbed because it has not limited its religious activities to officially prescribed places. In 1993, armed police put down a protest of 10,000 Muslims in Xining, Qinghai, over a children's book which showed a pig next to a praying Muslim. Mosque officials are required to cooperate with the government through the Chinese Islamic Association. Muslim militancy in the border state of Xinjiang fuels government fears of secession.

Roman Catholics

From 1949, Catholicism was identified with Western imperialism. Regulations were enacted to rid China of foreign missionaries, to sever foreign control of missions and to cut off funding from foreign sources. Priests, nuns and prominent Catholic lay people were imprisoned, nuns were forced to marry or become servants; missionaries were tried as spies, and foreign bishops and Catholic officials were required to resign or leave. For millions of Chinese the alternative to splitting with Rome was to go underground. Since the 1950s, underground churches have flourished in clandestine meeting-places.

Meanwhile, the official Chinese Catholic Patriotic Association (CCPA) was established, under duress, in 1953. Chinese Catholics who wish to call themselves so must belong to the CCPA. Those priests who refuse to join the Patriotic Association are forbidden to practise as priests. The boundaries of the dioceses in four provinces were changed in order to correspond with those of the civilian administration; any areas which did not have 'patriotic' bishops were given government-appointed 'heads of dioceses'.

Catholics living during the Cultural Revolution experienced much the same treatment as people of other religious denominations. Churches were destroyed, vandalised, closed down, artefacts were stolen or defaced, public worship was forbidden and more priests and nuns were imprisoned. After the Cultural Revolution, priests were released but were forbidden to practise and were still subject to constant surveillance.

In recent times, there have been improvements for Chinese Catholics to some extent. Hundreds of churches have been reopened or renovated and the text of the mass in Chinese, religious books and holy pictures are now available. A Catholic seminary has been set up in Shanghai, and since 1989, there have been over twenty guest lectures, given by foreign theologians. There are also teachers from overseas, and students are permitted to spend time overseas. The faithful in some areas have even been invited to solicit foreign funds for the rebuilding of churches, and in a few instances, priests openly faithful to Rome have said mass in public and received no reprimand. Masses have been said by foreign priests in recent times, despite official pronouncements forbidding this.

However, priests in the 'patriotic' church and seminaries undergo constant political indoctrination. China's Catholic population rarely agree with the fact that the CCPA accepts without question the government's directives on such matters as marriage, divorce, abortion and contraception. Secrecy and dissatisfaction have led some priests to refuse to hear confessions of people they do not know for fear they are government informers. Likewise, many Catholics hesitate to make confession to priests who are known to have collaborated with the government.

Repression has not stopped in the last decade. An 'illegal' Catholic seminary was accused in 1986 of loyalty to the Vatican; nuns were sexually assaulted when it was raided. There are also reports that Catholics and other Christians are being arrested in order to fill arrest quotas, alleged crimes including the holding of unauthorised church services and possessing Bibles which are not official publications. The legitimate Catholic Bishop of Shanghai, Gong Pin Mei – arrested in September 1958 and condemned to life imprisonment in 1960 on charges of being a 'counter-revolutionary' – was released in 1985 after much foreign protest, and then placed under house arrest. Since 1981, there has been a constant stream of arrested or imprisoned priests and there are also known cases of torture of priests. In 1993, six Catholics were tortured under interrogation by Public Security Bureau officials after a raid on a house in Fujian province where 250 youths were attending a class on religion and human quality.

These forms of repression have resulted in only 2–3 per cent of professed Catholics in Chinese cities frequenting the official churches, the underground movement absorbing the rest. In the countryside, especially in the north-west and some areas of the south-west, however, Catholics have an open and vigorous Christian life, travelling more than 100 kilometers to hear the mass of a foreign priest. Tourists to China note priests going around carrying small paper kits containing essentials for the Eucharist; villagers avoid compulsory abortions by arranging adoptions.

Protestants

Like Catholicism, Protestantism was seen as Western imperialism. Protestant priests and bishops were expelled if they were foreign or imprisoned if Chinese. When the PRC regime tried to strip Protestant leaders of credibility in their communities by setting them against each other, forty joined in a statement calling for cooperation with the government's goals of severing foreign relations and progress towards autonomy on Chinese soil. As a result, the churches became unable to survive financially without the support of the government.

The government policy was to unite all the Protestant churches in one denomination and in 1954 the Three-Self Patriotic Movement was established under the control of the state. Consequently, Chinese Protestantism became very rule-laden, overriding differences in teaching and practice among the churches and between the churches and the state. In 1980, a further organisation, the China Christian Council, was established to regulate the dissemination of Bibles, of publications and the training of new religious leaders. Compliance shielded Protestants from direct attack but churches were closed and children were questioned about their parents' activities and forbidden to attend Sunday school.

During the Cultural Revolution, all churches were closed down and the clergy were sent to factory jobs or farm work. However, the underground home gatherings became the mainstay of the Protestant Church, when several dozen million Chinese people attended clandestine church services and activities each week. When the Cultural Revolution ended, church properties were reclaimed and churches reopened but many Protestants had become accustomed to meeting in small groups. Unauthorised services are not permitted and some arrests have been made of Protestant house-gatherings. More young people are attending official places of worship, churches, bible classes and seminaries; the government has printed over a million copies of the Bible in four languages. The majority of 'meeting points' for Protestants – small, officially sanctioned groups (about 10,000) within communities – have joined the Three-Self committees.

Despite improvements for Chinese Protestants, many problems remain. In certain areas, the cadres of the state Religious Affairs Bureau do not allow Protestants to run their own affairs. The Three-Self Patriotic Movement itself has problems arising from its state origin but has, according to a report from a visit of the Council of Churches of Britain and Ireland, been engaged in rethinking its ideology in the context of today's greater partnership with the West.

The underground rural groups – although numerically stronger – are weaker than those groups which are officially approved. Cadres in some areas forbid youths under 18 to practise religion and actively police the underground movement. There is a shortage of trained ministers, and 'propaganda material' from Hong Kong or Macau, used by the underground groups, is confiscated whenever it is discovered.

Tibetan Mahayana Buddhists

The first recorded relations between Tibet and China were in the seventh century, when Tibet was made a tributary relation of both the Ming (1368–1644) and the Qing (1644–1911) Dynasties, although it maintained substantial independence. These early tributary relations provide the basis for modern Chinese claims to sovereignty over Tibet.

Tibetan Mahayana Buddhism combines the indigenous belief of Tibet with aspects of Buddhism introduced from India in the ninth century and later from Han territories. As well as lamas, there were many lay monks and nuns. Culture, religious practice and tradition combined in a depth of connection between religion and government which made Tibet vulnerable to exploitation. It was a hierarchical and harsh place to live for most Tibetans; corruption and hardship existed there before the Chinese communist invasion in 1950. Since 1950, Han Chinese have been relocated in Tibet in their millions, thus consistently changing the country's ethnic composition.

Despite gradualist policies in the beginning of communist rule, the year 1956 saw the beginning of a period of active persecution: torture and execution of lamas, rape of nuns, destruction and looting of temples and monasteries. In 1959, the general populace rose up in revolt and during an attack by the Chinese army in which 65,000 Tibetans were killed, their leader – the Dalai Lama – fled to India. His administration was replaced by the Preparatory Committee of the Autonomous Region of Tibet. By 1966, through persecution, neglect and destruction, the number of monasteries and religious personnel had been drastically reduced and many monks and nuns returned to secular lives.

During the early 1960s, the Chinese established a military apparatus to manage the affairs of monasteries and to control all religious expression. There were public trials, involving several beatings and coerced confessions of 'crimes', often ending in public execution. In the Cultural Revolution, many of the surviving monasteries and their libraries were damaged or destroyed and the already small number of practising monks and nuns further reduced. All religious activity and dress was strictly banned. The Dalai Lama was attacked in the official media. Destruction of the monastic system lowered education standards for monks; a Chinese education system was substituted.

After the Cultural Revolution, some of the monasteries were restored, principally for tourism purposes. Monks have to be approved by the Chinese Committee of Religious Affairs and are controlled by Democratic Management Committees (accountable to the local authorities) in each monastery instead of the traditional hierarchy.

In 1987, the Dalai Lama pushed for Tibet as a zone of peace and for an end to human rights violations. Tibetan monasteries and monks have called for an end to the Chinese occupation, taking their case to the United Nations and demonstrating in Tibet. Nationalist uprisings in 1987 and later years have been put down with violence, torture and executions; monks not in prison were 're-educated'.

Official Chinese statistics and those of Tibetans compiled on the basis of a wider area than the Tibetan Autonomous Region place the Tibetan population at 3–6 million. Since China invaded Tibet in 1950, over 1 million Tibetans have died – one-fifth of the Tibetan population – over 6,000 monasteries have been destroyed and an estimated US$80 billion in precious metal, religious artefacts and statuary has been extracted.

Dissidents in Tibet – usually involved in moves for independence – live in fear of the People's Liberation Army, the Public Security Bureau, and the People's Armed Police, all of which can enforce detention or prison terms for expressions of political opinion. Tibetan monks are among the many political prisoners. In 1989, a group of monks was sentenced to nineteen years' imprisonment for producing a Tibetan language version of the Universal Declaration of Human Rights. Detention orders for 're-education through labour' are issued by public security officers outside the judicial process and cannot be appealed to a court of law.

Those monks not in prison have to be constantly on guard. Local cadres continue to interfere with religious practices which are only allowed in designated places of worship. Religious gatherings or organisational activities beyond state control are not allowed. When the local population attempts to rebuild temples, they are arrested.

Underground opposition to the government is based in monasteries and temples. In 1994–95, Chinese authorities, besides closing down monasteries, attempted to reduce the independence movement by introducing regulations to limit the number of monks and nuns, to expel lamas from monasteries where there are 'too many', and not to replace them when they die. The authorities' preference is for monasteries to be headed by 'patriotic and law-abiding monks' and not by reincarnated lamas chosen by traditional divination. The regulations also severely discourage other traditional Tibetan religious practices such as spending a period as a lay monk or nun attached to a monastery or temple and supporting living Buddhas through donations. Some fourteen young Buddhist nuns in prison in Lhasa who sang songs about the Dalai Lama, alluding to the return of their spiritual leader, were recently reported to have been condemned to nine more years' imprisonment. Around 800 political prisoners are reported to be held in Tibet in 1996.

Most Tibetans do not accept the distinction the PRC draws between the permitted 'normal religious activities' and the prohibited political expression in the name of religion. The Dalai Lama symbolises both political and spiritual power and is still revered by the Tibetan population, although they are not allowed to display his picture, especially in temples, schools and other public places; this ban has been openly defied. Chinese authorities claim that the Dalai Lama would retain his religious position, if the people wanted him and if he returned to China. However, in early 1995 the Dalai Lama called for a referendum of Tibetans on independence for Tibet. In May 1995, the Dalai Lama announced that he had found the reincarnated successor to the Panchen Lama, who had died in 1989 in Beijing after many years under house arrest. Although the Chinese government had expressed its wish to help him in his search, the Dalai Lama used visions, dreams and omens in a spiritual quest, ending when he identified a 6-year-old boy in Tibet. The current tensions over the new Panchen Lama – the second most respected reincarnation in Tibetan Buddhism – have resulted in the disappearance of the child chosen by the Dalai Lama. Pro-Chinese Tibetans have been installed to run Tashilhunpo, the seat of the Panchen Lama in Shigatse, and a different child was enthroned there in December 1995 in a ceremony arranged by the state which involved senior monks in a ritual overseen by a top Communist Party official.

Customary beliefs and practices

Most minority ethnic customary religions feature worship of nature and ancestor gods. Perception of these gods has not changed much since ancient times, as gods, ancestors and ghosts are treated as real beings. When people go to temples they want sons, wealth, success and help in a practical sense. These beliefs play a vital part in the lives of millions of Chinese. The strong revival of traditional practices and festivals is related to the economic revival of China because these are occasions for great economic and social activity. The government takes a somewhat negative view of the festivals, possibly because it loses some direct power over economic affairs.

Women in religion and belief

The general outlook of all faiths and beliefs in China is ambivalent towards women. Strong patriarchal attitudes are obvious in the Confucian Analects and even as far back as 800 years before the common era, when texts explicitly compared the different celebrations for the birth of male and female children: 'For her no decorations, no emblems; her only care, the wine and food, and to give trouble to father and mother' (Shi Ching). Because the family is a sacred community, the miniature template of an ideal harmonious society reflecting Heaven, it is as mothers and wives that women achieved social status. However, it is important to note that, as in the complementarity and dynamism of yin and yang, male and female are not essentialised in China; all people are seen in relationship. However, the general association of the feminine with yin – the passive and yielding – is pervasive.

Although positions of power in all religions were reserved for males, many strong models for women emerged. Very early texts describing the 'Exemplary Woman' mention astuteness, benevolence, wisdom, moral excellence and intellect as well as the more usual virtues expected of women. Women were also the main practitioners of shamanism, divination and healing. Accounts of the lives of eminent women renunciants in Mahayana Buddhism in the fourth to the sixth centuries are preserved in texts and the Bodhisattva figure of Kuan-Yin as the embodiment of great virtue and power remains an inspiration wherever Chinese Buddhism has spread. It is significant that the 'Goddess of Democracy' in Tiananmen Square not only looked like the Statue of Liberty but also like a Kuan-Yin sculpture. It can be also be argued that the Confucian model with its requirements of discipline and respect for education and public service in some ways prepared women well for participation in the new Chinese state. Buddhist lay activities, especially by women, have increased in recent times: dharma assemblies, sutra chanting, meditation, elaborate home ceremonies and pilgrimage. Tibetan Mahayana Buddhism permits both men and women to become monks and nuns and there is a proud history of women saints and sacred feminine symbols. However, positions of power and monastic wealth have been in male hands.

The communist ideology incorporated women's participation, often to high office, even the Gang of Four. Many programmes were put in place to offer women equal participation in society, but not fully successfully, especially in the rural areas where the majority of the population resides. The implementation of the one-child family ideal has also meant enormous burdens for women, especially in view of the still pronounced preference for a male child.

In Catholicism, the CCPA tends towards Tridentine forms of worship and thus there is no talk of women's ordination although laywomen play many roles owing to the low numbers of priests. In recent years much more freedom has been allowed Catholics, including schools for training nuns.

Among Chinese Protestants, many older women act as preachers and prayer leaders and a new younger generation of women, some ordained, have just begun work in the parishes. Women are coming in large numbers to newly opened seminaries, one at Nanjing being founded and coordinated by a woman.

INDIA

India	
GDP (US$bn)	215
Population	884,400,000
Annual population growth (%)	2.2
Urban population (%)	26
Working population (%)	38
Literacy (%)	49.9
Ratifications	1; 2; 3; 4

India, with a population of 884.4 million, is the second most populous country in the world. It is a pluralistic, multi-ethnic, multi-religious, multi-cultural and multi-linguistic state with a substantial Hindu majority. The world's fifth largest economy, India began market liberalisation and structural reform in 1991. There are great inequalities in income distribution; 40 per cent of urban dwellers and 51 per cent in rural areas are extremely poor; half of India's people are illiterate.

Social composition

The basis of India's social structure is the very ancient economic and religious system of four classes – *brahmans, kshatriyas, vaishyas* and *shudras* – overlaid by a complex hierarchy of over 2,000 castes and many more sub-castes. From the lowest class (*sudras*) has devolved a large (about 200 million) group of 'outcastes', 'untouchables' or 'scheduled castes', whom Gandhi renamed *harijans*, but who prefer to be called *dalits*. These hierarchical divisions seem to be mainly economic in origin, linked to more or less socially significant employment. Religious sanction occurs in the way concepts of purity and pollution are used to indicate closeness to or distance from the 'sacred'.

India is also one of the few countries in the world where men outnumber women. This is not the process of natural selection. Despite the enactment of laws to improve the status of women in post-independent India, and ratification of the UN Convention on the Elimination of all Forms of Discrimination Against Women by India in 1992, the women of all religious communities are discriminated against. It is clear that religion is not the sole basis of sex discrimination and intolerance but is closely interwoven with a multitude of economic and political inequities.

Human rights groups estimate that at least 10,000 cases of female infanticide occur each year throughout the country. The source of this discrimination against girl children may be found at least partially in the value of a son for the wealth of the family and the spiritual welfare of the parents after death. In addition, the daughters of a family are only valuable for their contribution to the household before marriage. Marriage itself is costly for the bride's parents and may cost some brides their lives once they join their husband's family. Dowry deaths in India – 20,537 during 1990–93 – continue, despite government prohibition and the efforts of women's groups to overcome the practice.

Religious composition

India is the origin of several major world religions and others have established themselves over the centuries. There has been considerable interaction between their different world views, rituals and customs. Islam first came to India through Arab contact with the Malabar coast. In the eighth century, the Muslim conquest of Sind and Multan resulted in conversion through political pressure. Tradition has it that Christianity has flourished in south India from the first century. The arrival of the Portuguese on the Malabar coast in the fifteenth century brought conversions to Roman Catholicism, and with British rule from the eighteenth century, converts to Christianity increased.

There are eight main religious communities in India: Hindus (82.7 per cent of the population of which 15 per cent were formerly untouchables), Muslims (11.8 per cent), Christians (2.6 per cent), Sikhs (2 per cent), Buddhists (0.7 per cent), Jains (0.5 per cent), Zoroastrians (0.3 per cent) and Jews (0.1 per cent). The indigenous peoples (*adivasis*), whose beliefs, rituals and resources are uniquely associated with their ancestors and the forest, constitute 7.8 per cent of the population (60 million). While many indigenous people have a close affinity with Hindus, sizeable groups have converted to Christianity and some to Islam.

Sub-divisions based on doctrinal differences and details of ritual add to the complexity of Hinduism. Some divisions of Hinduism, such as Kabirpanth, Satnami, Lingayats, the Brahmo Samaj and Arya Samaj, have claimed to be separate religions but are usually regarded as variants of Hinduism. Buddhism, Jainism and Sikhism – which emerged as distinct from Hinduism – are considered by Indian state and society to be assimilable to Hinduism.

In other religions, Muslims are divided broadly into Sunnis and Shias, the Jains into two major sects and the Christians into Roman Catholics and Protestants of various denominations. Atheists, agnostics and rationalists have followings in India as do new religious movements, some of which originated there.

Political structure

India has a political system of federated states and territories. The Union Government sits in New Delhi and the national parliament is bicameral. The constitution describes India as a 'sovereign socialist secular democratic republic'.

The British colonial policy of 'divide and rule', in which the power-elites of some Indian communities were also complicit, shaped the behaviour and attitudes of the people of India today through significant policies and events. These include the partition of Bengal in 1905, the introduction of separate electorates for Muslims in 1909 – extending by 1932 to so-called untouchables, Sikhs, Europeans, Indian Christians and Anglo-Indians – and the partition of India itself in 1947, leading to the creation of Pakistan. Institutions and politics based on religious difference are considered at least partly responsible for communalising Indian society and its polity and for the persistence of intolerance and religious hatred.

Three kinds of ideological groups and political parties can be identified: liberal–democratic, Marxist and communist, and religious revivalist. People of many different religions can be found in all political parties except for rightist ideological groups affiliated with particular religious adherents: Hindus, Muslims and Sikhs. Communal parties or organisations have long been established in India: the Muslim League (1906), the Hindu Mahasabha (1907), the Rashtriya Swayamsevak Sangh (RSS, 1925), Bharatiya Jan Sangh (1951), Jamaa-e-Islami-Hind (1941) and Akali Dal (1920s).

The number of Hindu politico-religious groups has increased in recent years, among them the Bharatiya Janata party (BJP, which emerged in 1979 from the earlier Bharatiya Jan Sangh), Shiva Sena (Shiva's Militia), and cultural groups like Vishva Hindu Parishad

(VHP) and Bajrang Dal. Like the RSS, these groups believe in the establishment of a Hindu *rashtra* (state) and their leaders demand that minorities assimilate to Hindu culture and language, revere Hindu religion and glorify Hindu 'race' and culture. The role of women in supporting and inciting communalism is often unrecognised; many such groups have set up their own women's wings. Revivalism has sought legitimacy in recalling a Vedic 'golden age' of women's equality while not challenging male power.

Some Sikh and Muslim parties also use religion as their identity. The Indian Muslim League, a political party, is active mainly in Kerala and the Akali Dal is a Sikh political party confined to the Punjab. Among Muslims the only militant group is the Islamic Sevak Sangh (ISS) of Kerala, now banned. No other religious group has organised itself politically.

The Indian Council of Indigenous and Tribal Peoples was formed in 1987 and is affiliated to the World Council of Indigenous People. The Indian government has consistently taken a position in UN forums that *adivasis* (indigenous peoples) in India do not constitute indigenous populations. The 'national interest' is often used as the rationale for displacement of indigenous peoples from their traditional lands to allow for industrial development or the building of dams. There have been many insurgent and separatist movements in indigenous areas of the north-east region.

Protective discrimination law also reserves 7.5 per cent of government jobs and education places for *adivasis* for whom seats are also reserved in the national parliament and state assemblies.

In 1996 the long ascendancy of the Congress Party came to an end. The Hindu nationalist Bharatiya Janata Party, however, proved unable to form a working majority and was succeeded in government by the United Front, a centrist-left coalition supported by religious minorities and lower caste Hindus and Muslims. A ten-year programme of reforms proposed by the new government includes reserving for women a third of both parliamentary seats and government jobs, reforming laws which discriminate against women and eliminating illiteracy and poverty.

Legal system and constitutional guarantees

India is a common law country whose constitution contains detailed provisions on the protection of rights. The courts have power to declare invalid any laws passed by the parliament or state assemblies if they contravene the constitution.

The Indian state is secular in the sense that is it meant to treat all religions equally and keep its distance from every one of them. The former President of India, Dr Radhakrishnan, noted that in India 'secularism is not a positive religion or the state assumes divine prerogatives. We hold that no religion should be given preferential status.' Article 51A of the constitution imposes a positive duty on citizens 'to promote harmony and the spirit of common brotherhood amongst all people of India transcending religious, linguistic and regional or sectional diversities; to renounce practices derogatory to the dignity of women' but even harmful neglect of this 'positive duty' is not challengeable in the courts.

The right to freedom of thought, conscience and religion is included in the constitution and other legal codes. Article 25 of the constitution guarantees not only freedom of conscience, free profession and practice of religion, but also the right to propagate religion. Article 25(2b) provides that the state can make law for social welfare and reform or the opening of Hindu religious institutions of a public character to all classes and sections of Hindus. Buddhists, Jains and Sikhs are treated as 'Hindus' for the purposes of this provision and for other legal purposes, including the application of personal laws. Though Jains have not objected to this, Buddhists, especially neo-Buddhists (converts from low caste Hindus) have expressed disagreement. Sikhs have strongly protested; Akali Dal members publicly burned copies of the constitution in New Delhi in the 1980s.

The freedom to manage religious institutions and their property is constitutionally guaranteed (Article 26). Aid may be provided by the state as long as it is non-discriminatory while individuals are guaranteed freedom as to payment of taxes for promotion of any particular religion (Article 27).

Though India is a secular country in many aspects, it is not so in all. Article 48 makes it obligatory to prohibit the slaughter of cows and other cattle. Although this provision has never been implemented, cows remain a sacred Hindu symbol.

Article 28 stipulates that no religious instruction shall be provided in any wholly state-funded educational institution. Also prohibited is the imposition of religious instruction or worship on anyone attending an educational institution recognised by the state or receiving state aid, without the individual's consent or the parent's or guardian's if the student is a minor. The customary and codified personal laws of different communities also provide for the liberty of children to develop their own religious convictions.

Articles 29 and 30 of the constitution protect the cultural and educational rights of minorities. Any section of the citizenry with a distinct language, script or culture of its own has the right to conserve it. No-one can be denied admission into any educational institution, maintained by the state or receiving state aid, on the grounds only of religion, race, caste or language. Article 30 guarantees to minorities, both linguistic and religious, the right to establish and administer educational institutions. The state cannot discriminate against such institutions either in granting recognition or providing aid.

The Supreme Court has jurisdiction regarding conflict of law cases and cases that raise constitutional issues, such as those involving the human rights guarantees. In the influential Srirur Math case in 1954, concerning Hindu religious endowments, Justice B. K. Mukerjee set out the concept that a 'practice' or set of beliefs must not only exist but must be 'essential' to that religion, in order for it to be defined as one for constitutional purposes. The enormous variety of Indian culture and social situations is presented in case law and the judicial record on this issue alone is marked by variability.

Courts have also been criticised for expanding limitations and marginalising rights, thus allowing increasing state incursions on the autonomy of religious institutions, particularly in the area of public order. Almost any religious activity is subject to control because of enlarged concepts of secular management, public order, morality and health.

Owing to international criticism of India's human rights record, and to domestic pressure, the central government established a National Human Rights Commission in 1993. However, its capacity to act on allegations of human rights abuse is not unrestricted; for instance, other legislation prevents it investigating allegations against the armed forces.

Penal Code

The Indian Penal Code lists offences relating to religion, such as injuring or defiling places of worship with intent to insult the religion of any class, disturbance of religious assemblies and utterances intended to wound the religious feelings of others. Laws from the colonial era prohibit such religious practices as sacrifice of human beings, sacrifice of animals in a way deleterious to the well-being of the community at large, the practice of immolating a widow at the pyre of her deceased husband (*sati*) and the dedication of a young virgin girl as a *devadasi* (temple prostitute).

The Religious Institutions (Prevention of Misuse) Ordinance makes it an offence to use any religious site for political purposes or to use temples for harbouring persons accused or convicted of any crime. Although specifically designed to deal with Sikh places of worship in the Punjab, the ordinance technically applies to all religious sites. However, restrictions have not been placed on Sikh religious practices or on the management of their places of worship.

Personal laws

First the colonial government and then the Indian government enacted legislation covering the area of customary personal law. In the nineteenth century, this legislation reflected Brahman customary law, rather than local and lower-caste interpretations, resulting in new restrictions for many women. In some areas, such as Kerala State, the colonial government's laws were frequently enacted to abolish or reform what were considered the 'backward' or 'feudal' practices of a conquered nation. The men involved in the national movement opposed the demand of the All India Women's Conference to change the Hindu code in the areas of marriage, divorce and inheritance. The colonial government had been apprehensive about stirring communalist reactions if a uniform civil code were to be introduced and the current Indian state has also adopted a policy of non-intervention in the name of secularism or rights of minorities.

Before the promulgation of the constitution in 1949, Hindu personal law had its main impact on women in terms of lack of property and inheritance rights, permitted child marriage, lack of the right to adopt children, and (as widows) to be guardians of their own children, although limited rights in some areas were established by the colonial government. The 1956 Hindu Succession Act and other legislation removed some, but not all disabilities in relation to marriage, divorce, adoption and guardianship. The success of this legislation in changing actual practice has been limited in the majority Hindu population (including other religious communities subsumed into Hinduism for legal purposes).

Muslim personal law remains separate and distinctive for that community. The recognition of personal religious laws, intended as equality of recognition of religious difference in the secular state, has caused many problems recently for Muslim women. Muslim intellectuals have a long history of enabling the adjustment of Islamic personal law to socio-economic change, but the disempowerment of Islam in India after partition has reversed even this process.

In the Shah Bano case (1985), in which a divorced Muslim woman asked for reinstitution of maintenance payments ceased by her former husband, the Supreme Court upheld her right, quoting from the Qur'an without reference to Muslim scholars, and even recommending a uniform civil code, something which would have an impact on personal laws. Previous Supreme Court maintenance settlements for Muslim women had not been challenged, but because of the use of the Qur'an, the Shah Bano case was used by all political groups to debate the status of the Muslim minority community. Muslim conservatives stressed community fears of the loss of freedom of religious practice.

Finally, the government yielded to pressure and, without consultation, passed the Muslim Women's (Protection of Rights in Divorce) Act (1986) which granted less generous rights to women than prescribed by the Qur'an and Islamic jurisprudence. Worse, Muslim women are now precluded from the purview of Section 125 of the Criminal Procedure

Act which had originally protected Shah Bano. Specific requirements of the new Act also make it much more likely that a Muslim woman will be required to conduct a court case in order to obtain any maintenance at all.

The same kind of confusion operates in relation to divorce for Muslim women. The 1939 Dissolution of Muslim Marriages Act outlined liberal provisions, based on Islamic jurisprudence, for women to initiate divorce, a restoration of ancient rights eroded over time. But the 1956 Hindu Code Bill introduced a legal differentiation between Hindu and Muslim women and left intact provision for unilateral divorce by males only, as well as polygamy, however rarely it is practised. Such has been the increasing pressure by conservative Muslim leaders to stress community uniqueness that, in 1993, the All-India Muslim Personal Law Board upheld the privilege of unilateral divorce initiated only by the husband. In 1994, the Allahabad High Court in Uttar Pradesh ruled that this type of divorce was unconstitutional. These matters are unlikely to be resolved as long as the perceived need to assert minority differentiation at the expense of women's needs and rights continues.

Christians remain an anomalous group in relation to matters of marriage and divorce. In addition, they are legally excluded from the Hindu Code Bill provisions. Under the Indian Divorce Act 1869, it is virtually impossible for a Christian woman to seek divorce from her husband even if she is mistreated or deserted; men may divorce for adultery, but not women. In Kerala State, however, the High Court held the Act unconstitutional and allowed a Christian woman to divorce for any one of the grounds of cruelty, desertion or adultery. Until an amendment is passed at the national level, Christian women will not have the same rights in divorce as Hindu, Muslim and Parsee women. Zoroastrian (Parsee) women and men may apply for divorce before a jury of ten assessors from the Parsee community. Community tensions today have resulted in religious–personal law being used politically for establishing identity in terms of power and survival. Women have always had to carry the burden of specific cultural practices as markers of difference. These 'traditions' can be very differently interpreted, and even artificially rigidified, under the tension of political and economic exploitation.

Proselytising

Conversion has been an issue since colonial times. Hindu revivalism has focused opposition on Christian missions. Under the Hindu Code Bill, conversion in effect cuts off material and financial support and inheritance rights which would normally flow from being a member of a Hindu family. The impact is more severe in the case of women. Under the Hindu Succession Act 1956, none of the convert's children or their descendants would be entitled to inherit the property of any of their Hindu relatives.

Minority religions of non-Indian origin received an unpleasant surprise when the Supreme Court decided in 1977 that the constitutional right to propagate religion did not mean a right to convert any person to one's own religion. In 1992, there were 1,611 foreign missionaries in India, their entry barred to some of the north-eastern states. Former untouchables often convert to escape caste persecution. Indian religious organisations are allowed to maintain communications with co-religionists abroad but financial contributions from overseas are subject to scrutiny and licensing by the Ministry of Home Affairs.

From time to time unsuccessful attempts have been made to introduce bills in the national parliament restricting conversions of *dalits* and indigenous peoples to other religions, especially Christianity and Islam. However, Orissa State Assembly passed the Freedom of Religion Act 1969 and in 1978 Arunachal Pradesh State passed a similar Act which Christians and Muslims thought was directed specifically against them, as it ruled against converting but not against 'reconversion' to Hinduism. Through the *shudhi* (purification) movement, which started in the 1930s, Muslims and Christians may be reconverted to Hinduism. In November 1992, 2,000 Christians demonstrated in Ahmadnagar (near Bombay) to protest against the Shiva Sena's attempt to convert hundreds of Christians to Hinduism.

Most of the bills restricting conversion were aimed at preventing the use of force, inducement or fraudulent means in conversion but, in effect, they restrict the general practice of religious propagation. Roman Catholic and Protestant churches have worked together to counter these bills at national and local levels.

The restrictions have had an impact primarily on Islam and Christianity. When, for instance, Orissa authorities refused permission for Baptist missionaries from the USA to hold a faith-healing session in Badapada in May 1995, on the grounds that they might try to convert indigenous peoples, Orissa people protested and in the subsequent melee, ten missionaries were arrested as well as local Baptist organisers.

The role of Christian communities and orders in education and social welfare – Christian hospitals and schools are popular with Hindu families – has been associated by some with pressure to convert. In 1995, a Catholic nun was stabbed on a bus in Bhopal and 2,000 bishops and nuns were reported as having marched in protest.

Intolerance within and between religious groups

Although untouchability is not simply a religious phenomenon, discrimination on the basis of caste in Hinduism is associated with the concepts of purity and pollution, is strengthened by religious sanctions and has implications for a person's spiritual life. Increasingly since independence, positive discrimination quotas have operated for variously disadvantaged caste and religious groups. This has empowered many, but has also had the contradictory effect of making identity politics important; hence difference and competition between groups for economic advantage undermine communal cooperation.

The gradual establishment of a hereditary group of virtual slaves burdened with the most 'degrading' employment in society, even lower than the serving class of *sudras*, occurred during the first millennium of the common era. Although untouchability has been legally abolished and temples have been thrown open to former untouchables, the national parliament was informed in 1994 that more than 62,000 cases of atrocities against untouchable and indigenous people (52,534 and 9,579 respectively) were registered between 1991–93. Violence enacted by high-caste Hindus and the state police and bureaucracy includes the burning of *dalit* villages, rape, torture, murder and deaths in custody. *Dalits* are the poorest of the poor: 86.6 per cent of India's bonded labourers and 90 per cent of its child labourers.

In 1988, the bishops of Tamil Nadu noted that *dalit* Christians (about 60 per cent of Indian Christians), even after conversion, continued to suffer from segregation and violence. Within the Catholic Church, caste discrimination is practised through segregation in seating in church, reception of the sacraments, eating together, restriction of permitted marriage and funeral procession routes. *Dalits'* bodies remain outside the church for funeral rites and intermarriage with non-*dalits* is forbidden.

Despite India's history of reasonable tolerance of inter-religious difference and Gandhi's gift of the philosophy of non-violence (*ahimsa*) to the world, some Brahman and Muslim elites have in the past fostered violence on religious and other grounds. This problem has become dangerously widespread in recent decades. Inter-community violence has been practised on an unprecedented scale, especially between Hindus and Muslims and Hindus and Sikhs. The causes are rarely religious matters alone, but are complex knots of economic, political and religious discrimination. Some politico-religious organisations have misused popular religious sentiment for political gain. Although people of all communities have suffered, the minority religions may be said to have carried pro-portionally the greater burden.

Thousands of communal riots have occurred since independence, but since 1989 the scope and intensity of the violence have greatly increased. Many Sikhs died in the New Delhi riots following the assassination of Indira Gandhi in 1984. Hindu–Muslim riots include, in recent years, the Bhagalpur riots in 1989, Aligarh in 1990, Meerut in 1987 and the post-Babri Mosque demolition riots all over India in 1992 which left 1,200 dead and 4,000 seriously injured.

Actions provoking intolerance include confrontative electioneering and the setting up of quasi-religious structures paralleling the secular. A BJP 1991 election manifesto stated that if it came to power it was committed to the construction of the Ram temple by relocating the Babri mosque, while election slogans of the BJP–Shiva Sena coalition stated that 'Muslims have only two abodes – Pakistan or graveyard'. In the 1980s, a *dharam sansad* (religious parliament) was established by Hindu rightist organisations and in response, Muslim extremists established a *milli* (community) parliament in 1993.

In 1995 the Supreme Court ruled that speeches by Hindu supremacist Balasaheb Thackeray were intended to incite hatred between Hindus and Muslims, while in a second case, it rejected the BJP's challenge against a 1951 law barring politicians from seeking votes by appealing to religious sentiments. None the less, the Shiva Sena party continues to dominate politics in Bombay.

Sacred sites

Since 1991, the central government has taken certain legislative and executive steps to contain communal frenzy in disputes over sacred sites. After the VHP drew up a list of 3,000 mosques which they believe were constructed by demolishing temples during the era of Muslim rule, the Places of Worship Act 1991 was enacted to maintain the *status quo* of religious places as on 15 August 1947, the date of partition.

The Ram Janma Bumi-Babri Masjid was built in 1526 in Ayodya by a Moghul emperor. The site of the Babri mosque is said to be also the birthplace of Rama and is therefore significant to both Hindu and Muslim communities. Hindu devotees had worshipped near the disputed structure and, after 1949, the images of their deities had been placed within it – where devotees' worship continued – and even, after 1986, in the sanctum inside the shrine. Despite this, the mosque and the adjacent Ram chabutra were demolished by a communal mob on 6 December 1992. The central government then dismissed the BJP state government which had had the responsibility of defending the site from harm. The central government acquired adjacent land compulsorily for a Ram temple and a mosque. The statute allowing the government to acquire this specific religious property was found by the Supreme Court in 1994 to be constitutional on the ground of public order and not contrary to the constitution's secular and non-discriminatory principles.

Under the Unlawful Activities Prevention Act 1967, five communal organisations were banned in 1992, after the demolition of the Babri Mosque, although they are still active:

Bajrang Dal, VHP, RSS and the ISS; the ban on Jamaat-e-Islami Hind was later found to be unlawful. The central government also dismissed three more BJP state governments following the demolition of the mosque. The Supreme Court upheld this action, stating that under the constitution no party could simultaneously be a political party and a religious party.

In other incidents, the Hindu Munnani Community in Pondicherry, a former French colony, fomented unrest in 1994 to construct a Shiva temple at the site of the Immaculate Conception Cathedral which had been constructed in 1748 by French authorities. The Munnani people believe that this church was built by destroying a temple.

Management of religiously significant sites remains an issue. In 1995, half the members in the trust which controls the sacred Buddhist shrine, the Bodh Gaya temple (the place where the Buddha experienced enlightenment) were Hindu, one supporting the BJP. Buddhists have tried to secure an all Buddhist management. The former head of the trust, a VHP member, resigned as a result of Buddhist agitation which gained international prominence when monks from many parts of the world assembled in 1993 and demanded a change in the law. The non-Congress Bihar government supported their demand but failed to amend the trust statute before the end of its term of office. Furthermore, a report of the National Commission for Minorities, established in 1992, points out that despite the central government's taking over of the management of the Buddhist centre Nalanda Mahavihara at Patna, the centre and its buildings are in a state of neglect.

Discrimination, insurrection and disputed territory

In the Punjab, with each period of armed struggle by the Sikh religious minority since the partition of India in 1947, ever more repressive methods have been used by the central government to curb insurrection. Since the late 1970s, thousands of Sikh civilians have suffered at the hands of both armed opposition Sikh groups, and the police and security forces. The Temple of Amritsar (occupied by Sikh militants) was stormed by Indian troops in 1984; the Punjab has been under direct central government control since 1987. However, in 1996, after the deaths and disappearances of many thousands of civilians, terrorism is reportedly on the wane in the Punjab and the judiciary and the civil administration were said to be attempting to reclaim powers handed over to the police in previous years.

After independence, India was given limited control over the majority Muslim area of the Vale of Kashmir. As part of its 'duty of care' India undertook to conduct a referendum in which Kashmiris could determine their own political status in relation to India and Pakistan. This undertaking was not honoured. Lack of attention to the real problems involved and simmering conflict with Pakistan from the 1960s eventually resulted in open violence in 1989 when the secular Jammu and Kashmir Liberation Front (which now advocates independence) exploded a bomb in Srinagar. The Muslim Hazratbal Shrine in Srinagar was stormed in 1982 and in 1993 a large Indian government force laid siege to it with much damage to religious objects. In May 1995, both the town of Chrar-e-Sharief and its fourteenth-century mosque, a holy Muslim shrine, were burned down on the Muslim feast of Id-ul-Zaha. Guerrillas had occupied the mosque for several months. Many Kashmiris protested, including one demonstration by thousands of women, despite a shoot-to-kill curfew.

Pro-Pakistan Hizbul-Mujahideen militants have conducted their cause with violence and thousands of civilians have died in police or security force custody, in 'encounter killings' or have disappeared. The Indian government has regarded Pakistan as aiming to destablise it and both governments have talked of war. In June 1996, the incoming coalition government under Deve Gowda indicated a new willingness to enter into talks with Pakistan, foreshadowing maximum autonomy for Kashmir and Jammu.

The Pakistan–India People to People Forum for Peace and Democracy met in New Delhi in 1995. The conference concluded that local religious minorities (Hindus in Pakistan, Muslims in India) became the targets for chauvinism because they were held responsible for acts of their co-religionists over the border and because of the legacy of traumatic memories of partition and current experience of violence. Ending hostilities would help to bring about a tolerant and just society, and entrenched myths and prejudices fuelling religious intolerance should be tackled through education and the social sciences.

Education

Under the constitution, the state is the major provider of education, free and compulsory until the age of 14. Minority religions' educational institutions have been upheld by the Supreme Court as part of their cultural and educational rights, within an overall view – held by the assimilative and the pluralist secularists among Supreme Court judicial opinion – that state regulation of education is in the interest of both minorities and the public as a whole.

Protection of language rights has been an issue for minorities. For instance, state-run schools do not provide education to Muslim children in the Urdu language. In north India, Muslim children are compelled to study in Hindi, which is becoming highly Sanskritised owing to the policy of states dominated by Hindu revivalist parties. The former BJP government in the north Indian state of Uttar Pradesh has also changed the contents of the school history textbooks to give a communal interpretation of Indian historical developments, such as the era of Muslim rule. An account of the controversy over the Ayodhya mosque and temple, for instance, reflects the interpretation favoured by Hindu revivalism.

In a case involving conscientious objection by a Christian group, the Supreme Court recently struck down the expulsion from school of three Jehovah's Witness students who refused to sing the national anthem although they stood in silence when it was sung.

The media

Radio and television are state-controlled but the press is not. The English press is by and large balanced towards all religions, except occasionally during communal riots. The vernacular press, which is read by the poorest people, is more biased against minority religions and publishes provocative – sometimes conjectural – accounts of communal violence; the radio and television can be similarly biased. Media expansion into rural areas has unsettled previously tolerant communities.

While between 1990 and 1992 most Indian newspapers sought to legitimise the communal politics of the BJP, there was a sudden shift in their attitude following the demolition of the Babri Mosque; it was characterised as an event of national shame because the whole world was watching India on overseas networks.

In 1994, the government of the southern state of Karnataka introduced Urdu-language news broadcasts. Hindus protested, Muslims threw stones at them and the police opened fire and killed or injured over 200 people. The Congress-led state accused the BJP of organising the protests to arouse Hindu–Muslim hostility before the elections; it then suspended the broadcasts.

Women and religion

The Hindu scriptures contain complex and ambiguous representations of women. The detailed prescriptions of the Law Books (Manusmriti: 200 years before the common era to the end of the first century) reveal misogynistic attitudes and recommend control of women by father, brother and husband to ensure the ideal of the stable family and society. In addition, menstruation and childbirth are considered polluting in a religious sense. However, the same scriptures state that 'where women are honoured, there the gods are pleased'. Similar ambivalence can be found in other scriptures and in Indian history where warrior queens, rebellious saints, poets and scholars, political heroines and oral traditions of powerful women's rituals stand against numerous (religious) social and personal restrictions in many areas of women's lives. The priesthood and control of important public rituals are restricted to males, and male children have sole responsibility for parts of the death ritual which affect a parent's after-life. Only male children of the three upper classes are eligible for initiation into full religious rights and the view that marriage is the initiation ceremony for women increases the pressure on all women to marry. Indian women scholars and activists have been working for some time developing new exegeses of scriptures and new analyses of the complex interactions between religious, political and economic pressures on women. The complications of minority and caste identity, which affect both men and women, are also examined.

Muslim men and women share equality in spirituality. Islam established rights of inheritance for women far earlier than other religious cultures, but in practice these rights are not upheld. Women are not admitted to leadership positions although Sufi female saint-gurus are exceptions. A *maulvi* (religious scholar) in Kerala, P. K. Mohammed Abdul Hasan disappeared in July 1993. He had aroused the opposition of extremist Muslims because of his progressive views, such as saying that there is no place in the Qur'an for discrimination against women.

The tradition of withdrawal (*purdah*) of women from public scrutiny is not a religious or Qur'anic injunction. To some extent *purdah* for women is found in all Indian religious groups and is strongly associated with higher class and income groups and particular regions. In recent times, it has been used as a cultural symbol and marker of a particular community.

Muslim women in India are particularly affected by Islam's status as a minority religion faced with hostility, and the reduced and damaged condition of the community as a result of the violence of the 1947 partition process. The 1956 Hindu Code Bill also made their legal status controversial; unlike their Hindu counterparts, they are excluded from legal parity with males in their community.

Sikh women have enjoyed a strong measure of religious equality since the formation of the Sikh religion in the fifteenth century. They did not number among the Great Gurus and the scriptures are determinedly masculine in origin and interpretation, but women served as missionaries, play an important part in ritual including preaching and formal reading of the scriptures, and are initiated into the Khalsa equally with men. Lineage is traced equally through both parents, and widows act as heads of their households and are free to remarry. Veiling and *purdah* are strongly discouraged.

However, as with the not quite successful effort to abolish caste distinctions within the Sikh community, these forms of equality are not guarantees of women's well-being, especially under present conditions in the Punjab. The pro-women ideals of Guru Nanak have been eroded by general cultural influences, the status of Sikhism as a minority religion intent on resisting reacculturation into Hinduism, and the emphasis on masculine exegesis of the scriptures. The restoration of these ideals is the aim of women scripture scholars in overseas Sikh communities.

Women in the Jain community enjoy relative equality in their spiritual lives, but are at the centre of an ancient contradiction which encourages them to enter fully into one Jain ascetic sect, but not the other. The 'quality' and character of women were indeed the central issue propelling this sect division and parts of the Jain scriptures reflect perhaps the worst aspects of the misogyny associated with asceticism in all cultures.

Christian women remain subject to ancient western forms of exclusion from priesthood and liturgy. Many (previously Hindu untouchable) Christian women suffer also from exclusions related to caste.

Marriage outside the religious community usually brings penalties, especially to women. Although Parsees have over the years fought against polygamy and child marriage customs which had crept in under Hindu and Muslim influence, they still discriminate against women in the matter of marriage outside the community. While a man's marriage to a non-Parsee involves no disgrace and his children are accepted as Parsees, the same right is not given to the Parsee woman who marries outside the community. Even her right to enter the Fire Temple is not accepted.

The fierce publicity and debate surrounding the case of Roop Kanwar – a young widow who was forced to commit *sati* in 1987 in Rajastan – highlights the fact that *sati*, which was never widespread in India, is very rare now. When it occurs it is likely to be a matter of horrific criminality presented artificially in a 'religious suicide' context to disguise a young widow's murder for various reasons, including deflection of inherited property outside the husband's family or threatened removal of grandchildren from the influence or care of the husband's family. A large number of people gathered to glorify Roop Kanwar's *sati* as a 'religious' event, although it was a criminal offence; all efforts to bring possible criminals to justice have failed.

INDONESIA

Indonesia	
GDP (US$bn)	126
Population	188,700,000
Annual population growth (%)	2.1
Urban population (%)	33
Working population (%)	43[a]
Literacy (%)	82.5
Ratifications	4

Indonesia's cultural and social diversity is legendary. The world's largest archipelago, consisting of over 20,000 islands, is also its fourth largest nation with nearly 190 million people. Two-thirds of Indonesians are ethnically Javanese, while the rest of the 360 groups come from a wide variety of peoples, ethnic and linguistic groups, each having its own language, cultural practices and traditions. To facilitate and encourage national unity, Indonesian independence leaders introduced Bahasa Indonesia as the national language.

Indonesians have always lived by farming and agriculture, but now urban trade, industry and the large services sector form the daily occupation of most Indonesians; almost all have attended primary school. The shift to the city has had important consequences for the political and religious life of this increasingly complex society. The gap between rich and poor, widening rapidly, causes much tension.

Religious composition

According to the latest census, 88 per cent of the population are Muslims and therefore Indonesia is now the most populous Muslim nation in the world. A large number of other faiths are also found in Indonesia and Christianity, Hinduism and Buddhism are expanding.

From the third century of the common era, first Hinduism then Buddhism established powerful kingdoms in Indonesia. Islam came in the fifteenth century from Malacca via trading routes from the west and spread unevenly through the archipelago. Christianity was introduced in the sixteenth century from the east through the colonising efforts of European trading groups. Many of the inland areas of the larger islands (including parts of Java) were Islamicised only in the last 200 years. Confucianism, Chinese Buddhism and Taoism were introduced through trading contacts with China. Christians now dominate the private sector economy, especially the ethnic Chinese minority who have been the target of intolerance.

Jews form the smallest of all religious communities in Indonesia. The larger Sikh community was established through migration from India and the small Baha'i community through migration from Iran. Indigenous traditions form a small but significant group; however, many traditional belief systems have been taken over in the past two centuries by either Islam or Christianity. Indonesian mystical religious traditions form another group known collectively as *kebatinan*; they mix some elements of earlier indigenous religious doctrines with elements of Hindu, Buddhist or Islamic beliefs, particularly Islamic Sufi beliefs.

Political and legal context

Although caught up in the dynamic economic development of a modern state, Indonesian politics are still in transition from the post-independence era. Indonesia is a republic based on a presidential system of government. The Indonesian armed forces (ABRI) remain intrinsically important to an authoritarian state fearful of instability; they are used primarily to ensure internal security. They have committed documented human rights abuses by extra-judicial killings, torture, intimidation and false arrest.

The president is the head of state, leader of the government and the executive. The judiciary is subordinate to the executive and the military. The doctrine of 'dual function' (*dwi fungsi*) guarantees the army a block of parliamentary seats and allows military officers to assume senior government posts. Since the early 1970s only three political parties have been permitted to function: the ruling government party (Golkar) and two other parties which are oppositional only in name. In 1996 the government backed a congress which supplanted Megawati Sukarnoputri as leader of the Indonesian Democratic Party and in August, the armed forces fired on 300 people protesting against her ousting.

An indigenous national legal system is a government reform priority, to replace the legacy of the former Dutch colonial administration. While there is some pressure to Islamise the national law, the legal system already incorporates Islamic family law; the Marriage Act 1974 is implemented through an Islamic religious court established in 1989.

Presidential decree has established a Human Rights Commission which began functioning in 1994 with a mandate to investigate specific cases and review laws contrary to human rights promotion and protection. It may publish its findings though its powers are limited. However, in June 1994, increased political openness and freedom of speech in the media were dealt a blow by the government's banning of the news and political journals *De Tik* and *Tempo*. The Minister of Information's right to ban *Tempo* was upheld in 1996 by the Supreme Court.

Even though the armed forces' security approach has not much changed, widespread condemnation of human rights abuses committed by the military and scrutiny by the National Human Rights Commission and the media have resulted in some greater sensitivity in handling issues likely to generate civil unrest. The armed forces have been warned by General Tanjung that soldiers found guilty of such abuses will be brought to justice, as happened in 1995–96.

After nearly three decades, there have been increasing speculation – and political challenges – concerning the changes which may accompany the end of Suharto's rule, including a greater role for civilian leadership and opposition parties. Prospects for restoring the mutual respect of people of different religions, beliefs and cultural traditions in Indonesia remain inseparably linked to the process of democraticisation – gaining freedom of speech, the rule of law and equality before the constitution. In the official view these advances can only be made through progress in economic development and the eradication of poverty. In July 1996, Abdurrahman Wahid, the leader of the at least 30-million-strong Nahdlatul Ulama (Indonesia's largest non-government, and Muslim, organisation) was among those signing a public petition entitled 'Back to Indonesian Dignity'. The document claimed that the current 'situation is false unity. It is totalitarian, oppressing and will not provide space for the creativity of people.'

Religion and state

While one section of the Muslim community believes that all links between party politics and religion must be severed and another argues that they cannot be separated, most are undecided. This contention goes back to the Sukarno era – just before the proclamation of Indonesia's independence at the close of the Second World War in 1945 – when the decades-old political tension between those who strove to establish a secular state and those who endeavoured to establish an Islamic state resulted in a compromise in the Jakarta Charter of August 1945. Pancasila was established as the national ideology of the Republic of Indonesia and a Ministry of Religion was formed to oversee religious life.

Pancasila refers to 'the five principles' which are the belief in the Oneness of God, humanity that is just and civilised, national unity, democracy guided by the wisdom of representative deliberation, and social justice for all. The national motto is 'Unity in Diversity'. The government of Indonesia claims that the republic is neither a religious nor a secular state because the policy recognises the theistic convictions of many Indonesians. The policy has only been championed with vigour since Suharto came to power in the mid-1960s. Indonesia's many religious organisations and other non-government organisations are required by the Social Organisations Law 1985 to acknowledge the Pancasila as being the basis of their ideology or be disbanded. Pancasila has had a normalising effect on the exposition of doctrine and structure; hence all the 'official' religions have creeds acknowledging a Supreme Being, prophets, sacred texts and congregational forms of worship, no matter what their origin and traditional forms.

Freedom of religion

Under the constitution each person may freely practise their faith or religion in accordance with their own convictions. Freedom of religion is officially acknowledged to be one of the most fundamental of all human rights, having its origin in the command of God himself. In theory, the government is not allowed to concern itself with the internal issues of a religion such as matters of theology, forms of religious ritual or religious institutions. Religion is acknowledged as being a matter of personal conviction which has its basis in the relationship between an individual and God. In government legislation the right of all religions to exist and function in society is respected regardless of whether they are acknowledged as 'official religions' or not. For instance, the Church of Scientology has experienced no difficulties in gaining registration.

Although religious tolerance in Indonesian society is well developed, its multifarious nature leads to some community tensions from time to time. The government Department of Religious Affairs contains separate Directorates-General of Guidance for the Muslim, the Protestant and the Catholic communities and a combined directorate for the Hindu and Buddhist communities. Independent mystical groups are also supported.

Departmental policy encourages internal harmony within each religious community, harmony between each of the religious communities, and harmony between the religious communities and the government. For instance, the government has supported the Islamic obligation to make a pilgrimage to Mecca by facilitating the attendance of Indonesian pilgrims: 160, 000 in 1994. Organisations have been developed within each official religious group to bring a focus to their religious endeavours and promote internal harmony. Together they form the Joint Working Council of Religious Communities which, while providing a forum for dialogue on matters of mutual interest, has in reality little power to develop religious harmony among Indonesia's various faith communities.

Religious vilification

Legal action may be taken against activities thought to vilify religion. The mass media is forbidden to broadcast items which may have the effect of disturbing religious harmony, under a public discussion code governing people, group, religion, race and inter-communal relations. In 1990, a popular youth magazine ran a 'tongue in cheek' article on a reader survey of most admired public figures; the Prophet Mohammed was ranked eleventh. When Muslims objected, the editor was prosecuted, imprisoned for five years and the magazine was banned. In 1996, communal rioting in Situbondo, East Java, broke out when the prosecutor of a man charged with insulting Islam sought a penalty seen as too lenient. Over twenty churches and a Buddhist temple were burned down and five people killed.

Majority–minority relationships and proselytism

Religion is closely tied to ethnic identity, and has clear political and economic links as well. The two religious communities most inclined to feel threatened are the Muslim majority and the Christian minority communities.

The majority Muslim community commonly regard the Christian community as busy trying to 'Christianise' Indonesian society. This is an extremely sensitive issue in which levels of suspicion are high. First, Muslims who feel this way are generally unable to differentiate between the mainstream Christian community and the evangelistic practices of small splinter groups and independent churches, of which the mainstream community is also critical.

Second, there is a general perception among parents, Christian or Muslim, that Christian schools offer better discipline and higher academic standards. In both Protestant and Catholic schools it is generally obligatory for non-Christian students to participate in religious education classes teaching Christianity. This situation has given rise to a campaign encouraging Muslims not to send their children to Christian schools. An Islamic system of education (including many specialist universities) runs parallel to the state system. Full-cover Islamic dress for girls' school uniforms is not allowed.

Third, because of the suspicion about proselytism, both Protestants and Catholics frequently encounter difficulties in obtaining official permission to erect new church buildings. Church groups must secure neighbourhood approval for a new building project before official permission to build is granted. Fourth, some demand that inter-religious marriages be prohibited, and that Muslims not attend Christian celebrations of any kind, including Christmas parties.

As a reaction to evangelistic Christianity, demand has been made for the Penal Code to include punishment of death for converts from Islam to another religion. This and other examples of Islamic formalism are proposed in public speeches around the nation as answers to allegations of the so-called 'superiority' of Christianity, but most reject the theory of a Christian conspiracy.

Mystical movements

The mystical movements known as *kebatinan* are generally regarded within mainstream circles as representing deviant belief in competition with 'true religion'. These groups teach mystical practices to enable practitioners to attain certain spiritual states. Initially the Department of Religious Affairs tried to supervise and guide the groups through the departmental apparatus, a move resisted by the *kebatinan*. Tension developed because a number demanded official status. The government eventually acknowledged their existence alongside the official mainstream religions but at the same time distingishes between them in day-to-day matters. For example, the *kebatinan* have been denied permission to conduct wedding ceremonies or funeral services.

Humanists and atheists

It is extremely difficult for humanists or those with no particular religious convictions, let alone atheists, to openly declare their positions in Indonesian society. Since the crushing of the attempted coup in 1965, in which all known communists were killed or imprisoned as were hundreds of thousands of alleged sympathisers, atheism became synonymous with communism. There were few worse things to be in New Order Indonesia than a communist. After 1965, most people who previously had no clear religious affiliation took steps to declare one and both Christianity and Islam suddenly gained a large number of new adherents. It became generally accepted that to be a citizen, one needed to be a religious person, no matter how nominal.

Identity cards include information about the religious affiliation of the holder and it is impossible to obtain an identity card without declaring affiliation to one of the 'official' religions. People without identity cards find it almost impossible to deal with government departments or educational institutions, let alone obtain government jobs. Every child enrolling at school must declare a religious affiliation.

Prohibition of organisations, teachings and practices

Mainstream followers of any given religion are generally convinced that their under-standing of their religion is the correct one and they regard understandings that differ from theirs to be heterodox and misguided, if not actually heretical. Majority orthodox believers sometimes pressure the government to ban, or otherwise legislate against, groups holding heterodox views which generally have originated from 'reform' move-ments. Their range is diverse, their number and extent of membership are considerable. Some are messianic, others sufistic or political but all set up barriers against the broader society.

In 1962, a Presidential Decree outlawed a number of organisations on the grounds that they were contrary to Indonesian culture, that they were contrary to the process of ongoing revolution and that they were opposed to the principle of Indonesian socialism. Included were the Baha'i religion, the League of Democracy, the Rotary Club, the Divine Life Society, Freemasonry, and Moral Rearmament.

In the following and recent years, up to 400 organisations have been prohibited, as well as their teachings, practice and literature, for a variety of reasons. Although a ban may have been applied solely to organisations, in practice it has been followed by banning of teachings and devotional practices. Many of these bans have come about through protests of other religious leaders who, in the name of the danger of social unrest, called for the banning of certain religious groups, understandings or organisations which they regarded as deviant.

Islam Jamaah is a small exclusivist Muslim group. Because of demands from orthodox Islamic leaders, this group and its teachings were officially prohibited in 1972. Its followers then formed Lemkari, or the Institute of Islamic Professionals, which was granted affiliation with the official government party, Golkar. Further violent reactions from some orthodox Muslims to the activities of Lemkari led to a second banning, followed by the forming of a new organisation under yet another name.

The Jehovah's Witnesses have been banned since 1976 because of their refusal to salute or give respect to the Indonesian flag. Since 1978 the prohibition also includes their teachings. Jehovah's Witnesses have been arrested, brought to trial, and many sentenced to prison. They continue to actively press the courts to review the government ban.

Dar'ul Arqam is an Islamic religious movement based in Malaysia. On the grounds that its teachings deviate from orthodox Islam, it was prohibited first in West Sumatra and Aceh in 1992, and then in 1994 the Minister for Religious Affairs and the National Council of Ulama called for its banning throughout Indonesia. There were mixed reactions to this among the Muslim community. The Nahdlatul Ulama declared that Dar'ul Arqam did not seriously deviate from the teaching of Islam. Ultimately it was banned in a number of regions only, on the basis of allegations that a banned book was in use, one written by the movement's founder.

Initially the 1962 prohibition of the Baha'is only extended to Baha'i organisations. Consequently Baha'is remained free for a decade to practise their faith in private but not to organise publicly. Since 1972, however, their religious practices have also been banned and practising Baha'is have been arrested and jailed in Southern Sumatra. Baha'is were also forbidden to declare their religion to be Baha'i on their official identity card.

Some religions have not been recognised as distinct religions. One curious anomaly affects the indigenous Keharingan religion of the Dayak people of central Kalimantan where it is the second most important religion after Islam. Keharingan was initially treated by the government as a mystical movement. However, when its adherents objected that their faith should be regarded as an 'official' religion, the government could not easily fit it into the prevailing categories. The government also could not ban Keharingan because the religion had been adhered to by countless generations of Dayaks. Consequently, it has been officially categorised as a Hindu group (known as Hindu Keharingan) despite the fact that there is no link between the two religions.

Books may be banned if they are held to represent a deviation of teaching of true religions, disturb religious communities or upset religious harmony. As a result of a protest by the Prisade Hindu Dharma, all books relating to the teachings of the Krishna Consciousness (Hare Krishna) movement have been banned.

The crushing of the attempted communist coup of 1965 affected not only foreign relations but also the internal policies of Indonesia. Activities regarded as exclusively Chinese in character were prohibited, such as Chinese language schools for Chinese students and Chinese customary celebrations. While a Presidential Decree recognised the status of Confucianism as a religion in 1965, prejudice leads to the commonly held view that Confucianism is not a religion or not recognised by the state. Confucian adherents have not been allowed to declare their religion on their identity card nor to conduct traditional Confucian marriages. The teaching of Confucianism in schools has been banned, even where students are Confucian. Despite this, many continue to teach their children and conduct ceremonies.

In communal riots in 1996–97, social frustrations were taken out on Chinese Indonesians regarded as making profits out of the impoverished; colonial policies had not allowed ethnic Indonesians to establish businesses. At Rengasdengklok, on the edge of Jakarta, communal rioting damaged or destroyed several churches and Buddhist temples as well as about 150 businesses and dwellings in January 1997. Rioting reportedly began when an ethnic Chinese woman asked local children to make less noise when they woke up Muslim families before dawn during Ramadan. Some Muslims saved their houses by painting on the door 'True Muslims fight, the Chinese are disbelievers'.

East Timor

No United Nations-recognised act of self-determination has yet taken place in East Timor, formerly a Portuguese colony. Indonesia proclaimed East Timor a province in 1976. Since that time there have been various stages in the East Timorese struggle for independence and regular abuses of human rights – extra-judicial killings, torture, rape, disappearances – are well documented, establishing the existence of a culture of intimidation and violence.

The Catholic Church has played a major role in support of independence, calling in 1989 for a UN-conducted referendum on the issue, and supporting national aspirations. Under the Portuguese it was very prominent, and in the current conflict it has become a focal point for non-violent resistance to the Indonesian government. So much so that the number of people declaring their religion to be Catholic in the census tripled from 220,314 in 1974 to 676,402 in 1990 – four-fifths of the population – and absorbing the animists who found Catholicism more compatible with their beliefs than other Indonesian 'official' religions. In the same period, the number of Protestants also rose from 2,550 to 20,660.

The Catholic Church is outspoken on many issues in East Timor and overseas and church attendance provides a way for people to assemble in public without being arrested. In the course of its work on human rights and economic deprivation, the church conducts schools and seminaries with an East Timorese curriculum involving both Catholicism and indigenous languages and culture. Retaliation by the authorities involves constant surveillance of some church officials and other forms of intimidation. In July 1994, two Muslim soldiers pretending to be Christians committed acts of sacrilege while attending mass.

The government policy of 'Indonisation' of Timor and its culture includes transmigration from other provinces while 45 per cent of the East Timorese are unemployed or underemployed, and peasants are squeezed out of their lands. Although most migrants are Muslims, the government announced it would relocate 1,000 Indonesian Catholics to Timor in 1994 and erected a giant statue of Christ in Dili 1996.

Bishop Belo and José Ramos Horta were awarded the Nobel Peace Prize in late 1996. This has thrown the spotlight on how Indonesia handles the matter of East Timor autonomy. The Vatican has appointed a second bishop.

Irian Jaya

From the mid-1960s, colonisation of West Papua by Indonesia has been accompanied by repression of the indigenous population in the interest of economic exploitation and transmigration from Indonesian islands to the west, in which settlers were granted land seized from Melanesians. Human rights abuses have been reported; 43,000 indigenous people have been killed.

There are 1 million Melanesians in Irian Jaya, speaking a quarter of the world's languages; though many are Christians, the spirit world is still real for them. Concessions granted by the Indonesian government in Irian Jaya have permitted the Freeport copper and gold mine to destroy part of the highest mountains in West Papua, the home of the ancestral spirit of the Amungme people.

In 1995, the local Catholic bishop reported to the Indonesian Conference of Catholic Bishops on killings and torture inflicted on the Amungme people by Indonesian army units at the mine site; some had been protesting about loss of their lands. This report was confirmed by the government's Human Rights Commission. The bishop also drew attention to constant surveillance and intimidation of the Amungme people, even in churches and during prayer meetings. He also said that in Timika, some people celebrating Easter were injured and killed as authorities thought they were members of the independence movement.

Women in religion

Because Indonesian women belong to many different kinds of ethnic, geographical and religious communities, their participation in religion varies enormously. All areas of Indonesia have a history which includes politically powerful women; Aceh, Sulawesi, Bali, Minangkabau, the South Celebes and Java have all been ruled by women and the tradition of women's full participation in rural agriculture is strong in Indonesia.

Dutch colonisation reinforced aspects of Indonesian feudalism, including the feminine ideal of *kodrat wanita*, in which a woman is seen to excel above all in the domestic sphere. The perceived fragility of the post-colonial Indonesian state has resulted in an official ideology influenced by this ideal which stresses family stability, social harmony and women's roles as wives and mothers, with no mention of any economic function. The work of women as financial managers and their power in the private, domestic sphere are unacknowledged. The central religious ritual of the Javanese *kampung*, the *slametan* celebratory meal, reflects this dualism. The large part women play is not acknowledged as ritually important and ritual leadership is confined to male family members.

Balinese Hindu women are subject to a simplified caste system and stronger concepts of purity and pollution than elsewhere in Indonesia. A strong base of indigenous religions, however, allows women ritual status not acceptable in Indian Hinduism.

Orthodox Islam favours male leadership, but Muslim reform movements over the last century brought education in the scriptures and even some women-only mosques. In general, reform movements and women's associations benefit mainly women who have completed secondary education.

In her short lifetime (1879–1904), Raden Adjeng Kartini initiated resistance against polygamy, child marriage and other practices affecting the welfare of women, as well as the level of rural poverty in Java. The Indonesian nationalist movement included Muslim, Catholic and Protestant women's groups. After independence in 1945, women's organisations agitated for equality in matters of marriage and divorce, and were only partially successful in 1975 after long and heated parliamentary debate. In particular, proposed recognition of a Muslim marrying outside Islam was defeated (especially resisted was permission for women to marry out) and the final result of the bill was the enhancement of Islamic law. Limited forms of polygamy remained permitted and the regulation of marriage, polygamy, forced marriage and divorce is in the hands of the Islamic courts.

JAPAN

Japan	
GDP (US$bn)	3,671
Population	124,200,000
Annual population growth (%)	0.9
Urban population (%)	77
Working population (%)	52[a]
Literacy (%)	99
Ratifications	1; 2; 3; 4

Japan is at the same time a republic with a hereditary *Tenno* (a status approximating that of emperor) and a democratic country founded on the American-model constitution enacted in 1946 at the end of the Second World War. Japan's highly industrialised, modern nation, still close to the agricultural and fishing traditions of its islands, numbers 124.2 million people. The Liberal Democratic Party dominated the Diet (parliament) for thirty-eight years until it broke up in 1993, since when there have been several changes of government. Japan has ratified major human rights instruments. The CERD was ratified at the end of 1995.

Social structure

Japan has a long history of being isolated from other cultures. Most people of Japanese nationality are of Japanese extraction. About 50,000 indigenous people, the Ainu, live principally in the northern island of Hokkaido. In 1991, there were 1,218,891 foreign residents, about half of them Koreans, many of whom are permanent residents.

Japanese society places a high value on conformism and on an ideology of the homogeneity of the population forming the Japanese nation. One consequence is the discrimination experienced by minorities such as the Koreans and the Ainu, because of their race, ethnic origin or status as foreigners. The Buraku-min, on the other hand, are discriminated against for reasons more akin to caste and class, an enduring legacy of hierarchical social and economic classification. As recently as the last century the Buraku-min were classified as non-human.

Religious belief and practice

Shintoism is indigenous to Japan. Buddhism, Taoism and Confucian thought and practice came from China around the sixth century. Christianity was introduced by Franciscan and Jesuit missionaries who accompanied traders in the sixteenth century and then retreated after persecution by the shoguns in the seventeenth century. When Japan opened its doors to the West again in the nineteenth century, churches were rebuilt.

The religious consciousness of Japanese people is displayed in ways other than through acceptance of a particular system of belief. According to a newspaper survey in 1994, 72 per cent of Japanese people stated that they did not believe in any religion and only 11 per cent thought that everyday life should be carried on in the spirit of religion. But the survey also found that 86 per cent of the Japanese thought the spirits (*kami*) were always watching and protecting them. Most Japanese people pray at Shinto shrines or Buddhist temples, take their newly born babies to Shinto shrines, visit Shinto shrines on the first day of the year, have Christian or Shinto weddings and are buried in Buddhist funerals.

In 1990, the total number of declared believers in religion was 217 million, almost twice the population number. The discrepancy illuminates the pluralist approach which is taken to religion among the Japanese. While most people have a strong religious consciousness, they do not adhere to a single faith (such as Christianity, Buddhism or Islam), but combine practices and beliefs from several traditions.

Believing that there are many gods and spirits in every person – Buddhas and *kami* – most Japanese are tolerant of other people's religious beliefs provided that others acknowledge and respect their beliefs in turn. There have been no special hostilities between different religious communities and very few people are discriminated against because of religious belief. But should a religious group or an individual fail to show respect for other people's gods or spirits, that group or individual will be denounced as disturbing social harmony and will encounter considerable hostility.

Because the demands of exclusive belief systems are not understood or accepted, monotheistic believers are vulnerable to discrimination and hostility in circumstances dictated by the ceremonial and ritualistic character of Japanese culture. For example, people are often asked for a contribution to the local Shinto shrine or to join an annual Shinto festival. Refusal may bring social rejection.

Religion and state in the past and today

After 1873 – when the Meiji government rescinded the decree that had prohibited Christianity and the Buddhist Ikko sect in the days of the Tokugawa shogunate – every religion enjoyed formal equality. The 1889 constitution of the Empire of Japan guaranteed formal freedom of religion to all, provided that it was not 'antagonistic to their duties as subjects'.

The governmental system formed under the imperial constitution was essentially religious. The constitution declared that the emperor, the heart of the system, was a direct descendant of the sun goddess Amaterasu-omikami and was a divine being himself, his origins intended to unite the people. The *Tenno* served as the highest priest in Shinto.

Ise-jingu (the Ise shrines) which were dedicated to Amaterasu, took a special position above all other shrines. Each was given value according to its distance from the emperor and upper-level shrines had Shinto priests who were paid government officials. This union of Shinto and the state or the emperor was known as *kokka shinto*, state Shinto, conveniently developed as a national morality with a separate and higher status than religions. Thus, believers of other religions, as dutiful subjects, were expected to pay their respects at Shinto shrines and even Christian schools had Shinto altars. According to the scholar Minobe Tatsukichi, 'in carrying out one's duty to the state and to the Imperial line, one has the duty not to show disrespect to Ise Jingu, the Imperial mausolea, or shrines dedicated to the soul of the ancestors of the Emperor'. When some religious groups such as Omoto-kyo and Jehovah's Witnesses objected, they were deemed anti-social or anti-state and were suppressed by the government.

After the Japanese defeat in the Second World War, the General Headquarters of the Allied forces who occupied Japan ordered the Japanese government to separate religion from the state. The 1946 constitution contains several articles concerning freedom of thought, conscience and religion, some of which are guarantees of the liberty while others restrict the religion–state relationship.

The separation of religion and state is an important but disputed issue in present-day Japan. On the face of it, the constitution requires a strict separation of religion and state. Article 20 provides that 'No religious organisation shall receive any privileges from the State nor exercise any political authority' and 'The State and its organs shall refrain from religious education or any other religious activity.' In addition, Article 89 states that, 'No public money or other property shall be expended or appropriated for the use, benefit or maintenance of any religious institution or association.'

In spite of the strict principle of separation of religion and state, many practices may appear to violate it, none more resonant in disputes about religion–state division than activities centring on the Yasukuni Jinja, a Shinto shrine where those who had dedicated their lives to the state and had died during the past wars were deified. Although the Yasukuni Shrine Bill attempted to strip the shrine of its religious significance and hand it over to the state to be supported as a war memorial, this attempt was largely unsuccessful.

Religious groups have taken up opposing positions on the Yasukuni Shrine issue. Christian and new religions – which had experienced persecution before the war – insist that only strict separation will stave off a potentially dangerous combination of religion and state, while Shintoists interpret the constitutional provisions loosely, pointing to the inconvenience in everyday life if they were to be strictly applied. To many religionists, however, especially aware of damage done in China, Korea and other Asian nations, it remains a symbol of militarism and war.

In 1985, Prime Minister Nakasone publicly visited and worshipped before the Yasukuni Jinja, an action which was challenged in several courts and pronounced by some to be unconstitutional. Local governments have spent public funds as a contribution to the Yasukuni Jinja and have publicly offered sprigs of the sacred trees to the shrine. In 1994, despite a prime ministerial appeal for them to stay away, seven members of the Cabinet visited the shrine where the *Tenno* and his wife offered prayers for the dead. In July 1996, Prime Minister Hashimoto visited the shrine, a move understood as having both personal and political motivations.

Shinto altars may also be found in the warships of the Self-Defence Force, in public *kendo* (Japanese fencing) halls and on top of corporation buildings. The union between Shinto and the *Tenno* continues because he is the supreme ritualist in Shinto; public funds are expended to support his religious role. Such religious ceremonies and observances are apt to be seen by most Japanese as not particularly religious but part of everyday secular life.

The Supreme Court has taken a lenient approach in enforcing the constitutional separation provision. As a result, in different ways, a form of union between religion and government has been permitted, both at national and local level. The leading decision on separation of religion and state is the Tsu *jichinsai* decision in 1977. In this case, *jichinsai* in Shinto rites were sponsored by the city of Tsu. *Jichinsai* is a customary ceremony of purifying a building site before construction in order to protect against complications. In the Tsu case, the ceremony was performed by a local Shinto priest prior to inaugurating the construction of a new sports building. The city of Tsu paid 7,663 yen to the Shinto priest from public funds as payment for services and as an offering. The question was whether this sponsorship or *jichinsai* was a 'religious activity' violating the constitutional prohibition of state funding of religions.

The majority of the Supreme Court held that it was neither logical nor possible to effect a complete separation of religion from state. The Court adopted the so-called 'purpose and effect' judicial standard. The Court decided that the *jichinsai* was not a religious activity because the purpose of the ceremony was clearly secular and the effect would neither promote Shinto nor oppress other religions. Although the subject of criticism, this test has been followed by every court decision on similar matters since. For instance, attendance by local government officials at memorial services in Shinto or Buddhist rites before the Chukonhi, a sacred monument built in honour of soldiers who had died in past wars, was also judged a non-religious activity.

Lower courts occasionally take a stricter attitude towards the separation of religion and state than the Supreme Court. Thus, in March 1995, the Osaka High Court doubted the constitutionality of the public funding of Shinto ceremonies concerning the enthronement of the *Tenno*. In another important case, lower courts upheld a Christian widow's claim that it was an unconstitutional act of state for her husband, a Self-Defence Force officer who had died in a traffic accident, to be enshrined by fellow-serving soldiers' organisations in 1988, contrary to her wishes. She had requested that the ritual be stopped. However, on appeal by the government, the Supreme Court held that the soldiers of the liaison agency had acted as private citizens and that the enshrinement had been for the purpose of sustaining morale and had nothing to do with religion. The court agreed that the constitutional protection of freedom of religion extended to private organisations but stated that a spirit of tolerance was essential in a democratic society; just as the widow had the right to mourn her husband according to her religion, so her husband's colleagues had the right to cherish him in their own way.

Support of political parties by religious movements has lately been spotlighted and measures have been proposed to curtail the right of religious organisations to participate in politics. Rissho Koseikai has financially supported politicians predominantly from the Liberal Democratic Party. The Soka Gakkai movement established a large and influential political party in the 1960s and now supports the main opposition New Frontier Party. In 1996 an LDP member put up a bill for religious Basic Law (*shukyo kohin houan*) which redrew the parameters of Article 20 of the constitution and responded to multiple (often political) agendas. The Shirakawa Bill, which contains detailed prescriptions and proscriptions covering a wide range of religious activities in the public and private spheres of life, has yet to be discussed in the Diet.

Freedom of thought and conscience

The Japanese constitution guarantees freedom of thought and conscience separately from freedom of religion because freedom of thought and conscience had been so severely oppressed in the past. Article 19 states that 'Freedom of thought and conscience shall not be violated.'

In a case in 1973, an employee was dismissed for not telling the truth when he was asked about his political activities during his university days in a job interview. He claimed that the company's decision was based on the fact that he had not revealed his political thought, that he was a victim of discrimination because of belief and that his right to freedom of thought was infringed. The Supreme Court held that the constitution is limited only to state action and did not control private relations. The Court also suggested that the company was free to ask the job applicants about their thoughts. This has been criticised as opening the door to discrimination based on creed and to the violation of individuals' freedom of thought and conscience.

In practice, Japanese companies covertly discriminate against communist employees. The Public Security Investigation Agency was involved in phone-tapping of the Communist Party in the late 1980s and regularly investigates people it considers communist, socialist or right-wing in their convictions.

Conscientious objection

During the Second World War, dissidents and pacifists were imprisoned. They included some Christians, followers of Omoto-kyo and members of the early formation of Soka Gakkai. As a result of the war, the preamble of the constitution guarantees the right to live in peace. The constitution prohibits the raising of an army and therefore problems over conscientious objection to military service do not arise. Article 18 of the constitution prescribes that 'No person shall be held in bondage of any kind.' Involuntary servitude, except as punishment for crime, is prohibited. Compulsory conscription is therefore assumed to be prohibited in Japan. There is strong opposition among Japanese people to the existence of the Self-Defence Force and many Japanese scholars regard it as unconstitutional.

Freedom of religion

Article 20 of the constitution provides that 'Freedom of religion is guaranteed to all. . . . No person shall be compelled to take part in any religious act, celebration, rite or practice.' The scope of freedom of religion is treated as encompassing three main areas. In the first place, it means the absolute freedom to believe or not to believe in any religion. One can choose or change one's religion freely and should not be forced to confess one's belief or religion. This freedom overlaps with freedom of expression also guaranteed by the constitution.

Discrimination on the grounds of one's religious belief is forbidden as the constitution prohibits any discrimination because of 'creed' which includes religion, belief and thought. Discrimination by an employer against an employee in wages or other labour conditions because of one's creed is punishable under the Labor Standards Act. Although Japan has few Muslims, discrimination against Muslim women for wearing a head-covering in the workplace has been reported.

Second, freedom of religion also entails freedom of religious practice, such as setting up an altar, worshipping gods, attending divine services, administering religious ceremonies or rites, and missionary work. However, no-one is compelled to take part in such a religious act, celebration, rite or practice. Only when a religious activity takes on an anti-social character and threatens harm to someone's life and health, may it be restricted by law. Any restriction must be shown to be necessary and indispensable. Under the Aliens Registration Act, the government may restrict any foreign missionary it considers not acceptable or involved in an activity contrary to the public interest.

The Supreme Court has had to consider constitutional limits to the freedom of religious activities. In 1963, the Court held that the religious freedom clause did not render actions immune from prosecution when magico-religious rites and prayers intended to cure mental illness had subjected a patient to violence which resulted in her death. However, in 1975, a pastor who had hidden a suspected young criminal was judged not guilty because of his genuine pastoral activity. A cancer patient who refused a blood transfusion because of his beliefs as a Jehovah's Witness was held to have the right to refuse treatment.

Third, freedom of religion includes the freedom to establish religious organisations and to religious commitment through such organisations. There is no special governmental policy concerning religion in Japan. Although the Ministry of Education is the competent authority concerning religion, it has no power to interfere in the activities of religious bodies. A religious group can become a religious corporation by satisfying the conditions of the Religious Corporation Act. Such corporations are granted taxation privileges. A religious corporation may lose its status by the order of a court if it violates a law and injures public welfare or if it deviates clearly from its religious objects. But even after a religious corporation has had its tax status removed, it can remain as a religious body.

In late 1995, the Religious Corporation Revision Act was passed, transferring jurisdiction from local to central government and requiring greater financial disclosure. The law gives the state wide powers of investigation not only of religious groups' financial affairs but of their programmes, activities and membership. Concern has been expressed about the effect of this legislation on religious freedom in Japan.

In several cases courts have recognised the autonomy of religious bodies. When a Buddhist priest disputed the validity of his being dismissed, the Supreme Court held that it had no jurisdiction over disputes on religious positions in religious bodies.

Religious aspects of discrimination against the Buraku and Ainu

The contribution which religious groups make to racial discrimination (through doctrines of impurity, cause and effect, karma) as well as to its elimination has been acknowledged. In 1981, the Joint Conference of Religions Coping with the Dowa problem – segregation and discrimination against the Buraku-min – was founded. Some fifty-nine religious groups work together to counter (by promoting self-criticism) those actions, writings and speech, especially among religious groups, which incite religious and racial hostility.

Buddhism controls the rites under which most Japanese are buried. Because of the importance of ancestor worship, a religious name (*kaimyo*) is allocated posthumously by the Buddhist priest and it is carved on tombs. Derogatory names given to dead Buraku-min on graves all over Japan, such as *chiku-otoko* (animal man), indicate that Buraku origin was seen as an outcast or not human, thus publicly shaming their families and inhibiting their practice of worshipping their ancestors. The Buraku Liberation Movement has influenced many Buddhist groups to reflect and realise that true religion cannot exist unless all people are treated as fully human. Regrettably, however, the discrimination still persists. Although some Buddhist groups have held memorials to the dead and sealed old registers recording derogatory names, for others action has been tardy for various reasons, such as the reluctance of families to identify themselves as Buraku, to be associated with tombs which bear the names.

The indigenous Ainu people have beliefs which are associated with spiritual continuity to land and the natural world. Through modernisation policies conducted by the Meiji government, they were forced into agriculture, all land being confiscated if left un-cultivated. The majority culture attempted to dismantle Ainu culture through policies of assimilation, and prohibition of their language and traditional hunting and fishing practices. Development projects may destroy sacred sites and prevent the conduct of rituals. The Nibutani dam, for instance, would destroy landmarks associated with fox gods who traditionally warn villagers of impending fire and flood. The political status of the Ainu was enhanced in 1994, when the first Ainu was elected to the Upper House of the Japanese Diet, but the Former Aborigines Protection Act 1898 has not yet been repealed.

Ainu attempts to maintain or revive their traditions have been impeded by government regulations aimed at conserving species; the regulations do not also recognise indigenous rights. In 1982, applications for a special salmon fishing right for the ceremony to greet new salmon were granted but only through licences for a limited quantity of salmon. Ainu people have protested, pointing to the fact that the government justifies whaling on the ground that some whale meat is required for traditional religious ceremonies among fishing communities. In 1987, an application for permission to hunt for Blakiston's fish owls in order to conduct a traditional ceremony was denied. However, in 1995, Ainu in eastern Hokkaido were given permission for the first time to hunt deer according to traditional methods in a forest where hunting is usually prohibited. This hunt enabled the Ainu to conduct rituals including praying for the souls of deer killed by poachers.

Hokkaido University dug up sacred Ainu burial sites to amass bones for research purposes. After protracted negotiations over the bones, the university agreed to allow the Ainu to build an ossuary on campus where they hold an annual *icharpa* memorial service.

Education

Article 9 of the Fundamentals of Education Act states that to educate children about religion generally and to promote in them an attitude of mutual tolerance should be important goals of public schools. Ethics is taught from early grades onwards. Care is taken to educate children about the Holocaust and *The Diary of Anne Frank* is recommended reading. A Japanese filmmaker whose work has been dedicated to opposing war has now produced an animated film on her life (animation and cartoons are extremely popular in Japan for all age groups). However, students are not taught adequately to understand the history and the culture of the Ainu. Public schools are directed to refrain from specific religious education under Article 9(2) of the constitution. Muslims report that because public schools do not allow religious clothing, the head-covering cannot be worn by schoolgirls. There is complete freedom to establish religious schools, most of which are Christian.

One public school held a visiting day on a Sunday and recorded as absent on the school register a student who could not attend because he had to go to church. The Christian parent complained to the Tokyo District Court about interference with religious freedom, but in 1986 the Court decided that the requirements of public education could limit freedom of religious activity in this case. In 1994, the Osaka High Court, on appeal, reinstated a high school student who, as a Jehovah's Witness, refused to practise *kendo* and had been dismissed from school on the grounds of religious belief.

Sections of school textbooks containing accurate accounts and acknowledgement of human rights abuses by the Japanese Army in the Nanjing Massacre (1937) and other aspects of its invasion of Asia were censored by the Ministry of Education who ordered the scholarly author in the early 1980s to rewrite them to comply with the government's screening system. In 1993, the Tokyo High Court declared that certain directions by the Ministry were unconstitutional and unlawful though it upheld the validity of the screening system to maintain fairness, neutrality and quality of texts. The judge said he found it hard to understand that criticism of the actions of one's country was undesirable from an educational point of view. Non-government organisations supporting the case claimed that the education system was a crucial place in which to teach facts about the past in order to enable Japanese children to contribute to efforts for peace and human rights. The case has been appealed to the Supreme Court.

The media and publications

Article 21 of the constitution guarantees freedom of expression, assembly and association and censorship is prohibited. Any religious corporation or religious body can publish any newspaper, magazine or book freely. There is a wide array of religious newspapers, magazines and books published in Japan. Some religious bodies whose credibility had been strongly impaired by media coverage have successfully sued for defamation.

Although Jews in Japan are few in number, Japanese society is reportedly fascinated with them, both positively and negatively, as another highly distinctive ethnic group. This has given rise to a unique phenomenon, 'philosemitism', in which writers mirror the tenets of anti-Semitism by holding up the stereotype about Jewish money-making as a trait for Japanese to admire and copy.

The prime concern of Jewish organisations is the publication of anti-Semitic literature and media coverage, including advertisements for such publications which repeat anti-Semitic stereotypes. In 1995, a respected magazine publisher closed down a magazine it owned which aimed at young readers, because of a long article it published denying the Holocaust; the article had already been turned down by the national paper *Asahi Shimbun*.

'New' and 'new-new' religious movements

New religions or 'new-new' religious movements often become the target for severe criticism from the mass media and public opinion, attacked for pressuring converts into donating their money and properties to a religious body, for communal living and for selling goods at an exorbitant price as a fund-raising method. New-new religions are popular among university students.

Once the mass media have attacked a new-new religion, whatever the reason, there occurs something like mass hysteria in Japanese society and the religion encounters severe hostility. Iesu No Hakobune (Ark of Jesus), Toitsu Kyokai (Union Church) and Kofuku No Kagaku (Science of Happiness) have all been censured severely. Today, Aum Shinrikyo (Aum Supreme Truth), headed by Shoko Asahara, is the main target for criticism. Shoko Asahara, arrested in 1995 and charged with the sarin gas murders in the Tokyo subway, has denied in court that he was involved.

Aum Shinrikyo was disbanded by the authorities under Article 81 of the Religious Corporations Law, the first such order; the Supreme Court has held that the order did not contravene constitutional freedom of religion. Article 81 indicates that a religious organisation may be dissolved if it has been determined to have grossly impaired the well-being of the public and strayed significantly from the purpose of a religion. The Court's ruling indicated that the disbandment order was aimed solely at secular activities of religious organisations; it was not intended to regulate adherents' religious and spiritual activities. Aum Shinrikyo has been declared bankrupt and victims of the sarin gas attacks and their relatives are seeking compensation. However, in late January 1997, the public security commission decided not to use the Anti-Subversive Activities Law to outlaw Aum, as it seemed no longer a danger to society. However, Aum reportedly has some 8,000 followers and senior members have announced that they will continue religious activities according to the tenets of their leader.

In other matters concerning new-new religious movements, parents have been concerned about young believers leaving home and joining religious communes. Some parents have been prepared to go to extreme lengths to prevent young adults from staying with a new religious movement, justifying their actions as a response to alleged compulsion within the group. For instance, there have been a number of forcible deprogrammings of members of the Unification Church, involving the assistance of Christian clergy through the anti-cult movement established in the late 1980s. In unsuccessful deprogrammings, some young people have alleged that they were kidnapped and falsely imprisoned in order to coerce them into changing their beliefs. However, it is very difficult for Japanese lawyers, courts and society at large to conceive of coercive actions by parents as criminal acts.

Claims have been made of 'new-new' religions luring 'consumers' into 'spiritual sales'. A National Network of Lawyers Against Spiritual Sales has been formed which acts on complaints from disgruntled ex-members, particularly of the Unification Church, from which lawyers seek repayment of amounts loaned or donated; extensive civil damages are also sought.

In May 1994, the Fukuoka District Court ordered the Unification Church to pay 37.6 million yen compensation to two widows who had donated 32 million yen, saying that the church had illegally guided the widows by inducing in them feelings of despair and warning that the souls of their husbands would experience harm emanating from the spiritual world and ancestral karmas unless they donated sums of money. The judge said that in the context of religious donations, narratives about the spiritual world and karmas (whose existence could not be proved) might lawfully be used to solicit religious donations where such demands were based on 'socially appropriate objectives' and the methods used and results required for such donations are 'appropriate in light of social norms'. The ruling is being appealed.

There is wide public subsidisation of religion in Japan, and the focus by the Lawyers' Committee on Spiritual Sales on 'new-new' religions may have obscured the extent to which payment is solicited – and Buddhist temples supported by funds – for traditional prayers, votive offerings and statues commemorating the dead and promises of relief for the souls concerned. Special services (*mizuko kuyo*) may also be performed for the souls of unborn embryos of stillbirths, miscarriages and abortions. The manner of soliciting for spiritual services – including advertising – by some temples is reportedly somewhat in disrepute.

Inter-religious relations

It is not infrequent to find religious groups verbally attacking each other over their respective beliefs. There have been many altercations, for instance, between an existing religion (Nichiren sect) and a new religion (Soka Gakkai), between a new religion (Soka

Gakkai) and a new-new religion (Aum Shinrikyo), and between a new-new religion (Kofuku No Kagaku) and another new-new religion (Aum Shinrikyo).

On the other hand, different religions have often worked in close cooperation, such as through the World Conference on Religion and Peace, the International Association for Religious Freedom, the Free Religious Association of Japan (including humanists as well as Buddhists, Shintoists and Christians) and the Federation of New Religions in Japan. They have also sponsored many social movements in Japan such as the anti-nuclear bomb movement, the movement against Buraku discrimination and the movement against the *Tenno* system.

Women and religion

Women were central figures in religious aspects of ancient Japanese culture especially as shamanesses (*miko*), women of great spiritual power. The *miko*'s important role in political life was lost after the introduction of Chinese government structures and religions around the sixth century but, until the fourteenth century, imperial princesses served at Shinto shrines. A similar recognition of spiritually powerful women has occurred with the phenomenon of 'new' religions, many with roots in the pre-Meiji period. Many of the founders of these are female and each religious body has had many female leaders. As these new religions become 'institutionised', men tend to take over leadership and women, although over 70 per cent of practitioners, become marginalised.

Mahayana Buddhism at its highest level views male and female as similarly capable of enlightenment. The scriptures do contain, however, strong notions of women as impure and dangerous to men's spiritual progress (this being the fault of women, a typical aspect of ascetic traditions in all cultures). While Tantric Buddhism encouraged males to take over shamanistic roles, many folk practices were led by women. Women were also attracted to the religious vocation of ordination as nuns, as well as having more practical intentions, such as taking refuge from difficult marriages and for retirement; and through them has been perpetuated the female lineage of Buddhist ordination from India. From the ninth century, the Tendai and Shingon sects prohibited female ordination. Heian period women responded by creating their own form of monasticism, the Bodhisattva nuns. During the Feudal period, the status of all women, including Buddhist nuns, declined and during the Meiji Restoration, male priests were forced to marry but remained priests, while married nuns were stripped of their religious status.

Later, despite the support of their founder, Soto Zen nuns encountered a number of obstacles posed by a male-dominated training and power structure which favoured male monasticism and restricted women's. In the early nineteenth century, the nuns won the right to establish schools which offered higher levels of education and to grant officially recognised academic degrees. Post-Meiji, however, they were prevented from teaching, practising meditation without male supervision, initiating others, or performing mission work until the 1970s. Despite these achievements, discrimination persists in Japanese Buddhism because unmarried shaven nuns – though respected – are still not perceived to have equivalent ranking to men either in the *sangha* or in society. Because nuns are thought to be dependent on monks and play a complementary role, the decision to marry poses difficulties for women but not for men. Consequently there are fewer than 200 shaven nuns in the Nichiren sect of Buddhism, mostly elderly, though the number of unshaven, married nuns with families is slowly growing; in contrast, there are 10,000 monks.

Although Article 14 of the constitution prohibits discrimination on grounds of sex, like other provisions it only prohibits discrimination by the government or public authorities.

Religions such as Shinto or Buddhism may consider women to be polluting because of menstruation and childbirth. Women were forbidden to enter any sacred places and sacred mountains until 1873 and some are still forbidden them. The Sumo-wrestling ring is thought to be such a sacred place; recently, even the Minister of Education could not award a championship cup to the winner in the ring because of her sex.

In folk and family religion, belief in the dangerous spiritual power of women is declining, but these themes seem to have re-emerged in modern films and comics. Women retain their roles as healers and keepers of ritual knowledge, especially in the household, and the more sophisticated feminist groups still appeal to Amaterasu, the shamaness of rivers and the sea and later the sun goddess of ancient times: 'In the beginning was the sun, and she was woman'.

MALAYSIA

Malaysia	
GDP (US$bn)	58
Population	18,800,000
Annual population growth (%)	2.6
Urban population (%)	51
Working population (%)	38
Literacy (%)	81.5
Ratifications	4

After independence from British colonial rule in 1957, the federation called Malaysia was formed in 1963. The federation comprises the eleven states of the former federation of Malaya, and the states of Sarawak and Sabah in Borneo.

Malaysia is a multi-ethnic and multi-religious society and religious and ethnic affiliation are intimately linked. The indigenous Malays, who are Muslims, constitute a slim majority (55 per cent) of the population in peninsular Malaysia. Chinese (35 per cent) and Indians (10 per cent) who were first brought into the country as workers during colonial times – and thus of immigrant origin – form a large minority. Most Chinese are Buddhists or practise a form of traditional religion based on Confucianism and Taoism. Indians are principally Hindus, Sikhs or Muslims. A small proportion of Chinese and Indians are also Christians. The Orang Asli, most still practising their indigenous spiritual traditions, account for less than 1 per cent and are the poorest people in the nation.

Although large numbers of Malays and Chinese are also found in the east Malaysian states of Sabah and Sarawak, the largest ethnic groups in these two states are the indigenous peoples of Borneo, the Dayaks (45 per cent in Sarawak) and the Kadazan-Dusuns (35 per cent in Sabah) for whom land rights is an issue. Most are Christians, others Muslims or followers of their own indigenous spiritual traditions.

Muslims, therefore, account for 53 per cent of the total Malaysian population of just under 19 million, Buddhists 17 per cent, adherents of Chinese religions 12 per cent, Hindus and Sikhs 7 per cent, Christians 6 per cent, believers of folk religions 2 per cent and others, including non-believers, 3 per cent.

Colonial policy had introduced unequal treatment based on ethnic origin when it protected Malay land ownership by prohibiting Chinese and Indians from owning rice-growing land. As the Chinese developed urban enterprise to a high degree, they grew economically stronger. While many Chinese went to live in Singapore after it became independent in 1965, many stayed in Malaysia.

Ethnic bargaining and the constitution

The Constitution of Malaya 1957 was a product of ethnic bargaining and accommodation among the three ethnic-based political parties of the Alliance coalition: the United Malays National Organisation (UMNO), the Malayan Chinese Association (MCA) and the Malayan Indian Congress (MIC) in peninsular Malaysia.

The Malays agreed to liberal and common citizenship provisions which would benefit the non-Malays, while the Chinese and Indian leaders accepted provisions making Islam the official religion, Malay the national language, and the traditional Malay rulers heads of states. On the basis of Malays' disadvantaged economic position and their status as indigenous people of the peninsula, the leaders agreed to 'special rights' for the Malays in the allocation of scholarships, administrative appointments, and so on – the *bumiputra* policy. These arrangements were enshrined in the constitution and have now been extended to the indigenous peoples of Sabah and Sarawak, most of whom are not Muslims. However, the feeling of cultural exclusion and of being shut out from nation-building as equal and legitimate partners has contributed to non-Malay communalism over the past decades, notably racial violence in 1969.

Religion and state

Islam has a special status. Article 3(1) of the constitution states that 'Islam is the religion of the Federation; but other religions may be practised in peace and harmony in any part of the Federation.' Increasing numbers of Malaysians – though not all – have come to consider Article 3(1) a reasonable compromise. It reflects the aspiration of the Malays to see the stamp of Malay identity on the independent nation. The constitution, however, does not endorse the goal of an Islamic state, a defining characteristic of which is the implementation of Islamic *shariah* law upon all its citizens. Non-Muslims are not subjected to Islamic law. The *shariah* is only applied to Malaysian Muslims in personal law matters, such as family law, revised in 1989 to better protect property rights of Muslim women and to make their right to divorce more equitable.

Religious freedom is thus circumscribed by the unequal status of the different religions. Legal restrictions on the freedom of non-Muslims to promote their religion among Muslims are regarded as being in the interests of the whole society. There has, however, been no official attempt by the federal government to enforce Islam as a common religion. Neither has there been any federal policy of suppressing the religious beliefs of minority communities.

Since the early 1970s the Islamic revivalist movement has grown in Malaysia and UMNO began to promote the Islamic cause. Anwar Ibrahim, the founder-leader of the Islamic Youth Movement of Malaysia now seems likely to succeed Prime Minister Dr Mahathir Mohamed. New projects were launched, such as the Islamic Bank and banking system, Islamic insurance schemes, the introduction of Islamic values into government administration and the establishment of institutions such as the International Islamic University and the Institute of Islamic Understanding Malaysia, which play leading roles in promoting modernist Islamic discourse, including organising some inter-faith dialogue.

PAS, the other Malay Muslim party, remains committed to establishing an Islamic state in Malaysia through gradual constitutional means, whereas UMNO leaders have given greater emphasis to the infusion of Islamic values into society – leaving open to debate what an Islamic state implies for the future in a modern multi-ethnic setting like Malaysia.

Freedom of religion

The freedom to practise one's own religion is included as one of the fundamental liberties guaranteed under Malaysia's constitution. There is no specific protection under the constitution for freedom of thought, conscience and belief other than in the context of religion. The media have always been kept on a tight leash.

Article 11 of the constitution states as follows:

1 Every person has the right to profess and practise his religion and subject to Clause (4), to propagate it.
2 No person shall be compelled to pay any tax, the proceeds of which are separately allocated in whole or in part for the expenses of a religion other than his own.
3 Every religious group has the right:
  (a) to manage its own religious affairs;
  (b) to establish and maintain institutions for religious or charitable purposes; and
  (c) to acquire, own property and hold and administer it in accordance with law.
4 State law and in respect of the Federal territories of Kuala Lumpur and Labuan, federal law may control or restrict the propagation of any religious doctrine or belief among persons professing the religion of Islam.
5 This Article does not authorize any act contrary to any general law relating to public order, public health or morality.

Article 12 provides rights concerning education, allowing religious groups to provide for the education of their children; in Article 12(3), it is prohibited to require someone to receive instruction in or take part in any observances of a religion other than a person's own. Parents or guardians decide the religion of anyone under 18 years.

Article 8 provides for the equal protection of the law. Unless the constitution allows it, no Malaysian citizen may be discriminated against on various grounds including religion.

Federal penal laws

The federal Penal Code contains a number of offences relating to religion, not confined to Islam. In particular, Section 298A contains highly detailed provisions making it an offence to cause disharmony or to prejudice the maintenance of religious harmony, which make it risky for anyone, no matter how well intentioned, to interfere with or to criticise a religion without incurring the possibility of severe penalties.

The Malaysian government has taken such action against small groups of religious extremists who contravened the law. In 1978, some Malay Muslims, intercepted by Hindus in the act of destroying a temple in Kerling, Selangor, were killed and injured. Though the Hindus who defended their temple were charged with manslaughter, the Muslims who provoked that incident (among others) and survived were later tried and convicted. The government's handling of this sensitive episode was regarded as fair.

There have also been cases when Christians were fined and detained for conducting missionary work among Muslims. The UN Special Rapporteurs have asked the Malaysian government to respond to allegations by New Testament Church members, who are Chinese Malaysians, that their freedom of religion has been infringed. Their church had been deregistered, publications and banners confiscated and its members repeatedly arrested and detained for teaching the gospel. Some thirty members were arrested in 1991 on various charges of preaching illegally, illegal assembly using loudspeakers to attract the public, and illegal assembly when some protested against the arrest of their fellows. One, imprisoned for six months for preaching and for contempt in 1990 for reciting the scriptures in court, was said by the government to have disturbed Buddhist worshippers at a Chinese temple in 1980 by distributing pamphlets stating that idols were false gods. Buddhist and Christian groups had complained to the police about persistent disruption and belittling of their gatherings by church members.

State law and policy

The states have nine hereditary rulers who elect one of their number as king for five years. Rulers' powers are no longer limitless as their power to block legislation has been removed by Parliament. Rulers are head of the religion in their respective states, and the king is the head of the religion in the Federal Territories and the states of Penang, Malacca, Sabah and Sarawak.

The states have responsibility for matters of Islamic law, the *Shariah* Courts, and control the propagation of doctrines and beliefs among Muslims as well as the determination of matters of Islamic law and doctrine. The federal constitution allows for the operation of state and federal territory laws that may restrict the propagation of any religious doctrine or policy among persons professing the Muslim faith. State statutes on the control and restriction of the propagation of non-Islamic religions clearly state that missionaries of these minorities may not proselytise among Muslims.

Offences are detailed which prohibit many activities ranging between allowing, persuading, influencing and coercing someone to leave their Muslim faith. Using certain words (such as Allah, *ulama*, *kaabah*, *kadi*, *mufti*) in any public statements in association with non-Islamic religions is prohibited. A non-Muslim may only use such words by way of quotation or reference. This prohibition restricts the religious practice of the Baha'is, for instance. However, Muslim missionaries – many under the auspices of the state – are allowed to proselytise freely among non-Muslims.

Malaysia is unique in its plethora of detailed rules governing all matters, even prayer and fasting. Women are strongly affected in matters of inheritance, betrothal, marriage, divorce, dowry, maintenance, legitimacy and guardianship. These matters are enshrined in the legal system; for instance, in the early 1980s, in one state, failure to attend Friday prayers brought a fine of $25. The *khalwat* law prescribes strict conditions for social contact between the sexes with a similar fine for violation for both men and women. A woman can be fined for disobeying orders 'lawfully given by her husband' but more detailed and restrictive regulations have been suggested by Malay religious leaders, including forcing women to sit separately at the back of public transport.

Kelantan State penal laws

The Kelantan state government led by PAS, the Islamic party, passed the Syariah Criminal Code (II) Act 1993 to introduce *hudud* laws, prescribing punishments for six particular offences such as adultery and apostasy. It does not contain provisions relating to options available to non-Muslims, although the state government said they have a choice.

PAS's Majlis Ulamak (Council of Theologians) declared that any Muslim opposing the implementation of *hudud* laws is guilty of apostasy and the PAS leader stated that opposition would be seen as attempting to restrict Muslims from practising their beliefs.

Apart from Sisters in Islam, a Muslim women's group which is especially concerned that Muslim women would be discriminated against if *hudud* laws were to be implemented, no other independent Muslim group has openly opposed the PAS move. The PAS government had placed restrictions on women working at night and ordered women in government employment to cover their heads and bodies, thus restricting how they participated in public life. Sisters in Islam said that the Qur'an does not specify that women are inferior to men nor does it claim they are unable to be community leaders.

The UMNO-led federal government – whose consent was needed for the legislation to come into effect – rejected it, declaring that PAS's legislation reflects its own interpretation of Islamic teachings rather than the true spirit of Islamic teachings in a modern multi-religious context such as Malaysia.

Federal law and policy

Laws concerning association, assembly, security and expression can be used to curb free exercise of belief, such as the Police Act, the Societies Act, the Sedition Act, the Printing Presses and Publications Act (PPPA), the Internal Security Act and legislation controlling the use of land. In 1987, the government used the Internal Security Act (ISA) to detain 107 dissidents of many persuasions without trial because of their activism in pursuit of their beliefs. Some six Christians were detained for allegedly proselytising among Malays in defiance of the law; two former Muslims who had converted to Christianity were also detained and at least one was severely abused during detention. Reportedly, non-government organisations, opposition parties and the Bar Council have been questioning the need for the PPPA and ISA statutes.

The Prime Minister Dr Mahathir's anti-Zionist stance has been documented by organisations concerned with anti-Semitism. In 1994, the federal Censors Board banned the screening of the film *Schindler's List* on the ground that it favoured one race only. However, a review of the decision was announced by the deputy prime minister, stating that the government condemned all atrocities past and present.

In April 1996 Dr Mahathir criticised the judges in the Shariah Court for delivering unfair and even anti-Islamic judgments against women and for dismissing their problems as trivial. Women's organisations have criticised religious officials for delaying the implementation of domestic violence legislation – one judge had claimed it was a husband's right to beat his wife – and for an increase in the practice of polygamy. The Islamic Dakwah Foundation, supporting the prime minister's comments, called for the constitution to be amended if necessary to ensure that the Shariah Court dispensed justice according to the true spirit of Islamic law. The conservative views of state sultans and other religious officials are said to be likely to oppose reform. Federal Cabinet has approved the restructuring of the Shariah Courts, a move which will give the federal government new powers, including the appointment and promotion of Islamic affairs officers. Prime Minister Mahathir said in July 1996 that Islam in the modern age must be relevant to it.

Federal action to support Islamic orthodoxy

Malaysia officially countenances the Sunni version of Islam which embraces the four orthodox schools of Hanbali, Shafi, Maliki and Hanafi, with the Shafi school being dominant. Systematic infringement of religious freedom occurs in the government's treatment of those it considers 'deviant Muslims'.

The most recent case has involved Dar'ul Arqam, a sufistic and messianic Islamic missionary movement which was founded by Ustaz Ashaari in 1968. Arqam expanded rapidly in Malaysia in the 1970s and by the early 1990s it had established centres in sixteen different countries, operating over 200 educational institutions (including twenty religious schools), medical centres and various publishing and audio-visual outfits, trading, business and industrial activities in several countries, and establishing rural farming communities throughout Malaysia. An estimated 10,000 full-time activists and many more thousands of sympathisers were involved in the movement, at all levels of Malaysian life, including politics, potentially challenging UMNO's sway.

The Religious Affairs ministers of the six ASEAN nations (Brunei, Indonesia, Malaysia, the Philippines, Singapore and Thailand) met in Malaysia in early August 1994 to discuss what should be done. The following day, the National Fatwa Council (the official body in charge of declaring Islamic injunctions) ruled that the movement had deviated from Islamic teachings. Arqam was banned in Malaysia under the Societies Act and its activities curtailed.

In September 1994, Ustaz Ashaari (brought back from Thailand through the cooperation of the Thai police), his family and seven other leaders were detained without trial under the Internal Security Act. In October, after police interrogation, they appeared on television acknowledging that they had misled their followers and Ashaari recanted his messianic beliefs. They were released and have cooperated with the authorities in disbanding Arqam's centres. All wearing of insignia and special dress has stopped, although some Arqam members have been reported to have rejected the recantation and continue to live in their communes. The Islamic Office then announced it had developed a five-year plan, involving all levels of government administration, to get rid of all forty-seven 'deviant' Muslim movements the government had identified.

Discrimination against non-Muslims

Leaders of the non-Muslim religions set up the Malaysian Consultative Council of Buddhism, Christianity, Hinduism and Sikhism in 1984. Originally planned to include Muslims so as to promote inter-faith dialogue, the Council was unsuccessful in attracting Muslim participation and so has increasingly adopted the role of watchdog over the government's handling of religious matters.

The Council's complaints of discrimination against non-Muslims include the following:

1 Attendance at an Islamic Civilisation course is compulsory for all students, including non-Muslims, in schools and certain universities and colleges – the teaching has a strong religious bias as most of the teachers are Islamic religious teachers.
2 Adequate space is not provided for the future construction of churches and temples, as well as places for burial/cremation of non-Muslims in several major towns.
3 Non-Muslims have difficulties in acquiring permits from local authorities to construct churches and temples in certain areas, and when acquired, difficulties in getting building plans approved (often because of the display of non-Muslim religious symbols).
4 In contrast to increasing hours being given to Islamic programmes in the electronic media, very little air time – and only during festive seasons – is given to non-Muslim religions.
5 Distribution of tracts, videos and audio cassettes critical of and ridiculing non-Muslim religions is unrestricted in contrast to strict bans on similar materials critical of Islam.

6 The use of certain words in Malay-Indonesian (many derived from Arabic) by non-Muslims is prohibited.

7 Non-Muslims have difficulties with immigration authorities when applying for the entry or renewal of visas and/or work permits for foreign priests, monks and temple musicians.

8 The position of non-Muslims has been jeopardised by legislation restricting the promoting of their religions among Muslims in several states.

9 Several states have amended their constitutions regarding Islamic law with allegedly negative effect for non-Muslims as a result of a federal Supreme Court ruling that a girl under 18 years of age could not embrace a different religion (in her case, Islam) without the permission of her parents, even though she had attained the lower age of majority under Islamic law, since she had had her first menstruation and was of sound mind.

10 Non-Muslims cannot provide religious instruction for their children in schools, in contrast to the provision of such instruction to Muslim children.

Some of these complaints were resolved after confidential meetings with the prime minister in 1990 and with the deputy prime minister in 1993. Lack of jurisdiction over state laws on religion was acknowledged but problems involving federal agencies could be settled amicably.

The current situation

Islamic revivalism has had the unfortunate effect of arousing reactions among non-Muslims, leading to polarisation in the Malaysian community. Some non-Muslim religious movements have very narrow views. Religious festivals are also celebrated with greater gusto and increased use of symbolism. On university campuses, religious organisations of all kinds are very active, involving most of the students. Consequently, politicians of all faiths have allegedly exploited religion to mobilise communal solidarity against one another during electoral campaigns. None the less, the situation in Malaysia today remains stable because of the commitment of the federal government to a multi-ethnic, multi-religious approach and because of the pace of economic development.

Aliran, a leading Malaysian NGO active on matters of religion and human rights, considers that an inter-religious council which contains representatives from all the faiths is urgently needed to act as a safety valve if religious polarisation worsens. It should have government recognition and support but be independent and empowered to make recommendations to government. It also calls for a new education programme to build understanding and tolerance between Malaysia's religious communities.

PAKISTAN

Pakistan lies in a politically unstable area of South Asia, to the north east of India and Kashmir, and also shares borders with Iran, Afghanistan and China. It is a poor, predominantly Muslim nation with a high illiteracy rate, no compulsory education and 129.3 million people, 54 per cent of whom are under 20 years of age.

The dominant ethnic group is Punjabi (66 per cent) and other ethnic groups are Sindhi (13 per cent), Iranian (9 per cent), Urdu (8 per cent) and Baluchi (3 per cent). Official languages are Urdu and English; 48 per cent of the population are native Punjabi speakers.

Pakistan	
GDP (US$bn)	42
Population	129,300,000
Annual population growth (%)	3
Urban population (%)	33
Working population (%)	28
Literacy (%)	35.7
Ratifications	3

The creation of Pakistan

Pakistan, whose name means 'land of the pure', came into existence in 1947 through the partition of British India. The demand for Pakistan as a separate homeland for Muslims, put forward by Dr Mohammed Iqbal in 1930, was implemented by Mohammad Ali Jinnah. Dr Iqbal considered Hindus and Muslims to be two separate nations, able to be distinguished from each other by their religious and cultural differences, history having proved that they could not live together in harmony and peace. Partition eventually took place in the wake of a communal bloodbath.

The question of whether 'a Muslim state' was a state for Muslims or an Islamic state governed by *shariah* law has been the central debate in Pakistan's short history. The secularists and liberals argued that Islam was only used as a slogan to mobilise support among the Muslim masses and that the founding fathers wanted the state to be democratic.

The Muslim League remained the dominant political party with a strong nationalist but moderate religious programme during the transition to independence from 1947 to 1954. Agreement with India on the protection of minorities in both states was reached in 1950; in Pakistan a Ministry of Minority Affairs was established, largely to allay fears about the status of minorities. Parliamentary government with a multi-party system operating through coalitions was then followed by two periods of martial law (1958–69; 1969–71) and the secession of Bangladesh.

Islamisation

Since partition, popular demand continued for the incorporation of Islamic principles into the constitution and for the Islamisation of laws and society. However, it was not until 1973 that Islam was declared to be the state religion. Though Pakistan's various constitutions have each provided for Islamic principles to be the basis of all law, the degree of state commitment to achieving this has varied greatly. Pakistan's various governments have differed in their attitude towards implementing an Islamic ideology according to the influence of various segments of the ruling elite. Secularists, with Western-styled education and upper-class upbringing, have always insisted on a Pakistan modelled upon Western lines. Liberal reformists have always wanted to amalgamate Western and Islamic principles. Religious revivalists, mostly from the middle and poorer classes, have demanded a purely Islamic society. Today, though a few political parties have secular programmes, almost all other groups agree that society needs reconstruction on the basis of Islamic principles.

Personal law and religious community

The state's commitment to Islamisation has always been accompanied by the proviso that any Islamisation measures would not interfere in any way with the personal laws of non-Muslims and that the personal laws of distinct divisions within the Muslim community would also be protected. The 1961 Muslim Family Laws Ordinance has been controversial from its enactment. However, challenges to its conformity with Islam have proliferated since the late 1980s, following the insertion of Article 2A into the constitution. This article recognises that 'the Muslims shall be enabled to order their lives in their individual and collective spheres in accordance with the teachings and requirements of Islam'. It was argued by the Karachi High Court, in particular, that this article opened up the possibility of aspects of Muslim personal law being challenged as un-Islamic. The Supreme Court has since rejected this argument; however, petitions continue to be submitted condemning the ordinance.

The maintenance of a separate system of personal laws has thus been closely identified with the protection of separate religious identities, and although such a system has not been explicitly stated to be a corollary of the right to religious freedom, to date it seems to have been implicitly accepted in practice. Notably, the Shia community have repeatedly opposed proposals for *shariah* legislation and in particular, proposals to legislate within the field of Muslim personal law, on the ground that any such legislation would be likely to reflect the dominant Sunni interpretation of Islam. It has been suggested that this is the reason for the exclusion of Muslim personal law from the jurisdiction of the *Shariah* Courts.

Religious minorities

Non-Muslims constitute only 3.5 per cent of Pakistan's 117 million people, according to the 1981 census. Christians today, however, claim a higher proportion, some 10 million adherents. Minorities lack educational and employment opportunities and positive discrimination law allows a 6 per cent quota of minorities in employment.

Most Christians are descendants of converts from Hindu lower castes and they are still treated as being of a menial order of society. They are chiefly employed in low-level sanitary work which Muslims will not do and urban sanitary workers live in some segregation. The association with pollution continues because in some parts of Pakistan religious freedom organisations report that Muslims will not touch a utensil used by a Christian unless it is washed. Other work sectors are also closed to non-Muslims because of lack of educational and training opportunities to enable them to compete. Since Christian missionary educational institutions were nationalised in the 1970s, education access for poorer Christians has disappeared and their chances of admission to professional colleges are almost nil. The literacy rate among Christians – always low – dropped to 7 per cent in 1991.

Hindus have also experienced discrimination and intolerance in Pakistan. Christians and Hindus are reported to have a good relationship; both were attacked by Muslims as a result of the Ayodya and Bombay communal riots in India. The government has, however, rebuilt the churches and temples destroyed in the Pakistan riots.

Although Article 36 of the constitution says that the state shall 'safeguard' the legitimate rights and interests of minorities, it is clear that some groups declared to be non-Muslims are not adequately protected. Pakistan's Qadiani Ahmadis may profess belief in the Unity of Allah and the prophethood of Mirza Ghulm Ahmad, but they are not allowed to profess themselves to be Muslims or their faith to be Islam. Ahmadis have not been accorded acceptance as a division within Muslims. From the early years of the state, their beliefs have been at issue with those who held they had no place within an Islamised society and state.

The Punjab disturbances of 1953 were the result of the refusal of the prime minister to do what the *ulema* (religious leaders) demanded, which was for the state to declare Ahmadis a non-Muslim minority and for Ahmadis who held key state posts to be removed from office. The Ahmadis were finally placed in the category of non-Muslims in 1974 by a constitutional amendment which followed renewed communal agitation against them. Pakistan's government justified this in its reply to queries from the Special Rapporteur on Religious Intolerance as being necessary to safeguard majority religious sentiments and also to protect the Ahmadis. Ahmadis are free to form their own political parties, for instance.

The Zikris, a centuries-old minority Muslim group in Baluchistan province, are also regarded by the orthodox groups as non-Muslims because of different practices and belief that their leader is a prophet. They have also been harassed with a view to declaring them non-Muslims.

General Zia's Islamisation measures

Although the religious parties have kept up pressure on successive governments to incorporate Islamic principles in legislation, they have never gained enough electoral support to form a government by themselves. However, they gained enough support under the banner of Islam during the 1977 anti-Bhutto agitation to enable General Zia to impose martial law and rule in the name of Islam until he died in 1988.

General Zia's Islamisation measures included separate electoral rolls so that, since 1985, ten seats are reserved for non-Muslims in the National Assembly, the remaining 207 general seats being for 'Muslim' members. The voting blocs have been a source of grievance for the minorities; they are ineffectively protected as minorities and have little voice in a democratic process. In provincial assemblies, however, the legislation does not specify that general members shall be Muslim, and one Christian traversed a legal minefield to register his candidature for the Punjab Assembly after a Supreme Court decision which was later appealed by the Attorney-General.

In 1978, Zia proclaimed the enforcement of Islamic measures, such as prayers during government departments' working day, businesses and offices closing for Friday prayers, Islamic taxes for *zakat* (supporting the poor), eradicating the lending of money for interest, establishing *Shariah* Courts under the *ulema* (religious leaders) whose decisions could not be challenged, prohibiting alcohol, founding an Islamic university and setting up the advisory Council for Islamic Ideology to examine and study all aspects of Islamisation of law and society. The media were ordered to disseminate Islamic education and women had to cover themselves in public and observe *hijab*. Zia also amended the constitution and the criminal code. The judiciary were made subject to the president.

The Federal *Shariah* Court had the power to initiate the examination of the compatibility or otherwise of any law with the 'injunctions of Islam'. As well, any citizen could challenge the constitutionality of any law on grounds of 'repugnancy to Islam'. Although the jurisdiction of these courts is limited, they have broadened the sphere within which the *shariah* is implemented.

The constitution and freedom of religion or belief

Article 20 of the 1973 constitution protects the freedom to profess religion and to manage religious institutions:

> Subject to law, public order and morality, every citizen shall have the right to profess, practise and propagate his religion, and [every religious denomination and every sect thereof shall have the right] to establish, maintain and manage its religious institutions.

However, Article 20 does not protect all manifestations of religion. Only citizens of Pakistan are protected, and so foreign missionaries may face restrictions in propagating their religion. The right to change one's religion is not protected; it is considered apostasy for a Muslim to renounce Islam and so it is forbidden among Muslims.

Article 21 provides that people shall not be compelled to pay any special tax whose proceeds go to maintain a religion other than their own. However, *zakat* may be collected from all Muslims by the state. Article 22 makes attendance at religious instruction, ceremony and worship in educational institutions non-compulsory if it involves a different religion from one's own. This article also allows private religious and denominational schools maintained wholly by their community to give religious instruction to their pupils. Publicly funded educational institutions may not discriminate in admitting students on the basis of their race, religion, caste or place of birth. It has been held not unconstitutional for a public authority to reserve school places for students from socially or educationally disadvantaged classes.

The Enforcement of *Shariah* (Islamic law) Act of 1991 has imported the *shariah* into the general law; however, it protects constitutional guarantees to women and minorities from the effects of the statute. The 1991 Act did not change the jurisdiction of the *Shariah* Courts; it has been suggested that this is in order to protect the many varying interpretations of Muslim personal law in existence.

Such constitutional guarantees notwithstanding, it is important to note that the constitution has remained suspended for more years than it has been in operation. Although Pakistan has not ratified the ICCPR, it is a party to the CERD and the ILO Convention on Discrimination in Employment and Occupation. The treatment of the Ahmadis, other religious minorities and divisions within Islam has been severely criticised by the implementing bodies of these treaties as well as by the Special Rapporteurs on Religious Intolerance.

Legislation like the *Hudud* Ordinances, the Qadiani Ordinance and the Qanoon-e-Shahadat Ordinance are protected by the eighth amendment to the constitution and can only be removed by repealing it. This is significant as the discriminatory practices enshrined in that legislation are now deeply embedded in the state's constitutional system.

Sectarianism and discrimination

Although Sunni and Shia Muslims live and work amicably together in many parts of the country, the monocultural construction of Pakistan has made it vulnerable to the sectarianism and communal politics which so devastate its society today. All Pakistan's governments had turned a blind eye to extremist religious groups fomenting communal hatred, tendencies which were encouraged by lack of education and unemployment.

Communal violence against Muslims in India flowed over to Pakistan. With the destruction of the Babri Mosque in Ayodya, Pakistani Hindus were attacked and killed, temples destroyed, houses and shops looted and burned while police stood by without intervening.

The war in Afghanistan provided fuel for religious feelings, armed groups aligning themselves with different groups of Afghan *mujahideen*. Extremist parties also started exploiting sensitive religious differences between Sunni and Shia Muslims who constitute 77 per cent and 20 per cent of the population, respectively. After the Iranian Revolution at the end of the 1970s, Shias became more assertive and vocal, with violent clashes, armed rallies and the bombing of mosques belonging to opponent groups. Sunnis are also split by factionalism into various groups, such as Brelvis, Deobandis and Wahabis. Almost all these groups are fully armed and have no shortage of trained men from the Afghan war. Iran and Saudi Arabia openly finance their Shia and Sunni allies.

Sectarian tension is associated with the absence of effective democratic institutions. The Northern Areas of Pakistan have witnessed a number of clashes between Shia and Sunni communities, among other conflicts. The population is dominated by Shias (50 per cent) and Ismailis (35 per cent). Sunnis constitute only 15 per cent but the prevailing civil and military administration is dominated by Sunnis and Shias experience discrimination in their everyday lives.

Spokespersons for the Northern Areas communities have identified the absence of a democratic process within the region as a major contributory factor in arousing community tensions. No elections take place and the people in the Northern Areas have no vote in federal or provincial elections, owing to the status of the Northern Areas as a former part of Kashmir and the highly sensitive nature of politics within the region. Political agents are appointed by the government to administer the region, continuing British colonial structures. Opinion is divided over the future of this region, whether it should be part of Kashmir (independent or not) or a fifth state in Pakistan. Various proposals for administrative or political entities have been attended by fears that a Shia majority in a current entity would become a minority in a proposed amalgamation of territories inside state borders, or a Sunni majority become a minority.

Communal violence in which Sunni and Shia armed groups attack each other's communities continues to set the scene for the widespread unrest and disregard for law which is devastating the cities of Karachi and the Punjab both socially and economically. The government forces have also been in conflict with the Muhajir Quami Movement (MQM), a party representing Urdu-speaking Muslims who fled from India at partition and who have been seeking recognition as a distinct nationality within Pakistan, alongside Punjabis, Sindhis, Pathans and Baluchis. However, with the enormous influx of Afghan refugees into Karachi, the Muhajirs may no longer be in the majority there.

In an effort to counter the impunity with which sectarian forces were operating, Benazir Bhutto reportedly ordered the arrest in early 1995 of over 100 Sunni and Shia extremists allegedly responsible for communalist murders, some of people praying in mosques. In January she had also banned foreign funding for the religious schools in Pakistan as a first move to pinpoint schools responsible for preaching sectarian hatred. Extremist politicians, some of them religious leaders, also exploit the sentiments of a largely illiterate population. The authorities in May 1995 reportedly banned Muslim religious scholars from the Punjab from entering the province of Sind during the first month of the Islamic calendar, on the grounds that they were likely to incite hatred and ill-will between different religious divisions through 'inflammatory speeches'.

However, despite further periods of martial law, the government has often seemed powerless amid the spectacle of endemic human rights abuses; the weakness of its institutions has been seen as contributing to the dramatic increase in sectarian violence in Karachi. Benazir Bhutto's government was dismissed in 1996.

Penal legislation and its effect

Legislation prohibiting religious manifestations of particular minority groups has an adverse effect on all minorities. Chapter XV of the criminal code of Pakistan lists offences relating to the protection of the sensibilities of its religious communities. Up to 1980, the code referred to the use of words or actions and to disturbances of religious assemblies and burials in general terms applying to all religions. The Penal Code was expanded by Zia's military government to include provisions drafted in highly specific terms intended to restrict the activities of various Islamic sects considered not orthodox by the dominant clergy and also communities, such as the Ahmadis, who identified themselves as Muslim but were officially declared to be non-Muslims.

In 1980, Section 298A of the Penal Code made punishable by three-year imprisonment, fine or both, the use of words, images or any imputations 'defiling the sacred name' of certain personages related to the Prophet. This was intended to stop the preachings of those Muslims who do not recognise the three earlier Caliphs as legitimate and who question the role of one of the Prophet's wives.

In 1984, Sections 298B and 298C were added – the Qadiani Ordinance – prohibiting the manifestation of the beliefs of the Ahmadis, subject to three years' imprisonment and a fine. Section 298B prohibits Ahmadis from using specific Islamic religious terms for personages, places of worship and prayer in their own practices. Section 298C also makes it an offence for Ahmadis to call themselves Muslims or to propagate their faith, directly or indirectly, or to outrage the feelings of Muslims in any manner.

The application of these laws has resulted in widespread discrimination against Ahmadis and other minorities, not only in relation to their religious practice. In 1991 the government asked for details of all Ahmadis in government employment because cabinet had decided they were not allowed to remain in important positions. Despite the constitutional guarantee of no discrimination in government employment, thirty civil servants were sacked because they were Ahmadi between 1984 and 1992. Classified as non-Muslims on their passports, they cannot gain access to Mecca to perform the *haj*. A proposal to include religion on the national identity card would result in even more discrimination against Ahmadis.

In 1991, the Lahore High Court upheld the ban on Ahmadis holding their centenary celebrations. The Advocate-General argued that to allow the celebrations would be tantamount to giving Ahmadis the freedom to preach their faith, a crime (as blasphemy) punishable by death; even an Ahmadi preaching his faith to his child was seen as a crime. The court agreed on the basis of the public interest, majority disapproval of Ahmadi beliefs and the need to 'keep the mainstream of faith pure'. Several members of the Ahmadi community have been sued for inscribing Qur'anic phrases in their private letters and wedding cards or for calling themselves names like Mohammed. Two Ahmadis were stoned by a crowd in Peshawar in 1995 – one died – for allegedly trying to convert a Muslim.

Offences related to blasphemy and desecration

Under General Zia, life imprisonment became the punishment for the Section 295B offence of defiling, damaging, desecrating a copy of the Qur'an, using it in a derogatory manner or for any unlawful purpose; from 1982 such offences were tried by a special military court. But death or life imprisonment, plus a fine, were the punishments laid down for the Section 295C offence of blasphemy by 'whosoever by words, either spoken or written, or by visible representation, or by any imputation, innuendo, or insinuation directly or indirectly, defiles the name of the Holy Prophet'. When this provision was challenged before the federal Shariah Court, the court upheld the view – which still stands – that blasphemy must be punishable only by death; it should be noted that in Shariah

Courts, no non-Muslim may give evidence against a Muslim. In May 1991, the federal government, fearing backlash from the religious lobbies, withdrew its appeal to the Supreme Court against the judgment. In a further clarification, the Lahore High Court in 1994 reportedly laid down the principle that blasphemy against any prophet of God is tantamount to blasphemy against the Prophet. The Pakistan government reported that one Muslim was being tried for blaspheming against the Prophet Jesus Christ, as well as a Christian against the Prophet Mohammed.

The procedure for initiating blasphemy prosecutions has been open to abuse as anyone may be charged by the police under Section 295C and arrested without a warrant. It has been easy to register a false case for personal or political reasons and a person charged is immediately stigmatised as a blasphemer, facing the loss of honour, property and even life.

Since Section 295C came into force, the number of cases registered has escalated and in some cases the blasphemy charge has been added to other charges as an afterthought. At least four Christians and a Muslim have been killed, two without being convicted. Between 1987 and 1992, 106 Ahmadis were charged under the blasphemy law but none has been convicted. Several Muslims have also been charged. Two people, Christian and Muslim, were killed by mobs after rumours of blasphemy were circulated about them. Christian teachers and shopkeepers have been accused of blasphemy by people with various personal motives.

Rahmat, Manzoor and Salamat Masih – Christians – were accused of writing blasphemous remarks against the Prophet; Salamat was 11 years old and illiterate at the time of the alleged offence. All three were attacked in Lahore in March 1994 in front of the High Court, resulting in Manzoor's death. The remaining two were condemned to death in February 1995, the then Prime Minister Benazir Bhutto publicly expressing her displeasure with the verdict. Extremist groups called for their hanging outside the Lahore High Court during a successful appeal. Death threats were received by the judiciary and the legal counsel for the Christians was attacked. Released, the two flew to Germany, in the care of a Christian organisation. More than forty people now face the death sentence, mostly Ahmadis.

Repeal of the blasphemy laws is highly unlikely under current circumstances. Benazir Bhutto's proposal to amend the law merely to improve procedural points was opposed by religious groups, some issuing *fatwas* (religious decrees) calling for the death of those who proposed change. Amendments have been made which introduce greater procedural fairness in the application of the law. However, the law itself may be criticised for entrenching and validating intolerance. Christians have said that they are discouraged from entering into inter-faith dialogue with Muslims for fear that a simple statement of their faith would be held to be slandering the Prophet Mohammed.

Women and religious law and custom

Women have lower status in Pakistan, worse health and lower literacy rates than men. In 1992, 62 per cent of girls eligible to enrol did not start school. Pakistan has not yet ratified the CEDAW, but is at present said to be considering becoming a party to it with no reservations in relation to the supremacy of the *shariah*. Article 25 of the constitution grants women equal status to men.

In the *Hudud* Ordinances introduced by General Zia in 1979, the changes in the laws of evidence have had a significant impact on women, especially in prosecutions under the Zina (unlawful sexual intercourse) Ordinance governing the crimes of adultery, rape and fornication. In rape trials, where an attempt is made to impose the *hadd* (Qur'anic punishment of stoning to death or 100 stripes in a public place) punishment, Qur'anic standards of proof are required, that is, four male witnesses to the adultery or fornication. If *hadd* is not invoked, a lesser punishment (*tazir*) applies. However, rape cases are often presented by the defence as adultery on the part of the woman and because of the complexities of the Zina Ordinance, false charges of unlawful sex can be threatened as a form of blackmail. It is estimated that fewer than ten cases out of every 100 filed under the Zina Ordinance result in conviction; however, years may be spent in jail before a very long and unpleasant trial and no compensation is available to the innocent. Thousands of women were reported in 1990 to be in jail awaiting trial mostly on adultery charges. The *hadd* sentence of death by stoning has not yet been carried out.

Additionally, the Qanoon-e-Shahadat Ordinance of 1984 directly discriminates against women. It states that, 'In matters pertaining to financial or future obligations, if reduced to writing, the instrument shall be attested by two men, or one man and two women, so that one may remind the other.' Originally drafted to apply to all matters, after protests from women's groups and others the Ordinance was restricted to financial transactions in writing. Female lawyers in particular have been affected by it.

Personal law is dispensed through various systems of interpretation in matters of inheritance, succession and family matters. Lack of consistency and in-built discrimination against women in marriage and divorce matters are the cause of agitation for reform. However, such proposals are perceived as a threat to religious freedom, however damaging the unreformed law is to women. In April 1996, action began in the Lahore High Court to determine whether Islamic laws and principles allow Saima Waheed, a woman aged 21, to leave home, live independently and marry regardless of her father's opposition to the match. The woman's life is considered to be at risk in this highly charged case.

The Women's Action Forum and other women's groups in Pakistan work constantly for law reform and to create awareness of women's rights. Benazir Bhutto's government had identified laws which are discriminatory to women and was reviewing them. Women have been appointed to special police stations and as judges. However, their work is counteracted at the parliamentary level by electoral manipulation and by powerful religious groups who have firm views about the status and role of women.

Custom is also responsible for discrimination against women. In rural Pakistan, despite clear injunctions from both civil and *shariah* law enjoining the right of women to inherit, a family who wishes to keep control of a daughter's inheritance or to swell her brother's portion may 'marry her to the Qur'an', a practice not sanctioned by religion but enforced by custom legitimated by the name of religion. A woman 'married to the Qur'an' is kept in seclusion from any contact with men, even in her own family, after she reaches 14 years of age.

PHILIPPINES

The Philippines is the world's second largest archipelago. Luzon, to the north, makes up about two-thirds of Philippine territory. The second biggest island is Mindanao, to the south. Religious difference is only one aspect of the south, which is an area of vast ethnic and linguistic diversity, and complex problems.

The Philippine population of 63.4 million is mainly of Malay ethnic origin intermingled with others who arrived more recently: Chinese, Indians, Arabs and later, people of European origin. The small Chinese–Filipino community has preserved its close family

Philippines	
GDP (US$bn)	53
Population	63,400,000
Annual population growth (%)	2.6
Urban population (%)	51
Working population (%)	56[a]
Literacy (%)	94
Ratifications	1; 2, 2(a), 2(b); 3; 4

ties and customs; many have wealth and influence. Around 7 million people are members of indigenous communities. They maintain close links to their ancestral past and have been least influenced by colonial Hispanicisation and Americanisation of the lowland Christian majority. Indigenous people accounted for 17 per cent of Mindanao's 16 million population in 1992.

Economic and social structure

Despite its abundant human and natural resources, the Philippines has one of the worst poverty incidences in Asia, more than 45 per cent, and its economic performance lags behind that of other South East Asian nations, although its recovery is gathering speed. It is estimated that more than half of the country's wealth is enjoyed by only about 20 per cent of the population.

The Philippines economy is still mainly agricultural. Agrarian reform has been proposed since the 1930s by politicians, rural rebels, counter-insurgency experts, urban middle-class reformers and the Catholic Church; enacted by Congress in 1988, it has yet to be implemented. Jobs and resources are allocated through family, regional and patron–client political loyalties, making equality of access and participation an issue for the poor and for minorities.

Population pressure in the lowlands coupled with the rural landlord system have caused many Filipinos since 1945 to migrate to the cities and to 'public forest' land in the hills of less crowded Mindanao. The deforestation accompanying logging and clearing for settlement and development has displaced local indigenous peoples from their ancestral land, disrupting their customary practices. For instance, the Cubayon River dam will displace 18,000 Bugkalots. The assertion that the state owned all land not in actual cultivation at annexure was legitimated by the Spanish doctrine of land ownership which overrode ancestral land rights. Although the constitution calls for protection of indigenous peoples' ancestral lands and cultures, no laws give effect to this.

Political and legal system

Philippine constitutions have contained guarantees of human rights since the revolution against Spanish rule in 1898 and under the subsequent American occupation from 1900. The 1930s' independence movement culminated, after the Japanese occupation during the Second World War, in independence of the Philippines from the United States in 1946. After President Marcos was deposed from power in 1986, President Aquino decreed a temporary 'Freedom Constitution' which abolished all state institutions except the bill of rights. A new constitution, drafted by a constitutional convention, was ratified in 1987. The Supreme Court remains the final arbiter in the judicial system, except for matters which, in the court's opinion, are better dealt with by referendum.

The president is the chief executive and head of state. Law making is vested in a congress modelled on that of the United States, as is the electoral-based democratic tradition. The thriving multi-party system is made up of landowner and lawyer politicians recruited from the Filipino economic, social and political elite. Representatives of the middle class, the urban and rural poor, peasants, unions and ethnic minorities have no organised parties and thus little say in national affairs. However, some of a coalition of cause-oriented groups formed in the mid-1980s by anti-Marcos non-governmental organisations – several are connected with the churches – have survived the disillusionment of the 1980s to advocate democratic developments in line with human rights.

The Philippine government has ratified many international human rights instruments. However, documented reports of human rights abuses continue to attest to violations by the military and the rebels in the communist and Muslim insurgencies. Amnesties granted by the Aquino and Ramos governments to communist and Muslim rebels have made it difficult, in the context of a restive military, to prosecute the military and the police for human rights abuses.

Constitutional protection of freedom of religion or belief

The constitution states that 'the separation of Church and State shall be inviolable'. Article III (1) guarantees to everyone the equal protection of the laws. Freedom of religion is protected in the Bill of Rights, Article III (5) which states that:

> No law shall be made respecting an establishment of religion, or prohibiting the free exercise thereof. The free exercise and enjoyment of religious profession and worship, without discrimination or preference, shall forever be allowed. No religious test shall forever be allowed. No religious test shall be required for the exercise of civil or political rights.

Civil courts may resolve property disputes within religious groups but not internal disputes about matters of faith. Marriage and divorce are performed under civil procedures, religious ones not being legally binding. Churches, mosques, convents and other religious, educational and charitable institutions are tax exempt. Except to fund certain chaplaincies, no government revenue can be applied to support religious institutions or personnel. Educational institutions established by religious groups and mission boards may be foreign-owned but must be locally controlled and managed.

If parents or guardians indicate their wishes in writing, the constitution states that:

> religion shall be allowed to be taught to their children or wards in public elementary and high schools within the regular class hours by instructors designated or approved by the religious authorities of the religion to which the children or wards belong, without additional cost to the government.

Sanctions for the non-observance or the violation of the right can be found both in the revised Penal Code and in the civil code as actions for damages in compensation for intrusion on privacy, discrimination, harassment or humiliation because of religious beliefs. Public officials are constrained not to disturb religious worship or practices or to discriminate in their performance of marriages. No-one is allowed to offend religious feelings during worship or ceremonies. The state may only interfere with religious practice in cases where there is a paramount interest of public health, safety or morals.

The constitutional provision on the freedom of religion includes the freedom to reject, and the refusal to believe in a hereafter or in a supreme being. However, despite the fact that religious doubt, agnosticism and atheism are constitutionally protected, it is anathema to express atheistic beliefs openly. Two decades ago, one group openly advocated humanism, principally on more liberal school and university campuses. The Theosophical Society has held discussions and produces publications.

Religions and beliefs

The strength of the Roman Catholic Church is associated with more than three centuries of Spanish rule. The Spanish missionary friar was head of both the church and civil government in each town during the colonial period. Indigenous and Muslim rituals were dismissed as being only 'fit for pagans' and 'infidels', hence leading to eternal damnation. The church has played a major role in assimilating diverse communities into a single lowland Christian set of customs and traditions throughout the Philippines, creating the cultural majority. Although indigenous ways of life were eroded by the imposition of Roman Catholicism under Spanish rule and by the education system imposed by the Americans, family and linguistic group are still extremely important in Filipino society.

Most Christian Filipinos belong to the Roman Catholic faith; about 85 per cent of the population is nominally Catholic. The country proudly declares that it is the 'only Christian country in the region' and the church hierarchy is very influential in forming public opinion. Among Philippine Protestants are members of the Iglesia Filipina Independiente (Aglipayan) and the Iglesia ni Christo, 'born again' and charismatic Christians. There are also a number of small groups among the rural and urban poor which combine millenarian beliefs with veneration of national heroes as saints.

Because Islamic kingdoms flourished from about 1400 in the Malayo-Indonesian archipelago, Islam was brought to the Philippines by settlers and traders. Muslim Filipinos now number about 5 million, around 8 per cent of the entire population, inhabiting central and south-western Mindanao, Basilan, Sulu and parts of Palawan.

Until this century, indigenous peoples in the Philippines, such as the Igorot, the Mangyan, the Aetas and the Lumads, were animists; they venerated local spirits and ancestors as sources for continuing and sustaining life. Special burial practices are still followed by some groups. Non-Muslim indigenous cultural communities now amount to about 4 million people who live in the interiors of Luzon, Mindanao and Mindoro islands.

Christian–Muslim relations

Despite legal sanctions, prejudice in socio-cultural attitudes leads to discrimination. According to stereotypes underlying such prejudice, Christians perceive Muslim Moro society as feudal and backward, while Muslims and other groups consider the Christians to be exploiters and oppressors, land grabbers and opportunists. Lately, however, prejudiced attitudes among the Catholic Christian community are slowly being eroded through various educational initiatives by government and non-government institutions and inter-faith organisations.

Christian Filipino attitudes to the Muslim Filipino community originate in Spanish hatred for the Moors who occupied Spain for several centuries; all Muslims were categorised as 'Moro' (Moor), the Spaniards' national enemy. Whereas the Manila and Cebu sultanates were rapidly subdued by the Spanish, the sultanates of Mindanao were capable of organised and prolonged military resistance. 'Moro' pirates and raiders ravaged the coastal villages of Christian Philippines until the late nineteenth century, in part as resistance by the sultanates and in part for the profit from loot and slaves. The Spanish colonial power levied heavy taxes and labour conscription on the Christian Filipinos to build and man fleets to deal with the Muslim 'enemy'. Many items of folk religion, including the Moro-Moro plays enacted at fiestas, help to perpetuate the ancient enmity.

With superior arms and military organisation, the United States colonial power brought the Muslim areas under military control by 1915. Thereafter they began to be incorporated into the colonial state, then into the emergent nation–state. However, Mindanao's lightly populated land and its resources beckoned to the densely populated Visayas and to foreign and Luzon entrepreneurs. From about 1946 there was massive Christian migration to Mindanao. At first the Muslim *datus* (chiefs) welcomed more tribute-paying settlers but, by the 1960s, the Muslims were outnumbered by Christians on much of what had been traditional lands of Muslim ethnic groups. Christian majorities elected Christian village headmen, mayors, governors and congressmen. Christians then got jobs through patronage. State schools threatened Muslim cultural identity just as state land title threatened customary land claims and elections threatened Muslim political control. Combined with world-wide Muslim political activism in the late 1960s, young Muslims returning from education abroad, and encouragement in some cases from OPEC Muslim states, these problems generated ethnic conflict in Mindanao-Sulu.

Insurrection and conflict

Rural discontent with the Marcos regime supported the Communist Party of the Philippines and its military arm, the New People's Army (NPA), which in 1985 operated 'fronts' in more than two-thirds of the provinces. While the armed conflict between these rebels and the government in counter-insurrectionary forces escalated during the late 1980s and early 1990s, amnesties since 1986 plus ideological conflicts and splits have depleted rebel ranks.

In the south, the Muslim rebellion was led mainly by the Moro National Liberation Front, which mounted a war for a separate Islamic state after Marcos imposed martial law in 1972. The secessionist movement has slowly weakened, likewise plagued by splits and differences in its complex ethnic and political make-up, resulting in the emergence of groups and factions such as the Moro Islamic Liberation Front and, lately, the Abu Sayyaf.

Religion is just one aspect of social, economic and political complexity, an aspect which may be asserted by any of the parties in order to justify certain actions. The extremist Abu Sayyaf group, linked with Afghan and Pakistani guerrilla movements, have been said to be responsible for the bombing of San Pedro Cathedral in Davao and other churches. Abu Sayyaf has recently claimed responsibility for kidnappings not only of Christian missionaries and other religious personages, but also of businessmen and other citizens. In June 1994, the group killed sixteen out of a large group of Christians who were not able to recite passages from the Qur'an.

Nearly 8,000 families – mostly indigenous – were displaced in Mindanao by the fighting in 1993. Social and economic turmoil persists there; only business interests prosper as wealth is transferred to the north. Civilian militias, private armies, corrupt military officers and the police, acting in collusion with business interests and corrupt government officials, commit most of the human rights abuses, according to the Philippine Commission on Human Rights and prominent NGOs. Among organisations engaged in social welfare and human rights activities in the region are some Catholic religious orders.

The ideology of nation-building, cohesion and modernisation, promulgated by the Luzon-based elite, has contributed to the growth of communalism among Mindanao Muslims. The government has been hard-pressed to provide immediate and long-term solutions to the armed opposition groups that are actively engaged in rebellion. In June 1996, the government and the rebels agreed on a Southern Philippines Council for Peace and Development as a stage towards autonomous government for fourteen southern provinces. However, Christians in the region have been strongly opposed to the proposed rebel-led council.

Promotion of religion or belief and proselytising

The constitutional guarantee of protection for dissemination and propagation of a religion or belief has been upheld by the Supreme Court, in a case in which a municipal authority required a religious corporation selling Bibles and other religious articles to get a licence to sell them and to pay the corresponding fees. The court held that licence fees could not be imposed upon a foreign, non-profit, religious, missionary corporation for its distribution and sale of Bibles and other religious literature. The religious corporation was consequently granted exemption from municipal fees.

Catholics and Protestants have historically sent missionaries to non-Christian areas, sometimes providing medical, educational and development benefits as attractions. Animist groups have not resisted missionaries militarily in this century. However, Muslim groups have deeply resented and sometimes taken action against Filipino and foreign missionaries. Foreign Protestant groups with generous funds are unimpeded in evangelical work in which they use education, medical services and livelihood projects to attract indigenous people. There is an undercurrent of resentment against the groups of United States origin which proselytise to Catholics.

Education and the family

There is a high degree of literacy among Filipinos. Religious education is not part of the compulsory curriculum in public or state schools and universities. State funds cannot be used for the benefit or advantage of any religious group or community as the state might be seen to be favouring one religious group at the expense of another. However, religious instruction may be given by catechists or other orders as part of their ministry. Some Muslim children are educated in Muslim schools.

The family is highly regarded in the Philippines and protected by law. Adherence to a particular religion is like an heirloom, inherited and passed on through the generations, just like a family custom or tradition. Any effort to break this tradition is met not only with violent disapproval but could mean ostracism and the cutting of ties with other family members. Consequently, freedom to choose or hold a belief, or a conviction, may depend on how open a person's family is to accepting religious difference among its members.

The media

Freedom of expression – and freedom of the press – are among the most cherished of Philippine freedoms; the government can be criticised without fear of reprisal. Production and distribution of religious articles and publications are unhampered, readily observable by the number of religious pamphlets, articles and publications that are given away and freely circulated.

Under martial law, former President Marcos controlled all the media. The Catholic Church underground press and its Radio Veritas were among the few sources of criticism of the regime and Radio Veritas played a role in Marcos's overthrow in 1986. The

Protestant Iglesia ni Christo has its own press and radio. The media run by United States-funded evangelical churches have been accused of exacerbating ethnic tensions. Government media are relatively balanced in reporting but are imbued with a Christian perspective which has been considered offensive by some Muslims.

State relations with the Catholic Church today

The Philippines, although predominantly Roman Catholic, does not have an established state religion. The separation of church and state is a principle written in the constitution. The Catholic Church legally shared state affairs during the Spanish period. Today, lawmakers are careful how they tread in matters that are perceived to belong to the Catholic Church's sphere – such as divorce, contraception and abortion – whereas some church leaders have not hesitated to use their influence over their followers in order to pressure the government. Religiously affiliated political parties are allowed, such as the National Union of Christian Democrats (NUDC). President Ramos – a Protestant – rules by coalition between his party, the NUDC, and Laban, the largest opposition group.

Fiery debates between government and the Catholic hierarchy or the religious sector have been carried on in the print and broadcast media. The foremost example is the ongoing controversy over the government's population or family planning programme to which the Catholic Church has objected as it will endorse only the rhythm method of contraception. Department of Health campaigns for the use of condoms – especially in the government's anti-AIDS campaign – have been vigorously opposed.

During the preparation of the Philippine position for the International Conference on Population and Development, held in Cairo in 1994, the Catholic Church charged the government with endorsing not only artificial contraception as a means of population control but also with taking a pro-abortion stance, with accepting and promoting different family types (such as homosexual families and unions) as part of the government's population control programme. Several full-page newspaper advertisements were run by lay Catholic groups attacking what they claimed to be the government position. The church organised a Sunday rally of some 500,000 attended by government officials and politicians, including former President Aquino. The pressure was sufficient to have some impact on the government's position and on the composition of its conference delegation.

Women and religion

In the struggle for women's rights, for equality and non-discrimination, there is a long way to go before the rhetoric on equality is translated into positive action. Gender-based discrimination is prevalent although this is denied at all levels of law and policy.

One of the most sensitive issues is the access of women to positions of power, both within their own church hierarchy, groups or community, and in positions of responsibility in religious organisations. No woman member of a religious community may resort to the law for the enforcement of her fundamental right to equality. In the Philippines, as in other countries, the Roman Catholic Church still rejects the ordination of women as priests. In other Christian denominations, women have become ministers, performing religious rituals, but positions in church hierarchies are still beyond their reach.

Although the Catholic Church hierarchy is extremely conservative, there are a number of reformist priests who assist in the formation of basic religious communities in which women have more voice and theological education. The Catholic reformist movement is also aggressive in confronting the state on matters of poverty and corrupt practice. These latter affect women's lives to an extraordinary degree, leading to the 'export' of women as very poorly treated – often criminally victimised – servants, prostitutes and wives for foreign families and men who expect the stereotype of female Catholic servitude which has unfortunately been promulgated by the official church. The Catholic Church has also been criticised for doing little to assist the quite large number of young women and girls whom poverty forces to become part of the sex trade for foreign tourists.

SINGAPORE

Singapore	
GDP (US$bn)	46
Population	2,800,000
Annual population growth (%)	1.7
Urban population (%)	100
Working population (%)	49
Literacy (%)	89.9
Ratifications	4

The Republic of Singapore, a tiny city–state of 2.8 million people and founded on multi-racialism, is the most outspoken among Asian nations of the view that human rights is an essentially Western concept which has been imposed on ancient civilisations whose traditional values would be more suited to their cultural ethos, sense of community and method of achieving economic goals.

Singapore has successfully maintained high economic growth rates for most of the past twenty-five years and has been transformed from a colonial entrepôt into a modern, high-tech city with almost full employment, a very high per capita income of over US $11,800, good housing, health services and clean water supply.

Singapore has not ratified any of the major United Nations human rights agreements and appears to have no intention of doing so. Singaporean society is tightly disciplined. There is no pretence that the full substance of civil and political rights is granted to citizens; rather, the state continually justifies the circumscription of rights as necessary for the survival and security of the nation. The only social behaviour permitted is thus that which conforms to the political and economic goals of the state. However, Singapore's material success has encouraged a personal independence, individualism and mobility which also may not necessarily accord with the state's interests. To counter Westernisation and the prospect of cultural values eroded by materialism, in 1991 a government White Paper identified four core values in a National Ideology of Shared Values: community over self, the family as a basic building block of society, using consensus to resolve major issues and stressing racial and religious harmony. In 1994, a set of Family Values was propagated, more precisely related to the government's anti-welfarist stance. Among other things it stresses women's obligations in the family for all ethnic groups. This has led to differential benefits for women who produce children and condemnation of those among the highly educated elite who choose to have no children, small families or not marry at all.

Ethnic and religious composition

Most Singaporeans are Chinese (78 per cent) and most Chinese are either Buddhists (31 per cent) or adherents of Chinese traditional beliefs and Taoism (22 per cent). The next largest affiliation is Islam (15 per cent). Virtually all Malays are Muslim and form 14 per cent of the population, the remainder of Muslims being mostly Indian. Christians make up 13 per cent of the population – most Christians are Chinese and some Indian – followed by Hindus with 4 per cent. Christians form a wealthy elite; 41 per cent of university graduates are Christian.

Malays, who are the indigenous people of the region, form the lowest socio-economic stratum of Singapore society and suffer institutional discrimination at many levels of an essentially Chinese polity. Malay religious homogeneity based on the Islamic faith is regarded with wariness by the Singapore government which keeps a close eye on external influences.

The Singapore Muslim Religious Council, a statutory board advising the president on all Muslim religious matters, has over the years acted to centralise and standardise Islamic practice. From 1957, the *Shariah* Court has had jurisdiction over divorce and inheritance matters, and in 1989 the Council took direct control over subjects taught in Islamic schools and of Friday mosque sermons.

The government is concerned not to allow minorities to dominate in enclaves and has legislated to preserve a balance in a multi-religious and multi-racial society. The government established a Presidential Council for Minority Rights which advises the government on legislation to ensure that no ethnic or religious minority is disadvantaged unintentionally by laws or regulations. The Council is chaired by the Chief Justice of the Supreme Court and its membership includes Senior Minister Lee Kuan Yew, the Attorney-General, the Roman Catholic Archbishop and other representatives of minority faiths and communities.

Political structure

The island of Singapore forms an enclave of Chinese immigration within the formerly British-ruled Malay peninsula. The People's Action Party (PAP), formed in 1954, won the 1959 elections and gained state power in the transition to independence in 1965. The Lee Kuan Yew faction's cooperation with the British and then the Malaysian governments led to its undermining of the PAP's broader-based left wing which had dominated the anti-colonialist movement.

Singapore's political structure, deriving from British parliamentarism based on universal suffrage, has gradually been adapted to the imperatives of a one-party republican state. There is a formal commitment to parliamentary democracy; however, the PAP's determination to remain in power has ensured that it has had either a monopoly of seats in the legislature or – despite almost 40 per cent of the vote going to opposition parties – faced only one or two opposition members in parliament. Opposition political parties have been kept weak by systematic suppression of dissenting opinion in the wider society.

The civil service has acted as the organisational base of the ruling party because of the conflation of government and party during thirty-five years of single party rule. Government and party apparatuses are also merged at the community level through a pervasive network of official bodies, cementing in place a comprehensive system of intelligence gathering and social control. Members of such committees are recommended by their PAP members of parliament, security vetted and then appointed by the prime minister's office.

From 1991, the president of Singapore has held wide powers. The power of veto gives the president the final say in all major financial, political, and personnel matters. Lee

Kuan Yew is Senior Minister in the Prime Minister's Office, after retiring from the post of prime minister.

The legal system

Singapore's constitution states that it guarantees citizens the protection of entrenched fundamental rights such as equality before the law, freedom of speech, assembly and association, the right to profess, practise and propagate one's religion, the right to protection from discrimination on the grounds of religion, race, descent or place of birth (Articles 12, 14–16). However, these provisions are heavily qualified in the constitution and substantively overridden by other legislation as the constitution does not act as the supreme law.

The president appoints all Supreme Court and subordinate court judges. Legislation also precludes government decisions being open to judicial review, including the president's executive actions. Ties with the Privy Council in London have been severed.

A number of laws and administrative measures have in effect restricted freedom of expression and association, prerequisites for free exercise of thought, conscience and religion or belief.

Freedom of expression

In Singapore, personal space is by no means private space. There is an extensive system of surveillance throughout the housing estates. All citizens are finger-printed when they reach the age of 12 years. This is recorded on an identity card which is used in all dealings with the state, including all services such as pension scheme, state housing, utilities, telephone, schools, hospitals, income tax, driving licence and passport.

The Singapore government carefully controls the domestic media and restricts the foreign media while allowing some modulated criticism of selected policies in the press and occasional brief reports of the highly critical opinions of opposition politicians. The independence of the domestic media was effectively ended by the PAP in the 1960s and 1970s. As well as the Sedition Act, the Internal Security Act (ISA) was invoked to suppress any material deemed prejudicial to the 'national interest, public order or society of Singapore'. The restructuring of the domestic press during the early 1980s established a government-controlled conglomerate which incorporates all the major newspapers.

The Broadcasting and Television Act (1963) gave the government the sole right to establish radio and television stations. The Singapore Broadcasting Corporation (SBC) is a statutory board which cooperates closely with the Internal Security Department.

Freedom of expression through academic research and debate is also severely limited in Singapore.

The Internal Security Act and the Societies Act

The Internal Security Act (ISA) has been used against PAP's political opponents since the party came to power. In 1963, 133 opposition members, trade unionists, educators and journalists were arrested. It gives the government extraordinary powers of executive detention and extensive abuses of human rights have been documented. The use of the ISA should be seen in the context of a criminal code which has increased the power of discipline on anyone exhibiting behaviour held to be non-conformist. The criminal law mediates a high level of violence, regularly increasing penalties, especially through flogging and hanging.

The most recent ISA mass arrest took place in 1987 when twenty-two young Roman Catholics were detained, accused of being involved in a Marxist conspiracy to overthrow the state. Vincent Cheng's televised acknowledgement of Marxist contribution to liberation theology was considered by an international mission of jurists in 1987 to reflect his concern for the underprivileged and a wish to see a more just and equal society. Those arrested had been providing free legal assistance, running church welfare centres and involved in the Catholic Justice and Peace Commission's activism on social inequality and poverty. The PAP government pressured the church leadership to disband the Commission by threatening to bring it under the Societies Act if the Archbishop, in the words of Lee Kuan Yew, 'could not put his own house in order'.

The effect of the Societies Act has been to suppress all political activity at the community level except that which is supportive of the government or politically non-controversial. It prevents registered organisations from developing into community pressure groups; some religious groups and organisations have been affected by it. Heavy penalties are also laid down for organising processions or assemblies without a police permit.

The Societies Act was among the legislation used in the 1950s and 1960s to suppress political opposition from trade unions, educational institutions, journalists and newspapers. In 1987 the international headquarters of the Asian council of churches (the Christian Conference of Asia or CCA) was suddenly dissolved under Section 24(1) of the Societies Act, its accounts frozen, property seized and affairs wound up; its international staff were expelled. The government claimed the CCA had breached its undertaking 'not to indulge in any political activity or allow its funds to be used for political purposes'.

The Watch Tower Bible and Tract Society (Jehovah's Witnesses) was deregistered in 1972. The Unification Church is also banned.

Freedom of religion

The PAP government has retained its firm commitment to a secular state and has consistently encouraged good relations between religions. It has also assisted with the formalities of self-regulation of religious bodies. The government established the Council for Muslim Religion as an advisory body to the President of Singapore to regulate the affairs of Muslim organisations and to oversee the administration of Muslim family law (through *shariah* courts under the Administration of Muslim Law Act 1966). Similarly, the considerable number of private Acts and Ordinances which legally establish the administrative structures and processes of other religious bodies assists in their self-regulation.

The long-established faiths of Singapore (Christianity, Hinduism, Sikhism, Buddhism and Islam) negotiated tax exemptions with the government many years ago. However, 80 per cent of tax exempt donations must be spent openly and accountably in any one year, any unspent surplus being taxed at the full rate. Only 20 per cent is allowed to be kept aside, in order to prevent religious groups accumulating wealth which might be used to undermine the state. Smaller religious groups must also be registered but have no tax exempt status.

Although there has been some disagreement and bad feeling between religious communities from time to time, mainly due to aggressive evangelisation or an act of particular insensitivity, inter-religious relations in Singapore can generally be described as harmonious and positive. Mechanisms have long been in place to resolve any sensitive problems and smooth regulation of religious affairs by each community assists positive interaction. Furthermore, the Inter-Religious Organisation (IRO) – founded in 1949 – which is an association of individuals of different faiths who work for religious understanding and cooperation and organise inter-religious observances, can be called on to exercise its 'good offices' to relieve small-scale community tension.

Education

Religious education no longer takes place in state-run secondary schools but the government has considered a number of ways in which approved values and attitudes to society could be instilled in the young. From 1980, the government, to provide a form of moral education in schools, had included Muslim, Hindu and Buddhist studies, along with Bible Knowledge for Christians. However, it eventually abandoned this approach because of unintended consequences of creating division with the Muslim community and facilitating the conversion of English-speaking Chinese to Christianity. Its Confucian Ethics programme failed to attract more than a small percentage of Chinese students.

Maintenance of Religious Harmony Act

From 1986 to 1987 concerns about fundamentalist Islam and the allegiance of Malay Muslims had been raised by the government and, after the detention of Roman Catholic activists in 1987, the government commissioned academic research on religiosity, conversion and anomie among Singaporeans. On the basis of this and its White Paper on Maintenance of Religious Harmony, tabled in parliament in 1989, the government proposed legislation and elicited consensus from religious leaders. The Maintenance of Religious Harmony Act was passed in 1990 to maintain religious harmony and to establish a Presidential Council, two-thirds of whose members are representatives of the major religions of Singapore. The president may veto appointments.

This legislation has been criticised as moving beyond the sphere of inter-religious co-existence into the area of preventing social activism and political dissent from emerging through religious institutions, effectively confining religion to the private sphere of life. The state's view is that religion should be rigorously kept separate from politics in this secular state. Apart from its neutrality towards religion, according to the White Paper, the state views religion as a positive factor in society and encourages religious groups' socially beneficial activities.

The Act gives the government discretionary power to suppress by executive decision almost any activity by a religious group or leader. Section 8 of the Act empowers the Minister of Home Affairs to issue a restraining order against any religious office-bearer if he is satisfied that the person, after ignoring a preliminary caution, has committed or is attempting to commit acts:

(a) causing feelings of enmity, hatred, ill-will or hostility between different religious groups;
(b) carrying out activities to promote a political cause, or a cause of any political party while, or under the guise of, propagating or practising any religious belief;
(c) carrying out subversive activities under the guise of propagating or practising any religious belief; or
(d) exciting disaffection against the President or the Government of Singapore while, or under the guise of, propagating or practising any religious belief.

An order for up to two years (renewable) may restrain a person from a wide range of expression and publication of views without the prior permission of the Minister. Representations against such an order can be made and the President's Council for Religious Harmony may make recommendations to the Minister concerning orders. Those contravening a prohibition order may be fined or imprisoned.

Conscientious objection

Singapore's regional insecurity as a small island between the Muslim nations of Malaysia and Indonesia has been invoked to justify the extensive militarisation of Singapore society. National service is considered by the government to be the cornerstone of the country's survival and security. On the Swiss model, all males over 18 are placed under military discipline through compulsory military service for two years followed by regular active participation in the military reserves until middle age. Many paramilitary organisations are formed at the community level. There are no provisions for excepting any person from military service on the grounds of conscience, religion or belief. Those who refuse to serve are imprisoned. Jehovah's Witnesses, because of their religious beliefs, oppose military service, will not perform national service, salute the flag or swear oaths of allegiance to the state.

First established in the colony in 1940, the Witnesses' Watch Tower Bible and Tract Society was registered in 1962 but deregistered in 1972 when the government dissolved it as prejudicial to public welfare and good order. More than 100 Witnesses have been detained and court-martialled for conscientious objection since 1972. The police have reportedly estimated that Witnesses number about 2,000 in Singapore today; thirty-two complaints about their proselytising were received between 1989 and 1991, and thirty-one complaints have been received since 1992. Japanese Witnesses had been reported as proselytising in housing estates where many Japanese lived.

In 1994, four Witnesses were fined for possessing banned literature and appealed to the High Court to have the deregistration considered by the Court of Appeal. Chief Justice Yong Pung How, rejecting the application, stated:

> People who enjoyed the benefits of living in Singapore have an obligation to abide by the law of the land and do national service. Any organisation, whose members are bound by its own rules not to do national service, whether it be Jehovah's Witnesses or a mere society to promote the playing of tiddly winks or something else, must have to face de-registration.

The Chief Justice also said:

> Singapore is a secular country and its citizens are free to practise their faiths, but only so long as their actions do not impinge on the freedom of others to practise their religions. Aggressive proselytising, especially when directed against those devoted to their own faiths, may provoke a violent backlash that threatens the very basis on which religions co-exist here: mutual understanding and tolerance. The Maintenance of Religious Harmony Act is clear on this point. The action against the Jehovah's Witnesses is a reminder of the need for vigilance against sects and cults, the scope of whose convictions is equalled only by the reach of their irresponsibility. Singapore cannot afford them.

In 1995, the police arrested a further sixty-nine Jehovah's Witnesses who were at meetings at 9 p.m. on 24 February at four residential addresses. Most were later charged with attending the meetings of an unlawful society. The prosecution stated that the purpose of deregistration was to prevent societies of Jehovah's Witnesses in Singapore. Defence submissions that the deregistration and consequently the arrests were contrary to freedom of religion under the constitution drew the response from the prosecution that the constitution also made the right to religion subject to the general law. In February 1996, thirteen of the Witnesses were jailed for up to a week for possessing Bibles and other 'undesirable publications', materials from the Watch Tower Bible and Tract Society and the International Bible Student Association, both prohibited. Appeals to the High Court have failed.

SRI LANKA

Sri Lanka	
GDP (US$bn)	9
Population	17,700,000
Annual population growth (%)	1.8
Urban population (%)	22
Working population (%)	41
Literacy (%)	89.3
Ratifications	1; 2, 2(a); 3; 4

The island of Sri Lanka – separated from the Indian subcontinent by only twenty-two miles – has a population of 17.7 million, affected by fluctuating refugee movements resulting from fighting between government and Tamil secessionary forces. Displaced people number 600,000 officially, mostly women and children victims of war and refugees.

The economy, disrupted by violent political conflict, is rapidly accelerating as a result of the most liberal market-oriented policies in South Asia. Unemployment (at 13.6 per cent) and underemployment remain high. The budget deficit was 8 per cent of GDP in 1993; military expenditure drains government resources and there is a high external level of debt. Inflation ran at the rate of 11.7 per cent in 1993. The literacy rate is high.

The constitutional and legal system

After a long period of Buddhist and Sinhalese revivalism in which political *bhikkhus* (monks) played a major role, Sri Lanka became independent of British rule. Its first constitution was drafted in 1948 and has been superseded by the 1973 and 1978 constitutions. A new constitution is in preparation.

The legal system of Sri Lanka is a complex mixture of customary law and laws introduced through Western colonialism. In the first category fall the laws of the Sinhalese, the Tamils, the Muslims, the Mukkuvars, the Chetties, the Parsees and the Paravars. Of the three colonial powers in Sri Lankan history, only the Dutch and the British introduced their laws. The English common law system predominates, the Roman–Dutch law applying as residuary law.

In Muslim marriage and divorce matters, Muslims have access to *qazi* courts in which all officials are male. A Muslim Law Reform Committee (composed of women) is reviewing areas of Muslim personal law which appear to discriminate against women. The Muslim Mosques and Charitable Trusts or Wakfs Act 1956 (and later amendments) governs the registration of mosques and sets down the duties of trustees, importing into Muslim *wakf* administration the terms and concepts of English law.

Ethnic composition

Sri Lanka contains many ethnic groups: Sinhalese (74 per cent), Tamils (18 per cent) and Moors (7 per cent). The remainder is made up of Burghers, Malays and Veddahs. The Sinhalese are concentrated in the south west, the Tamils in the north and east, concentrated in the Jaffna peninsula. One third of the Tamils – descendants of labourers imported from India in the nineteenth century to work tea plantations – live in the central hills. The Moors are descendants of Indian Muslim traders. The city dwelling Burghers are descended from European colonists and the Malays are descended from mercenaries brought in by the Dutch in the eighteenth century. The Moors and the Malays are Muslims; the former are Tamil-speaking while the latter are multi-lingual urban dwellers. The Veddahs are indigenous hunter-gatherers, small in number to begin with and steadily assimilated into other groups.

Religion, language and ethnicity

Religion, language and ethnicity are interwoven in Sri Lanka. Buddhists constitute 69 per cent of the population, Hindus 15 per cent, Muslims and Christians 8 per cent each. Some 3 per cent of the Tamils are Christian, mostly Roman Catholic. Buddhism was introduced in the third century before the common era by the Indian Emperor Asoka, known for his tolerance. Islam arrived with Muslim traders in the fourteenth century as did Christianity with the Portuguese who made converts to Catholicism. The Dutch brought the Reformed Church in the following century, and the British introduced the Anglican Church in the nineteenth century along with other Protestant groups.

Centuries of existence side by side have resulted in a significant degree of intermixture, influence and exchange between and within Sinhalese and Tamil Sri Lankan society and its two major languages of quite different derivations. Similarly, Tamil Hindus, especially those concentrated near the centres of Buddhist worship, participate in the rituals and ceremonials of the Sinhala Buddhists. Through the centuries there has been much intermarriage. In ethnically different adjacent regions, ethnicity, religious identity and language of the one group merge with those of the other. People have names that are part Sinhala and part Tamil; they may adopt each other's dance forms. Furthermore, the Sinhala caste system is closer to that of the Tamils than to the 'classical' form found in India.

Sri Lanka's current ethnic and cultural intermixture stands in contrast to puristic conceptions of identity and separateness that both Sinhalese and Tamils constructed no earlier than the mid-nineteenth century in response to rapid social and economic change brought about by colonial contact with the West. Centuries of peaceful immigration from India contrast with periodic invasions over the centuries from South India. These invasions contributed to the siege mentality of the Sinhalese polity and Buddhist monastic historians (whose institutions were the object of pillage) typified the South Indian invader as the enemy. Although peaceful immigrants were not so stereotyped, tensions arose between the Sinhalese and the Sri Lankan Tamils after the Sinhala Buddhist nationalist revival in the mid-nineteenth century. Tension focused on religion and language obscured the underlying factors of competition for jobs and economic advancement.

Emergence of ethnic conflict

The origins of the current conflict in Sri Lanka lie not only deep in the past but in the actions of its governments reinforcing ethnic division over recent decades. Following independence in 1948, the United National Party (UNP) government, in order to disenfranchise supporters of Marxist parties, enacted a statute denying citizenship to 1 million Tamil labourers of Indian origin who had been working tea plantations for generations.

The national coalition government (MEP) was elected in 1956 through the force of the political *bhikkhus*, on whose agenda was the removal of funding from missionary schools. The Bandaranaike government asserted the dominance of Sinhala Buddhists through a number of measures, thus alienating minorities, especially Tamils, and ultimately pushing their radical youth towards the cause of a separate state. Sinhala was made the sole official language, in which public servants were required to gain proficiency or be dismissed. In response to Tamil protests, the prime minister negotiated an agreement with the Tamil leader but was forced by the nationalist lobby to abandon it. Relations between Sinhalese and Tamils then deteriorated. There were riots in 1958 because of the language issue, antagonism which was compounded by the government making Sinhala the language of the courts and official announcements in 1960, leading to Tamil-led civil disobedience quashed by the army and police. After her election in 1960, Mrs Bandaranaike abolished funding to Christian denominational schools and brought them within the government system dominated by Buddhism. The new constitution of 1973 reaffirmed the status of Sinhala as the official language and gave a position of primacy to Buddhism. There were more riots in 1977 and 1981.

The nationalist United Front government of 1971 (which included traditional Marxist parties) further alienated Tamil youth through a policy of 'standardisation' which dramatically reduced admission of Tamil students to university science, medical and engineering faculties. Tamil youth considered their hopelessness to derive from the discriminatory policies of a Sinhalese majority government. In 1983, the Liberation Tigers of Tamil Eelam (LTTE) took control of most Tamil or Tamil-speaking areas of the north and east of the island, attacking non-Tamil or non-Hindu villages adjacent to territory they claimed as theirs by right.

The Janata Vimukti Peramuna (JVP), a revolutionary organisation of Sinhalese youth, was formed, committed to the idea of armed rebellion to achieve equal opportunity by means of a socialist state. Their first revolt in 1971 was put down but by the late 1980s the group, assisted by some of the similarly youthful radical *bhikkhus* in the MSV (Buddhist organisations), had managed to paralyse the government and society. The terror unleashed by both the armed youth groups was matched in turn by that of the government's Special Task Force, continually generating violence and counter-violence.

Limitations on human rights enacted in the 1978 constitution and other legislation, such as the widely drafted Prevention of Terrorism Act passed in 1979, combined with the concentration of power in the president to lead to extreme human rights violations. An atmosphere of authoritarianism and intolerance characterised UNP rule of the island between 1977 and 1994. Politicians and the media fomented hatred on both sides. The once lively culture of free speech in Sri Lanka was replaced by an 'alternative' press, of low budget although thriving. Editors, journalists and others were harassed, threatened, assaulted and killed. The major newspapers, the radio and television are state-controlled and acted as mouthpieces of the government, focusing on the president. The suppression of free speech was one symptom of the extensive rupture of Sri Lankan society's moral fabric, an inner crisis. President Premadasa was assassinated in 1993.

The new government of the People's Alliance in 1994 under President Kumaratunga was publicly committed to finding a peaceful end to the civil war and to safeguarding the freedom of the individual in a viable system of checks and balances restraining government power and also protected by independent expression of public opinion. A cease-fire in early 1995 did not hold and Tamil Jaffna fell in December to government forces. Revisions to President Kumaratunga's federal-style plan for reforming the constitution weakened the support of the mainly Sinhalese opposition and, by granting Buddhism a form of constitutional primacy, they also alienated moderate Tamils. In June 1996, the United National Party indicated that they wanted the unitary state to remain intact while the Tamil parties still wanted greater regional authority; the president announced plans to rebuild Jaffna as a Peace City. But the violence continues.

Freedom of religion and belief

Article 9 of the 1978 constitution provides for Buddhism 'the foremost place' and charges the state with the duty of 'protecting and fostering' the religion, while assuring the rights of all other religions. Article 10 guarantees the right of every person to freedom of thought, conscience and religion, including the freedom to have or to adopt a religion or belief of his choice. The constitution further assures the citizen of 'the freedom, by himself or in association with others, and either in public or in private, to manifest his religion or belief in worship, observance, practice and teaching'. The Sri Lanka Press Council Act 1973 makes it an offence for a newspaper to publish any matter (deemed 'profane') which is intended to insult any religion or its founder, or any deity or saint venerated by the followers of a religion.

Children must be taught the religion of their parents and so religion is a compulsory subject at school taught by religious organisations conducting their own programmes. The system has been criticised for failing to contribute to value formation and moral education. Private schools (including denominational schools) are neither funded nor controlled by the state. Temple schools, funded by the state, provide education for Buddhist monks, admitting only male lay students at 14 years.

The primacy of Buddhism has assumed a largely ceremonial form. 'Protecting and fostering' Buddhism has involved the Ministry of Buddhism in allocating funds for minor-scale building and restoration of religious structures and attempting to build a central organisation for the monkhood (*sangha*) to deal with matters of adjudication. However, the monkhood has a code of discipline of its own and any lay interference with monastic behaviour is deeply resented. Disputes relating to their property, governed by ordinances set up under British rule, are dealt with in the secular courts.

Women in religion

The position of women in Sri Lankan society is influenced by the high rate of literacy, low mortality and good life expectancy. The caste system is less rigid than in larger caste societies and there have been no traditions of untouchability, of banning remarriage of widows, *purdah* or child marriage. All the religious traditions are patriarchal in nature, with no formal leadership allowed to women, but women have access to healing and shamanic leadership within the flexible framework of 'popular' Buddhism and Hinduism.

Portuguese, Dutch and English colonisation resulted in stricter codification of previously flexible marriage laws which removed much of the initiative allowed to women. On the other hand, education for girls began much earlier than in other Asian countries. Although marriage is generally assumed important for all women, ancient traditions of renunciation for women are still strong.

A Sri Lankan *bhikkhuni sasana* (order of nuns) was established in the third century before the common era and lasted 1,000 years. The ordination lineage was not re-established in Sri Lanka but survives in China. Its acceptance back into Sri Lanka is impeded by the objection that the Chinese Bhikkhuni Sangha is Mahayana, the other great division of Buddhism. Whether there should or can be a female *sangha* is an issue in Theravada Buddhism which has an all-male *sangha* accused of hanging on to outworn traditions. Some groups of Buddhist women are claiming that the option of renouncing worldly life and practice as taught by the Buddha is an inalienable right of all Buddhists. Whether the 2,500 women who are *dasa sila matas* (non-ordained renouncers), with a lower level of formal education than monks, should be accepted as *bhikkhunis* (ordained nuns) is a live issue in Sri Lankan Buddhism. Many of the *dasa sila matas*, however, are ambivalent about being brought more closely under the jurisdiction of the monks. Meanwhile the government is assisting in raising the level of *dhamma* education for the *sila matas*.

Inter-faith relations

The Christian churches have refused an offer of state support to be administered by the Ministry of Cultural Affairs. In the 1960s the state had withdrawn support of Christian denominational schools which then had to either finance themselves or hand over their administration to the government. This action led to bitterness between the Christian churches and Buddhist nationalists at the time, reviving old animosities based on the Buddhist response to aggressive missionary activity in the early colonial era. The ethnic crisis had led to Sinhalese seeing themselves as Sinhalese rather than as Buddhists or Christians. Today, changes within the Christian churches have promoted a different attitude towards other religions. Progressive sections of all major religions in Sri Lanka united in their opposition to the Premadasa government's policies of the 'open economy' as neo-colonialist and destructive of indigenous values and conceptions of the moral economy.

Long-established Christian churches are making common cause with Buddhists against more than 200 well-financed new evangelical groups, who in their turn have reported encountering considerable hostility and physical harassment in the community and local media which the government has shown no sign of remedying. Although there is no ban on proselytising as such, long-standing tensions between Buddhists and the Catholic Church can be seen in the fact that new Jesuit priests have remained banned from entry to the country for the last thirty years.

Christian churches' alleviation of poverty among marginal Buddhist communities has been criticised as insensitive missionising – a sore issue in view of the colonial past – but Buddhist monks have also been criticised for their interest in gaining donations and endowments and for the incomes they derive from property without there being any tradition of using these for social service to the needy among their laity. However, the opening of secular education has led to a generation of university-educated young monks who wish to emulate the social involvement of Christian churches; they possess a medium for Buddhist–Christian dialogue which has only existed since the 1980s. They have also been active in protests against the implementation of government policy deemed contrary to the social good in Sri Lanka.

Inamaluve, a senior monk, led local protests in 1991 against a plan to build a tourist hotel near a major Buddhist site, the Dambulla cave temple. When the monks threatened in April 1992 to boycott a state occasion in which they normally appeared, the president phoned Inamaluve and threatened him with reprisals; later that month, the monastery archive was burned down by arsonists. Protests were attended by representatives of many religions, but the government response was to launch a campaign to discredit Inamaluve in the eyes of Christian supporters by rousing inter-religious antagonism. This tactic backfired, and further protest meetings had the effect of uniting religious groups.

Hinduism and Buddhism remain closely related in their worship. Hindu gods have been adopted into popular Buddhism, and official rituals at major Buddhist sites are modelled on a Hindu ritual. Similarly, many Hindus participate in major Buddhist festivals like the annual Asala pageantry in Kandy, in which, indeed, two of the four major deities propitiated are Hindu. Catholic youth help to make Buddhist constructions to celebrate the birth of Buddha in May.

Tamil Hindu priests were attacked by Sinhala Buddhist mobs in 1983 while, in 1992, a temple which sheltered thousands of refugees was bombed and pilgrims gathering at another temple were shelled. However, such attacks represent organised political violence not religious intolerance. No attack on any place of worship by members of any religion has occurred since then. Buddhist–Muslim tensions too have been minimal since early in the century.

Complaints about the noise of ceremonies, rituals and amplified calls to prayer in already noisy, overcrowded cities provide an occasional minor irritant within the picture of widespread inter-religious tolerance. Every year, Buddhist, Hindu, Christian and Muslim devotees worship together at the festival at Kataragama, and, during a four-month season lasting from January to April, climb together the 6,000-feet high Adam's Peak to worship the imprint there which to Buddhists is the footprint of the Buddha, to Christians that of Adam and to Muslims that of the Prophet.

VIET NAM

Viet Nam	
GNP	72[b]
Population	69,700,000
Annual population growth (%)	2.2
Urban population (%)	20
Working population (%)	49[a]
Literacy (%)	91.9
Ratifications	1; 2; 3; 4

The Socialist Republic of Viet Nam was established after the unification of North and South Vietnam at the end of the Vietnam War in 1975. A fast-growing state of nearly 70 million people, Viet Nam is essentially an agricultural country; only 20 per cent of the population live in the towns, the largest of which are Ha Noi, Hai Phong and Ho Chi Minh City, formerly Saigon. Although its economy has been invigorated by recent reforms and urban living standards increased, over half its people live in poverty.

Because it is located at the cross-roads between India and China, a rich diversity of ideas, beliefs and religions have flowed into Viet Nam from neighbouring civilisations. Viet Nam itself has given birth to innumerable popular beliefs and religions during its 5,000-year history.

Ethnic and religious composition

Most Vietnamese (88 per cent) are ethnic Viets, or Kinh people. There are over fifty ethnic minorities living mainly in the mountainous and frontier regions. Most important are the Tay, Thai, Nung, Giay and Hmong peoples and the Khmers of Cambodian origin based around the Mekong Delta. The other large group is the ethnic Chinese, or Hoas, concentrated mainly in the cities. Many Hoas left Viet Nam after its break with China in 1979, but a few million still remain. The influence of this community is steadily increasing in pace with Viet Nam's opening towards a market economy.

Traditionally, Viet Nam's religious communities have lived in harmony. The oldest religion is Buddhism, which came to Viet Nam from India over twenty centuries ago and has impregnated the thinking and cultural expression of Vietnamese daily life. Today, over three-quarters of the population are Buddhists. Buddhist monks helped to found the first independent Vietnamese state in the tenth century, after 900 years of Chinese domination which had also brought Chinese Mahayana Buddhism, Taoism and Confucianism. Buddhist monarchs of the eleventh and thirteenth centuries presided over a civilisation in which Buddhist pagodas were centres of learning, worship and community activities. Most Buddhists in Viet Nam follow the Mahayana school. The Mahayana Buddhist who attains enlightenment may become a *boddhisattva*, someone who has achieved Nirvana but vows to remain in the world to save fellow human beings. Theravada Buddhism is strong near the Cambodian border.

The French military occupation of Indochina occurred in 1887. During the colonial period and up to the early 1960s, Buddhism was not allowed to function as a religious institution. The Federation of Buddhist Associations in Viet Nam, established in 1951, was limited to the status of an association under colonial decree. After the fall of Ngo Dinh Diem and the abrogation of this decree, the first nation-wide Buddhist congress was held in 1964 and the Unified Buddhist Church of Viet Nam (UBCV) was established. The UBCV combines the Mahayana and Theravada schools into one Buddhist congregation.

Two religious groups indigenous to south Viet Nam are the Cao Dai and the Hoa Hao, which have followings of 3 million and 2 million respectively. The Cao Dai religion, founded in 1926, reconciles Western beliefs with traditional Asian religions and has a constellation of deities ancient and modern. It allied itself with the nationalist movement for independence, like the Buddhist-inspired Hoa Hao, founded in 1939. The Hoa Hao became anti-communist when the Viet Minh assassinated their prophet and founder in 1947. After 1975, both groups were banned by the communist government of Viet Nam; all church property was seized, rituals forbidden and followers persecuted. Only in the late 1980s did the government even begin to tolerate a revival of their religious activities.

Roman Catholicism, which was introduced into Viet Nam by Portugese Dominican missionaries in 1615, has a following of some 6 million people today, making it the second largest Catholic Church in South East Asia. The Vietnamese Catholic community is close-knit and influential with its ties to the Vatican. Although persecuted during short periods of Vietnamese history, the Catholic Church grew most rapidly under French colonial rule.

Protestantism was introduced in 1911 by American missionaries. The Vietnamese Protestant Church has 300,000 followers, about one-third ethnic minorities living in the central highlands. There is also a small Muslim community of about 50,000 people and Hinduism is practised by the Cham people on the southern coast of Viet Nam.

Ancestor worship is an ancient indigenous belief uniting all Vietnamese, whatever their beliefs. It forms the basis of Vietnamese ethics, enshrining the central importance of the family and the sacred bonds between individuals and the land on which their ancestors were born. Incense burns alongside the photographs of parents, grandparents, and other departed members of the 'clan' going back five generations. These altars may be juxtaposed with Buddhist or Christian shrines. The linkage with the land is most important; souls wander forever if bodies are not buried, such as those of soldiers missing in action after the Vietnam War.

Political system and its background

Politically, Viet Nam is a one-party state, controlled at all levels by the Communist Party of Viet Nam (CPV). Party members are not allowed to adhere to a religion. Despite Viet Nam's ratification the ICCPR in 1982, its constitution and laws still subordinate all forms of individual political, cultural and religious thought and expression to the ideology of the state.

The Socialist Republic of Viet Nam was established after the National Assembly ratified the unification of the Democratic Republic of (North) Viet Nam and the former Republic of (South) Viet Nam following the military victory of the communists in April 1975. The 1980 constitution was established on lines of a proletarian dictatorship. This principle was deleted from a revised constitution adopted in 1992, but the role of the Communist Party is still enshrined as 'the only force leading the society and the state' (Article 4). The 1992 constitution affirms the institutionalisation of the relationship between the nation's goals of transition to socialism 'in the light of Marxism–Leninism and Ho Chi Minh's thought'. Religion and other 'superstitious practices' have always been viewed with hostility by Viet Nam's Marxist leaders.

After the end of the war against the French administration of Indochina, the country was partitioned at the seventeenth parallel by the 1954 Geneva Agreement. All forms of religious expression were repressed by the government of the Democratic Republic of (North) Viet Nam. During the land reforms of the mid-1950s, thousands of monks and priests were subjected to 'struggle campaigns' and publicly executed. The government set up 'patriotic' religious organisations under the control of the party. The Federation of Buddhist Associations was outlawed and replaced by an 'Association of Unified Vietnamese Buddhists'. To escape persecution, over 800,000 North Vietnamese, mostly Catholics, left for the south after partition. They supported Ngo Dinh Diem, a Catholic from central Viet Nam, who had been installed as premier of the state of Vietnam by France and the USA. Diem – under whose administration the Buddhists were also persecuted – declared a republic and redistributed land to the original landlords. His assassination in 1963 was followed by a series of corrupt governments leading to the intervention of the USA and the Vietnam War.

After the fall of Saigon in 1975, the Provisional Revolutionary Government in South Viet Nam instigated widespread repression against the Buddhist, Cao Dai, Hoa Hao, Catholic and Protestant communities alike. Pagodas and churches were confiscated and closed down, clergy detained without trial in re-education camps or forced to do 'civic duties' such as compulsory military service in disregard of their non-violent beliefs. Many hundreds of priests, monks and nuns died from ill-treatment in the camps in the first years of communist rule.

Buddhism became the primary target of the revolutionary authorities' campaign. Twelve monks and nuns immolated themselves in protest in November 1975. The authorities confiscated and dismantled the vast UBCV network of Buddhist pagodas, medical centres, orphanages, schools and universities, and arrested its leaders, one of whom died under torture in 1978. In 1982, An Quang Pagoda was taken over by the authorities and the UBCV was formally banned.

After 1975 the government also embarked on a campaign of discrimination and harassment against Catholics. As in the case of the Buddhists, decrees forbade priests from teaching outside their parishes, limited the number of new priests ordained and forbade church construction or repair. Priests returning from re-education camps were automatically stripped of their civil and sacerdotal rights. In 1978, the Communist Party instructed party cadres to infiltrate the church and create a schism. Catholic priests protested, such as the Archbishop of Hue who was placed under house arrest.

The government further established state and party control over all religious activities by setting up state-sponsored religious institutions, the only organisations to receive official recognition. In 1981 the Viet Nam Buddhist Church (VBC) was established; the government campaigned widely to persuade all Buddhists to join. Because the leaders of the Unified Buddhist Church vigorously opposed the VBC's creation, two prominent UBCV monks were arrested in 1982 and banished to their native villages. Similar policies were applied to the Catholics and other religious communities. Although the Government did not formally ban the Roman Catholic Church, a 'Committee of Patriotic Vietnamese Catholics' was established in 1983, and other 'patriotic' bodies of Cao Dais, Hoa Haos, Protestants, and so on were set up.

Mechanisms controlling thought, conscience and belief

Mechanisms of surveillance and control ensure that little of personal or family life is unknown to the authorities which can use the information received to suppress dissent. The mechanisms themselves also inhibit free expression of belief. The state's most formidable means of control was the two-fold system of the obligatory residency permit, and the precinct security warden. These two institutions, which are still operational today, form the basis of a vast security apparatus. The powers of the precinct security warden extend far beyond those of an ordinary police officer. Usually a member of the CPV or the Communist Youth League, the security warden has charge of about thirty to fifty extended families, must be aware of all that goes on in the precinct and is entitled to enter and search anyone's home without warning or permission.

Every citizen must possess a residency permit which must be produced for every administrative procedure, for employment, admission to school or hospital or requesting a travel permit. Personal details on the permit include religious or any former political affiliation. Only the security warden can issue (or confiscate) the permits. People without residency permits are illegal citizens and can be arrested. Monks and priests returning from re-education camps are not issued with permits and so live in a state of permanent insecurity.

In 1993, for example, security police expelled Venerable Thich Hanh Duc from Son Linh pagoda in South Viet Nam on the grounds that he did not have a residency permit although he had been living undisturbed as Superior Monk of the pagoda under the auspices of the state-sponsored VBC for over ten years. However, when he began to publicly support the UBCV in 1992, he was threatened with expulsion and in 1993 he was arrested with 100 Buddhists and twenty-five other monks and imprisoned for three years.

Buddhists wishing to be ordained are required to submit full personal information to the Board of Religious Affairs. Future monks and nuns are required to provide details of their 'past activities and contributions to the Revolution', including names and addresses of associates, information on 'the political opinions . . . before and after the revolution' (i.e. 1975) of all family members and their whereabouts.

The *doi moi* policy and legislative change

In 1986 the Sixth Party Congress launched a new policy of *doi moi* or renovation, a major change in which Viet Nam began to open up to the outside world and started to transform itself into a 'socialist-orientated market economy'. Criticism of corruption and mismanagement was encouraged in the official press, restrictions on travel within and outside the country were eased and moves were made to reform the legislative framework; penal legislation was issued. A new Decree on Religions was adopted (1991) and a new constitution was introduced in April 1992 replacing the one of 1980.

The 1992 constitution laid the foundations for wider protection in the field of human rights. Religious freedom is guaranteed. Article 70 provides that 'the citizen shall enjoy freedom of belief and of religion; he can follow any religion or follow none. All religions are equal before the law.' However, this article also states that 'No-one can violate freedom of belief and of religion', nor can they 'misuse beliefs and religions to contravene the law'. The exercise of religious freedom thus becomes a matter of official interpretation of the new codes, sanctioning discriminatory policies and reclassification of prisoners of conscience as common criminals. Human rights and religious organisations have documented regular human rights abuses in the repression of dissenting opinion and practice of beliefs through the use of charges under the codes.

Thousands of people have been convicted of offences under the Criminal Code, among them four Buddhist monks convicted of 'disturbing public order' for their part in a non-violent demonstration for religious freedom in Hue in May 1993 and a Catholic Hmong who was imprisoned on charges of 'slander' because he made a complaint against local security police and district authorities of discrimination against Catholics in the mountainous regions of North Viet Nam.

Two Buddhist scholars, arrested in 1984, were condemned to death under the code in 1988 for 'activities aimed at overthrowing the people's government', as were human rights activists distributing leaflets calling for human rights and democracy. Their sentences were commuted to twenty years' hard labour as a result of international protests. The government is reportedly working on revisions of the Criminal Code, particularly the chapter on 'national security', as part of its commitment to build a society grounded on the rule of law.

Decree 69 on Religious Activity and National Interests was made public in 1991. All religious activities now required the approval of the authorities: the opening of religious schools and seminaries, the holding of retreats or meditation periods, the publication of religious books, travel abroad by Vietnamese clerics or visits by representatives of foreign organisations to Viet Nam. The decree made all religious appointments subject to approval by the state authorities or the Council of Ministers. Decree 69 was followed by a spate of directives and regulations as the authorities struggled to control an upsurge of religious activities. In 1993 one directive ordered a clampdown on the publication of unauthorised religious books and stipulated that a criterion for choosing new clergy must be 'the satisfactory accomplishment of their civic duties'.

The right to freely select new clergy and ordain monks and nuns on the basis of religious, not political, criteria remains an unresolved issue. There has been serious conflict between Viet Nam and the Vatican, and Catholic bishops have been imprisoned for long periods or placed under house arrest. In September 1993, the government rejected the Vatican's appointment of an apostolic administrator of Ho Chi Minh City. No new priests have been ordained since the beginning of 1995.

Pragmatism versus ideology

During the 1990s, however, a significant change in the government's approach to religion occurred. With increasing claims for the right to religious freedom in defiance of government restrictions and with the rise in social problems, a pragmatic recognition of the 'utility value' of religion was incorporated in party policy. The Seventh CPV Congress report acknowledged that religious belief was an inescapable component of the people's mentality and endorsed the utility of religions in civil society.

With the influx of foreign capital and the rapid development of the tourist trade, religion has also become a potential source of revenue. Many ancient Buddhist pagodas were restored and allowed to celebrate regular religious services. As the number of monks had significantly diminished under communist governance, there are now more pagodas than monks, especially in the north. Even in the south, which had over 40,000 monks and nuns before 1975, only 13,538 remained for a total of 4,433 pagodas. None the less, pagoda restoration is appreciated and believers and non-believers alike make the annual pilgrimage to the Perfume Pagoda.

State–Buddhist conflict

Religion and variety of belief as a whole are on the increase in Viet Nam. While some religious communities accommodated to governmental pragmatism, glad of the opportunity to promote their faiths in relative peace, the government and Buddhists of the UBCV, however, continued to confront each other over religious freedom and state control of the Buddhist Church.

The Han Noi authorities have been locked in conflict with the UBCV since a dispute over the funeral of the former UBCV Patriarch whose will designated his successor. Thich Huyen Quang, the current Patriarch, then openly called on the government to recognise the UBCV and release imprisoned Buddhists. The state arrested and harassed those found in possession of speeches by the Patriarch and other unlawful documents.

Hue has become the centre of Buddhist dissent. In May 1993, self-immolation was followed by hunger strikes and a demonstration of over 40,000 people – the greatest public protest in Viet Nam since 1975 – which was violently repressed. A nationwide vilification campaign in the state-controlled media preceded a brief, closed trial and the deportation of four monks to a forced labour camp in early 1994.

Protests culminated in the arrests of the two UBCV leaders, Patriarch Thich Huyen Quang and Thich Quang Do in late 1994 and early 1995 so that virtually all the UBCV leadership is now under arrest. Party leaders perceive the UBCV's demands as a challenge to its authority, equating them with 'peaceful evolution' which they see as an internationally supported conspiracy to erode the party's authority by attacking it from within, as has happened in Eastern Europe.

Minority religions

Tight control over religion still affects the structures, organisation and practice of religion among Christian and indigenous minority believers in Viet Nam. The Puebla Institute has noted that recent reforms have benefited mostly the urban religious minorities while those without influential international connections have continued to suffer. Protestant house church leaders have been fined for unauthorised meetings. There is still harassment, persecution and arrests of Hmong Christians in the mountains, and of indigenous Cao Dai and Hoa Hao believers who cannot easily mobilise outside help. Vietnamese returning to the country to celebrate their faith at Cao Dai and Hoa Hao sacred places have also been harassed, interrogated and arrested on their journeys. The government has also reportedly opened meat restaurants in the holy grounds around the vegetarian Cao Dais' Great Temple.

In 1994, Han Noi allowed one Vatican appointment of a Catholic bishop but then announced it might veto more. Limitations on numbers of seminaries and their entrants and on ordinations have resulted in a severe shortage of priests and pastoral activities have been limited to celebrating mass in prescribed places.

The media

Freedom of the press, opinion and speech is guaranteed by the 1992 constitution and *doi moi* introduced a wider scope for diversity and debate in the official press. In 1993 the Vietnamese bishops asked for the right to set up their own publishing house and run their own independent Catholic paper. However, the country's 300 or more newspapers are state-controlled. Directives on religion specify that all religious publications must be printed on state-run presses. In general, however, the publication and distribution of religious material in Viet Nam have witnessed a cautious increase since *doi moi*. In 1994, the government allowed the printing of 2,000 missals for the first time since 1975 and allowed Bibles – still scarce – to be imported for the Protestant churches.

Education

Primary and secondary schools and universities formerly run by the Christian and Buddhist churches were closed down after 1975 and there are now no private religious schools. Families are free to bring up their children according to their own convictions but they cannot organise their own schools. Religion is not taught in state schools, which have maintained the secular value system enculturated under the French colonial administration.

The question of religious education has also been the cause of discontent in Viet Nam. The state-sponsored VBC has recently been allowed to re-open a number of seminaries and schools, closed down after 1975, for the formation of Buddhist monks. But the political content of these schools' curricula and their discriminatory enrolment criteria have caused widespread protests. The government detained a VBC Buddhist dignitary and several novices for several days for 'working sessions' for protesting about having to teach 'civic studies' as well as Buddhist scriptures. The authorities also may veto teacher appointments in these schools.

Women in religion

The lower status of women in Confucianism, Chinese Mahayana Buddhism and Theravada Buddhism is often blamed solely on the religions, but it is clear that the politicians of feudalism used the religious traditions to maintain social order and women's subservience. Vietnamese women have a long pre-feudal history of martial figures and rebel activists, and in the last 150 years, a tradition of literary achievement, especially in poetry. Many women intellectuals and activists lost their lives in the struggle for independence before 1964.

In modern Viet Nam there is no gender discrimination in terms of legislation and, while the state formally encourages the participation of women at all levels, it plays no part in the participation of women in religious life. However, Viet Nam's feudal and Confucian legacy has given women a 'back-seat' role in terms of formal representation at the highest level in both Cao Dai and Hoa Hao groups and in Buddhist organisations. There are very few women dignitaries at the top executive level of either the state-run or traditional Buddhist churches. However, before 1975 and in the United Buddhist Church of Vietnam charter, the Bhikkhuni Council managed its own administration, training and ordination, although by long-established Buddhist tradition, monks must co-ordain nuns. *Bhikkunis* manage their own social and educational institutions and the elected Head of the Council is a member of the UBCV Ecclesiastical Council. Many nuns are invited to manage charity and welfare activities at all levels. Nuns outnumber monks in some districts.

Women do not play a prominent role in religious affairs in Vietnamese Catholicism and both Catholic women and men have experienced discrimination in not being allowed by the state to establish convents or novitiates.

Europe

REGIONAL INTRODUCTION

Old and new regional international organisations are following common policies to build democratic security and human rights throughout the continent. The values for which the Council of Europe has worked for fifty years, pluralism, human rights, democracy and inter-cultural tolerance, are now central to the mandate of the Organisation for Security and Cooperation in Europe (OSCE) and the European Union. The interest in and imperative for increased cooperation has been promoted partly by traumatic memories of Europe's past conflicts and even genocides, but also by a sense that Europe has developed its culture from many sources, including Jewish, Christian and Muslim principles of humanity and tolerance.

Where religious identity coincides with nationhood, ethnicity, minority status, linguistic heritage or regional predominance, one finds religion quickly exploited, even by erstwhile atheistic politicians, to justify struggles for self-determination or independence. Too seldom do they enlist – or do religious leaders and people assert – the capacity for religion to promote cooperation, harmony and reconciliation.

The religious component in many European tensions and conflicts is sometimes incidental or contrived, but it can become explosive, especially as atavistic emotions or traumatic memories are revived. The atrocities perpetuated in the Bosnian conflict now being examined by the UN War Crimes Tribunal at The Hague offer a grim illustration. One of the contrasts of Europe is that such a secular and materialistic climate can still sustain primitive, exclusivist, ignorant and arrogant manifestations of religious hate. Northern Ireland is a recurrent depressing example.

It is one of the great paradoxes of the present decade that, even as virtually all constitutions across the continent guarantee freedom of religion, conscience and belief, there are new possibilities of misusing or reducing such liberties. There is growing concern that freedom to preach and to choose one's religion can be misused, both by established or majority religions and by new religious movements, and can become a licence for violent or insidious forms of proselytism or sectarianism. However, it is still possible for some governments to invoke principles of 'national unity' or 'laicity' in order to inhibit or even to persecute authentic forms of religious or cultural self-definition, especially those practised or expressed by minorities.

With the establishment of constitutional guarantees of protection, at least for majority religions, throughout Europe, the debate about religious liberty has largely shifted away from how governments practise tolerance to how religious communities show tolerance and afford freedom of conscience and belief to their own members and to their neighbours of other faiths or ideologies. Ecumenism among adherents of the various confessional forms of the same religion has developed widely throughout Europe but is often affected, although not determined, by widely varying church–state relations.

Still greater contrasts of practice appear when the issue widens beyond cooperation and reciprocity among Christians to relationships among people of various religions in Europe and their relations with the state. Rights which had been protected for Christians and Jews are being extended to Muslims and others, but not without considerable resistance or reluctance on the part of many in the majority communities.

Since Muslims constitute the largest religious minority in most European countries, and the majority in Albania and Turkey, many issues of freedom of religion, conscience and belief in Europe involve the complex history of Christian–Muslim rivalry and hostility (and of their positive and fruitful interaction). Both educational and political efforts are needed to sustain the liberal and open elements in a European Islamic society which is too often caricatured and demonised in the press and from fascist political platforms.

Jews continue to be victims of intolerance in Europe. Anti-Semitic acts have been widely reported. It is a mark of how vulnerable a religious minority in Europe can be that, despite so much information and education about the Holocaust, revisionist historians and manipulative politicians can still be active. Historical memory can also be very short about, for example, the sufferings of Armenians, Serbs or Roma-Sinti people.

Religions in Europe, so long marginalised and manipulated, too often weak and self-serving as their adherents' own self-criticism makes clear, are still part of the human dimension and the 'soul' of Europe. They need to be protected and given their rights, but they should not misuse those rights by sowing discord or enmity. They need to exercise their responsibilities to show tolerance within their own communities and between their various communities, but also with those neighbours who may ignore or reject religious beliefs.

ALBANIA

Albania	
GDP (US$bn)	3.3[b]
Population	3,400,000
Annual population growth (%)	2.3
Urban population (%)	36
Working population (%)	48[a]
Literacy (%)	85
Ratifications	1; 2; 3; 4

The Republic of Albania offers the most vivid example of transition in the former communist world on the issues of freedom of conscience. Albania was the poorest, smallest and most isolated of the former communist European states. It was a prison state with many thousands of political prisoners; the President of the Ex-Political Prisoners Society, Osmar Kazazi, spent almost forty-two years in prison or detention, almost the entire span of the Hoxha regime. For nearly four decades, the Albanian government attempted to eliminate all forms of religion from society, substituting an atheistic ideology. Enver Hoxha died in 1985. Since 1990, Albania has sought to establish a democratic state with guarantees of basic human rights, including the freedom of religion or belief. A measure of its success was acceptance of its application to join the Council of Europe in 1995. However, elections in May 1996 were reportedly marked by allegations of irregularities and police assaults on socialist supporters.

The atheist state

In November 1944, the Communist Party initiated a new constitution in which Article 15 stated: 'Freedom of conscience and belief is guaranteed to all citizens . . . Religious communities are free to exercise and practise their religions.' A few months later an agrarian reform bill was passed which deprived religious institutions of much of their property. The Jesuit and Franciscan orders were closed and foreign Catholic priests, nuns and monks were expelled from Albania. Dozens of local clergy and intellectuals, Catholic, Muslim and Orthodox, were accused of 'propaganda against the state', tried and sentenced, imprisoned and tortured because of their beliefs; many were executed or died in prison or in suspicious circumstances.

Religious persecution became a tool in the hands of the dictatorship whose aim was to reshape the spiritual life of the believers according to communist patterns. Centuries of Ottoman and other foreign rule made the new government feel vulnerable to external influence and internal dissent. In 1949, the Presidium of the People's Assembly ordered each of the four principal religious communities – Muslim, Bektashi (Shia Muslim), Orthodox and Catholic – to prepare draft statutes in which a pledge of loyalty to the state was to be expressed. Once the decrees were in force, penal sanctions protecting the constitutional guarantee of freedom of religion were removed.

The atheisation of Albania was achieved through the closing down of all foreign religious communities, orders, associations and missions, a mass persecution of clergy, the closing of mosques and churches, confiscation of property and religious objects and public ridicule of religion as 'the opiate of the people'. According to personal testimonies of those who survived, the years 1966–67 were the worst as the ethos and methods of the Chinese Cultural Revolution were transplanted to Albania. At the Fifth Party of Labour Congress in 1966, the dictator Enver Hoxha called for an offensive against religion and religious institutions which began with the closing down of St Nichel's Church in the Lezha district in December 1966; the village priest was dismissed and the church building was adapted into a house of culture. By the end of the 1960s, the government had wiped out all forms of organised clergy in Albania.

Hoxha's 1967 circular, entitled *On the Fight Against Religion, Religious Prejudices and Customs*, guided all the district party committees to

> spearhead our struggle against religion, concentrating on religious dogmas, its philosophical principles, especially its idealistic and mystic contents, as well as against religious rites which have become part of the daily life of the believers, and of the unbelieving, too.

At the end of this period, 2,169 religious institutions, including 740 mosques, 508 Orthodox churches and monasteries, 157 Catholic churches, 530 *tekkes* and other holy Muslim places, had been closed down or demolished.

The 1976 Albanian constitution and the 1977 Penal Code laid down in statute the Albanian regime's campaign against religion. The country's laws now openly sanctioned the theory and practice of discrimination against freedom of thought and basic human rights. Article 37 of the 1976 constitution stated: 'The state recognises no religion whatever and supports atheistic propaganda for the purpose of inculcating the scientific materialist world outlook in the people.'

Article 55 of the Penal Code on agitation and propaganda against the state provided an anti-democratic legal framework:

> fascist, anti-democratic, religious, warmongering, anti-socialist agitation and propa-
> ganda, as well as the preparing, distribution and keeping of literature of such
> content with the intention and purpose of weakening or undermining the state of
> the dictatorship of the proletariat is punishable with privation of freedom from three
> to ten years.

The catalogue of abuses lists severe penalties for owning a Bible or Qur'an, the enforcement of the name-change programme – religious names were excluded from 'suitable' national names for new-born infants and religious place names were altered – and a total prohibition of religious symbols and sharing one's religious beliefs and customs. The atheisation programme proved ineffective in so far as a diminished form of private religious sentiment and practice survived in Albania. However, the impact of the repression on the expression of beliefs among Albanians was so profound that it has been noted that the clandestine nature of such religious practice as survived resulted in its lacking reference to public and institutional religion, thus often depriving practitioners of its religious meaning. Fearing that their children would reveal family religious practices, as they had been taught to do in school, adults were inhibited from practising religion in the privacy of their homes, which in turn prevented them from handing their beliefs down to the younger generation.

Restoration of freedoms and constitutional initiatives

In 1990, the wind of freedom and democracy which swept across Eastern and Central Europe also swept through Albania. Two constitutional initiatives have supported restoration of guarantees of freedom of conscience, religion or belief. First, Albania's 'temporary constitution' in 1991 was supplemented by a Charter of Rights in 1993. According to Article 7, 'The Republic of Albania is a secular state. The state respects freedom of religious faith and creates conditions to exercise it.' Second, the draft constitution of the Republic of Albania, 'the new Albanian constitution', received nation-wide discussion but was rejected in a national referendum in November 1994.

Albanians quickly adjusted to the new reality. Even before the 'temporary constitution' was voted in, church bells in Shkodra and Korca were ringing again and a visitor to Tirana was able to hear prayers said from the city's central mosque. Soon, at the request of Albanian authorities, the international community began helping the country's 'revolutionary' politicians in drafting new legislation and the world of religion moved in. Public 'evangelism' and restoration of religious buildings accelerated.

There have been several efforts to draft law on religions. In 1991 a proposal would have required leaders of religious groups to be of Albanian nationality and approved by the President of the Republic on the recommendation of the particular religious community. Seen as an Albanian reaction to fears of Greek influence, this sparked sustained protest. A different law was published in 1993, but not acted upon.

A 'Law on Communist Genocide', passed in 1995, excludes from politics anyone who held a Communist Party post before March 1991 and appears intended to help strengthen the present government's hold on power. Elections held in spring 1996 were condemned by foreign observers as unfair.

Social and religious composition

Albania contains three traditional religious groupings among its 3.4 million people: 65 per cent Muslim, 23 per cent Orthodox (predominantly to the south) and 12 per cent Catholic (to the north). The Muslim-descended population, two-thirds of Albanians, reflects the influence of centuries of Ottoman rule. Reluctantly, the traditional communities are admitting the limitations of these statistics as another, major group needs to be included as well: the non-believers, many of whom are atheists. More than twenty, mostly Christian, denominations have prepared statutes and filed requests for official registration with the state in recent years; their presence is not reflected in the traditional divisions of Albanian religion.

The Greek minority is the largest ethnic minority; others are Vlachs, Roma and Slav speakers and small numbers of Armenians. During the communist period Greeks (along with other national minorities) were subject to serious discrimination and human rights abuses, particularly in terms of religious freedom, education in their mother tongue and freedom of publication. Today, political radicalisation in the Greek minority has led to confrontations and a much criticised trial in 1994 of activists of the Democratic Union of the Greek Ethnic Minority People of Albania (OMONIA).

Religion–state relations

The new religious freedom and democratic reality exposed a genuine difficulty for many Albanians. In the words of the Muslim representative of the Secretariat for Relations with Religious Communities of the Council of Ministers:

> We have a dilemma here. How to operate in this new situation by protecting religious liberty for every religion, yet maintaining religious harmony among the three main religions. We may be violating human rights if we impose restrictions, yet we feel like protecting the existing order.

Political machinations present obstacles in the way of codifying guarantees of freedom of conscience; these are reminiscent of the recent infamous past and supported by a rhetoric of intolerance both in parliament and in the public media. Parliamentarians admit that the proposed law and the new constitution reflect the political preferences of the majority religious group, Muslims. The case of the Greek minority's autocephalous Albanian Orthodox Church – after the enthronement of the Orthodox Archbishop who is of Greek nationality – has been handled with political expediency. The Albanian government considered the appointment of a Greek national as a 'temporary' appointment 'until an Albanian priest is prepared to assume his functions'. Four Greek bishops appointed by the Archbishop were refused entry to Albania because of their nationality. Most of the Christian denominations in Albania, whose clergy were almost wiped out during the decades under communism, are currently headed by expatriates, not Albanian nationals. The much smaller Sv Jovan Vladimir Orthodox Brotherhood, related to the 45,000 Serbs, Montenegrins and Govanci living in Albania, has been promised registration after threatening to complain to the Organisation for Security and Cooperation in Europe.

The issue of requiring Albanian citizenship and nationality of a leader of an Albanian religious community is thus perceived as a limitation of religious freedom, and the particular matter of the Orthodox Church and the Greek community was taken up with the government by the Special Rapporteur on Religious Intolerance in his 1994 and 1995 reports.

Tensions also exist within the constitutional, governmental and social context between applying the provision of 'separation of religion (church) and state' and attempts to re-establish Albania as a religious state. Sociological data available today disprove the notion that the majority of Albanians are in fact Muslim. It is evident that the majority of Albanians are non-believers. The intellectual and non-Muslim communities are afraid that monopolies of the past are being turned into new monopolies, often supported by politically motivated foreign religious forces. This confusion was amplified when President Berisha brought the country into the Islamic Conference, as a member of the World Organisation of Islamic States. Religious pluralism and harmony were suddenly confused by the declaration of Albania as a secular state. President Berisha has denied that the joining of the Islamic Conference is other than a pragmatic step directed at economic development. At the same time, Albania, in June 1995, joined the Council of Europe and ratified the European Convention on Human Rights.

Promotion of religion or belief

Religious communities, other than the three main religious bodies, are concerned that their attempts to establish or re-establish themselves freely in the new Albania are fraught with obstacles. Some religious leaders label all who are not Muslim, Orthodox or Catholic, as 'new religious sects', for which, as intolerant comment has it, 'there is no place in Albania'. Albania today has more than forty different religious groups operating with relative freedom. However, the state does not provide the legal basis to allow the churches or religions (with the exception of Islam) to reclaim successfully all alienated properties, to acquire building permits or to protect one religion against the attempts of another to subject their organisation and its members to harassment and social discredit. Religious communities cite numerous cases of obstacles placed in the way of their establishing their religious identity and ownership of property. The issue of tax exemption for religious institutions has not been resolved and religious organisations operate at best as tolerated yet outside the law.

Conscientious objection and holy days

According to the Ministries of Defence, Education and Labour, government is not yet ready to regulate issues of conscientious objection and freedom to choose a day (or days) of worship according to precepts of one's faith. The Ministry of Defence upholds freedom to abstain from military service, based on religious conviction, as a matter of principle but has not addressed the issue of specific regulation on this matter.

Education, the family and social issues

Different state ministries are involved in discussions about issuing regulations regarding the religious or ethical education of children as well as the provision of a legal basis for religions and churches to operate private schools with or without state funding; this includes providing financial assistance to pay salaries to teaching staff for legally recognised religious groups. Theological seminaries are already in operation. The question of Albania 'becoming a religious (i.e. Muslim) state' is an issue which is often cited when 'foreign financial assistance' is accepted by the state from the Islamic states to propagate Islam, while no state provisions have been made to allow all religious communities to establish their own religious schools.

Women's equality in law is affirmed without restriction and women participate in public life and work in large numbers. Arranged marriages, early betrothal and dowry practices remain in Albania.

Freedom of expression

The state guarantees and makes provisions to allow religious organisations to promote themselves through publications, media and advertising. While in 1991–93, there were numerous examples of media access given to churches to advertise religious functions and transmit religious festivals and ceremonies, in 1994–95 Islam has been given preferential treatment in the media and access for the Roman Catholic and the Orthodox Church has been limited. Minority churches cite cases that access to the media is denied to them to propagate their religious beliefs, though radio and television are willing to negotiate time-slots on commercial terms. The Protestant churches use their own radio transmitters for their religious programming. Currently there are no restrictions on printing and promoting religious literature and church information in Albania.

Questions for the future

Albania has made a real attempt to re-establish freedom of conscience and to recognise the internationally accepted documents on religious liberty. The limited resources of the state do not bode well for human rights education in the country although seminars, symposiums and workshops promulgating freedom of conscience have been held by the state universities and also through grants and functions organised by the international community. Literature on international standards in the area of human rights is available in state and university libraries.

However, a number of questions remain:

1 Will Albania continue to pursue a traditional view that the religious harmony can be based on recognising only three main religious communities: Muslim, Catholic and Orthodox? Religious minorities continue to push for treatment on equal terms, not just benevolent treatment as 'other religious groups'.
2 Will the non-religious beliefs such as humanism and atheism be protected by law? The drive to democracy and re-establishment of religion in the country has created a polarised predicament with non-belief and atheism becoming synonymous with communism.
3 How will the influence of the Albanian diaspora – in Kosovo, in Macedonia, in Greece – influence Albania's quest to uphold human rights and truly reflect the statement from its 'temporary constitution' that Albania's legislation 'considers, recognises and respects the generally accepted principles and norms of international law'?

ARMENIA[1]

In 1991, with the collapse of the Soviet Union, Armenia regained its independence. The country had to build its independence in the catastrophic context of war and blockade, caused by the conflict with neighbouring Azerbaijan over the Armenian-populated enclave of Nagorno-Karabakh.

Despite the severe economic conditions at independence, Armenia had one advantage other former Soviet nations did not have: its diaspora spread throughout the Middle East, Western Europe and North America. More than half the world's Armenians live outside the Armenian Republic as a result of the emigration under stress of their ancestors. The new republic gained a window to the outside world, a cross-fertilisation of talent and an advocate in the international community.

Armenia	
GDP (US$bn)	3
Population	3,400,000
Annual population growth (%)	1.9
Urban population (%)	68
Working population (%)	48.9[c]
Literacy (%)	98.8
Ratifications	1; 2, 2(b); 3; 4

This advantage in modern times has come as part of the complex legacy of the Armenian genocide at the beginning of the century. The Armenian peoples carry memories of major persecution under the Ottoman Empire early in the twentieth century – when Armenians were sent on long death marches through desert areas – and withdrawal of support by Western European colonial powers. It is estimated that about one-third of the total world Armenian population died in horrific conditions between 1895 and 1920. Whereas no external power came to the defence of Gregorian Armenian Christians, Catholic Armenians were defended by Western European Catholic powers. Diaspora Armenian communities exist in many countries.

Population and ethnic composition

According to the 1989 Soviet census, there were 3,304,353 inhabitants of the Armenian Soviet Republic, 93.25 per cent of them Armenians; Armenia was a fairly mono-ethnic and mono-cultural society. In 1989, only 2.57 per cent of Armenians were Azeri, with smaller Kurdish, Russian, Ukrainian, Assyrian and other communities. Since then, the war with Azerbaijan has seen the expulsion or flight under stress of the entire Azeri population of Armenia (about 85,000 people), almost all the Muslim Kurds (perhaps two-thirds of the nearly 60,000 Kurds in Armenia) and the influx of almost the entire Armenian population of Azerbaijan (with the exception of those in Armenian-controlled Nagorno-Karabakh), some 400,000 people.

The severe economic climate and the lack of opportunity in Armenia have led to the departure of some of the Slavic population and have also caused a dramatic exodus of nearly half a million Armenians, some of it temporary, some permanent. Many Armenians have gone to work in Russia since independence; others have left for North America.

Today Armenians form 96 per cent of the population. In addition there are small minorities of Russians, Yezidi Kurds, Greeks, Jews and Assyrians. As many of the Armenians expelled from Azerbaijan in the same period settled in Armenia or in Armenian-controlled Nagorno-Karabakh, Armenia has thus become more homogeneous.

Socio-economic structure

Armenia remains a fairly traditional, cohesive society, with relatively conservative attitudes to the status of women and family relations. The blockade by Azerbaijan and Turkey has brought the economy of Armenia – formerly one of the richest of the Soviet republics – almost to its knees. It is cut off from traditional markets in the former Soviet Union, has almost no energy sources and has difficulty getting access to the outside world. Most of the population has been living at little more than subsistence level. The Armenian government has pledged itself to a market economy through privatisation of industry and agriculture, but has been hampered by the collapse of the economy.

Political and government system

In the transition from independence, Armenia had a presidential system of government, with a single-chamber parliament. A new constitution, granting greater presidential powers, was also approved when multi-party elections were held in 1995.

Armenia's relationship with the self-declared Nagorno-Karabakh Republic, ruled by the local Armenian population, is close, but the government of Armenia has no formal jurisdiction over the enclave which, until the end of the Soviet era, was an autonomous region with the Azerbaijan Soviet Socialist Republic. Armenia has not recognised the independence of Nagorno-Karabakh. Azerbaijan is determined to regain control over the breakaway enclave.

Religious composition

The Armenian Apostolic Church is one of the oldest Christian churches. The Armenian state became the first Christian state in the world when it adopted Christianity in 301 of the common era. There is a close link between nation and church, and almost the entire nation has nominal membership of the church. However, persecution and state control of religion during the Soviet era have left the church weak in practice, despite the privileged position it later managed to gain after the Second World War; active participation remains low.

The head of the Armenian Apostolic Church, the Catholicos, is a national figure and his residence in the monastery at Echmiadzin, outside Yerevan, is a national centre. Catholicos Vazgen I, who ruled the church from 1955 until his death in 1994, had to work closely with the communist regime but managed some independence for the church. Reluctant to welcome independence for Armenia, he was the first to be honoured as National Hero of Armenia. Clerical and lay delegates from Armenian communities around the world chose Karekin Sarkissian, formerly Catholicos of Antelias (Beirut), as Catholicos of All the Armenians at elections in Echmiadzin in April 1995. Karekin I became the 131st Catholicos. The symbolic importance of the office means that the Armenian government, like its Soviet predecessor, will always keep a close eye on the choice of incumbent. The 1991 legislation required the person elected as Catholicos to become a citizen of Armenia if he is not already.

For women, a contradiction exists in that the church is the guardian and persecuted defender of a much-prized culture yet women do not enjoy equality in access to leadership positions – all the clergy is male – nor in other matters in which they enjoy equal status under civil law.

In the north, a long-established community of Armenian Roman Catholics has revived since independence. Although there is tension with the Armenian Apostolic Church in the Middle East, the Catholics in Armenia have stressed that they are not seeking to poach converts from the Apostolic Church. The Armenian government established full diplomatic relations with the Vatican in 1992.

In the capital Yerevan and other cities there are also communities of Protestant Christians, who have become active in the past century. The Russians are mainly of Russian Orthodox background; the Greeks are likewise of Orthodox origin, while the

Assyrians have their own ancient Christian church. There is also a small Jewish group. None of these groups could practise their faith openly under Soviet rule.

Towards the end of the Soviet era new religious movements appeared; Krishna Consciousness was persecuted by the authorities. Later came the Mormons, the Jehovah's Witnesses and Transcendental Meditation, and Western-financed Protestant groups also started working in the country. However, these movements have remained relatively small, although, after the disastrous earthquake in 1988 and the outbreak of hostilities with Azerbaijan, informal Christian fellowships flourished for a short time.

Laws affecting freedom of religion or belief

Under previous Soviet legislation, tight controls made all religious activity outside worship within a registered place of worship a criminal offence. They were administered through a branch at the local level by the USSR's Council for Religious Affairs (CRA). A Council for the Affairs of the Armenian Apostolic Church, attached to the Armenian Council of Ministers (based in Yerevan), acted in parallel with the CRA and handled matters specifically related to the Armenian Church. The USSR's Law on Freedom of Conscience, in 1990, was mirrored in individual Soviet republics.

Armenia adopted its Law on Freedom of Conscience and Religious Organisations in 1991. The law guarantees freedom of conscience (to believe or not to believe) and profession of faith (to conduct religious rites individually or with others). It also guarantees the equality of all citizens before the law, regardless of religious belief or affiliation. Proselytism is banned (Section 3.8), as is compelling citizens to adopt any religious belief or participate in any religious activity (Section 1.3). The only restrictions on religious freedom are those affecting public order, the 'health and morality of citizens' and the defence of the rights and freedoms of other citizens (Section 1.3). Equality before the law notwithstanding, the 1991 law gives a special status to the Armenian Apostolic Church and differentiates between religions in the matter of eligibility for official recognition.

While acknowledging freedom of conscience and expressly adhering to Article 18 of the International Covenant on Civil and Political Rights, the preamble states that the law recognises 'the Armenian Apostolic Church as the national church of the Armenian people and as an important bulwark for the edification of its spiritual life and national preservation'. Section 2.6 specifically mentions the existence of the Armenian Church, separate from 'other religious organisations'. The law also specifically reserves to the Armenian Church the right to 'preach and disseminate her faith freely', to 'recreate her historical traditions, structure, organisations, dioceses and communities', to build new churches, conduct religious education in state educational institutions and to expand charitable work. The Republic will also protect the Armenian Church's activities abroad (Section 6.17).

Other religious groups may receive official recognition if they satisfy specific criteria. Section 2.5 states that only groups 'based on historically-recognised holy scriptures' and whose 'doctrines form part of the international contemporary religious–ecclesiastical communities' can be officially recognised. Groups need to be dedicated to religious, not material, ends and to have at least fifty members. The ambivalence of this section and the vagueness of definition leads to discrimination against newer religious movements. However, religious organisations for 'ethnic minorities with their national doctrine' do not need to conform to the Section 2.5 limitations.

Legal status and registration of religious bodies

In order to gain official recognition, eligible groups must present their statutes to the Council for Religious Affairs (attached to the Council of Ministers) (Section 5.14), with details of structure, membership and activities (Section 5.15). Council decisions may be challenged in the courts; the courts can wind up a religious organisation if it violates the law (Section 5.16); however, there remains a strong element of subjectivity in the decision-making process. The Council may respond to requests by religious organisations for help in resolving disputes with government entities and, at the government's request, mediate between religious groups (Section 6.23).

The law declares that there is absolute separation of church and state, that the state must not interfere in the internal affairs of any religious group (Section 6.17) and must finance neither religious nor anti-religious activity (Section 6.18). The state does, however, take responsibility for preserving historical monuments of whatever affiliation (Section 6.21).

The law permits recognised religious groups to own property in accordance with the law on private ownership (Section 4.9). They may hold services on their own premises or on the premises of members, as well as in state institutions (such as hospitals, prisons and military camps) at the request of members in those institutions. It also permits them to organise religious education for their members (and children with the consent of their parents), to train clergy, to use the mass media, to engage in charitable work and to maintain contact with their religious centres abroad (Section 3.7). It permits religious groups to raise money (tax free) from their members (Section 4.12). However, it bans religious organisations 'whose spiritual centres are outside Armenia' from receiving money from those centres or political organisations abroad (Section 4.13).

The 1991 law thus seems to be an uneasy alliance of three competing and contradictory elements: traditional Armenian belief that the Armenian Apostolic Church should be the protected national church; Soviet tradition that every organisation, including religious organisations, must be registered and have official approval before undertaking any activity; and international norms regarding religious freedom and human rights.

In addition to the privileged position accorded to the Armenian Apostolic Church, it is notable that unrecognised groups are not accorded protection under this law. It appears that such unrecognised groups may not own property, rent premises for meetings, publish newspapers, sponsor broadcasts, collect money, conduct charitable work or sponsor visas for visitors to Armenia.

Legal developments affecting religious freedom

Despite the privileged status granted to the Armenian Apostolic Church, the 1991 legislation came under increasing pressure from the Armenian Apostolic Church which resented the freedom allowed to incoming religious groups, many financed from abroad, to provide what it believed to be unfair competition. In late 1993 the president issued a decree in effect restricting the freedom allowed to denominations other than the Armenian Church. The 1993 decree asserts that foreign and unregistered religious groups, and even some registered religious organisations, have violated the 1991 legislation: 'They affect the moral and psychological atmosphere in the republic, sometimes fostering a lack of respect toward military service, and hinder the smooth work of religious organisations, thus arousing their justified complaints.'

The decree accords the Armenian Apostolic Church the right to 'build and strengthen the religious consciousness of the Armenian people'. The Council for Religious Affairs is to investigate registered religious groups to see whether any have been proselytising in violation of the law; if so, they are to be dissolved. The Council is to 'terminate the activities of representatives of foreign religious organisations who, visiting Armenia at invitation, carry out activities not sanctioned by their status' and to 'establish proper oversight' of religious publications. The decree specifies that only registered religious groups can 'conduct religious propaganda' or rent premises for religious meetings from enterprises or institutions, in both cases keeping the Council informed. All foreigners invited for religious purposes must be invited via the Council. Only teaching based on that of the Armenian Church is permitted at state educational institutions. The Council must also be informed of an invitation abroad of any Armenian citizen by a foreign religious organisation, whatever the purpose of the visit. Penalties for violating legislation on religion were to be amended and the Council's work made more efficient.

Some religious groups were required to re-register in the wake of the decree and to include new clauses in their statutes banning their members from proselytising. Some groups, such as the Mormons, were quietly discouraged from applying for registration; they have kept a low profile.

The role of the Council for Religious Affairs, a continuation of the Soviet tradition established by Stalin during the Second World War, appears to have changed somewhat in practice, despite the extensive powers granted to it in the 1991 legislation and expanded in the 1993 decree. Some politicians and believers wish to see it abolished, feeling that it should have no role in a secular and democratic state. Some complain that despite the provisions of the law banning it from interfering in the internal affairs of religious groups, it continues to do so. Senior members of the Armenian Church have, however, supported it as a sympathetic government ally against newer religious groups.

While the Law on the Legal Status of Foreigners, passed in 1994, stresses that resident foreigners must observe Armenia's laws and 'respect the national customs and traditions of its people', it also guarantees them 'freedom of thought, speech, conscience and confession' in accordance with Armenian legislation. The 1995 constitution has since strengthened citizens' rights to freedom of conscience and belief.

Religious minorities

In practice, 'traditional' religious faiths that do not threaten the dominance of the Armenian Apostolic Church and which do not proselytise outside their own circle are accepted. Despite the conflict with Azerbaijan – which is popularly seen as a Christian–Muslim war – Muslims themselves, although very few, are not threatened. The small community in Yerevan is mostly made up of diplomats from Iran and elsewhere and the former mosque in the capital is being renovated with Iranian help.

Newer religious groups within Armenia have encountered hostility from the Armenian Church and some obstruction from state officials. Especially affected have been Protestant Christians from groups affiliated to foreign (mainly American) missions. Despite being officially registered in 1990, the Krishna Consciousness movement is still unwelcome, though communities exist in a number of cities. Following a fire at their temple in Yerevan, apparently started by relatives of a young convert, devotees alleged that the state authorities were uninterested in establishing the identity of the culprits and bringing them to justice. The state authorities have also obstructed the import of Krishna Consciousness literature, interpreting the import of the books as a sign of proselytism. Members also complain of hostile media coverage of their activities.

In public statements on the occasion of representations by the Armenian Apostolic Church in November 1993, the vice-president Gagik Arutyunyan assured it that 'within the legal framework, the state would struggle against every extremist and illegal phenomenon in the spiritual sphere'. He stressed that he 'regarded the Armenian church as the mainstay of the state, because it unified all Armenians in Armenia and the diaspora'. This openly partisan approach by such a senior politician, came just three weeks before the presidential decree tightening the 1991 legislation, and shows the sympathy the Armenian Church enjoys at the highest levels of government.

Conscientious objection

There is no separate legislation guaranteeing the right to conscientious objection to military service, although the 1991 law provides that in cases of 'conflict between civic duties and religious convictions', government entities and religious organisations may come to a mutually agreeable alternative form of service. Members of religious groups maintaining pacifist beliefs often leave the Republic to avoid having to perform military service; Armenian members of such groups expelled from Azerbaijan in 1988–90 chose to resettle in Russia or elsewhere.

Note

1   See also the entry on Azerbaijan.

AZERBAIJAN[1]

Azerbaijan	
GDP (US$bn)	5
Population	7,300,000
Annual population growth (%)	2
Urban population (%)	55
Working population (%)	39.4[c]
Literacy (%)	96.3
Ratifications	1; 2; 4

In 1991, after the collapse of the Soviet Union, Azerbaijan regained its independence. However, by then the conflict had already broken out over the Armenian-populated enclave of Nagorno-Karabakh, which had declared its intention to secede from the new republic and join Armenia. Azerbaijan's failure to crush Armenian separatism in Karabakh has led to constant political turmoil.

A sense of national identity has been difficult to establish in the post-Soviet era. Azeris have been torn between a religious identity as Shias (and thus close to Iran), an Azeri identity (together with the Azeris of Southern Azerbaijan in Iran), racial identity as Turks (and thus close to Turkey) or a pan-Turkic identity (encompassing not only Turkey, but the four Turkic states of Central Asia). Current issues are thus the development of Azeri Islam as an expression of Persian cultural heritage and justice in the treatment of the Armenian minority, which involves the future of the culturally isolated area of mountainous Karabakh.

Population and ethnic composition

According to the 1989 Soviet census, the population of Azerbaijan was 7,019,739. This included the 4.1 per cent of the people who lived in the enclave of Nakhichevan and the 2.69 per cent in Nagorno-Karabakh. In 1989, Azeris formed 82.6 per cent of the population. The Slavs, mostly Russians, composed the largest minority, followed by the Armenians (5.56 per cent, including the 2.07 per cent in the mainly Armenian Nagorno-Karabakh). Lezghins, Avars, Tatars, Jews (and Mountain Jews), Turks, Tsakhurs and Kurds were the other main minorities. The current population is estimated to be 7.3 million.

The war with Armenia has seen the expulsion or exodus of almost the entire Armenian population of Azerbaijan (with the exception of the estimated 150,000 in Nagorno-Karabakh) and the small Assyrian population, and the influx of almost the entire Azeri population of Armenia. The estimated 18,000 Armenians and part-Armenians who remain in Azerbaijan itself (mostly in mixed marriages) have sometimes been prevented from leaving and often live very restricted lives.

The Karabakh forces in the self-declared Nagorno-Karabakh Republic have expelled the entire Azeri population, and Karabakh victories around the enclave have resulted in the expulsion of the Azeri and Kurdish residents there as well. In all, some 600,000 Azerbaijani citizens are internally displaced within the republic, as well as all the Azeri refugees from Armenia. There are also Meskhetian Turk and Azeri refugees driven out of Central Asia by ethnic riots in the last decade. War, economic crisis and an uncertainty over their fate in an independent Azerbaijan have also led to an exodus of Slavs and Jews since independence.

Socio-economic structure

Azerbaijan remains a fairly traditional society. Although the country is mainly Muslim, smoking and alcohol consumption are widespread. The official weekend is still Saturday and Sunday.

Azerbaijan used to be a prosperous region of the USSR but the collapse of the Soviet Union and the rupture of trading relations, together with the Karabakh war and internal upheaval, have had a serious effect on the economy. Inflation has eaten away at personal savings. Many people have been reduced to poverty and refugees from the battle zone have especially suffered.

Oil has been a major component of the Azerbaijan economy since commercial exploitation began in the last century. Since independence, successive governments have sought international cooperation to exploit this wealth.

Political and government system

In the Soviet era, Azerbaijan contained two autonomous entities: Nakhichevan (an enclave between Armenia and Iran, with a short border with Turkey) was an autonomous republic and Nagorno-Karabakh (enclosed entirely within Azerbaijan) was an autonomous region. Nakhichevan retains its autonomous status, but the Azerbaijani government unilaterally abolished Karabakh's autonomous status in November 1991, a decision which provoked the Karabakh Armenians to declare full independence.

After independence, two presidents of the republic followed in rapid succession and then the former Azerbaijan KGB chief and Soviet Politburo member Heidar Aliev was elected unopposed as president in October 1993. President Aliev has ruled with a strong hand, crushing revolts, isolating political opponents and banishing them from Baku. Few decisions are now taken without his personal approval.

In 1992 the previous Soviet entity had been obliged to hand over its legislative powers to an unelected Milli Mejlis (National Assembly). A new parliament was due for election in October 1995 under a new system with a two-chamber National Assembly. The 1991 constitutional law on independence had included some guarantees of human rights; a new draft constitution has been in preparation. Some political parties have been banned or severely restricted in their activity, although opposition parties do function. An Islamic Party of Azerbaijan was formed in late 1992 (one of two current Islamic parties), but it has not become a significant force.

According to a law passed by parliament in April 1994, the president must take his oath of office on a copy of the Qur'an. President Aliev – who soon after his return to power in 1993 declared that he had been led to a faith in God – made a pilgrimage to Mecca in late 1994. Azerbaijan joined the Organisation of the Islamic Conference in December 1991, the first of the majority-Muslim republics of the former Soviet Union to do so.

Religious composition

Most Azeris – perhaps three-quarters – are Shia Muslims. The rest are Sunni of the Hanafi school. Also of Muslim background are most of Azerbaijan's minorities; the southern districts are almost exclusively Shia, while the central area is mixed (although with Shia dominance), and the north is predominantly Sunni.

During the Soviet era there was fierce persecution of Muslims, and most of the 2,000 mosques and all of the nearly 800 Qur'anic schools were closed. Until *glasnost* and greater openness towards religion in 1987, there were just sixteen registered mosques in Azerbaijan, fourteen of them Shia and two Sunni. However, unofficial places of worship continued to exist, boosted after 1979 by Islamic broadcasts beamed from across the border in Iran.

The Muslims of Azerbaijan are led by the Spiritual Board of Transcaucasia, based in Baku, a mixed Shia–Sunni body. The Board was founded in May 1944 during Stalin's wartime reconciliation with religious groups. It has been headed since 1980 by a Shia Sheik-ul-Islam; his deputy is always a Sunni Muslim.

There are now some 200 mosques in Azerbaijan, with at least forty in Baku. In 1989 a *madrassah* (theological school) was built next to the Taza-Pir Mosque in central Baku. After independence, and with financial support from Saudi Arabia, it became the Islamic University, admitting both Shia and Sunni students; students who espouse religious extremist views are reportedly expelled from the university. There are also other, smaller religious schools.

The Board formerly had jurisdiction over all the Shias of the Soviet Union, as well as Sunni Muslims in Transcaucasia as far as the southern edge of the Caucasus mountains. Since the break-up of the Soviet Union, however, the Board's authority outside Azerbaijan has been confined mainly to Azeris living in Georgia; few Muslims now live in Armenia after the expulsion of the Azeris and the Kurds.

The Russians are mainly of Russian Orthodox background; those believers in Azerbaijan came under the jurisdiction of the diocese of Stavropol and Baku, until 1994, when a separate diocese of Baku was established. The small Georgian community in the Kakhi region gained its first legal Georgian Orthodox church in 1989. Although up to half the

Jewish community has emigrated to Israel since independence, some synagogues exist and community organisations function. There are a few Protestant Christian communities (mainly Baptist and Adventist) of mixed Russian–Azeri composition. The Baha'i community in Baku has revived in recent years. Although there are hardly any Catholics in Azerbaijan, the state established diplomatic relations with the Holy See in 1992. None of these groups could practise their faith openly under former Soviet rule.

Inter-religious reconciliation

The Karabakh conflict, although not strictly a Muslim–Christian conflict, none the less reflects the different religious background of the protagonists. On a popular level religious differences are stressed, although most combatants on both sides are secularised. The Azerbaijani forces have been reinforced by Muslim fighters from other countries, including veterans of the Afghan war. The Karabakh Armenians have likewise counted on the sympathy of traditionally Christian countries, notably Russia.

Various reconciliation meetings have taken place between leading Azerbaijani Muslim and Armenian Christian clerics. In 1993 Sheik-ul-Islam Allahshukur Pasha Zade met Catholicos Vazgen, then head of the Armenian Apostolic Church, at a meeting in Switzerland sponsored by the World Council of Churches, the Conference of European Churches and the Islamic Association of Dawa and Relief. In 1994 Patriarch Aleksy of the Russian Orthodox Church hosted a reconciliation meeting in Moscow, attended by the Sheikh-ul-Islam and the Armenian bishops of Karabakh and of Moscow.

The Sheikh-ul-Islam has been instrumental in establishing the Higher Religious Council of the Peoples of the Caucasus, aimed at bringing together believers of different religious groups. Armenian church leaders boycotted a conference held in Baku in 1992, at which the Sheikh-ul-Islam personally attacked Catholicos Vazgen as being behind the Karabakh war. The Russian Orthodox Bishop of Stavropol and Baku attended the conference, as did Muslim leaders from Chechnya and other parts of the North Caucasus. The Georgian Orthodox Church sent only a priest as an observer.

Laws affecting freedom of religion or belief

Under previous Soviet legislation, tight controls made almost any activity outside worship within a registered place of worship a criminal offence. The USSR's Council for Religious Affairs ensured compliance with legislation and granted registration to approved religious communities through branch offices at the local level. The USSR's Law on Freedom of Conscience, in 1990, was mirrored in individual Soviet republics. Azerbaijan adopted its own law, the Law on Religious Freedom, in August 1992. The 1992 law follows Soviet practice in spelling out what is or is not permitted for a religious group but leaves a number of key areas undefined. However, it does clearly state the separation of the state from religious groups and forbids state favouritism for any one group. If provisions in international agreements to which Azerbaijan is a signatory conflict with those of the 1992 law, international agreements take precedence.

The law states explicitly (Article 5): 'In the Azerbaijan Republic, religion and religious organisations are separate from the state. The state does not prescribe the fulfilment of any affairs by religious organisations in relation to it and does not interfere in their activity.' The same article declares that different religions are equal before the law and that the state can have no preference for, nor limitations on any one religion. Religious organisations are allowed to take part in public life and make use of the media. However, they are banned from taking part in the activity of political parties or contributing money to them. Any 'servant of cult' (the old Soviet term for a cleric) must suspend activities as a cleric for the duration of any service in a state body.

In the law, the freedom to worship and believe what one wishes is emphasised strongly (Article 1). This applies to both individuals and religious organisations, on which no restrictions are placed, whether they are local in origin or international. Parents or guardians are allowed to bring up children in their own faith. Obstructing the performance of religious rites or teaching of religion is forbidden. All citizens, regardless of religious affiliation, are equal before the law (a provision which echoes the 1991 constitutional law on independence), and reference to a citizen's faith can be made in official documents only at that person's request (Article 4).

The only restriction placed on religious practices is specified in Article 1, which states that: 'The practice of freedom of religious belief can be restricted only for considerations of state and public security and in cases of necessity for the protection of rights and freedoms in accordance with international commitments of the Azerbaijan Republic.' The meaning of 'cases of necessity' remains undefined.

Religious rites may be conducted without restriction in places of worship belonging to a religious group, in places of pilgrimage, in graveyards, in religious education institutions and in citizens' homes (Article 21). In hospitals, homes for the elderly and the handicapped, hostels and prisons, inmates may invite clerics to conduct prayers and religious rites. The administration of such institutions must cooperate in facilitating this. Only in 'exceptional circumstances' (not defined further) can commanding officers in military units obstruct soldiers from participating in religious rites in their free time. Clerics are allowed to function in military units with the approval of commanders. Public religious events take place in accordance with the law on public meetings and demonstrations. Individual believers and groups are free to take part in international religious activities and attend meetings held abroad (Article 24). Officials and citizens who violate the law on religious freedom are to be punished in accordance with legislation of the Azerbaijan Republic (Article 30).

Legal status and registration of religious bodies

The law defines religious organisations – which must be voluntary and made up of adults – as 'religious communities, institutions and centres [i.e. central bodies], monasteries, theological educational establishments and their associations' (Article 7). They are represented by their central bodies and must be run according to approved statutes. These statutes must detail the organisation's type, denominational affiliation, location and numerous other details of how it functions and what property or media it owns (Article 11). Internal documents do not require registration with the state. Through registration, religious organisations gain legal personality.

To gain registration for an individual community, ten adult citizens must apply to the 'local organ of executive power' with a declaration and a statute they have drawn up (Article 12). The decision taken must be notified to the religious affairs organ of the Azerbaijan Republic which provides registration documents with the approval of the Ministry of Justice. In certain 'necessary cases' (undefined) the organ granting registration may consult the appropriate local authorities and 'specialists'.

Registration of a statute can be refused if the 'goals and tasks' set out in it are against the law (Article 13); a refusal may be challenged in court. A religious community can be 'liquidated' at its own request or if it violates the 1992 law or any other law of the

275

Azerbaijan Republic (Article 14). This too may be challenged in court according to the civil code.

Each religious community has the right to affiliate with any religious central body inside or outside Azerbaijan, and to change this affiliation (Article 8). If the religious centre is outside Azerbaijan, religious communities can function provided the statute does not contradict Azerbaijani law (Article 9).

Clerics and others employed by religious organisations have their wages and conditions set out in a contract between the two sides (Article 25). Employees may be members of trade unions. Their conditions of work are subject to legislation on employment and their wages are subject to tax (Article 26).

Religious groups are permitted to own buildings, 'objects of cult', money and other property necessary for their work (Article 18). They may raise voluntary contributions from individuals, as well as from organisations and the state. Donations are not subject to tax. Donations for charitable activity conducted by religious organisations are likewise not subject to tax (Article 23). Religious groups may also use state property, or property belonging to social groups or individuals in accordance with direct agreements (Article 16). Land is used by religious groups in accordance with the Land Code of the Azerbaijan Republic.

Religious groups are permitted to set up publishing houses, restoration and building firms once they have legal personality, as well as homes for orphans, boarding schools, hospitals and other institutions (Article 19). Income from manufacturing firms is subject to tax applicable to firms belonging to social organisations. Religious literature and objects can be produced, exported and freely distributed only in accordance with agreements with state religious affairs bodies (Article 22).

Education

Azerbaijan's schools are separate from religion (Article 6 of the Law on Religious Freedom). However, state educational establishments are permitted to teach 'theology, religious–gnosiological and religious–philosophical disciplines and the familiarisation with sacral/cult books'. Religious groups are allowed to conduct teaching for children and adults in their own educational establishments or outside, using their own property. Article 10 adds that they may establish institutions to train religious personnel, where students enjoy the same rights and state support as those in state institutions. The Jewish Women's Organisation of Baku, operating out of the Mountain Jewish synagogue, runs Jewish schools and Hebrew teaching projects, partly state-funded.

Council for Religious Affairs

After independence, the Soviet-era Council for Religious Affairs was replaced by a department for religious affairs within the Cabinet of Ministers. This department handles liaison between the government and religious groups. However, much of the spirit that imbued the old Council remains. Responsibility for registering communities has passed from the Council to the Ministry of Justice.

Article 29 of the Law on Religious Freedom covers the activity of the body prescribed by the law to handle religious affairs on behalf of the state. At the request of religious groups it must provide assistance in reaching agreement with state bodies. It must 'help the strengthening of mutual understanding, tolerance and respect for each other between religious organisations of different faiths'. It is required to handle the registration of statutes, as well as amendments to them. It is to work with local authorities in the application of the law on religious freedom. It maintains links with similar institutions in other countries – presumably with the successors to the Council for Religious Affairs in other former Soviet republics and with religious affairs ministries which exist in Middle Eastern countries and elsewhere – and holds information on religious groups in the country and on the application of the law.

There are some, including Haji Sabir Gasanly, the rector of the Islamic University in Baku, who would like the Council for Religious Affairs to be restored as a separate entity, a view which some fear could see a return to strict control over minority religious communities.

The state and minorities

Successive presidents of independent Azerbaijan have proclaimed the government's religious tolerance, a tolerance that extended to all religious groups except the Armenians. In 1992, then President Elchibey declared on television:

> The religious and ethnic policy of the leadership of Azerbaijan will follow the traditions of the Azerbaijani Democratic Republic of 1918–20, traditions laid down by its founder, Muhammad Amin Rasulzade. This is a democratic republic and we cannot live any more in conditions other than those of a democratic republic. We do not accept the idea of a mono-ethnic republic.

He stressed that there were several Christian churches in Azerbaijan which the government was working to restore, and that synagogues were being returned to believers. He specifically denied that Azerbaijan was constructing an Islamic 'fundamentalist' state.

Elchibey's successor, Heidar Aliev, has repeated assurances that Azerbaijan is a country tolerant of religious minorities. Congratulating Orthodox Christians at Easter 1995, he declared that Azerbaijan has always been the motherland for all peoples, irrespective of nation, religion or race.

Despite the constitutional guarantees against religious discrimination, numerous acts of vandalism against Armenian Apostolic Church property have been reported throughout Azerbaijan. These acts are clearly connected to anti-Armenian sentiments brought to the surface by the war between the two countries. There used to be an Armenian diocese in Azerbaijan with the cathedral in central Baku but by 1990 the bishop and all the priests had fled Azerbaijan in the wake of attacks and the diocese was abandoned.

Other religious communities, such as the Baha'is, have not been able to regain their former places of worship confiscated during the Soviet period. Baptists in Shemakha have complained of harassment from the local authorities. Three Muslim clerics from Sheki have reportedly been arrested and sentenced for their preaching.

Some Christians complain that, despite the secular nature of the state, they fear the imposition of Islamic rule, with second-class status for members of other religions. So far there is no evidence that government leaders are contemplating this. However, Muslim papers often make derogatory references to Christians and Christianity, probably sparked by tensions over the conflict with Karabakh.

Conscientious objection

The situation for those objecting to military service is confused. The 1992 Law on

Religious Freedom – in an apparent reference to conscientious objection – allows the state to offer alternatives to civic duties by agreement with religious groups.

Article 9 of the Law on the Armed Forces of the Azerbaijan Republic, passed in October 1991, offers believers and others who object to serving in the armed forces on grounds of conscience the right to conduct alternative service. Young men between the ages of 18 and 25 called up for military service can opt for alternative service of two years' duration (six months' longer than the term set out for military service). However, subsequent law on military service in 1992 does not make provision for an alternative service for believers and others whose conscience does not permit them to serve in the armed forces.

The internal instability and the ongoing conflict with the armed forces of the Karabakh Armenians have brought chaos to the recruitment process. Draft evasion is widespread, helped by the ease of bribery. There are periodic sweeps through the streets of Baku and other cities to press men of military age into service in the forces.

It is not clear whether alternative service has been put into practice. Some conscientious objectors and those who are unwilling to give bribes to evade military service have left Azerbaijan for Russia.

Armenian-controlled Karabakh

The Armenians of Nagorno-Karabakh have declared their own Nagorno-Karabakh Republic, which remains unrecognised by the outside world (including by Armenia itself). The Karabakh authorities control not only the disputed enclave itself but a swathe of territory around it. As an unrecognised state, the Nagorno-Karabakh Republic is not eligible to sign international human rights instruments. However, it claims to abide by provisions in international law protecting basic human rights.

Although religious representatives from both sides have denied any religious motivation to the Armenian–Azeri war, many people on both sides view it as continuing ancient Christian–Muslim rivalry. The Karabakh Armenians allege that Azerbaijani forces have deliberately targeted Christian churches. They cite two air raids on Sunday mornings a week apart in August 1992, the first on the Gandsasar monastery (the bishop's seat), the second on the Holy Cross church in Shusha. The Karabakh Armenians claim they have deliberately avoided damage to mosques in areas they have seized. However, in Agdam, for example, the historic mosque was in a sorry state in 1994 after Karabakh troops had seized and systematically wrecked the town.

In the 1930s all the Armenian Christian churches and Muslim mosques in Karabakh were closed by the Soviet authorities. It was not until 1988 that the Armenian Apostolic Church was able to re-establish a diocese of Artsakh (Karabakh) and appoint a bishop who brought in priests from Armenia to re-open churches and to serve the local population.

The Nagorno-Karabakh government tacitly accepts the Armenian Apostolic Church as the national faith. Bishop Martirossian is close to the Karabakh leadership and on occasion opens official events with a prayer. The Karabakh authorities took action in 1993–94 against missionaries from Armenia representing Krishna Consciousness and Protestant Christian groups who began charitable work in the enclave. Some preachers were detained and premises used by these missionary groups were attacked and closed down. One preacher was sentenced to three years' imprisonment on charges of draft evasion. Robert Kocharian, the leader of the Karabakh government, denied this was religious persecution. He claimed that these missionaries were spreading pacifism among the soldiers.

Women in Azerbaijan and Karabakh

Because the Azeri peoples have been subjected to the influence of Iranian revolutionary Islam in the south, this has affected women's freedom. As in other upheavals in this area, women are used as cultural markers in terms of dress and behaviour and, in persecution, they suffer sexual violence, enforced exile and refugee status. Azerbaijan society's conservative attitudes in family relations especially affect women. In some rural areas women do not venture much outside the house and at elections the head of the household votes for the entire family. Total head-covering is not practised; rural women wear head-scarves.

Both the majority group of Muslim Turkic-speaking Azerbaijan women and the Christian Armenians have traditions of major women poets, including the gifted nineteenth-century Azeri poet Kurshidbanu Natavan (the latter name assumed by her, and meaning 'powerless').

Note

1 See also the entry on Armenia.

BULGARIA

Bulgaria	
GDP (US$bn)	11
Population	8,900,000
Annual population growth (%)	0.4
Urban population (%)	69
Working population (%)	50[a]
Literacy (%)	93
Ratifications	1; 2, 2(a), 2(b); 3; 4; E

Since the collapse of communism in 1989, Bulgaria has been undergoing a slow and painful transition from a totalitarian state with a centrally planned economy to a democratic political system and a market economy. This transition has affected all aspects of social and personal life in the country, not necessarily for the better. Economic reform has been very slow and piecemeal. Democratisation, with political life still dominated by the former communists, has been painful. There has been huge social dislocation and loss of habitual security, especially in employment, health and education. In addition, there has been a very unfavourable international environment, an unprecedented exodus of the active population and an acute sense of spiritual and moral crisis.

As for living standards, 85 per cent of the population now earn less than the basic cost of living, 75 per cent are below the poverty line and 55 per cent below even subsistence level. Over half a million people – mostly young and skilled – have left Bulgaria since 1989. By the end of 1996, inflation was very high and the nation was in uproar.

Some ethnic groups fared considerably worse than others under the economic reforms. Thus the unemployment among the Roma Sinti (gypsies) reached 70–90 per cent – the Roma are the poorest of the poor and the least educated in Bulgarian society – while the stated reason for many of the Turks leaving the country is the destruction of their traditional livelihoods. In the mountainous regions of the south, too, unemployment has reached almost 90 per cent. The overlapping of ethnic differences with economic deprivation provides no fertile ground for tolerance.

Ethnic and religious composition

There is considerable overlap between the ethnic and religious composition of the country's main communities: Bulgarians and Turks. According to the 1992 census, ethnic Bulgarians constitute 85.8 per cent of the population of around 9 million, ethnic Turks 9.7 per cent, Roma Sinti 3.4 per cent and all other ethnic groups, including Pomaks, 1.1 per cent. As for languages, there are 86.3 per cent Bulgarian-speakers, 9.8 per cent Turkish-speakers and 3 per cent Roma-speakers. Over 90 per cent of ethnic Bulgarians live in urban areas. Over 80 per cent of the ethnic Turkish population live in rural areas; they are concentrated in the Burgas region and in the regions of Kurdzali, Razgrad, Silistra and Shumen. A parliamentary commission is investigating claims that pressure was applied to Muslims to declare themselves Turkish. Pomaks, for instance, are ethnic Bulgarians who are Bulgarian-speaking Muslims.

Several years before the collapse of the former communist government in 1984–85, a forcible assimilation policy (the 'revival' campaign) tragically attempted to make Bulgarian Turks change their names. Bulgarian Turks left in their hundred thousands for Turkey in 1989 and continued to do so after the policy was rescinded, although many have since returned. In 1993, almost 600,000 applications by Turks, Roma and Pomaks for the restoration of their family names were granted, according to the Bulgarian government.

Census statistics on religious composition show that 86.2 per cent of Bulgarian citizens are Eastern Orthodox, 0.6 per cent are Catholics and 0.2 per cent are Protestants; 12.7 per cent are Muslims (predominantly Sunni Muslims).

The Bulgarian Orthodox Church has played a major role in the nation-building process and has traditionally enjoyed a rather favoured status. The first 'national' history was written in the late eighteenth century by a monk; the church achieved its independence in 1872 before the independent Bulgarian state was created. The Eastern Orthodox Church split into two synods in 1992 after much recrimination. The dispute concerned the allegation of subservience to the communist regime by the leaders of the clergy.

The Muslim community is governed by a Chief Mufti's Office and was subject to the same rigid governmental control before 1989 as the Orthodox Church. There have recently been internal divisions within this supreme body of Muslims, and the Directorate of Religious Affairs intervened to endorse local and central leading bodies composed of people the authorities trusted. An order issued by the Council of Ministers in February 1955 was subsequently upheld by the Supreme Court as within the scope of the competent body.

There have been communities of Catholics in Bulgaria since the seventeenth century and several Protestant denominations, mainly Pentecostal churches, were established in the nineteenth century. There are also small Jewish and Armenian communities. In the last five years dozens of new religious groups have also established themselves. Although the Roma have their own religious framework, many practise Christianity or Islam.

More than thirty religious organisations were until recently registered with the government's Office of Religious Denominations and reportedly more than 300 associations undertake activities of a religious nature.

As far as relations between the governing bodies of the different denominations are concerned, there is a clear need for an institutionalised forum for dialogue. A council of religious denominations has been proposed but never formed and the links between the different communities are maintained on an exclusively informal basis.

In a 1992 survey of religious believers, fewer ethnic Bulgarians said they believed in God (37 per cent) than did members of the minority Turkish, Pomak and Roma groups. Notably, 73 per cent of ethnic Turks surveyed said they believed in God while the proportion of Bulgarians who did not believe in God or were uncertain was 35 per cent and 28 per cent, respectively, much higher than the minority groups. Surveys of religious practice confirm this picture. Only 6 per cent of Christian believers are daily churchgoers and 16 per cent go to church once a week. One-third of the Muslims declared that they perform the five prayers every day. Of the Roma respondents, 38 per cent declared themselves to be Orthodox Christians, 40 per cent Muslims and 3 per cent adherents of other denominations.

The survey found that the highest levels of prejudice were directed at the Roma by other groups. Many of those surveyed were in favour of segregating them and characterised them negatively, as a 'lower' race, unfit to be educated and inclined by nature to laziness and deviant behaviour. Further, the dominant prejudice about Turks was that they were 'religious fanatics, cruel' and communally minded.

These stereotypes and prejudices none the less co-exist with a high degree of interaction between the main groups, mostly in work and celebrations. Joint festivities are quite common, especially in rural areas, but cross-community marriages remain extremely few. Anti-Semitism has apparently not been much of a problem for the Jewish population of up to 7,000, living mainly in Sofia.

Political and legal structure

According to the new constitution of July 1991, Bulgaria is a parliamentary republic based on the principles of the rule of law, the separation of powers, constitutionally entrenched rights and an independent judiciary. Political pluralism is enshrined in the constitution. Since until 1989 the dominant position of one political party and its ideology was constitutionally protected, the new constitution specifically prohibits the establishment of a dominant ideology.

There is an enduring legacy of Marxism and anti-individualism but it can be said that all ideologies are competing in the market-place of ideas at present. There are more than 100 political parties registered, from ultra-right to ultra-left. Ideological divisions do not, however, mean a great deal to people in the streets.

The president is directly elected but has limited powers. His sphere of power includes defence and foreign policy but his prerogatives in most areas clash with those of the Council of Ministers (the government) and are subject to constant disputes. The president has a suspensive veto over legislation passed by parliament which, however, can be overridden by a simple majority.

The country is divided into regions, headed by appointed regional governors, and municipalities with directly elected mayors and directly elected councils. Bulgaria is a unitary state and autonomous entities are specifically prohibited in the constitution.

The 1991 constitution introduced a Constitutional Court which interprets the constitution and can rule on the conformity of legislation to the constitution and to the international obligations of the state.

Article 11.4 of the constitution stipulates that 'there shall be no political parties created on [an] ethnic, racial or religious base, nor parties which seek the violent usurpation of

281

state power'. This provision is criticised by non-nationalist commentators but supported by most Bulgarians. The constitutionality of the Movement for Rights and Freedoms (MRF), which effectively represents Bulgarian Turks, has been challenged unsuccessfully before the Constitutional Court.

There have been numerous attempts at creating an umbrella organisation to represent the interests of the Roma but still no agreement has been reached among their leaders; thus the Roma do not have organised political representation.

Constitutional protection of freedom of religion or belief

In the constitution of 1991, a general principle of equality of dignity and rights is enshrined in Article 6, which also prohibits any restrictions on rights or privileges on the grounds, *inter alia*, of race, ethnic self-identity, religion and opinion.

Freedom of religion or belief is protected in Article 13, which states:

1 The practice of any religion shall be free.
2 The religious institutions shall be separate from the state.
3 Eastern Orthodox Christianity is the traditional religion in the Republic of Bulgaria.
4 Religious denominations and institutions and beliefs shall not be used to political ends.

Article 37 further states:

1 The freedom of conscience, the freedom of thought and the choice of religious or atheistic views shall be inviolable. The state shall assist the maintenance of tolerance and respect among believers from different denominations, and among believers and non-believers.
2 The freedom of conscience and religion shall not be practised to the detriment of national security, public order, public health or morals, or of the rights and freedoms of others.

Article 37.2 has been criticised by a member of the (UN) Human Rights Committee as being too vague for citizens to know clearly what is implied.

The constitution also protects freedom of expression. There are no restrictions on publication of religious materials apart from the availability of funds. Broadcast religious programmes are few and mostly of Orthodox Christianity. There are no restrictions on imports of books and materials.

Legislation affecting freedom of religion or belief

The legislation which governs the exercise of freedom of religion or belief pre-dates the constitution. It consists mainly of the Religious Denominations Act 1949 (RDA) and the governmental decrees on the Office of Religious Denominations (ORD). The RDA reflects an extremely restrictive approach towards the practice of religion or belief and a desire for total control by the state over any religious activity. It was one of the first legislative acts to be challenged for its unconstitutionality after the adoption of the 1991 constitution. The Constitutional Court, however, in June 1992, only declared certain provisions to be unconstitutional, those that gave the executive the right to hire and fire priests, that prohibited links between local religious organisations and related ones abroad, and that prohibited religious missions, aid or health institutions or religious orders. These provisions have not been formally repealed.

Certain offences against freedom of religion or belief are contained in the Penal Code. Part III, entitled 'Crimes against citizen's rights', contains (in Chapter II, 'Crimes against denominations') provisions against 'preaching hatred on religious basis by means of speech, the press, acts or other activities' (Article 164), against impeding the free exercise of religion – but only those manifestations which conform to the laws of the country, public order and public morals – and against coercion to take part in manifestation of religion (Article 165).

Article 166 prohibits the founding of political organisations based on religion and the use of the church or religion for propaganda.

Education

Article 20 of the 1991 constitution proclaims that 'the education and organisation of children and young people are exclusively a task of the state'. After the collapse of communism, however, there has been a proliferation of private educational establishments, especially at primary and secondary level, which have effectively destroyed the monopoly of the state on education.

As far as the contents of the educational material taught in state schools is concerned, according to the regulations on the application of the 1991 Education Act, the education in public schools is secular and 'religious or ideological indoctrination' is prohibited. What is considered to be indoctrination is determined by experts of the Ministry of Education which has control over the curriculum and textbooks. According to the Ministry, in the classes on literature, philosophy, history and ethics, religious values which 'have won recognition in European culture' are emphasised.

Parents are free to send their children to private schools. The Ministry exercises control of the curriculum of those for children under 16 (it can also close such schools down) but there is provision for classes in religious instruction. There are Islamic secondary schools.

There are also numerous Sunday schools which offer religious instruction and religious organisations operate religious high schools for the training of future priests. There also exists a Faculty of Christian Orthodox Theology in the Sofia State University and an institute of Islamic studies in Sofia. All the restrictions on the education of priests abroad have been lifted.

State registration of religious organisations

The communist regime left a legacy which influences relations between the state and religious groups today. The Religious Denominations Act 1949 was intended to place all religious activity – deemed to be inherently dangerous to the totalitarian state – under total government control. Remnants of this attitude still linger in recent legislative enactments, especially when religious issues are used to further political or economic interests.

One of the most controversial issues has been the issue of registration of religious denominations, especially the many new religious groups, often referred to as 'non-traditional' denominations or 'sects'. Up to 1989, only the Orthodox, Muslim, Jewish and Gregorian denominations had been registered.

In all bills on religious matters, the use of public space (buildings, parks, street processions) is conditional on a religious organisation's being registered. A list of registered organisations is established by the ORD; those which are not on it have allegedly been refused access to assembly halls by local authorities. Other difficulties of non-registered entities may also be envisaged, such as refusal to open bank accounts, to own property, different tax status, and so on.

Under the system which existed until early 1994, there were two ways to operate as a legal entity: as a 'religious denomination' registered with the ORD, or as a non-profit organisation under the Persons and Family Act 1951. Under registration of denominations with the ORD, operating under the 1949 Act, the Director of the Office assessed an application for registration and the Council of Ministers made the final decision. This procedure lacked essential procedural safeguards in the form of defined procedures, criteria on which a decision should be based and no time limits for the executive decision. The procedure before the courts under the 1951 Act was fairer, less onerous and much quicker, and some organisations which run Sunday schools or other religious activities have opted for it.

The government then consolidated its hold over religious activities and organisations in 1990 by giving the ORD power to 'supervise' the religious organisations registered under the Persons and Family Act, and created an 'expert' standing working group in the ORD to give opinions on registration applications for the status of 'denominations'.

Then in early 1994 – after more than a year of hostile press coverage of the activities of new religious movements – a campaign was initiated ostensibly to straighten out the registration procedures and to encourage all organisations undertaking religious activities to register under the RDA. At the same time all groups 'which have religious or related activities or perform religious education' and were registered under the 1951 Persons and Family Act were required to re-register with the ORD after 'positive vetting' by a commission of the Council of Ministers. Some thirty denominations and twenty-two associations and foundations were then registered, including Krishna Consciousness.

The applications of twenty-four of the formerly registered denominations were not successful under the new procedures, the government stating in response to a query from the Special Rapporteur on Religious Intolerance that their statutes and activities were considered to infringe Bulgarian legislation. The registrations of the White Brotherhood, Angels of Salvation, Soldiers of Christ, Soldiers of Justice, Wassan, Emmanuel, Gedeon, Salvation and the Jehovah's Witnesses were revoked on 17 June 1994. Many are contesting the legitimacy of this decision.

Like the original procedure for registration, the new one also lacks important elements and safeguards and has produced results widely criticised by the human rights community. It leaves total discretion to government officials, there is no definition of which activities are deemed to be 'of religious or related' nature, the procedures are not defined and it does not provide for any appeal. Effectively, the executive had acquired a right to determine what the courts would or would not register and to cancel previous court decisions on registration without any hearing.

The Director of the ORD has associated himself with the 'struggle' against the 'sects' (acknowledged by the government in correspondence with the Special Rapporteur for Religious Intolerance) by reportedly saying that the changes in the law are 'an attempt to counter the activity of sects with legal means'. In various interviews the Director of the ORD – the official most directly responsible for state–church relations – has publicised its opinion that decisions should be taken not only on legal grounds but also on grounds of expediency. He is also believed to support the establishment of Orthodox Christianity as a state religion and to have claimed that in Bulgaria the spectrum of the twenty-one recognised Protestant denominations is complete and everyone can express their longing for God within the already existing churches. The Bulgarian government regards the constitutional freedom of religion as protecting solely the rights of individuals.

New legislative proposals

As well as the registration legislation, there has been a recent flurry of legislative proposals aimed at making Eastern Orthodox Christianity the dominant religion in Bulgaria. Two Orthodox priests who are members of parliament have called for the changes and Protestants have objected. The following are some of the main proposals: to establish compulsory teaching of Eastern Orthodox Christianity in state schools; to establish a department in the public media (radio and television) to broadcast religious programmes; to ban the use of public buildings by 'non-traditional religious denominations', and to prohibit missionary activities and proselytism.

It must also be noted, however, that there are other legislative proposals which aim at creating conditions for meaningful exercise of freedom of religion or belief, among them a bill suggesting the abolition of the ORD altogether and the registering of all religious organisations with the district courts.

Intolerance

Although Bulgarians like to think of themselves as tolerant, hospitable and open towards foreigners, this has not been supported by social surveys such as the one mentioned above. Negative stereotyping and intolerance towards Bulgarian Turks may be scars left by the so-called 'revival' campaign in 1984–85 – the forcible change of the names of Bulgarian Turks from Turkish to Bulgarian ones, with unconfirmed reports of many deaths – and the fierce nationalist campaign surrounding it. The press recorded great satisfaction when whole villages – forcibly made Muslim centuries ago – were christened.

These incidents are still deeply felt in Bulgarian minds and hearts. History and geography have not been generous to Bulgaria, with its history of being subject to Ottoman rule and being the closest ally of the former USSR. Popular opinion fears the spreading of wars in the former Yugoslavia eastwards and there are suspicions about the policy of Turkey towards fellow Turks in Bulgaria. Indeed, the fear of a 'Cyprus' variant was widely cited as one of the reasons to initiate the 'revival' campaign.

However, greater consideration might be given to the part economic collapse has played in promoting intolerance. Its social consequences have been unevenly distributed among the different ethnic groups, with a concomitant rise in hatreds towards 'the other'. Mass media and political and economic groups thrive on these phenomena and only unsettle the now rather fragile inter-ethnic and inter-confessional equilibrium.

However, despite the present economic situation and the lack of well-functioning friction-eliminating institutions, coupled with splits within the large religious communities of Orthodox Christians and Muslims, no major outbursts of religiously motivated violence have occurred. This is most often explained as deriving from traditional tolerance in interpersonal relations and also from horror at atrocities in former Yugoslavia. 'At least we are not Yugoslavs . . .' is a nationwide morale-boosting catchphrase. Some political forces also whip up nationalist feelings when elections approach.

Another disturbing feature is the recent proliferation of avowedly nationalist organisations. The leader of one of them in a newspaper interview proclaimed as one of the aims of his organisation the separation of ethnic groups and the creation of ghettos, which in his opinion were not anti-democratic and existed in all democratic countries. He also supported the struggle against 'the sects' which to him are a 'spiritual narcotic' for the nation.

The issue of registration of denominations also turned into a wholesale hostile campaign against 'sects', or 'non-traditional' religions, a strong reaction of intolerance towards non-traditional forms of Christian religious beliefs on the part of some state agencies and non-governmental entities, supported by a vicious and markedly uniform media campaign. In 1995, religious literature was seized by police from members of the Word of Life group and the Jehovah's Witnesses. The ORD may intervene to resolve a dispute when officially registered religious groups become the target of such hatred – as happened with Krishna Consciousness when some members were attacked in the street in Sofia.

In 1995 there were instances of employment discrimination and harassment of people belonging to minority religious groups (such as the Word of Joy and Word of Life groups) reported by the press and by non-government organisations (NGOs). In addition, in disputed custody cases, mothers belonging to the Jehovah's Witnesses and Warriors of God were not awarded custody of their children.

Two recently created NGOs advocating freedom of religion or belief operate now: the Citizens for Religious Tolerance Project of the Bulgarian Helsinki Committee and the Bulgarian Association for the Protection and Promotion of Religious Freedom. The campaign against 'the sects' is reminiscent of times not too distant of intolerance towards dissidents; it has also targeted the human rights organisations engaged in advocating tolerance and, in particular, the Bulgarian Helsinki Committee.

Conscientious objection

Some religious conscientious objectors may experience extreme intolerance. According to allegations in the 1995 report of the Special Rapporteur for Religious Intolerance, the Jehovah's Witnesses have been the object of smear campaigns in the media as well as threats of death and imprisonment and assaults which the police allegedly refused to report. In response, the Bulgarian government stated it had no information about these particular incidents but added:

> It should be explained that the prohibition of blood transfusions contained in their [Jehovah's Witnesses'] doctrine constitutes a direct threat to the health of Bulgarian citizens, while refusal to take an oath to the Bulgarian flag infringes the Universal Military Service Act and thus affects state security.

The 1991 constitution explicitly states that no-one is entitled to be relieved of their constitutional and legal obligations on the basis of their religion or belief. However, in practice, military conscripts who raise conscientious objections are likely to be sent to the construction forces. In 1995 instances of sentences of imprisonment have been reported regarding 'total objectors'.

CYPRUS

The island of Cyprus's location in the eastern Mediterranean, forty miles from the coast of Asia Minor, has given its inhabitants thousands of years of turbulent history. The present *de facto* partition of the island between Greek and Turkish Cypriots – enforced by 30,000 mainland Turkish troops – is a legacy of over 300 years under the Ottoman Turks, eighty-two under the British and thirty-three under the independent Republic. By introducing mainland Turkish settlers and converting local people to Islam, the Ottomans began the demographic division of an island inhabited mainly by Orthodox Christians

Cyprus	
GDP (US$bn)	Greek area:6.7[b]
	Turkish:550mn[b]
Population	700,000
Annual population growth (%)	0.7
Urban population (%)	53
Working population (%)	46
Literacy (%)	94
Ratifications	1; 2, 2(b); 3; 4; E

of Greek culture. The Ottoman *millet* system of administration gave Turkish Muslims and Greek Christians responsibility for their own communal affairs and from 1878 British policy preserved communal separation and exploited communal differences.

In 1960 the present constitution, along with a Treaty of Guarantee providing for the security of the island's Greek and Turkish communities, was imposed on the Republic as a condition of independence. The three guarantor states were – and remain – Britain, Greece and Turkey. The Treaty effectively neutralised the Republic militarily, and the provisions granting the minority Turkish Cypriot community veto powers on all matters of substance – as well as the right to separate municipalities in the island's five major cities – made it virtually impossible to govern the Republic.

As a result, in 1963 the government of the then president, Archbishop Makarios, proposed amendments to the constitution which led to violent Turkish Cypriot opposition, Turkish intervention under the Treaty and the creation of separate Turkish Cypriot enclaves. Following the Turkish military invasion in 1974, in response to a coup against Makarios's government by the military junta in Greece, virtually the entire Turkish Cypriot community – and 37 per cent of the territory of the Republic – came under *de facto* administration headed by the Turkish Cypriot communal leader, Rauf Denktash.

In 1975 Denktash proclaimed a Turkish federated state in northern Cyprus and in 1983, supported by Turkey, an independent Turkish Republic of Northern Cyprus. This amounted to a violation of the treaty establishing the independent Republic of Cyprus agreed at Zurich on 11 February 1959. In 1985 Turkish Cypriots adopted the 'Constitution of the Turkish Republic of Northern Cyprus'. This document supplanted the 1960 constitution which remained in force on the rest of the island.

The Republic of Cyprus is thus internationally recognised; only Turkey recognises the Turkish Republic of Northern Cyprus. UN forces monitor the welfare of Greek Cypriots and Maronites in the north and of Turkish Cypriots in the south. In 1983, the European Commission of Human Rights (in a complaint made by Cyprus against Turkey) reported that Turkey was responsible for preventing the Republic from exercising its own jurisdiction over the northern part of the country occupied by Turkish forces. The Commission found that 'the acts [of Turkey] violating the Convention were exclusively directed against members of one of the two communities in Cyprus, namely the Greek Cypriot community'. The Commission concluded that Turkey had failed to secure rights and freedoms without discrimination on the grounds of ethnic origin, race and religion as required by Article 14 of the Convention.

The Republic of Cyprus is a pluralist democracy with a presidential system; the executive, legislative and judicial branches are separate. The legal system is strongly influenced by the British tradition. In the Republic, human rights are guaranteed for the whole of the population; Turkish Cypriots living in the Republic enjoy equal rights, privileges and the law's protection. The Turkish Cypriot administration maintains a multi-party parliamentary structure; its citizenship is largely restricted to a single ethnic–cultural–religious community.

The GDP of the Republic vastly exceeds that of the Turkish Cypriot area and the per capita income of Greek Cypriots is three times more than that of Turkish Cypriots. While there is full employment in the Republic, there is considerable unemployment in the Turkish Cypriot area. The economy of the north, dislocated by the 1974 invasion and the occupation, has been integrated into the much larger economy of mainland Turkey which provides an annual subsidy. In 1988 the Republic concluded an agreement for full customs union with the European Union.

Ethnic and religious composition

Following the Turkish invasion, 180,000 Greek Cypriots living in the northern part of the island were driven south while 47,000 Turkish Cypriots in the south moved north. Thus, virtually the entire Greek Cypriot community now lives in the southern 63 per cent of the island and almost all Turkish Cypriots reside in the north.

Each side provides different pictures of the demography of the island. According to the Republic's statistics, its population is 629,800 while the Turkish Cypriots are estimated to number 93,000, or 14.9 per cent of the island's people. According to a 1992 report for the Council of Europe, mainland Turkish settlers number 40–45,000.

Tradition holds that Orthodox Greek Cypriots form 80 per cent of the population of the island, Sunni Muslim Turkish Cypriots form 18 per cent and Christian minorities – Maronite and Latin Catholics and Armenians – about 2 per cent. There is also a number of newer religious groups and movements.

Religion and state in the Republic

The 1960 Republican constitution contains guarantees of human rights and freedoms and protection to all communal groupings and individuals. The Republic ratified the European Convention on Human Rights in 1962; it has superior force in the country over all legislation except the constitution.

Article 18 of the 1960 constitution guarantees 'every person . . . the right to freedom of thought, conscience and religion' and states: 'All religions whose doctrines or rites are not secret are free' and 'All religions are equal before the law.' In reply to a question from the Human Rights Committee in 1994, the Cyprus representative said that Freemasonry was not considered a 'secret sect'. Articles 19 and 20 of the 1960 constitution, among other things guarantee free speech, association and assembly, thus ensuring the freedom of all religious groups to proselytise.

While the Republic's citizens are free to choose and practise their religion, or to reject religion outright, Greek Orthodoxy is the predominant religion of Greek Cypriot Christians and the Autocephalous Greek Orthodox Church of Cyprus (the Cyprus Church) has the character of a state institution. Although there may be no legal discrimination against other religious groups, the church has a privileged place in every sphere of activity: religion, communal affairs and education, land ownership and taxation.

The identity of the 'Greek Cypriot' people, historically, has been defined by ethnicity (Greek birth), Hellenistic culture and membership of the Orthodox Church which, as the first of the Christian churches, continues to assert its claim to primacy as an institution and to a monopoly of the truth, in terms of Christian doctrine. Church dominance and its secular role were reinforced during Ottoman rule, when the Greek community was administered by its bishops. After the outbreak of the Greek freedom struggle in 1821, Orthodox leaders headed campaigns for the liberation of Cyprus, first from Turkey and then from Britain. Archbishop Makarios's assumption of a leading role in the rising against Britain and his elevation to the presidency of the Republic were both consistent with his role as 'Ethnarch' ('Leader of the Nation') of his community.

Although the Orthodox Church has lost a considerable amount of power and influence since the establishment of the Republic, it retains a dominant position in society and a determining role in education and, until recently, was the sole means of marriage and divorce. The church has maintained this position because it is the guardian of Greek tradition and because the Greek Cypriot people are still conservative in their outlook, although few Greek Cypriots now respect the church as an institution or its bishops and priests as a clerical caste; weekly services are largely attended by elderly women, usually widows. None the less, tradition is still strong when it comes to family groups' observance of the Lent fast and attendance at Easter services. Greek Cypriots from all backgrounds – including ultra-secular, old-style communists – generally baptise their children, marry in the church and are buried by the church.

Greek Cypriots who leave the Othodox Church to join one of the Protestant or other religious groups established on the island since British rule are considered to have lost a key dimension of their religio–cultural–national identity, an essential part of their 'Greekness'. Thus the church opposes – and the community in general disapproves of – proselytising by newer churches and religious groups, although their right to proselytise is guaranteed by the constitution and guarded by the authorities. Conversion does not remove Greek Cypriots from being considered members of the Greek Cypriot community, as defined in the 1960 constitution.

The Orthodox Church is not affiliated with any Greek Cypriot political party although the clergy, the archbishop and bishops, have, on occasion, enjoyed special relationships with and promoted particular politicians, some rising to ministerial posts.

The Cyprus Church and social change

In the Republic, both the Cyprus Church and the conservative nature of society discriminate against women. This discrimination, in the words of Kate Clerides, one of the two women currently serving in the House of Representatives, stems from the 'deep-seated tendency of the three monotheistic religions to place women at a lower level' than men. As a result 'women's issues are trivialised by both men and women' and it is very difficult to raise such problems as domestic violence and sexual harassment in the workplace which the male- and church-dominated society prefers to ignore. The same is true of the issue of homosexual rights. The politicians refuse to repeal legislation outlawing homosexual relations, because of strong pressure by the church; however, the authorities choose not to enforce it.

However, the 1960 constitution was amended in 1989 to remove 'matters of personal status' for Greek Orthodox Cypriots from the exclusive governance of the Autocephalous Greek Orthodox Church. Greek Cypriots may now have the option of civil procedures: registry marriage and separation or divorce through family courts. Also provided for are equal rights for children born out of wedlock, and other rights for men and women in marriage, custody and divorce including penalties for and protection from marital violence. This combination of legislation, in effect, severed the link with the church on family law matters and loosened the hold of patriarchical traditions.

The amendment was vigorously opposed by the Orthodox Church which has refused to name one of the three-judge panel specified for divorce cases. The church does not allow a remarriage in the church to a person with a civil divorce. The policy of non-cooperation adopted by the church serves as an impediment to general acceptance of civil marriage and divorce.

The new family law covers only marriages of Greek Cypriots and Orthodox Christians. The family relations of cross-community marriages are under the old Marriage Law and those of Turkish Muslims under the Turkish Family Law.

A bill providing the right to civil marriage and divorce to members of the Catholic (Maronite and Latin) Churches and the Armenians is before parliament, supported by parliamentary representatives of the Maronite and Latin communities but opposed by the churches.

The Ministry of Interior licenses representatives to perform marriages recognised by the state. In addition to the Greek Orthodox, Maronite and Latin (Catholic) Churches, eighteen representatives of five 'foreign' churches were chosen on the basis that they had a stable following. Others may perform religious ceremonies which, to be recognised by the state, must be confirmed by a municipal registry service.

Religion and state in the Turkish Cypriot entity

Fundamental rights and liberties, spelled out in the constitution of the Turkish Cypriot entity, include guarantees of 'freedom of conscience, religious faith and opinion' and freedoms of thought, opinion and expression; compulsion in religion is prohibited.

Turkish Cypriots are militantly secular, in line with the ideology of Ataturk, the 'father' of modern Turkey. Although 99 per cent of Turkish Cypriots are Sunni Muslims, Islam is not the state religion. Secular legal codes apply in all spheres of personal and civic life, including marriage and divorce which come under the 1959 Turkish family courts rather than Islamic Shariah Courts.

Turkish Cypriot policy and Cypriot religious practice

In the Turkish Cypriot entity, former Greek Cypriot inhabitants – 517 largely elderly people – have been denied their rights to property, freedom of movement and worship in their churches and religious sites. The Turkish Cypriot authorities regulate travel into and out of the Turkish Cypriot area, barring from entry Greek Cypriots, Greeks and third-country nationals of Greek origin and preventing Turkish Cypriots from visiting the Republic. The Turkish Cypriot authorities also regularly prevent Turkish Cypriots from attending meetings organised in the UN-controlled buffer zone or in the south, intended to bring individuals from the two communities together.

Greek and Turkish Cypriot communities in the Turkish-controlled entity are thus deprived of access to their respective places of worship. Under the control of the Turkish Cypriot administration are hundreds of Greek Orthodox churches and religious properties: modern buildings and premises administered by the Orthodox Church itself including churches, monasteries, chapels and shrines, and premises designated as 'ancient monuments'. All of these properties have, in theory, been transferred to the Turkish Cypriot authorities in accordance with Article 159 of their constitution. Although this article prohibits the transfer of these properties 'to real and legal persons', some have been transformed into mosques by the Turkish Cypriot Evkaf and many have been used or are being used by individuals or municipalities as storehouses, clubs, cinemas and museums. Others have been looted and desecrated and despoiled by neglect.

At present, only six Greek Orthodox churches and one monastery (all in the Karpas) are functioning and there is only one active priest who takes services in these churches by turn. A retired priest who is over 90 years old assists by officiating at christenings and funerals. One of these churches is located at the Saint Andreas Monastery at the tip of the Karpas peninsula, formerly a particular place of pilgrimage for all Greek Orthodox followers in Cyprus. At present only the small Greek Cypriot community enclaved in the Karpas are permitted to attend services at the monastery on feast days. No-one is allowed to go there without a police permit.

The Turkish Cypriot authorities also deny their own people the right to visit and worship in the four mosques located in the Republic, which have been preserved and maintained by its authorities. Among these sites is the Tekke of Hala Sultan, a shrine housing the tomb of an aunt of the Prophet Mohammed who arrived in Cyprus in 694 with the invading Arab armies, died there and was entombed at Larnaca. The tomb is said to be revered by Turkish Cypriots as the 'third holiest site in Islam'.

Women in religion

The Cyprus Orthodox Church, the Maronite and Latin Catholic and Armenian communities do not permit women to join the clergy. Although a number of Protestant and other religious groups accept, in principle, the elevation of women to positions in the clergy or as elders, in practice there are very few if any. Women are not elevated to the *umma*, the class of religious judges and *imams* among Turkish Cypriot Muslims.

Religious minorities

Legislation on freedom of religion and religious organisation is strictly observed in both the Republic and the Turkish Cypriot area. Although there are no accepted religious minorities in the Turkish Cypriot area other than the Baha'is, new religious movements have multiplied in the Republic, all of them competing to convert Greek Cypriots.

The only religious grouping to gain converts in the Turkish Cypriot north is the Baha'i faith, which first came to the island in 1868. There are at present about 500 Baha'is in Cyprus: 100 residing in the south (only eleven are of Greek Cypriot origin) and 400 in the north, almost all Turkish Cypriots. Baha'is in the two areas of the island maintain contact, celebrate festivals together and bring their children together in summer schools and camps.

The Jehovah's Witnesses conduct house to house campaigns throughout Cyprus. First on the island in 1930, the Jehovah's Witnesses now number 3,000 members and baptise sixty to seventy adult converts a year. They own a dozen 'Kingdom halls' and rent other premises.

Education

Greek and Turkish Cypriots, under Article 108 of the 1960 Republican constitution, have the right to 'receive subsidies from the Greek or the Turkish Government respectively for institutions of education, culture, athletics and charity'; 'schoolmasters, professors or clergymen' can also be recruited from Greece or Turkey.

The Greek and Turkish Cypriot educational systems and curricula have thus been patterned on those of Greece and Turkey and have promoted the separate national identities of the two communities. In spite of this, it has been widely accepted that Greek and Turkish Cypriots have, in terms of character and outlook, more in common with each other than with their respective mainland communities.

Article 18 of the 1960 constitution guarantees the right of parents to bring up their children according to their convictions while Article 20 gives the right to persons and institutions to give instruction 'in accordance with the relevant communal law'. Throughout the Greek Cypriot state education system, religious instruction is compulsory for every child whatever their family's beliefs. At secondary level children receive twice-weekly instruction in Greek Orthodoxy; some lessons in comparative religion are also given.

Although many textbooks come from Greece, more texts produced in Cyprus are now being used in schools. Illiberal ideas and negative images of other religious groupings and of the Turks as former colonial masters may be transmitted by an older, more conservative generation of teachers who have been trained in Greece; the younger generation is reportedly more open in its attitudes.

The only organised opposition to the Hellenocentric character of Greek Cypriot education comes from the Communist Party which considers it an obstacle to reconciliation with the Turkish Cypriots. In July 1994 the party presented proposals for the reform of an educational system criticised by the party as cultivating 'hatred, fanaticism and chauvinism'. The Education Minister replied by saying that Hellenocentric education aimed to cultivate the values of Hellenism (democracy, freedom, justice, dignity, responsibility) and the Orthodox Church (tolerance, compassion, solidarity and self-sacrifice). 'These are the roots of our tradition and the basics of modern European civilisation,' she said.

In the secular Turkish Cypriot north, weekly instruction in 'Religious Culture and Ethics' is compulsory in the two final years of primary school and through most of secondary schooling. Teachers of religion at the elementary level are trained locally while those in the secondary schools are generally graduates of theology faculties in Turkey. Most but not all school books come from Turkey; most teachers are Turkish Cypriots, many educated in Turkish universities.

Although Islam does not play as large a part in the acculturation of Turkish Cypriot children as does Christianity in that of Greek Cypriot children, the secular 'Turkish identity' is inculcated and 'Turkish nationalism' promoted. As a result, more secular Turkish Cypriot nationalists find it difficult to understand the importance of religion in the make-up of the Greek Cypriots while Greek Cypriots believe Islam has far more importance as an influence on the Turkish Cypriot personality than it in fact does.

Publications and the media

In both the Republic and the Turkish Cypriot north the press is free and engages in vigorous debate including criticism of the authorities, and religious books and texts are published. Religious groups freely import books and texts for the use of their communicants and for proselytising.

When the Republic deregulated radio and television broadcasting in 1990, the Orthodox Church set up its own stations with religious services and a limited amount of religious programming. Minority religious groups have access to state-controlled media even though, since these groups have such small congregations, they do not avail themselves of it.

The Turkish Cypriot authorities maintain a monopoly over radio and television. Friday mosque services and Muslim religious programmes are aired.

Communalism in military service

In the Republic and in the Turkish Cypriot north, eligibility for compulsory conscription for military service has been based on the ethnic origin of the rulers, a legacy of Ottoman times when only the ruling Muslim community provided military conscripts while Christians and Jews paid taxes to fund the military. When the Republic gained its independence, the Greek Cypriot majority and Turkish Cypriot minority were given the right to form separate communal security forces and Greece and Turkey were given the right to base specified numbers of troops on the island.

In the Republic, all men of Greek Cypriot origin, irrespective of nationality, are liable for military service. Turkish Cypriots are exempt and men from the Maronite, Latin and Armenian communities may elect not to serve. The Maronites and Armenians have always pressed for exemption, the Latin community less so. In the north, all Turkish Cypriot citizens are liable for military service although in practice only males serve.

Conscientious objection

The Republic legally recognised conscientious objection in January 1992. As an alternative to twenty-six months of mandatory military service, a conscientious objector may choose either forty-two months of unarmed military service (out of uniform, outside a military area) or thirty-four months of unarmed military service (within a military area).

This law was adopted after considerable pressure from international human rights groups to provide an alternative to military service to conscientious objectors, all of whom have been Jehovah's Witnesses. Jehovah's Witnesses' elders have been granted exemption from military service. Until the amendment, all conscientious objectors were fined or imprisoned, some repeatedly as conscription or reserve duty is compulsory until the age of 50.

However, as the amendment did not give exemption from conscription by the military but simply relief from serving in military units, the Witnesses continue to refuse performing any service under the Ministry of Defence. Elders say their members would perform service if it was supervised by another ministry, such as in hospitals under the Ministry of Health. Furthermore, the Witnesses claim that the alternative periods of service are 'punitive' as twenty-six months plus one-third – 34.6 months in all – is accepted as an international norm.

As of June 1993, 128 Jehovah's Witnesses were imprisoned as conscientious objectors. Another twenty are estimated to have become involved in court cases or been sentenced since then. Amnesty International has repeatedly called for the release of 'all conscientious objectors imprisoned for refusing to perform military service'. Following appeals in April 1994, concerning these 'prisoners of conscience' and the conditions on which alternative civilian service was made available, the Ministry of Defence has promised a review of the 1992 law.

There is no provision for conscientious objectors in the Turkish Cypriot north. The first Turkish Cypriot to claim relief from conscription as a conscientious objector did so in 1993 and was sentenced to three years of imprisonment; his case has been raised with Amnesty International.

FRANCE

France	
GDP (US$bn)	1,320
Population	57,300,000
Annual population growth (%)	0.7
Urban population (%)	73
Working population (%)	43[a]
Literacy (%)	99
Ratifications	1; 2, 2(b); 3; 4; E

France, a major industrial nation with a diversified economy, is a multi-party democratic republic, headed by an elected president. The judiciary is independent and the law is conducted under the Napoleonic code. The highest administrative court is the Council of State.

Social, religious and belief composition

The population of Metropolitan France is 57.3 million, while that of France overseas numbers nearly 2 million. One-third of French people have some foreign ancestry. Nearly 4 million foreigners have permanent residence in France; Algerians, Moroccans and Tunisians together comprise nearly 1.5 million people. An estimated 90 per cent of the population are Roman Catholic, 2 per cent Protestant, 1 per cent Jewish, 1 per cent Muslim (mostly from North Africa) and 6 per cent unaffiliated to any religion. Several secular organisations exist, such as the Ligue d'Enseignement, the Union Rationaliste, the Cercle Condorcet.

Women have always participated in France's long history of effective protest and intellectual influence outside the major public institutions. Although women were not enfranchised until 1944, they have enjoyed the highest rate of tertiary education in Europe.

The state, religion and belief

Article 2 of the 1958 French constitution states that:

> France is a Republic, indivisible, secular, democratic and social. It shall ensure the equality of all citizens before the law, without distinction of origin, race or religion. It shall respect all beliefs.

The history of French law on freedom of religion and secularity has its origin in the philosophy of the Enlightenment and the principles invoked in the Revolution of 1789. The secular state evolved as the church's relationship to the state was diminished but its privileges were not entirely removed. Indeed, the 1790 Decree, issued by the National Assembly, stated that the Assembly respected religion and was linked to the Roman Catholic Church, which was the only one supported by public monies, that the Assembly could not and ought not debate a motion on the Catholic religion and that it would continue the customary ecclesiastical privileges.

The fundamental principles and laws of the Republic, passed in 1789, stated in their preamble that: 'The French people solemnly affirm the laws and rights of man and the citizen set down in the Declaration of Rights of 1789 and the fundamental principles recognised by the laws of the Republic.' Freedom of thought and opinion, including religious opinion, was affirmed by the Declaration of 1789.

The concept of secularism (*laïcité*) is central to this first of the emerging nation–states. In his speech in 1875 – introducing his plan for a secular education system – Minister Jules Ferry invoked the spirit of the French Republic, 'created by the citizenry acting in unity and imposed equally on all people, even those who reject it', to confirm the principles of elected public authority and the secularity of the state. He reminded members of the National Assembly that

> Religious matters are matters of conscience and, consequently, of liberty. The French Revolution's major enterprise was to emancipate politics and government from the shackle of various religious beliefs. We are not theologians; we are citizens, republicans, politicians and civilians.

He called on Assembly members

> to uphold the principle which is the principle of freedom of conscience, independence of civil authority, independence of civil society in relation to religious society . . . A hundred years ago . . . civil authority was secularised. Two hundred years ago, the greatest minds of the world – Descartes, Bacon – secularised human knowledge, science and philosophy. Today, we are to follow in this tradition, we are only submitting to the logic of this great movement begun so many centuries ago, when we ask you to make the education system secular.

Secularism was confirmed in the 1946 French constitution, and in the revised constitution of 1958, after overwhelming votes in referendums.

Traditional liberties and social or associational rights – subsequently reaffirmed by specific legislation – include the freedom of the press (1881) and freedom of association (1901), among others. Freedom of conscience and worship was ensured under the 1905 Laws of Separation which formally ended the privileged position held by the Catholic Church. Article 2 states that, 'The Republic does not recognise, remunerate or subsidise any religion.'

The 1905 laws were the result of a complex compromise between the Catholic Church and other religious and non-religious groups, which all differed among themselves. The legislation was both infused with the spirit of free enquiry while at the same time it exercised vigilance against the possibility that one religion or a majority of religions might try to exercise some sort of moral authority over society. The law covers a wide range of beliefs. Specific legislation passed for congregations and associations in the laws of 1901 extends to Buddhists. Although the Muslim minority has not yet formed itself into a representative body, it has complete liberty of religion and worship.

There are some variations based in the regional history of the departments of Bas-Rhin, Haut-Rhin and Moselle where pre-1905 regulations continue to distinguish between recognised and non-recognised religions. The recognised religions are the Catholic Church, the Lutheran Church of the Augsburg Confession and the Reformed Church, and the Jewish faith. Non-recognised religions are Islam, Orthodoxy, independent Protestant churches not attached to the two recognised Protestant denominations, and various new religious movements. Non-recognised religious associations acquire legal personality and capacity by registering with the records office of the local court. While administrative authorities may refuse such registration, the Council of State has confirmed that the authorities cannot refuse registration except on grounds of public order. Consequently, the 'unrecognised' faiths in practice now operate within the general system of church–state separation.

The state ensures freedom of worship but does not intervene in religious internal affairs. Only ceremonies which occur in public places or processions on the public highway are subject to regulation. Today, administrative matters are handled by the Ministry of the Interior through the Central Office of Religion and Worship.

Protection against discrimination and intolerance

Religious and racial discrimination, among other bases for discrimination, is prohibited by law and incitement to racial hatred is a criminal offence. Desecrating grave sites of a specific ethnic, religious, national or racial group is a criminal offence punishable by imprisonment and fines.

Stigmatising of difference has over past centuries led to discrimination and intolerance. Jewish organisations have noted that a variety of secular anti-Semitism dates from the revolutionary period, associating Jews with religious obscurantism and fanaticism and equating them with financial power. These attitudes had contributed to the persecution of Jews in twentieth-century France. Today they are mostly manifested by members of extremist movements. Holocaust denial and distribution of associated literature continue despite the restrictions on its publication under the Gayssot law of 1990 and the fining of offenders. Paul Touvier, the first French citizen to be convicted of crimes against humanity, died in 1996 after two years in prison; he had ordered Jewish prisoners to be murdered fifty years previously. Touvier had been sheltered by the Catholic Church hierarchy in Lyons; the church had supported the Vichy government against what were seen as the encroachments of socialism.

While racist incidents doubled between 1992 and 1993, anti-Semitic incidents tripled in the same period, according to the National Consultative Commission on Human Rights. Jewish school children, students and school buses have been targets for harassment. In 1994, about twenty Jewish and Muslim graves were desecrated. Security has been arranged for Eid and Yom Kippur celebrations and religious buildings have been put under protective surveillance from time to time. Government-initiated programmes against racism and anti-Semitism have raised public awareness and brought together local officials, police and concerned associations; anti-racism campaigns have taken place in public schools. Anti-racism NGOs are very active.

The policy of assimilation

France welcomes all who have citizens' rights from its former colonial territories, whatever the colour of their skin, as long as they submerge their cultural identities within the dominant French secular culture and ideology. Assimilation is seen as the goal appropriate to the French nation. The Anglo-American model of communities which consult and negotiate with the government through democratic representatives is widely rejected as 'ghettoisation' – particularly if religion is allied to community – because it does not allow people their rights to opinion as individuals. The institutionalising of 'race relations' (common in the Anglo-American model) is also seen as separating people on the basis of particular characteristics instead of integrating them into the whole society. Michel Rocard has set up a Haut Conseil à L'Intégration to institutionalise the French model of social relations.

French nationality is seen as a privilege, and, especially in right-wing politics, one which should be deserved, not only by living in France and speaking the language but by adopting its political beliefs, obeying its laws and serving in the army. Although 81 per cent of Algerian French youths do serve in the army, their ethnic background and cultural conditioning alone ought, in the opinion of the far right-wing, to disqualify them.

Because Islam is considered to be more than a religion, North African (*maghrébin*) immigrants are thought by some to be incapable of accepting French values of republicanism, institutional pluralism, gender equality and secularism. This view of immigration has been a recurring phenomenon in the past hundred years of French history. During the Spanish Civil War, settled Spanish immigrants were accused of being too religious and were called 'Christos'.

From the beginning of the 1960s, immigration policy became more interventionist as North Africans came to represent a 'social problem' and temporary workers stayed on in France. Since the early 1970s, mistrust of the capacity of non-Europeans (especially North African Arabs) to assimilate has characterised immigration policy, so much so that the concept of 'immigration' has been robbed of legitimacy and the word 'immigrant' has become a euphemism for non-European, especially the *maghrébins*. Fears that cultural and religious difference will combine with more rapid population growth than the French average have led to the fear of 'ghettoisation' of North African immigrants.

Pressure for change

In the last twenty years, the emphasis on 'la République une et indivisible' has been under scrutiny, as an ethic called on when nation was perceived to be under threat. The ideology masks real ethnic, regional and other differences. Difference is regarded with ambivalence: conveniently recognised when it is a matter of needing to employ foreign workers, but otherwise considered more or less as an obstacle to social cohesion and national values.

Separate entities have been rejected as counter-evolutionary, that is, contrary to Enlightenment concepts of personal, individual freedom within a framework of the human march of progress. The 'evolutionary potential' of men and women in equality cannot be fully pursued if it is constricted by the identity needs of the groups and faiths from which they come. Where feelings of superiority have been expressed towards groups which, because of their cultural identity and history, are considered to be backward or to take an inferior place in the progress towards enlightenment, these feelings have contributed to inequalities in France today.

There has been pressure for change, for recognition of the position of minorities in France. Since the 1968 civil unrest, indigenous and territorially scattered minorities (Alsatians, Basques, Bretons and Catalans) have been pressing the state to adopt a pluralistic definition of French nationhood. They were soon joined by the Muslims. Those supporting a multi-cultural France as in the nation's interests argued that one could be politically and culturally French while being subculturally and subpolitically a member of an identifiable group. Immigrants should be given a full and equal place in the nation they have helped, as workers, to build. The term 'French Islam' refers to different things depending on whether it is used by the partisans of secularism or by the members of the Muslim community.

According to Jacques Robert, a state of reciprocal recognition and mutual respect exists, for which the fixed and uncompromising affirmation of a secular framework – brought into being by a history in which Muslims have not participated – is not adequate. The Muslim religion and its culture are 'newcomers' and their reception may well require changes which do not in themselves flow from the basic concepts of secularism.

The debate in France today is therefore over whether the state should move from an alleged strict neutrality towards a more 'balanced' secularism. Some religions – such as Catholicism – have, because of their history and influence in French life, a more favoured existence than others. The principle of religious neutrality sits awkwardly with the religious culture of France, as the legacy of Catholicism is still prominent in many aspects of French public life, something clearly felt by the Protestant minority. The question of how far the state should provide facilities and resources for religious minorities – especially Islam – has also been raised. A new secularism could take difference into account. However, French law and policy have not yet interpreted the secular principles of equality and non-discrimination as requiring the active accommodation of the cultural, linguistic and religious characteristics of minorities.

Religious influence on social issues

What could be interpreted as the Catholic Church's influence on the law in relation to women's concerns remained until the mid-1960s when contraceptives were first legally sold. Although the famous 1971 Bobigny trial – in which a raped girl was charged with the crime of terminating her pregnancy while the rapist was not brought to trial at all – may be interpreted as revealing church influence on the law, rape has since been reclassified as a crime. Matters of equal pay, equal parenting, divorce by mutual consent were all settled by the mid-1970s, and an obligation on hospitals to perform termination of pregnancy was enforced in 1982.

Individual clergy within the Catholic Church have up till now been critical of the Catholic Church's response to the spread of AIDS in France, saying that the church regarded it as some form of divine retribution and that it was condemning people to death by prohibiting the use of condoms. However, in February 1996 the Catholic episcopate released a document prepared by the church's social commission, *Aids: Society in Question*, which contained testimony from Catholic specialists in AIDS research, prevention and treatment, as well as from sociologists and theologians. The church document passed on the view of medical specialists that 'The use of a condom is comprehensible in cases where an individual with an established pattern of sexual activity needs to avoid a serious risk.' The document has been welcomed as a step towards overcoming the ambivalence of the French authorities towards AIDS in France.

Education

Since the introduction of secular education in the nineteenth century, Catholic schools have been in the private sector. The secularism of the public education system was confirmed by the 1946 constitution, and there is no religious instruction, children being freed from other classes on Wednesday afternoons so they can go to catechism classes. Children may have crosses and rosaries at school and attendance at Christian ritual is sufficient reason to suspend homework requirements. Non-Catholic Christians required to attend church on Saturdays and Jewish children (*Shabbat*) are not required to attend Saturday school. Jewish children may also wear the *kippah*. Religious practice is thus widely respected in French schools. Only the wearing of a head-scarf (*hijab*) by Muslim girls has aroused a national storm. In one of the clearest examples of religious–cultural discrimination in relation to women, they were made once more the markers of cultural boundaries.

The *hijab* case (*l'affaire des foulards*)

In September 1989, three girls were expelled from a public secondary school in Creil for wearing the *hijab* in class. The principal of this school similarly objected to Muslims requesting exemption from physical education and sex education classes and Jews being absent on *Shabbat*. There was a furore; debates followed in the National Assembly and political opinion was divided. The media reaction was anti-Islam. *Le Monde* saw things in polarities: through the French school, children could be saved from the obscurantist particularism of religion, which impeded their progress towards the rational, neutral principles embodied in the Republic.

A significant sector of the French intellectual elite considered that the school should be an 'emancipatory space' in which ethnic, religious or political allegiance should be left at the door. This is where people of different origins become French and symbol-wearing would impede this process as well as encourage discrimination and divisiveness in the community. School, therefore, was a place of liberation and the *hijab* was seen as a symbol of women's oppression and of the denial of sexual equality and equal opportunities to Muslim girls. The *hijab* was seen as a symbol of patriarchal power, as if the father in the house were to accompany the girl into her school. Muslim women, it was thought, ought to have access to other ways of living and alternative ways of seeing the world so that they could freely choose whether or not to wear the head-scarf in the world beyond school. Development of critical awareness and freedom of choice should be part of the role of education. The mission of the education system to contribute to the development of a student's personality and to favour equality between men and women was recalled by the Administrative Court of Nantes in February 1992.

Those criticising the *hijab* reportedly saw Islam in terms of fundamentalism and obscurantism, although some thought that prohibiting the *hijab* might drive Muslim parents to choose segregated education in Muslim schools. The segregation and marginalisation of the Muslim community were viewed as incompatible with Republican values and ideals.

Other views of the *hijab* were voiced on both sides of the political spectrum. A leading member of the New Right, Alain de Benoist, argued in favour of the girls' right to express their cultural difference while SOS-Racisme's president, Harlem Desir, said that students who wore expensive clothing brought more inequality into the classroom than did those wearing the *hijab*.

In November 1989, the Council of State declared that while there can be no general and absolute prohibition on wearing the veil or any other religious symbol, it could be restricted under certain circumstances:

> Freedom of expression and freedom to manifest religious beliefs stated under the Constitution do not allow students to wear religious symbols which, by their nature, by the conditions under which they are worn either individually or collectively, or by their ostentatious or assertive character, amount to acts of pressure, provocation, proselytism, or propaganda, which could affect the dignity or freedom of the student or of other members of the educative community, thus compromising their health or security, disturbing teaching activities and the educational role of teachers, [and] finally, upsetting order in the school or the smooth running of the public sector.

There was to be no exemption from parts of the curriculum, such as sex education, as all students were expected to take part in every aspect of school life. The court's decision, it was generally agreed, continued the spirit of compromise of 1905 by recognising the contemporary evolution of French secularism.

In 1991, the Paris Administrative Tribunal held that the wearing of religious symbols could be the subject of regulations to be determined by a secondary school's board of directors. The board of the College of Montfermeil thus forbade the wearing of the

Islamic scarf in class, on grounds of the 'danger of fanaticism', and ordered the permanent expulsion of students who had contravened the regulation. This decision was, however, reversed in November 1992 by the Council of State, which held that expulsions of students on the basis of wearing the head-scarf were contrary to the law and beyond the powers of the educational authorities. The principle of secularism commanded that 'education be provided in respect of, on the one hand, the neutrality of its curriculum and teaching and, on the other hand, the freedom of conscience of its students'. The court recalled France's national and international commitments forbidding any discrimination based on religious beliefs and convictions of students. Students had 'the right to express and manifest their religious beliefs within the school, while respecting pluralism and the freedom of others'.

A circular by the Minister of National Education distributed in December 1993 framed the court's decision in slightly different terms:

> Students must not wear any ostentatious distinguishing sign, in clothing or otherwise, which aims to promote a religious belief; also proscribed is any proselytising behaviour which goes beyond simple religious convictions and aims to convince other students or members of the education community and to serve as an example to them.

Finally, in September 1994, the Ministry of Education issued a directive prohibiting the wearing of 'ostentatious political and religious symbols' in schools, leaving the matter of determining what they might be to the discretion of school administrators. Reportedly about eighty students have been prevented from wearing the *hijab*, though several hundred others continue to wear theirs. As a result of the *hijab* incident, Muslims looked for and found allies among Catholics and Jews to work for a new secularism in which religion could return to the public space.

The *hijab* incident had some symbolic aspects. An issue of *Le Figaro* magazine in 1985 bore on its cover a picture of Marianne, the quasi-sacred symbol of Republican France, veiled. It was a potent image, conveying the seductiveness and the threat of 'the other' right to the heart of the French nation. Invasion by would-be usurpers of Marianne must be resisted; hence the fear of allowing religion, any religion, too near the political space and the ambivalence over allowing individuals to express 'too much' difference, from the struggles of the Breton community for recognition of its language to the issue of Muslim schools which might establish counter-identities at the heart of the nation.

Fear of Islam as 'the other' is exacerbated by sensationalism in the media. A poll reported in *Le Monde* in 1989 revealed that 60 per cent of those surveyed associated Islam with violence, 66 per cent considered it anti-progressive, and 71 per cent associated it with fanaticism. In a 1993 poll, 63 per cent feared the consequences of the development of Islam in France, and 68 per cent feared trouble caused by immigration in general. While 61 per cent agreed that the Islamic faith was as respectable as the Christian faith, 23 per cent disagreed.

Marriage, divorce, homosexuality and religious institutions

In the area of marriage and divorce, a number of legal judgments have been made in cases which involve religious institutions and religious law. For instance, a parish priest and a vicar-general were convicted for allowing a religious marriage ceremony to be held although no civil ceremony had taken place. Further, in the matter of the delivery of the document of religious divorce – by which a husband may release his wife from a Jewish marriage and without which, she cannot remarry in the Jewish faith – the Court of Cassation in 1990 decided that the delivery of the divorce was a matter of freedom of conscience for the husband and that his abuse of his right could give rise only to an action for personal damages.

In a case in which a religious school dismissed a teacher for remarrying after divorce, the Court of Cassation in 1978 upheld the school's decision. An employment contract existed between the teacher and the school in which the religious convictions of the teacher were considered, although such considerations usually fall outside working relations. These considerations were voluntarily included, and accordingly, became an integral part of the contract. After pointing out that the school, bound by the principle of indissolubility of marriage, had acted to safeguard the smooth functioning of the school and to maintain its unique characteristics and reputation, the Court dismissed the teacher's petition for damages for breach of contract.

Similarly, in a 1991 decision, the Social Chamber considered articles of the Labour Code which prohibit an employer from dismissing an employee on the sole ground of the employee's morals and religious beliefs. The provisions also indicate that an employee may be dismissed for sufficient cause when it can be shown that his or her conduct – taking into account the nature of the duties and the goals of the employer organisation – created problems within it. The Social Chamber decided that an association that dismissed an assistant sacristan after learning that he was homosexual violated the above mentioned articles.

However, the Court of Appeal reversed the decision, stating that homosexuality had always been condemned by the Catholic Church and that the employee had deliberately failed to comprehend his obligations, quite apart from the scandal to which such conduct could have given rise. It was irrelevant whether his behaviour was known only to a small number of believers and was revealed to the employer by indiscretions.

Children and choice of religion or belief

French courts have considered in a number of cases the matter of the interest of the child and the adoption of a religion. In a case where one parent opposed the baptism of their child as a Jehovah's Witness, the judges pointed out that she had been born of Catholic parents and baptised; consequently, she should be obliged to wait until her majority to make her own choice. In 1992, the Montpellier Appeal Court rejected an approach which might oblige it to compare the merits or demerits, advantages or disadvantages, of a dominant religion with those of a minority religious group. Instead, the court stated, it should 'look whether . . . the father's and mother's activities within a church, sect, political party or any other group of religious, cultural, political or philosophical character present advantages or disadvantages with regard to the interest of the child'. Each parent should work to overcome any tendency to sectarianism and together give the child a religious education compatible with that given by the other, knowing that if there was any instance of excess or intolerance, the access arrangements for the non-custodial parent would be restricted.

Similarly, the Court of Appeal in Nîmes in 1991 opted for the joint exercise of parental authority as a method of protecting a child against a possibility that its Jehovah's Witness parent might refuse a blood transfusion and jeopardise the child's health. The court also commented that 'any type of education, in that it necessarily imposes and inculcates ideas, beliefs and principles, is in itself an indoctrination of which only the content (and even the methods used) may give rise to concerns'. Further, in a 1993 decision, the District Court of Appeal of Rennes referred to the Penal Code and the Convention on the Rights of the Child to confirm that the French law upheld the right of parents to inculcate their beliefs in their children, as a matter inherent to the fundamental freedom of thought which could not be questioned unless it affected the child's health, security or morals.

New religious movements

New religious movements have been the subject of political debate and investigation in France. The issue was first raised in the National Assembly in 1978 by Deputy Alain Vivien, whose report has been criticised as unscientific and inaccurate. The National Consultative Commission for Human Rights considered it inappropriate to take legal measures to restrict new religions.

Anti-cult organisations continued to press for investigation and regulation. In June 1995, after another deputy's report, the National Assembly established a commission of enquiry into 'the liberty-destroying effects of certain associations known as sects', which reported on 10 January 1996. The report of the commission (the Guyard Report) has been criticised as containing largely unsupported allegations against the so-called 'sects', allegations of criminal or anti-social behaviour which are vague and ill-defined, insufficient differentiation between groups labelled as 'sects', inaccurate and out-of-date information about the groups identified in the report and as making no attempt to present objective (and readily available) academic assessment of the groups and issues involved. Scholars in the field have also expressed concern that the commission overlooked ready sources of information in the form of court decisions in France and elsewhere which could have thrown quite a different light on some aspects of its investigation.

The report did not propose and the National Assembly reportedly will not pursue specific legislation against new religious movements in France. However, other recommendations have given cause for concern to specialist academic commentators – notably the Center for Studies on New Religions – about precisely who is accorded religious freedom in France, and who is not. The report employs a definition of 'sect' which is prejudicial, as it is based on mere suspicion that certain vaguely described activities occur in a group's practices. It lists and describes religious groups in terms of popular misconceptions and is not accurate.

While the report recommends no specific new legislation, it has recommended an official campaign to denounce new religious movements, an education campaign in schools to foster rejection of new religious movements and the selective enforcement of the existing law against them, as most allegations seem to have been rejected by the authorities. The parliamentary reports may result, however, in fostering intolerance in general, which may have wider ramifications for French society.

Where complaints have substance, they have been dealt with by the ordinary law. The judge investigating the deaths of members of the Order of the Solar Temple in the Vercors in late 1995 reached the conclusion that they had been murdered by two members who then committed suicide. In March 1996, the police arrested, questioned and released forty disciples of the Order on suspicion that another such episode might take place, based on claims by a psychologist 'sect expert'.

Conscientious objection

Every young male citizen of France must perform ten months' national military service unless, because of their conscientious objection, they choose to perform twenty months' civil service instead, according to Article L 51–60 of the National Service Code. In 1993 the Brussels-based NGO Human Rights Without Frontiers estimated that between 700 and 1,000 Jehovah's Witness youths were prisoners of conscience because they had not applied for alternative civilian service on religious grounds and so had been sentenced to one year in prison. The dimensions of the problems associated with conscientious objection in France may be gauged by the number of Witnesses imprisoned between 1950 and 1992: 7,593 people.

This conflict was eventually resolved in 1995 through efforts of this NGO, interested lawyers, the Jehovah's Witnesses and the French Ministries of Justice and Defence. Clarification of the specific nature of the religious objections played an important role in formulating a resolution. The particular situation which differentiates the Witnesses' objections from those of other conscientious objectors is that they adopt a position of neutrality and do not challenge militarism. They are law abiding, objecting only to wearing military uniform and handling arms. Their particular conception of civic duty manifests itself in the fact that they have never refused to do civilian service so long as two conditions were met; they would do only tasks which had no connection whatsoever with military requirements and they refuse to choose civilian service voluntarily as a way of performing military service.

The French authorities decided that, from February 1995, when a young man is called up for military service, and responds by indicating in writing that he has religious objections, he is to be sent a formal 'decision' requiring him to carry out his national service obligations in the manner of conscientious objectors, that is, civilian service for twenty months. From that point on, the young objector is to be treated in exactly the same way as any other conscientious objector.

The last Witnesses were imprisoned for their beliefs in January 1995; the 200 still behind bars in June were released in September by presidential decree. Young Witnesses who have been performing civilian service have expressed themselves thankful to be serving their country in a useful manner, the privacy of their religious convictions assured because there is nothing to distinguish their civilian service from that of other conscientious objectors. A criminal record would also have been an impediment to employment in the teaching profession and the public service.

In 1996, President Jacques Chirac, as commander in chief of the armed forces announced that conscription, which had been in force since 1905, would be phased out over a period of six years.

GERMANY

Germany	
GDP (US$bn)	1,789
Population	80,400,000
Annual population growth (%)	0.3
Urban population (%)	86
Working population (%)	38[a]
Literacy (%)	99
Ratifications	1; 2, 2(a), 2(b); 3; 4; E

The Federal Republic of Germany (FRG) re-united in 1990 the former West Germany and East Germany. A multi-party democracy dominated by a conservative coalition, its capital is once more being established in Berlin. Despite the sudden fall in the standard of living in the east after unification and the amount of assistance flowing from the west, economic integration of the east with the advanced industrial economy of the west is proceeding. Though economic recovery is strong in the east, unemployment is high (13.5 per cent in 1994); in the west, society is urbanised and skilled, with high living standards and welfare benefits. With significant post-war movement of people within its borders from east to west, and from Eastern Europe, Germany is still a society in transition.

Ethnic composition and intolerance

United Germany's population is around 80.4 million. German citizens have invoked their constitutional right of return to Germany as being ethnically German (*Aussiedler*). Recognised minorities (*Minderheiten*) are restricted to such groups as the slavic Sorbs of eastern Germany and the Danes and Friesians in the west. The Roma (gypsies) were specifically excluded from *Minderheit* status even though they have been present for centuries. About 8 per cent of the population are foreigners who are not permitted to become German citizens and remain foreign in status; their children born in Germany may apply for citizenship, but it is not automatic on birth.

German society does not readily admit a composition of many cultures; instead, it continues to search for a traditional 'Germanness' which is at odds with the reality of the composition of modern Germany. The fact of immigration is still not recognised within government structure, there being no specific body responsible for it. There is not only unequal treatment but widespread, systematic discrimination against non-dominant groups, on both the legal and social levels. The distinction between citizens and foreigners is felt by immigrants to be a humiliating one. The fact that discrimination because of skin colour and foreign descent is experienced also by those who are German citizens shows that 'hostility against foreigners' contains strong elements of racism.

Of foreigners who have lived there for over a decade, 66 per cent are Turks and higher proportions come from Spain, Italy and the former Yugoslavia. Even Chancellor Kohl said in 1993 that 'those who have come' now 'belong as part of us'. They were originally brought to Germany to overcome a temporary labour shortage, and were intended to return to their home country. However, Turkish people living in Germany now number around 2 million, 40,000 of whom hold a German passport. There are over 40,000 Turkish companies and 13,000 Turkish university students; 150,000 Turks live in Berlin. Generational change has occurred as the children of 'guest-workers' have become adults in Germany. The feeling of primarily being Turkish has become mixed with the reality of decades of living in Germany. Intercultural societies have facilitated immigrant entry and participation in German life. In 1994 the first person of Turkish descent was elected (as a member of the Green Party) to the Bundestag (Parliament). Immigrant leaders have been calling for recognition of their communities as national minorities.

Arson attacks have been made on 'guest-workers' and immigrants' hostels and other violence also perpetrated against ethnic or religious minorities, asylum-seekers from many lands. Most of the reported cases of such atrocities are committed by individuals and right-wing groups of individuals.

Xenophobia and hatred of 'foreigners' and other minorities is also sometimes found within the institutions of state. Amnesty International in 1995–96 highlighted numerous reports of ill-treatment of asylum-seekers, refugees and members of ethnic minorities by German police and other officials.

Violence and arson attacks have been condemned by the Parliamentary Assembly of the Council of Europe. But, along with in their thousands German people who show solidarity against racism, the German authorities strongly condemn racist violence and seek to arrest and prosecute the perpetrators.

Church and state: background

Until the late Middle Ages, the Roman Catholic Church was the sole lawful religious body in Germany. During the Reformation and Counter-Reformation, religious wars laid the country to waste. In a political compromise, the principle of *cuius regio, eius religio* was adopted – the state religion accords with that of whoever rules – first accepted in 1555 in the Peace of Augsburg and confirmed in the Peace Treaty of Westphalia of 1648, which ended the Thirty Years War in Germany. The principle of *cuius regio* required the subject to conform to the religion of his sovereign. Freedom of religion thus consisted of the freedom to choose between the only two recognised denominations; Protestant and Catholic Germans were allowed to move to a state in which their religion was the official one. Religious minorities were at best tolerated, if unobtrusive. The formula remained in force until the formal secularisation of the German Reich in 1803; prohibition of all 'sects' remained in force until 1806.

Church and state were formally separated in 1918. Although freedom of conscience and religion had been acknowledged in the constitutions of the different German states during the nineteenth century, the two main denominations retained their privileged positions, remnants of which remain.

In 1871 the German leadership passed from the historical Catholic power, Austria, to Prussia, the chief of the Protestant states, which united all the German states (except Austria) into one Germany. Under Bismarck this led to a campaign of discrimination and persecution against Catholics, the so-called *Kulturkampf*, under which, among other things, the Jesuits were expelled.

Ideology in the twentieth century

After the First World War, the Weimar Republic was established, based on the most liberal of German constitutions. The Weimar constitution stated that 'There is no state church' (Article 137); its Article 136 read:

> No-one is required to reveal his religious beliefs. The authorities only have the right to inquire into membership of a religious association to the extent that rights or obligations flow from this or when the collection of statistical information, prescribed by statute, requires this.

The liberal and democratic constitutional order of the Weimar Republic was, however, soon to be undermined and finally destroyed by the emerging National Socialists under Adolf Hitler. Having been democratically elected, Hitler soon trampled on the Weimar freedoms and in 1933 established the National Socialist one-party state and dictatorship to bring into being a 'Third Reich', an empire with a distinct millenarian focus.

National Socialism was based on the fundamental denial of the equality of human beings and of the validity of inherent human rights; its core values were the belief in the supremacy of the Aryan race, and in the 'leadership principle' under which the nation, the state, and the Leader were combined: *ein Volk, ein Reich, ein Fuhrer*. Tolerance was weakness; intolerance was state policy, and persecution of Jews and other 'inferior' races a joy and a sacred duty. Discriminatory laws and regulations were instituted which severely circumscribed Jews' social, cultural and economic lives and legitimated public and state hostility. Then, from 1939–45, Hitler and his followers dragged the rest of

Western civilisation into their dark abyss. What had once been proudly proclaimed, under German European leadership, to be the 'Christian culture' of the West was left to smoulder in the ashes of Auschwitz and the other concentration camps.

Initially, Hitler sought an accommodation with the churches; however, an actual alliance was never forged. Pope Pius XI, after agreeing to a concordat with Hitler in 1933, in 1937 warned against the evils of Nazism in his encyclical, 'With a Burning Anxiety'. Even so, some German Christians at least initially supported Hitler and most failed to stand up to his inhuman and fundamentally anti-religious ideology. They, like most Germans, remained silent as millions of Jews, together with Jehovah's Witnesses, communists, socialists and political opponents, and other so-called 'sub-human' groups such as gypsies, homosexuals or people with disabilities were led away to the camps where medical experimentation and extermination were justified under a 'therapeutic' imperative. 'Inferior' races, such as the Slavs, were enslaved.

Even after Hitler realised that he could not obtain the active support of the major churches, and became more openly anti-religious, most Christian churches provided, at best, a body of passive resistance to the Nazis. Not only the Nazi hierarchy and bureaucracy but many ordinary Germans, for centuries steeped in the culture of anti-Semitism, assented to and participated in persecution and killings with few conscientious scruples relating to their own humanity. There are, however, the shining exceptions: Bonhoeffer, Niemoller (inspired by Barth), the Jesuit Father Delp, and others, including many local pastors and priests. Protestant opposition to totalitarianism and oppression led to the founding of the 'confessing church' (*die bekennende Kirche*), a movement which still plays a major role in the Lutheran churches. In 1996, the Pope's first visit to reunited Germany provided the occasion for discussions on the church's silence during the Holocaust.

Post-war ideologies

Following the defeat of Germany in the Second World War, the experience of the 1930s and 1940s impressed on Germans, first, a determination to disavow forever the ideology of National Socialism, and second, an equal determination not merely to avoid the errors of the past, but also to ensure that the conditions would never again arise under which Hitler had come to power.

In eastern Germany, the communist German Democratic Republic (GDR) saw itself as the embodiment of ideological opposition to fascism and National Socialism; many of its founders and early prominent politicians had fought the Nazis in the communist resistance. The GDR saw itself as a bulwark against fascism, which it believed remained dormant in the Western 'bourgeois' democracies. Soon, however, the East German state turned into its own Stalinist dictatorship; of all the Eastern European communist states, it became perhaps the harshest and most doctrinaire.

Although Jehovah's Witnesses and other small religious communities were banned, the communist regime was not able to suppress the main churches. In the end, the churches in the GDR were among the main protagonists in the events that led to the fall of the Berlin Wall. The old GDR, however, has little history of formal or practical tolerance.

In western Germany, too, the new legal order presented a clear ideological break with the past. Unlike the GDR, the Federal Republic of Germany accepted blame for the atrocities of the Nazis and sought to atone for them. However, although the leading Nazis were punished or side-tracked, others remained in office or were allowed to rise to prominence again, provided they abjured their former Nazi sympathies.

While the new constitutional order was based on respect for fundamental rights and a denunciation of totalitarianism, that order felt itself under direct threat from the communist east and its system of civil and political liberties was moulded in the Cold War. During the 1950s and 1960s, the strident anti-communism of the FRG did not foster an atmosphere of political tolerance. In the 1970s, similar strains were placed on the formal commitment to tolerance and adherence to the rule of law by the emergence of the left-wing urban terrorism of the Baader-Meinhoff Group and the 'Red Army Faction'. These developments created political and legal precedents for present-day issues of contention in the field of tolerance.

The federal constitution

The Federal Republic of Germany sees itself as a 'democratic and social federal state under the rule of law'. This concept of the state applies throughout re-united Germany. The three core concepts on which the FRG is built are these: the concept of the state as a state under the rule of law (*Rechtsstaat*); the concept of the state as a social welfare state (*Sozialstaat*); and the concept of the state as a federal democracy (*demokratischer Bundesstaat*). The twin concept of the 'social state under the rule of law' (*sozialer Rechtsstaat*) hinges on the principle of freedom of the individual being reconciled with the principles of social justice.

The 1949 constitution (Basic Law or *Grundgesetz*) was formed in a context dominated by two factors: first, as a reaction against the National Socialist dictatorship and also against the liberal democratic Weimar Republic, and second by its formation in the context of the Cold War. The Weimar democracy was seen as a 'suicidal democracy' and the new, post-war order was established to guard against the danger of such 'suicidal' tendencies recurring. The German constitutional order consequently perceives itself as not 'free of [moral or ideological] values' (*wertfrei*). Rather, the fundamental values of the new democratic order are to be actively protected against threats from outside and within, whether moral or ideological as well as military or physical.

In the 1970s, the authorities suppressed and outlawed communists and their supporters regardless of whether or not they committed violence or incited it. In recent years, controversy has arisen over certain religious minorities which the German authorities feel foster ideas or an ideology 'contrary to the spirit of the constitution'.

Protection of human rights

The constitution attaches fundamental importance to human rights. Article 79(3) states that these rights are 'eternal' and cannot be denied – even by the legislator – without violating the constitution. Moreover, *in extremis*, the constitution expressly grants to every German citizen the right to resist 'anyone' (including the organs of state) who might seek to overthrow the constitutional order of the FRG (Article 20(4) of the constitution).

Legal remedies are available against violations of human rights, including appeals to the German Constitutional Court. However, constitutional guarantees of non-discrimination (including grounds of religion and race, language, country of origin or descent, but not status as a foreigner) are limited in two ways: to interactions between the individual and the state itself – not any third party – and to direct discrimination only.

There is increasing concern over the activities of individuals and groups which openly preach racism, xenophobia and intolerance, and which at times openly espouse Nazi ideologies. Neo-Nazi propaganda is forbidden under the federal Penal Code; it is also a crime to deny the Holocaust. The authorities strongly condemn racist material and incidents. Race hatred sources are not confined to Germany, as anti-Semitic material has also been imported and disseminated.

Freedom of religion or belief

Article 4(1) of the 1949 constitution guarantees freedom of religion, of belief and conscience, and the freedom to express one's religious or philosphical convictions. Article 4(2) guarantees 'the undisturbed practice of religion'; the Constitutional Court has ruled that this extends to the practice of non-religious, 'philosophical' beliefs. The right to freedom of religion, belief and conscience has been held, in conjunction with other articles in the constitution, to entail the principle of 'philosophical–religious neutrality' of the state.

The state and religions or beliefs

Under Article 140 of the 1949 constitution, a detailed statutory arrangement for the churches was taken over from the Weimar constitution. These provisions declare that the civil and political rights of the citizen may not be determined or limited on the basis of religion; that the enjoyment of those rights, and access to the civil service, may not depend on the confession of religion; and that no-one can be obliged to declare their religious beliefs or to participate in religious manifestations or to take an oath based on religious formulae.

The provisions stipulate that 'there is no state church', and that each religious community is free to organise and arrange its own affairs independently, within the law. Religious communities are entitled to legal personality according to civil law, except that some religious communities are given, or may be granted, recognition as public legal entities. This status is granted to those religions which already had that status at the time of adoption of the Weimar constitution. Other religious communities must, if they request this, be accorded this status, but only 'if they can guarantee permanency by their constitution and by the number of their adherents'. The latter phrase requires a measure of internal organisation, adequate financing, and a certain period of existence; in practice, existence for thirty or forty years is required before a religious community can be considered to have shown sufficient 'durability'. Within this framework, these matters are determined on a state by state basis. The main advantage of public law status is that the religious entities concerned may raise taxes according to the law of the state in which they are established.

The primary beneficiaries of automatic public law status throughout the FRG are the Protestant and Roman Catholic churches, the former state churches. Other religious communities have also been held to have the right to this status automatically, at least in some states: for instance, the Jewish community in Berlin and the New Apostolic Church in Hamburg. Others elsewhere have been granted this status on request and supply of information about 'durability': for instance, the Salvation Army, the New Apostolic Church, the Seventh-Day Adventists, Christian Science and the Mormons in Berlin. A request by the Jehovah's Witnesses to be recognised as a religion with public law status in Berlin was opposed by the authorities but is being reviewed in the courts which have, so far, held that they should be granted it. The Muslim community has not yet been successful in its attempts to gain it.

The provisions apply equally to 'philosophical' communities (*Weltanschauungs-gemeinschaften*). Within this overall framework, the states may also adopt more detailed laws regulating religious (and philosophical) communities.

Religious education

Under Article 7(3) of the constitution, religious education in state schools is a constitutional duty for most states; this must be provided 'in accordance with the principles of the religious communities'. Article 7(4) and (5) grant the right to establish private schools when certain conditions are met. Islam is to be taught in schools in some federal states.

The use of Christian symbols in state education has been challenged. In the formerly Catholic state of Bavaria, a law requires that the crucifix be displayed in every state school classroom. In Nittenau, Ernst Seler – a man whose beliefs reportedly favoured Rudolph Steiner – objected to the presence in his daughter's classroom of a crucifix with an image of the bleeding body of Christ. Although the local priest agreed to replace it with a plain wooden cross, Seler pursued his campaign against the Bavarian law and its administration in the face of considerable opposition, including harassment and, after claiming to the local council that he would defend his children with his 'spiritual sword', forcible admission to hospital for psychiatric treatment.

Appealing against decisions in lower courts, Seler eventually reached the Constitutional Court which in August 1995 ruled that Bavaria's law was unconstitutional. Public campaigns to keep the crosses, fuelled by memories of their removal during the Nazi era, resulted in a new draft law confirming the obligation to display the cross but setting up an appeal system. This has also been seen as likely to be unconstitutional. Meanwhile, no crosses are displayed in the classrooms of Seler's three children.

Protestant and Roman Catholic churches

The Federal Republic of Germany has approximately 80.4 million inhabitants. The largest religious communities remain the Evangelical Church (Protestant) with 45 per cent of the population and the Roman Catholic Church with 37 per cent. Protestants predominate in the east; more Catholics live in the Rhineland and the south than elsewhere. Adherents are registered as belonging to one or other of these two main churches, that is, as a baptised or confirmed member. In practice, only a minority regularly attend religious services. The average number of churchgoers among the members of the Evangelical Church was 1.2 million per Sunday; among the Roman Catholics, on average 5.5 million attended mass each Sunday.

In the states belonging to the former GDR, most of the population is not registered at all as members of either church. The former East German government had systematically harassed the churches and in 1969 forbade eastern Protestant churches from participating in the German Evangelical Church which united east and west. However, when baptisms increased, freedom of religion became guaranteed in 1976.

Despite some decline in adherents of the two main churches, they remain pre-eminent in German society, involved in education, social work and Third World development aid. After the state, they employ more people than any other organisation: nearly 1.2 million employees. In some areas of social welfare, the role of the main churches and their charitable institutions rivals that of the state itself.

The finance for this extensive work is raised through the church tax. The tax is collected by the state, on behalf of the two main churches and other religions recognised as institutions of public law. The tax is mostly raised as an additional surcharge of 9 per cent or 8 per cent on income tax. The money is collected by the state and transferred to the churches or religious communities, as appropriate. Liable for this tax are all baptised members of the church concerned who are resident in the relevant area. If a German citizen who has been baptised into the Protestant or Roman Catholic Church (and who has therefore been registered as a member) does not wish to pay this tax, he or she must make a declaration to that effect to a state authority. Some choose not to pay tax. In particular, people who live in the east of Germany have been used to giving directly to their local church and do not trust more remote administration. The number of people 'opting out' of the church tax system in this way has increased. The special status conferred by the church tax system is likely to come under increasing strain as the number of registered (church tax paying) members declines and as other groups seek to attain equal status and benefits.

Christian minority groups

Apart from the Christian denominations granted public law status, there are a wide range of other, smaller Christian groups. These include the Methodists, the Baptists, the Old Catholic Church, the Jehovah's Witnesses, the Orthodox Church and the Religious Society of Friends (the Quakers). Most of these, while not enjoying the special privileges of the two main Christian churches, are left free and unhindered. They complain, however, that they do not enjoy equal status with the main churches because they do not benefit from the church tax system and must find their own financial support.

Jews

The Jewish community is recognised as an institution with public law status and has taxes collected on its behalf. The community has about 50,000 members. About half are immigrants from the former Soviet Union and more have applied to come to Germany; the Central Council of Jews estimates that only half have a Jewish mother. New members of the Jewish community of Eastern European descent are often regarded as 'foreigners' and immigrants.

In recent years, there have been attacks on Jews and on synagogues and other Jewish targets by anti-Semitic groups and individuals. The President of Israel, Ezer Weizman, during a visit to Germany in 1996, told parliamentarians that he found it difficult to understand how Jews could live in Germany. He urged the parliamentarians to look to the future with the knowledge of the past and smash every stirring of racism and neo-Nazism. However, Ignatz Bubis, leader of the German Jews, disagreed to some extent; he considered that since 1945, a new and very different German society has emerged.

Muslims

Apart from the Jews, the main non-Christian religious community consists of the Muslims, mostly Turks or Kurds. Their first generation came to Germany in the 1960s and 1970s as migrant workers, but there is also an increasing, second-generation German-born population of ethnic Turks and Kurds. It has been estimated that there are around 1.7 million Muslims in Germany. Muslims are the subject of intolerance and discrimination. Although Turkish workers considerably outnumber Turks of pensionable age, older immigrants do not receive benefits because of their foreign status and social services have been criticised for not meeting the special needs of Muslims.

While not all of the Turks and Kurds are Muslims, or practising Muslims, Islamic organisations play an important part in their social and cultural life. Some Turks – a minority among the predominantly secular Turkish Muslims – espouse nationalist and Islamist ideologies stemming from religious revival movements.

Other religious minorities and new religious movements

The authorities have targeted some minority religious groups, pejoratively referred to as 'sects'. Recent years have seen an astonishing and, for post-war Western Europe, unique policy of official, and officially endorsed, vilification of and discrimination against certain of these groups including the Jehovah's Witnesses and, most particularly, the Church of Scientology.

The reason for the official policy of discrimination against certain 'sects' lies in the view taken by the authorities, that these groups are a danger to the inherent dignity of the individual who may be 'reduced' by them; in the authorities' view, these groups, in their ideological foundations, are also in a more general (indeed, political) sense 'contrary to the values of the constitution'. The government's latest, detailed statement criticises them for having 'teachings and ideologies which stand in flagrant contradiction to the consensual democratic values'.

The federal government has named in parliament twenty-five (mostly very small) organisations and groups, while adding that some – including the Jehovah's Witnesses – cannot be mentioned by name since they have started legal proceedings against their inclusion in the list. The Church of Scientology (referred to as 'Scientology-organisation' or SC in government publications and thus not recognised as religious) is singled out.

The Jehovah's Witnesses

The Jehovah's Witnesses have been established in Germany since 1897. Recognised as a religious community in the Weimar Republic in 1927, they were declared illegal in the 1930s. Jehovah's Witnesses were persecuted by the Nazis and incarcerated in concentration camps, where many perished. In the GDR, they were first registered, but in 1950 the Minister of the Interior of the GDR ordered that they be struck off the list of registered religions. The Witnesses were told that all activities of the community were prohibited and punishable by law. This situation lasted until January 1990 when, in the last days of the GDR, the Jehovah's Witnesses were again added to the list of recognised legal religious communities.

Although the Jehovah's Witnesses were not declared illegal in the Federal Republic, they were – and still are – not regarded as entitled to consideration as a religion, as is clear from the views expressed about them by the FRG authorities. When recently the Jehovah's Witnesses sought public law status in Berlin, the state argued that the application should be rejected on the basis that the Jehovah's Witnesses constituted a 'totalitarian coercion-system'. The religious community was said to have 'discredited the principle of democracy, which is one of the founding, structural principles of the Federal Republic of Germany', for instance by prohibiting its members from participating in, or standing for, elections to public office or from respecting official holidays or national symbols. It was said to have led to splits in families, especially concerning education. This, and its strict refusal to allow blood transfusions for children and babies, was said to have violated constitutional guarantees of the right to life and physical integrity, and the right to family life. They were said to have rejected all contacts with other religious communities and all inter-faith cooperation. Finally, the Witnesses' 'minutely detailed' rules on payment for work for the WatchTower Society were said to have 'contradicted all the basic principles of labour and social legislation'.

These arguments notwithstanding, the courts held in both first instance and on appeal that the Jehovah's Witnesses were entitled to be granted public law status now, since they had shown that they were adequately organised and financed, had sufficient members, and had shown 'durability'.

The Appeal Court accepted that religious communities, in order to qualify for public law status, also had to show 'loyalty to the law', and that associations which are unlawful because they are against the legal order of the state could also not be granted public law status. However, constitutional requirements went no further. The Jehovah's Witnesses had, over several decades, not acted either deliberately criminally or contrary to the constitution. The allegations against them – which they denied – had no direct effect on matters of state and the principle of state neutrality in religious matters prevented the state – and the court – from assessing the internal merits of the community's beliefs or indeed their compatibility with the principles of democracy. The constitution did not demand a 'total democratisation' of all activities within the state but, rather, respect for autonomous elements of social activity. The Jehovah's Witnesses were therefore, the Appeal Court decided, to be granted public law status. The state of Berlin has lodged a further appeal.

In the meantime, the official attitude of the executive authorities remains extremely hostile. They continue to describe the Jehovah's Witnesses as a totalitarian, anti-democratic and dangerous 'sect' and to condone discrimination against Jehovah's Witnesses in many fields of life.

The Church of Scientology

Scientology is regarded as far the most dangerous 'sect' by the German authorities and has been subjected to far-reaching measures by the state. All ministries of federal and state governments are asked to take whatever steps are possible within the law to counter the activities of Scientology, in the fields of taxation, social and labour law, medical law, competition law, criminal law, and even under local by-laws regulating the handing out of leaflets on the street.

The Church of Scientology has made repeated documented submissions to the United Nations and other international bodies on the matter of religious discrimination and intolerance by the German authorities and the private sector, by individuals and communities. The Special Rapporteur on Religious Intolerance, Mr Abdelfattah Amor, has taken up the matters referred to him with the German authorities.

The reports include cases of Scientologists having been dismissed from jobs or appointments in the public sector, in particular in teaching. Others were disciplined. A trainer for the German national fencing team was dismissed for stating in an interview that he enjoyed the books of L. Ron Hubbard. The Federal Minister for Labour has issued a decree barring all Scientologists from operating an employment agency; all permits to operate such an agency, granted to Scientologists, were revoked. The permits of a Scientologist who ran an au pair agency were withdrawn when she refused to sign a form declaring that she was not a Scientologist.

In some towns or states, Scientologists are barred from renting public halls or other spaces. In 1993, a concert in which the American jazz musician, Chick Corea, was to perform was cancelled by the Baden-Würthemberg state Government when it learned that he was a Scientologist. More recently, it was reported that his invitation to perform at a concert in Bavaria was withdrawn; the promoter was informed that he would not receive state subsidies for any event involving this artist's performance.

Scientologists were banned and, indeed, expelled from the main political parties until this policy was held to be unlawful by the courts. Since then, however, some parties have resolved to exclude Scientologists in defiance of court rulings. The authorities also actively sponsor 'enlightenment' campaigns in which the public is warned against Scientology (and other 'sects'). In some states, such 'enlightenment' has been made compulsory in schools. The information handed out in these campaigns is couched in vituperative language and, according to the Church of Scientology, contains numerous factual errors, as well as pejorative value judgements. Politicians have called for social ostracism of Scientologists.

The authorities condone and actively support discrimination against Scientologists in the private sector, with the aim of excluding Scientologists from economic life and reducing the social and financial support for members and their families which comes from earning income or engaging in business. The Federal Minister of Labour has called for a ban on all Scientologists from all occupations which 'intersect with society', such as schools, the government and business companies. Several state and city governments send out forms to all private contractual partners of such public bodies, requiring them to declare in writing that they have nothing to do with Scientology or the teachings of L. Ron Hubbard. The authorities warn that Scientology tries to 'infiltrate' business and commercial interests.

The private sector has responded to states' initiatives by trying to exclude Scientologists from all business activities, initiating a further round of discrimination and intolerance. Board members, company directors and employees have been dismissed from their jobs after being 'exposed' as Scientologists. Banks refuse to allow Scientologists to open bank accounts; several will not do business with Scientologists. Trade associations and Chambers of Commerce issue leaflets, based on official information, warning businesses against Scientology. Conferences are organised which explain how businesses can 'spot' Scientologists (and Jehovah's Witnesses) and what action they can take to exclude them, such as the issuing of forms similar to the government-issued ones. Lists of companies allegedly owned or run by Scientologists are distributed in business circles.

Self-declarations and dissociations are part of the intolerance. Some companies have taken out advertisements stating that they are not Scientologists and would never have anything to do with Scientologists. A well-known television talk-show host, Thomas Gottschalk, after being 'accused' of being a Scientologist, announced that he had nothing to do with Scientology and would sever his relationship with a Scientologist friend.

The official policy provides a context of intolerance in which particular instances of toleration are to be viewed as exceptions to the general rule. For instance, the Hamburg state prosecutor, while concluding (after extensive investigations) that the Church of Scientology was not unlawful, approvingly quoted the Munich state prosecutor's view that, none the less, 'the ideas, aims and practices of the Scientology-organisation are in many ways incompatible with the values of the Basic Law'.

Scientology is denied its identification as a religion or belief system, official policy maintaining instead that religion is simply a cover for a purely commercial organisation which is not entitled to the constitutional protection of religious freedom and is a threat to democratic values. The duty of the state is to protect the general public against perceived dangers by ensuring that 'sects' do not 'infiltrate' the organs and institutions of the state or the private economy. Some therefore call for the Church of Scientology in particular to be placed under surveillance by the secret service. The government keeps the question of whether the Church of Scientology should be declared a prohibited association under active review.

The Federal Labour Court has ruled that Scientology is not a religion and not entitled to the protection of the constitutional freedom of religion; however, this matter has yet to be finally determined. Indeed, the authorities have called for the law to be reviewed and amended if current law cannot stop the activities of Scientology. Some individual cases are now pending, or about to be lodged, with the Constitutional Court.

Women and religion

The influence of the Catholic and Protestant Churches has been linked with political and legal conservatism and authoritarianism which has had an impact on women's status in German society. Many women left the churches in the early 1960s. After a long struggle for the right to safe abortion, a key amendment put before the federal court in 1975 failed; changes to divorce and family law and restricted access to abortion date from 1976. Renewed and bitter debate over abortion occurred when Germany was re-unified because of the liberal provisions of the former East Germany.

As regards the place of women within religion, the Evangelical Church has long admitted women to the highest levels of its clergy. Debate on the Catholic Church's refusal to admit women to the ranks of the clergy has been strong among German Catholics but Pope John Paul II has opposed female ordination. However, Germany's 30,000 Old Catholics reject papal authority, as the Old Catholic Church was founded in 1873 to protest against the First Vatican Council's declaration of papal infallibility in 1870. In 1996, two married women were ordained as priests in a service attended by representatives of the Evangelical Church and the Anglican Archbishop of Canterbury.

Conscientious objection

Adult males are eligible for military service. Article 4(3) of the constitution guarantees the right to conscientious objection to military service.

GREAT BRITAIN AND NORTHERN IRELAND

Great Britain	
GDP (US$bn)	903
Population	57,800,000
Annual population growth (%)	0.3
Urban population (%)	89
Working population (%)	49[a]
Literacy (%)	99
Ratifications	1; 2, 2(a); 3; 4; E

England, Scotland and Wales are the three 'national' communities of the oldest major parliamentary democracy, Great Britain. (Northern Ireland is discussed separately, see p. 323.) The freedom of thought, conscience and religion which contemporary Britain enjoys is the result of a long series of pragmatic adjustments by which an older tradition of institutionalised religious privilege and discrimination was replaced by increasing respect for religious freedom and liberty and its practical implications.

The transition from a 'confessional state' to a 'religiously plural' society was a piecemeal development, more the product of a gradual dismantling of a mass of specific discriminatory laws against Catholics, Jews and Protestant nonconformists – and other laws which had the same impact – than the result of a deliberate assertion of religious equality or freedom of conscience and belief. Non-dominant groups were allowed to find a place within a framework established by the terms, structures and character of mainstream Christianity. This situation has been described as one of 'tolerant discrimination', a step away from assimilationism but still not quite that pluralism which is conducted through dialogue and mutual change on the basis of respect and acceptance.

The legal system and human rights

Britain not only does not possess a written constitution, bill of rights or other written provisions for fundamental rights and freedoms, but also lacks any systematic statement or body of legal or constitutional protection for religious liberty or against religious discrimination. Precedents established in British courts which have maintained freedom of religion, belief and opinion, expression and association under the common law are considered by a substantial body of opinion (which includes Law Lords, senior judicial members, politicians and human rights NGOs) as no adequate substitute for positive guarantees in law to protect human rights. Incorporation of the European Convention on Human Rights is favoured by many as the means to provide such guarantees.

Although there have been a number of occasions when the religious practices of a particular group have been upheld by the courts on the basis of legislation designed to prevent racial discrimination, this application can by no means be relied upon as an avenue for seeking redress. Discrimination against Muslims, in particular, was described as quite blatant by the UK Action Committee on Islamic Affairs in 1993 as it campaigned for laws which specifically addressed religious discrimination, vilification and ridicule of religious beliefs, practices and sanctities, and incitement to religious hatred.

Religious composition

Christianity, through its many denominations, is still the dominant religion in Great Britain. According to the *UK Christian Handbook*, in 1990 'active church members' constituted some 11 per cent of the population in England, 17 per cent in Wales and 30 per cent in Scotland. However, 65–66 per cent of the British population still identify with Christianity or a Christian church to some extent.

Other religious communities may number perhaps 1 million Muslims, 330,000 Jews, 300,000 Hindus and 400,000 Sikhs, as well as smaller numbers of Buddhists, Jains, Zoroastrians, Baha'is, Rastafarians, Mormons, Jehovah's Witnesses and Christian Scientists. There is also an extremely diverse spectrum of new religious movements, New Age or 'alternative' spiritualities whose influence is highly diffuse and whose membership numbers are difficult to estimate.

Ethnic composition and religion

There is no direct correlation between ethnic background and religion in the United Kingdom; the relationships are complex and dynamic. The 1991 census revealed that the population of almost 55 million included 1.6 per cent who identified as black, 2.6 per cent as Indian, Pakistani or Bangladeshi and fewer than 1 per cent as Chinese or Asian. For many Muslims, Hindus and Sikhs, membership of strongly differentiated religious groups and their associated cultures constitutes a distinction possibly more important than ethnic differences. But not all who described themselves as 'Indian', 'Pakistani', 'Bangladeshi' or 'Asian' were necessarily Hindu, Sikh or Muslim by religion; there is an

Asian Christian presence in contemporary Britain as well as Asian adherents of a number of other religious traditions.

While the Afro-Caribbean believers are mostly Christian – a majority belong to recently founded 'black-led' Christian churches and a minority to traditional denominations – there are other Afro-Caribbeans whose religious allegiance is to Rastafarianism. But for many more, probably a majority of the Afro-Caribbean population in Great Britain, religion is a matter of indifference, which is the characteristic religious posture of the majority of the white population of contemporary Britain.

Further, a number of Muslim groups protested strongly against the discussion of Islamic perceptions and requirements in the area of education in terms of 'ethnic' educational issues and needs. The issues, they protested, were fundamentally religious in nature and decisively transcended the wide variety of 'ethnic' backgrounds among Muslim children in Great Britain.

While the principal religious tradition remains Christianity, Great Britain is thus also inescapably a religiously plural society. Contemporary discussion of issues relating to the distinctive religious customs and values of minority groups in British society and the extent to which such customs should be respected, tolerated, accommodated, defended or protected has inevitably become intimately bound up with similar discussions and debates over race, racism, 'multi-culturalism' and the rights of racial as well as religious minorities.

Neglect of women's rights and freedoms often results when anti-racist concerns are expressed through an uncritical multi-culturalism and culture and religion are simplistically equated. There are tensions in a religiously plural society between respect for the distinctive customs and beliefs of religious and ethnic minority groups and the freedom of women within those minorities to dissent from their communities' traditionally conceived religious and cultural demands.

Religion, belief and state

Historically, Great Britain is not only a country whose society and culture were crucially shaped by Christian traditions and values but one in which particular Christian churches were once accorded a highly privileged status within national life.

The (Anglican) Church of England and the (Presbyterian) Church of Scotland remain nominally 'established' and retain a particular prominence and salience in the religious life of England and Scotland. In England, the Archbishop of Canterbury is, in formal terms, the highest ranking non-royal person. The sovereign, who is Head of the established Church, must be a member of the Church of England and, under the 1701 Act of Settlement, cannot marry a Catholic. The monarch appoints the bishops of the Church of England on the advice of the Prime Minister, who in turn, by convention, chooses from two names nominated by the Church itself. The Church takes the leading role in national and civic religious occasions.

The Church of England is also represented in the House of Lords – the second and non-elected chamber of the British Parliament – through the presence of the two Archbishops, the Bishops of London, Durham and Winchester, and the twenty-one most senior of the remaining diocesan bishops. However, senior members, both lay and clerical, of various other denominations and religious traditions are now routinely nominated as peers.

Although clergy of the Churches of England and Scotland and the Roman Catholic

Church are disqualified from election to the House of Commons – the lower chamber of the British parliament – there is no bar to the election of the clergy of other denominations. Broad correlations between particular religious and political allegiances have today virtually disappeared.

The (Anglican) Church in Wales was disestablished in 1920. However, the (Presbyterian) Church of Scotland has played an important role in sustaining Scottish identity since the union between Scotland and England in 1707. The sovereign is represented at the Church of Scotland's General Assembly but plays no role in appointing senior clergy.

In practical terms the continuing establishments are now so residual and symbolic that they give rise to very little active opposition. Indeed, paradoxically, while some members of the Church of England wish to 'free it' from the remaining obligations and constraints of its traditional role, recent defenders of its established status have included prominent members of the Roman Catholic, Jewish and Muslim communities. Other Christian denominations and other faiths are now regularly included in national and civic religious events. The religious 'establishment' of contemporary Britain has actually come to be more an 'ecumenical establishment', including all the major Christian denominations and increasingly extending to include the Jewish community. In November 1995 the Queen attended the centenary celebrations of Westminster Cathedral, the centre of Roman Catholic religion in England. She was the first reigning monarch to do so since the 'Protestant' Revolution of 1688.

All religious groups are free to associate, worship, publish, promote their views and proselytise on behalf of their beliefs and world views. Similarly, non-religious groups (such as the British Humanist Association and the National Secular Society) are free to promote non- or anti-religious views and opinions. There is also a tradition of official concern for the promotion of inter-religious dialogue and cooperation and for the fostering of good relationships between religious groups. Within the predominant Christian tradition, ecumenicism and inter-denominational collaboration have become the norm, as has the wish to establish positive relationships with 'people of other faiths'. Groups such as the Council of Christians and Jews, the Inter-Faith Network and the Callamus Foundation, an ecumenical Islamic group, seek to advance the cause of religious pluralism and tolerance, working in both national and local contexts. Occasional inter-religious services are held both at local and national level although there are also pressure groups opposed to such inter-religious initiatives.

Successful discussions between religious minorities and the British authorities have secured adjustments, exemptions or compromises over regulations in a variety of matters, such as the following:

- the exemption of turban-wearing Sikhs from legislation requiring the use of protective headgear;
- accommodations in matters relating to burial customs;
- the extension of the right – legally as well as religiously – to solemnise marriages, to Hindu, Sikh and Muslim institutions;
- the continued right of Jews and Muslims to practise animal slaughter according to the requirements of Jewish and Islamic religious law, despite pressure from animal rights groups and organisations such as the Royal Society for the Prevention of Cruelty to Animals (RSPCA) and the Farm Animal Welfare Council, to make such slaughter illegal.

However, in spite of pragmatic toleration, there still exist some areas marked by inequity or discrimination and intolerance.

Education Reform Act 1988

The 1988 Education Reform Act sought to make the requirements concerning religious education in state schools more specific than those in the 1944 Education Act. From the 1960s onwards, the development of non-confessional religious education syllabuses had emphasised the study of world religions and avoided advocating any particular religion; there had also been a shift away from explicitly Christian acts of worship. In contrast, the 1988 Act required that syllabuses for religious education in state schools should 'reflect the fact that the religious traditions in Great Britain are in the main Christian whilst taking account of the teaching and practices of the other principal religions represented in Great Britain'. Similarly, the 1988 Act reaffirmed the requirement for a daily act of worship and further specified that the worship should be 'wholly or mainly of a broadly Christian character'. The 'conscience clause' was also retained, whereby children might be exempted upon parental request. Provision was also made for particular schools to be exempted from the requirements that collective worship should be mainly of a Christian character. Local Standing Advisory Councils on Religious Education were to include representatives of 'such Christian and other religious denominations as . . . will appropriately reflect the principal religious traditions of the area'.

The Act thus explicitly privileges the Christian religion. In 1995, the Association of Teachers and Lecturers recommended that the legal requirement to hold Christian collective worship in state schools should be removed. One teacher reportedly said, 'There should be regular assemblies to bind schools together to help in the development and growth of spiritual issues, but not an imposition of worship.'

State funding for religious schools

Apart from the state system of education, parents may send their children to private schools. The balance between a now religiously plural society and the continuance of Christian privilege is reflected in the range of schools enjoying 'voluntary aided' status, that is, receiving state funds though retaining a denominational background and character, including the right to present denominationally specific religious education. Most such schools are run by Christian denominations and a small number by Jewish organisations.

Religious communities may also establish schools with an overtly religious syllabus and orientation, but wholly without state funding. A number of Islamic schools have applied for 'voluntary-aided' status but have been refused, an anomaly criticised by the Commission for Racial Equality as well as by Muslim groups and others concerned to see equality of treatment for various religious traditions. Certain Muslim, Christian and Jewish schools which have been refused funding in the past have now formed an alliance to press for funding. One reason that applications have been unsuccessful was that there are surplus places at nearby schools. However, as the alliance's coordinator said, 'If you are going to have choice, you have to have spare places.'

Blasphemy

Blasphemy and blasphemous libel remain criminal offences in Great Britain. From 1922 to 1977 no case was brought before the courts and it was widely assumed that the law against blasphemy had become an anachronism.

However, in 1977, the magazine *Gay News* was prosecuted for blasphemy by Mary Whitehouse, a conservative Christian campaigner, against what she perceived as 'moral decline' in British society, especially in relation to the publication of sexually explicit material and the broadcasting of irreverent, violent or sexually explicit material on television. *Gay News* was prosecuted for the publication of a poem entitled 'The love that dares to speak its name' in which the centurion at the crucifixion was portrayed as having homosexual fantasies in relation to the dead Jesus. Whitehouse was successful in her prosecution, a decision subsequently upheld in both the Court of Appeal and the House of Lords, whose majority judgment took the view that the crime of blasphemous libel did not require the deliberate intention to upset or offend others, but only that the material published should have had that effect.

Blasphemous libel was defined as follows:

> any writing concerning God or Christ, the Christian religion, the Bible or some sacred subject using words which are scurrilous, abusive or offensive and tend to vilify the Christian religion and therefore have a tendency to lead to a breach of the peace.

Lord Scarman argued that the law still served a useful purpose and should be extended to protect the religious beliefs and feelings of religious believers other than Christians. In an increasingly plural society, he argued, it was necessary 'not only to respect the differing religious beliefs, feelings and practices of all but also to protect them from scurrility, vilification, ridicule and contempt'.

Subsequently, in 1985, a Law Commission Report on Offences Against Religion and Public Worship presented a divided report. The majority argued solely for the abolition of the offence of blasphemy and blasphemous libel. A minority wanted it to be replaced by a new offence of publishing 'grossly abusive or insulting material relating to a religion with the purpose of outraging religious feelings'. No change was made.

However, in 1989 the controversy which erupted over the publication of Salman Rushdie's novel *The Satanic Verses* refocused the issue with renewed urgency. The controversy over *The Satanic Verses* centred precisely upon the discriminatory nature of the existing legislation in a religiously plural society. Muslims could not bring a prosecution under the blasphemy laws in respect of their outrage over *The Satanic Verses* in the way that Christians had been able to in the *Gay News* case. This privileging of Christianity by not allowing the space for dialogue and consideration of other religious sensitivities may well have contributed to the fervent but ill-judged demonstrations of anger by small groups of British Muslims. After Ayatollah Khomeini's *fatwa* in February 1989, the author was in hiding because of a religiously motivated call for his death on account of what he had written. Therefore, calls to reform the law in a way that would facilitate his prosecution for causing religious offence aroused fierce reactions, and provoked responses in the name of free expression which also vilified Islam and the Qur'an.

The controversy thus raised acute questions concerned with the overlap of freedom of expression and opinion with the freedom of thought, conscience and religion or belief, which were involved in the rights of dissenters from and protesters against religion as well as those of believers in religion. The complexities and the many levels of debate showed that the issues were by no means trivial or marginal.

New religious movements

The status of new religious movements again illustrates the ambiguity and tension inherent within British attitudes to minority religious groups. New religious movements in Britain have, since the late 1970s and early 1980s, been subjected to substantial and sustained criticism and to repeated attempts to have their activities officially investigated, condemned or curtailed, and their religious and charitable status removed. However, these have in the long term failed, such as a ban on the entry to Britain of foreign members of the Church of Scientology which was lifted, after twelve years, in 1980.

Criticism of new religious movements has frequently been both severe and pejorative to the point of being derogatory, often describing them as 'cults', 'spiritual counterfeits' or not 'genuinely religious', among other allegations. Such criticism has flourished in the press and broadcast media, has been restated in parliament under cover of parliamentary privilege and has been actively fostered by 'anti-cult' organisations such as Family Action Information and Rescue and the Deo Gloria Trust.

In October 1995, the home secretary, Michael Howard, refused entry to the Rev. Sun Myung Moon who had planned to visit Britain to hold a service for 1,200 people, including the 700 UK members of the Unification Church. He had several times before been refused entry, but had subsequently been cleared. The home secretary had reportedly acted on the basis of information received about the church. Mr Justice Sedley in the High Court stated that the home secretary had the power to exclude people if that was in the public good, but that power he had to exercise fairly; the Rev. Moon had not been asked to put his views forward and therefore the matter should be reconsidered. The home secretary, however, refused; the Rev. Moon would have to apply again.

In November 1995, a High Court judge confirmed that a member of The Family could retain custody of her son – so long as she put his welfare before her devotion to The Family – against an application for custody by his grandmother. Lord Justice Ward was quoted as saying:

> They have come in from the cold. They carry some mud on their coat, but if they choose they can wash it off. They can sit at society's supper table, eccentric guests perhaps, but welcome . . . We must all be ready to welcome the return of the prodigal son.

The Home Office has indicated an awareness of the need for a non-polemical approach to new religious movements and the issues which they pose. It contributed to the foundation of INFORM (Information Network Focus on Religious Movements), an organisation which was set up to conduct research into new religious movements and to provide objective and balanced information concerning them. INFORM has already published a practical guide.

The media

Although only receiving a minority share of the time available for religious broadcasting on British radio and television, Jewish, Muslim, Sikh and Hindu concerns have gradually received increasing attention, in contrast to the overtly Christian emphasis of the earlier religious focus of BBC broadcasting. Since 1977, however, the religious broadcasting of both the BBC and the major independent television channels has been required to 'reflect the worship, thought and action of the principal religious traditions represented in Britain, recognising that those traditions are mainly, though not exclusively, Christian'. The first Christian radio station was launched in 1995.

Religious minorities have experienced continuing hostility, caricaturing and negative stereotyping in large sections of the press and media. Muslims consistently protested in the wake of the 'Rushdie affair' that the British media caricatured and negatively stereotyped Muslim opinion in sensational and exaggeratedly controversial terms.

Pressure groups

Religious–political pressure groups have emerged as lobbyists on religious or moral issues. From the early 1970s, Christian groups – combining both evangelical Protestants and conservative Roman Catholics – developed a network committed to a conservative agenda, generally attempting to reverse perceived 'permissiveness' and to promote 'traditional', 'Christian' and 'family values'. Some pursued overtly Christian aims in public education and in areas of medical ethics.

Re-assertion of conservative and traditional religious teachings in relation to women caused the emergence of other lobby groups such as Women Against Fundamentalism, founded in 1989. This coalition includes women from a wide variety of both ethnic and religious backgrounds and seeks to identify and protest against the ways in which women in various traditions and communities suffer discrimination as a result of the policies and demands of religiously conservative (and usually male) leaders.

Internal religious affairs

Women are generally in a minority in positions of authority in religious hierarchies. In many Christian churches, numerous women have also felt unfulfilled in their traditionally supporting roles. In the last twenty years – with campaigns starting much earlier – there has been often bitter controversy over the ordination of women in the Church of England, an issue eventually resolved in favour of ordaining women; 1,200 women were ordained in 1994. About a quarter of the Church of England's 12,000 clergy are thought to remain opposed to women priests, and the priesthood in Wales is entirely male; policy and procedures have been devised to accommodate such differences in the church. Some married clergymen who have felt unable to remain in the Anglican confession because of the ordination of women have been ordained as non-celibates in the Catholic Church.

The institutional dominance of Anglicanism and Catholicism has tended to overshadow the existence of other churches and religions where women have been admitted to positions of authority, such as Reform, Liberal and Progressive Judaism, the Sikh religion, the Western Buddhist Order, the Free Churches, some other Christian churches and some new religious movements. The Religious Society of Friends (Quakers) was founded on principles of sexual equality; the Brahma Kumaris, a Hindu-based group, have a female-dominated leadership; and Wiccans – the contemporary witchcraft movement – focus on the Great Goddess who appears in many forms in historically ancient Middle Eastern and European traditions as well as living religious traditions in Asia.

Women from the Indian sub-continent have immensely influenced religious practice on another level in Britain by replicating the religious custom and practice of their families and villages, by stimulating the growth and diversification of their religions and by maintaining particular traditions to keep them distinct within the wider group. They organise and control this alternative public sphere through which they also transmit their religious culture to the next generation.

One particular issue for Jewish, Christian and Muslim women has been the matter of inclusiveness in the liturgy, as in scripture, doctrine and theology. Language which expresses and describes humanity primarily in male terms has been seen as excluding women's religious perceptions and needs, as well as depriving religious concepts (including that of deity) of their female aspect and therefore of wholeness or as masking the gender-neutrality of transcendent interpretations of the divine. Thorough revaluation and critical reading of the Hebrew scriptures, the New Testament and the Qur'an have been undertaken by Jewish, Christian and Muslim women. In 1988, the Anglican General Synod published a report on inclusive language for use with the Alternative Service Book.

On the matter of sexuality, there is tension between precept and practice. The presence of many homosexual people in British churches has been acknowledged. Major issues are recognition, visible participation and full acceptance as spiritual equals of hetero-sexual men and women. One Anglican priest has said that, 'To be a lesbian or gay man in the Church is to live a continual act of forgiveness.' Rabbi Lionel Blue, a religious broadcaster who came out publicly in 1989, has said, 'I used to feel very angry about the difficult hand God has dealt me, but being Jewish and gay has given me a great sense of empathy with all outsiders.' The Anglican Church accepts priests whose sexual orientation is gay, but demands that they be celibate, while heterosexual priests are encouraged to marry. The question of whether high-ranking officials, by keeping their sexuality concealed, have thus supported homophobia and hypocrisy in the Anglican Church, was raised by the gay rights pressure group OutRage, which in 1995 named certain prominent church members as homosexual. This invasion of privacy has been criticised by the Lesbian and Gay Christian Movement which encourages lesbians and gay men to reveal their sexuality as they choose.

Following the resolution of the matter of ordaining women, that of the place of lesbians and homosexual men in the Anglican Church and their ordination is likely to engage the church in debate over the next decade. One bishop has already said that he may ordain priests living in stable homosexual relationships. Members of the world-wide Anglican communion issued a statement in March 1995, saying:

> Within the Church itself there are those whose pattern of sexual expression is at variance with the received Christian moral tradition but whose lives in other respects demonstrate the marks of genuine Christian character. The issues are deep and complex. They do not always admit of easy, instant answers. A careful process of reflecting on contemporary forms of behaviour in the light of scriptures and the Christian moral tradition is required.

Cardinal Hume, leader of Britain's Catholics, has confirmed the traditional church stance that while love between two human beings is to be treasured, homosexual practice remains 'disordered'. However, he stated in 1995 that any systematic failure to respect the dignity of homosexuals should be tackled by legislation and that Catholics should not be homophobic. The Gay and Lesbian Humanist Association then called on him to challenge a Vatican 1992 document advising churchmen not to be 'manipulated' into supporting homosexual anti-discrimination laws.

Reforms in Jewish religious divorce procedure were proposed by the Chief Rabbi, Jonathan Sacks, in late 1995, to ease the problems encountered by Jewish women whose husbands refused to give them the *gett* (Bill of Divorce). Husbands' resistance to granting divorce has been countered to some extent by the rabbinate's making of an order (*nidui*) prohibiting practising Jews from speaking to or coming near the recalcitrant husband.

NORTHERN IRELAND[1]

In the past twenty-five years, over 3,000 men, women and children have died violent deaths in Northern Ireland and countless numbers have been maimed, bereaved and emotionally scarred. Despite the revocation of the Irish Republican Army (IRA) cease-fires in February 1996, with renewed bomb explosions and open conflicts, efforts none the less to establish peace continue.

Northern Ireland[1]	
GDP (US$)	1,965,240
Population	1,577,336
Annual population growth (%)	2.65
Urban population (%)	see Great Britain statistics
Working population (%)	41.39
Literacy (%)	99
Ratifications	as for Great Britain

A question which is crucial for future peace, however, is: how much of the conflict was (and is) due to religious intolerance? Atrocities like the Darkley Gospel Hall and Milltown Cemetery massacres – if not Bloody Sunday – point to deep and intractable religious hatred, an impression confirmed by an unending catalogue of bigotry and sectarianism between people who nearly all profess to be Christians. Yet Protestant and Roman Catholic leaders and many of their followers claim that there is more that unites than divides them. That there is also a vigorous ecumenical movement in Northern Ireland is also beyond doubt.

Socio-political aspects

Between 1920 and 1972, Northern Ireland was a self-governing region of the United Kingdom with a parliament under the Government of Ireland Act 1920 modelled on the Westminster system. Political power was held by Unionists for almost fifty years. The United Kingdom Parliament retained ultimate responsibility but did not intervene under the 1920 Act until 1972. After complaints of civil rights abuses and discrimination against Catholics in local government, housing and policing and a series of confrontations between civil rights campaigners and the police and local militia, devolved government was suspended and the Westminster government took direct control. A campaign of violence by the IRA to secure British withdrawal of sovereignty continued for a quarter of a century until a cease-fire which lasted from 31 August 1994 to 9 February 1996.

The Northern Ireland Constitution Act 1973 provided for a new devolved power-sharing assembly elected by proportional representation. This, however, was a short-lived experiment brought down by a 'Protestant Workers Council' strike in 1974. A second attempt to set up a devolved power-sharing assembly in 1982 also failed.

Subsequent efforts to provide a more balanced framework for a devolved power-sharing government have also so far failed to bear fruit. The Anglo-Irish Agreement 1985 acknowledged the existing status of Northern Ireland while also giving formal recognition to the legitimate interest of the Irish government in the concerns of constitutional Irish Nationalists. However, it failed to secure cooperation between unionists and nationalists. Nor is there any clear indication yet that the peace process will result in an agreed form of government.

Ethnic, religious and cultural factors

Historically, the primary connotation of 'ethnicity' in Northern Ireland has been religious denomination. Nearly 90 per cent of Northern Ireland's over 1.5 million people claim affiliation to a Christian denomination. In the 1991 census, 38.4 per cent of the population claimed to be Roman Catholic and 50.5 per cent were mainly Protestant (21.4 per cent Presbyterian, 17.7 per cent Church of Ireland and 3.7 per cent Methodist) or

Evangelical Christian (7.7 per cent). Of the remainder, 11 per cent do not state an affiliation or claim to have none and 0.02 per cent claim a non-Christian faith or beliefs. Church attendance in Northern Ireland is high: 58 per cent of respondents in a survey said they attended church frequently, compared with 15 per cent in Great Britain. Attendance is highest among Roman Catholics (94 per cent).

However, the strength of communal, religious or cultural identity which this picture implies depends on a number of more complex historical and demographic factors. First, all Northern Ireland citizens have British nationality, but the minority Catholic population have an Irish identity and most hold dual citizenship with the Republic.

Second, more than half the population lives in segregated areas (enumeration districts which are either 90 per cent Protestant or 95 per cent Catholic). At a regional level there are relatively more Protestants in the east and north compared with the south and west. Communal segregation in more localised rural areas or small towns reflects influences ranging from communal violence and para-military activity to apparently voluntary patterns of social and residential segregation reinforced by almost mutually exclusive participation in church and school-based sporting, social and cultural activities.

Third, religious identity in Northern Ireland has a significance that is unique in Western Europe. Both nationalists and unionists in their separate collective histories can refer back to a historical link between their own ideas of religious freedom and national self-determination which pre-date independence and the partition of Ireland. Both also tend to presume their separate origins and destinies and ignore or deny any shared economic or social interests.

Fourth, it has become clear that separate identities have been maintained to a much greater degree than was at first appreciated by the physical segregation and separation of institutional structures in education, health, sport, local community affairs and communications as well as in religious affairs. Most important of all, in response to uncertainty and violence in the last twenty years, each community has developed a unique collective solidarity, shown most obviously in hostile attitudes and perceptions of members of the 'other' community.

Economic structure

Economically, Northern Ireland is less developed than many other regions of the United Kingdom. Occupational segregation along ethno-religious lines, once a significant feature of the economy, has changed over the last ten years. Skilled manual employment, where Catholics were poorly represented, has declined and new non-manual administrative, professional and service employment, particularly in the public sector – with a more balanced ethno-religious profile for both men and women – has grown. However, in the private sector, two-thirds of small-scale employment is still effectively segregated.

Many of the disadvantages of the Northern Ireland economy have fallen to a dis-proportionate degree on the Catholic–nationalist population. Catholics are much more likely to be among the young and long-term unemployed. Many continue the tradition of emigration.

Continuing occupational segregation in part reflects the high degree of educational segregation. Of Northern Ireland school pupils, 96 per cent attend segregated schools, although the proportion in integrated schools is nearly 4 per cent and growing rapidly. There is some correlation between academic achievement and religion, in that the highest percentage of pupils leaving school without any qualifications is among

Catholic boys. But there is an even stronger correlation between social class and educational achievement.

Inter-religious intolerance and discrimination

There is little doubt that differences of belief between the Catholic Church and Protestant churches have contributed to sectarianism and intolerance. Spiritual authority for Catholics derives from the Pope and bishops. For Protestants, the authority of the Bible is supreme although the precise emphasis varies and evangelical Christians tend to emphasise the role of personal spiritual conversion. The colliding absolutisms which distinguish the Catholic–Protestant divide are apparently irreconcilable conceptions of religious truth and authority which are more manifested than discussed in theological terms.

The extent of religious intolerance among Christian denominations in practice is difficult to assess, but many observers, both within and outside the churches, acknowledge that it is considerable. The effects of numerous influences, from folk memories of past persecutions and proselytising, significantly different religious and quasi-religious signs, symbols and ceremonies to constantly reinforced stereotypes and prejudices, have been meticulously recorded, as have the mechanisms by which they are passed on in everyday contact, as well as avoidance.

The late Professor John Whyte argued that the 'two factors which do most to divide Protestants as a whole from Catholics as a whole' are separate education and separate marriage. Separate education may also undermine religious adherence. A recent study of religious attitudes found that almost half of secondary school pupils in Northern Ireland, both Catholic and Protestant, found Christianity hard to accept because of the Catholic–Protestant divide.

Religious intolerance is not confined to intra-Christian relations. Intolerance by Christians towards non-Christian and humanist ideas and their adherents is sometimes manifested in hostility. People of other religions in Northern Ireland constitute a small minority but perhaps for this reason their beliefs and practices are often subject to much more overt intolerance. For instance, Chinese people have found that their religious duties and practices may be ridiculed or ignored in institutions such as hospitals, while Pakistani people have been the subject of racial attacks and abuse in housing estates. Travellers (gypsies) also experience hostility, abuse, attacks and official neglect.

Church and state

While there is no established church in Northern Ireland, the main Christian churches are involved informally to a significant extent in many areas of political and administrative life. The spiritual capital of both Irish Roman Catholicism and the Church of Ireland is Armagh and both spiritual leaders are regularly consulted by the government. Together with the Presbyterian and Methodist churches, they constitute the largest institutions in the island of Ireland outside government. In the United Kingdom there is no religious bar on holding public office, except that the sovereign by the Act of Succession must be Protestant, and no formal bar on members of the clergy seeking political office. Only Protestant clergymen in Northern Ireland have stood for election and been returned as members of the Westminster Parliament, but to varying degrees clergymen of all Christian denominations are involved in non-elected public office at a local level.

There is a close association between membership of particular Christian denominations and membership of political parties, most notably the Free Presbyterian Church and the Democratic Unionist Party led by the Reverend Ian Paisley MP and, to a lesser extent, the mainly Catholic Social Democratic and Labour Party, mainly Catholic Sinn Fein and the mainly Protestant Official Unionist Party. Only the Alliance Party claims significant cross-denominational membership. Although no political party is formally linked to a specific church, denominational teaching on ethical issues has influenced party policy in resisting the extension to Northern Ireland of United Kingdom legislation on controversial or liberal issues such as abortion, Sunday opening and gender and sexual rights.

Most churches in Northern Ireland own property and their clergy or nominees are involved in managing many statutory community facilities and voluntary organisations which are grant-aided by government, including nurseries, youth, sports and cultural clubs, hostels, nursing and old people's homes, and hospitals. The Roman Catholic Church acts as agent of the government by providing education for pupils in Catholic schools.

As a result of government attempts to keep funds out of the hands of para-military organisations, the Roman Catholic Church is currently the largest provider of Action for Community Employment jobs (an economic regeneration programme funded partly through the European Social fund) in Catholic West Belfast. Its role has sometimes led to conflicts with local community groups, and in particular with Sinn Fein, who see their exclusion as discriminatory and anti-democratic. More generally, however, there is some evidence to support the view that the Catholic Church as an organised institution has come to act as a crucial bridge between the state and the Catholic population.

Inter-church cooperation

Prolonged conflict has inevitably forced the main churches in Northern Ireland, often under pressure from the world religious community, to address the issue of inter-church relations. Changes have taken place but often are as much due to personal initiatives in reconciliation as to developments in inter-church relations.

In the wake of Vatican II, the Catholic Church adopted the Declaration on Religious Liberty recognising religious freedom as a universal right in 1965. In response, the Church of Ireland adopted more reconciliatory language. Since 1973 the four main churches (Roman Catholic, Church of Ireland, Presbyterian and Methodist) have taken part in the Ballymascanlon Inter-Church Talks. Their *Violence in Ireland Report* (1977) advocated a number of integrated religious education and joint-church projects. They came together under the auspices of the Department of Education to agree on a statutory 'common core' religious education programme which all schools would be required to teach. They also supported the implementation of cross-curricular themes in Education for Mutual Understanding and Cultural Heritage, a compulsory part of the Northern Ireland curriculum which aims to teach understanding and tolerance for 'the other side'. However, other religious groups or people with non-religious beliefs have not been included in curriculum drafting groups and their ideas and beliefs are largely ignored in the resulting religious education programmes.

Both the Church of Ireland and the Roman Catholic Church have none the less been hostile to other forms of joint-church educational provision. For example, they have refused to make joint chaplaincy appointments in integrated schools, or to make nominations to boards of controlled integrated schools as provided for in the legislation. In some instances, religious representatives on semi-official public bodies have been obstructive.

On the question of attitudes towards 'mixed' or cross-community marriages, the four main churches have been somewhat more flexible. The proportion of cross-community marriages has increased in recent decades, from 1.2 per cent in 1943 to 9.7 per cent in 1978–82. The most recent study of cross-community marriages in Northern Ireland found that most couples wish to maintain their links with their churches. However, while there has been a shift away from the traditional notion that one partner must surrender the religious upbringing of the children to the other partner, the promise the Catholic partner must make remains a bone of contention. Clergy, however, are increasingly being encouraged to develop joint pastoral care of cross-community marriages.

Constitutional recognition of freedom of conscience and religion

An official commitment to the principle of non-discrimination was written into the constitution of Northern Ireland at its foundation. The Northern Ireland Constitution Act 1973 which replaced the 1920 Act empowered the courts, or the Judicial Committee of the Privy Council on referral by the Secretary of State, to review and if necessary strike down any Northern Ireland legislation which discriminates against

> any person or class of persons on the grounds of religious or political belief (Section 17) or to issue an injunction against such unlawful discrimination by any minister of the Crown, a member of the Northern Ireland Executive or other person appointed by them (Section 19).

However, the 1973 Act provides only limited protection against discrimination. The provision does not cover normal Westminster Acts of Parliament and it does not extend to indirect discrimination, even though this was covered with respect to employment in the subsequent 1989 Fair Employment Act.

The current restriction of exemptions from the fair employment legislation to the general occupational exception – for the employment of teachers in schools and for the purpose of safeguarding national security, public safety and public order – have generally operated to preserve segregated employment. An exemption in respect of policies designed to promote balanced integration of both communities in employment might provide, it is thought, a more effective way of dealing with serious cases of imbalance.

More generally, however, while it is desirable to maintain a positive approach to equality of opportunity between the two communities in employment and to monitor progress in terms of the perceived affiliation to one of the two 'main' religious groups, none the less there remain difficulties in ensuring that those of other, or no real or perceived religious beliefs, are not disadvantaged and that people brought up in one of the two 'main' religious groups are effectively free to adopt or change their religious beliefs.

Policy and programme measures

Following a series of highly critical international reports on the conflict in Northern Ireland, a number of policy and programme measures (apart from fair employment legislation) were implemented in order to remedy apparent discrimination in government policies and to promote 'parity of esteem'. In 1987 the Central Community Relations Unit was established to advise the Secretary of State. As a result, Policy Appraisal and Fair Treatment and other economic and social programmes to deal with areas of special need, such as the Making Belfast Work, and Targeting Social Need initiatives, were introduced. Soon after, in 1988, a new Community Relations Council was established to foster cross-community understanding, and financial support was given to community relations programmes initiated by district councils and other local voluntary groups with an acceptable level of cross-communal involvement.

Additional measures were also directed at achieving equality of educational provision for the Catholic and Protestant communities. An influential Standing Advisory Commission on Human Rights report (for 1991–92) had been highly critical of the Department of Education, arguing that high unemployment levels experienced by Catholics were linked to long-standing discrimination in educational funding.

Education

Up to 1989, Northern Ireland only recognised the educational rights of parents to the extent that provision and funding were made for two categories of effectively mono-denominational, segregated schools. These were the voluntary schools owned by trustees (but maintained in most cases by the state) which were predominantly Catholic, and the controlled schools which were owned by the state and controlled and managed by an area board.

The main difference between Catholic schools and controlled 'state' schools managed by area boards was that the latter received 100 per cent capital funding compared to 85 per cent for Catholic schools. This had been justified on the basis that the Government of Ireland Act 1920 prohibited the endowment of religion. The Northern Ireland Catholic bishops challenged the discrepancy when the Education Reform (NI) Order 1989 created the option of a new category of grant-maintained integrated schools, eligible for 100 per cent capital funding. Though the bishops' case was rejected in court on the grounds that there was no direct discrimination under the provisions of the Constitution Act of 1973, the law was subsequently changed.

In addition, the Department of Education accepted the argument that the number of Catholic grammar school places was less than proportionate to the number of Catholic primary school pupils and, in 1992, the Department sanctioned capital provision for two new Catholic grammar schools, one in Belfast and one in Derry.

All schools except special and nursery schools are required by law to provide religious education, collective worship and allow clergy access to pupils. Provision is made for pupil withdrawal in recognition of parents' right of conscience and, in the case of controlled schools, religious education is to be non-denominational. Only teachers in controlled schools may in principle opt out of religious education teaching on conscientious grounds.

The Education Reform (NI) Order 1989 imposed a duty on the Northern Ireland Department of Education to encourage and facilitate the development of integrated education, and contained specific provisions for the creation of new integrated schools or the transformation of existing ones by means of parental ballot. However, the 1989 Order was open to criticism on several counts. The Order did not provide genuine freedom of choice for parents by imposing a statutory requirement to ensure adequate provision throughout Northern Ireland of primary and secondary schools for those who wanted integrated education, or by requiring education and library boards to facilitate integrated education. Nor was provision made for initial capital funding of integrated schools on a par with segregated schools.

Other provisions in the Education Reform Order also threatened religious pluralism and diversity. The creation of a statutory basis and funding for a Council for Catholic Maintained Schools, a body catering for a single denomination, arguably discriminates against other denominations and also against the freedom of conscience of parents and teachers. The functions of the Council include statutory rights in the appointment and employment of teachers, in the planning of Catholic schools and in nominating members of school boards, but there is no requirement for the Council to facilitate integrated education where Catholic parents support it. Further, the government has so far resisted calls from the other main Protestant denominations who are represented on 'state' schools for a statutory administrative body with similar powers and funding.

In this respect the exception of the employment of teachers from the fair employment legislation has been of concern. Discrimination in the appointment of teachers in publicly funded denominational schools ensures that parents have the freedom to choose, and (some) denominations have the right to provide, denominational education. Furthermore, the provision which permits teachers in controlled schools to contract out of any religious duties on conscientious grounds does not apply to voluntary and grant-maintained schools. There is thus a limit on the religious freedom of teachers in schools other than controlled schools, which arguably contravenes the Northern Ireland Constitution Act.

Conscientious objection

There is no legal provision for the recognition of conscientious objection on grounds of religious or other belief in Northern Ireland except in the case of teachers and pupils in controlled schools. A test arose in Northern Ireland in a case brought under the Incitement to Disaffection Act 1934 when Pat Arrowsmith was charged and convicted of attempting to seduce soldiers from their duty or allegiance in relation to service in Northern Ireland. An acknowledged pacifist, she argued that she was exercising her right under Article 9 of the European Convention on Human Rights to manifest her beliefs. The European Commission rejected her claim on the ground that the leaflets did not express her pacifist views.

Women and religion

Although Catholic women in the north have borne the huge burden of widespread unemployment, loss of male members of their families through violence and imprisonment and relative poverty in terms of the Protestant majority, they have enjoyed more legal freedoms under United Kingdom law in matters of reproduction than women in the south. The famous 'contraceptive train' of protest in which southern Irish women travelled ceremonially to buy contraceptives in Belfast is an illustration. Protestant women have also suffered in the violence of the north and it is notable that Catholic and Protestant women joined to form the first effective peace movement in Ireland and are the main supporters of suggestions concerning the integration of the two separate education systems.

Note

1 See also the entry on Ireland.

GREECE

Nearly two-thirds of Greece's population, estimated at 10.3 million, live in urban communities. Athens is the major focus of manufacturing and services; about one-third of the Greek population lives in Greater Athens. After the Second World War, many

Greece	
GDP (US$bn)	67
Population	10,300,000
Annual population growth (%)	0.7
Urban population (%)	64
Working population (%)	39[a]
Literacy (%)	93.8
Ratifications	1; 3; 4; E

Greeks from impoverished rural and island communities emigrated, so much so that Melbourne, Australia, is called the second largest Greek city in the world. The Hellenic diaspora maintains close ties with its communities. However, immigration is now increasing.

Legal and political system

A long period of political upheaval and constitutional crisis culminating in the 1967 *coup d'état* which brought Greece under military rule came to an end with the collapse of the military dictatorship in 1974, when democratic institutions were restored. Return to a constitutional monarchy was rejected.

The 1975/1986 constitution stipulates that Greece is a parliamentary democracy, based on popular sovereignty, the rule of law, the separation of powers and the welfare state. The constitution also provides for the independence of the judiciary, authorises the judicial review of acts of parliament, statutory instruments and administrative acts and guarantees citizens' access to the courts. The 1986 amendment diminished the power of the president.

Freedom of expression and freedom of association, as well as the rights to found and to belong to political parties, are guaranteed and censorship is prohibited. Today, political parties represent views across the political spectrum. The two main parties New Democracy and Panhellenic Socialist Movement (PASOK) have been in and out of power following the regularly held democratic elections. For the last twenty years, the country has enjoyed a period of political stability unparalleled in its history.

Because of the experience of dictatorship, the 1975/1986 constitution ensures a more complete and effective protection of the individual than did its predecessors by providing all the guarantees of individual rights that characterise the modern legal regime of rights. The constitution sets out the principles of equality, protects the dignity and worth of the human person and the right to self-development, and entrenches human rights. Economic, social and cultural rights, as well as the right to the environment, are also legally entrenched, although the exercise of these rights is subject to social restrictions. Greece has ratified some international human rights instruments and regional ones as part of the European Union. Under the constitution, their generally accepted norms prevail over any contrary provision of municipal law. The Council of State is the Supreme Court which deals with civil and administrative matters; its rulings are binding on the state.

Ethnic and cultural background

Greek society is extremely homogeneous ethnically, culturally and linguistically. One of the underlying causes of this homogeneity is the decisive role played by the Christian Eastern Orthodox Church in maintaining Greek language and culture during nearly four centuries of Ottoman rule and its involvement in the struggle for liberation. The Greek Orthodox faith became the focal point of Hellenic identity and has provided a point of reference for the Hellenic diaspora across the world. Owing to its widespread influence and presence at all social levels, as well as the relative absence of other traditions, serious religious conflicts have been few in Greece.

A further complexity in the matter of religion, nationality and ethnicity was added with the Lausanne Treaty of 1923, which ended the Greco-Turkish war. The convention provided for the compulsory exchange of Turkish nationals of the Greek Orthodox religion (living in Turkey) with Greek nationals of the Muslim religion (living in Greece). Only two groups were exempted from the exchange of population: Greeks living in Constantinople, and the Muslims living in Western Thrace who form the only officially recognised Greek minority group.

Religious composition

Despite lack of reliable data, it is said that the overwhelming majority of the population (about 97–98 per cent) are members of the Eastern Orthodox Church. Other religious groups also present in Greece include Muslims, Jews, Catholics, various Protestant denominations, Orthodox Old Calendarist, Jehovah's Witnesses, Mormons, Krishna Consciousness and Baha'is.

Although the Greek Jewish community dates back to classical times, the largest Jewish communities date back to 1492, when Sephardim (Ladino-speaking Jews) expelled from Spain and later from Portugal were allowed to settle in the Ottoman Empire and were recognised as a separate *millet* by its authorities. A small group of Ashkenazim also arrived in the 1830s, at the time when the Bavarian, Othon, was made the first king in the newly formed Greek state.

Since the late nineteenth century, Jewish numbers have dwindled. Thessaloniki used to be a very large Jewish town, its trades (shipping, sailing and chandlery) dominated by Jews. After 1913, the Jewish population began to decline, due to a catastrophic fire in 1917 and emigration to Palestine. Later, as a result of the Nazi occupation and associated atrocities during the Second World War, the total Jewish population of Greece was reduced to about 10 per cent of its original, dropping from about 63,200 Jews in 1928 to 6,325 in 1951. Only 4–6,000 Jews now remain.

The 120,000-member Muslim minority in Western Thrace is composed of people of Turkish, Pomak and Roma (gypsy) origin. Greece has 140,000 Roma, including 45,000 nomadic Muslims; there are intermittent campaigns by the Orthodox Church to convert them. A limited number of Muslims live on the island of Rhodes.

Greek Catholics live mainly in those areas which centuries ago were under Venetian, Genoese and later Italian rule, such as the Cyclades, Dodecanese and Ionian Islands. Today, according to the Catholic Archbishop of Athens, there are about 52,000 Greek Catholics of the Latin, Byzantine and Armenian rites. A further 139,000 Catholics living in Greece are of Polish, Filipino, German and French nationalities.

There are up to 18,000 Protestants, mainly evangelical and Pentecostal, in about 130 congregations, concentrated primarily in Athens, Thessaloniki and Patras. The Jehovah's Witness movement first appeared in Greece in the beginning of the twentieth century, opening its first office in 1922 in Athens. Witnesses number in the tens of thousands, in 338 congregations.

Women and religion

Greek Orthodox Christianity espouses very conservative values in relation to women. Women can be seen as morally inferior to men, responsible for original sin and unclean because of menstruation and childbirth. Hence all female living creatures are banned on Mount Athos, the monastery complex in northern Greece (which has autonomous status), where there are no distractions or temptations from the quest for 'the closest to Godliness which mortal man can attain', according to one commentator.

However, moves for the strengthening of women's status began as early as 1804 when Greek women founded institutes and schools for girls. Feminist magazines and organisations for women's rights date from 1835 and consistent feminist activities (including the founding of the Panhellenic Union of Women in 1945) have continued throughout Greece's long history of political instability, cruel wars, occupations and dictatorships. But it was not until the PASOK government under Andreas Papandreou (whose wife was a prominent feminist) came to power in 1981 that real progress for women was possible.

Relationships between the government and the Greek Orthodox Church then deteriorated because of direct government intervention in church affairs and major intended changes in family law and women's rights. In 1985, the clergy marched in protest against educational reforms and the proposed nationalisation of monastery property in 1987, an issue which was taken to the European Court.

Some success for women was achieved in 1983, with a new family law allowing women to work outside the home, freeing them from the legal obligation to carry out domestic work and establishing equality in all marriage matters. Reproduction issues were also settled against a background of church protest, with easy availability of contraceptives and the most advanced abortion laws in Europe.

There still remain large differences in social traditions between rural and urban Greece. Dowry, arranged marriage and the male honour system operate in large areas of rural Greece. The Orthodox Church continues to exert pressure against the breaking down of discrimination against women but is continually confronted by women's groups which are among the most influential and best organised in Europe.

Constitutional guarantees of freedom of religion or belief

The Greek constitution specifically recognises freedom of conscience only in respect to religious matters, primarily freedom of worship, under Article 13. Nevertheless, a constitutional basis for a general freedom of conscience can be identified by referring to the provisions pertaining to the worth of the human person and other provisions. Article 13 also guarantees the state's neutrality towards the religions practised in Greece. The state should not intervene, either by hindering or by imposing a specific direction, in the process of forming as well as in manifesting religious convictions. The protections of Article 13 apply equally to both Greek citizens and aliens, and may not be amended nor suspended in any period of emergency. Article 13 of the constitution states:

1 Freedom of religious conscience is inviolable. The enjoyment of civil rights and liberties does not depend on the individual's religious beliefs.
2 Every known religion shall be free: each form of worship may be practised without hindrance under the protection of the law provided that it is not incompatible with public policy or accepted moral standards.
3 The ministers of all known religions shall be subject to the same supervision by the State and to the same obligations toward it as those of the prevailing religion.

4 No person shall be exempt from discharging his obligations to the State or may refuse to comply with the laws by reason of his religious convictions.

5 No oath shall be imposed or administered except as specified by law and in the form determined by law.

Article 13.2 guarantees freedom to practise any 'known' religion. The term refers to any religion that does not require initiation, whose doctrines are authentic and whose worship takes place in public. It does not mean that a religion must be officially recognised; it simply means that a religion is accessible, that is, it can be known to anyone who so chooses. According to the jurisprudence of the Council of State, there are no further requirements for a religion to be 'known' or 'recognised' and acquire constitutional protection, apart from the above. A religion does not have to be approved or otherwise recognised by the state or the Eastern Orthodox Church. According to the Council of State, it is irrelevant whether or not a religion is considered a heresy by the church, whether its believers have established religious authorities or not, or that its ministers are not recognised as such by the Orthodox Church.

However, the constitution's protection of freedom of religion is not absolute but relative. Article 13.4 stipulates that no-one may be exempted from discharging his obligations to the state, or 'refuse to comply with the law by reason of his religious convictions'. It has been established, on the one hand, that the fulfilment of obligations towards the state has priority over religious freedom and, on the other hand, that religious freedom is conditional on compliance with the laws, especially those that pertain to education, health, public safety and national defence.

Church–state relations

Greece is the only Orthodox state in the world. Article 3.1 of the constitution states that the Eastern Orthodox Church is the 'prevailing' religion:

> The prevailing religion in Greece is that of the Eastern Orthodox Church of Christ. The Orthodox Church of Greece, acknowledging our Lord Jesus Christ as its head, is inseparably united in doctrine with the Great Church of Christ in Constantinople and with every other Church of Christ of the same doctrine, observing unwaveringly, as they do, the holy apostolic and synodal canons and sacred traditions. It is autocephalous and is administered by the Holy Synod.

The constitution sets up a regime where there is neither an established church nor complete church–state separation. However, in *Kokkinakis* v. *Greece*, the European Court of Human Rights noted in 1993 that 'according to Greek conceptions, it [the church] represents *de jure* and *de facto* the religion of the State itself, a good number of whose administrative functions . . . it carries out'. The involvement of the Greek Orthodox Church in areas of public life which come under state regulation has been institutionalised by means of the provision of Article 2 of the Charter of the Church of Greece, which constitutes a law of the state. Its integrative function has been institutionalised through the Ministry of Education and Religion, by which it exercises administrative control over all religious affairs in Greece. The state also pays the salaries of Orthodox clergy and for the functions which other ministers of religion perform as public officials in civil matters, such as marriages (for which there also exist civil ceremonies).

However, the prerogatives of the 'prevailing religion' with respect to other 'known' religions have been tempered by other provisions of the constitution. Thus everyone can enjoy their individual and political rights, irrespective of their religious convictions

(Article 13.1); all religions are subject to the same restrictions with respect to freedom of worship (Article 13.2); proselytism is prohibited (Article 13.2); ministers of 'known' religions have the same obligations towards the state and are subject to the same state supervision as the ministers of the 'prevailing' religion (Article 13.3). The President of the Republic does not have to be Orthodox, even though apparently he has to be a Christian (Article 33.2) and he no longer swears 'to protect the dominant religion of the Greeks' as the former King had to do under the 1952 constitution.

According to the parliamentary debates during the drafting of the 1975 constitution, the term 'prevailing religion' should not be taken to suggest the predominance of the Greek Orthodox Church over other religions. The distinction is to be understood as acknowledging only that almost all Greeks adhere to it. However, in practice, the term 'prevailing' is taken to indicate a privileged status for the Orthodox religion and its ranking above all other religions, based on the numerical significance of the Orthodox population and, most importantly, on the nexus between Orthodoxy and Hellenism.

Indeed, legislative, administrative and judicial practice often diverges from the standard set by the new, more secular and egalitarian constitutional framework. Bonds between the state and the Orthodox Church, privileging the church over all other 'known' religions, have been strengthened instead of relaxed whenever state officials and others have not given full weight to the constitutional guarantee of freedom of religion, by interpreting it to mean freedom from any religion except the 'prevailing' one.

One example of the complexity of the issues of identity and affiliation came when the government proposed to make optional the compulsory information about a person's religious affiliation on the identity card every Greek must carry. The Catholic and Jewish representatives successfully lobbied for this proposal as the religious information could provide an opportunity for discrimination and harassment by anybody who had to see the card. However, the amendment was denounced by the Greek Orthodox Church and continued provision of compulsory information about religion on identity cards was supported in parliament in 1993 by a coalition across the political spectrum, on the basis that Orthodoxy was integral to national identity.

The Muslim community apparently contains differences of opinion on the matter of state appointment of some of its *muftis*. Two of the Thracian *muftis* have been appointed on the recommendation of a committee of local Muslim scholars, religious authorities and community leaders; others have been elected. In accounting for its involvement, the government has referred to the judicial functions which the *muftis* exercise in relation to marriage and other matters covered by Muslim personal law. They are solely responsible for ensuring their decisions are in line with Islamic law.

In a number of cases, the government has refused entry to religious officials and theologians from other countries, sometimes alleging a political aspect to their proposed visits.

Virtually all the top posts in government, the military, the judiciary and schools are allegedly restricted to registered members of the Orthodox Church, thus ensuring the dominance of majority views and assumptions in matters of public life.

Proselytising

'Proselytism and any other action against the dominant religion' were prohibited for the first time in a clause added to the first constitution (1844), during the reign of Othon I, after persistent complaints from the Greek Orthodox Church that Orthodox children had been proselytised by members of a German Bible society (Othon I had come to Greece from Bavaria). Subsequent constitutions reproduced this clause. The 1952 constitution prohibited proselytism, as well as 'any other interference', but only if aimed 'against the prevailing religion'. The 1975 constitution widened the prohibition of proselytism to protect all 'known' religions from proselytism, not only the Greek Orthodox.

Furthermore, in 1938, during the dictatorship of Metaxas (1926–40), proselytism was made a criminal offence by Article 4 of Act 1363/1938 and the following year the term 'proselytism' was defined in Article 2 of Act 1672/1939:

1 Any person found guilty of practising proselytism shall be liable to imprisonment and a fine between 1,000 and 50,000 drachma and shall be placed under police supervision for a period of time, from six months to one year, to be fixed by the judgement of the Court. The term of imprisonment may not be commuted to a fine.
2 By 'proselytism' is meant, in particular, any direct or indirect effort to intrude on the religious beliefs of a person of a different religious persuasion, with the aim of altering those beliefs, either by any kind of inducement, or promise of an inducement, or moral support, or material assistance, or by fraudulent means, or by taking advantage of his inexperience, trust, need, low intellect, or naïveté.
3 Where such acts are carried out in an educational establishment, training centre, or charitable institution, this shall be regarded as a particularly aggravating circumstance.

The European Court of Human Rights' decision in 1993 in the Kokkinakis case – a major case concerning freedom of belief under Article 9 in European human rights law – established that the application of the Greek law on proselytism had infringed one Jehovah's Witness's freedom of belief when he was convicted of proselytising his religion to a Greek Orthodox woman in her own house. She had invited Mr Kokkinakis and his wife into her house. Her beliefs had not been altered by the short encounter; her husband, a Greek Orthodox cantor, had called the police. Mr Kokkinakis had previously been arrested more than sixty times for proselytising in Crete since 1936, and imprisoned on several occasions. He provided the Court with statistics to show that 4,400 Witnesses had been arrested for proselytising between 1975 and 1992, of whom 1,233 were committed for trial and 208 convicted. In the years before democracy was restored in 1975, Witnesses had been among those convicted under laws for preventing communism and its effects, and for preserving the public order.

The US Department of State reports only one prosecution in 1994 for proselytising: a Jehovah's Witness in Volos, central Greece. Many already convicted have appealed to higher courts and in recent years to the European Court. The Greek government's view, forwarded to the Special Rapporteurs on Religious Intolerance, has been that all the cases of religious discrimination and intolerance referred to it were related to an 'individual's rights to oppose, by legal means, repressive action of their fellow-citizens directed against their religious conscience'. However, arrests usually involve third parties as well: allegedly, Orthodox priests, family members or people in the village. The laws prohibiting proselytism have not yet been amended or repealed.

The Kokkinakis case decision

The European Court of Human Rights saw the Kokkinakis matter as concerned with Article 9 of the European Convention on Human Rights, concerning freedom of thought, conscience and religion: a precious asset for all people whatever their religion or belief and indispensable for 'the pluralism indissociable from a democratic society'.

However, the Court stopped short of considering whether the Greek legal provisions against proselytism as such (with their penal sanctions) were compatible with the Convention. The Court assessed only the matter of whether the application of the Greek law in this particular case had overstepped the mark. The Court did not examine the general issues further than to say that the legal measures were in pursuit of a legitimate aim under Article 9(2), namely the protection of the rights and freedoms of others and that therefore the Court needed to consider only whether the restriction on the Article 9 freedom was 'justified in principle and proportionate'.

Greek law distinguishes between 'proper' and 'improper' proselytism. The European Court did not define the latter but offered some *obiter dicta* distinguishing between 'bearing Christian witness and improper proselytism' in terms of offering material inducements and social advantages, pressuring people in distress or need, and use of violence or 'brainwashing'. The Greek courts had not proved that Mr Kokkinakis had proselytised in an 'improper' manner; the conviction met no 'pressing social need', was not proportionate to 'the legitimate aim pursued' nor was it 'necessary in a democratic society . . . for the protection of the rights and freedoms of others'.

Not all the Court's judges agreed with its reasoning in this case. Judge Pettiti, while concurring with the Court's conclusion, criticised the vagueness of the charge and the lack of any clear definition of proselytism on which to determine criminal penalties. He also stated that in his view:

> The expression 'proselytism which is not respectable', which is a criterion used by the Greek courts when applying the law, is sufficient for the enactment and the case-law applying it to be regarded as contrary to Article 9.

> The Government themselves recognised that the applicant had been prosecuted because he had tried to influence the person he was talking to by taking advantage of her inexperience in matters of doctrine and exploiting her low intellect. It was not therefore not a question of protecting others against physical or psychological coercion but of giving the State the possibility of arrogating to itself the right to assess a person's weakness in order to punish a proselytiser, an interference that could become dangerous if resorted to by an authoritarian State.

Religious establishments

The Metaxas legislation also introduced the need for a special permit issued by the 'competent ecclesiastical authorities' – usually the local Orthodox bishop – and the Ministry of National Education and Religion, as an obligatory requirement 'for the establishment, or operation of a church belonging to any religious denomination whatsoever'. This requirement applies only to places of worship belonging to religions or faiths other than the Greek Orthodox. Any such building erected without permission is liable to be closed and sealed by the local police, further use prohibited and those who put them up or operated them liable to both a fine and imprisonment of two to six months.

Permission has allegedly been difficult or impossible to obtain, or unreasonably delayed, according to documented cases from minority religions. Prosecutions have followed when congregations continue to practise their religion in locations without official approval. Two such cases were reported by the Special Rapporteur for Religious Intolerance in his 1995 report, concerning the Jehovah's Witnesses in Alexandroupolis and in Gazi-Maleviziou in Crete. In the Alexandroupolis case, when the leaders of the congregation had been acquitted of the charge of illegally using a house of prayer, the police who had been ordered to remove the seals from the building were unable to do so before the prosecutor appealed the decision to a higher court. It sentenced the leaders to imprisonment, commuted to fines, a sentence confirmed by the Supreme Court on appeal.

Education

It is noteworthy that the Ministry for Education is combined with Religion. Religious instruction in schools is compulsory for all students unless their parents declare that they do not adhere to the Greek Orthodox religion. None the less, some Jehovah's Witness pupils have reportedly been made to attend Orthodox observances by their teachers, and have been harassed and physically attacked for their beliefs. Books used for religious instruction are said to denigrate the religion of the Witnesses.

There have, however, been some positive developments. Religious education has benefited from exposure to ecumenical thinking in recent years and secondary school textbooks have a stronger emphasis on social issues. The new textbook on other religions gives more objective detail than previously, approaching religions from the standpoint of their believers' understandings rather than through invidious comparison with Christianity. The texts reportedly also attempt to provide information about Islam as objectively and extensively as possible.

Teachers in primary schools were required to be members of the Greek Orthodox Church until 1988; Catholics, among others, had been denied teaching appointments as primary teachers were expected to conduct religious education in the Greek Orthodox faith. In 1988 legislation was passed allowing the appointment of persons of any religion or faith as public schoolteachers in primary schools with more than one teacher. Despite this change in the law, however, Jehovah's Witnesses and Baha'is who have teaching qualifications have been unable to obtain positions in schools, even in private tuition centres, such as English language schools. In one official letter sent to an applicant, a departmental circular was quoted in which it was stated that the reason for rejection of Witness and Baha'i applicants was that 'the purpose of elementary and secondary education is, among other things, to contribute towards and to encourage students to cultivate faith in their country and in the genuine elements of the Greek Orthodox tradition'. There are some indications from reports that non-Orthodox teachers are more likely to be rejected now than they were in the 1980s.

For the Muslim minority in Thrace, there are schools where Qur'anic teaching takes place. Their teacher training school has been raised to university status by the government; students would be able to pursue a full course of university studies by choosing either the teaching track or the theological–Islamic track.

The media

While public discourse is outspoken and vigorous in Greece, there is said to be a certain amount of self-censorship on matters of national security and the national identity. Since the repeal of the law against 'insulting authority' in late 1993, however, a number of prosecutions involving restrictions on freedom of expression – including the cases of five Trotskyists and two journalists – have apparently been dropped.

The Special Rapporteur on Religious Intolerance noted that the evangelical community had not been allowed to continue broadcasting from its private religious television station, Hellas 62. Many private stations operate without licences.

The Church of Scientology, as the Greek Center of Applied Philosophy, is not recognised as a religion. The media call it 'a dangerous heresy' or the group 'new Satans'. In January 1997, an Athens court ordered dissolution of the Center, describing its activities as incompatible with its licence as a non-profit public interest organisation.

Conscientious objection

Military service is compulsory in Greece. Conscientious objection is an offence for which there is no alternative service available. The Council of State confirmed in 1990 that all ministers of religion were exempted from military service, not only Orthodox, Catholic and Protestant Christians, Muslims and Jews, but also all other 'known' religions and faiths whose doctrine, teachings and rites are accessible. Traditionally, Jehovah's Witnesses were not granted this exemption and had to serve prison sentences. The history of conscientious objection in Greece, as charted by Amnesty International in its 1993 report, is such that between 1938 and 1992, Witnesses had collectively spent more than 5,000 years in military and civil prisons.

The military recruiting section has apparently taken the view that the decision of the Council of State about the Jehovah's Witnesses being a 'known religion' had no greater status than referring to the case of one individual. Consequently its policy of not recognising the eligibility of Witnesses for exemption has not been altered. The recruiting section continues to rely on the opinion of the Ministry of Education and Religion which takes the Orthodox Church's view that the Witnesses do not constitute a 'known' religion. Consequently, Witness ministers have had to spend up to a year in jail while waiting for their appeals against convictions to be heard.

In 1994, the Special Rapporteur on Religious Intolerance asked Greece to respond to the situation where 400 conscientious objectors who were Witnesses were allegedly being held, and often ill-treated, in military prisons on four-year prison sentences.

HUNGARY

Hungary	
GDP (US$bn)	35
Population	10,300,000
Annual population growth (%)	0.1
Urban population (%)	63
Working population (%)	45[a]
Literacy (%)	99
Ratifications	1; 2, 2(a), 2(b); 3; 4; E

Hungary, lying at the meeting point of east and west in Europe, has had diverse ethnic groups, religions and beliefs for centuries. Jews have been present since the era of the Roman Empire, Christianity since the third century and eastern Christianity in the late ninth century after the Magyar conquest. Hungary has been swept by religio-political forces, first of the Reformation under which Protestant groups flourished, then of Ottoman rule over all but Transylvania where the Act of Torda mandated religious tolerance in 1568, the earliest such legislation in Europe. After the victory of the Counter-Reformation in the seventeenth century, Catholicism was the only public religion allowed until 1781 when the Austro-Hungarian Emperor Josef II pronounced the Edict of

Toleration. On this basis, the Protestant half of Hungary's population regained their rights to public worship and religious organisation but the Catholic Church remained identified with the state. By the end of the nineteenth century there was greater religious toleration of minorities, although social and economic anti-Semitism persisted.

At the end of the First World War, Hungary's boundaries were redrawn and significant Hungarian minorities found themselves living in neighbouring states. Between the wars, the semi-fascist Horthy regime persecuted and eventually prohibited smaller Protestant groups; Jews were also persecuted. In March 1944 the Nazi occupation of Hungary began; 600,000 Jews were massacred or deported to concentration and labour camps from which few returned. With liberation in 1945, all laws of the Horthy and previous regimes which discriminated against Jews were repealed but many survivors emigrated. Forty years later, the Hungarian Jewish population was no more than 100,000.

The Roma (gypsies) were deeply discriminated against. Just in the area of women's rights alone, while the communist state enjoined equal rights and responsibilities for all citizens since 1949 and gave women access to participation in political life and all areas of the workforce, the depth and extent of discrimination and intolerance, coupled with a life of poverty and ill-health brought about the situation where Roma women had fifteen years' less life expectancy than women in the rest of Hungary.

Hungarian women have a long history of women's activism and played a central part in the 1956 anti-Soviet rebellion. In the pre-*glasnost* years, women's freedom was not inhibited by the church because it had little influence in a socialist state. However, a state population policy was implemented in 1974 which restricted access to abortion.

No reliable statistics on religion or belief have existed since 1948. However, it is generally accepted that today Hungary's population of 10.3 million is nominally 60 per cent Catholic, 20 per cent Reformed and 10 per cent Lutheran but, in fact, 40 per cent of Hungarians do not even call themselves Christian, according to a fact-finding mission by the churches' East–West European Relations Network in the 1990s. About 5 per cent of Hungarians belong to one or another of the 30–35 smaller religions, the majority of which are Protestant groups; 1–2 per cent are Jews and a smaller proportion are Muslims. There are also Buddhist groups and a small Baha'i community.

Freedom of thought under communist rule

After the war, Hungary became a socialist state. As collective economic, cultural and social rights were considered primary rights, the subordination of individual freedom and rights was held to be permissible. The Hungarian constitution of 1949 stated that citizens could only use their human rights lawfully, that is, in harmony with the interests of socialism.

As a 'soft' dictatorship, Hungary did not have formal censorship but state monopoly of telecommunications, book and newspaper publication and editorial control of book publication ensured that ideas disapproved of by the Communist Party would not appear in the media. Freedom of thought and expression was limited by the practice of 'silencing'. For any period of suspension, nothing by the author to be punished could be published or broadcast. Silencing was addressed not only to the person punished but to all intellectuals unless they wished to be 'silenced' in their turn.

Freedom of religion under communist rule

Freedom of religion and conscience was also curbed under communist rule. While no genuine opposition party was allowed to operate, it was accepted that the existence of churches was historically justified in socialism – even if temporarily – and for this reason, the limitation of religious freedom was different. According to Marxist thought, religion met certain social demands, providing consolation (however illusory) for those who were unable to see that real liberation lay elsewhere. Faiths were thus considered necessary evils but, as rivals to Marxist ideology, their activities needed to be restricted.

All efforts were made to place Marxism at the forefront. There was compulsory tuition in Marxism in higher education for many hours a week, as 'the only scientific ideology'. As religious views were false ideals, 'pseudo-science', they had no place in universities and schools. Marxism also dominated the media.

All religious orders were dissolved in 1949 and religious communities were deprived of legal personality. Church social services were eliminated or drastically cut; nuns were not allowed to care for patients, and priests were barred from consoling prisoners and soldiers. Church-owned schools were secularised. The autonomy of the churches was terminated and a state Secretariat of Religious Affairs controlled the financial and ideological activities of religious organisations and participated in clerical appointments. The clergy were state-funded; theological training was allowed to continue, although on a smaller scale. Confiscated religious property was often used for higher education facilities or student hostels.

In the 1980s, along with the freeing of the economy, the restrictions on religious and other freedoms also eased in Hungary. Wider possibilities opened to spread religious ideas and it was gradually acknowledged that the different religions could play a positive role in the management of unsolved social problems. Dialogue between the churches and the state began, on the basis that religious teaching contains basic moral values desirable to society.

Hungary after communism

After 1989 the new democracy brought fundamental change in the relations between the state and its citizens. In the multi-party parliament, a number of parties reflect religious concerns. The Christian Democratic People's Party openly advocates Christian ideas, and the Hungarian Democratic Forum and the Independent Smallholders' Party also identify themselves with Christian values, but no faith is attached to any political party. In May 1994 a Socialist–Liberal coalition government was elected.

The Hungarian constitution was changed radically in 1989 and 1990 to bring it into harmony with major international and European human rights instruments. In 1990 Hungary joined the Council of Europe and ratified the European Convention on Human Rights. The legal guarantees of the Hungarian constitution are enforced through the newly established Constitutional Court. The constitution now states that 'everyone has the right to freedom of thought, conscience and religion'. This right includes free choice or acceptance of religion or any other conviction according to one's conscience, and the liberty to express, or refuse to express, to exercise or teach one's religion and conviction through the performance of religious acts and rites, either individually or together with others, either publicly or in private. The constitution provides for separation of church and state. Everyone has the right to declare views and opinions freely, to have access to information of public interest, and also the freedom to disseminate such information.

Freedom of the press is also protected. However, Jews remain concerned about the undercurrent of anti-Semitism in the media and public discourse, in references to the 'Jewish question'. Racial and religious stereotypes – such as the concept of 'true Christian ethnic Magyars' espoused by ultra-nationalists – contribute to intolerance.

In 1993, Parliament adopted the Rights of National and Ethnic Minorities Act which states that discrimination against minorities violates the constitution and is punishable by law. The Roma are Hungary's largest ethnic minority, numbering 600,000; in 1995, they became the first gypsies in central and eastern Europe to gain autonomy as a national minority. The Jewish community decided not to seek such status, though noting that they could apply in the future.

On the initiative of an inter-party parliamentary committee against anti-Semitism, the Parliament in 1993 adopted a statement which

> in the spirit of humanity and in accordance with the international treaties and the Hungarian constitution condemns and rejects extremism, wherever and with whatever content it may appear, particularly hatred against national and ethnic minorities, xenophobia, anti-Semitism and manifestations which offend national and religious feeling.

Contemporary problems for women include living with the contradiction of valuing a persecuted church now struggling towards full freedom of expression, while being adversely affected by defensive, conservative theologies which are typical in Eastern European Christian institutions as a result of decades of repression and isolation.

The new freedom of religion

Two laws were passed in 1990 and 1991 concerning religious freedom. The 1990 Law on the Freedom of Religion and Conscience in its preamble expressly rejects the Marxist view of the role of religion by stating that the religions in Hungary are 'outstanding factors in upholding values and promoting community in society. Apart from their activity in religious life, they work in the fields of culture, education, nurture, social welfare and health.' As a consequence, Hungary protects by law and promotes the operation of religion. The law also states that religious organisations can be involved in any activities which are not exclusively a state duty, and it lists the spheres where such activity is especially desirable, including religious activities in prisons and hospitals. In 1993 the Constitutional Court held that state neutrality towards religion did not require it to be indifferent towards religion.

Religions are now able to re-establish federations and organisations (the operation of religious orders was regulated in 1989). Under the new law, a religious group needs only 100 declared adherents to be eligible to register with the county courts as a religion and share the funds set aside for the religious groups. The 1990 Act also states that no organisation can be established to supervise religious groups, thus guaranteeing the autonomy of religious institutions. The Act makes it a criminal offence to violate freedom of conscience or religion by force or threats, punishable by up to three years' imprisonment.

Property compensation

Despite the fundamental changes since 1989, the consequences of the restrictions on religious freedom under communism have not yet disappeared. During the socialist period, the Christian churches lost their economic basis, assets and schools. Although it states that legal violations in the past have to be remedied, the 1991 Law on the Settlement of the Ownership of Church Assets primarily addresses functionality, to ensure the material conditions needed for the now unrestricted churches to carry out their multifarious activities. Because of the use to which much property had been put in the previous forty years, its immediate return could create social tensions. The Catholic Church used to own 2 million hectares but return of large landed property is impracticable. The 1991 Law now provides that buildings that belonged to the churches must be returned to their former owners within ten years or, if not given back, resources have to be ensured from which buildings of an equal value can be created or other property of equal value handed over.

The committee established to coordinate church–state relationships in the Ministry of Culture and Education was to settle the issue of church property expeditiously. The return of church property is a massive and complex process. While in 1948, 60 per cent of the elementary schools were owned by churches, the proportion today is 2 per cent. Even though the former Christian–national conservative government (1990–94) put an emphasis on the return of church property, by 1993 only a few properties and other assets had been handed back. The main reason for this is said to be the state's budget deficit.

The Jewish community has received some compensation for the loss of property seized in the 1940s through legislation passed in 1992. Jewish groups have urged the state to pay the estimated amounts into a Jewish reconstruction fund for building hospitals, public centres and schools.

Recent religious developments

Since 1989, the newer religious groups have developed rapidly; this has caused some tension with the traditional groups. Antagonisms have arisen in part out of resentment towards those who claim to be spreading Christianity as if it had not been present in Hungary for centuries. On the other hand, the stagnation of religion under communism meant that traditional churches did not experience the internal changes resulting from developments post-Vatican II and in Western Protestantism. Consequently, the newer groups found ready audiences. Parliament has also considered allegations by a pastor of the Transylvanian Community of Reconciliation that the Unification Church, the Church of Scientology, Krishna Consciousness and the Jehovah's Witnesses were 'destructive' organisations because they allegedly break up families and 'Americanise' Hungarian society.

One of the conflicts between older and newer religious groups has concerned state support. All the historical churches are ensured state support – without which they would be unable to survive and function – even if they have to apply to parliament annually for it, a humiliating process in their view. In 1993, Parliament debated whether every religion deserved state support – fifty-four have so far registered – and as a result, funding applications by three religious minorities (the Unification Church, the Church of Scientology and the Jehovah's Witnesses) were denied. State funding was given to thirty-two groups while the remainder did not seek it.

It was proposed to modify the 1990 law to include criteria on the basis of which an institution can be considered and registered as a church. Members of traditional churches wished the law to require a membership of 10,000 supporters and only allow registration of groups established before 1991. The opposition parties did not agree with the withdrawal of the state subsidy. They said lists of members constituted an invasion of privacy and it was discriminatory not to allow newer groups to operate. It would also make the traditional churches too dependent on a secular government in order to survive in an unfamiliar pluralist environment. Thus there are currently no limitations on the opportunity of religious groups to operate freely, including the dissemination of ideas and missionary work. Jehovah's Witnesses, for instance, a group which was registered in Hungary in 1947, are free to construct their churches.

Education

Parents are free to decide whether their children should receive religious education or not. In contrast with the previous period when religious parents were at a disadvantage and when it was difficult to get into universities of social sciences from certain church schools, today there are no such limitations. Children whose parents want them to receive religious education may receive it in state schools but out of school hours; it is state-funded. Most denominational schools are Catholic. There are also eighty Reformed schools and a newly established Reformed university.

In two Constitutional Court decisions in 1993–94, the Court ruled that the state is not obliged to and, indeed, may not itself establish or maintain confessional schools; however, it must make it legally possible for such schools to exist.

Compulsory religious education was the subject of a long debate in parliament in 1990. Representatives of the ruling coalition were of the opinion that, as religious freedom had been severely restricted in the previous forty years, it would be necessary to introduce compulsory religious education in the elementary and secondary schools. While the opposition parties agreed that the restoration of balance was necessary and there was indeed a moral crisis, they argued that it would not be appropriate to introduce compulsory religious education because that would contravene the right to freedom of conscience as well as international human rights norms. Eventually most parliament-arians voted against the proposal. More than three-quarters of the parents surveyed in 1990–91 were against the introduction of compulsory religious education. The govern-ment has since been formulating an obligatory moral education programme which will not have an explicit link to Christianity; the inclusion of information about the teaching and history of religion is also under consideration.

The media

All faiths are free to disseminate their views. Every Sunday morning, a religious service is broadcast. Secular Hungarians think that the churches' share of programming is too large, while religious representatives find the time allocated to them too little. They claim that the electronic media are anti-clerical and under a strong liberal and former communist influence. Some television programmes made by the Hungarian branch of the International Association of Religious Freedom have been screened.

Conflict may also develop between the churches about media share. During the visit by the Pope to Hungary in summer 1990, representatives of the Protestant churches claimed that too much weight was given to the details of the visit in the electronic media which made it appear as if Hungary was a Catholic country, the country of Mary, whereas in reality a significant proportion of the people are not Catholics.

Inter-faith relations

Ecumenical movements have been developing, especially in humanitarian fields where there is some cooperation between the churches, and inter-faith services are held regularly. None the less, ecumenical development, which started with Catholic–Protestant cooperation in the 1980s, is still in its infancy. The Hungarian Ecumenical Council brings together all the churches except the largest, the Catholic Church. Catholics, however, regularly take part in inter-church services. Reconciliation is also a daunting task when memories of colluding or compromising with the socialist state are still fresh. Many prefer to give priority to rebuilding and renewing their church's spiritual life; there is a serious shortage of religious leaders, teachers and workers. There are two Christian–Jewish dialogue organisations.

Conscientious objection

Conscientious objection to compulsory military service was formerly a criminal offence. Since 1991, a new law has allowed young men not to take part in armed service on the basis of conscience but to perform unarmed service in the army or work in social institutions instead, although for a longer period of time.

IRELAND

Ireland	
GDP (US$bn)	43
Population	3,500,000
Annual population growth (%)	0.7
Urban population (%)	57
Working population (%)	38[a]
Literacy (%)	99
Ratifications	1; 2, 2(a), 2(b); 4; E

Ireland is a democratic republic of 3.5 million people governed by a directly elected, although largely titular, president and a two-chamber parliament under a constitution adopted by referendum in 1937. There is a lively political culture, with a high turn-out at elections and a sophisticated electorate accustomed to a complex voting system.

What makes Ireland unusual in Europe is not only its religious homogeneity – nearly 92 per cent are Roman Catholics – but the high proportion of its people who practise their faith; 80 per cent weekly attend church. Religious allegiance has been a pervasive force in modern Irish society. The traditional nationalist allegiance and identity of almost all its people were built to a considerable extent around the Catholic Church, owing to alienation from the pre-1922 British state. Many people still equate being Catholic with being Irish, and being a member of the Protestant minority with being British.

This historical background continues to exert a dominant influence on Irish society's organisation and ethos. The conflict in the other part of the island of Ireland, the United Kingdom province of Northern Ireland, between a Protestant majority, most of whom want to stay part of the UK, and a Catholic minority, most of whom want a united Ireland, is a constant destabilising factor in the public affairs of the Republic. At the same time, important sectors of civil society in the Republic continue to be controlled by the Catholic Church; most schools and many hospitals – although 85–100 per cent funded by the state – are controlled by Catholic boards of management.

Equally, the Catholic underpinnings of Ireland's nationhood have had a huge impact on its attitudes towards freedom of thought, religion and belief, affecting ideas about the role of that church in public life, the importance of the family *vis-à-vis* both the state and the individual, the particular role of women as mothers and wives, and the desirability of limiting expressions of sexuality and censoring books and films. For most of the seventy-year existence of the independent state, Irish official thinking on most of these sensitive areas has been greatly influenced by the late nineteenth- and early twentieth-century teaching of the Roman Catholic Church, although in recent years this influence has started to decline dramatically.

In Ireland the struggle for freedom of thought and conscience over the past seventy years has been a struggle of small numbers of individuals – writers, intellectuals, some minority religious groups – against a monolithic Catholic Church whose edicts were until fairly recently not contradicted by a compliant state. Over the past thirty years a number of factors have combined to weaken this dominance. the new government policies of attracting foreign investment as a means towards faster economic growth in the 1960s, which did much to weaken international isolation; the advent of television, bringing with it the demand for a more modern Western lifestyle, with more liberal attitudes to personal freedom and sexual morality; the equivalent liberalising effect of the Second Vatican Council within the Catholic Church; and, in 1973, entry to the European Community, an opportunity to open up internationally which the Irish seized enthusiastically, and which moved them culturally into the more pluralist and secular mainstream of the Western world.

The Irish constitution

Ireland's 1937 constitution was one of the most liberal constitutions of its day; its guarantees of civil and political freedoms were inspired by the United States constitution. In turn, its inclusion of communitarian values, especially the state's duty to promote economic and social rights, inspired other post-war constitutions, including that of India. However, the constitution's preamble is theocratic, acknowledging the Irish people's 'obligations to our Divine Lord Jesus Christ' and several of its articles in effect legislate Catholic social teaching.

Article 41 begins by declaring that the state 'recognises the Family as the natural primary and fundamental unit group of Society, and as a moral institution possessing inalienable and imprescriptible rights, antecedent and superior to all positive law'. While this text presaged the formulation of the nature of the family in the Declaration of Human Rights, it went on to prohibit divorce. This ban lasted until 1995 when it was removed, by a wafer-thin majority, in a referendum. In 1995 the Constitutional Court also was to rule that the references in the constitution to natural law had no judicial meaning.

Article 44 guarantees freedom of conscience and religion, and the free practice of religion subject to public order and morality; that the state shall not endow any religion; that the state shall not discriminate on the grounds of religious profession, belief or status; that state aid for schools shall not discriminate between schools under the management of different religious denominations, nor affect the right of any child to attend a school receiving public money without attending religious instruction there; and that each religious denomination shall have the right to manage its own affairs, own and acquire property, and maintain institutions for religious and charitable purposes.

Under this article, the state also acknowledges that 'the homage of public worship is due to Almighty God. It shall hold his Name in reverence, and shall respect and honour religion.' The clause recognising 'the special position' of the Roman Catholic Church as 'the guardian of the Faith professed by the great majority of the citizens' was in 1972 deleted by a large majority of the electorate in a referendum, with the support of the Catholic Church itself. The following clause, giving state recognition to four named

Protestant denominations, the Jewish faith, and other unnamed religious denominations, was deleted with it.

The partition of Ireland had encouraged the confessional ethos of the Republic because the Catholic elements in Ireland's constitution were an expression of the democratic will of the overwhelmingly Catholic electorate in the formative decades of the independent nation which emerged out of a guerrilla war with the British colonial power. Political parties could not oppose the views of the Catholic hierarchy without alienating the electorate.

Church influence on social legislation

The legislature has in the past shown considerable deference to the Catholic hierarchy views on social and family policy. Ireland was unique, for example, in having no provision for legal adoption until 1952 because of Catholic Church opposition. In 1974 the High Court held that the legislative requirement that both adoptive parents be the same religion as the child's parents or natural mother was in breach of the constitution because it discriminated against a 'mixed' (i.e. Catholic–Protestant) married couple who sought to adopt a child. The new Adoption Act now permits adoption irrespective of the adoptive parents' religion, provided that their beliefs are known to the child's natural mother. However, adoption remains difficult for 'mixed' couples and for atheist or agnostic couples, since most adoption agencies are church-based.

Similarly a 1935 law totally banning the sale or import of contraceptives lasted until 1979 when it was amended to allow their sale by medical prescription, following a Supreme Court ruling that the 1935 Act was unconstitutional (the McGee decision). By this time, with a more conciliatory approach post-Second Vatican Council, change in the law was opposed but the Catholic Church did not insist that the civil law should reflect Catholic social teaching. A number of years went past before a government felt able to introduce – and pass in 1985 – a law allowing the widespread sale of contraceptives.

Until its relaxation in the late 1960s, heavy-handed censorship of publications legislation, strongly influenced by Catholic moral teaching and policed by its priests and lay activist organisations, succeeded in banning a wide range of literature, including educational literature on birth control. Such censorship is rare now: the ban on the last novel from a serious Irish writer was lifted in 1988. However as recently as 1992 copies of the British *Guardian* newspaper were seized by customs officials who believed it contained an advertisement for an abortion clinic. Later that year a new clause was inserted into the constitution guaranteeing freedom of information about services lawfully available elsewhere in the European Union.

Towards the end of the 1970s, Catholic conservatives expressed concern at the increasing liberalisation of Irish society. The powers of judicial review of legislation particularly worried them because they sanctioned radical change in the law which could not have been brought about by the legislature because of its fear of Catholic reaction. Following Pope John Paul II's triumphant visit to Ireland in 1979, conservative Catholic lobby groups pressured the two largest political parties to hold a referendum – passed in 1983 – on incorporating into the constitution a clause protecting the life of the foetus. In 1986 the electorate, by almost two-thirds, declined to remove the prohibition on divorce from the constitution.

On the surface, the results of both the 1983 abortion referendum and the 1986 divorce referendum appeared to indicate that most people in the Republic, despite paying lip-service to the national aim of eventual unification with the Protestant majority in

Northern Ireland, had adopted a conservative stance and had ignored, for example, the wishes of the Protestant churches in the Republic, who were both strongly opposed to the 1983 amendment and in favour of limited civil divorce. However, only a minority had in fact come out to the polls to support the Catholic Church's doctrine on abortion and divorce, despite the immense pressure put on people from pulpits to vote according to Catholic doctrine.

The granting of the vote to 18 year olds in 1972 – Ireland is Western Europe's most youthful society – only added to the numbers who no longer listened to the once-powerful majority church when it came to taking decisions on sexual, social and political matters. Only four years after the 1986 divorce referendum, young and women voters, in particular, came together to elect as President Mary Robinson, a feminist and liberal constitutional lawyer who had been one of the earliest advocates of women's rights, the liberalisation of the contraception laws and the introduction of divorce.

The ban on divorce was again put to a referendum in 1995. Since the 1986 referendum, successive governments had brought in a considerable body of legislation to deal with marriage breakdown, separation and division of property. The 1995 campaign was emotive and often bitter. An alliance of conservative Catholic lay groups used evidence from Britain and the United States to claim that divorce led to the undermining of families, and thus society, and to argue that the spouse and children of first marriages were effectively abandoned. As in 1986 it was these arguments, rather than the moral arguments of the Catholic Church, which were at the centre of the campaign. However, this time the electorate voted very narrowly to amend Article 41 of the constitution in order to allow 'no fault' divorce for married couples who had been living apart for at least four years.

Another change which Irish governments would have hardly dared to contemplate even a few years ago was the legalisation of homosexuality. With little public debate or controversy, legislation was introduced in June 1993 decriminalising sexual activity between consenting adults over the age of 17.

In a 1995 judgment, the Irish Supreme Court was faced for the first time with a claim that the constitutional invocation of natural law placed a limit not only on the legislature but on the people's competence in a referendum to approve a rule that the competent Roman Catholic experts claimed was contrary to natural law. In one devastating sentence this argument was dismissed by the Court: 'The Court does not accept this argument.' The Court thereby rejected the argument that natural law was superior to the constitution and the corollary argument that the power laid down in the constitution of the Irish people to amend the constitution was limited in any way, except by reference to the relevant procedures for consulting the electorate under the constitution.

Religious minorities

The Protestant religious minorities in Ireland in the past seventy years have occupied a relatively privileged economic and class position; successive governments have been careful to guarantee their control over their own schools and hospitals. Little discrimination against individual Protestants has been reported. Until recently Protestants formed the only significant minority in the state; their numbers have declined steadily to around 3 per cent of the population, affected disproportionately by emigration and until recently by cross-community marriages. Recent research suggests that Protestants chose emigration less because of religious factors than because their British–Irish political identity was eclipsed by the policies pursued by the new Irish state of dismantling links between Britain and Ireland.

Until the early 1970s the Catholic Church required a written pledge from the Catholic partner that the children of a cross-community marriage would be brought up and educated as Catholics. In the past two decades this has been replaced by a verbal promise, often ignored, but the Protestant churches still view such a promise as damaging and discriminatory.

The state has been scrupulous in upholding the right of the Protestant community to its own schools. The Department of Education provides funds for scholarships and transport costs. Dublin's two Jewish schools are similarly supported, and when the Muslim community in the Irish capital became large enough to warrant its own primary school, it received the same state assistance as all other denominational schools. Overt anti-Semitism has been rare in modern Ireland, partly due to the very small size of the Jewish community. Leaders of the small but growing Muslim community also speak warmly of their good relations with the Irish state and public, emphasising their preference for the respect paid to religion in Ireland compared to the secular atmosphere of a country like Great Britain. In a 1972 Supreme Court judgment, Ireland's distinguished reforming judge, Brian Walsh, made clear that the constitutional recognition that worship was due to God did 'not confine the benefit of that acknowledgment to members of the Christian faith'.

Education

Ireland's denominational system was inherited from the British who had tried and failed to introduce a universal non-denominational primary school system in the 1830s; it was maintained and strengthened by the new Irish state. The voting majority on primary and secondary schools' management boards has continued to be appointed by the appropriate Catholic bishop, religious order or minority religion body.

Almost all primary schools in the Republic of Ireland are denominational and most under the patronage of the local Catholic bishop (there is a Jewish primary school). Over 60 per cent of secondary schools are run by Catholic religious orders, with the rest multi-denominational in theory, but usually Catholic in practice. Allegations of discrimination have come from a small but growing number of parents who wish their children to have a more pluralist or secular form of religious and moral instruction. Humanist parents have had to have children baptised to ensure their enrolment in local schools, and there has been pressure on parents not to absent their children from religious instruction classes owing to lack of teachers to supervise them.

Until the early 1960s secular and religious instruction were largely separate. Parents, however, exercised their constitutional right to withdraw their children from the latter very infrequently. However, in 1971, the Department of Education, in line with the then current thinking on child-centred rather than subject-centred courses, integrated the primary school curriculum so that religious and secular instruction were interwoven throughout every class and subject, so that 'a religious spirit should inform and vivify the whole work of the school', according to the primary school rule book. The Department has only recently acknowledged that this is discriminatory; its removal was foreshadowed in government proposals in 1992.

Another complaint by atheist, agnostic and humanist parents is that because the control of teacher training is in the hands of the Catholic Church, apart from one small Protestant college, only practising Catholics are employed as teachers in the great majority of the state's schools. In 1988 a teacher who was living with and had a child by a married man in a small town in County Wexford in the south of the country was dismissed from her teaching post because her conduct was a 'rejection' of the school's Catholic norms of behaviour. The High Court ruled that she had not been unfairly dismissed.

In the early 1970s parents in the suburbs of the capital, Dublin, worked for the establishment of a number of multi-denominational primary schools. At first they faced resistance from both the Catholic and the main Protestant churches and received little assistance from the state, but now there are thirteen such schools – compared with over 3,200 denominational schools – which are funded by the state on the same basis. In January 1996, the High Court ruled that state funding of Catholic chaplains in some state-run secondary schools was constitutional.

The real test of whether profound structural reforms affecting church interests in education can take place in contemporary Ireland will come in the next few years. A government plan for education foresees at least some of the control of both primary and secondary schools being taken away from the churches and vested in democratically accountable regional education authorities. It also proposes to separate the teaching of religion from other subjects at primary level. Both these changes have provoked the alarm of the Catholic Church, and it has joined with the main Protestant Church to resist any attempts to dilute church control over the management of schools. Conscious of Protestant sensibilities in Northern Ireland, the government may not want to lay itself open to the charge of forcing change through against the wishes of the Protestant churches.

Health and welfare services

The secularist group, the Campaign to Separate Church and State, has expressed concerns about the provision of health and welfare services. When the Irish state took over the health system from the British, it turned to the Catholic Church – particularly orders of nuns – to run large parts of the services, as the church had already been doing this in its own hospitals since the previous century. The result was effectively a Catholic takeover.

Few complain about the quality of Ireland's Catholic-run health services, particularly the nursing care they offer, or about the Catholic Church's taking on of welfare services for the poorest and most marginalised sections of society ignored by state and secular society alike. It is unheard of for anyone to be turned away from any of these institutions on the grounds of religious affiliation. But some point to the anomaly of 100 per cent state funding for hospitals and other institutions which supply health services in accordance with Catholic medical ethics, ethics which all staff (including trainee doctors and nurses) must agree to abide by. Thus, in the past, powerful ethics committees ensured that in both Catholic and state hospitals no female sterilisations were carried out. This has changed radically in recent years, with around half the country's hospitals now offering such procedures; individual consultant views now decide the issue. The forms of contraception offered in state-run family planning clinics are often limited, with Catholic-approved 'natural' methods being those most often advocated.

The 'x' case and abortion

In February 1992 came an extraordinary legal case whose impact on the country's legal, political and moral attitudes will continue to be felt for a long time to come. The Attorney General went to the High Court and was granted an injunction, using the clause inserted into the constitution nine years earlier to protect the foetus, to prevent a 14-year-old girl from having an abortion in England. The Supreme Court overturned the decision, ruling that a correct interpretation of that clause meant that abortion – and the right to travel abroad to have an abortion – would be legal if there was a substantial and grave risk to the life of the mother. In the case of the 14 year old, the court had heard that she was suicidal.

A lengthy political, constitutional and moral crisis followed, as the government and public tried to come to terms with the fact that in Ireland abortion was now lawful in certain limited cases. A series of referendums the following November further confused the issue. Even the Catholic bishops were confused, announcing that Catholics could vote either 'Yes' or 'No' in the referendums in good conscience, provided that their vote was meant to express their abhorrence of abortion.

Priestly celibacy, sexual scandals and abuse

Among the key developments encapsulating the change of atmosphere must be numbered the sensational resignation of a leading Irish bishop, Eamonn Casey, in May 1992 together with the revelation that he was the father of an 18-year-old son in the United States. But even more damaging to the authority of the Catholic Church as the main source of moral leadership for most Irish people was the extraordinary rash of clerical child sex abuse scandals which erupted from the middle of 1994 onwards. These started with the case of a religious order priest who was convicted in Northern Ireland on dozens of charges of sexually abusing children in his care over nearly forty years. When it became known that the Republic's chief law officer had failed to act on an extradition warrant for this man, the resulting public outrage and series of political rows led to the resignation of the Republic's prime minister and the collapse of his government.

In the following year, there were several more court cases and newspaper exposés involving priests abusing children. For a people which had placed such a near-absolute trust in its priests, this had a shattering effect on the Catholic Church's traditional moral authority. Bishops came under increasing public attack for their perceived attempts to 'cover up' the crimes of some priests, and the morale of priests, long used to being the almost unquestioned leaders of the community, particularly in rural areas, slumped. Opinion poll evidence indicated that weekly mass attendance had fallen by up to 20 per cent, largely as a result of the scandals. The Catholic hierarchy's spokesman admitted it was the worst crisis experienced by the church this century.

Impact of change on religions and beliefs

The new liberal atmosphere has had a direct effect on the freedom to practise religion in the Republic of Ireland. The 1991 census showed a striking 400 per cent rise over the previous decade in the number of people stating that they were followers of 'other religions', even though the total was only 1.3 per cent of the whole. This figure is largely accounted for by increases in those who have joined evangelical Protestant churches and groups, new religious movements and groups following Eastern religions, as well as by an increase in the Muslim population. Evangelical Christians convey the impression that there is a new freedom to preach and even to proselytise that would have been unthinkable even twenty years ago, when there was deep suspicion, and even hostility, to any kind of non-Catholic religious group seeking members, particularly in rural areas. Similarly, humanists and secularists have been able to organise and lobby freely.

This climate of increasing tolerance has been helped by a significant increase in ecumenical contact between the Catholic and main Protestant churches at leadership level. In the mid-1970s, reacting to the deepening divisions caused by the conflict in

Northern Ireland, the heads of the Catholic, Anglican, Presbyterian and Methodist churches – all-Ireland bodies – started meeting formally and regularly to discuss practical and theological difficulties, a procedure which they claim is unique in the Christian world. The personal relationship between the current Catholic Primate and his counterpart as Primate of the Anglican Church of Ireland, the largest Protestant denomination, is particularly close. In the early 1970s an Irish School of Ecumenics was opened in Dublin, with a Jesuit and a Presbyterian as its first two directors. Although at first the church leaderships gave it only their begrudging imprimatur, it is now seen as a model of its type.

Ecumenical initiatives at grass-roots level have proved more problematic, partly because of the scarcity of Protestants in the Republic, but also because many leading Catholics and Anglicans see the country's religious divisions as a purely Northern Ireland problem. Although in general personal relationships between Catholics and Protestants have improved greatly in recent decades, there are still deep divisions over theology and Christian practice. Few Catholics have ever been at a Protestant church service, for example, and the Church of Ireland's enthusiastic espousal of women priests – three years before the Church of England – is seen by the Catholic hierarchy as having put another obstacle in the way of moves towards Christian unity.

Despite overall high levels of religious commitment, it is generally accepted that among the urban young, and among deprived working-class communities, religious adherence has slumped in recent years, with fewer than 10 per cent of people in more marginalised areas of Dublin and Cork now attending church on a weekly basis. Large sections of Irish society are culturally Catholic but becoming religiously indifferent. It is a challenge that the Irish Catholic Church, with a conservative hierarchy which has been accustomed for the past 150 years to being accepted as the unquestioned religious leaders of the broad mass of the people, is singularly ill-equipped to confront.

The Catholic Bishop's Commission for the Laity, in a report published in late 1995, has called for a new model of the church to stem its decline. They concluded that people's experience was that the Irish church was perceived as a 'clerical church, male and hierarchical'. The Catholic Church, it said, had taken the faith of the nation for granted and the Commission called for a church which 'honours holism, inclusiveness and democracy', as well as 'the giftedness of women and their unique contribution'.

NORWAY

Norway	
GDP (US$bn)	113
Population	4,300,000
Annual population growth (%)	0.6
Urban population (%)	73
Working population (%)	50[a]
Literacy (%)	99
Ratifications	1; 2, 2(a), 2(b); 3; 4; E

Christianity is part of Norway's national tradition; the nation's flag is designed as a cross and Norway is considered a Christian country. Norway has a state church and yet it has freedom of religion and belief. Christianity came later to Norway than to many other parts of Europe; its 1,000th anniversary was celebrated in 1995. Although the change from the old Viking religion was gradual, it was finally forced on most of the population by militant Christian kings such as Saint Olav, who has an altar in the Vatican in Rome. In the Reformation, Norway changed to Protestant Lutheran Christianity – in spite of some resistance from the clergy – by the decree of King Kristian III in 1537. Since then Norway has remained Lutheran.

Norway is a homogeneous society in ethnic and religious terms. The only real exception until recently was the small indigenous Sami population. Even with immigration, the foreign-born population still numbers less than 5 per cent of the total population of 4.3 million (1991).

Political structure

Norway's monarchy in modern times dates back to the constitution of 1814. Today the king has only a symbolic role in politics but is a sign of the nation's unity in a time of crisis, such as during the Second World War when the king was the central symbol of resistance against Nazi occupation. The king is still the formal head both of the state and the Church of Norway, but this formality no longer has legal significance.

Norway today is a parliamentary democracy based on a multi-party system. The constitution was amended in 1994 to give greater effect in national law to the country's numerous international human rights commitments. The welfare state is broadly accepted as the common framework for the nation. It is lawful in Norway to establish political parties on a religious basis. The Christian Democratic Party, since 1936, is the only such party; it aims to promote Christian ethics and values in the political arena. It attracted 6–8 per cent of the voters in recent elections, as it has for many years, and has taken part in the coalition government's alternative to the Labour Party governments.

The long Christian tradition in Norway's homogeneous culture has made it not only desirable but almost necessary for the main parties to pay tribute to Christian norms and ideals when they formulate programmes according to their differing ideological bases.

In international policy, Norway has been an advocate for a strong United Nations. It has seen its role as a bridge-builder between north and south, east and west. The Nobel Peace Prize and its achievements as facilitator for important negotiations in regional conflicts are part of this role. Norway is one of the few countries to meet the UN goal of giving 1 per cent of GDP to development aid.

Religion and state

The relation between state and religion and religious freedom is set out in Article 2 of the constitution: 'All inhabitants of the state have freedom to practise their religion' and 'The Evangelical Lutheran religion remains the official religion of the state. Those inhabitants who confess this religion are obliged to educate their children in it.' Article 2 thus contains both the freedom of religion for the inhabitants and the proclamation of an official religion for the state. While this might be seen as a contradiction, the official point of view in Norwegian politics and legislation is that this is both desirable and possible. There is no explicit constitutional prohibition of discrimination on grounds of religion or belief but it is commonly viewed as implicit in the first sentence of the article.

Norway has a state church which in a formal sense and in practice is ruled to a degree by the government. The cabinet has the right to appoint its bishops. However, the right to appoint other clergy has recently been transferred from the state to the diocesan councils of the church. While this transfer reflects a general trend towards more self-government for the Lutheran Church, there is not at present a strong drive either on the political level or within the church to separate state from church. The church also does not wish to exploit its position as the dominant religious institution in society. This attitude is strongly rooted in Lutheran theology. Luther developed his doctrine of the distinction between 'the two kingdoms' – the spiritual and the secular – in opposition to a theocratic model where the church also claims authority to rule the state.

It is accepted that the state has legitimate authority in political affairs except in a situation where the state demonstrates systematic and massive violations of human rights. Such an exceptional situation occurred in Norway during the Nazi occupation when all the bishops and almost all the clergy together resigned from their positions in the state church and established a temporary 'free church'; they were all imprisoned. When the war was over, the state church was re-established.

Article 4 of the constitution provides that the king must confess and protect the Evangelical Lutheran religion. Article 12 requires that more than half of the cabinet belong to the official religion of the state. Ministers who do not confess the official religion cannot participate in decisions about the state church. There is a joint ministry for church, education and research; the minister must belong to the state church, so that a Roman Catholic cannot become minister for this department. The obligation to confess the official religion is, however, in practice limited to the requirement of formal membership of the church.

This constitutional heritage raises the question of the rights of persons not belonging to the state church – within a minority faith or without any religious affiliation – and also the question of religious freedom within a church which is to some degree controlled by the state.

Other religious faiths and humanist organisations, whether they are formally registered or not, receive by law the same economic support per capita from the government as does the state church. Only established organisations of a religious or humanist nature are eligible for this support.

Religious composition

Almost 90 per cent of the population in Norway are members of the Evangelical Lutheran state church, a decline over the last thirty years from more than 95 per cent. Other faiths are principally Christian denominations such as Pentecostals, Roman Catholics, Evangelical Lutheran Free Church, Methodists, Baptists and others. The Christian denominations have been ecumenically united since 1993 in a common council; the Roman Catholics joined but the Pentecostals decided to stay out.

The Sami population who for a long time had their own indigenous religion – like the Vikings – are today Christians through conversion in earlier times. The original Sami religion and culture were considered 'pagan' by the clergy in medieval times and, indeed, into this century. However, in recent years there has been growing understanding of the injustice towards the Sami people and measures have been taken to recognise their rights as an indigenous people through policy and legislation. Some claims over natural resources are linked to indigenous religious beliefs.

The fastest growing religious confession in Norway over the last twenty-five years is made up of various types of Islam; there are now twenty-five mosques in Oslo. The Muslim community has grown from 1,000 in 1970 to 40,000 in 1995. This is larger than the

Roman Catholic Church (32,500), which also has grown considerably in the same period owing to immigration mainly by refugees and asylum seekers. In comparison, Pentecostals number about 44,000 members, the largest religious group outside the state church. There are about 1,000 Jews, 1,300 Sikhs and 1,650 Hindus. Jehovah's Witnesses number about 15,300.

About 6 per cent of the population are not members of any religious community. Among these are about 60,000 members of a humanist association (Human-Etisk Forbund). This organisation offers alternative rituals for baptism, confirmation, weddings and burials to people not wanting a religious ceremony. Internationally it is considered the strongest national humanist organisation, though it only accounts for 1.4 per cent of Norway's population.

Most members of the state church are not active adherents, except for the rituals of birth, confirmation, weddings and burials. Some 3 per cent on average attend church on Sunday. Christmas and Easter services attract a high attendance and a relatively high percentage tune into religious programmes on radio and television. While the term 'secularised' has often been used to describe the religious situation in Scandinavian countries, this stereotype takes no account of empirical evidence which shows that almost 80 per cent of Norwegians believe in a god or a divine power and more than 50 per cent believe in God. However, members of the minority Christian churches and Muslims are significantly more regular participants in their faiths.

Church and community

The Lutheran Church in Norway has a distinctive expression of commitment through a number of active church organisations. First, few countries have sent so many missionaries to the world outside Western Europe as Norway, relative to the population. While some of these organisations are conservative and emphasise spiritual mission, an organisation such as Norwegian Church Aid mostly concentrates on work directed towards famine and health care in the developing world. The various missionary organisations have brought information to Norway about the religious and cultural diversity of other parts of the world and have opened the Lutheran Church to influences from other Christian churches in music, liturgy and ethical thinking. Thus liberation theology from churches in Latin America and Southern Africa has influenced Norwegian theology and missiology.

Although some have seen missionary work as an expression of cultural imperialism, generally there is a positive attitude towards the missionary organisations. The common view in the organisations themselves is that missionary work both in the spiritual sense and as development aid in health and education is not only legitimate but a Christian obligation.

Second, organisations for internal missionary work strengthen the spiritual life and fight against secularisation in Norwegian society. These are active in education, the media, cultural life and the church.

Third, there are organisations working in the general social field like health care, social work and education. These organisations run institutions which either supplement the welfare state or do work on behalf of the state with total public funding.

Inter-faith relations

There is peaceful co-existence among Norway's religious communities and few examples of conflicts although some minority religions occasionally complain that the state church is somewhat privileged. The Christian churches have been in the forefront of combating racism and religious intolerance from the far Right. The Bishop of Oslo was central in a big demonstration where thousands of Norwegians literally turned their backs on an outdoor meeting of nationalistic racists in Oslo, as a silent, peaceful protest clearly indicating massive popular rejection of such tendencies. The most striking example of this attitude was the fact that almost 700 asylum seekers – most of whom were Muslims – were given sanctuary in Norwegian churches in 1993 to protect them from being expelled from the country by the state authorities.

Education and the family

Parents have a legal right to educate their children in their own belief with due consideration taken for the best interest of the child. Children have the right to decide in religious matters and choose their own education from the age of 15. The subject of religious education has been much discussed recently in Norway.

In the public schools for children in the first nine grades (ages 7–16), the teaching of religion is obligatory and based on the Evangelical Lutheran confession. Factual and objective teaching about other religions must also be given. A proposal to make the teaching non-confessional was rejected by a majority in parliament in March 1995 who argued that a knowledge of Christianity is necessary to understand Norwegian society and its cultural heritage. A minority pointed out that Norway is the only Nordic country with confessional teaching of religion in its public schools; neutral teaching of culture, values and beliefs would be more appropriate.

Pupils whose parents do not belong to the state church are exempt if they so wish. They have the right to free time for religious education in their respective denominations, as guaranteed by the Education Act 1969.

In a recent court case in Hardanger, the parents of a 15-year-old boy in the ninth grade of public school sued the state for his right to be exempt from the teaching of Christianity. At the age of 15 he had resigned his membership in the state church and wanted to attend the teaching of the alternative belief subject at his school, a choice with which his parents (both members of the state church) had agreed. But the school authorities acting on instruction from the Minister of Education had refused. The court in March 1995 concluded that the boy at the age of 15 had full self-determination in matters of religion and education. The court referred both to national legislation and to international human rights standards.

For the past twenty-five years, it has also been possible for students to opt to take a general belief subject with an emphasis on ethics and general knowledge of religion and humanistic beliefs. In practice, this option is chosen almost exclusively by children of the organised humanists and other people with no religious affiliation. The general belief subject, however, will be deleted from 1997 from the school curriculum because of a decision in Parliament at the end of 1995.

In May 1995 a committee appointed by the Ministry for Church, Education and Research recommended the introduction of a new, open and inclusive Christianity subject, which would in principle be common for all pupils and therefore compulsory; the optional subject would not be continued. In addition to knowledge about Christianity, the new course would contain teaching about other religions and accentuate the teaching of ethics and philosophy. Nevertheless the teaching would still have its basis in the Evangelical Lutheran confession rather than, say, Catholicism. However, the committee stressed that the subject is not the baptismal education of the state church and that the model of teaching should not be dogmatic. The committee, however, admitted that parts of the content of the course may be problematic for some pupils and their parents. Parents who are not members of the state church may get exemption for their children from specific parts only, but not from the whole course.

The new model is meant to be a viable compromise in line with the cultural situation in modern Norway, to contribute to a harmonious, well-integrated and more multi-cultural society. None the less, it has evoked strong opposition both from humanists and leaders of faiths outside Christianity. From 1997, it will be more difficult to gain exemption from the teaching of religion.

Special legislation secures the right to establish private schools based on religious or other grounds. These schools normally get public recognition and financing on the same basis as public schools. Less than 2 per cent of pupils attend private schools; of these, the majority go to schools for minority Christian churches or for Christians within the state church who are not happy with the teaching in the public schools.

In 1994 the Social Democratic government, supported by two other parties, rejected an application for public funding of a Muslim elementary school in Oslo. The Christian Democratic Party objected to this decision; however, the government cited the need to integrate the immigrant population into Norwegian society and the objection to attitudes within Muslim communities with regard to the role of women in society. Separate classes for boys and girls were mentioned and it was claimed that evidence from other countries shows that Muslim boys go to the state schools, while the Muslim schools are used almost exclusively by the girls.

The contrary argument invoked respect for religious freedom; separate classes for boys and girls are compatible with international human rights law. The government replied that Muslims are free to establish their schools without public funds but Muslim spokespersons have stated that they cannot afford to establish private schools and so there are at present no Muslim schools in Norway. Two minority Christian groups also had their application for public funding for schools rejected in 1994.

Promotion, proselytising and religion in the media

Promotion and proselytising are legal for religious and non-religious groups and denominations. Humanists, Christians and Muslims are active, as can be seen on the main street of Oslo every Saturday.

All the major media cover religious issues in many forms. Everyone has, in principle and in practice, access to the media and freedom to publish, print and distribute their own material. Religious and anti-religious material is freely published. Old legislation on blasphemy has fallen into disuse. Christian organisations have many publications which they freely disseminate. Some television stations actively propagate Christian belief although they do not draw many adherents.

Conscientious objection

Conscientious objection to compulsory military service is recognised in law both on religious grounds and for a general ethical conviction. There have been some cases of conflicts in the grey zone between religious or ethical objection and political reasons of a more temporary nature. This was particularly so during the Cold War when some objectors claimed exemption from military service because of Norway's NATO member-ship. Some claimed that this meant a risk of being commanded to take part in an unjust military action. Such objections founded on political analyses were only recognised if the objection to carry arms was permanent.

Discrimination on grounds of religion or belief

Ideals of equality and non-discrimination are strongly rooted in Norwegian culture and political life. Strong and persistent examples of discrimination on grounds of religion or belief are therefore not often seen. But some incidents of conflict have emerged from time to time.

The formal status and name of the state church, its size and dominance are to some symbolic expressions of discrimination. In public ceremonies and great national events the church draws the focus of the media while others tend to be overlooked. The official name of the state church is 'The Church of Norway' and it is seen to misrepresent the fact that other churches exist in Norway. Though some criticism is voiced from time to time, these problems are not seen as hot issues in society, not even among the minority religious communities.

Immigration, however, is a live issue in Norway where new rules and regulations have had to be adopted in order to meet a more multi-cultural situation with respect for differences of religion or belief. For example, in the military, religious minorities have the right to the same number of free days for religious purposes as have military personnel belonging to the state church; they also have a right to a special diet if needed for religious reasons. After some discussion, Sikhs may now wear turbans in the military forces.

As in other societies there are more subtle and indirect forms of discrimination which are hard to combat by legislation alone. It is clear that ethnic minorities have more difficulties in work, education and housing than other groups in Norwegian society. This is not discrimination on grounds of religion in an open and exclusive sense, but more related to indirect discrimination. The problem is integrated in a wider context of ethnic, cultural and religious differences between some groups of immigrants and the mainstream of Norwegian culture and society. Muslim immigrants seem to encounter more difficulties than others, probably because of a complex mix of factors.

Internal religious affairs

The status of women varies from group to group, both among Christian denominations and among others. Equality legislation does not apply to the internal affairs of religious communities.

The state granted the ordination of women in the state church in 1938, but only 9 per cent of the clergy are female, such has been the resistance of the male clergy. The government in 1993 appointed the first female bishop, one of very few female bishops in Lutheran churches throughout the world. However, many of the clergy hold to their theological conviction that only men may legitimately be priests. The fact that the state appointed a female bishop and also the first female priest in the state church is seen by some as a violation of the freedom of religion. The state cannot interfere with such appointments in other religious communities. There is also an intense conflict in one of the country's leading missionary organisations about the right of women to have a vote in their general assembly; up to now only the men have had this right.

The situation of homosexuals in the state church has also been the subject of intense debate. Although Norway grants homosexuals the legal right to register as couples and gives them the same social and civil rights held by heterosexual couples, the synod in

November 1995 prohibited lesbians and gay men in homosexual relationships from holding positions in the Church of Norway.

Three of the ten bishops in the church have argued for the full acceptance of homosexuals in the church. Bishop Köhn, who considered that responsible, caring and loving behaviour by homosexual people should be supported by the church, wrote to Archbishop Tutu for personal guidance on the issue, given his experience with social justice and discrimination issues in church and society. Replying to her letter, the archbishop stressed that he could not comment on the way the church had dealt with the issue, but he expressed support for 'various groups campaigning for gays and lesbians to be treated on an equal basis with all baptised persons' and further stated that, 'It is baptism which gives us our special character, and to exclude anyone from the church is to deny God's grace and our interdependence as members of the Body of Christ.'

POLAND

Poland	
GDP (US$bn)	84
Population	38,300,000
Annual population growth (%)	0.8
Urban population (%)	63
Working population (%)	49[a]
Literacy (%)	99
Ratifications	1; 2, 2(a), 2(b); 3; 4; E

In the few years after the fall of communism, Poland had become a parliamentary and multi-party democracy, the right and ability to change the government guaranteed in the constitution. Most of the new Polish political parties have their roots in the official parties of the old communist regime or in the 'Solidarnosc' movement. A few religious associations became co-founders of several Christian Democratic parties.

Although an industrial country, Poland has a significant rural population, nearly two-fifths of its 38.3 million people. The private sector is developing towards a market economy but there is still some social and economic dislocation.

In recent elections, most of Polish society expressed its disappointment with the anti-communist bloc which had been in power for more than three years. In September 1993, the Democratic Left Alliance (SDRP), a successor to the Polish Communist party (PZPR), won a comfortable majority and formed a coalition government with the Polish Peasant Party (PSL), also the successor of a party from the communist past. In 1995, Aleksander Kwasniewski, a member of SDRP, was elected president, replacing Lech Walesa who had played a vital role in the fall of communism in Poland.

Legal system

Poland still functions under the communist constitution of 1952, fashioned on the Soviet model. The political and economic system codified in what is known as the 'Little Constitution' has been transformed. The armed forces and the internal security apparatus are subject to governmental authority and under civilian control. A new constitution is in preparation.

Economic and legislative harmonisation with Western Europe and eventual membership in the European Community – fundamental goals of Poland – determine the strategy guiding reforms. An Association Agreement between Poland and the EC has been in force since February 1994; formal application to join the European Union was made in August 1994.

Protection for human rights

The Ombudsman (the Office of the Commissioner for Civil Rights Protection, established 1987) monitors human rights in Poland. In 1993, the Helsinki Committee reported that the Polish Government displays a generally positive and helpful attitude towards human rights investigations. Poland has been a member of the Council of Europe since 1990 and has subsequently ratified the European Convention on Human Rights as well as the European Social Charter.

Poland's 1952 constitution provides for the separation of church and state, for freedom of conscience and belief, and also the freedom to practise any religion. Religious groups may select and train personnel, solicit and receive contributions, publish and engage in consultations without government restraints. There are no government restrictions on establishing and maintaining places of worship. The Penal Code stipulates that offending religious sentiment is punishable by a fine or a two-year prison term.

Freedom of speech and the press is generally provided for; Poles may generally express their opinions publicly and privately. The Penal Code, however, states that anyone who 'publicly insults, ridicules, and derides the Polish Nation, Polish Republic, its political system, or its principal organs' may be imprisoned, a law which has been used by the non-communist government against its critics.

The rich jurisprudence of the Constitutional Court, the Supreme Court and other bodies emphasises the importance of human rights treaties in Polish law.

Ethnic and religious composition

Poland is a very homogeneous country ethnically with the exception of small Ukrainian, Belorussian, Slovakian, and Lithuanian minorities in the south-east and east, and a small German minority in the south-west. Teachers and language training are provided for minorities groups in schools. Members of ethnic minority parties have been elected to office; such parties are not required to win 5 per cent of the vote nationwide. This provision reinstates principles of the 1921 constitution guaranteeing minority representation.

For the Ukrainian, Russian, and Belorussian minorities, their national Orthodox churches are symbols of ethnicity and national links. However, cross-community marriages are common and the children of these marriages tend to grow up speaking only Polish and attending Roman Catholic services.

Polish society is characterised by a traditional, socially conservative form of Roman Catholicism. Of the non-Catholic denominations, the Orthodox Church has been active in Poland since the fourteenth century. Lutherans and Calvinists appeared in the sixteenth century, as well as Moravian Brethren, Mariavites, the Polish National Catholic Church and others, mostly as religious or political refugees from Western Europe. During the Second World War, members of Polish evangelical reformed churches, particularly those of German descent, became the target of repression by the Nazis; numbers are now lower than after the First World War when there were more than 900,000 Protestants. In 1994, there were eighty churches and religious groups officially registered in Poland.

Muslim and Jewish communities, officially numbering 4,000 and 1,560 respectively in 1992, have lived in Poland since medieval times. Anti-Semitism was part of the platform of Polish nationalism before the First World War and was deeply embedded in the attitudes of the general population and the social and political establishment between the wars. The sufferings under Nazi policies of Jews in the Warsaw ghetto culminated in the extermination of the Jews carried out systematically on Polish land at Auschwitz and Treblinka. Although at the time of the Second World War Polish Jews had numbered 3.5 million, very few survived. A pogrom in 1946 and anti-Semitism under the communist regime followed; it was used by the Communist Party as a tool against intellectual opposition in March 1968. Today's tiny Jewish community in Warsaw lacked even a rabbi until 1989, when one came from Israel especially to minister to a predominantly ageing population.

Since 1990, other Protestant churches and new religious movements such as the Unification Church, the Church of Scientology and the Krishna Consciousness movement have appeared.

The real power of the Polish Roman Catholic Church is embodied in national tradition, cultivated by a religious educated intelligentsia, as well as in rural life. In a primarily industrial society, the church continues to promote the ideal of a 'rural civilisation' based upon private property and the integrity of the family. Deep in the countryside, Poland's holiest shrine and focus of religious life, the Jasna Gora monastery, draws pilgrims from far and wide.

Roman Catholic institutional life had been allowed to continue under communism, such as the Catholic University of Lublin (the only non-state university in the former COMECON countries) and the Academy of Catholic Theology in Warsaw, which also trained Evangelical clergy. Teaching of religion to children and adults was also permitted in public, through thousands of churches. There were relatively independent Catholic publishing houses, five Clubs of Catholic Intelligentsia and, between 1967 and 1976, the Centre for Documentation and Social Studies. Furthermore, there were the 'Oasis' summer camps, which had begun as a Christian family outdoors programme in the 1950s, and evolved into the 'Light and Life' movement. Over 300,000 Polish youth received spiritual formation through this movement in the 1980s, resulting in over 40 per cent of the country's vocations to the priesthood. Thus the Roman Catholic Church entered the 1990s with a nationwide network of immense social influence.

The Evangelical Reformed Church also carries out activities among children and young people, such as Sunday schools and youth camps and social work. The Methodist Church, established in Poland in 1921, has founded orphanages, boarding houses for poor students and English language schools.

Together, the Augsburg-Evangelical Church, the Evangelical Reformed Church, the Methodist Church, the Polish Church of the Baptist Christians, the Polish Autocephalous Orthodox Church, the Polish Catholic Church, and the Mariavite Old Catholic Church form the Polish Ecumenical Council, active since 1946. This Council maintains an official relationship with the Roman Catholic Church, establishing the Mixed Commission and the Subcommittee for Dialogue, which drafts constitutional proposals concerning church–state relations.

Under communism, there were thirty-three Catholic newspapers and religious publishing and distribution remains vigorous in Poland today. The Evangelical Reformed Church monthly *Jednota* (Unity), which is marked by a high standard and sensitivity to ecumenicism, reaches many readers particularly among the Catholic intelligentsia.

The Roman Catholic Church and the state

After 1945, the Polish Roman Catholic Church was seen as an institution embodying national continuity. Consequently, its hierarchy became the chief political anti-communist competitor. During the communist period, the hierarchy of the Polish Roman Catholic Church acted as negotiator between society and the communist rulers. The hierarchy presented itself as a domestic policy expert, able to offer critiques of alternative options, thus enabling it to be a participant in balancing democratic interests and authoritarian force in the state. During the 1970s, the church and the secular opposition began to work together for the defence of human rights. A turning point came in 1978, when a Polish priest became Pope John Paul II. The religious attitudes of most Polish people were affirmed by this and solidarity displayed around the Roman Catholic Church culminated in the radical movement 'Solidarnosc'.

The formal relationship between the church and the state goes back to the end of the First World War with the revival of an independent Polish state in 1918. Poland adopted some of the socio-political doctrines of the Catholic Church, particularly the encyclicals of Pope Leo XIII, which set out the obligations of a capitalist state towards workers and also endorsed state intervention in the social and economic sphere. The 1925 concordat, violated by the Holy See during the Second World War, was terminated by the new communist government in 1945. For the next fifty years the relationship between the church and the state remained basically unregulated although there were diplomatic relations with the Vatican. Between 1946 and 1950, the communist authorities took over about 180,000 hectares of land and thousands of properties from the church.

In July 1993 the government signed a new concordat with the Vatican which specified that the church and the state are 'autonomous and independent'. This concordat, which has aroused much controversy, has not yet been ratified by parliament.

Church and state interests have not coincided for significant periods of time. After 1944, the communists encouraged an exodus from the countryside to accompany the development of industry and sought to remove the traditional bases for the church's power by reorganising the peasantry around new institutions which embodied a communist ideology. Because it was against communism, the church refused to involve itself openly in the national rebuilding process and the hierarchy supported a political agenda of free elections and majority voting.

After the transition to democracy, 'Solidarnosc' and the Catholic Church quickly detached from each other. The function of negotiator between ruler and society which had been the sole province of the church for many years, became formally institutionalised in a completely secular and democratic parliamentary system and thus was taken back into society as a whole. Nevertheless, the church hierarchy continued to speak out and made use of its civil agents, such as political and social organisations, which in turn benefited from declaring themselves to be Catholic.

Within the Roman Catholic Church today, the attitudes and activities of the hierarchy contrast with those of ordinary members of the common church, that is, most Poles, who look for social justice at all levels of social life in a new Poland and now reach for their dreams even more impatiently. In June 1991, 74 per cent of people polled in a survey believed that the role of the church in political life is too great and 57 per cent suggested that the church should not participate in political life at all; 71 per cent required a strict separation of church and state. Three years later, in March 1994, in a similar survey, only 17 per cent of the population accepted the concordat of 1993 as signed.

By the early 1990s, the church's position on abortion, religious instruction in schools, and the media was largely rejected by the public. However, pro-church deputies who enjoyed a slight majority in the 1991–93 parliament, but were mostly not re-elected, were able to secure the passage of legislation conforming to church views on these subjects. Abortion, though widely practised and the subject of several trials, is now practically illegal; Catholic religious instruction has been introduced into the public schools; religious symbols have been restored in the military – there have been controversies about military ceremonies and the role of Catholic chaplains; and the term 'Christian values' has been inserted into media legislation. Change to this law was resisted by the then president, Lech Walesa.

While no general restitution legislation has been introduced, the Catholic Church has been able to reclaim its property. The church also took this opportunity to claim property of which it had been dispossessed by the Tsarist government last century.

The process of secularisation of Polish society is underway today. Thus, in a society where Catholicism is traditionally strong and where Pope John Paul II enjoys the position of a charismatic national leader, there are the first symptoms of an open confrontation between religious conservatism, represented by Catholic activists, and a still growing social demand for independence in politics.

The most serious problem, especially after 1990, has been the gap between the clergy and the laity in the Roman Catholic Church because the Polish Church cannot give any institutional patronage to social change, as the hierarchy has not felt impelled to make church doctrines and their own attitudes more directly relevant to the lives of ordinary citizens. The growth of secularity is thus accompanied by anti-clericalism.

The Polish Church hierarchy has also greeted the new wave of poverty following the downfall of communism with incomprehension. It has faced a historic choice, like the church in Latin America, to make the preferential option for the poor and denied it, despite papal urging. Religious professionals displayed their lack of interest in the physical health of Polish society, seeing it as the general task of society to continue to make financial contributions to the church. In the current crisis affecting the savings and economic future of the ordinary people, the dedication of church finances to building a massive new cathedral has been seen as particularly insensitive.

Education

The 1952 constitution and other communist regulations allowed crosses to be placed in churches and places of worship, but not in state and public institutions such as schools. During the communist period, religious instruction was held on a voluntary basis in church buildings.

In the 1990–91 school year, religion was introduced in state schools on the basis of an instruction prepared by the Joint Commission of the Government and Episcopate. Under pressure from the church hierarchy, the Minister of Education signed a controversial ordinance regulating religious education in schools, from April 1992. The ordinance introduced grades in religion on school certificates and public funding for priests who teach in schools. The Ombudsman challenged this directive before the Constitutional Tribunal as violating separation of church and state. In April 1993, the Tribunal decreed, first, that it was unlawful to demand declarations from parents or older schoolchildren that the child was not going to take part in religion classes at school or that he or she attended religion classes elsewhere; and second, that it was unlawful to give a grade in religion or 'ethics' on the official school certificate if the subject was taught outside the school, as minority beliefs were. The Tribunal ruled that the provision whereby a bishop's withdrawal of recommendation for a religion teacher could mean that a teacher would lose his or her job was unconstitutional. However, the hanging of religious symbols in classrooms was held to be lawful, as was a prayer at the beginning of classes. Debate in parliament over the future of the directive was suspended after the then president Walesa dissolved parliament in May 1993, leaving the rest of the directive in effect.

The 1993 concordat confirms the Roman Catholic Church's right to 'maintain religious instruction in schools'. The state is obliged to organise these classes. While the Ministry of Education regards them as part of religious activity and thus not to be remunerated by the state, the Ombudsman regards every position as needing to be remunerated.

The media

For thirty-five years, the mass media in Poland had been dominated by the state; no information on religious matters was provided. The Catholic and other religious press had been allowed to operate, but the state authorities limited the circulation of religious newspapers and journals. Official programmes celebrating anniversaries, state holidays, and other special occasions contained no religious element.

Since 1980, however, a Sunday service has been broadcast every week on Polish Radio's First Programme. The Roman Catholic Church currently has airtime on state-run radio and television. As a result of the 1989 'round table' negotiations, only the Roman Catholic Church is authorised to issue licences to radio and television stations which are equivalent to those by the National Broadcasting Council; it holds eighteen radio licences. The church also publishes numerous newspapers and other publications. State authorities now participate in church services and celebrations.

The law stipulates that programmes should not promote illegal activities or those contrary to Polish state policy, morality, or the common good. All broadcasts must 'respect the religious feelings of audiences and in particular respect the Christian system of values', a controversial requirement. The church and some of its supporters have dismissed the objections of the media and other critics as 'communist revenge', using the term 'communist' to condemn liberal views. Attempts to use this law to suppress broadcasts, such as rock songs, the film *The Last Temptation of Christ* and satirical pictures using religious imagery, seem largely to have failed.

Elections

In the post-communist era, the Roman Catholic Church is reverting to its traditional ambivalent attitude towards modern civil society. During the first free elections of 1991, prominent Polish churchmen, many ordinary priests and lay advocates of conservative Catholic attitudes warned of the growing influence of values 'alien to the Polish nation and tradition', implicitly referring to social-democratic and liberal ideas. In the 1993 elections, ignoring a law prohibiting political campaigning on election day, Polish country priests and bishops told their congregations which political party to support and, in 1995, overt church support for Lech Walesa was found to be one of the reasons for his defeat at the presidential polls.

The 1993 concordat

The concordat signed in July 1993, in the view of commentators, seems to contravene the Polish constitution. First, the state and the Roman Catholic Church in Poland are like partners, as two legal subjects of equal rank. The abandoning of church–state separation would have negative consequences for other religions and beliefs in Poland, as well as for declared non-believers. Further, Roman Catholic priests would gain more privileged status than other citizens in the civil and penal law. If government and parliament ratify the concordat of 1993 without radical changes, as a basis for the future constitution of the state, Poland may drift towards a constitutional Roman Catholic state. On the other hand, if they do not ratify it, inconsistency in the crucial legal issues of the state is likely to continue and cause instability.

However, because of Catholic–patriotic sentiments, the situation in Poland is made even more complex because there is no rights-oriented political culture and the representatives of the church hierarchy show little sensitivity to others; on the other hand, there is also the national tradition of protesting spontaneously when government attacks the church. Both these factors contribute to the Polish stalemate.

Concerns of other religious groups

The other religious groups in Poland each have their own concerns about religion–state relations. To Ukrainians in Poland, it remains extremely important that the Greek Catholic Church should be allowed to function openly; some Ukrainians declare their ethnic identity and attachment to their church in religious terms, as 'Greeks'. Others have accepted the Orthodox Church, on the grounds that this was their original church, and distinguishes them clearly from Poles. The attitude of local Ukrainians towards Poles can be described as tolerant and resigned.

Despite the small number of its members, the Evangelical-Reformed Church demonstrates particular sensitivity to political and social issues. It was an outright critic of martial law in 1981 and an original and courageous voice in the public debate on abortion in the 1990s.

A Council for Polish–Jewish Relations has been established, attached to the presidential chancellery. Some anti-Semitic vandalism of Jewish cemeteries and other incidents have been noted. In 1996, President Kwasniewski conducted a ceremony which for the first time commemorated the deaths of Jews in a pogrom at Kielce in 1946. Post-war pogroms in several Polish cities were a subject long unacknowledged under communist rule.

A long-standing dispute between the Jewish community world-wide and the Polish Roman Catholic Church has been the presence of a Carmelite convent in the grounds of Auschwitz, the place primarily associated with the Holocaust of millions of Jews in the Second World War. After years of efforts to persuade the nuns to move from Auschwitz, a new convent was consecrated in May 1993 and they left in July. The campaign against their move, spearheaded by the National Party Szczerbiec, raised the spectre of 'Jewish Communism'.

All the minority religions have expressed negative views on the 1993 concordat which excludes them from the relationship between the state and the Roman Catholic Church. The concordat treats them as 'the other beliefs', which, to some extent, have similar rights in the state dominated by the two major partners, but the precise nature of the relationship between the state and the 'other churches' is to be regulated only in an undefined future.

There is also the significant matter of the attitude of the Catholic Church hierarchy towards other religions in Poland. Even though the church was constrained during the communist period, it still did not act to prevent the destruction of Ukrainian churches. The Vatican's 'new evangelisation' seems only to be understood as its duty to convert the 'others', in particular the Orthodox religions. For example, in Komancza in 1981, the sole obstacle to the holding of a Greek Catholic service was the attitude of the Roman Catholic bishop of the diocese. Despite the protest of Catholics and several appeals to the Pope, it seems likely that many more may transfer to the Orthodox Church if this is the only way that they can participate in eastern rite services. In May 1989, with reference to the law (1596) of Polish King Zygmunt III, the Polish Roman Catholic Church required the subordination of Greek Catholic churches and the Uniates in the territory of Lithuania and the Ukraine and subsequently nominated Polish bishops, provoking political conflicts with the new states.

Women and religion

Despite great esteem for the Blessed Virgin Mary, women in the Polish Roman Catholic Church are, like all Catholic women, excluded from the priesthood. There is at present no pro-ordination pressure. Generally, the state promotes the rights of women and stresses their equality, giving equal rights to education, work and an active role in society. Conservative Catholic women played their part in the church's campaign against abortion during the years of transition to democracy when a chapel of the Warsaw Cathedral was dedicated to this cause.

ROMANIA

Romania	
GDP (US$bn)	24
Population	23,100,000
Annual population growth (%)	0.7
Urban population (%)	54
Working population (%)	47[a]
Literacy (%)	96.9
Ratifications	1; 2, 2(b); 3; 4; E

Communist rule since 1947 ended in Romania with the violent overthrow of the dictatorship of Nicolae Ceausescu in December 1989. The degree of repression and the extent to which the communist regime had sought to mould Romanian society around Marxist–Leninist ideas had singled out Romania from other Warsaw Pact countries. Political insiders, mainly out of favour with Ceausescu, quickly filled the political vacuum. The National Salvation Front (NSF) acquired popularity by lightening the burdens of daily life for hard-pressed citizens. In May 1990 it won a sweeping mandate to draw up a new constitution, assisted by control of state assets, especially the electronic media, and by its promise to shield workers from the adverse effects of a transition to a market economy. Genuine liberalisation has been accompanied by sporadic government harassment of opponents. Political competition is allowed but it is unclear whether a genuine transfer of power from the NSF to its opponents is possible. Since the 1992 elections, the NSF has ruled in alliance with extremist parties nostalgic for the communist era and openly contemptuous of human rights and toleration for minorities.

The communist period did enormous damage to the material, physical and psychological well-being of the Romanian people. Recovery is proving slow and painful. The years 1990–92 witnessed a 32.1 per cent fall in real GDP growth. Much of the command economy remains intact; privatisation has been supervised by former members of the ruling elite and external investment remains weak.

Romania's hybrid regime thus contains elements of autocracy and democracy. The government is poorly placed to resolve the totalitarian legacy of ethnic, economic and religious conflicts. Profound insecurity over the political deadlock at home and conflicts in the Balkans makes it difficult to resolve internal disputes, not least inter-ethnic and religious ones. Romania in 1993 was the last of the Warsaw Pact satellites to join the Council of Europe, after persistent doubts about its capacity to protect human rights adequately.

Ethnic and religious composition

According to the 1992 census, the main ethnic groupings of Romania's population of 23 million were Romanians (89.4 per cent), Hungarians (7.1 per cent), Roma (1.8 per cent) and Germans (0.5 per cent). The Hungarian minority claim that their number was underestimated at 1.6 instead of 2 million in order to weaken their case for collective minority rights in the areas of education and culture. Estimates of the size of the Roma (gypsy) minority have also been much higher than official figures.

Before the Second World War, religious minorities used to constitute more than a quarter of the population. Permitted emigration to Israel in the 1960s and to Germany in the 1980s has steeply reduced the numbers of Jews and of German-speakers attached to Western Christian faiths. This has boosted the prominence of the Romanian Orthodox Church, whose followers constituted 86.8 per cent of the population in 1992. Minority Christian groups include Roman Catholics (5 per cent), Reformed (3.5 per cent), Uniate and Pentecostal (each 1 per cent) together with smaller Protestant, Catholic and eastern Christian groups. Muslims constituted 0.2 per cent. Only 0.2 per cent of Romanians formally declared themselves to be atheist.

These figures do not reflect the extent to which a faith is practised, especially after forty years of communist rule. Certainly new Protestant faiths regard Romania as missionary terrain and have enjoyed some remarkable successes in converting nominally Orthodox or atheistic Romanians.

Inter-ethnic disputes have placed Romanians and Hungarians at loggerheads and highlighted the inadequate protection enjoyed before the law by the Roma. But generally religious disputes have not reinforced these conflicts. The Hungarian minority's beliefs are diverse, Roman Catholics and several large Protestant denominations exercising considerable influence and generally enjoying harmonious relations with one another.

The Romanian and Hungarian wings of Catholicism (as represented by the Orthodox- and Latin-rite churches) enjoy close ties that stem in part from their experience of common suffering. In the absence of their own churches, Uniates were secretly baptised in Hungarian Catholic churches during the communist era. Since 1990 influential nationalists have objected to such links, claiming that Uniates support Transylvania's secession from Romania.

The Orthodox–Uniate conflict

The main confessional quarrel in the 1990s is an intra-Romanian one that has placed the Orthodox Church on a collision course with the Uniate Church. For ethnic Romanians who possess a nationalist outlook, this embarrassing quarrel contradicts the view that the Romanians are bonded together in unity.

Majority identification with the Orthodox Church (however nominal it might be in some cases) stems in part from a controversial act carried out by Romania's communist rulers during their first months in power. In December 1948, the Uniate Church (also known as the Eastern Rite or Greek Catholic Church) was abolished, its congregations and many of its church buildings (numbering between 1,800 and 2,000) being transferred to the Orthodox Church by the state. The Uniates who numbered 1,427,391 or 7.9 per cent of the population in the 1930 census, were the main church of the ethnic Romanian majority in the province of Transylvania which had become part of Romania in 1918 following the breaking-up of the Austro-Hungarian Empire. While retaining the Orthodox liturgy and married clergy, the Uniate Church differs from the Orthodox Church by recognising the Roman Catholic Pontiff as its spiritual leader and by having been exposed to rationalist and liberal traditions. From its emergence in the 1690s, the Uniate Church played an important role in awakening Romanian national consciousness, stressing similarities both in language and ancestry between the Roman and Latin civilisations (Romanian is a Romance language). For these reasons it was anathema to the communists who wished to insulate Romania from Western influences and minimise differences that placed Romanians apart from Russians.

The communist presence in Romania was sustained by the Soviet Red Army until the 1950s. Initially, Romania's new rulers sought to exercise control over a mainly peasant population through the Orthodox Church which, in this country, was largely compliant to state rulers. As Romania left Moscow's orbit in the 1960s while remaining rigidly communist in its social system, the Orthodox Church enjoyed more visibility but it remained heavily policed by the state. Other Christian faiths whose adherents mainly belonged to the Hungarian and German minorities were even more stringently policed and it was Laszlo Tokes, a dissident pastor of the Hungarian Reformed Church, whose defiance sparked off the revolt that led to the 1989 overthrow of Ceausescu.

On 31 December 1989, the provisional government lifted the ban on the Uniate Church. In 1990 the interim parliament fully legalised the Uniate Church but failed to resolve the question of Uniate property acquired by the Orthodox Church in 1948. The Uniate demand for its property to be returned unconditionally and in its entirety was viewed as unrealistic by the Orthodox Church; it claimed that many descendants of former Uniate families preferred to remain Orthodox and it insisted that every believer should be offered the chance to opt for one church or another by means of local plebiscites. This proposal was and remains supported by the government. Some eighty churches have been restored to the Uniates, according to the Romanian government's response to enquiry from the Special Rapporteur on Religious Intolerance in 1993, and the remainder of the property dispute is, it said, to be resolved by Christian cooperation and dialogue according to the 1990 law which requires a committee of the representatives of clergy of both de-nominations to take into account the wishes of local parishioners. But the Uniates have rejected a local plebiscite, believing that the outcome could be manipulated by the Orthodox Church in alliance with the local authorities who, in most localities, have not greatly altered since the period of full communism. Uniate spokesmen argue that in the Transylvanian countryside there is a climate of intimidation which prevents people exercising a free choice about which faith they should worship in. Violent incidents in which Uniate believers have been disturbed at their worship in farms and homes, or in which Uniates have tried to repossess their former churches, have featured in reports published by the Special Rapporteur.

The suffering which the Uniates experienced under communism gives this inter-confessional dispute a bitter edge. Some seven Uniate bishops died in prison, and one, secretly appointed a Cardinal by Pope Paul VI in 1969, died later under house arrest. The current Uniate leadership accuses the government of practising communism through its unwillingness to undo the wrongs committed by its communist predecessor. In May 1991, the Metropolitan of the Uniate Church was appointed a Cardinal by Pope John Paul II. Earlier that month the Uniates had regained possession of their cathedral in Blaj, the undisputed centre of the faith for over 200 years. Shortly afterwards, Teoctist, the Romanian Orthodox Patriarch, appealed to Orthodox faithful everywhere 'to break off their theological dialogue with the Catholic Church during the pontificate of Pope John Paul II, since he favours Uniate proselytism all over Eastern Europe, which means the expansion of Catholicism at the expense of Orthodoxy.'

A few pro-government deputies have spoken in similar vein. Petre Turlea accused Pope John Paul II in 1993 of inciting war against Serbia and claiming that 'all bad things in Romania are connected with the Catholic reality here'. The Catholic Archbishop of Bucharest, Ioan Robu, was later received by President Iliescu who dissociated himself from the outburst and denied the existence of an anti-Catholic spirit in Romania.

The political and legal system

On 21 November 1991, the bicameral Constituent Assembly approved a new constitution later endorsed by referendum; Romania is now a republic with a president and prime minister. The 1991 constitution created a Constitutional Court.

In 1991, the National Peasant Party added the adjective 'Christian' to its title and became the National Peasant and Christian Democratic Party. It is the largest opposition party, the driving force behind the opposition alliance known as the Democratic Convention, and enjoys close ties with German and Italian Christian Democrats.

The constitution permits parties with a religious or ethnic basis. Radical nationalist parties are opposed to the existence of the Hungarian Democratic Federation of Romania which represents Hungarians in the Romanian parliament (having obtained 7.45 per cent of the vote in 1992), claiming that citizens of the state possess only a Romanian nationality.

One seat is set aside in parliament for national minorities which fail to obtain the number of votes for representatives in parliament. The Roma, despite being the second largest minority, have been unable to build up effective political organisations, though some have been elected to office at municipal level.

Constitutional guarantees and minorities

Romania has ratified the major human rights instruments. The 1991 constitution guarantees fundamental human rights, including freedom of religion or belief; it overrides international law in cases where the two may conflict. Freedom of religion or belief is covered in Article 9:

1 Freedom of thought, opinion, and religious beliefs may not be restricted in any form whatsoever. No-one may be compelled to embrace an opinion or religion contrary to his own convictions.
2 Freedom of conscience is guaranteed; it must be manifested in a spirit of tolerance and mutual respect.

3 All religions shall be free and organised in accordance with their own statutes, under the terms laid down by the law.

4 Any form, means, acts or actions of religious enmity shall be prohibited in the relationship among the [religious organisations].

5 Religious [organisations] shall be autonomous from the State and shall enjoy support from it, including the facilitation of religious assistance in the army, in hospitals, prisons, homes and orphanages.

6 Parents or legal tutors have the right to ensure, in accordance with their own convictions, the education of the minor children whose responsibility devolves on them.

Article 30 states that 'any instigation to ... religious hatred, any incitement to discrimination, territorial separatism, or public violence ... shall be prohibited by law'. The Penal Code lays down penalties for persons who attempt to prevent the clergy and believers from enjoying the religious rights and freedoms guaranteed by the constitution.

Article 6.1 recognises and guarantees the rights of persons belonging to national minorities, to the preservation, development and expression of their ethnic, cultural, linguistic and religious identity. However, Article 6.2 requires that protective measures towards minorities should 'conform to the principles of equality and non-discrimination in relation to other Romanian citizens'.

In 1993, the (UN) Human Rights Committee expressed concern about the government's lack of activity in combating the level of discrimination against minorities, and in particular offences committed as a result of incitement to ethnic or religious intolerance. The Committee noted the vulnerability of the Roma (gypsy) minority which has had a long history of discrimination and persecution by the authorities and the general populace.

Although the Roma have always suffered low status and deprivation of rights, there was little direct violence against them under Ceausescu. They were virtually ghettoised in areas of very poor housing, with lack of water supply and garbage collection, and Roma children were automatically defined as slow learners, supposedly inheriting a culture defined by the government as having 'retrograde traditions and mentalities'. The background to this ethnic and religious hatred is a centuries-long history of formal enslavement in Romania, especially as servants of the clergy and nobility. The monasteries were the largest owners of gypsy labour and although the Roma were liberated in mid-nineteenth century, the pro-Nazi government during the Second World War systematically destroyed huge numbers of the Roma population. Since the end of the Ceausescu dictatorship, the Roma community has suffered increasingly direct violence (burning of homes, expulsion from some neighbourhoods) which has not been curbed by the authorities.

The increase in 'pogroms' against the Roma in recent years has also aroused the fears of the small Jewish community. In the nineteenth and early twentieth centuries, Romania was extremely anti-Semitic; Jews were reluctantly granted citizenship only in 1923. Anti-Semitism imbued the programme of the Iron Guard; persecution of the Jews was legislated before the Second World War and enforced under the Antonescu military dictatorship; at least 250,000 Jews perished during the Second World War. Nationalist ideologies reclaiming an allegedly glorious imperial past in continuity with the Roman Empire played their part in underpinning Ceausescu's regime, in which anti-Semitism was condoned, and are revived today in campaigns to rehabilitate Antonescu and the Iron Guard.

Church and state

Notably, the Romanian Orthodox Church was not accorded a special place in the 1991 constitution; it has been much criticised for allowing itself to become an instrument of the avowedly atheistic Ceausescu regime. Indeed, the current Patriarch, Teoctist, temporarily retired for a few months in 1990 amidst fierce criticism, some of it within the church, about his role during the last years of the regime.

Ion Iliescu who was architect of the post-1989 transition, was not affiliated to any church and is a freethinker. Some evangelical Protestants, especially the new Protestant faiths who have won many converts among nominally Orthodox Romanians, have said that they feel more secure under a head of state who is a freethinker than under one affiliated to a Christian denomination, such as Orthodoxy, who might be disposed to advance his church at the expense of others.

An informal alliance did spring up between the National Salvation Front (NSF) and the Orthodox Church, these being two institutions which do not wish to disrupt existing power alignments in church and state. In the 1990 elections, Orthodox support contributed to the NSF victory, one of its parliamentarians being an Orthodox priest. Nationalists, who have been represented in government since 1994, have demanded that the special status of the Romanian Orthodox Church be formally recognised.

There was a Ministry of Religious Affairs from January to July 1990 after which the Ministry was reduced to a sub-secretariat.

The Religious Denominations Bill

The Draft Law on Worship and Religious Freedoms was published in 1992 by the State Secretariat for Religions. By early 1995 it had been submitted to parliament. Sharp objections from various religious quarters may have deterred the government from moving speedily in this area.

A clause of the Draft Law describes the Romanian Orthodox Church as the 'National Church'. Objections to this formulation have been lodged by the Catholic, Reformed, Lutheran and various new Protestant churches. A system of state registration of faiths is proposed; fourteen religious faiths are listed as having fulfilled the conditions for recognition by the state. Other religions applying for state recognition are obliged to 'respect the constitution, the laws, and conventions' of the Romanian state. Concern has been voiced that the requirement that 'religious faiths will have central and local organisations in conformity with their statutes' may impose an organising model with which decentralised religious groups, such as the Baha'i faith, may be unable to comply. Doubts have been expressed about the constitutionality of the proposed arrangements.

The government, in correspondence with the Special Rapporteur on Religious Intolerance in 1994, has cited fifteen denominations and more than 250 religious associations. Concerned about the influx of foreign preachers, the authorities have admitted only those who had been invited by Romanian organisations, under the condition that they did not promote 'religious propaganda or proselytising activities which could offend the religious faith of Romanian believers'. The government has also pointed out that Article 4 of the Draft Law provides that:

> the religious denominations are equal between themselves, before the public authorities without any privilege or discrimination. The State will not promote or stimulate any privileges or discriminations [*sic*] among religious denominations, through administrative measures, domestic or international law.

Education

The Draft Law on Worship and Religious Freedoms enables churches to organise their own educational institutions, provided 'legal provisions are respected'. New Protestant faiths which set great store on operating their own church schools have, in some cases, expressed fears that their freedom of action may be curtailed quite significantly in the educational domain.

Education is a matter of particular concern to the religious minorities, particularly those which belong to the Hungarian minority. Confessional schools were the first to be established in Romania and, today, some Hungarian schools attached to Catholic and Protestant faiths go back several centuries. German and Romanian confessional schools were established in the sixteenth century.

In 1948, the communists nationalised 1,600 confessional schools. The Draft Law on Education, proposed in 1992, would leave them under state control, a resolution which is unacceptable to the Hungarian minority's church leaders who have been critical of the government's proposals, claiming that only return of these schools to confessional control will prevent the loss of minority cultural identity. Despite government assurances about adequacy of language availability, Hungarian language teaching remains a concern to them.

There is also a strong appeal for financial compensation for the buildings of those schools which it is impractical or inappropriate to return. For instance, what was once the main Reformed college in Cluj no longer has Hungarian students and compensation would help to cover the costs of new religious institutions, such as the nursing school of the Reformed Church there.

The government states that religious education is protected by law and is available through the state school system; however, this occurs only when at least ten children of a particular denomination are in one class. Confessionally-based seminaries and institutes of theology at secondary and tertiary levels have been established in Romania, some since the revolution (Seventh-Day Adventist and Pentecostal). For example, in Cluj, Reformed, Lutherans and Unitarians jointly sponsor one seminary.

Women

Women in Romania still suffer from the disastrous effects of Ceausescu's policy of pro-natalism. Although a number of Orthodox Church clergy became courageous dissidents, many colluded in pro-natalist policies which enacted absolute bans on contraception and abortion for any reason. The state instituted monthly gynaecological examinations of all women in the workplace to police the bans, a gross invasion of women's privacy and personal freedom. The medical profession became isolated from the outside world and from each other and appalling breaches of ethics became commonplace in relation to women and children and also in relation to the spread and treatment of AIDS. The result of pro-natalism was the birth of large numbers of children who could not be supported by the poverty-stricken population. Many mothers had little option but to place their babies, both healthy and handicapped, in the care of the state, in institutions whose barbarous conditions only became known after the fall of the regime. Although pro-natalist policies were annulled, continued medical malpractice and the effects of malnutrition, disease and neglect are still a major burden for Romania's women and children.

THE RUSSIAN FEDERATION[1]

The Russian Federation	
GDP (US$bn)	388
Population	148,100,000
Annual population growth (%)	0.7
Urban population (%)	75
Working population (%)	53[a]
Literacy (%)	98.7
Ratifications	1; 2, 2(a), 2(b); 3; 4

Russia continues its difficult period of economic and political transition. By the 1970s Marxism–Leninism, the only permitted ideology in the Soviet Union and Soviet-dominated Eastern Europe, had ceased to function as a visionary creed motivating people to work for a better future. Rulers and ruled alike paid lip-service to the ideology as the price for social stability and job security. Nevertheless, the system was barely able to meet basic needs, and citizens were compelled regularly to resort to the corrupt black economy. At the same time the state security system required the cooperation of a considerable proportion of the general public in helping to maintain the political *status quo*. The social climate was thus characterised by low self-esteem as a result of having to 'live a lie', suspicion and fear, a combination of disdain and envy for any who stood out in the crowd in any way, and an absence of personal initiative and responsibility in the public sphere.

The vastness and diversity of Russia can be seen from the saying that when viewed from the Western perspective, Russia is a Slavic state, while from the perspective of the Middle East and Central Asia, it is an Islamic state. The Russian Federation is composed of over 100 nationalities in twenty republics and eighteen autonomous regions. Ethnic Russians comprise 85 per cent of the population of nearly 150 million, the rest being principally Tatars, Ukrainians and Chuvash, with over 100 other ethnic groups including an estimated 650,000 Jews. The ethnic Russians – whose birth-rate fell in the last quarter century and dropped again because of economic hardship since the end of communism – have traditionally been afraid that they will eventually be outnumbered by non-Russians from the east. These feelings have fuelled, for instance, the current conflict of the Russian Federation with the Muslim Chechnyans, halted by treaty in 1996.

President Boris Yeltsin's New Year Message for 1996 promised Russians that their living standards would improve and counselled patience, as well as threatening severe punishment for corruption. The end of communism has not produced a society in which human rights, dignities and freedoms are obviously being promoted and protected. The market economy had rapidly turned sour; between January 1991 and May 1994, industrial output in Russia fell by 64 per cent. Though unemployment levels remain lower than expected, the experience of transition to capitalism in Russia has been particularly harsh and has not been improved by the effects of massive internal displacements of people, including the return to Russia of many from surrounding, newly independent countries.

Political and constitutional system

During 1992–93 President Yeltsin and his government, committed to rapid marketisation, proved increasingly unable to work with the Congress of People's Deputies, which had been elected while the Soviet Union was still in existence. Stalemate ended in the storming of the White House in October 1993 and the forcible dissolution of the Congress. A new constitution for the Russian Federation was promulgated in December 1993. The president, elected for up to two four-year terms, appoints the prime minister and must approve ministerial appointments. Succeeding to the Congress of People's Deputies, the Federal Assembly consists of two houses: the Federation Council and the state Duma. The Duma has little power, however, compared to the office of the president. Elections to the Duma in December 1995 did not result in whole-hearted support for reform. President Yeltsin was elected for a second term in July 1996 but is ailing.

The 1993 constitution confirms that ideological pluralism is to be recognised in the Russian Federation; that no ideology is to be established as state or compulsory ideology; that the Russian Federation is a secular state; that no religion is to be declared an official or compulsory religion; that all religious associations are to be separate from the state and equal before the law. International treaties shall be part of the Russian legal system, which shall conform to international legal standards. If an international undertaking differs from Russian law, the former shall prevail. Human rights and freedoms are inalienable and belong to each individual from birth, and are to be recognised and guaranteed in accordance with international law.

Religion in the Soviet period

In the Soviet period, legislation on religion restricted religious believers to acts of worship inside the very few buildings specifically registered for that purpose. Religious believers who tried to relate their faith in any way to their daily life could expect systematic discrimination and even persecution. The churches and other religious bodies were totally excluded from involvement in social activity, charitable work, education, politics, public life and public comment in general, even sermons.

From the 1960s the major denominations were allowed to retain a hierarchy and a very limited number of theological, educational and publishing facilities in return for explicit support for all aspects of Soviet domestic and foreign policy, including denial of the existence of discrimination. The majority of believers opted for the path of 'discretion'; a significant minority for whom this type of compromise was unacceptable chose or were forced along the path of 'valour', suffering discrimination or persecution as a direct result of their religious witness.

Religious composition of Russia today

The Russian Orthodox Church and Islam are the two major faith groups of Russia, comprising, respectively, around 75 per cent and 15 per cent of its people. Although the Russian Orthodox Church sees itself as the mother church of the Russian nation, religious nominalism is more the norm in Russia today, the result of over seventy years of communist rule. The majority of Russians regard themselves as Orthodox without necessarily knowing anything about the faith or doing more than attend baptisms and funerals. Citizens of the Russian Federation who are of Central Asian origin tend to regard themselves as Muslims, though again this is usually a nominal allegiance.

The third largest religious group, about 1 million people, is probably the Baptist Church. This denomination arose in Russia out of Protestant-type movements in the Russian Orthodox Church and nineteenth-century missionary activity from the West. As well as ethnic Russians, Baptists include Russian citizens of German origin.

Other smaller Protestant denominations include Pentecostals, Seventh-Day Adventists, Methodists and Mennonites. There is a small number of Roman Catholics, largely in the capital cities and in parts of Siberia.

Only a small minority of the large number of ethnic Jews in Russia practise their faith, as teaching in Hebrew used to be forbidden, even in private homes, so that children could not be taught the faith. Emigration (once it was allowed) has further reduced the number of practising Jews in Russia. Most Russian Jews live in Moscow or St Petersburg.

The number of new religious movements is burgeoning. These include the Unification Church, the Church of Scientology, The Family, the White Brotherhood, and the largest Aum Shinrikyo branch outside Japan.

While the population shows a hunger for spiritual values, there is almost total public ignorance about what the various denominations represent and about what demands a particular faith may make on its adherents. A Radio Free Europe survey in 1994 revealed that 39 per cent of Russians considered themselves religious, although only 6 per cent attended church and only 4 per cent said they had strong beliefs.

Laws affecting freedom of religion or belief

In the Soviet Union, the restrictive Law on Religious Associations of 1929 was repealed in 1990 and replaced by a Law on Freedom of Conscience which guaranteed believers a very wide range of religious liberties. The Russian Federation's version of the same law, passed later in 1990, was even more liberal. Efforts are now being made to modify the law in order to protect 'home-grown' Russian religions from foreign competition. Since the end of communism there has been no restriction on proselytising, preaching, publishing, social work or political activity by or on behalf of any religious group. The Soviet state's Council for Religious Affairs (CRA) was formally dissolved in January 1991 in accordance with a clause in the 1990 Law on Freedom of Conscience to the effect that no organisation might be set up to decide on questions linked to citizens' religious rights.

A few days before the nationwide referendum on his presidency and the reform programme in April 1993, President Yeltsin invited to the Kremlin the religious leaders of the Russian Orthodox Church, the Russian Baptist Union, and leading representatives of the Old Believers, Muslims, Jews and Buddhists. Yeltsin acknowledged the guilt of the state for past persecution of religion and confirmed his opposition to discrimination against individual believers and whole denominations. He promised to continue to allocate state funds for the restoration of religious buildings and announced a decree inaugurating a programme to return property confiscated from religious bodies by the Soviet regime. Finally, he urged believers to support his reform programme. Invited to put their concerns to Yeltsin, the patriarch and other denominational leaders spoke of the authorities allowing too much freedom to foreign missions; even the Baptist leader complained that television and radio were dominated by foreign preachers. Traditional religious groups have been concerned that legal personality may be gained by any group able to register an association – and thus gain privileges available to religions – with only ten signatories; they say that parishes on paper have been created overnight.

Consequently, amendments to the 1990 Law on Freedom of Conscience concerning the accreditation of individuals were passed by the Congress of People's Deputies in July 1993. While individual foreign religious believers would continue to enjoy full freedom of worship with Russian fellow-believers and to preach if invited, the law would require representatives of foreign religious organisations, as well as foreigners working for Russian religious organisations and Russians working for foreign ones, to receive state accreditation before engaging in religious work. Individuals representing foreign religious organisations who were not Russian citizens would no longer have the right to engage in missionary activity or publishing.

Father Gleb Yakunin, Orthodox priest, veteran religious rights campaigner and former prisoner of conscience, was the only person to oppose this measure inside the congress. His protests were backed by the Russian branch of the International Religious Liberty Association, which sent a letter to Yeltsin signed by Baptist, Pentecostal and Adventist leaders worried that foreign religious organisations that had given them aid in the past would henceforth be prevented from doing so; they complained that they had not been shown the draft law. However, Patriarch Aleksy II, who had been shown it, wrote to the congress saying that it fully satisfied the wishes and needs of the Russian Orthodox Church.

Yeltsin told the congress that the proposed new law contradicted the Russian constitution and did not meet standards laid down by international law on human rights and religious liberty; it was redrafted. However, new disputes arose after the congress introduced a new amendment requiring the state to 'support religious organisations whose activities preserve and develop historical traditions and customs, national–cultural originality, art and other aspects of the cultural heritage of the peoples of the Russian Federation'. The wording appeared to allow positive discrimination in favour of the Russian Orthodox Church within the Federation, and in favour of Islam and Buddhism in those autonomous republics where they are the majority national religion. Yeltsin's veto sent the law back to the congress; it has not yet been debated.

Problems with the past

Since the onset of *glasnost* and *perestroika* in 1987, there has been much tension in the churches between those who 'compromised with the authorities' – particularly as revealed through KGB files opened briefly to the government's Committee on Freedom of Conscience in 1991 – and those who 'suffered for their faith' in the communist period. Bitterness and recrimination have drained the energies of the denominations and have hampered their capacity to respond to the new freedoms.

The question of where individual believers stood in the 'discretion–valour' spectrum is further complicated by the fact that the fall of communism has revealed very different agendas amongst those who were formerly on the same 'side'. Did a religious activist who resisted communism do so because the communist system was totalitarian or because it was atheist? If the former, political and ideological pluralism will be defended, as it is by Father Yakunin in the Duma. If the latter, the revealed truth of religion will be defended and democracy, liberalism and the market will be regarded as harmful products of the secular Western enlightenment just as the communist system, a Western import had been spurned previously. Metropolitan Ioann of St Petersburg, who died in 1995, was notorious for his anti-Western and anti-Semitic chauvinism.

The deteriorating economic and political situation in Russia led to a widespread resurgence of anti-Semitism, encouraged by conservative elements in the Russian Orthodox Church and by extremist secular organisations claiming to defend Orthodox values, many of whose statements would certainly constitute 'incitement to racial hatred' by international standards. Over the past few years there has been mounting criticism of the Orthodox Church leadership for its failure to issue an explicit condemnation of anti-Semitism. A spokesman for the Patriarchate explained in 1993 that the Orthodox Church did not in fact have a 'position' on anti-Semitism since the church fathers themselves were divided on the issue.

Inter-religious relations

There has been a marked deterioration in inter-church and inter-faith relations. The response of the Russian Orthodox Church to sudden religious freedom has been a mixture of the triumphalist and the defensive. It has had to defend its jurisdiction against rival Orthodox churches and also against the Ukrainian Catholic Church. The dis-orientating influx of religious groups from West and East has alarmed the indigenous Russian denominations which resent 'religious imperialism' on the part of well-funded and well-resourced Western and Eastern religious organisations, both traditional and modern. The younger intelligentsia show great interest in Catholicism; the Russian Orthodox Church is deeply suspicious of the alleged proselytising intentions of the Vatican within Russia.

In the Soviet period, the Catholic Church had been allowed no structures of any kind and was officially confined to one church in Moscow, but by 1990 the Vatican was able to appoint a pro-nuncio. However, it omitted to inform the Russian Orthodox leadership of this move in advance. The Holy Synod was already traumatised by the re-emergence of the Ukrainian Catholic Church and in 1991 Patriarch Aleksy II, on an official visit to London, launched a bitter attack on 'Catholic proselytism'. In June 1992 the Vatican's Pontifical Commission for Russia sent a letter to all Catholic dioceses in Eastern Europe urging sensitivity; apostolic structures were intended to respond to the needs of Catholic communities present there and not to bring the Catholic Church into conflict with the Russian Orthodox Church or with other Christian churches present in the same territory.

Nevertheless, problems and tension continued. In April 1993, priests of the newly formed Orthodox dioceses of Magaden and Kolyma in eastern Siberia bitterly criticised a Catholic plan to build an ecumenical centre in Magadan with American Catholic donations. The Archbishop in Alaska had sent priests and money to the region's Catholic community and also provided humanitarian aid to all the population.

At its third congress in St Petersburg in June 1992 the Union of Orthodox Brotherhoods expressed anxiety at the intention of the Orthodox leadership to renew dialogue with the Vatican in view of the 'proselytising activity of Catholicism', especially in Ukraine; the congress also stated that it was inappropriate for the Russian Orthodox Church to remain a member of the World Council of Churches.

There have, however, been some progressive inter-faith events. In 1992 an inter-faith Religious Liberty Association was founded with Adventist, Baptist, Methodist, Orthodox, Lutheran, Pentecostal and Muslim participants. In September 1993, representatives of the major Christian, Muslim and Jewish bodies assembled in Moscow for the first inter-religious dialogue since the fall of communism. The conflict in Chechnya has also resulted in some drawing of Christians and Muslims together, as the Patriarch and the Mufti made joint appeals for a peaceful and negotiated settlement.

Dispute over religious jurisdiction

In 1943 Stalin abolished the several million-strong Ukrainian Catholic Church and gave its parishes and property to the Russian Orthodox Church. Mikhail Gorbachev, on the eve of his visit to the Pope in December 1989, announced that legal rights were henceforth restored to the Ukrainian Catholics. More than 500 priests promptly renounced the jurisdiction of the Moscow Patriarchate whose local representative was Metropolitan Filaret of Kiev. Filaret then denounced the alleged 'violence' of the Ukrainian Catholics in their attempts to regain control of their churches; the Ukrainian Catholic Church has wide popular support, particularly in western Ukraine.

A 'Ukrainian Orthodox Church' was then set up as a subsidiary of the Moscow Patriarchate; early in 1990 Filaret received the title of 'Metropolitan of Kiev and All Ukraine'. The failed political coup in Moscow in August 1991 was followed by Ukraine's declaration of independence and by allegations about collaboration with the KGB by Filaret and other Metropolitans. Filaret was defrocked in April 1992 and replaced as head of the Russian Orthodox Church in Ukraine by Metropolitan Vladimir of Rostov. Filaret then gained the support of the Ukrainian government and became the deputy of successive patriarchs of the recently re-legalised Ukrainian Autocephalous Orthodox Church.

Relations between the Russian Orthodox Church and the Ukrainian government were thus at a low ebb, the former perceiving the latter as allied with two usurping jurisdictions, the Ukrainian Catholic Church and the Ukrainian Autocephalous Orthodox Church.

Meanwhile in Russia, the Moscow Patriarchate was witnessing hundreds of its parishes going over voluntarily to the jurisdiction of the American-based Russian Orthodox Church in Exile or of the True Orthodox or 'Catacomb' Church (illegal during the Soviet period) on the grounds that these churches were untainted by collaboration with the Soviet authorities. In the city of Oboyan in the early 1990s, the Orthodox priest Fr Ioasaf and his parish transferred themselves to the jurisdiction of the Russian Orthodox Church Abroad. Barred by his archbishop, Yuvenaly of Kursk, from his church buildings, Fr Ioasaf and his parishioners eventually got back into their church in August 1994 only to be evicted by a Kursk court official assisted by special branch ('OMON') troops summoned by the archbishop, the secular authorities thus cooperating with the Russian Orthodox Church.

Religion and the state

In line with the new Russian constitution, both President Yeltsin and Patriarch Aleksy II have made it clear that they are opposed to the idea that the Russian Orthodox Church should become any kind of state church. Nevertheless, local bishops and clergy as well as the local secular authorities often find that their interests coincide. Groups with political or economic investment in a local area will sometimes symbolise their cooperation in a prestigious religious project. In 1993, the regional government in Vladivostok voted to rebuild the city's cathedral with the assistance of a consortium of local interests. The gigantic Cathedral of Christ the Saviour – built to commemorate the defeat of Napoleon in 1812 and blown up by Stalin in 1931 – is being rebuilt in Moscow as an all-Russian enterprise to symbolise the stabilisation and raising up of Russia, according to President Yeltsin.

More generally, religion – Orthodoxy in particular – may be recruited to give legitimacy and credibility to novel political, social or economic undertakings, such as priestly blessings at the opening of the Leningrad stock exchange. In January 1994 the new offices of the Russian government in Moscow were blessed by Bishop Arseny of Istra and members of the Moscow diocesan council of the Russian Orthodox Church. On behalf of Patriarch Aleksy II, the bishop presented Prime Minister Chernomyrdin with an icon of the Mother of God, symbolising, he said, 'the renewal and rebirth of Russia'.

Religion and politics

For most of the twentieth century no individual or institution in the Soviet Union was allowed to express a religious view on any aspect of political life. In general the leadership of the Russian Orthodox Church sees the church's role as attempting to effect reconciliation in conflict situations. More than once, for example, most recently in April 1994, the Patriarch has joined other religious leaders (of the Armenian Church and of the Muslims of Azerbaijan) in calling on the presidents of the three countries to put an end to the war between Armenia and Azerbaijan.

Towards the end of the Soviet period, it became possible for religious believers to be elected to public office. Patriarch Aleksy II and two other bishops were members of the last Soviet parliament elected in March 1989. Since then dozens of religious activists, both lay people and clergy, from a wide range of denominations have been elected to the highest organs of government. They have stood for an equally wide range of political parties and groupings.

Since 1989, a number of Christian Democratic parties have been formed, some committed to pluralism, Western-style democracy and ideological tolerance and others, such as the Christian Democratic Movement of Viktor Aksyuchits, with an exclusivist and chauvinist agenda. An unresolved question for all Christian Democratic parties was how far they were 'Christian'; some welcomed not only Christians of all denominations but also non-Christians and non-believers as members; others were in fact, if not explicitly, 'Russian Orthodox' parties. The parties also varied on the question of claiming – or even wanting – the support of the Russian Orthodox Church. As in all areas of political life in Russia, issues of personality proved just as divisive as issues of policy and by late 1993, Christian Democracy looked a spent force in Russia.

Religion and nationalism

Orthodoxy, as 'the soul of the people', is closely linked to national aspirations. The late Metropolitan Ioann of St Petersburg was quoted as saying, 'If Russia isn't your mother, God can't be your father'; he represented an extreme of opinion in the Orthodox leadership. The Patriarch Aleksy II himself rejects national exclusiveness, having a long record of involvement with the Conference of European Churches and activity in the world-wide ecumenical movement. Chauvinist programmes are most often found among newly formed lay organisations of enthusiastic new converts to Orthodoxy, such as the Union of Orthodox Brotherhoods, founded in 1990.

The question of the relationship between religion and nationalism regularly arises in those regions of the Russian Federation which are seeking autonomy or independence and which have a Muslim majority. The Russian Orthodox Bishop of Kazan protested in 1992 against what he claimed was discrimination against the Orthodox Church by the pro-Muslim authorities of the Tatar Autonomous Republic. Despite repeated applications in the previous three years not one confiscated Orthodox church had been returned. While numerous churches and monasteries were standing empty, the existing churches were overflowing and there were no facilities for charitable work.

Religious education and training

Parents now have the right to bring up their children according to their own convictions. Religion may be taught in state schools, out of hours, or in parish schools; private denominational schools, colleges and institutes are proliferating. Since the collapse of communism, the secular authorities have encouraged initiatives to educate citizens in civic virtues and moral standards.

In Moscow and St Petersburg, many new religious educational establishments have been set up by laymen and laywomen, often with the backing and participation of individual priests or bishops but not of the church as an institution. The secular authorities tend to be very supportive of such private enterprises.

The major denominations are responding more slowly to the new opportunities for increased theological education. The Department for Education and Catechesis within the Russian Orthodox Church is now doing effective work; new theological training establishments have been opened by the Baptists and Seventh-Day Adventists.

Jewish educational and cultural organisations have been re-established, including day schools, seminaries (including one for women), and several Jewish universities.

The media

There is no restriction on religious publishing; in 1989 the Russian Orthodox Church published its first newspaper, the *Moscow Church Herald*. There is a proliferation of publishing initiatives by clergy and lay people at local level. Since the late 1980s, many dioceses and parishes have started publishing newsletters, scriptures and teaching materials. There is no restriction on importing religious literature and every kind of religious material can be had on the street.

It is in the secular press rather than the religious press where debate on issues affecting the inner life of churches tends to take place. The secular press have covered religion eagerly ever since the abortive coup of 1991, including the revelations about collaboration between clergy and the KGB and the public airing of disputes between the different Orthodox jurisdictions. Generally speaking, the liberal democratic press writes sympathetically about all religions, while the conservative and right-wing press concentrates on news about Orthodoxy and mentions other faiths merely to belittle them as alien and dangerous to Russia. However, there is sometimes sympathetic coverage of Islam, reflecting the friendly relations between certain Russian nationalist groups and anti-Western Muslim leaders like Saddam Hussein.

The articulation in the media of popular anti-Semitism has been of serious concern to Russian Jewry. In May 1993, a *Pravda* article 'Satanic Tribe' resurrected the blood libel, among other allegations about 'ritual killings'; the paper eventually printed an apology. Jewish organisations regard Russian courts as ineffectual in enforcing Article 74, the law which prevents the spread of racist and fascist propaganda.

Social welfare work

Church social work, though still banned, began in 1988 when the head of Moscow's biggest psychiatric hospital welcomed volunteers from the local Baptist church. Since then this area of activity has proliferated among the denominations with active encouragement by the authorities, both secular and religious. Teams of volunteers from churches of all denominations work in hospitals, mental institutions, children's homes, and prisons. In towns and villages, the theological academy, the local monastery or nunnery, even the local church parish will be running a soup kitchen, an old people's home, a hospital or a clinic, usually with the help of Western money, equipment and expertise.

In spring 1991, the new director of the once notorious Serbsky Institute of General and Forensic Psychiatry in Moscow appointed an Orthodox chaplain to its hospital. Russia's newly founded Christian Medical Association (CMA) has now called for the introduction of chaplains into all state hospitals. The CMA call would not favour any particular denomination: believers should be able to have access to priest, pastor, mullah or rabbi. Chaplains of all denominations are now also to be found in the more progressive Russian prisons.

In 1994 the Roman Catholic Archbishop became the first Christian leader in Russia to speak out against abortion when he issued a pastoral letter calling for the protection of unborn children. Authoritative statements on issues of public morality have never been part of the tradition of the Russian Orthodox Church.

Religion and the army

The army, one of the staunchest bulwarks of Marxist–Leninist orthodoxy and a powerful institution under communism, remains almost the only area of public life where the contribution of religion is unwelcome. A defence ministry survey in 1992 revealed that 64 per cent said there was no framework within the army for expression of freedom of conscience. Among the officers, 38 per cent were opposed to the idea of army chaplains and 41 per cent were against forming religious societies in the army. The Cossacks, who have always seen themselves as defenders of Orthodoxy, now have priests attached to their military units.

Women in religion

The question of women's rights is very low on the agenda of all religious denominations in Russia. Right across the denominational spectrum it is widely regarded as one of the fashionable 'modern' preoccupations typical of the 'secularised' churches of the West and not a problem for churches coping with all the more important challenges of freedom. Ordination of women in the Church of England has been a major factor in the loss of momentum in the post-war Anglican–Orthodox dialogue.

Note

1 See also the entry on Ukraine.

SPAIN

Spain	
GDP (US$bn)	575
Population	39,500,000
Annual population growth (%)	0.8
Urban population (%)	76
Working population (%)	39[a]
Literacy (%)	98
Ratifications	1; 2, 2(a), 2(b); 3; 4; E

Spain is a largely urban-based industrial democracy. Its 39.5 million people have few ethnic differences apart from the 600,000 Roma minority (gypsies) and the immigrant population. In the last few years, there has been a notable increase in people coming from the Maghreb countries, especially Morocco and Algeria, and Senegal, as well as from Latin America and the Philippines. Unemployment is rising faster in Spain than elsewhere in Europe, affecting 22 per cent of the labour force in 1995.

The religion of the majority of the Spanish population is Catholic. About 17,686 male religious live in ninety-eight Catholic orders. The number of women religious is considerably higher: some 56,008 living in 282 Catholic communities. There are smaller Protestant, Muslim and Jewish (20,000) populations. Evangelistic Christianity is making adherents among the much discriminated against Roma minority.

Spain in its last sixty years has been the field for major conflicts between ideologies. General Franco rose to power when in 1936 he led a mutiny against the then socialist government, starting a civil war which lasted until March 1939; the states of Nazi Germany and Fascist Italy supported Franco while the Soviet Union and international socialists defended the Republican government. General Franco, whose forces were victorious, continued as head of the Spanish state until he died in 1975. He presented himself as a Catholic and as a supporter of traditional values against 'godless atheism'; dissenting Catholics and Protestants as well as people with secular philosophies experienced great difficulties during his thirty-six-year rule.

Legal and political system

Spain's democratic constitution was adopted at the end of 1978. Spain is a parliamentary monarchy; the king has ceremonial functions only. The government is answerable to the legislature (Cortes Generales). The president, as head of the executive, is elected by the Congress of Deputies. Spain is a unitary state which is politically decentralised. The constitution recognises political autonomy for nineteen historical nationalities and regions incorporated into the Spanish state.

Article 1.1 of the constitution recognises political pluralism; Spain has no official ideology. Its multi-party political system covers the range of views typical in Western Europe. On the one hand, the Spanish Labour Socialist Party (PSOE) has socio-economic policies which are a synthesis of social democratic and liberal. Another party is the successor to the former communist party. At the other end of the spectrum is the right-wing Partido Popular (Popular Party), of more conservative ideology as far as social traditions and the influence of religion are concerned; some members belong to Opus Dei, the highly conservative Catholic lay organisation founded in 1928 in Madrid.

In the case of Catalonia and the Basque Country, local parties have the majority: a coalition named respectively, Convergencia I Unio and the Basque Nationalist Party. They respond to a political spectrum of central liberal to right-wing opinion, with some Catholic influence which brings them close to the European Christian Democrat parties. In the Basque Country, radical nationalism defends the use of armed struggle in pursuit of its ideology. This is the situation that produced the coalition between Herri Batasuna and the armed group ETA.

Spain has many NGOs presenting various ideological stances, generally alternatives to those in power, such as the Green Party and groups which are anti-racist, supportive of developing countries, nationalist, anti-immigration, anti-Semitic, and so on. The legacy of the authoritarian past can be seen in the multifarious spectrum of far Right opinion and association.

Racism and xenophobia

Islamophobia and anti-Semitism have ancient roots in Spain. Spanish national identity was formed as anti-Muslim in the four centuries-long Christian Reconquista of peninsular Spain from the Muslim Moors. Both Muslims and Jews were brutally treated by the Inquisition. Granada, the last Muslim stronghold, fell in 1492, the same year in which the Edict of Expulsion – until implicitly revoked in 1869 – also cleared Spain of almost all its Jews. In 1492, the triumphalist Spanish throne blessed the voyages of Christopher Columbus to carry the Christian standard forward into the New World. The 500-year anniversary of the fall of Granada and the voyage of Columbus was marked by great celebrations as well as protests from minorities to whom reconciliation activities were designed to give some cultural acknowledgement.

Racism and xenophobia are still an issue in Spain today. Such incidents increased in 1993, mainly towards non-white immigrants. Anti-Semitic literature and other manifestations also appeared and were on sale on Spanish streets, according to the Anti-Semitism World Report. The Roma (gypsy) minority have long been discriminated against and disadvantaged; they are among the poorest Spanish people.

A poll of teenage students in Spain, published in 1994, has shown that racist attitudes are substantially increasing among young Spaniards, in comparison to a similar poll in 1986. Asked if they would expel certain kinds of people from Spain, if they could, the students nominated Gypsies (31 per cent), North Africans and Arabs (26 per cent), black Africans (14 per cent) and Jews (13 per cent).

Spain has supported European education initiatives to counter racism among the young. Racial discrimination, hatred and xenophobia are prohibited by law. The major political parties have supported the reform of Spain's Penal Code to include prohibitions on racist and Neo-Nazi activities, including the dissemination of ideologies promoting racism. Since 1989, there has been a Special Advisor for Human Rights in the Ministry of Justice and the Interior to promote human rights law and to train senior law enforcement officers.

Freedom of thought, conscience and religion or belief

The Spanish constitution contains a general principle of non-discrimination. Article 14 states that:

> Spanish people are equal before the law, and may not be discriminated against in any manner on grounds of birth, race, sex, religion, opinion or any other condition or personal or social circumstance.

Article 16 of the constitution recognises freedom of thought, ideology and belief in these terms:

> Freedom of ideology, religion and worship of individuals and communities is guaranteed with no other restrictions regarding its expression, than those required for the maintenance of public order as protected by law.

Thus this widely defined freedom protects not only individuals but also groups, those organised on the basis of affiliation, as are religious groups. The provision allows individuals the right to be part of any religion or none. The constitution also declares that 'No-one can be forced to declare his/her ideology, religion or beliefs.'

Constitutional jurisprudence

Article 10.2 of the constitution provides that ideological freedom, religious freedom and the general rights to conscientious objection must be interpreted in the light of the Universal Declaration of Human Rights and the international human rights agreements to which Spain is a party. The jurisprudence of the European Court of Human Rights has direct effect, as has been recognised by the Constitutional Court from 1981 onwards.

Freedom of religion is regulated by Organisation Law 7 of 1980. Religious liberty is there defined as the right of any person:

- to freely choose to either profess a religious belief or none at all;
- to manifest religious practice and worship and receive the religious assistance of his/her own faith;
- to receive and impart religious education and information;
- to meet or make public manifestations for religious purposes; and
- to associate in order to develop religious activities as a community.

Through its jurisprudence, the Constitutional Court has interpreted the meaning of ideological and religious freedom, in decisions which define the content of this right:

1 The right to freedom of ideology, religion and worship belongs not only to individuals but also to communities, meaning the social groups to which a person affiliates according to doctrine or religious practice.
2 Ideological liberty does not protect acts that fail to recognise the obligations derived from the exercise of public duty.
3 Religious liberty requires that no-one may be forced to declare his/her religious convictions; in employment matters, an employer must scrupulously adopt a position of neutrality. However, the particular requirements of a certain religion which has feast days that differ from employment regulation may generally be permitted as a reasonable exception, but may not be imposed on the employer.
4 Religious assistance to Catholics in the armed forces does not violate freedom of religion.
5 The basic principles which govern the relations between the state, the churches and other religions are essentially two-fold:

   (1) religious liberty understood as a subjective right of a fundamental nature, which is made manifest in the recognition of a sphere of liberty of the individual;
   (2) the equality provisions of the constitution (Articles 9 and 14) mean that it is not lawful to establish any kind of discrimination or different legal treatment of the citizen by reason of their ideologies or beliefs. Actions of public officials may be invalidated if they violate the right to ideological or religious freedom.

6 In education, the respect for ideological freedom implies that mere disagreement by a teacher with the philosophy of an educational establishment cannot be a lawful reason for dismissal, if it has not been externalised or made visible in any of the institution's activities.
7 Ideological freedom allows criticism of the state's institutions, including the monarch.

Religion and state

Spain's imperial and colonial past was as a confessional state. The 1978 constitution specifically indicates that Spain is no longer so: 'There shall be no state religion. The public authorities shall take account of the religious beliefs of Spanish society and shall accordingly maintain relations of cooperation with the Catholic Church and other faiths.' In this way the constitution represents a radical break with the state as it was during the Franco period. However, it recognises the extent to which the Catholic religion is interwoven with Spanish society.

The state, bearing in mind the religious beliefs of Spanish society, can establish cooperative agreements with any faith; these must be ratified by parliament. Among them is the treaty with the Vatican on legal matters, religious assistance to the armed forces and military service by priests and religious orders, and educational and cultural matters. Similar agreements were signed with Protestant, Jewish and Muslim representatives in 1992. A regime connecting Jewish and Protestant marriage ceremonies with civil marriage requirements was established. Though Catholicism is state-funded, Protestant and Jewish leaders are said to have refused the government's offer of financial support.

Legislation in 1980 set out the rights of churches, faiths and religious communities and their federations. They have legal personality once registered with the Ministry of Justice; registration is automatic. In 1989, 510 organisations were so registered: Catholic organisations, Calvinist, Anglican, Evangelist, Baptist, Lutheran, Pentecostal, Jewish, Islamic, Orthodox and other organisations.

The Catholic Church's social teachings on sexuality and marriage are no longer reflected in Spanish law. Access to divorce, abortion, equal rights for unmarried and homosexual couples, are all now available to Spanish people. Religious programmes in the media are monopolised by the Catholic religion whose religious ceremonies are transmitted by public television channels.

Education

In the agreement signed by the Spanish state with the Vatican on the 3 January 1979, the Catholic Church and its religious orders are entitled to set up schools. This monopoly regarding religious provision was paralleled in the armed forces by an agreement in the same year. There are also some private universities – all Catholic – in Spain. Other privately run schools may also be established.

Under the constitution and in other pieces of legislation, the liberty of parents to ensure the religious and moral education of their children in conformity with their own convictions is assured. The Right to Education Organisation Act of 1985 states that 'all state schools shall undertake their activities in conformity with Constitutional principles, the guarantee of ideological neutrality, and respect for the religious and moral beliefs referred to in article 27 (3) of the Constitution'. The curricula of both Protestant and Catholic religious education for primary and secondary schools was established in 1993, according to their agreements with the state.

New religious movements

In Spain, new religious movements have encountered considerable opposition. Two incidents in particular have concerned the Church of Scientology and The Family (formerly the 'Children of God'). In 1988, an international convention of Scientologists in Madrid was raided by the Spanish police on the order of a local Judge of Instruction to arrest all foreign Scientologists. Seventy-two were arrested and interrogated by the judge on the basis of allegations made about the practice of Scientology and the work of the drug rehabilitation agency run by the church. Eleven, including the president of the Church of Scientology International, an American, Rev. Heber C. Jentzsch (who had arrived in Spain the same day that he was arrested), were kept imprisoned; the rest were released and twelve foreigners among them deported. Rev. Jentzsch was imprisoned for three weeks, then released on bail but not allowed to leave the country for a further three months. In 1991, the National Court found no evidence of fraud or financial crimes and remanded the matter to the local Madrid Court. In 1994, a new Judge of Instruction sent twenty-one people to trial, including Rev. Jentzsch, on various charges which did not concern specific incidents or conduct linked with the individuals named. The case is pending and is expected to be challenged on grounds of constitutional rights and freedoms.

In the matter concerning the new religious movement The Family, Spain has stated to the (UN) Human Rights Committee that protection is given against 'pseudo-religious' organisations which cause harm to children. In 1994, the Special Rapporteur on Religious Intolerance reported that, following complaints by representatives of 'anti-cult' associations, police had arrested members of the new religious movement in Barcelona in 1990; twenty-two children were then held in child welfare centres for over a year. On their release, Catalan authorities allegedly demanded that their parents send them to a state school and that each family in the community should undertake to reside in their own home. Schooling is compulsory in Spain; The Family's home-schooling arrangements were informal.

In a lengthy and considered response to the query from the Special Rapporteur, the Spanish government stated that The Family had not applied for registration as a church, faith or religious community and therefore had no legal status as a religious entity; nor had it established itself formally as an association. The investigation and arrests had been made in the pursuit of the legitimate aims of public authority and at the order of the competent courts. Allegations of neglect and ill-treatment of the children were denied; Catalan authorities had provided schooling, social, psychological and medical care of which, they claimed, the children had been deprived.

In May 1992, a Barcelona judge, reportedly describing the police action as an error, ordered the acquittal of the adult members – who had been charged with unlawful association, setting-up an unlawful teaching establishment, psychological injury and fraud – and the return of the children to their parents' custody. Appeals followed. In June 1993, the Barcelona Provisional Court acquitted the accused and declared the preservation measures adopted null and void. The Court stated that it does not and cannot judge 'beliefs' except in cases where the closed, dogmatic and disciplined communities to which they give rise are harmful in character. In October 1994, the Supreme and Constitutional Courts also upheld the acquittals.

Conscientious objection

Spain's constitution also recognises the right to conscientious objection to compulsory military service. According to the 1984 legislation which regulates conscientious objection, alternative social service is provided for – of twice the length of military service – if for reasons of conscience related to religious, ethic, moral, humanitarian, philosophical or other convictions of a similar nature, those who are called up object to doing military service. Anyone who absents themselves from alternative service for more than three days running, without due cause, is liable to up to six years' imprisonment. Conscientious objection that occurs after recruitment into military service is not accepted.

In public hospitals, where terminations of pregnancy may be performed, according to legal precedent, doctors may invoke a right of conscientious objection.

Women and religion

Spain's fascist past under Franco is vividly kept in mind by women in considering matters of religion. For about forty years after 1936, legislation was based on nineteenth-century models and restrictions for women were re-introduced into Spanish society with strong support from the majority of the clergy and a structure of elite families. Ecclesiastical tribunals arbitrated all marriage, family and sexual matters. Struggle against the power of the clergy has been a constant theme in Spanish feminism.

During the last years of the Franco regime, a new generation of young priests pressured the Catholic Church to liberalise its views in advance of the state. Gradually such measures as the requirement that wives obtain husbands' permission to work outside the home were removed from the law. In areas associated with the family and reproduction, change has been difficult. In 1976, about 30 per cent of women prisoners were there because they had had abortions. Feminist demonstrations resulted in a very limited permission for legal abortion in 1982, but the policy was demonstrated against strongly by the Catholic Parent Confederation. Because of a conscientious objection clause for medical personnel, even the most recent amendments do not ensure that termination of a pregnancy is reasonably available.

The high incidence of violence in Spanish marriages has only begun to be addressed; incest and sexual abuse laws are virtually unenforceable, as are the very punitive laws against rape which both define rape such that most rapes do not fall within the parameters, and encourage 'forgiveness' by the victim and consequent lack of prosecution of the perpetrator. In spite of the achievements of the Spanish women's movement in the short time since the demise of fascism, the particular attitudes of the Catholic Church towards women, sexuality and reproduction remain powerful and tend to confirm rather than reform the pervasive codes of honour and shame that restrict women.

TURKEY

Turkey	
GDP (US$bn)	100
Population	58,400,000
Annual population growth (%)	2.4
Urban population (%)	64
Working population (%)	35
Literacy (%)	80.5
Ratifications	4; E

Turkey is at once a European, Asian, Balkan, Mediterranean, Black Sea and Middle Eastern country, as the successor to the Ottoman Empire which had its territories on three continents (Europe, Asia and Africa) and embraced many peoples of different faiths. After the Republic of Turkey was established in 1923, it became the only Islamic country to adopt secularism, against a background of the dominance of Islam at all levels of state and society. It is currently a member of all European organisations, has made a Customs Union with the European Union and is an active member of the Organisation of the Islamic Conference.

Ethnic and religious composition

Today, nearly 59 million people live in Turkey; 99 per cent of the population is Muslim, the rest consisting primarily of Christians and Jews. Although the largest ethnic group in Turkey are the Turks, after the Empire was split up, many Muslims – mainly from the Balkans and the Caucasus – moved or were expelled to Turkey, defining themselves as Muslims or being so defined by others: Bosnians, Albanians, Pomaks, Georgians, Circassians, Abkhazes, Ossets, Tartars, Uzbeks, Turcomen, Kazhaks and Azeris. Kurds and Arabs are indigenous Muslims.

The estimated 8 million Kurds form the largest, though mostly unacknowledged, ethnic minority. A major conflict between Kurdish militants (the Kurdestan Workers Party or PKK) and the Turkish military forces has continued in south-east Turkey since 1984. An estimated 20,000 people have been killed and at least 2 million Kurdish people have been driven from their homes and villages by the security forces.

Turkish Muslims include the 80 per cent Sunni majority, in four main schools of which the Hanafis are the largest group. The remainder are Alevis and Shias, groups which in particular disagree about the political organisation of Islam. Alevis are vigorous defenders of Turkish secularism and have liberal religious practices, including a refusal to segregate women in prayers and social life.

Turkey's a small non-Muslim population – less than 1 per cent – has various divisions of Greek Orthodox adherents, Armenian Christians, Jews, Roman Catholics and Assyrian Christians. Many now have taken Muslim names.

Differences in ethnic background and religious tradition have resulted in a complex interplay between majority and minority in Turkey. For instance, the Alevis are a minority among fellow Muslims but are of majority Turkish origin, while the Kurds – a minority in ethnic terms – are among the Sunni majority.

Turkish revolutionaries – Kemalists, followers of Kemal Atatürk – in the early 1920s themselves adopted a minority view of Islam which holds that Islam does not need to organise itself politically since the true Khalifate disappeared at the end of the Orthodox Khalifate when the Umayyads transformed it into temporal rule. According to this understanding, the observance of Islamic normative order in its entirety may be left to individual believers, while the state may be organised according to secular principles.

Religion and state in the Ottoman Empire

The history of relations between the state and Islam in Turkey may be traced back to the Islamic theocratic state, from the thirteenth to the mid-nineteenth century, when the Ottoman Empire rapidly declined. A Westernisation reform process was launched in 1839; secular movements gained momentum while Islam remained the official, dominant religion. The secular period began with the establishment of the Republic in 1923 when the state assumed control over religion.

The Ottoman Empire became a fully-fledged religious state in the early sixteenth century after Selim I took over the Khalifate from the Mamluks, the ruling dynasty of Egypt. Until the mid-nineteenth century Sunni Islam remained the state ideology throughout the Empire. The Sultan was not only the head of the Empire but also the highest spiritual leader of all Muslims, the Khalif, earthly deputy of the Prophet.

Sultan Mehmed II, in accordance with Islam, established a semi-autonomous status for non-Muslim communities as *millets* (nations). *Millets* were free to rule their communities according to their own beliefs and traditions through a leader who was responsible to the Sultan. Thus, all *millets* had their religion-based autonomy, governed by their patriarchates, which in turn accounted to the Sublime Porte for all members of their faith. The patriarchs were granted the status of a *vazir* (Minister) with access to the *divan* (Council of Ministers). They had their own courts with jurisdiction over their members in religious matters. Judgments given by such courts were executed by the Ottoman government; some patriarchates had their own prisons. The *millet* system was continued by later sultans although, as the Empire expanded, more non-Muslims came under the jurisdiction of the Sublime Porte. There were as many as fourteen *millets* in 1914.

The freedom of religion of non-Muslims was, however, subject to some constraint. Bells could not be rung outside the church or during the prayer time of Muslims. New churches could not be built without permission and their repair was subject to strict supervision. Extension of churches was not allowed. Construction of such institutions as hospitals, schools and orphanages was also subject to government approval. Non-Muslims were not admitted to public employment and their testimony in the courts, in favour of or against Muslims, was not allowed.

Some of these restrictions were lifted during the nineteenth-century reform period, when secular (*nizami*) courts were introduced which adjudicated disputes of a non-*shariah* nature, especially if they involved non-Muslims. Laws passed by parliament were meant not to violate the *shariah*.

At the splitting up of the Empire after the First World War and the end of the war between Greece and Turkey, the Lausanne Treaty of 1923 recognised the fully independent status of the Republic of Turkey and abolished the organisation of the Empire, including the *millet* system in its original form. All citizens were given equality without distinction by race or religion. Minority status, however, was given to non-Muslims under the guarantee of the League of Nations.

The development of Turkish secular ideology

Turkish secularism was designed to disestablish the centuries-old religious state and to transform, along Western lines, political and social structures of a state and society shaped by Islam over centuries. As the Constitutional Court has put it, secularism has been given the function of transforming the structure of opinion and thought in Turkish society. In a sense, this has been achieved. Secularism is the most important pillar of the state and nation, protected by the constitution as well as by numerous laws and regulations. Established as an ideology at the expense of Islam, it particularly restricted freedom of religion in the Republic's early years.

In 1924 the Turkish Grand National Assembly was presided over by the Republican People Party, the party dominating political life until 1950. The Khalifate was abolished, as was the Ministry of Sharia and Avqaf endowment. The educational system was secularised; all educational institutions, including hundreds of theological ones (*madrassas*), were transferred to the Ministry of National Education (MNE). All religious schools were closed down. A Directorate of Religious Affairs administered all mosques, *masjids*, dervish orders and convents, and appointed and dismissed, as the case may be, *imams*, sheikhs, preachers, prayer-callers, and other similar religious functionaries; religious services could only be performed in designated places. The Swiss Federal Civil Code was adopted as the Turkish Civil Code in 1926; it replaced Islamic law in personal status matters of marriage, divorce and inheritance. *Shariah* courts were closed down. The references in the constitution to Islam as the religion of the state and to the parliament as the chief executor of the Islamic system were deleted.

Culture and religion were deeply affected by the change. In secularising education, the Arabic alphabet was replaced by the Latin, cutting off the nation from its past in an attempt to integrate it with the West in particular and the world in general. Numerals, measurement units, the Islamic calendar – all were replaced by Western ones. Prayers, called for centuries in Arabic, began to be called in Turkish in 1932; this alienated many Muslims from the mosques. Traditional Ottoman dress made way for European headgear and styles of dress and in 1934 it was made illegal to wear religious clothing outside religious places. On the other hand, women were given the vote in the same year and allowed to stand for election. The imposed process of modernisation was thus both liberating and traumatic.

Political developments under secularism

With the introduction of multi-party democracy in 1946, the ruling party allowed more religious freedom in the predominantly Muslim electorate; the dance of the whirling dervishes was once more permitted to establish the Sufi mystical continuum with God. However, the state bureaucracy continued to dominate political life. In 1950, the Democrat Party set about undoing the excesses of secularism during the single party era; for instance, it restored Arabic as the language of worship, reopened religious (Imam-Hatip) schools in 1951 and allowed the Qur'an to be recited on state radio. The number of religious institutions increased rapidly while the strict grip of the state over religion was relaxed in almost all spheres.

For a long time the place of the parties on the political spectrum was defined by reference to attitudes to religion or secularism. The Right was labelled anti-secularist, while the Left was associated with secularism. For the intelligentsia, a religious person could not be progressive or modern, but most people were religious and voted for the Centre-Right.

By the late 1960s, the established parties could offer no more to the religious Right without departing substantially from the essence of secularism. The National Order Party was then established by the Islamists; it was hardly sympathetic to the Kemalist reforms and its activities were closely watched and it was closed down by the Constitutional Court in 1972. Shortly afterwards the religious Right was reorganised as the National Salvation Party, which formed a coalition government with the Republic People Party in the late 1970s. It was also closed down, along other political parties, after the 1980 military coup.

However, the religious movement had gained enough momentum to continue and in 1983 the Islamic revivalist Welfare Party was established. In late 1995 the Welfare Party, already successful in municipal elections, won the general elections, promising a 'just order' for the poor and alienated. By July 1996, a coalition eventually formed between the Welfare Party and the secularist True Path Party in which the Welfare Party leader pledged to uphold the democratic and secularist principles of the Turkish state. Although the party has a religious approach and has expressed dislike for secularism as it stands today, the Welfare Party and the Centre-Right parties channel most Islamist concerns into the democratic system. Militant Muslim organisations have gone underground. Hizbullah is believed to be responsible for terrorist activities against prominent secularists and Islamic Action and Islamic Jihad have also made their presence felt.

Protection of secularism

The principle of secularism is unassailable and permeates the structure of the state and the constitution. The Constitutional Court has clarified the meaning of secularism: 'from a legal point of view, in the classical sense, secularism means that religion may not interfere with state [affairs] and the latter not with religious affairs'. According to the Court, Turkish secularism consists of the following elements:

> First, that religion is not to be effective and dominant in state affairs;

> secondly, that in such parts of religion as relate to the spiritual life of the individual, a constitutional guarantee recognises unlimited freedom, without any discrimination;

> thirdly, that in such parts of religion as go beyond the spiritual life of the individual

and as relate to actions and behaviours which affect societal life, restrictions may be imposed, and the abuse and exploitation of religion may be prohibited, with a view to protecting public order, public safety and the public interest;

fourthly, that as the guardian of public order and public rights, the state may be given a power of control and supervision with respect to religious rights and freedoms.

The Court has applied these criteria very strictly, with a view to maintaining the system as it was established in the 1920s.

Although the secular legal system has become entrenched, in recent years some provisions restricting freedom of thought and opinion have been repealed. Articles 141 and 142 of the Criminal Code had prohibited activities which might sound like communism and Article 163 had made a criminal offence of activities violating the principle of secularism. Under Article 163, Nourists had been prosecuted for publishing and distributing the teachings of the Kurdish man of wisdom Said-i Nursi, whose writings became known as the Nour Collection; they were seen as weakening Turkish nationalism and secularism. In cases involving hundreds of judges, one by one those prosecuted on account of these books and pamphlets were acquitted. Nourists publish extensively today.

After the adoption of the 1982 constitution, courts allowed greater freedom of expression, permitting behaviour they considered related to individual belief. It is now possible to talk more freely about all aspects of Islam, including those covered by secularism, but political organisation of Islam is still forbidden. Political parties, trade unions and associations may also be closed down if they are held to violate the principle of secularism.

To curb Muslim militance and Kurdish separatism, the authorities now have recourse to the 1991 Anti-Terror Law. Article 8 of that law which prohibited forms of expression 'regardless of method, intention, and ideas' which would damage the 'indivisible unity' of the state has been modified to require an intent, but human rights activists are sceptical about the changes enlarging freedom of speech. A number of publications have been closed down and editors and journalists arrested or harassed for issuing what has been seen as 'separatist propaganda'. In 1996 hundreds of journalists, demonstrators and human rights activists were reportedly detained and beaten by the police. More than 130 academics, journalists and writers are in prison for Article 8 offences.

The removal of restrictions on freedom of expression with respect to religious matters has not yet led to an environment of greater mutual toleration. In 1993, thirty-seven secularists were burned to death – allegedly by religious extremists – in a hotel in Sivas, where they were attending an Alevi arts festival which Aziz Nesin, a boldly atheist satirist, who had previously published parts of Salman Rushdie's novel *The Satanic Verses*, had organised. Leading up to the catastrophe were incidents indicating insensitivity to religious feelings during the period of Friday prayer and some religious incitement to violence; extremists were indicted. In March 1995 tensions between Alevis and Sunnis erupted into riots in Istanbul. Alevis who were demonstrating against the growing popularity of the Welfare Party, seeing a potential for imposition of Islamic law, had come under gunfire reportedly from extremist Sunni groups.

Other Muslims have accommodated both Islam and secularism. They practise Islam, exercise tolerance in religious matters and consider that religion is a matter for the individual alone.

Protection of freedom of religion

Article 24 of the 1982 constitution states:

> Every one has the freedom of conscience, religious belief and opinions.

> No-one may be compelled to worship, to participate in religious rites and ceremonies, to [disclose] manifest his religious belief and opinion. No-one may be reproached and accused for his beliefs or opinions.

> Religious and moral education is to be conducted under the state control and supervision. The instruction of religious culture and morals shall be included among the compulsory courses taught at the primary and middle education institutions. Further religious education shall be given only on the request of the persons concerned and, in the case of minors, on the request of their legal representatives.

> No-one may abuse or exploit religion, or religious sentiments, or things that are considered sacred by religion in any way whatsoever for the purpose of founding in any way the social, economic, political or legal order of the state, in part, or in whole, on religious rules, or of gaining political or personal interests or influence.

All religions enjoy the same constitutional protection (Article 10) and the state has no power to define, create or change any religion. On this basis, in the late 1980s, the Court of Cassation overturned a lower court's decision that the Jehovah's Witnesses were not entitled to constitutional protection because they were considered a secret organisation with a religious appearance (Article 24).

Blasphemous acts against any religions – without discrimination – and interference with the exercise of the freedom of any religion are punishable offences in the Turkish Criminal Law:

> Any one who blasphemes [vilifies] Allah or any of religions or any prophets or holy books or sects of such religions, or who condemns or defames or insults any other person because of his religious beliefs or of complying with or failing from complying tenets of his religions, shall be punished.

Discrimination and prejudice

A person's religion or belief has to be disclosed under certain circumstances. All citizens have to have their religion or faith entered into their family register and indicated on their identity cards, according to the Census Act 1971; details may be amended only by a magistrate. The Constitutional Court has held that the requirement to reveal one's religion or belief for such purposes does not amount to coercing belief. The legislation does not require information about subdivisions such as the Sunni and Shia; since most people are Muslim, compulsory revelation of faith has thus not caused discrimination among Muslims. However, atheists, for instance, might experience social discrimination.

The Alevi have experienced prejudice and discrimination. They felt that they could not manifest their belief openly in a Sunni-dominated society and considered their belief to be misrepresented and misunderstood. It still may not be accepted and Alevis are constrained to practise their beliefs by violating the law. For instance, the Welfare Party mayor of Istanbul reportedly has tried (so far unsuccessfully) to close the houses of worship which the Alevi use for prayer.

In a similar way, *tariqas* (Sufi brotherhoods) that have been known, rightly or wrongly, as fundamentalists or anti-Kemalists may have difficulties in revealing their particular beliefs. For example, during the period when Nourists were prosecuted for expressing their beliefs, it required courage for a Nourist then to manifest his attachment to the teaching of Said-i Nursi.

State functions concerning religion

The Directorate of Religious Affairs is attached to the Office of the Prime Minister. The functions of the Directorate include enlightening Muslims as to worship and morals, conducting religious affairs and managing and supervising religious institutions. They do not extend to temporal matters; in accordance with the principle of secularism, the constitution deprives the Directorate of any political role.

The Directorate is assisted by its Supreme Religious Affairs Council, the functions of which include undertaking research on religious affairs, writing or translating religious works, advising the Directorate about publications, preparing opinions on religious questions and determining the essentials of Friday *khutbas* (sermons).

The Directorate's 90,000 personnel are civil servants and its president is appointed by the government. Its current budget is more than 1 per cent of the state budget; it manages 68,000 mosques, organises pilgrimage (*hajj*) affairs and provides religious education through 5,600 Qur'anic courses.

The Directorate has its critics. A large group of the secularists, including many Shia Muslims, are against the state's ever having had such religious functions, seeing them as the result of political concessions to the religionist groups, members of such *tariqas* or movements as Nakhshibandism, Nourism, Suliaymanism, Khadirism who have attained important positions in the state.

The composition of the Directorate is also predominantly Sunni Muslim; one Alevi leader sees this as evidence that Turkey is not a secular state. The Directorate tends to see Alevis as a cultural, not a religious, grouping. The US State Department reported that in 1993 no Directorate funds went to the Alevi community. Most of the Alevi population is Kurdish and there are no state-funded Alevi religious leaders in south-east Turkey. In Tunceli province, almost entirely Alevi and Kurdish, there have been well-attested reports of forced evictions and burning of Alevi villages by security forces. The government has built a large mosque in the centre of Tunceli which is used solely by Sunni employees of the central government.

Some would prefer to see the Directorate have a bigger role and be given autonomy, like universities. Others would prefer that religious affairs be left to the respective communities and removed from state control. The bureaucratic view is that, although ideally the state should not give any place to any religion in its mechanism, the special historical position of Turkey requires that it should control religion for a while longer, for many reasons. Leaving religious affairs to their belief communities would be risky as such issues could be open to abuse in a multi-faith society and politicians would exploit religious differences and sentiments. An open, uncontrolled market of faiths might be dominated by oil-rich 'fundamentalist' neighbours or states in the region. It might become difficult to sustain secularism as the state ideology, and internal conflicts among the Muslim divisions and movements would arise.

Religious and secular education

Religious education is a controversial issue and remains under state control. Article 266 of the Turkish Civil Code states:

> Parents have the right to determine the religious upbringing of the child. Any contract calculated to restrict this freedom of the parents is null and void. Those who have reached their majority are free to adopt a religion of their own choice.

After the introduction of secularism, religious schools which had been run by the Ministry of Sharia and financed by special foundations were transferred to the Ministry of National Education (MNE). To train personnel needed for religious services, a Faculty of Theology and Imam-Hatip schools (*lycée*-level religious schools) were established. These took the place of the abolished religious schools, but in 1930 they were closed down because the government feared they might undermine the newly established secularism. Furthermore, after the use of the Arabic alphabet was banned in 1928, the Qur'an could not be taught. In 1930, religious courses were removed from primary school curricula.

Thus between 1925 and 1950 the teaching of religion was effectively banned in Turkey, with the result that by the late 1940s it became apparent that many religious services could not be conducted because of the lack of religious personnel. Imam-Hatip schools were thus reactivated in 1951 together with a Faculty of Theology in Ankara and a Higher Institute for Islamic Studies in Istanbul. The scale of these secondary and tertiary educational institutions has grown substantially up to the present. The schools are run and supervised by the MNE; private Imam-Hatip *lycées* cannot be opened. They have the same curriculum as secular *lycées*, with additional religious courses and are partly state-funded. Some Imam-Hatip schools are also open to female students. Not all graduates of Imam-Hatip schools perform religious service. Many have gone on to university studies. However, secularists, concerned about the number of Imam-Hatip graduates who work in state administration, demand that they should have no access to higher education other than to the faculties of theology. Government permission to open 200 new Imam-Hatip *lycées* has not yet been given. Opponents consider that the secular state is preparing its own demise and that the increase should be frozen. The number of faculties of theology, however, has increased.

Between 1950 and 1982, religious education in schools was optional; parents had the right to have their children exempted. However, in the 1982 constitution, a secular provision has been added; Article 42.3 states:

> Training and education shall be conducted under the supervision and control of the state, pursuant to the Atatürk principles and reforms, and in accordance with the contemporary standards of science and education.

The MNE has reportedly decided that Kemalism must be taught in every lesson at elementary school level. In religious classes Atatürk's devotion to freedom of religion and secularism will be taught and in music courses students will be taught Atatürk songs.

None the less, Article 24.3 of the 1982 constitution still makes instruction in religious culture and morals compulsory. Other religious education can be be given only on request by older children, or by their parents or guardians. Secularist circles, in particular the Alevis, demand that religious education should be optional; the curriculum contains no reference to Alevi beliefs. The MNE has exempted non-Muslim students from the constitutional requirement.

The Directorate of Religious Affairs organises Qur'anic courses for those who want to have further religious education. These short-term courses, partly state-funded, teach the Qur'an and train *hafidhs*. All such courses must be authorised and taught by authorised teachers; an *imam* of a village cannot teach the Qur'an to children in his village if he is not authorised, without risking prosecution.

The status of non-Muslims

While non-Muslim citizens of Turkey have the same fundamental rights and freedoms as the majority Muslim population, they also enjoy a minority status granted by the Lausanne Treaty of 1923. Its provisions cannot be amended unilaterally and are superior to national law; thus it has shielded non-Muslims against the rigidity of the early applications of secularism. The Treaty defines the minorities by their faith, as 'non-Muslims'. The legal regime it established is also applicable, according to Article 45, to 'Muslims' in Greece. It is also confirmed in Article 42 of Turkey's constitution.

Turkey has recognised, according to the treaty, the religious identity of the communities as well as individual and minority rights. However, the communities have no juridical personality *vis-à-vis* the state. They retain part of the autonomy they had during the Ottoman period, in the sense that they manage their religious, social and charitable institutions, schools, and hospitals.

Minority status gives to those communities under the jurisdiction of Turkey equality before the law without distinction as to religion, and the right to free exercise, in public or in private, of all aspects of belief, religion or sect, provided that it is not contrary to the public order and public morals. Religious or sectarian differences are not to constitute an obstacle for such a Turkish national to enjoy civil rights, political rights, and in particular admission to public employment, getting promotion, honours, taking up any profession or doing any work. On their religious holidays, however, non-Muslims do not have to appear before the national authorities or courts, though they are not exempt from the law affecting public order.

The Lausanne Treaty provides a special regime for non-Muslims in family and personal status law. According to Article 42, this must be provided in accordance with their traditions and customs. However, when the Swiss Civil Code was adopted and Islamic law ceased to apply to personal status matters, the representatives of three non-Muslim communities (Jews, Greeks and Armenians) renounced their right to form separate commissions, as they considered the Civil Code – a secular law, adopted from a Christian country – applied to both non-Muslims and Muslims. The Turkish government also undertook to give full protection to churches, synagogues, cemeteries and other religious institutions of the communities, as well as to facilitate the establishment of new religious and charitable institutions. The patriarchates run various religious, educational, health and welfare institutions which the state must none the less approve; school curricula are tightly controlled.

The Ecumenical Patriarchate of Orthodox Christianity – 'first among equals' of the Orthodox around the world – is based in Istanbul (as the former Constantinople) and ministers to a dwindling number of the Greek faithful. Even though the erosion of this power base began long ago, the Patriarchate has been accused in the press of trying to establish an independent state on the lines of the Vatican or of wishing to revive the Byzantine Empire. The Patriarchate has been trying to have its seminary reopened, on the island of Halki in the Sea of Marmara, but the authorities have refused, saying, among other things, that the Greek minority is too small. In 1995 the Chairman of the Turkish

Parliament was alleged to have threatened to convert the Patriarchate into a museum 'as we did in the past with the Church of Saint Sophia' if it continued to 'act as an independent state'. Church property has been stolen, vandalised and damaged.

Some of the traditional non-Muslim communities are now smaller than they were when the Treaty was signed in the 1920s and fear that places of worship may revert to government possession under Turkish law because they have difficulty staffing local religious councils.

The Jewish community, well integrated into Turkish society, is still concerned about incidents of anti-Semitism in Turkey and an increasing number of anti-Semitic publications.

Non-Muslims who are not covered by the Treaty include evangelical Christians. There is no law prohibiting proselytising and charges of disturbing the peace are usually dismissed. However, evangelical Christians are watched and may be detained. In 1993, fourteen Spanish Protestants were ordered to stand trial for singing hymns and distributing religious pamphlets outside a mosque at Friday prayers. One of the most prestigious educational institutions in Istanbul, Roberts College, was founded by American Protestants but is now administered in a non-confessional way.

Women, religion and secularism

Turkey was the first Islamic state to negate the legal influence of the *shariah* in 1923–24 by abolishing religious courts and the Islamic religious education system. Sufi religious orders were banned and other reforms were introduced which benefited women. However, the mode of the new militant secularism was authoritarian; it attacked the Islamic symbol system and included almost compulsory injunctions to wear modern Western dress. Muslim women had generally worn a veil, urban lay male Muslims a fez, while the *ulema* (scholars) and religious leaders had their own specific dress. The fez was strictly banned and the wearing of veiling strongly discouraged. The 'hat law' is still commemorated annually as a symbol of Atatürk's reforms.

However liberating were the reforms, they embodied a national vision that discouraged women's action on their own behalf, as evidenced by the suppression of autonomous women's organisations. The gains made in women's participation in public life, especially in the professions, slowed after twenty years and many rural women did not benefit at all.

Gradually, more stress was placed on women's importance as mothers and home-makers and in the 1980s there has been a strong revival of conservatism at the same time as Turkey is negotiating to meet the requirements of the European Economic Community. Conservative Islamic intellectuals condemn modern secularist industrial technocracy and what they see as a confusion of roles in family and wider social life.

The struggle between the new conservatives and the secularists is epitomised in the current debate about appropriate clothing. Generally free to dress as they wish, including mini skirts and jeans, some female university students, teachers, nurses, and attorneys have begun dressing in head-scarves and turbans both for study, at work and in other public places. This is vehemently opposed by secularists especially in universities, which has resulted in refusal of admittance to classes and exams, or suspension of such students, thus preventing them completing their professional training. The question has engaged the parliament, the Constitutional Court, the Council of State and the public at large.

It is thought that a major influence is the increasing number of conservative families allowing their daughters to attend higher education institutes. It is also possible that the dress innovation reflects an environment of freedom which has made it possible for a new generation to assert themselves in ways not possible before. But secularists argue that the move is a symptom of *shariah*-based fundamentalism.

According to a recent public survey, a great majority of the Turkish population believe that the female students have the right to attend their classes with their scarves or turbans and that it is not against secularism. Secularist circles see it as a symbol of anti-secular thought, and as such, a step towards the establishment of the *shariah*, with the perceived risk of abolition of fundamental rights and freedoms. Others see it as a symbol of provincialism and peasant backwardness. Some take up a legal approach, arguing that a public institution which offers a public service has the right to set conditions for benefiting from such services. Thus, students, like civil servants and soldiers, should not dictate to the authorities by wearing dress of their own choice.

The official response to this problem has varied. The Council of State has refused to give relief to students who cover themselves. In a case brought by a female medical student against a decision of the university administration to suspend her for a month for wearing a head-scarf during classes, the Council of State ruled that the head-scarf or turban had come to symbolise a world view contrary to the freedom of women and the basis of the Republic. The Court stated:

> Some of our girls who have not received adequate education cover their hair, without any specific [i.e. ideological] thought, under the influence of the customs and traditions of the social environment in which they live. But some of our girls and women who have received enough education not to submit to the pressure of the social environment, or to the customs and traditions, are known to cover their heads, contrary to the principle of secularism, for the purpose of showing that they prefer a religion-based state. For these people, using a head-scarf is no longer an innocent habit; it becomes a symbol against the freedom of women and the basic principles of our Republic. Whereas the applicant is now receiving education at the university level, she is supposed to know the importance of these principles in the establishment and protection of our Republic.

Parliament then attempted to resolve the issue in 1988. All turban-wearing students who had violated university restrictions on dressing and had been subjected to disciplinary actions were pardoned, and the Higher Education Law was amended to read as follows:

> It is obligatory to have contemporary appearance and dress in Higher Education institutions, their classrooms, laboratories, clinics and corridors. [There is freedom, however, for women] to cover, due to religious belief, the neck and hair with a head-scarf or turban.

This caused indignation among secularists, including Kenan Evren, the then President, who successfully sought before the Constitutional Court to have this clause annulled. The Court recalled that where religion affected society's life and social behaviour, under the constitution religious freedom may be restricted for the purpose of protecting the public order, public safety and public interest. The Court also said that in a secular system laws cannot be enacted on a religious basis, whereas the statute under review was enacted on such a basis.

In commenting on the issue of women covering their heads in universities, the Court said that to allow female students to cover their heads on university grounds might adversely affect the public security and unity of the nation because the head-scarf or turban shows who belongs to which religion. This action, it said, would prevent students from studying together and cooperating in their attempts to reach scientific truth; it would lead to differences and eventually to religious conflicts. The Court also thought that the freedom to wear a turban in the university grounds contravened the principle of equality of all faiths before the law, as to allow the head-scarf would be to grant certain students a privilege not granted to others. Religious clothing which was not contemporary was, it considered, incompatible with secularism.

In the event, universities have adopted individual and conflicting policies on the matter of covering forms of dress.

Holidays and days of religious observance

For Muslims, Friday is the day of congregation in mass prayer, a sacred day according to the Qur'an; until 1935 it was the official weekly day of rest and observance. Since then, work days and the weekend have become aligned with those in the West.

In the arrangement of working hours, there is no allowance for prayer time in general and Friday prayer time in particular, not even in Ramadan, although there have been demands for it. Attempts by local authorities to accommodate religious practices have been opposed not only by secularists, but by the Council of State which quashed, for example, a circular of the General Directorate of Roads, which had changed working hours so that employees could attend Friday prayer. The Court considered that public sector administration had to be independent of religious rules. There was a duty to refrain from exerting any pressure of a religious nature on individuals. Further, changes in working hours on Friday to accommodate Friday prayer had, in the Court's view, nothing to do with the public interest.

However, *masjids* have recently been built in some official workplaces and state institutions in order to meet the religious needs of employees for prayer in private; this has been criticised by secularists. Because government policy has not changed, the Directorate of Religious Affairs has recently proposed that the Friday prayer time itself should be changed so as to adapt it to working hours and make it possible for officials to pray during their lunch time.

On the other hand, two major Muslim feasts, the Feast of Ramadan (Id al-Fitr) and the Feast of Sacrifice (Id al-Qurban), are official holidays. Other religiously significant days are celebrated by praying in mosques and reciting the Qur'an, which is broadcast on the state radio and television, as well as on private electronic media.

Conscientious objection

Military service is a requirement and there is no provision for conscientious objectors in Turkey. Even children have been known to be drafted as soldiers.

UKRAINE[1]

For almost 350 years Ukraine was a colony in the Russian Empire. Ukraine, newly independent in 1991, is experiencing a national renaissance and seeking to create a democratic state. A by-product of transition from communism to democracy has been serious religious conflict between the three churches of the Eastern Byzantine tradition: the Ukrainian Catholic or Greek Catholic, the Ukrainian (Autocephalous) Orthodox Church and the Russian Orthodox Church.

Ukraine	
GDP (US$bn)	95
Population	51,600,000
Annual population growth (%)	0.6
Urban population (%)	69
Working population (%)	51[a]
Literacy (%)	95
Ratifications	1; 2, 2(a), 2(b); 3; 4

After the First World War, the Ukraine was divided between Poland and the Soviet Union, and was fully reintegrated in 1945 under the Soviet protectorate. A national revival crystallised during the period of *perestroika* into the Rukh movement which brought together a democratic opposition. The failure of the Soviet Communist coup in 1991 led to the declaration of Ukraine's independence on 24 August 1991 and the banning of the Communist Party. Two weeks later, Ukraine's first president was elected and the political divisions of the new state emerged; democratic parties came out of the Rukh while the communists consolidated. In the 1994 parliamentary elections, the post-communists gained a substantial majority while the Rukh became a marginal political power.

Ukraine is an industrial country, with a rural population of 32.6 per cent (1991), but structural change in industry is only beginning and privatisation is stagnating. Ukraine ended the first year of its independence in a serious depression, on the edge of hyper-inflation with its budget deficit ballooning to 44 per cent of GDP. The country is dependent on Russian energy sources and the price of imported fuel has been raised.

Historical background

The adoption of Christianity (Byzantine order, the patriarchate of Constantinople) by the Rus-Ukrainian state in 988 was a major development in Ukrainian history and has remained the means of preserving national identity. From the fifteenth century, however, under Polish rule, many Ukrainians of the upper social class adopted Roman Catholicism. For patriotic reasons, others became zealous defenders of Orthodoxy. From the seventeenth century, under Russian pressure, Ukrainian Orthodoxy was taken over by the Russian Orthodox Church (patriarchate in Moscow), integrating it into the Tsarist Empire. By the beginning of the nineteenth century, the Ukrainian Orthodox Church hierarchy had become totally Russian.

Russian dominance over Ukrainian culture and religion continued under the Soviet Union. By the 1970s, the percentage of Russian-speakers in the Ukraine had increased to almost half the population. In 1965 and 1972 there were waves of arrests of Ukrainian cultural figures, historians, journalists and those who had tried to protest against what they described as repression of their nation. During the 1970s and 1980s, the issue of Ukrainian language and beliefs and opposition to Russian Orthodox Church dominance became critical elements of Ukrainian identity.

Religion and state under communist rule

Under Soviet rule, churches and religious societies were deprived of the rights of legal entities and land; most properties were nationalised. In the Ukraine, legislation on religious denominations was based on Lenin's Decree on Freedom of Conscience, 1918. Its main principles were the following:

- all possible limitations on the activities of religious organisations, including the deprivation of their socially important functions;
- discrimination against believers, especially in the sphere of education, culture and public activities;
- preference to those confessions which manifested their loyalty and adaptability to the communist order and ideas;
- prohibition of all forms of public religious education;
- deprivation of all rights of religions to provide the material basis of their churches and activities.

During the 1930s, most Ukrainian villages lost their church, their priest and their leading farmers, all of which had been important elements in the national culture. In the period from 1917 to 1937, communist authorities in the Ukrainian Soviet Socialist Republic executed or deported 35 bishops, 2,500 priests, thousands of monks and nuns, most of them members of the Ukrainian (Autocephalous) Orthodox Church. Clergy became classified according to the degree to which they were 'loyal to socialist society'. Under severe pressure, during the Synod of Lvov in 1946, the Ukrainian Catholic Church declared its 'self-liquidation' and its 'reunification with the Russian Orthodox Church'.

However, from the 1970s the voices of those who worked for religious freedom in the Ukraine began to be heard through underground publications and chronicles. In 1988 the Ukrainian Orthodox Church joined the campaign. In February 1989, Ukrainian Catholic and Orthodox priests celebrated a service together outside the Cathedral of St Yuri in Lvov attended by 30,000 believers. Unofficial millennium celebrations were held in Kiev, Kharkov and Odessa. Two weeks earlier, the Initiative Committee in Support of the Revival of the Ukrainian Orthodox Church had been launched, and the policies of the Russian Orthodox Church towards Ukrainian religious aspirations were openly criticised.

Legal and constitutional system

Ukraine's parliamentary and multi-party democracy is still governed by the 1978 Constitution of the Ukrainian SSR, modified by the addition of legal guarantees for the institutions of democratic government and an open economy. A redrafted constitution has been in preparation since 1992. The capacity of the legislative and juridical branches to function independently from the executive branch is limited. The armed forces have largely remained outside politics.

Laws passed in 1991 and 1992 on the rights of ethnic and national minorities guarantee their rights to schools and cultural facilities and the use of their languages in business and official correspondence. Yet restrictions on freedom of the press and the prison and legal systems continue from the Soviet era. Ukraine is now a member of the Council of Europe.

Ethnic and social composition

The population of Ukraine was 52 million in 1992. In 1989, there were 44.2 million Ukrainians in the USSR; of these 37.4 million lived in the Ukraine on the day of independence in 1991. In the formerly Soviet diaspora, 3.7 million Ukrainians mostly lived in Russia and in the border regions of Kursk, Voronezh, the Don basin, and the Kuban.

Ukraine is 72.4 per cent ethnically homogeneous. The Russians (22.1 per cent of the population) form the largest minority, concentrated in eastern and southern Ukraine.

There are also smaller Jewish (490,000), Moldovan and Romanian (460,000), Bielo-russian (444,000), Bulgarian (234,000), Polish (219,000), and Hungarian (160,000) minorities, living mostly in the south and south-west. The large Russian minority reinforces separatist tensions; Russians, concentrated in industry sectors which have no future under the market economy, show little interest in the independent Ukrainian state.

Citizens of the Ukraine are thus deeply divided by region, national expectations and also by religion. In the west, where the Ukrainian (Greek) Catholic Church has historically been dominant, the independent state is strongly supported. In the east and the Crimea, where Orthodoxy predominates, support for independence is weak. The Ukrainian government recognises that its chief task is to keep the state from splitting into two, or even three, independent parts.

Religious composition

Ukraine is situated on the frontier between the West and East European cultures of Catholicism and Orthodoxy, Christianity and Islam. Beside the Orthodox Church with partriarchates in Moscow and in Kiev, there exist other Christian denominations: Greek Catholicism and Roman Catholicism, the Old Believers, various Protestant communities. Judaism and Islam are also represented.

The largest religious communities are the Orthodox, 70 per cent of which belong to the Ukrainian Orthodox Church, 20 per cent to the Ukrainian Orthodox Church of the Kiev Patriarchate, and 7 per cent to the Ukrainian Autonomous Orthodox Church. Of all religious communities, 18 per cent belong to the Ukrainian Greek Catholic Church (most located in Galichina and the Transcarpathian region). Every fifth community is a Protestant community, sometimes very small.

If, in the recent, communist past, only 5 per cent of respondents in Ukraine declared themselves to be believers, now this figure is 70 per cent, numbers increasing particularly among young people and the intelligentsia in this now multi-denominational country. Religious activity and organisations have flourished in recent years: clergy, centres, schools, missions, monasteries, and publications. The period 1988–94 saw a rapid increase in the number of religious communities; on average they increased by 20 per cent per year, particularly in the west.

Five years ago, only ten religious denominations were officially registered; now more than seventy different religious organisations are registered. The number of religious communities has increased from 4,500 in 1990 to 16,500 in 1995. Newer faiths and religious groups include the Christ Church, the Union Church, the New Apostolic Church, the New Evangelical Church, the Church of Jesus Christ of the Latter Day Saints, Jehovah's Witnesses, various charismatic and Marian movements, Buddhism, Baha'i, Krishna Consciousness and the Unification Church.

Today, several problems in religious life have been dealt with pragmatically, such as:

- the activities of confessions prohibited in the past (such as the Ukrainian Autonomous Orthodox Church and the Ukrainian Greek Catholic Church) have been resumed;
- all confessions have the freedom to conduct their canonical and preaching work freely and without obstruction;
- the local Orthodox Church, the Kiev Patriarchate, has been established;
- religious properties taken by the communist regime are now being returned;
- many religions have restored links with religious communities abroad;
- religious education classes are permitted in public schools as an extra-curricular

activity; the Greek Catholic and the Orthodox Churches have seminaries; Jewish religious schools operate in Kiev, Lvov, Odessa, Kharkov, Uman and Vinnytsia.

The following problems are in the process of resolution:

- the granting of privileges for religious communities in the sphere of taxation and payment for public utilities;
- publication arrangements for religious literature, newspapers and magazines;
- creation of religious and theological training institutions and programmes of religious education and awareness;
- construction of new religious buildings and the repairing and restoration of old ones;
- state registration of the main faith communities.

In the Ukrainian Orthodox and Catholic Churches and in their practice, women still stay in background, excluded from becoming priests. Most Ukrainian women seem to accept traditional roles in religious life.

Legal protection of freedom of religion and belief

In the Soviet period, legal decrees on freedom of conscience played only a cosmetic role. Communist Party bodies at every level were the law. Even in its more liberal phase, after the Party Congress in June 1988, Soviet religious policies were applied by means of administrative instructions rather than by legislation. In independent Ukraine, there is still no detailed law which guarantees freedom of religious organisation and the rights of believers. However, at the constitutional level there are important provisions with respect to civil rights: freedom of speech and press, freedom of peaceful assembly and association, and freedom of movement within the country, foreign travel, emigration and repatriation.

A Freedom of Conscience statute of 1991 has proved a failure and is being revised. The 1991 statute provides for registration and numerous rights for religious organisations, but these rights have proved hard to realise in practice. By the end of 1995, the Soviet-style National Council on Religious Affairs had been abolished by presidential decree and a new department of religious affairs planned for the Ministry of Nationalities, Migration and Religion.

An Inter-Church Council exists, but it consists only of the representatives of officially registered religions; newer religious minorities are not represented. Nevertheless, this body has the power to regulate the activities of all religious organisations.

The law does not provide for a state church, but it does not prevent local governmental bodies from being confessionally aligned, as in the Galichina region of Ukraine where Greek Catholicism enjoys a privileged position.

Registration of religious organisations

Although it is not stated in the existing law, registration of religious organisations is viewed by some authorities as the only legal basis for groups of Ukrainians to engage in religious activities such as worship and propagation of their faith to others. In Ukraine the government has continued to take the former Soviet approach, that all religious activity must be registered; foreign groups have been deported due to failure to register.

Registration of religious organisations involves the acquisition of the status of a legal entity which can own property, have a bank account, issue official visa invitations, hire employees and enter into contracts. Under the 1991 statute, any religious group supported by ten citizens may be registered. In practice, however, registration is a confusing and lengthy process. The criteria are not made known to applicants. Personal discretion is often exercised by officials; decisions are made on the basis of personal relations, and the political and religious preferences of those in charge. For example, national registration has been denied to the Ukrainian Autocephalous Church, despite the fact that it has been allowed to register many local congregations. In contrast, another religious group was told that it could only register a national entity if it had local chapters in at least eighteen locations, a requirement which cannot be found anywhere in the applicable law. However, the authorities have not interfered with the registration of minority religions such as Islam, the Mormons, the Jehovah's Witnesses, and the Church of Nazarene.

By contrast, creating a civic association in the Ministry of Justice in Ukraine is a model of normative process. A set of written instructions is posted for all to see, listing the required documents, filing fees and dates the office is open for applications. Properly filed documents are promptly approved and a new entity can begin operations. Similar procedures are followed for religious organisations in Russia and in Kazakhstan.

Foreign support for religions

In the current economic climate, virtually all Ukrainian religious organisations receive some form of financial, material and personnel assistance from abroad. However, there are no rules governing how this assistance is to be delivered. For example, financial donations in the form of transfers of hard currency have unlawfully been required to be converted into local currency (donations are also currently taxed at the rate of 37 per cent). Exorbitant customs duties have been levied on religious items from abroad; there are complaints that such items may also be pilfered or lost in customs storehouses.

Foreign religious workers have been subject to harassment depending upon the whims of local authorities. The Law on Freedom of Conscience and Religious Organisations required special advance approval from the National Council on Religious Affairs for any foreign visitors engaging in preaching or evangelism. For a long period, it was unclear on what basis the Council would decide who should or should not be admitted and it is still unclear how this law will be implemented since the Council has been abolished. Even visitors who took the trouble to obtain these special visas encountered problems in exercising their rights. The law places particular limitations on the religious activities of foreign religious workers. Groups with foreign religious centres have not been given the same rights as those locally established; concepts such as the requirement of a loyalty oath to Ukraine by the leaders of such religious groups appear to be unwarranted, unacceptable as they are to foreign citizens, and may violate international law.

The national spiritual renaissance has also been accompanied by the involvement of external spiritual centres – in particular, those of the Moscow Patriarchate and the Vatican – in the religious life of their subordinate confessions. The problem of finding a solution in the law to the connections between Ukrainian churches and the corresponding foreign centres is urgent as it is important to determine the status of residence in Ukraine of the Orthodox communities which are affiliated to the Russian Church.

In order to exercise religious freedom, Ukrainian religious groups need either to lease or to buy public property or they need property confiscated in the past to be returned. Leasing or buying such property is permitted under current law but it is not always available, allegedly because of discrimination. There are no procedures, judicial or administrative, to enable groups to obtain redress when routinely denied the right to meet for no just cause. The complex issues involved in the return of confiscated property, ideally through a nationwide consultative basis, have not yet been addressed.

In general, there is a clear need for the restoration of the rule of law in the regulation of religious organisations. There is also a need to state in the law expressly that registration is required only in order to obtain the rights of a legal entity, not in order to engage in meetings and other group activities of a religious nature.

Inter-religious relations

Both the Ukrainian Orthodox Church and the Ukrainian Greek Catholic Church have had long experience of state and state-validated persecution. Some Ukrainians have claimed that the policies of the Russian Orthodox Church not only continue Stalin's immense pressure but also the Tsarist policy of Russification; the revival of the Ukrainian churches would result in the loss for the Russian Orthodox Church of some two-thirds of its parishes and income.

At independence in 1991, each church proclaimed itself to be the sole traditional, national church in Ukraine. Subsequently, they started and continue to accuse each other of past collaboration with the communist regime. The greatest struggle developed between the Orthodox Church hierarchy of the Kiev Patriarchate and the Orthodox hierarchy of the Moscow Patriarchate. The religious situation in Ukraine is made more complex by the generation gap in the priesthood in Ukrainian Orthodox churches. The priests in control are all very old men in their eighties or nineties, while the new priests are fifty years younger and have different ideas about how the church should be managed.

Relations between and within the three major churches in Ukraine have been marked by misunderstandings and even open conflict between the churches and among their adherents. In the Lvov region alone, inter-religious conflicts affect over 600 settlements. Violent incidents associated with religious intolerance have occurred elsewhere. For instance, during the funeral of Patriarch Volodymyr of the Ukrainian Autocephalous Orthodox Church in November 1995, followers demanded that he be buried in St Sofia's Cathedral in Kiev. When the government rejected this and the body was taken to a cemetery, a riot ensued and the crowd buried the patriarch in a makeshift grave on the pavement outside the cathedral; fifty people were injured in the riot. Other general manifestations of intolerance have included reports that evangelical and Pentecostal meetings have been attacked by armed Cossacks who threatened those attending with bodily harm, that foreign worshippers have been assaulted when attending traditional churches, and that church services have been disrupted in Kiev.

Anti-Semitic views promoted by ultra-nationalist Ukrainians and Russians continue to cause concern. The Council of Nationalities of the Rukh party monitored anti-Semitism and in 1993 pressure from Rukh led to charges of incitement to national hatred being laid against two people whose writings had stirred up ethnic tension.

Religion and politics

Religious struggles are strongly reflected in political campaigns in Ukraine, so that, together with the deteriorating economy, they are also responsible for creating instability and social confusion.

For the last four years, each one of the three dominant Ukrainian churches has competed for a privileged position for itself *vis-à-vis* the state, continually promoting its pre-eminent importance for social co-existence and the significance of its part in the battle for national independence in the 1980s. The Orthodox Church of Kiev Patriarchate, for example, claims to speak as the state religion of the whole of the Ukraine, while in the western Ukraine, it is Greek Catholicism that takes this position, supported by local political power. Religious problems and issues are often biased in favour of the dominant faith when presented in the Ukrainian media.

However, all religious institutions regardless of their disagreements have in fact been pushed out of the field of political action. New political elites do see religion as an instrument of political or ethnic mobilisation, a means to achieve political goals or to help create national culture. But for many reasons Ukrainian political associations have not found any platform for a stable cooperation with the churches – notwithstanding the role played by the Ukrainian churches in the demise of communism and the creation of democracy – and in political party programmes religious background has become irrelevant.

The new pluralism

Although some Ukrainians argue for a return to one or more state churches, others see that this would be attended by serious risks: division of the nation, institutionalisation of power in the hands of those installed in power by party structures, dampening of a nascent spiritual revival, and the imposition of a new form of intolerance in the name of faith. One reality is that the opposition of the traditional confessions in Ukraine to the newer religious groups has become more determined. The traditional churches appear eager to establish their own representative bodies with links to state institutions in order to limit the activities of the new religious groups.

These attitudes stem from the period of state persecution and domination which resulted in the crippling of church hierarchies and led to today's schisms and disagreements. Traditional churches were robbed during the communist period of the ability to grow and change at a time when the world experienced spiritual innovations such as Vatican II. Thus, the new pluralism may have a stimulating and energising influence, providing ideas and challenges for spiritual renewal.

Note

1 See also the entry on the Russian Federation.

FEDERAL REPUBLIC OF YUGOSLAVIA

After the death of President Tito in 1980, tensions increased among the republics of the Yugoslav federation until the federation collapsed. The Federal Republic of Yugoslavia was one of the successor states, others including Croatia, Bosnia-Herzegovina and Macedonia. The subsequent long war in the former Yugoslavia has been marked by a rarely rivalled degree of internecine savagery and, with the 1996 elections in Bosnia, a fragile structure for the area may only just be starting to emerge. The Federal Republic of Yugoslavia consists of two republics, Serbia and Montenegro, Serbia having much the larger territory and more people. The constitution was promulgated in 1992; the government claims international legal continuity with former Yugoslavia.

Since May 1994 the republic has been subject to international sanctions, since somewhat reduced.

Serbia[h]	
GDP (US$bn)	10[e]
Population	10,093,314[e]
Annual population growth (%)	0.54[e]
Urban population (%)	48[d]
Working population (%)	23.26[c]
Literacy (%)	89[d]
Ratifications	1; 2; 3; 4 (Serbia and Montenegro)

In 1991, Serbia and Montenegro had over 10 million inhabitants and the following ethnic composition: Serbs (62.57 per cent), Albanians (16.49 per cent), Montenegrins (5 per cent), Yugoslavs (3.36 per cent), Hungarians (3.31 per cent), Muslims (3.23 per cent), Roma (gypsies; 1.38 per cent), Croats (1.07 per cent), and other smaller minorities. Being Muslim, not only in terms of religion but as a national affiliation, had been allowed under the 1974 constitution of the Socialist Federal Republic of Yugoslavia but not under the 1992 federal constitution.

These data no longer reflect reality. Hostilities in former Yugoslavia have caused large-scale migrations. Many non-Serbs, especially Hungarians and Croats from Vojvodina and Muslims from Sandzak, have left the country. Some 500,000 refugees (predominantly Serbs) have come into Serbia from Croatia and Bosnia and a further estimated 250,000 Serbs arrived, mainly from Krajina, in mid-1995; meanwhile, about 200,000 younger Serbs have emigrated in search of better life opportunities.

The federal republic's parliament has been controlled from the beginning by a coalition of the Socialist Party of Serbia (SPS) and its Montenegrin counterpart, the Democratic Party of Socialists (DPS). Both are reformed national branches of the League of Communists of Yugoslavia. Although the federation has its government and its president, real power lies in the republics, especially in Serbia and with its president, Slobodan Milosevic. The SPS and DPS are the strongest political parties on the republican level as well, not only in terms of parliamentary deputies, but also in terms of the army, police, media and control of foreign policy. Pressure for democracy increased at the end of 1996 when two months of demonstrations by opposition supporters won a few grudging concessions over biased local election results.

The political situation in the country is dominated by the disintegration of the former Yugoslavia and the war in Bosnia and Herzegovina. When the multi-ethnic, multi-cultural and multi-religious Yugoslav society was divided along national lines, this emphasised the role of the different religious affiliations of ex-Yugoslav nations.

The fact that the three major warring parties in Bosnia have been associated with three different faiths – Croats are, or are expected to be, Roman Catholics; Serbs and Montenegrins, Orthodox; ethnic Muslims, Muslims – has had important implications for religious tolerance in Serbia and Montenegro. On the other hand, the fact that the ruling political parties in Serbia and Montenegro, owing to their historical background, still support atheist attitudes – although not too loudly – has prevented Orthodoxy from becoming a form of state religion in the federal republic. However, this is not the case in the Republika Srpska, the political 'entity' of Bosnian Serbs. Its ruling political party, the Serb Democratic Party (SDS) of Radovan Karadzic, shows much more sympathy and respect for the Serbian Orthodox Church whose dignitaries have frequently been invited to offer prayers and deliver messages at assemblies of Bosnian Serbs.

The constitutional and legal system

All relevant constitutions – the federal republic's in 1992, Serbia's in 1990 and Montenegro's in 1992 – have sections on basic human rights and fundamental freedoms. The federal constitution generally prohibits discrimination on any ground. Incitement to national, racial and religious hatred and intolerance is unconstitutional and punishable. Freedom of thought, conscience and belief is guaranteed in Article 35, while religious freedom is guaranteed in Article 43:

1 Freedom of belief, freedom to manifest religion in public or in private as well as freedom to manifest religion in worship is guaranteed.
2 There is no duty to declare religious beliefs.

According to the Serbian and Montenegrin constitutions, religious communities are separated from the state and free to conduct their religious practices. They can establish religious schools and voluntary organisations. The state can provide material assistance to religious communities.

However, the constitutional provisions are not fully in accordance with the international standard embodied in Article 18 of the ICCPR. First, the lack of reference to the right 'to have or to adopt' a religion or belief, which necessarily entails the freedom to choose or replace one's current religion or belief, is not without practical consequences, as in the case of conscientious objectors in the military reserve. Second, the liberty of parents or legal guardians to ensure that their children receive religious and moral education in conformity with their own convictions, has not been provided for by Yugoslav legislation. Religious education remains a controversial and unresolved issue.

Third, none of the constitutions states clearly that freedom of thought and conscience should be protected unconditionally. Given the role of political police in the socialist federal republic and the secretiveness and importance of the same service in its successor, this omission is not without relevance.

Serbia and Montenegro have recently repealed laws governing the legal status of religions. Under the former communist authorities, religious organisations had to be registered and all religious activities were closely monitored. Religious organisations may now register with the federal Ministry of Religion but this is not compulsory. Since 1991 both Serbia and Montenegro have had Ministries of Religion to 'develop harmonious relations' between the government and religious communities. At the federal level the same role is played by the Commission for Relations with Religious Communities.

Religious and belief composition

Serbia had a very secularised society until a decade ago when revival of religion was the result of a profound crisis in its society's system of values and of the gradual disintegration of socialism and its previously effective ideology. In a 1993 survey, more Serbs (42 per cent) declared they held a religious belief than they had since 1945; of Montenegrins, only 25 per cent held a religious belief. Ethnic minorities in the federal republic have a higher proportion of believers: Albanians (70 per cent), Hungarians (68 per cent) and Muslims (56 per cent). Yugoslavs from cross-community marriages had only 20 per cent of believers.

The dominant religion in the federal republic is Orthodoxy. The 1991 census was the first after 1945 to include data on confession. As Orthodoxy represents tradition, national origin and culture, many people, when asked about their faith at the moment of the collapse of socialism, declared themselves to be Orthodox, despite the fact that many still were non-believers. As a rule, even Orthodox believers have not been regular churchgoers.

The Serbian Orthodox Church actively maintains a relationship with the Ecumenical Patriarch and, since 1971, an essentially consultative membership of the World Council of Churches and Conference of European Churches.

There are some fifty religious communities in the federal republic. According to the 1991 census there were 6,988,901 Orthodox followers, 533,369 Roman Catholics, 468,713 Muslims, 89,369 Protestants, and 1,008 Jews; there were also 170,528 non-believers. Given population displacements since 1992, the proportions in these figures will now have changed. The number of Muslims was understated by at least 1 million; Albanians from Kosovo had boycotted the census.

As in all former Yugoslav republics, relations between different nations are compounded by simultaneous distinctions in terms of the dominant religion. The situation in Bosnia and Herzegovina with its three main national–religious groups is particularly complex. The central problem in Croatia had been, until the military events of 1995, the relation of the Roman Catholic Croat majority and the Orthodox Serb minority. In Macedonia, the Orthodox Macedonian majority has largely yet to come to terms with the predominantly Muslim Albanian minority.

The non-Serb population in the federal republic is now in an uncomfortable minority position, made worse by Serbian nationalistic excess, which is often tolerated – sometimes instigated – by the authorities and aggravated by the war in other parts of the former Yugoslavia. The different religion of national minorities and their demands for religious rights and freedoms have usually been seen as the best evidence of their potential disloyalty.

Relations between the 'fraternal' Orthodox churches have also been far from perfect because all nations with Orthodox traditions aspire to have their own independent (autocephalous) churches. The Serbian Orthodox Church does not accept the independence of the Macedonian Church, which in Skopje has been regarded as an important element of Macedonian statehood. In Montenegro, too, a local assembly to establish (or re-establish) an independent Montenegrin Orthodox Church was swiftly countered by the Serbian Orthodox Church which annulled its election of a bishop; the Montenegrin committee was also removed from the republic's register of legal persons.

An important social consequence of growing nationalism and of war in the former Yugoslavia has been the identification of every nation with its traditional religion and pressure for religious conformity, so that existing religious diversity, nominal adherence and secular belief became subsumed into particular religious–national blocs.

The Serbian Orthodox Church and politics

The Serbian Orthodox Church has played an important national and political role throughout history. During the long period of Ottoman rule – with intermissions, from the Serbian defeat on the Kosovo Field in 1389 to the nineteenth century, when Serbia gradually became independent and was formally recognised in 1878 – the church was the only national institution to preserve and foster national culture and identity. Many Serbian prelates fought in uprisings against Turkish rule; political slogans of the Serbian national revolution (1804–30) did not differentiate between the struggle for independence and the campaign for religious rights.

The Serbian Orthodox Church and its theologians have generally opposed the modernisation and Westernisation of Serbian society. Before the Second World War the church owned substantial lands. Religious instruction was compulsory in primary schools. However, after 1945, during the dominance of the Communist Party, the church, as were all other religious communities, was put on the margin of social and political life, and most of its property was nationalised. Although almost all political parties in 1990 promised that this property would be returned to the churches, this has not happened yet. The Orthodox Church started to return to the political sphere in the late 1980s, when the future Serbian president Slobodan Milosevic discovered the enormous political potential of nationalism. He mobilised Serbians for his populist platform by appropriating the nationalistic ideas and slogans of a part of the Serbian intelligentsia, especially that around the Serbian Academy of Arts and Sciences. At the same time, he grasped the importance of the Serbian Orthodox Church as a traditional national institution and allowed it abundant access to government media and to public prominence.

Carefully orchestrated by the church and the state, the celebration in 1989 of the 600th anniversary of the battle at the Kosovo Field has been generally regarded as the start of their unannounced nationalist coalition. This relationship then passed through various phases but the presence of the Serbian Orthodox Church in many aspects of public life remains clearly discernible.

The Serbian Orthodox Church does not allow its clergy to participate in politics. However, the church considers it its duty to make its views known any time when the 'destiny of the people' is at stake. Many bishops thus take an active part in public life and some have presence and influence above that of the average party leader.

The Serbian Orthodox Church's official positions are discussed at the meetings of the Holy Synod and of the Holy Assembly of Bishops. Both have issued several general statements in the last five years, almost all on major political issues concerning war and peace, the fate of the Serb people outside Serbia, elections, statehood, self-determination or foreign policy.

On the eve of the 1990 multi-party elections in Serbia, the church stated that it was not 'a party but a patriotic institution' and expressed its hope that 'elections would be fair'. When the war in Croatia broke out, in November 1991, the Orthodox Church called 'for the unity of all Serb people' and recalled that 'the Serbian Orthodox Church condoned only defensive and liberating, but not aggressive, war'.

Before the 1992 elections in Serbia, the church invited people not to vote for parties and programmes which support 'non-believing attitudes about man and the world'. Together with its famous statement, also made in 1992, that 'no-one's position is more important than the freedom and destiny of the entire nation', this was interpreted as a distancing from Slobodan Milosevic and his Socialist Party of Serbia.

The church has resisted territorial settlements which would in its view be detrimental to Serbians. Thus in 1993 it warned the authorities that no settlement could be reached without the blessing of the church. In August 1994, when the federal government decided to break all ties with Bosnian Serbs because they had refused to accept the settlement for Bosnia and Herzegovina offered by the Contact group of five nations, the church condemned 'the blockade and sanctions against brothers', 'the media campaign against them' and demanded 'self-determination for Serbs in Bosnia'. However, in August 1995, Patriarch Pavle publicly witnessed the decision which recognised the competence of President Milosevic to represent all Serbians in peace negotiations.

While the Serbian Orthodox Church has repeatedly expressed its support to the Serb side, it has not flinched from criticising Serbian violations and expressing sympathy for Croat and Muslim victims; church representatives also took part in several peace or mediation efforts. The aged Serbian Patriarch, Pavle, who generally enjoys great respect, has been an advocate of love and forgiveness. His attitude stands in contrast with that of some bishops who have narrow nationalistic views.

In January 1997, Patriarch Pavle led a 300,000-strong procession through Belgrade on St Sava's Day, the patron saint of education and students. The church-led march, to protest against election fraud, supported the role students have played in pressure for democracy in Serbia.

Religions and war in the former Yugoslavia

The fact that warring sides in former Yugoslavia traditionally belong to the three different faiths has often been used to explain the conflict as a religious war. Some religious leaders had contributed to the already existing ethnic tensions, or simply accepted the tragic reality, but the real causes for civil war in former Yugoslavia are more complex. Conflict in Croatia and Bosnia and Herzegovina has had devastating consequences for all three major religious communities.

The destruction of places of worship has been particularly barbaric. According to some independent sources in the war zones, 154 Orthodox churches were completely destroyed and 175 damaged; 652 mosques were destroyed and 153 severely damaged; some 450 Roman Catholic churches were destroyed or damaged.

The disintegration of the former Yugoslavia has caused changes in the internal structures of the major religious communities as well, especially the dissolution of the Muslim central leadership. Serbian Orthodox bishops whose seats lay in some Croatian cities (such as Zagreb and Sibenik) have found it difficult or impossible to return or visit, while some Roman Catholic bishops have had great difficulty in being allowed to visit Serb-controlled areas in Croatia, such as Knin until it was 're-integrated' into Croatia in mid-1995.

Representatives of the Serbian Orthodox Church, the Roman Catholic Church in Croatia and the Islamic religious community have met on several occasions to appeal for peace and reconciliation. Patriarch Pavle, the Croatian Catholic Archbishop of Zagreb and the Russian Patriarch Aleksy II together signed 'the Sarajevo declaration for peace' in May 1994. The religious leaders stated that the 'tragic conflicts on the Balkans were sins against every religion' and that 'the use of religion to justify hostilities was immoral'. These efforts were supported by the speech which Pope John Paul II made while visiting Croatia in September 1994. To the chagrin of many Croatian nationalist dignitaries, and undoubtedly to the displeasure of some of his Croat co-religionists, he referred to the shared heritage of the South Slavs and to the need to separate nationalist intolerance from religion.

Unfortunately, all major churches in former Yugoslavia, and in particular some of their high dignitaries and theologians as well as many priests, have been guilty of unpardonable acts of supporting and condoning intolerance, atrocities and ethnic cleansing, if committed by 'their' side. For instance, the Serbian Orthodox Church's *Communiqué concerning the false accusations against the Serb nation in Bosnia and Herzegovina*, issued in December 1992, dismissed as propaganda designed to 'satanise' the Serbs the accusations that systematic or officially instigated policies had promoted violations in concentration camps and advocated rape as a method of 'ethnic cleansing'. In this respect the church was more indulgent than the officials, who only refused to believe that atrocities had been committed by regular army units. Subsequently, church statements – especially the messages of the Patriarch – contained many condemnations of Serbian violations, but some saw this as 'too little, too late'.

Inter-faith relations

Despite the unfavourable circumstances, the major faiths in Serbia and Montenegro have co-existed reasonably well. The Belgrade *mufti*, however, has drawn attention to psychological pressure placed on people with Muslim names and the Catholic Archbishop of Belgrade has referred to a general 'anti-Catholic' or 'anti-Vatican' atmosphere.

Roman Catholics and Muslims in Serbia and Montenegro have been victims of so-called 'soft ethnic cleansing'. Among other acts of violence against Croats and Hungarians (in Vojvodina) and Muslims (in Sandzak and elsewhere), extreme nationalist para-military bands have attacked mosques in Belgrade (1992) and Podgorica (1992) and Catholic churches in Beocin (1991), Petrovaradin (1992) and Subotica. The authorities have not always prevented or investigated these and similar outrages, although the state did find resources to enable the Belgrade mosque to be extended in 1994.

The Serbian Orthodox Church has campaigned against some smaller religious communities because of their alleged proselytising among Orthodox Serbs. In June 1994, the Holy Assembly saw 'an army of diverse sects arriving from the same places as sanctions and bombs', considering them to be 'the threat of spiritual genocide of the Serb nation'. The bishops and the church press have accused newer religious organisations generally of exploiting humanitarian aid as a proselytising tool. Seventh-Day Adventists, Jehovah's Witnesses, Mormons, Baptists, Buddhists, Evangelicals and other smaller religious groups in Serbia have denied these accusations. Their followers say that they do not feel the less Serbian because they are not Orthodox. Representatives of the federal Commission for Relations with Religious Communities have tried to reassure the Adventists who had been the target of accusations against their humanitarian aid agency, ADRA.

Since state authorities act in a neutral way and do not back the state church aspirations of the Serbian Orthodox Church, the individual right of non-Orthodox Serbs to practise their religion has not been in serious legal or political jeopardy. Vuk Draskovic, leader of the strongest nationalist opposition party, the Serbian Renewal Movement (SPO), has since 1990 developed a firm anti-war stance and criticised some prelates of the church for encouraging war and intolerance.

While being very critical of religious communities which spread their beliefs among Serbs, the Serbian Orthodox Church has been conducting a 'mission for the renaissance of Gypsy spirituality' to Roma in Serbia. Religious books have been translated by the church and religious services are conducted in Roma language; new churches in Roma agglomerations have been built. While Roma have their own traditional beliefs, some also practise a form of Roman Catholicism or Islam.

No Christian religious community in the federal republic, including the Orthodox Church, can be held directly responsible for the outbursts of anti-Semitism which have come as a surprise in Serbia and Montenegro, traditionally tolerant towards Jews. These incidents have included two editions of the translation of *The Protocols of the Elders of Zion*. The authorities did not, however, treat this as incitement to racial and religious hatred. After some hesitation they instituted proceedings against the editor of the bulletin of an extreme rightist party in Bijelo Polje (Montenegro), which in July 1994 had published an ugly harangue against Jews. The Anti-Semitism World Report 1994 points out that close contact between nationalists and their Russian counterparts may account for these manifestations.

In the area of inter-religious dialogue, consultations with the theme of reconciliation were convened in February 1996 in Belgrade by the Theological Faculty of the Serbian Orthodox Church and the Conference of European Churches, based in Geneva. Among the participants were representatives of churches in Serbia, Slovenia, Croatia and Bosnia, as well as others from Europe and North America.

Education

The freedom of parents to teach children their religion or belief exists in practice even though federal legislation does not explicitly mention it. All religious communities are free to organise religious education. The three major faiths have developed their systems of religious education and training, from primary to university level.

Religion is not taught in state schools, not even as an optional subject, although all three major faiths would like this to happen. In December 1993 the federal parliament rejected a draft law on religious education in primary schools submitted by the opposition party. Private religious schools are allowed, such as the two Muslim secondary schools, but the state does not subsidise them. In 1993–94, the Serbian Orthodox Church provided religious education for younger people in youth centres, cultural centres or in some state schools, outside school hours. Serbian bishops especially welcomed the fact that Republika Srpska and Krajina – the two self-proclaimed Serbian entities in Bosnia–Herzegovina and Croatia – had included compulsory religious instruction in their primary schools in September 1993.

New buildings for the Orthodox Theological Faculty, long delayed by financial difficulties and international sanctions, were finally opened in January 1996.

The media

Religious books and religious publications are printed and distributed free within the country for all faiths. The Serbian Orthodox Church has become more dependent on the media and vulnerable to government pressure and manipulation because low regular attendance at Sunday liturgies has made the use of the media more effective in spreading the church's messages than traditional contact at parish level.

The dominant religion is far more favoured than other faiths in its access to the state-controlled broadcasting media and its influence over the media in general. Orthodox services have been broadcast in detail during recent years while non-Orthodox faiths are usually presented negatively; as former communists, the state authorities are trying to change their past image. However, the Serbian Orthodox Church cannot effectively control television news editors when important political issues are reported and discussed. State television usually reports official church positions only when they accord with government policy.

The programming of the state-controlled TV Belgrade regularly involves the demonisation of certain ethnic and religious groups. Owing to the war in Bosnia, the treatment of Islam and the Muslims in official media has been very unfavourable. Islam is often presented as an inherently aggressive religion aimed to destroy all 'non-believers' in a holy war or *jihad*.

Women and war in the former Yugoslavia

The impact of the civil war on women in Bosnia–Herzegovina and Croatia has been immense as communities have been shattered and scattered, families destroyed and individuals 'disappeared' or were imprisoned, raped, tortured and killed.

Contemporary analysis of the politicisation of rape, especially in Bosnia, shows that the discourse of threatened or imagined rape began in the media in Kosovo as early as 1987. Ethnic conflict between the majority Albanian population and Serb and other minority groups seems to have its origin in poverty and underdevelopment in association with differential emigration and reproduction rates, which unbalance previously 'comfortable' proportions of different ethnic groups sharing scarce resources. In Kosovo, the Albanian population increased while the Serbs emigrated in large numbers and the remaining Serbs found it difficult to adjust to lower minority status.

Media persecution of Albanians centred on the perceived threat to Serbian women by a stereotype of Albanian men as violent rapists, fuelled by the Fadilgate affair in which a prominent Albanian politician was said to have implied that the 'rape phenomenon' could be solved by the import of Serbian prostitutes. It is far from clear whether Fadil Hoxha actually made this explicit suggestion; he made a public explanation and apology, but was later indicted for fostering 'national, religious and race hatred'. Later statistics compiled by the Independent Commission of the Yugoslav Forum for Human Rights and the Association of the Yugoslav Democratic Initiative, show that the occurrence of rape at the time was much lower for Albanian males in comparison with the Yugoslav average and also in comparison with every other ethnic group. However, the separation and binding of the different ethnic communities using women as boundary markers proceeded to crisis proportions and mutual aggression and retaliation.

The Serbian government introduced a new category of rape into law: inter-ethnic rape, with more severe penalties than intra-ethnic rape. According to Yugoslav feminist scholars, this period of rape discourse was accepted because the level of culturally tolerated familial violence in all groups in Yugoslavia is high and because nationalist mythologies stress epic battles of great violence in which ethnic and religious difference is crucially involved. These scholars link this earlier period of conflict, expressed in 'honour' terms of supposedly threatened populations of women, with the later development of a policy and practice of violent rape by the Serbian military in Bosnia.

Further, analysis shows that different population growth, including reproduction rates in specific regions of Bosnia, is clearly linked with rates of military rape. In particular, the reproduction rate of Muslim groups in areas of Serbian minorities was very high and the Serbian government collected statistics which categorised 'Muslims as an ethnic group'. Intermarriage with Muslims by any contiguous non-Muslim individuals was viewed increasingly negatively and when civil war broke out, the concept and practice of 'ethnic cleansing' were instituted massively in areas where Serbs were a minority and Muslims a relative or absolute majority.

Pregnancies of raped women ensured that they were publicly marked as having been raped, and thus shamed and dishonoured as well as physically injured. These women's connection with their community can rarely be re-established; most were raped in the presence of relatives and neighbours, and many were young girls aged between 7 and 14 years who either died or became permanent invalids.

There remains little doubt that rape has been used systematically for 'ethnic cleansing'. It is also clear that religious, as well as ethnic discrimination is in complex relationship with population movements in societies under severe political and economic stress. In strongly patriarchal cultures such as those of the Balkans, women have become completely overpowered and violently made into victims even in situations where they have been organised in protest and resistance.

In the course of action at the international level to deal with gross violations of human rights and war crimes, the issue of rape is being developed and defined. In mid-1996, the War Crimes Tribunal was investigating whether rape was a form of torture; it remains to be seen how the Tribunal and the International Court of Justice will deal with the issue of rape in relation to genocide.

Women and religion

Except on abortion matters, the Serbian Orthodox Church has no consistent stand on the position and rights of women, although its patriarchal bias remains obvious. It supports the new, more conservative and nationalist version of the Circle of Serbian Sisters, a venerated organisation of women devoted to charity and traditional 'female' values. Women cannot be ordained; there has not even been any debate on the matter.

Conscientious objection

After a lively debate in the late 1980s on 'civilian service' in the then Yugoslav People's Army and after the traumatic experiences of the civil war in former Yugoslavia, the individual right of conscientious objection was legally recognised in the federal republic in 1994. Conscripts who refuse to carry arms on the basis of 'religious or other beliefs' may serve for twice as long a period (two years) in social services. Conscientious objectors have the same legal status as other conscripts. However, the relevant procedure has not yet been developed and put into practice.

Middle East

REGIONAL INTRODUCTION

The general political and economic context is particularly important in this region which effectively spans both North Africa and the Middle East. These are countries where the religious question is closely linked to the political and social aspirations for democracy and development. Both the elites and those struggling for power from below invoke religion, which also affects social issues; for example, there are issues of sex discrimination which are religiously defended, such as inheritance laws and rules of evidence.

This region is above all the region of Islam. The Islamic faith, which spread from Mecca with the victory of the Prophet throughout the Middle East, has known enormous conflict and social turmoil throughout the twentieth century. However, the continuing presence of Christians in many countries and the establishment of the state of Israel are a reminder of the religious pluralism in the region. A clear distinction must be maintained between Islam as a world religion capable like any other religion or belief of adapting its tenets to changing world and regional situations, and some tendencies within it which project its message in intolerant and reactionary directions.

In some countries of the region people are not free to exercise their unbelief because of religious constraints or terrorism. In many Middle Eastern societies, there is a complete gulf between the formal guarantees of rights and the practice of respect for these rights, although this is also true of a great many societies and cultures in other parts of the world. The significance of formal guarantees is that they do at least represent the official position and need to be scrutinised in terms of conformity with the international standards. In the Middle East there is no regional international system of protection of human rights and freedoms; nor is progress in this direction likely in the foreseeable future.

Free expression and freedom of thought, conscience and religion or belief are closely related rights. It is important to note the role of the media in stimulating expectations about and frustrations with the given order especially among young people, and the role of Islamic influences in the media spreading Islamisation, often contrary to the elites' formal wishes.

Today, the Middle East is characterised by dislocation, massive urbanisation and population growth, with economic failure and environmental degradation. The wealth of oil of some states is in stark contrast with the poverty of others. In this context comes the long struggle over Israel and the Occupied Palestinian Territories. Many countries have known colonialism and nationalism but now seek an option in Islam. Islam is often a political vehicle to voice distress and anger at failures of modernisation, and the inability to provide the security of life and standard of living which are held out by satellite television as attainable. Dislocation of people and the degree of poverty and insecurity lead to the search for stability in the elements of identity which Islam provides. In such conditions, the capacity for tolerance is very limited.

The pre-eminence of Islam as an answer to the West is of fundamental importance. The West is blamed for both the injustices suffered by the Palestinian people, and for the economic failure of the countries in the region. The memories of colonialism are strong, and deeply influence responses to human rights concepts. Many countries can be said to be looking for a fresh formula of government; states are fragile, civil society is weak and the long tradition of autocratic rule is a culture which inhibits the development of democratic political systems.

Societies may be seen in a spectrum of response to common problems and the question of Islam. Broadly there are those which seek to implement a full Islamic vision, convinced that it will be the answer to the need for self-respect and prosperity. There are others who seek to follow Islam but do not want an Islamic state. The recognition of international norms on freedom of thought within countries depends on the position within that spectrum. The resources of Islam and its own tradition of tolerance towards other religions are a neglected side of the usual depiction of the region. Similarly, both Jews and Christians, leaders and communities need not look only inwards at their 'minority' situation but increasingly should be seeking ways to relate to their Islamic neighbours.

IRAN

Iran	
GDP (US$bn)	110
Population	62,500,000
Annual population growth (%)	3.4
Urban population (%)	57
Working population (%)	26
Literacy (%)	64.9
Ratifications	1; 2; 3

Despite the high hopes of so many people around the world for the Iranian revolution of 1979, the ruling system that resulted from that major upheaval has proved a great disappointment. Judging by the annual reports of such human rights organisations as Amnesty International and Human Rights Watch, the repressiveness of the previous regimes has paled into insignificance compared to the systematic suppression of not only political dissent, but also artistic creativity, women's liberation and free thought. It is within the context of that general oppression that the treatment of religious minorities in the new Islamic Republic needs to be seen.

When Iran's supreme leader, Ayatollah Ali Khamenei, on 4 June 1994, spoke during a memorial service for the late founder of the state, Ayatollah Khomeini, he set out Iran's attitude to human rights in the following terms:

> The Islamic Republic is accused of violating human rights, by which they mean [we implement] Islamic laws. We certainly prefer the text of the Holy Qur'an to the

products of the failing minds of western lawyers. We aim towards full implementation of Qur'anic laws.

The Islamic Republic of Iran occupies an anomalous position in the world today. On the one hand, it appears to value its membership of the United Nations. On the other, it openly denounces most declarations and conventions of the UN, which it has signed and ratified, including the Universal Declaration of Human Rights, as contrary to the will of God. It claims that most charters and protocols of the UN are imposed on 'the dispossessed' of the world by 'the arrogant powers', meaning the West.

The Universal Declaration is particularly excoriated. Iranian leaders often denounce it as a charter for the criminal and the corrupt, and claim that Islam, the principles of which rule all their counsels, has a morally superior and intellectually more valid system of rights for humankind. As a result, Iranian officials are not offended when charged with being totalitarian.

This illustrates the depth of the break with the previous regime, the monarchy of Shah Mohammad-Reza Pahlavi, which the clergy helped to overthrow in February 1979. Whereas the monarchy, repressive as it was, saw its mission as modernising the country along Western lines, the leaders of the Islamic Republic say that they derive their inspiration from classical Mecca. They say they wish only to borrow the technology of the modern world and none of its habits of mind.

Perhaps the term 'totalitarian' ought to be used with caution in the case of Iranian leaders; for while they act with extreme severity towards anyone who might call into question the principles of Islam, they sometimes disagree among themselves as to precisely what Islamic law decrees in certain situations, a falling out which inflicts upon the country's legal system a degree of indecisiveness and even chaos, which can appear as weakness at the centre.

The country's legal system is further affected by a fierce power struggle between President Ali-Akbar Hashemi Rafsanjani, who is formally in charge of the executive and has international responsibilities, and Ayatollah Ali Khamenei, the official spiritual leader, who is constitutionally empowered to set the overall moral guidelines for policy and intervene in executive matters, when need be. The lack of a clear dividing line between the powers of the two leaders of the republic provides an environment for administrative vacillation. Government officials and the judiciary tend to carry out their tasks, not always according to the state's formal laws or policies, but according to their own perception of which political faction may be the stronger. The ideological and political differences between the leaders of Iran's Islamic state perhaps explain why they have not been able to take any real steps towards creating their successor, as have similar ideological systems before them.

This degree of unsettledness in the wake of a revolution – and the proud boast of standing outside, and above, the legal framework of the world – make it difficult to see what pressures might prove effective on Iranian leaders to make them implement those declarations and covenants of the United Nations which their country has ratified. Resistance is doubled against implementing international treaties entered into by the deposed monarchy.

Socio-economic structure

Only about 10 per cent of Iran's surface is capable of agriculture, the rest being deserts, marshes and mountains. Iran's population is 62.5 million and, in 1995, the average per

417

capita income stood at only 440 US dollars. When compared to the average per capita income of 2,400 US dollars in 1979, the year of the Islamic revolution, these figures show a staggering fall in the standard of living of Iranians over the previous sixteen years.

In the twenty-eight years between 1966 and 1994, Iran's official population more than doubled. The figure is now expected to jump to 100 million by 2010, and illiteracy and poverty now afflict more Iranians than at any other time. The movement of millions of rural unemployed into overcrowded towns has been a primary factor behind the political turmoil of recent decades.

Other factors contributing to a lowering of the average standard of living in the country have been: the political upheavals of the late 1970s which interrupted industrialisation; the war with Iraq from 1980–88 which consumed a great portion of the country's resources, destroyed thousands of border villages and saw young boys dedicated as martyrs to the cause; the diplomatic isolation of the country's new leadership with its consequent dearth of foreign investment; and the slide in the price of oil in the late 1980s, oil providing over 90 per cent of the government's foreign currency.

Ethnic and religious minorities

A precise breakdown of ethnicity is not available and the data are not collected in the census. It is likely that the true sizes of the non-Persian minorities are larger than is officially acknowledged.

The number of Azerbaijanis living in several north-western and central provinces has been estimated at 27 per cent of the total, official population, or over 16 million. This would amount to more than twice the population of the former Soviet republic of Azerbaijan in the Caucasus.

With the number for other minorities estimated at about 25 per cent, the dominant Persian-speaking community itself becomes a minority. It must be noted, though, that the Azerbaijanis share the Shia branch of Islam with the Persians, which brings the two largest blocks of population closer together in mental attitudes.

By contrast, the great majority of Kurds, who live in several western provinces, are not Shias. They belong either to the Sunni branch of Islam or to semi-secret mystic orders with their roots in Zoroastrianism and other pre-Islamic religions. Chief among these are the Yarsan (the Disciples), also known as the Ahl-e-Haq (the people of the truth), who may number up to 1.5 million among the Kurds of Iran alone. With a long history of persecution at the hands of Muslims, the adherents of Yarsan keep a low profile and are not recognised as a separate religion by the state.

The Kurds are estimated at just over 6 million in Iran. Up to a million of them might be Shias, concentrated in and around the city of Kermanshah. Thousands of Kurds have died in western Iran as a result of their attachment to their national culture. In July 1996 Iranian armed forces conducted raids into Iraq in pursuit of 'counter-revolutionary' exiled Iranian Kurds.

The third largest ethnic minority are the Baluchis in the south-east, bordering on Pakistan and Afghanistan and numbering about 1.2 million. The Baluchis largely belong to various types of Sunni Islam, as do the smaller ethnic communities of Turkomans, Tajiks and Pathans, in the north and the north-east.

About 1 million Shia Arabs along the coast of the Persian Gulf and several semi-migratory tribes of Qashghais and Bakhtiaris in the highlands of central and southern Iran constitute the rest of the non-Persian peoples that make up the Iranian mosaic.

Altogether, perhaps between 5–6 million of the total population belong to the Sunni branch of Islam.

Non-Muslim minorities

All official figures for non-Muslim minorities in Iran must be similarly treated with caution, but for different reasons. Non-Muslims are required to state their religions on census forms, but due to persecution or economic hardship after the revolution, or both, their ranks are constantly being depleted through emigration abroad, legal or otherwise. Compared to Muslim Iranians, Christian and Jewish citizens have found it easier to obtain immigration visas from foreign states, particularly in the West.

There is evidence that some adherents of unrecognised religions have described themselves as Muslims in censuses. If they could be shown to have been born Muslims, they would officially count as apostates deserving execution. Some have, nevertheless, declared themselves as belonging to one of the recognised minority religions, for instance, Zoroastrians, even though no-one born into Islam is allowed to convert to these either.

The biggest community among Iran's non-Muslim religions is formed of Christians of the Armenian Apostolic (or Catholic) Church, of great antiquity. Informed Armenians say that, as a whole, their community numbers about 150,000, mainly concentrated in the large cities such as Tehran, Isfahan, Urmieh and Tabriz. A small fraction have in recent years converted to various Protestant denominations.

'Assyrian' Christians are divided into two branches, the (Catholic) Chaldeans and the (Orthodox) Assyrian Church of the East. They number up to 50,000, according to their own spokesmen, and are concentrated in Tehran and around the western city of Urmieh, where many of them are farmers. Mainstream Roman Catholics, adherents of the Episcopal Church of Jerusalem and the Middle East (Anglicans), and several small evangelical Protestant churches make up the rest of the Christian community of 250,000 people.

Iran's Jewish laity, which dates back to Babylonian times, has dwindled by more than half from the 80,000-strong community it was in 1979, but the Zoroastrians are thought to be stable at around 40,000.

The 300,000-strong Baha'i community of pre-revolutionary years appears to have been decimated through ferocious persecution. Its organised hierarchy has been completely destroyed and thousands of its laity have been forced to flee the country or renounce their faith. Others have been driven underground in small, isolated groups. No-one is quite sure about the extent of their survival.

Sikhs, Hindus and Buddhists are present in very small numbers and mostly related to foreign embassies with diplomatic immunity.

Legal and political structure

The constitution of the Islamic Republic of Iran was formulated in 1980 and slightly altered in 1989 after the death of Ayatollah Khomeini, the state's founder. It sets out the ideological concepts of Shia Islam, as described by Khomeini in his various writings, and aims at ensuring the permanent 'ijtihad of the fuqaha', the jurisprudence of the Islamic clergy, and 'jihad (holy war or struggle) in Allah's path' to extend the domain of the *shariah* law throughout the world

It provides for an elected parliament, the Islamic Majlis, but with crucial limitations. Supreme power is vested in the person of a senior cleric chosen by an elected Assembly of (Islamic) Experts, the Khobregan. The elected leader is called the Vali-ye Faqih, or Theologian Holyman, who then sets the overall guidelines for the parliament and the government according to his own interpretation of Islamic principles. He has also been given widespread powers of intervention in executive matters.

Furthermore, candidates for election to the Majlis (parliament) are subject before election to the scrutiny of the Ministry of the Interior 'for Islamic piety', and a committee of twelve senior clerics, the Council of Guardians of the Constitution, appointed jointly by the supreme leader and the parliament, vets all legislation for compatibility with the teachings and the laws of Islam. No act of parliament would thus become law unless approved by the Council of Guardians and the supreme leader. The 1996 elections returned to power the more traditionalist of the two right-wing Islamist movements, the Association of Militant Clergy.

The need for complete compatibility with the teachings of Islam means that the Republic recognises as valid religions only those that had a sizeable presence in the Arabian peninsula in the seventh century and were mentioned in the Qur'an. They are Judaism, Christianity and, to a lesser extent, Zoroastrianism, the main religion of Iran in pre-Islamic times.

Accordingly, Iranian citizens who adhere to any of these 'Religions of the Book' are guaranteed freedom of worship, though in private gatherings only, and are allotted representatives of their own in the Islamic Majlis. Thus the Armenian community is allowed two members of parliament, the Assyrian and Chaldean Christians one, and the Jews and the Zoroastrians one each. Protestants and Roman Catholics are not mentioned. By implication, Hindus, Buddhists, Sikhs and others are classified as heathens deserving the traditional forced conversion to Islam or expulsion from the Islamic realm, but, perhaps out of fear of retaliation by other countries, are left unmentioned and no measures are recommended against them.

Women are accorded full electoral equality with men. They are allowed to vote in Majlis elections and to be chosen as its members. To date, however, their membership of parliament has been on a token basis; only women supporting the new order have been allowed to stand (though this applies to males, too), and none has been made a minister. Faiza Hashemi Rafsanjani, the President's daughter, won a seat for the Servants of Reconstruction party in the 1996 elections. Feminists have pointed out that no member of the Guardians Council is a woman. Elsewhere, women are subject to limitations placed on them by Islamic laws and traditions, but within clerical circles there has been increasing debate about whether the Islamic government has been unnecessarily harsh to women.

Constitutional protection of human rights

The constitution stipulates that the government should ensure freedom of expression for citizens, allow them the right to form political parties and assume them innocent until convicted by a legally constituted court. All forms of torture are banned, though the term is interpreted to exclude traditional types of beating under interrogation.

Everywhere, the citizen's constitutional freedoms are crippled by references to such vague considerations as 'the need to safeguard the interests of the state' or to 'uphold the honour of the clergy'. These qualifications allow the authorities to impose their own interpretations on the concepts concerned. The citizen's freedom of expression excludes the freedom to shed doubt on the divine nature of Islam, to declare adherence to any humanist belief or even to indicate a preference for the other, non-Muslim religions, albeit the recognised ones. Only the expression of preference for Islam is allowed in print or in public speaking.

The Iranian press is severely censored, both by the government and by its proprietors who are required to be devout Muslims and who also fear the closure of their businesses. All broadcasting stations are fully state-owned and their directors appointed by ministers to carry out state policy.

The legal system

In the early stages of the revolution of February 1979, almost every Shia cleric in the country felt empowered to set himself up as an Islamic judge and summarily execute people he identified with the monarchy or regarded as 'corrupt on earth', a Qur'anic expression. This was sometimes to cover the clergy's own tracks, as a majority of them were believed to have cooperated with the monarchy and been on its pay rolls. The most notorious of such judges was a middle-ranking cleric, Ayatollah Sadeq Khalkhali. Gradually, however, attempts were made to formalise the legal system and judges such as Khalkhali, who had set up personal fiefdoms and acquired wealth in the process, became an embarrassment. The Ministry of Justice, with its staff of Western-oriented judges and lawyers, was placed under the supervision of senior clerics and told to implement the *shariah* penal laws themselves.

This was beside a parallel system of Islamic Revolutionary Courts that were kept on for cases involving political dissent. In November 1994, the Islamic Revolutionary Courts were re-instituted after a period in abeyance, on the grounds that many legal cases had remained unresolved for too long. For this, some of the legislation passed under the monarchy proved indispensable.

Nevertheless, on rare occasions, Islamic judges, particularly in the provinces, still assert their traditional autonomy and impose the *shariah* regardless of the consequences for the government, giving rise to legal confusion. They always find champions among the clergy to support them, with the net result that, in Islamic doctrinal matters, the government appears not to be fully in charge.

One of the traditional Islamic laws enshrined in Iran's legal system is the practice of stoning to death people accused of adultery and a number of other sexual offences. Though the ruling clergy exhibit signs that they are embarrassed by it and try to reduce its implementation, they are unable to remove it, as to do so would appear to fly in the face of religious doctrine. In December 1994, the daily newspaper of the Tehran municipality, *Hamshahri*, reported a case of stoning that showed the practice was still continuing in the country. Furthermore, the way the punishment is implemented is biased against women. In only one incident from the last sixteen years, were both a man and woman reportedly stoned to death in public in the southern port of Ramhormoz for killing the woman's husband.

Altogether, the general perception at home and abroad is that the Iranian regime is among the most authoritarian in the world, and that it regularly violates its own laws in order to intimidate its critics and opponents.

The current situation

After the death of Ayatollah Khomeini in 1989, it was widely hoped that his younger successors would take steps to rein in the zeal of the early years of the revolution in order to reduce their government's diplomatic isolation abroad and attract foreign investment to the war-shattered economy. Unfortunately, this did not come to pass, perhaps because the hopes of President Rafsanjani to become Iran's paramount political leader did not materialise. With the passage of time, Ayatollah Khamenei, the nominal successor to Khomeini, claimed more of the powers he had formally inherited and appeared to aspire to be the same kind of religious and revolutionary leader as had been his predecessor. The widening rift, which often humiliated Rafsanjani in public, reached such a point that, by the middle of 1994, Rafsanjani was no longer regarded as particularly influential in Tehran.

With this shift in political fortunes, and bearing in mind that notable clergymen in the provinces had reclaimed some of their lost autonomy since the death of Khomeini, the precarious position of the religious minorities further deteriorated.

Such was the degree of chaos in the country's administration of justice in July 1994 that the chief legal inspector resigned. Ayatollah Mostafa Mohaqeq Damad, who had been in the post for thirteen years, told the Tehran press that too many powerful quarters interfered in the affairs of the courts to make his position tenable. 'Without immunity from interference,' he said, 'it is impossible to solve the country's other problems either, such as official corruption and economic regression.' Reports of torture have been confirmed by reports published by human rights organisations and by the Special Rapporteur of the UN Human Rights Commission, Mr Galindo Pohl, in November 1994.

In the previous month, Ayatollah Hussein-Ali Montazeri, the former designated successor to Ayatollah Khomeini who was dismissed in 1989, denounced the Special Court of the Clergy, a secretive court set up to investigate charges against clerics only, as unconstitutional. He accused the state of setting up the court 'to intimidate clerical dissidents and to whitewash the crimes of its own members'. Most ordinary citizens regarded the Special Court of the Clergy with disdain as it implied special privileges for clergy.

Ayatollah Montazeri, who was under house arrest in the shrine city of Qom and whose home and office had been ransacked several times, said that, generally, Iran was now ruled 'not through the law, but through force'. Two months later, the Ayatollah was nominated as 'the Source of Emulation', or the holiest man of the Shia branch of Islam, by influential clerics inside the ruling establishment, to the dismay of Ayatollah Khamenei, the official leader, who attempted to rally clerical supporters to block the nomination. Observers believed that the rift showed the disunity afflicting Iranian Shiism as a result of its involvement in political power.

Limitations imposed on 'the Peoples of the Book'

Christians, Jews and Zoroastrians are recognised in the Qur'an as valid religions, or the Religions of the Book. As such, therefore, they are entitled to a separate existence, provided they do not attempt to convert Muslims to their faiths, on the grounds that their holy books had been superseded by God's latest, unadulterated message, the Qur'an.

In the constitution of the Islamic Republic of Iran, no restrictions are formally imposed on Christians, Jews and Zoroastrians but more subtle pressures have been consistently exerted on them in their daily lives, both by secret government circulars and by individual influential Muslim clerics. Thus they have not been able to be promoted in government offices, to distribute any publications in Persian that might fall into the hands of Muslims, to hold any public worship ceremonies, to dress in any way in public that might be judged contrary to the Islamic norm, and so on.

In the first years of the revolution, a number of young women belonging to the minorities were abducted by powerful Muslim clerics and forced to write to their parents, asking that they not communicate with them on the grounds of conversion to Islam. Minority schools were also placed under official control and churches told to worship in Persian. Furthermore, some churches were ransacked by mobs, priests were arrested and beaten for being 'counter-revolutionaries', and a number of believers were murdered.

Some of these tactics continue to be used, particularly against Protestants, but, on the whole, the leaders of the recognised religions say that they have been treated better than expected. Examples may be given of Armenian, Jewish and Zoroastrian communities.

The Armenians

Among Iran's estimated 250,000 Christians, the Armenians are the most privileged. This is mainly due to their ancient roots in the region, which means they have learnt not to proselytise among Muslims, and because they are not linked to a hostile foreign state like Israel or the United States. In the early 1990s, they were also helped by Iran's rivalry with Turkey. The newly independent former Soviet republic of Armenia was seen by Tehran to be blocking Turkey's push for influence in Central Asia.

Nevertheless, general economic hardship and Islamic restrictions on public and private life have caused at least 50,000 Armenians to leave Iran in recent years. The remaining 150,000 or so Armenians are allowed to maintain their own institutions, including mixed-sex swimming clubs, and even to produce alcoholic drinks for sale to one another.

In the early 1990s, zealots tried to persuade the government to force food shops owned by Armenians and other non-Muslims to display signs to the effect. This was to help Muslims who did not wish to touch food processed by non-Muslims not to buy at the premises. But it did not succeed, due to resistance inside the government of President Rafsanjani.

In December 1994, the Tehran daily newspaper, *Salam*, reported the complaint of a group of Armenian university graduates who had been denied jobs in government offices. 'Wherever, we go,' *Salam* quoted them as saying, 'we are told that it is forbidden to employ non-Muslim graduates.' The newspaper's tone was sympathetic and implied that such discrimination was rampant.

All Christians have known, however, that in the army, for one government institution, they are never made commissioned officers. In less sensitive departments of the executive, they are not promoted to higher positions. Everywhere, they are made to feel that they do not belong, that they are inferiors compassionately tolerated on Muslim land.

The Assyrians

Spokesmen for the estimated 50,000 Chaldean Catholics and members of the Assyrian Church of the East express, somewhat diplomatically, gratitude to Iranian authorities for their treatment. While it is true that the two churches have been allowed to carry out their religious duties without harassment, they have had very little freedom in any other sphere. They have had to be extremely careful not to appear to be proselytising; they have been compelled to give up their previously Western mode of dress; and their joint member of parliament in the Majlis has regularly had to denounce the United States in public, even though many Assyrians have been seeking immigration visas from Washington.

The Jews

Fearing a strongly anti-Zionist government coming to power after the Shah, leaders of Iran's 80,000-member Jewish community sent secret emissaries to Ayatollah Khomeini in exile in Paris in 1978 to assure him of their goodwill before the revolution of February 1979. Nevertheless, a dozen of the most prominent Jewish businessmen were executed in the first year of the revolution, while many others fled. The situation subsequently improved for Iranian Jews after the Iraqi invasion of September 1980. Under a heavy Western arms blockade for its taking the staff of the American embassy hostage, Ayatollah Khomeini's Iran badly needed modern weapons compatible with its stock of American arms, which Israel is believed to have supplied on a large scale.

Jews, too, like the Armenians, have ancient links with Iran and their relationship with the country has seen many storms. In early 1995, a *modus vivendi* was re-established which allowed the community to go about its business largely unmolested. In return, its representative in parliament had regularly to denounce Israel. The Jews' former commercial prominence had also been reduced to a considerable extent due to discrimination in awarding government contracts.

The Zoroastrians

Even though many of the most prominent Zoroastrians have felt it necessary to emigrate, rather than live under a strictly Islamic order, the community believes the situation might have been far worse. Zoroastrians, like members of other non-Muslim religions, are not allowed to be buried alongside Muslims. Since before the Second World War, their 'Towers of Silence', on which corpses were laid for vultures to reduce to bare bones, have been made illegal in Iran.

A curious phenomenon came to light after the census of 1991. The Zoroastrians were suddenly found to be 89,000 in Iran, more than twice the community's own information. The explanation was that some Muslims who had converted to Christianity, Baha'is and others had passed themselves off as Zoroastrians to escape persecution. Some 10,000 such 'Zoroastrians' were found to be living in the eastern province of Khorasan, where they had not been suspected to be.

The Baha'is

The most important among the religious minorities not accorded any legal status are the Baha'is, a nineteenth-century offshoot of Shiism which has now established communities all over the world. In its original homeland, it is one of the most ferociously persecuted religions in the world, partly because it is perceived as a threat, having proved attractive to sizeable areas of Iran in former times, and also because some of its members or alleged adherents achieved high positions under the last Shah, notably the fomer prime minister, Amir Abbas Hoveida, executed in 1979. This was despite the persecution of the religion in the earlier years of the Shah.

The Baha'i community in Iran has now been virtually annihilated. Over two hundred of its leaders are known to have been executed in government prisons after long periods of torture. An unknown number have been killed by mobs. Others have emigrated and the bulk of the laity has been driven underground or forcibly converted. Dozens languish in gaols under extreme conditions, despite repeated protests from international human-itarian organisations and human rights groups.

The Iranian regime's ferocious enmity towards Baha'ism was revealed by the statement that an official felt he had to make in September 1993. Hojjatoleslam Mohammad Ghazavi, the Islamic judge of the south Tehran suburb of Shahr-e-Ray, said that he had just freed two brothers who had burned to death a third man during a robbery. He said that, under Islamic law, he had been powerless, for the killers had been Muslims and their victim an unbeliever, a Baha'i. Thus the *shariah* is applied literally in Iran.

Sunni Muslims

Iran's estimated 5–6 million Sunni Muslims have, as a religious community, generally been wooed by the government since 1979. This was both to ensure a greater degree of political unity in the face of such enemies as Iraq, and to impress other Muslim states which are predominantly Sunni.

However, there have been many cases of overbearing behaviour, discrimination and even outright aggression against Sunni communities around the country, often by local Shia zealots or military commanders whom the government has not punished. As a result, relations between the two branches of Islam remain tense.

Perhaps the most important event of recent years in this respect was the death of the Friday prayer leader of the southern port of Bandar Abbas in July 1994. The beheaded and mutilated body of Mohammad Ziai was found beside his car five days after being called to a police station for interrogation. With a long history of criticising the regime's excesses, he had been imprisoned several times. Most recently he had denounced the destruction of the only Sunni mosque in the eastern city of Mashhad. The act had caused major demonstrations in several eastern and southern towns with a majority Sunni population. A large bomb explosion in the shrine of the eighth *imam* of the Shias, Imam Reza, in the spring of 1994 in which hundreds were reported killed and injured, was thought to be related to the tension between the two communities.

Efforts inside the ruling establishment

Efforts have been made inside the ruling establishment to persuade it to moderate its zeal. For a number of years, a group of members of the Majlis have set up a human rights committee, headed by a former ambassador to the UN, to promote 'fair treatment' for Iranian citizens in their encounters with the authorities. While the committee often denounces the Universal Declaration of Human Rights as inferior to what the committee sees as human rights under Islam, there are signs that it occasionally becomes embarrassed by incidents of blatant unfairness in the treatment of dissidents and religious minorities in Iran.

The committee is regarded as close to the faction of President Rafsanjani and conscious of the need to improve Iran's image abroad in the face of efforts by the United States to isolate it commercially and politically. It is possible that, behind the scenes, it may have succeeded in preventing at least some abuse, although it does not seem to have much influence among zealots close to Ayatollah Khamenei.

Women and religion

Women have been the critical centre of Islamic political projects in Iran from colonial times, through the Pahlavi period to revolutionary Iran from 1979 to the present. Equally involved is the image of the European woman which was a limited model at some stages and a despised figure at other times. In 1936, conditions for Iranian women were improved by the Pahlavi Shah, but by dictatorial means. Unveiling was compulsory as were other measures; women were never consulted and at the same time as the state instituted reforms, all independent women's societies and journals were shut down. The reform process was solely in the charge of Islamic male scholars, politicians and some of the clergy.

Similar features mark the revolutionary period; women played an important part in the struggle and were initially successful in refusing suggested new limitations of their freedoms. However, the religious leadership gained political power over the fragmented secularists and in a project to establish an Islamic society based on the 'rule of the jurist', they stressed the family and women's roles. The positive model was Turkey, although the Iranian reforms were more limited and implemented more brutally. The negative model was the perceived moral corruption of the West, especially visible in women. In general, the approach was based on particular Shia schools of *shariah* interpretation presented as the essentials of Islam, although this would be disputed by many Islamic scholars in other branches and *shariah* schools who would judge that many of the measures implemented by the revolutionary government are in fact anti-Qur'anic.

Beginning with the gradual enforcement of compulsory veiling, discriminatory features of the revolutionary state included the excluding of women from the judiciary and their disadvantage as witnesses in court, segregated public transport and a strongly gender-differentiated school curriculum. The marriage age for girls was lowered from 18 years to 13 years and there was a revival and encouragement of the much disputed (especially by Sunnis) temporary marriage tradition in which the minimum age for women is 9 years. High school males have been particularly targeted as 'needing' temporary marriage. Disenfranchisement of women has been discussed from time to time.

Large numbers of women demonstrating against veiling were physically attacked by members of Hizbullah (Party of God). One woman member of parliament, herself a daughter of a prominent Ayatollah, protested vigorously, to no avail. Reports of violence against women by individuals and by the state have been frequent over the last two decades. The effect of the Iran–Iraq war was to bring more women into the workforce and public space. Far from releasing women from duress, it has been established that the more women have moved into the public arena, the more strictly have moral codes been enforced. This in turn has aroused passionate opposition from Iranian feminists, but many women fervently support the ideology of the Republic and accept what they see as genuine Islamic restrictions in their lives.

Not all militant female opposition to the Republic is specifically feminist. Different ethnic–sect–religious groups such as the Kurds and Turcomans who belong to Sunni Islam demanded autonomy during the final stages of the revolution. They resisted repression by the new government by means of guerrilla warfare in which many women took part. Women also bear the burden of extreme poverty in the Kurdistan region of the Republic. Azeri Muslims and Baha'is have also become persecuted minorities. In addition, the guerrilla groups Fida'i and Mujahideen, originally fighting together with other anti-Pahlavi movements, eventually became opposed to the new state. The Fida'i espoused socialism and assumed that women's rights would be taken care of automatically; they refused to consider any separate movement for women's rights. The Mujahideen wished to break the clerical monopoly over religion and advocate a progressive Islam with full equality for women. Both groups, however, recommend the veil for women; neither has any women in leadership, and the Mujahideen is notable for its glorification of martyrs including young women killed by groups loyal to the Republic.

IRAQ

Iraq	
GDP (US$bn)	38[b]
Population	19,000,000
Annual population growth (%)	3.2
Urban population (%)	73
Working population (%)	24
Literacy (%)	54.6
Ratifications	1; 2; 3; 4

Since the Arab Ba'ath Socialist Party seized power in 1968, Iraq has been a single-party state under tight security control. The Special Rapporteur of the Commission on Human Rights, Mr Max van der Stoel, came to the conclusion that there are no freedoms of opinion, expression and association in Iraq. An insidious, intrusive climate of intolerance, repression, surveillance and silencing through fear of informants among community leaders, friends and family supports a culture of human rights abuses perpetrated and sanctioned by the state and its agencies. Freedom of thought and conscience is meaningless in such an environment and religious persecution a constant reality.

The Special Rapporteur on Iraq has drawn attention to the impact on Iraqi society of Iraqi Ba'athist policy:

> Those in power in Iraq have used the politico-legal structure to bolster an order which permits the secure enjoyment of essentially no human right or freedom . . . This order is justified by a revolutionary logic and a militarism which requires severe restrictions of human rights and seems to require an enemy. The continuing effect of such an order is a complex of abusive acts which seem impossible to catalogue or calculate. Insidiously, those in power are able to obtain the compliance of others in carrying out abusive acts under damnation of themselves, their loved ones and their spiritual integrity. In effect, those in power damn the people and then, in the worst way, make people damn themselves, damn their children, damn their families, damn their neighbours, damn their tribes, damn their religions and damn their futures: the people are stripped of all dignity, shamed and rendered compliant, 'guilty' and hopeless. They are pacified.

Social, ethnic and religious composition

Iraq's population was estimated at 19.4 million in 1991. In 1989, 71 per cent of the population lived in urban areas; 21 per cent lived in Baghdad in 1990. Among Iraqis, 75–80 per cent are estimated to be Arabs, 15–20 per cent Kurdish, 5 per cent Turcoman, Assyrian and other ethnic groups. As for religions and beliefs, 97 per cent of Iraqis are estimated to be Muslim (60–65 per cent Shia and 32–37 per cent Sunni Muslims).

Christians (mainly Assyrians and Chaldeans) make up 3 per cent of the population comprising both Arabs and a smaller number of Christians in the north. Other smaller religious groups in Iraq are the Yezidis in the north and the Sabeans (or Christians of St John) who live in the Basra region. Of the once thriving Iraqi Jewish community numbering 120,000 prior to 1948, only a few hundred still remain; there is a synagogue in Baghdad.

The mountainous north and north-east is dominated by the mainly Sunni Kurds; the centre-west is predominantly Sunni Arab and the south, below Baghdad, is predominantly Shia Arab. The three zones meet and intermingle in greater Baghdad where over the course of the twentieth century large numbers of mostly tribal Shia Arabs have migrated from the rural south; over 1 million Shia Muslims live mainly in the poorer areas of the city.

Sunni Arab minority rule

Before the twentieth century, sectarianism was not an issue. The main social division was between town and tribe, the former being dominated by Sunni Arabs, the latter by competing tribal leaders, Shia Arabs and Kurds as well as Sunni Arabs. This situation of semi-autonomy began to change in the late nineteenth century as Ottoman-trained officials were recruited from the Sunni urban elite and power became increasingly centralised.

The First World War ended over four hundred years of Ottoman control of the Arab Middle East; the region was subsequently partitioned according to British and French interests. Iraq was awarded to British Mandatory power in 1920. The creation of the new nation-state of Iraq over the following decade welded together the disparate ethnic and religious groups that had formed majorities in the former Ottoman *vilayets* (provinces) of Mosul, Baghdad and Basra.

Sunni advantage crystallised under the British mandate when British and Sunni interests converged, at the expense of the Shias. In 1924, a law was promulgated distinguishing between Iraqis of Ottoman origin and those of other origins, principally Persian. This distinction was maintained by successive governments, the Ba'athist state sharpening them further in terms of perceived loyalty and disloyalty to the regime. Notably those of 'Persian origin', primarily Shias, were presumed to be disloyal.

Sunni Arab minority rule in Iraq took on an added significance against the background of the Iranian revolution in 1979. The destabilising potential of revolutionary Islam was feared both regionally and internationally. The West and the Gulf States supported Iraq during the Iran–Iraq war (1980–88) because Saddam Hussein's regime was viewed as the main bulwark against Iranian domination of the Middle East and its vital oil reserves.

The impact of the 1991 Gulf war on the three main ethnic and religious groups in Iraq – the Kurds, Sunni and Shia Arabs – has been immense. The savagery of the Iraqi regime's repression of the subsequent popular uprising in southern and northern Iraq has deepened animosities, increasing the likelihood of future sectarian strife.

Sunni minority rule may have suited external interests but it has proved to be catastrophic for the people of Iraq as a whole. It has led to the suppression of political pluralism and blocked the development of the political and legal institutions that create the foundations of civil society. One viable alternative to the long tradition of autocracy and repression in Iraq is a transition to a federated state that would accommodate the diverse interests of Arab Shias, Sunnis and Kurds. However, to make this transition possible, the right to freedoms of expression, opinion and association, as well as to freedom of thought, conscience and religion or belief, is needed to lay the foundations of tolerance.

Economic and political development

The Iraqi economy is dependent on the production of oil which provides 98 per cent of its revenue. Iraq has some of the world's largest oil reserves. In July 1990 (before the

1991 Gulf War), oil production stood at 3.3 million barrels per day. Oil wealth facilitated Iraq's development into a militarily powerful state, the development of its nuclear capacity and the purchase of sophisticated weapons from the former Eastern bloc, from Europe and from the United States.

When the Ba'ath Party took control of Iraq in 1968, it adopted a planned economy. The nationalisation of the Iraq Petroleum Company in 1971 allowed the government to take full advantage of the sharp and repeated increases in world oil prices following the Arab–Israeli war of 1973. The increased revenues from the newly nationalised oil industry were used by the Ba'athist government to consolidate and gradually extend political power throughout every aspect of Iraqi society. It is estimated that 30 per cent of the working population is engaged in the public sector. By the 1970s the government controlled virtually all jobs, prices, trade and communication.

Popularity – or at least acquiescence – was bought by increasing wages and salaries, via infrastructural and industrial projects, and by extending health, welfare and educational services. But while the middle classes expanded, relatively little of Iraq's oil wealth was directed to the poorest sectors of the population.

There is little evidence that the proclaimed Ba'athist ideals of 'Arab unity, freedom and socialism' have guided party decision-makers. The economy did not become socialist, ultimately featuring state capitalism and the wooing of foreign investors.

In the 1980s the enormous human and economic costs of the Iran–Iraq war (1979–88) left Iraq with a significant external debt, and although living standards did not fall drastically, development projects were delayed or cancelled. The destruction caused by the 1991 Gulf War, combined with UN economic sanctions, has led to a reduction in essential services (such as health and education) and a sharp drop in living standards for most of the population except for the party and military elite. In May 1996, the UN allowed Iraq to sell oil to buy food and medicine for its people, while sanctions remained in place.

Women

The value of the family as the centre of security (to the benefit of the state) is fostered strongly among women and children, especially by the General Federation of Iraqi Women. The education system has addressed illiteracy and given equality to women. The model 'new Iraqi woman' is Arab, employed outside the home and well educated, but in the service of state ideology and one-party control. In 1978, modest changes were made to personal and family law; aspects of both Sunni and Shia *shariah* law were used to give women wider rights to divorce and child custody, and to place restrictions on second wives for males. However, women have been disappointed with the scope of personal law reform and the tendency of the state to take over family matters.

Women were granted equal franchise in 1980 and enjoy generous child-care and maternity leave provisions in a pro-natalist framework, as well as subsidised low-income housing for which women can apply independently. However, Shias, Sunni Kurds and secular groups who oppose the ruling elite are suspicious of state-sponsored programmes.

The Special Rapporteur to the UN Commission on Human Rights reporting on violations of human rights in Iraq has also stated that a Revolution Command Council Decree of February 1990 grants immunity to men for honour killings of female family members ('mother, daughter, sister, aunt, niece or cousin'). Mr Max van der Stoel commented: 'The absence of judicial control over such important matters causes the Special Rapporteur to marvel at the scope for abuse that such laws clearly afford.'

Women's freedom of movement has been restricted by requirements that they cannot gain approval to travel abroad without the approval of their husband, father or brother(s). Unmarried women without living male relatives cannot gain approval to travel abroad.

Many families have been deprived of principally adult male family members in the course of war, repression and acts of human rights violation such as arbitrary and extra-judicial executions, torture and disappearances. The consequences of the 1991 Gulf War have also been disastrous for the welfare of women and children as health and education networks have been deprived of resources in a deteriorating economy. Families of people who have been executed or disappeared have also been deprived of state benefits.

Political and governmental structure

The outstanding characteristic of government in Iraq is the extent to which power is centralised in a minute number of institutions and persons. According to Article 1 of the 1970 Provisional Constitution, Iraq is a 'people's democratic and sovereign Republic, the basic aim of which is to achieve a unified Arab State and to establish a socialist system'. Until this ideal of Arab unity is reached, Article 2 stipulates that 'the people is the source of authority and its legitimacy'. The free participation of citizens in the government of the country is extremely limited, given the power vested primarily in the Revolutionary Command Council (RCC) and the President.

The institutions of government are largely defined in the 1970 Provisional Constitution (subsequently amended several times) together with the National Assembly Act No. 55 of 1980. The constitution may be amended by a decree promulgated by a majority of two-thirds of the RCC in closed session, without being obliged to consult any other institutions. Since there is no Supreme Constitutional Court or any form of review procedure, it is possible for the RCC to enact legislation contrary to the Provisional Constitution.

The Republic is composed of these principal institutions: the Revolution Command Council (RCC) of the President of the Republic, the National Assembly, the Council of Ministers and the judiciary. An examination of the legal structures of these institutions reveals the extent of the powers vested in the RCC and the President of the Republic and how little power rests in the National Assembly, the Council of Ministers and the judiciary. The RCC has absolute legislative power enabling it to bypass the judiciary and control all aspects of political, social and economic life in Iraq. It also has sole control over the armed forces and the extensive security apparatus.

However, the Revolution Command Council is ultimately only 'an advisory body' to the President of the Republic whom it elects by two-thirds of its members according to Article 38(a) of the constitution. Apart from being the Chairman of the RCC, the President also acts as Head of State, Commander-in-Chief of the Armed Forces and Secretary-General of the Ba'ath party. Like all members of the RCC, the President – Saddam Hussein – is designated by name in the constitution. He has no fixed term of office and can only be dismissed by a two-thirds majority of the RCC. In effect the president is sole *de facto* ruler of the country.

Freedom of religion or belief and government policy

Article 25 of the 1970 constitution guarantees freedom of religion and belief, as well as freedom of religious observance, provided that such freedom is neither inconsistent with the provisions of the constitution and the law nor incompatible with public order and morality.

The constitution stipulates that Islam is the religion of the state (Article 4). However, the Sunni ruling elite of Iraq has never espoused a narrowly *shariah*-ruled Islamic state. The Iraqi authorities respect the observances of other divinely revealed religions and do not prevent non-Muslims from engaging in religious worship.

The hallmark of government policy towards religious communities which pose a political threat is that of the carrot and the stick. The authorities have spent large sums of money on the construction and renovation of mosques in an attempt to win over the *ulema* (religious leaders) to the regime. However, membership of politically active movements such as the Islamic Da'wa Party – as well as the Arab Socialist Party, the Communist Party and the Patriotic Union of Kurdistan – merits the death penalty. Baha'i activity is prohibited under Iraqi law and members of the Baha'i religious group are liable to a penalty of imprisonment, or even the death penalty in the case of a person who returns to the Baha'i faith after leaving it.

In line with government policy to conduct an all-out assault on the Shia religious establishment in the wake of the Iranian revolution and the start of the Iran–Iraq war in 1979–80, the Ministry of Awqaf (endowment) was extended to encompass Religious Affairs. This Ministry (unlike any other) was directly linked to the presidential office and its manpower and authority increased. The Ministry was charged with supervising the curricula of all schools. It is also responsible for the creation of a network of committees for religious indoctrination. Run by Ba'ath party officials or members of the religious classes cooperating with the regime, the committees now supervise the very mosques and religious processions which Shia Islamist groups such as the Da'wa Party had used to spread their ideas.

The government states that it encourages religious education and training at home and abroad (which includes sending priests and monks for theological study in European universities) and the publication of religious books and magazines, and that it supports the importing of holy books and gospels. However, this takes place solely within the context of compliance with state objectives. Over 1,000 religious books are, according to the Special Rapporteur on Iraq, said to be prohibited. The state has total control of information media in Iraq. There has been a virtual ban on Shia religious programmes on television and radio.

The Special Rapporteur of the Commission on Human Rights, Mr Max van der Stoel, in his 1994 report, has noted that the government consistently exploits and subverts tribal and religious community institutions. He noted instances of severe degradation and humiliation by the state which were intended to highlight the impotence of resistance, such as arranging a mass marriage celebration on the Shia solemn holy day of Ashura, on which Shias mourn the martyrdom of Imam Hussein. Members of the Islamic Da'wa Party have also been required to carry out the executions of their own members.

Shia Arabs

Despite Sunni political dominance, the persistently Shia character of southern Iraq is attributed to the following factors: the staying power of religious belief enhanced by feelings of oppression and injustice; the presence of the Shia shrines at Najaf and Karbala and the Shia theological colleges at Najaf and Hilla; and the commercial and religious intercourse maintained over time with Shia Persia. The great waves of Bedouin tribes that migrated into the region from Arabia during the course of the nineteenth century gradually adopted the beliefs and practices of Shi'ism.

The differing development of Shia Islam in Iraq and in Iran (where Shias constitute a very large majority) in the twentieth century reflects the essentially different characters of Shia religion and society in the two countries. In contrast to Iran, the Iraqi Shia *ulema* (religious leadership) did not emerge as a powerful player in national politics and were unable to mobilise large numbers of people for political action. The Shia Arabs have never achieved political representation commensurate with their numbers. Despite the religious inheritance of Shia Islam which stressed injustice and the illegitimacy of temporal power, political withdrawal rather than activism characterises the history of Shi'ism up to the Iranian revolution.

The intellectual inspiration for militant Shi'ism in Iraq is found in the writings of an Iraqi Shia Ayatollah, Mohammed Baqer al-Sadr. By 1979 Sadr was explicitly fusing political appeal with Shia cultural references in the first ever call in Iraq for the religious leadership to guide the political destiny of the nation. The growing popularity of Sadr's views seriously alarmed the Ba'athist leadership. President Saddam Hussein warned that anyone who attempted to politicise religion and challenge the secular ideology of the Ba'ath ruling party would be brought under the 'iron fist of the revolution'. The summary execution of Sadr in April 1980 and the unleashing of a policy of terror against the Shia opposition ended this threat to Saddam's one-man rule until the uprisings of March 1991.

The Special Rapporteurs on Religious Intolerance and on Iraq, together with other reports, have noted systematic discriminatory and repressive policies adopted by the state towards Iraqi Shias following the Gulf War. The late Grand Ayatollah Abul Qasim al-Musawi al-Khoei was arrested and the regime has failed to account for the disappearances of 105 Shia religious scholars and family members arrested in March 1991. Deportation and threats of deportation of Shias have taken place. The state has also interfered with Shia clerical selection processes. In 1994, the death – not an accident from accounts of the circumstances – of the late Grand Ayatollah's son, Muhammad Taqi al-Khoei, who directed a world-wide network of educational and charitable foundations, attracted international comment. The Special Rapporteur on Religious Intolerance received information in October 1994 that the al-Khoei family had been evicted from the late Grand Ayatollah's home and that confiscation orders applied also to other houses belonging to members of their clerical families. Religious endowment properties allocated for schools and mosques and administered by Muhammed Taqi al-Khoei were also said to have been confiscated.

Desecration and destruction of Shia holy shrines took place and only the most famous, the shrines of Imam Hussein and Imam Ali – the Prophet's grandsons and the most revered *imams* of Shia belief traditions – have been restored. Under government 'modernisation' programmes, houses and religious buildings in the Shia holy cities have also been bulldozed.

A large number of other mosques, libraries and *Husseiniyas* (religious community centres) have not been restored. Those *Husseiniyas* which have been approved for restoration are not allowed to be identified as *Husseiniyas*, thus depriving them of their identification as Shia centres of learning and worship. Kulliyya al-Fiqh, the main theological school in the holy city of Najaf, has not been allowed to reopen as an academy or centre of instruction and reportedly operates as a public market. Its students have been transferred to the Shariah College in Baghdad where no Shia philosophy or jurisprudence is said to be taught. Traditional Shia texts held in major public collections have reportedly been withdrawn from circulation or put on permanent reserve, and Shia scholars are often refused permission to publish their books. The government stated in reply that the Karbala and Najaf theological schools have continued to publish despite the effects of the economic embargo on supplies of paper and printers' ink. The government has been reported as transferring the legal title and administration of the thousands of *Husseiniyas* and other Shia properties to the Ministry of Awqaf and Religious Affairs, which is changing their names, functions and identities.

The Shia version of the call to prayer is reportedly still prohibited in some districts where Shias live, such as Sayyed Mohammed and Samara, and parts of Baghdad. The Special Rapporteur on Iraq noted that freedom to worship through prayer had thus been outlawed, Shias being forced into small clandestine meetings. Public manifestations of Shia traditional practice, such as the ritual preparation and distribution of food during the holy month of Muharram have been prohibited.

The Special Rapporteur on Iraq, Mr Max van der Stoel, considered that government policy systematically violated the right to freedom of religion or belief of the Shia community. He saw a clear need, because of systematic threats to Shia clergy and the assault on the community's religious heritage, to reassure the community that their religious beliefs and practices would be respected and their historical traditions and institutions safeguarded.

The Kurds

The 1970 Provisional Constitution defines the Iraqi people as consisting of two principal ethnic groups: Arabs and Kurds. Article 5(a) recognises the ethnic rights of the Kurdish people, as well as the legitimate rights of all minorities within the framework of Iraqi unity. Article 7(b) states that 'the Kurdish language shall be an official language in addition to Arabic in the Kurdish region' and Article 8(c) states that 'the region in which the majority of the population are Kurds shall enjoy autonomy in the manner provided for by law'. In practice, the egregious nature of human rights violations in the Kurdish regions of Iraq epitomises the failure of the Iraqi constitution to safeguard the rights and freedoms of its citizens.

The Kurds are one of the major peoples of the Middle East. Their origins are uncertain but, despite regional and tribal differences, they have retained a distinct identity for at least 2,000 years. Relations with peoples of the surrounding plains – whether Arab, Turk or Iranian – have always been complex and often contentious. In Iraq the Kurds have fought for autonomy for decades.

The introduction of national borders between Turkey, Iran and Iraq following the First World War imposed formal political barriers between the different groups of Kurds who live mainly in the mountainous areas of eastern Turkey, northern Iraq, north-western Iran and the south-east of the former Soviet Union.

Although religious belief is not a major component of Kurdish distinctiveness, Kurdish peoples are marked by religious diversity. Before the Islamic conquests of the seventh century, tree and solar cults, Zoroastrianism, Judaism and Christianity had competed in the region and are still extant in the Yezidis' compound religious tradition. Most Iraqi Kurds are Sunni Muslims. A minority (the Faili Kurds) are Shia Muslims and have been subjected to expulsions from Iraq, particularly in 1980. Religious difference is expressed in practice, through adherence to religious brotherhoods, particularly the Qadiriya and Naqshbandiya.

The Madan (Marsh Arabs)

The vast area of permanent lakes and marshes surrounding the Tigris and Euphrates rivers in south-eastern Iraq is inhabited by a unique people whose way of life is thought to constitute an unbroken link to the Sumerian fishing culture of 5,000 years ago. The Madan are followers of Shi'ism but low literacy levels and the distances from Shia centres of learning meant that their knowledge of Islam was often poor. Tribal ties and custom remained intact within the marshes and along with the Madan's unique and self-sufficient lifestyle, differentiated the Marsh Arabs from the urbanised sector of southern Iraqi society.

For centuries, the remoteness and inaccessibility of the marshes made the area a refuge for bandits and political rebels. The presence of the current Shia opposition in the region (like the earlier presence of deserters during the Iran–Iraq war) has not been of the Madan's choosing; however, it has had consequences that are leading inexorably to their elimination as a discrete group. The Madan have traditionally held aloof from external politics, but the deliberate draining of the 6,000-square-mile marshes of southern Iraq on which their water-borne way of life depends has forced many of them to take up arms against the regime. Thousands have fled to the Iranian border and thousands have been forced into so-called 'model villages' described as concentration camps by the opposition. Massive fire-power used by the Iraqi regime against the displaced Marsh Arabs has resulted in environmental and human disaster.

Christians

The Christian population includes both Arabs and a smaller number in the north who feel close cultural links with the Kurds. Despite family and tribal allegiances, Christian relations with Muslim Kurds have varied at different times from cooperative to hostile.

The Nestorian or Assyrian Church is the largest Orthodox church and has approximately 40,000 adherents in Iraq. The Assyrian language is also spoken in parts of northern Iraq. Among the Uniate churches, the Chaldean Church is the largest of the Christian denominations with some 250,000 members. There are also Latin and Syrian churches and a very small Armenian Catholic Church.

Following the 1991 Gulf War, Iraqi Christians have felt increasingly vulnerable and thousands have attempted to leave Iraq. Rising communal tensions are possibly exacerbated by the regime. Closer ties with the West, including families living abroad (particularly in the United States) have led to the Christians being labelled as pro-United States government, whatever their real views are. Local church hierarchies deny that religious persecution is occurring and urge Christians not to flee.

Turcomans

The Turcomans are descendants of the Turkic-speaking nomads who migrated from central Asia centuries ago. They are predominantly Sunni Muslims, although a small minority are Shia Muslims, and live mainly in the governorates of Mosul, Arbil, Kirkuk and Diyala. Kirkuk, situated at the epicentre of the oil industry of northern Iraq is a major centre of Turcoman population. Turcoman *mullahs* are reportedly forbidden to speak or lead prayers in the Turkish language; this policy has been carried through as the *mullahs* are all state employees. Shia Turcomans have experienced greater discrimination and repression, destruction of religious community property and other abuses of human rights than Turcomans in general.

Conscientious objection

Military service is compulsory. Iraqi citizens are expected to contribute to the development of the country through work and military service, which are seen as 'sacred' duties.

ISRAEL[1]

Israel	
GDP (US$bn)	70
Population	5,000,000
Annual population growth (%)	2.7
Urban population (%)	91
Working population (%)	39
Literacy (%)	95
Ratifications	1; 2; 3; 4

The issue of freedom of religion or belief in Israel is complex because it is inseparable from the underlying Arab–Jewish conflict, even though, in general terms, freedom of religion and belief for members of all faiths in Israel is safeguarded. At all levels, however, the clash of ethno-religious–national principles and terrorism impacts on civil rights, including the observance of Article 18. The link between state and religion in Israel means that further major issues rather concern freedom from religion than freedom of religion. Above all, there is a lack of a clear constitutionally guaranteed system in the state–religion relationship, not only for Orthodox and secular Jews but for all religions and denominations, as well as non-believers.

It had been hoped that the developments initiated by the peace process, especially with Palestinians, might result in a new harmony within the state of Israel's ideals of being both a Jewish and a democratic state. However, President Yitzhak Rabin was assassinated in November 1995 by a *yeshiva*, a student at a Jewish religious seminary, who had reportedly discussed the proposed killing with rabbis, though he failed to gain their blessing for it. This and the renewal of suicide bombings in Israeli cities in 1996 by members of the Palestinian group Hamas and Islamic Jihad (financed by Iran) have restored confrontations and repression on both sides, and slowed the peace process to a crawl. When the leader of the Likud Party, Benjamin Netanyahu, was elected prime minister, it was not clear whether or how the peace process would be resumed, but in July Israel eased its closure of the West Bank and Gaza and, after a fraught process of negotiation, Israeli troops largely withdrew from Hebron in January 1997.

Ethnic and religious composition

Among Israel's over 5 million people, 81 per cent of Israeli citizens are Jewish, the remaining 19 per cent are Arab, consisting of Sunni Muslims, Christians, Druze and other minority religions. Official statistics give the ethno-religious breakdown of population as follows: Jews (81 per cent), Muslims (14.4 per cent), Christians, Arabs and foreigners (2.9 per cent), Druze (1.7 per cent). Christians are divided into a large number of churches and denominations. The largest are the Greek Catholic and Greek Orthodox churches followed by the Roman Catholic and Maronite churches. Most Muslims are Arab and Sunni; there are a small number of Circassians and Ahmadis. The Druze are not Muslim, although their religion originated as a Shia sect. The headquarters of the Baha'i faith is in Haifa and there are about 300 members in Israel.

Arab-Israeli citizens are mostly descendants of those who lived in Palestine before the creation of the State of Israel. Tolerance of different beliefs can be seen in a variety of forms. Travel to visit religious sites or performance of religious obligations both within and outside Israel is widely permitted; for example, in 1991, over 1,500 Israeli Muslims were able to go on *hajj* to Mecca. Missionary activity is allowed in Israel although a 1977 law prohibits the offering and receipt of material benefits as an inducement to conversion.

A complex inter-relationship between ethnic, racial and religious factors is the cause of discrimination and violent intimidation of minority groups. The massive and ongoing problem of the resented presence of Muslim, Christian and other Palestinians in Israel and its occupied territories affects the lives of these groups severely. Together with Jews from Arabic-speaking countries, as well as the *falasha* (Ethiopian Jews), Palestinian Arabs are low on the social scale, working as unskilled labour and domestic servants, and comprise the largest number of poor people in Israel.

The Jewish state and the non-Jewish Arab minority

The legal and institutional structure of the State of Israel derives from the history of the Jewish people, for centuries in diaspora and persecuted, and from the history of Zionism which kept hope alive for a land where the diaspora communities would be at last gathered together. Zionism gathered momentum as a political movement in the late nineteenth century, to the point where the UN General Assembly in 1947 ordered the British Mandate of Palestine to be portioned. Israel and the Arab states fought in 1948–9. With the founding of the State of Israel, many Jewish people arrived from around the world after 1948, coming after the Holocaust from the position of being in diaspora as minorities to join the Jews living in Israel to become, as a collective group, the majority in the new state. Many Palestinian Arabs living within the boundaries set by the Arab–Israeli war fled under pressure to neighbouring states.

Israel, in common with other countries which have a major ethno-nationalist and religious diversity, has not fared well in securing equality between its Jewish majority and Arab minority. All citizens of the State of Israel are formally equal in the eyes of the law. Although there is no written constitution or bill of rights, the Declaration of Independence, proclaimed on the establishment of the State of Israel in 1948, provides that the state will 'maintain equality of social and political rights for all its citizens, irrespective of race, religion or sex'. It also included an appeal to the non-Jewish (Arab) population 'to take part in the building of the state on the footing of full and equal nationality and appropriate representation of all its organs'. Palestinians living inside the pre-1967 borders of Israel are Israeli citizens, hold Israeli passports and theoretically enjoy the same rights as Jewish citizens.

However, the Declaration also proclaims the state to be a 'Jewish State in Eretz-Israel' which would 'open its doors to every Jew'. It has been criticised, therefore, as establishing a contradiction between democratic ideals of 'equality' on the one hand and its Jewish character on the other. The state's basic goals are conceived exclusively in Jewish terms, thus excluding the Arab population. In practice, Jews and Palestinians live apart politically, administratively and socially. The result for Arab-Israeli citizens is substantial economic and educational disadvantage and discrimination.

Israel's Basic Laws, being constitutional in nature, define the state of Israel. Thus, the Basic Law on Human Dignity and Freedom states as its purpose 'to protect human dignity and liberty in order to establish in a Basic Law values of the State of Israel as a Jewish and democratic state'. The ideological basis of the state, with its emphasis on Jewish identity, raises the sensitive issue of determining who is and who is not a Jew for a multiplicity of religious, social and legal purposes.

The Law of Return (1950) grants any Jew in the world the right to settle in Israel and automatic citizenship and one-third of the Jewish diaspora has already been ingathered. The Nationality Act (1952) provides the basis on which citizenship is defined. It applies different rules to the acquisition of Israeli nationality by Jews and non-Jews. Whereas most states combine two methods of obtaining citizenship – birthplace and consanguinity – Israel gives preference to consanguinity, with the result that a person born in Israel does not receive citizenship on the strength of birthplace alone.

The Nationality Act, legislated out of religious–nationalistic considerations, has led to discrimination against the Arab minority. It accords any Jewish immigrant automatic citizenship, whereas even for those Palestinian Arabs living in what became Israel in 1948, citizenship was not automatic. The law was subsequently amended so that the children of non-Jews, who previously were not entitled to citizenship, can apply for citizenship at a certain age and subject to certain conditions. However, no citizenship provision exists for those who were absent when the state was established yet would qualify owing to birthright. In its present form, the law grants citizenship to all Arabs presently living in Israel; however, their spouses, unlike those of Jews, are not automatically entitled to Israeli nationality.

Land laws define the land as being the property of the Jewish people; 92 per cent of Israel's agricultural land and water is restricted to Jews alone. Other laws authorise the expropriation of non-Jewish (Arab) land for military or Jewish settlement purposes; one such law in relation to public purposes dates back to the British Mandate in Palestine.

Key quasi-governmental organisations – the Jewish Agency, the World Zionist Organisation and the Jewish National Fund, infrastructure established decades before the State of Israel – serve only the Jewish sector and are responsible for immigration and settlement, education, social welfare and the purchase and development of land in Israel. For instance, referring to the purposes and founding of the state, the constitution of the Jewish Agency states that title of lands taken in the name of the Jewish National Fund 'shall be held the inalienable property of the Jewish people'. The organisations provide a structure of service delivery which by definition benefits Jewish citizens while excluding non-Jews. The resources on which they draw come from the Jewish diaspora as part of the continuing commitment of world Jewry to support the Jewish homeland.

Discrimination against non-Jews, therefore, for historical reasons is systemic and structural and these inequalities have had a cumulative effect. The unequal allocation of budgets and resources by government bodies to Jewish and non-Jewish localities affects the housing, education and services available in those localities. Funding to local Arab councils is 25–30 per cent of that given to Jewish councils. In the mixed Jewish–Arab cities of Haifa, Acre and Jaffa, for example, government-owned houses occupied by Arabs are in disrepair through government neglect, while those of Jewish residents are properly maintained. Public housing projects in Jewish areas far outnumber those in Arab areas.

The tensions inherent in the definition of the state as both Jewish and democratic have been demonstrated within the democratic and legislative process itself. An amendment to the Knesset Basic Law in 1985 – predicated on another amendment (aimed at Meir Kahane and his Kach Party) to prevent racist parties from participating in parliamentary elections – banned any party which 'denies the existence of the State of Israel as the State of the Jewish People'. This served as the basis of an attempt to disqualify the Democratic List for Peace (DLP), a predominantly Israeli Arab grouping that also had Israeli Jewish members; it campaigns to transform Israel into a state both of Jews and Arabs. By a vote of twenty to nineteen the Central Election Committee decided not to disqualify the DLP, a decision later upheld by the Supreme Court. The Political Parties Act 1992 then restored the clause justifying the banning of a party 'which denies the existence of the State of Israel as a Jewish and Democratic state' in place of the 1985 amendment.

Education

The State Education Law provides that: 'The object of state education is to base elementary education in the State on the values of Jewish culture and . . . on love of the homeland and loyalty to the State and the Jewish people.' The education curriculum subordinates Palestinian Arab identity to the Jewishness of the state. Thus, while Palestinians are required to study Hebrew, Jews are not obliged to study Arabic (the second official language of the state). Palestinians must study Jewish religion and history, while Jewish children are not required to study the Qur'an, the Gospels or Arab history.

The two separate educational systems (Jewish and non-Jewish) have different budgets. Primary and secondary education for Palestinians is poorly funded and overcrowded. Palestinian children generally receive only one-third of the national average per capita allocation; as a result, the provision of teachers, buildings, facilities and equipment is inadequate in quantity and quality, compared with Jewish schools.

The role of religion in Israel's educational system is a subject of bitter debate. Shulamit Aloni, Minister of Education in 1992, was removed from her post when the religious parties led by the National Religious Party threatened to leave the government in response to her proposed reform of the state education system. Mrs Aloni – putting forward a secularist view – lamented the fact that Darwinian theory was not taught in schools and questioned the biblical account of creation. Criticising the over-emphasis of the secular syllabus on Jewish traditions and national values, Mrs Aloni declared herself 'opposed to the conservative religious establishment which sees the woman as an object to be fruitful and multiply, which is xenophobic, which is afraid of progress, culture, science and even afraid to talk about evolution'.

Orthodox and secular Jews

In Israel, the controversy between orthodox and secular Jewry is not over freedom of religion but over freedom from religious coercion in matters of belief and practice. The issue has been the subject of bitter social, political and ideological conflicts. This stems from the '*status quo*' agreement made between secular mainstream Zionists and the religious parties before the establishment of the state. According to this agreement, the Sabbath is the official day of rest, with no public transport allowed; institutional kitchens must follow Jewish dietary laws; Jewish law has jurisdiction in matters of personal status for Jews; and the religious educational system enjoys full autonomy.

Increasingly, the agreement has been invoked to justify religious gains at the expense of the secularists: El Al, the national airline, discontinued its Sabbath flights; television and radio broadcasting on Yom Kippur (the Day of Atonement) has been banned; cable-TV broadcasting is under threat. In 1994, under pressure from religious parties, the Knesset passed the Import of Frozen Meat Law, which prohibits the import of meat that has not been certified as kosher. This Act reversed the decision of the Supreme Court that restriction on meat imports on religious grounds was in contravention of the Basic Law of Freedom of Occupation.

The ultra-Orthodox lobby wields considerable power in particular locations, such as Jerusalem, where it has forced the closure of certain areas to traffic on the Sabbath in opposition to secular Israelis. Recent years have seen vociferous demonstrations organised by both secular and religiously observant Jews over the opening of cinemas, bars and clubs on Friday evenings. Secular Jerusalem-dwellers want the city to be a symbol of a modern state, whereas for the religious, it is predominantly a 'Holy city'.

Such is the power of the ultra-Orthodox lobby that prominent figures, like Members of the Knesset (MKs) Shulamit Aloni and Yael Dayan, have been held to public account for private actions, such as allegedly eating non-kosher food and 'violating' the Sabbath and Yom Kippur. The late prime minister, Yitzhak Rabin, was accused of 'unacceptable behaviour' after it was revealed that he ate non-kosher food in public while visiting Japan. The former prime minister, Shimon Peres, was forced by religious MKs to apologise publicly for saying that 'not everything [the biblical] King David did . . . is acceptable to a Jew or is something I like'.

Within the Knesset, the religious parties hold a crucial position as a result of the Israeli electoral system. Since no single political party has sufficient electoral support to enable it to form a majority government, the religious parties have been called on to join successive coalition governments. In this position, they are able to make demands on the government and exercise a degree of power that far outweighs their own electoral support. In the 1996 elections, religious parties took twenty-three out of the 120 Knesset seats and through coalition with the ruling Likud Party, gained representation at senior levels of government. Pressure for greater religious orthodoxy through government policy has been the result. For instance, the Transport Minister, an Orthodox Jew, ordered in July the Sabbath closing of Bar-Ilan, a road running through an ultra-Orthodox neighbourhood. However, the High Court reversed the ban after left-wing parliamentarians claimed that it imposed religion.

Women and religion

Women in Israel are affected most strongly by their ethnic–religious identity as well as by the control of the various Jewish, Druze, Christian and Muslim religious courts. Depending on the strictness of religious observance, the majority population live by some or all of the 613 commandments in the Jewish tradition, only two of which apply to women: responsibility for the keeping of dietary laws and the keeping of the Sabbath. Another set of laws applies to married women's menstruation. In general, the most Orthodox position is that women have major domestic religious responsibilities, but cannot be serious scripture students or become rabbis and have only limited participation in synagogue ritual.

Alternative interpretations and schools of Judaism allow more religious freedom to women, including access to membership of the Rabbinate and less onerous personal legal restraints. When the state was established, there was considerable debate over the part women should play in settlement of the land. Migrants came from very different cultures and Jewish women already in the region had a different experience from all migrants, particularly those who had survived the Holocaust. Finally, in the struggle to establish the state with politico-religious Zionists, on one hand, and 'classical' Jewish views, on the other, the need to deal with the perceived threat of the indigenous Arab population and to develop desert agriculture and an industrial base, the matter of gender and women's rights dropped to the bottom of the hierarchy of concerns.

The classical role of the 'woman of valour' in the home became the basis of early promulgation of personal law, but general state law gave Israeli women excellent legal protection in other matters, such as enshrined in the Equality of the Sexes Act (1951) and the Equal Opportunity in Employment Act (1982). The resultant contradictions are clearest in the legal profession. Women may become judges, but not in a family court where they may not even be witnesses.

Personal status and religious laws

Matters of personal status – principally marriage and divorce – are governed by religious law. Each recognised religious community in Israel has legal authority over its members in matters of marriage, divorce, conversion and inheritance: Rabbinic Courts, Shariah Courts, Druze Religious Courts, and Courts of the Christian Community.

Orthodox religious authorities have exclusive control over marriage and divorce of all members of the Jewish community, whether or not they are Orthodox. When the state was established, the system of personal law and religious jurisdiction under the British Mandate was retained. Therefore religious courts have exclusive jurisdiction in matters of marriage and divorce for their respective communities.

Those who advocate separation of state and religion argue as follows: that religious law is imposed on Jewish citizens who have no other recourse but to the religious courts in matters of personal status; that Orthodox religious courts do not recognise alternative movements in Judaism; that a direct violation of civil rights is inherent in a religious test that distinguishes between first- and second-class Jewish citizens (the 'who is a Jew' issue); and that there can be no freedom of conscience in matters of religion when the state deprives some of its citizens of basic rights like the right to valid marriage.

Those who support the present system contend that not all religious legislation constitutes coercion. They admit that the Law of Marriage and Divorce may violate the freedom of conscience of the secular individual, but do not see it as religious coercion since broad sectors of the secular public are willing to accept it.

In their turn, the religious claim that their demands for religious legislation are motivated by altruism, by an obligation to look after the whole Jewish population and preserve the Jewish nature of the state. Orthodox leaders struggle against what they perceive as secular intervention in religious spheres, or 'anti-religious coercion', in such matters as religious education, the conscription of religiously observant women, and the Law of Anatomy and Pathology, which limits organ donations and the use of corpses in medical studies.

Marriage

The Rabbinic Court Jurisdiction Law (Marriage and Divorce) (1953) provides that for Jewish citizens or residents of Israel, marriage and divorce are under the exclusive jurisdiction of the Rabbinic Courts. Thus, neither inter-religious nor civil (or non-Orthodox) marriage is available in Israel, despite lengthy campaigning for change.

However, in practice, ways of allowing a couple to cohabit legally, even though Israeli laws forbid them to marry, have been developed. Thus, the High Court has sanctioned marriages that take place abroad (so-called 'Cyprus marriages'), including those between Jews and non-Jews, or conducted by Jewish Reform, Conservative or Reconstructionist rabbis. Private marriage ceremonies are also recognised, affecting Jewish couples forbidden to marry by Jewish law. Common-law marriages are also recognised, although the children are considered illegitimate if the woman has not received a divorce document (the *gett*) from her former husband.

In December 1994, the Religious Affairs Ministry was accused of keeping a secret computerised blacklist of 10,000 Israeli citizens who are prohibited from marrying other Jews. The list includes about 2,000 people identified as *mamzerim* (illegitimate) and ranges from women lacking proper divorce papers to the alleged descendants of sinners from several thousand years ago. The issue emerged when a Rabbinic Court in Tiberias annulled the twelve year marriage of a woman whose distant ancestor was said to have married a divorcee 2,500 years ago; he was a member of the Cohen (priest) tribe who are prohibited from marrying divorcees. Israeli civil rights activists, led by Shulamit Aloni MK, called on the government to override the Orthodox rabbis and permit civil marriage. The blacklist also affects many of the 500,000 immigrants from the former Soviet Union, about a fifth of whom are considered non-Jewish and are therefore unable to marry Jews in Israel.

Divorce

Religious law ascribes a passive role to women in both marriage and divorce; it is the husband who agrees or refuses to give a divorce. This has resulted in a major problem of divorce 'refuseniks'. Although women's rights groups estimate that in Israel there are between 8,000 and 10,000 *agunot* ('chained women') living in the limbo of separation without divorce and thus prevented from remarrying, official sources claim that the total number of *agunot* is 400 and that the courts are working to solve this problem.

The Rabbinic Courts, according to Jewish law, can order a defiant husband to give his wife the *gett* and can obtain an arrest warrant. However, they have done so only thirty times in the past forty years. Even then, the husband must grant it 'of his own free will'. In cases of such a 'compulsory divorce', the district court has the authority to imprison the husband until he grants a divorce, although some men have continued to refuse even after release. A new law recently passed in the Knesset gives the religious courts powers to take punitive measures against 'refusenik' husbands with imprisonment of up to ten years.

According to traditional Jewish law, a husband who separates from his wife can live with another woman and have children without any stigma attaching to himself or them. In certain cases, he is even allowed to commit bigamy; the rabbis have granted at least ninety husbands this right in the last five years. However, a wife who begins a second relationship is branded as an adulteress and can lose custody of her children. Any children born from that relationship are regarded as *mamzerim* (illegitimate) who can marry only other illegitimate children.

Abortion law

The Abortion Law of 1977 approves abortions for physical or mental health reasons, when pregnancy results from rape or incest, if the mother is unmarried or the father not her husband. Article 5 of the law also allows abortion for socio-economic reasons. Religious parties argue that abortion is 'anti-Jewish' since such 'permissiveness' would decrease the already low birth-rate of the Jewish population. Despite protests, an amendment to Article 5 was passed in a coalition agreement between the Likud Party and the religious parties in the Knesset in 1977. The debate over the bill concerned the status of women in Israel and the right of the state to interfere in the life of a woman and her family in the name of politics and religion.

Conscientious objection

National service in Israel is compulsory: three years for men and one year for women. The army is the foundation for adulthood in Israel and military service has a direct effect on future employment and career prospects. No issue in Israel enjoys a broader consensus than army service and obedience to military orders. The social stigma attached to refusal is great and not serving in the army involves surrendering a sense of belonging. Imprisonment is the official, though perhaps not the worst, punishment; Israelis ostracise those who will not serve.

There is no provision for conscientious objection in Israel. The only possibility of release from the army without going to jail is to plead psychological unfitness by persuading an army Medical Health Officer that the stress of serving against one's conscience might lead to irreversible emotional damage. The dismissed individual receives a certificate stating that the bearer has emotional problems and is labelled with the lowest medical profile, Profile 21. Although bound by the principle of confidentiality, military sources admit that data on persons with Profile 21 are freely available. Profile 21 also affects work prospects, particularly in the government sector, Israel's largest employer. Every employment questionnaire asks for a military profile. Thus, a person unfit for the army is also considered unfit for civilian positions such as teacher or telephone operator.

A conscientious objectors' support organisation, Yesh Gvul (There's A Limit) was founded in 1982 at the time of Israel's three-year war in Lebanon. Israelis who objected to serving as an occupation force in a foreign country and in a war they did not support, took the unprecedented step of refusing army service, questioning the unchallenged motives of the army and terms like 'security' and 'self-defence'. After Israel's (partial) withdrawal from Lebanon and after the start of the Intifada, Yesh Gvul's work extended to include support of the growing number of objectors refusing to serve in the Occupied Palestinian Territories. Yesh Gvul members have been harassed and imprisoned; by July 1990, 111 objectors had served prison sentences and 1,500 people have signed Yesh Gvul petitions.

A recent judicial decision has held that conscientious objection based on religious or philosophical convictions will be recognised by courts.

Religious exemptions

The Military Service Act 1949 allows for the deferment of military service for *yeshiva* (Jewish religious seminary) students and exemptions for young religious women who, according to the original Act, were exempt for reasons of conscience rather than religion. The Association for Civil Rights in Israel protested about this inequity and argued that young men for whom military service was against their principles should also be exempt.

An agreement between the ruling Likud Party and the religious parties in 1977 led to the amendment of the Military Service Act and ended all provision for army exemption for reasons of conscience. However, a young woman could be exempted from military service on the strength of her declaration that she was religiously observant. Today this constitutes one of the most bitter subjects of controversy between religious and secular sectors in Israel. The Orthodox justify this release in terms of the religious tradition which argues that the study of the Torah helps the security of the people of Israel no less than fighting on the front lines.

The release of *yeshiva* students from military service has grown as more concessions are made to the religious parties by coalition governments. Army 'service deferrals' in order to study the Torah grew from 7,000 in 1982 to over 20,000 a year by 1992.

Religious sites

Israel officially guarantees full access to holy places for all faiths under Basic Law: Jerusalem, Capital of Israel and the Protection of Holy Places Law 1967, which also prohibit their desecration. Israeli officials and archaeologists say that every effort is made to preserve artefacts and relics of religious value.

None the less, Christian patriarchs and bishops believe that Christian antiquities have been disregarded as part of Israel's campaign to assert its right to Jerusalem. Since the establishment of the state, mosques and other Muslim holy places have reportedly been expropriated and placed under state jurisdiction. Some have been demolished or put to alternative uses, as shopping centres or even night-clubs; some cemeteries have been appropriated over the years by public utilities.

Three important recent treaties concern the status of holy places: the agreement between the Vatican and Israel for the establishment of diplomatic relations, the Peace Treaty between Israel and Jordan and the agreements between Israel and the Palestinian Authority. However, difficulties over Jerusalem remain between all parties and confrontations continue there. The Vatican has also refused to endorse Israel's declaration in 1980 that Jerusalem is its 'united and eternal' capital.

Inter-religious understanding and cooperation

There is an Inter-religious Coordinating Council in Israel that works with the World Alliance of Inter-faith Organisations. Its guide to inter-religious activities lists a range of bodies: Bridges for Peace, Clergy for Peace, Melitz Center for Christian Encounter with Israel, Rabbis for Human Rights, The Tantur Ecumenical Institute for Theological Studies and many others. There are also other initiatives in which communities live together, villages of Jews and Arabs, such as Neve Shalom/Wahat al-Salam, which was established to preserve both people's traditions and national identities while they live together and to maintain respect and tolerance for each other.

Note

1 See also the entry on the Occupied Palestinian Territories.

THE OCCUPIED PALESTINIAN TERRITORIES[1]

Palestine, the holy land of the three great monotheistic religions of the world – Judaism, Christianity and Islam – is at the same time a land of great contention, where religion, ethnicity, economics and politics have intertwined and battled for many centuries.

The contemporary political history of the Palestinians is long and complicated, making any evaluation of their exercise of freedom of religion, or any other right for that matter, quite difficult. From the moment around the turn of the century that the Zionist movement began its efforts to establish a Jewish state in Palestine, the line between religion, ethnicity and political identity began to be drawn thin. The line disappeared altogether when the State of Israel was established. Israel's 1948 Declaration of

The Occupied Palestinian Territories	
GDP (US$bn)	2.840[g]
Population	2,291,086[g]
Annual population growth (%)	3.1[g]
Urban population (%)	see Israel statistics
Working population (%)	see Israel statistics
Literacy (%)	87[e]
Ratifications	see Israel

Independence affirmed it as the birthplace of the Jewish people where 'their spiritual, religious and political identity was shaped' and proclaimed 'the establishment of a Jewish state in Eretz-Israel, to be known as the State of Israel'.

It is a matter of debate, at least from the Palestinian perspective, whether or not the Jewish state has fulfilled the other promise in the Declaration of Establishment, that of ensuring 'complete equality of social and political rights to all its inhabitants, irrespective of religion, race or sex' and 'freedom of conscience, language, education and culture . . . [and to] . . . safeguard the Holy Places of all religions'. This synthesis of religion, ethnicity and politics has informed the laws of the state as well as its policies throughout the years of confrontation with the Palestinians and with their Arab neighbours from 1948 to the present.

Arab national and political identity, on the other hand, is also intertwined with religion, as Islam has been since the seventh century the driving force of Arab identity. This is compounded by the fact that Islam is not only a personal religion, but a system of life which provides laws for most aspects of individual and social behaviour. The Palestinian Christians as well have for centuries perceived themselves to be part of Arab Islamic civilisation as an expression of their national and cultural sense of identity.

In the Occupied Palestinian Territories every political decision has had religious implications, and vice versa. One extreme example is the Israeli settlements, illegally established in the West Bank and Gaza, many of which are inhabited by armed extremist Orthodox Jews motivated by religious ideologies. These settlements, and settler behaviour, have been the source of much political friction in the Territories. The fact that many religious sites are holy to at least two of the three monotheistic faiths has further exacerbated the situation and the tensions created fertile ground for conflict. Another problem is the extreme Muslim groups Hamas and the Islamic Jihad, who perceive religion and political struggle to be one and the same.

The political environment in the Occupied Palestinian Territories remains extremely volatile, its continuing instability affecting all aspects of life, including the exercise of the freedom of worship and manifestation of faith. Exacerbated by the political activities of religious extremists, excessive measures taken by those in authority continue to place these freedoms in jeopardy for the foreseeable future.

Historical and current context

This entry concerns itself with that part of Palestine which was not included in the territory declared as the State of Israel after the war of 1947–48, which broke out consequent to Security Council Resolution 181 (29 November 1947) partitioning Palestine into a Jewish state and an Arab state. An Arab state was never constituted, and what was left of its proposed territory was geographically divided by Israel into two: the

West Bank with an area of around 5,500 sq kms which came under Jordanian control, and an additional 360 sq kms (known as the Gaza Strip) which was taken and administered by Egypt. From that point on these two areas developed differently in terms of legal systems and administration.

In the 1967 war, both the Gaza Strip and the West Bank (including the eastern part of the city of Jerusalem) came under Israeli occupation. Israel unilaterally annexed East Jerusalem. This annexation was protested and remains unrecognised by the international community until today. Nevertheless, Israel extended its own civil law to East Jerusalem and the Palestinians living there have been subject to that law. However, on 13 September 1993, as a result of negotiations between Israel and the Palestine Liberation Organisation (PLO), a Declaration of Principles on Interim Self-Government Arrangements for Palestinians was signed in Oslo. After this, other implementing agreements were made and in May 1994, the PLO took up limited autonomy in the Gaza Strip and the city of Jericho on the Jordan River. In August 1994, another agreement was signed transferring responsibility for five specific civil authorities to the Palestinians: health, education, social welfare, tourism and direct taxation.

PLO leader Yasser Arafat was elected president in 1995. In April 1996, the Palestine National Council made an historic decision to remove all references in the Palestine Covenant which call for an armed struggle against Israel. While the then Labour Government in Israel hailed the decision as an important ideological shift, the leader of the former opposition Likud Party called for the new PLO charter to recognise Zionism and the State of Israel. Palestinian hopes to have Jerusalem as a capital have been steadily rejected by the new Likud government.

Economic and social factors

In 1993, there were 1,084,400 Palestinians living in the West Bank, 748,900 in the Gaza Strip, and more than 150,000 living in East Jerusalem. At least 14 per cent of Palestinians live in extreme poverty; indeed, the poor constitute most of the population. Unemployment is very high, as Israel in thirty years of rule has made the Gaza labour force dependent on employment within Israel while constraining and weakening Gazan domestic economy by, for instance, controlling its borders and consequently its trade. The closures of the border with Israel as security against suicide bomb attacks have had what is seen as a punitive impact on everyone in Gaza.

In Gaza, over half the population is under 16 years old and 70 per cent is under 25. Children have been the most severely traumatised by the six years of the Intifada and literacy rates have dropped. Education in the Occupied Palestinian Territories has fallen far behind the historical norm in which Palestinians were reputed to be the most educated in the Arab world. Closures of the Israeli border have made it difficult for Gaza students to travel to West Bank universities.

Ethnic and religious composition

The vast majority of Palestinians are Muslim, with a small minority of around 4 per cent who are Christian and belong for the most part to the Eastern Orthodox Church, with fewer numbers of Melkites, Catholics and Anglicans. The size of the Christian minority varies from area to area. Most Christians (90 per cent) live in East Jerusalem where they constitute 15 per cent of the population. In the Gaza Strip, Christians are about 0.2 per cent of the population.

President Arafat has declared major religious holidays, both Christian and Muslim, as national holidays, and has since added the dates on which Orthodox and Catholic Christians celebrate their two main feasts.

Freedom of religion, equality and non-discrimination

The freedom to have or to hold religious beliefs is generally respected in Palestine. While Muslims constitute the vast majority of the population, there is a history of religious co-existence amongst the various religious communities, and this history has been affirmed in law. In practice, however, the exercise of freedom of religious belief is hampered by the political impact of the Israeli occupation, by the fine lines between religion, ethnicity and politics, and by societal modes of behaviour that place certain limitations on that right.

Article 2 of the Constitution of Jordan, which forms part of the local law in the West Bank, states that the official religion of that area is Islam. However, in the Gaza Strip, legal arrangements under Egyptian administration, which do not include this edict, guarantee complete freedom of belief (Article 11). Both sets of laws guarantee equality and prohibit discrimination on the basis of religion, as well as the right to manifest belief (respectively, Articles 14 and 11) within the normal limitations as found in the ICCPR.

Further, the Declaration of Independence of Palestine, in 1988, states that religious beliefs are to be safeguarded, assures non-discrimination, *inter alia*, on the basis of religion, and promises 'total commitment to Palestine's spiritual and cultural heritage of tolerance and tolerant coexistence amongst religions'. Although the Palestinian Declaration of Independence does not have the force of law, it does carry within the Palestinian community strong moral force. The Palestinian (Draft) Basic Law now under discussion, on the other hand, has stronger and clearer protections of the freedom of religion and belief. The draft Basic Law does not propose Islam to be the religion of Palestine.

Personal status law

Within the Palestinian community itself, there are strongly entrenched practices and traditions that affect freedom of conscience and belief. It is common practice in the society that a person is identified as either Christian or Muslim whether or not that person is religiously observant or even an atheist. Children automatically follow the religion of their parents, and are registered as such at birth. Personal status issues are determined by religious law in accordance with each denomination's precepts and rules. Marriages normally occur between couples of the same religion, and the parents' right to determine the religion of their children is considered sacrosanct.

In the West Bank and Gaza, Muslim Shariah Courts and Ecclesiastical Courts (Christian) exercise jurisdiction over many functions related to marriage and divorce, inheritance and general family status laws. These courts have functioned since Ottoman times and have established continuity throughout the changes in administration and authority over the area. Each of these courts apply the personal or family status laws of its community's religion; within the Christian community, five of the denominations have their own specialised ecclesiastical courts and laws.

Women, religion and equality

Women in the Occupied Palestinian Territories suffer discrimination and violence in double degree. There are considerable numbers of Palestinian women political prisoners. Because the Palestinian community is under severe stress, this has resulted in the family being the key to personal security and ethnic–religious confidence. The cultural practice of honour and shame in relation to the behaviour of women – widespread throughout the Mediterranean and the Middle East – tends to result in violence against women of all religions in communities at war and struggling for survival. Certain interpretations of *shariah* law tend to reinforce the ideology of women's honour. It has often been remarked that in conditions of warfare, matters of women's autonomy and survival are the least of anyone's concerns and women's protest is seen as trivial in view of supposedly larger questions of national survival.

The establishment of the Gush Emunim, consisting only of Jews observing Jewish religious law, had as its purpose Israeli settlement of occupied territory. Much of the movement's success has depended on women's initiative in establishing households and also in women's participation in vigilante activity against Palestinians.

Discrimination between Jews and non-Jews

Israeli military orders indirectly discriminate between the Jewish and non-Jewish communities because, while appearing neutral, in practice they have an adverse impact only on Palestinians. Military orders have been passed, designed to protect the sanctity of holy places of worship. For example, Military Order 327 (1969) assures the protection of holy places from 'desecration or any other damage and from anything that might impede the free access of religious followers to their holy places or which might offend their sentiments towards these places'. However, these orders only effectively protect holy places against Palestinian but not Israeli incursions, as the illegal Jewish settlers cannot be prosecuted under West Bank military law. Consequently only Palestinian Christian or Muslim offenders may be prosecuted and sentenced to imprisonment, while Israeli Jewish offenders may only be prosecuted under Israeli civil law.

Religion is listed in birth certificates and in the Israeli-issued personal identity card required by law to be carried by each resident of the Occupied Palestinian Territories. This opens the way to tangential discrimination on the basis of religion in a number of ways, such as in granting of permits to enter Jerusalem to attend religious events there. While the Israeli authorities claim such measures to be for the purpose of guaranteeing access, the result is often the reverse. Even before permits were required for entry to Jerusalem, Muslims, for example, were often not allowed into the city on Fridays, in order to reduce the number of worshippers.

The recording of religious identification also facilitates different treatment on the basis of religion in the provision of a number of services, including family reunification, travel and other permits, and within Palestinian society itself in employment, school registration (particularly in private schools) and other services.

Change of religion or adoption of secular belief

While there is no law that prohibits anyone from changing religion, there is nevertheless strong societal resistance to it. In Islam, this stems specifically from *shariah* precepts prohibiting *ridda* (apostasy), a Muslim's repudiation of Islam which is a crime commonly recognised as punishable by death. Although *ridda* is condemned in the Qur'an in the strongest terms, yet the Qur'an does not in fact define a punishment. Palestinian Shariah Courts have only indirectly addressed the issue of *ridda*, usually in the context of inheritance disputes where they have stopped 'apostates' from inheriting, but such cases are rare. For Christians a similar problem exists with respect to societal disapproval of changing one's religion, although there are no specific laws against it.

447

Problems arise in cross-community marriages, where the right to maintain one's religion comes under threat. According to *shariah* law, a Muslim man is allowed to marry a Christian woman, with the latter allowed to maintain her faith, but a Muslim woman can only marry a Muslim. Consequently, Christian men wishing to marry Muslim women must become Muslim themselves. Christian women marrying Muslims are sometimes ostracised by their families and it may take years, or never, for reconciliation to take place.

Although there is no official policy or law that prohibits atheism, to declare atheism publicly is generally unacceptable. Most professed Palestinian atheists are linked to Marxist political groups, but even they have not challenged societal norms of religious custom and tradition. In fact, many members of these groups are devout and observing Muslims or Christians, and do not perceive a contradiction between their faith and their political ideology. While the current response to atheism does not reach the level of ostracism, present attitudes may change since Islam has become the organising basis of movements which enjoy considerable strength in Palestinian politics.

Discrimination in manifesting religion – access to religious sites

The right to manifest one's religion is most affected by the political dynamics of the occupation. The extent to which anyone in the Occupied Palestinian Territories is allowed to manifest their belief in practice depends on whether the practice is, or is perceived to be, an expression of religious or of political sentiment and need by the Israeli authorities. They have limited religious practice through measures such as closure of mosques, the storming and desecration of mosques and churches, confiscation of religious material, interference with burial ceremonies and religious processions, military closures and curfews.

The most significant measure at present which restricts Palestinian Muslims' and Christians' right to worship and manifest their faith is the closure of East Jerusalem to the rest of the Occupied Palestinian Territories. Muslim and Christian holy places are found in almost every corner of the city. From the Old City of Jerusalem, both Jesus Christ and the Prophet Mohammed ascended to heaven, making the city the holiest city for Christians and the third holiest place in Islam.

Following the Gulf War in 1991, a general order banning the entry of West Bank and Gaza Palestinians to East Jerusalem was issued. Since that time, entry to Jerusalem has been granted only through individual permits. In the past two years, these permits have been extremely difficult to obtain and are very often suspended *en masse*. While this and other measures are promulgated for security reasons – broadly defined by the Israeli authorities – and not specifically as an attack on freedom of worship, they have nevertheless severely affected the right of both Christians and Muslims to worship in the holy city. At present, nearly all Palestinians, with the exception of residents of Jerusalem (0.075 per cent of the Palestinian population), are unable to worship at their holy places in Jerusalem.

Even within the Old City of Jerusalem, Israeli forces often restrict worship by blocking entrances to these sites and preventing worshippers from entering freely. It has been an Israeli practice, most frequently on security grounds, that soldiers stand at the entrances to mosques and especially to the Al-Haram Al-Sharif compound in Jerusalem checking the identity cards of worshippers, harassing some in the process. As a result, worshippers are frequently prevented from going into the compound for prayer. Such measures severely restrict the right to collective manifestation of faith, particularly as Muslims are required to pray five times a day.

Israeli soldiers blocked the entrance to the Church of the Holy Sepulchre in the Old City of Jerusalem on 22 April 1995, the Saturday preceding Easter for the Orthodox Churches.

On that day, worshippers traditionally arrive from distant towns and villages, so that they can return to their homes and towns with candles lit from the Tomb of Jesus. The Israeli authorities said they were organising worshippers' entry to the church in order to prevent overcrowding, but some clashes erupted and Israeli soldiers started beating people, injuring several. A large number of pilgrims from all over the world were also prevented from praying in the church.

Restriction of access to religious sites is not limited to Jerusalem, however. A number of sites revered by Muslims and Jews alike are scattered throughout the Occupied Palestinian Territories, and the Israeli authorities have taken over the administration of these sites. The authorities organise access for members of both faiths in a manner which purports to guarantee access while at the same time to maintain the security of Jewish worshippers in particular, most of whom are residents of the illegal settlements in the West Bank. The political tensions between Jewish Israeli settlers and Palestinian local residents often erupt into open confrontation and violence, engendering Israeli army measures which in turn restrict Palestinian access to religious sites.

For example, Israeli settlers began praying at a site in Nablus believed to be Joseph's Tomb and in 1982 established a school for the Torah at the site. Confrontations intensified between the Jewish settlers and local Muslims and the Israeli military consequently divided the site between the two religious groups, with the larger space accruing to the Jewish settlers. However, the tensions remain and few Muslims dare worship there any longer.

On 25 February 1994, twenty-nine Muslim worshippers were massacred at al-Haram al-Ibrahimi Mosque in Hebron. Baruch Goldstein, a settler from the nearby Kiryat Arbaí settlement in Hebron, opened fire on Palestinians kneeling in prayer inside al-Haram, until he was killed himself by those Palestinians present. While investigating the incident, the Israeli authorities closed the shrine to all worshippers for seven months. The recommendation of the investigative commission to divide the shrine's space between Jewish and Muslim worshippers, giving approximately two-thirds to Jewish ones, was adopted by the Israeli government. In January 1997 Hebron was handed over to the Palestinian Authority. The holy site, however, remains under Israeli control, as does the area surrounding Jewish settlements nearby.

An earlier violent incident took place on 8 October 1990 in the occupied Old City of East Jerusalem, at the Al-Haram al-Sharif compound. The Temple Mount Faithful, a Jewish extremist group advocating the destruction of the al-Aqsa mosque over the Dome of the Rock for the purpose of rebuilding the Third Temple, had announced their intention to lay the cornerstone of their temple on that day. Tensions were high, with around 5,000 Muslim worshippers within the Al-Haram walls. The Israeli police and army were present in force, on top of and around the walls of the compound. The tension exploded into riot during which Israeli security forces used excessive force; seventeen Palestinians were killed and at least 150 injured due to indiscriminate use of live ammunition.

Israeli forces occasionally raid mosques and sometimes churches for purposes stated invariably to be the seizure of 'seditious and inciting literature' or weaponry, in response to information on alleged demonstrations, or for general security investigations including the arrest of wanted persons. As well as deaths and injury, these incidents are followed by the closure of mosques, the confiscation of religious books and other literature, and even the confiscation of loudspeakers used by *muezzins* for calls to prayer. Soldiers have on occasion fired live ammunition inside mosques, killing and wounding worshippers. Several such incidents were documented during the Palestinian Intifada.

Israeli soldiers and illegal Jewish settlers have obstructed services, raided mosques, churches and religious processions, and interfered with burial rites and funeral processions. Religious property has been destroyed, including copies of the Qur'an, a deeply offensive act. Israeli soldiers are said to display lack of respect and a callous disregard for religious sentiment. Soldiers have marched into mosques with their weapons and with boots on and exhortations by mosque *imams* and sheikhs not to violate the sanctity of a house of worship have gone unheeded.

There have also been a number of assaults on clergy, both Christian and Muslim. During 1993, for example, over thirty *imams* were arrested, detained, interrogated, and many imprisoned in the Bethlehem and Jericho areas alone. One example took place on 12 April 1990, when the Greek Orthodox Patriarch Theodoros I was rendered unconscious due to tear gas thrown by the Israeli police as he visited St John's Hospice, a Greek Orthodox building which housed a clinic. The hospice had been taken over forcibly by extremist Jewish settlers.

The cycle of intolerance, protest and repression

In Israel's unrelenting war against Islamist political groups such as Hamas and Islamic Jihad, any activity interpreted to be political by the authorities can result in raids and assaults. Between December 1992 and August 1993, twenty-one mosques were ordered closed for periods between three weeks and six months. In 1994, the number of mosques ordered closed was reduced to five, while at the same time raids on mosques and the arrest of religious personnel began to rise again.

In actions against Muslim militants the Israeli government has enforced punishment collectively without assigning responsibility to identified individuals. On 14 December 1993, the dead body of Israeli border guard Sergeant-Major Toledano was discovered and the militant Islamist group Hamas claimed responsibility. Three days later, the Israeli government deported 413 alleged Hamas or Islamic Jihad activists and the Israeli Supreme Court sanctioned the implementation of those deportations prior to appeal. The deportations were made in composite orders with an attached list of names. The charge against the deportees, twenty-six of whom were sheikhs and mosque *imams*, was that they were 'inciters . . . who endanger lives by their activities'. The government's interpretation of its security needs and of perceived threats to that security has thus resulted in broad and collective punishment of Muslims, many of whom were, by force of duty, *imams* and public speakers in their mosques and communities.

Not only the Israeli government has been involved in actions responding to threats or perceived needs about security. From the first year of the Palestinian authority's rule in Gaza and Jericho, the Palestinian police have made efforts to curb Hamas and Islamic Jihad attacks against Israeli military and civilian targets. A number of measures introduced have tangentially resulted in restrictions on freedom of expression and religion. In May 1994, the Palestinian police issued a notice calling on mosques not to use their loudspeakers for 'propaganda and information which may do harm rather than good' and asking that such information be reviewed by security in the relevant area. Another order, issued in April 1995, more specifically prohibited 'any attempt to use mosque platforms to incite and create conflict' and ordered the removal of posters and written material from mosque walls, as such activities are seen as being 'in contradiction to the teachings of our correct Islamic faith'. During the following month, Palestinian police stormed mosques in the Gaza Strip, removing posters and published material which the police considered 'inciting against the Palestinian Authority'. In April 1995, the police claimed to have found weapons and dynamite in Qabaaí Mosque in the Jabalya district.

In one incident, Palestinian security forces killed fourteen and injured many more in the Gaza Strip, when riots broke out after Friday prayers at Palestine Mosque in Gaza City. Tensions were high as Hamas had announced its intention to conduct an illegal march through the streets. When worshippers came out after prayers, riots broke out and were met with indiscriminate shooting by security personnel. This incident created an environment where any religious Muslim became suspect; many were beaten and ill-treated on the streets and in detention afterwards.

Waves of mass arrests of alleged Muslim activists by Palestinian and Israeli authorities took place after suicide-bombing incidents in Israel for which Hamas and Islamic Jihad have claimed responsibility.

From August 1994 to April 1995, more than 680 individuals were arrested by the Palestinian and over 1,500 by the Israeli authorities. Many of those arrested, however, had not been directly connected to political groups working under the guise of Islam with any connection to the bombings. According to documented evidence, many of the detainees were subjected to torture and ill-treatment by both authorities for the purpose of extracting confessions; one alleged Hamas suspect died as a result of torture. A number of documented incidents of torture and ill-treatment by the Palestinian authorities include beatings and the shaving off of beards, an act offensive to religious sentiment.

Israeli government action against those families whose members have been involved in bombing incidents notably includes the dynamiting of the house in which the family lives, thus forcing the family to scatter. Extreme poverty, destruction of family and dis-possession, coupled with religious and ideological training to a narrow focus, play a large part in making martyrdom attractive. One Palestinian study of the lives of the suicide-bombers has shown that many of the young men were children during the Intifada, had lost parents and other members of their devout Muslim families, had spent time in Israeli gaols themselves for street protests, and had been held without charge and beaten. Most came from refugee communities and were unable to find work. The rewards of martyrdom are reportedly promised by Islamic Jihad members and by armed militant members in the nationalist movement Hamas (the Islamic Resistance Movement) which has the infra-structure of a large political party and a considerable measure of popular support. Hamas has a social welfare wing which provides educational, health and recreational services.

After a series of suicide bombings linked to Hamas in early 1996 and a subsequent lull, Hamas announced, on 10 March 1996, that it was withdrawing its suicide-bombing cease-fire against Israel as a result of the actions of the Palestinian authorities. On the following day, Yasser Arafat had three leading members of its military wing arrested. Reportedly 600 Islamist militants have been arrested by the Palestinian police and the Palestinian authorities have taken over mosques, schools and charities run by Hamas. Also in March, the Islamic National Salvation Party was announced, a new political party made up of former Hamas militants and supported by Yasser Arafat. The party abjures violence while seeking to express Hamas's ideological ends by legal political means; two of its leaders are women.

Religious education

Religious education is compulsory in West Bank schools. Students are required to study Islam in government schools, but Christian students are exempted and can study Christianity if offered at the school. The same holds true in private schools, many of which are owned and managed by religious communities within and outside the Occupied Palestinian Territories. Many of these private schools are Christian, having been established by missionaries around the turn of the century. In these schools, both Islam and Christianity are taught and, in some, an additional or a substitute class called 'Ethics' may be taught.

In the West Bank, passing an examination in Islamic studies is a requirement for Muslim students in order to pass the *Tawjihi*, the Jordanian matriculation examinations. Today, under the Palestinian Authority this is no longer a requirement, and it has become an elective subject for both Muslim and Christian students in the West Bank.

Schools in the Gaza Strip follow the Egyptian system, but there as well religious education is mandatory, in accordance with the student's religion. Gaza students taking the General Secondary Education Examination are required to pass a test in religion in order to qualify for graduation.

Religious education within the purview of mosques and churches continues unhampered, except in cases where the institution itself has come under pressure or attack by the Israeli military authorities or the Palestinian police. This education stops, for example, when a mosque is closed by military order, or when a curfew is imposed on a town or village for an extended period of time. A number of religious educational institutions, particularly institutions of higher learning, have been subjected to harassment and closure by the Israeli military authorities. These measures are imposed on the basis of the same criteria as the closure of mosques, such as suspicion of security-related activities or hostility to Israel, charges of incitement and 'hostile propaganda'.

Religious media and publications

There are no laws preventing the publication and distribution of religious information or other material. However, broadly defined political criteria can be used to impose censorship or bans on certain publications from circulation. Around forty religious books and books dealing with religious matters have been banned by the Israeli military authorities since occupation began in 1967. These represent only around 1 per cent of the total books banned under Article 88(1) of the British Defence (Emergency) Regulations of 1945, reinstated by the Israeli authorities.

In protest over recent raids on mosques by Palestinian police, an editorial was published in *Al-Watan* newspaper, known to be sympathetic to Hamas, and in May 1995, the Palestinian police arrested the editor-in-chief, Sayyed Abu Msameh, and brought him one day later before the newly formed State Security Court, which sentenced him to two years' imprisonment for incitement. *Al-Watan* itself was ordered to be closed for three months.

Note

1 See also the entry on Israel.

SAUDI ARABIA

Ever since the oil crisis of the mid-1970s, Saudi Arabia has been a focal point of interest for the world community. Its dominant position in world oil markets has led to economic and financial influence, and the country also exerts religious and political leadership in the Arab world and among other Islamic countries. Saudi Arabia is the centre of the Islamic faith, world-wide. The holy cities of Mecca – the birthplace of the Prophet Mohammed, the seat of the Great Mosque and the Shrine of Ka'ba – and of Medina, the burial place of Prophet Mohammed and the second sacred city of Islam, are located there. All devout Muslims, world-wide, try to make at least one pilgrimage (*hajj*) to the holy cities.

Saudi Arabia	
GDP (US$bn)	111
Population	16,800,000
Annual population growth (%)	4.5
Urban population (%)	78
Working population (%)	29[b]
Literacy (%)	69.7
Ratifications	nil

Saudi Arabia occupies the south-western corner of Asia. Most of its 2.24 million sq kms are desert: the Empty Quarter, al-Nafoudh and al-Dahna. Declining oil revenues and rising unemployment are bringing new challenges to the traditional society and its rulers. More than 60 per cent of Saudi Arabians are under 19 years old, the education system needs reform if the country is to enter the modern age and the 'Saudisation' of the job market has become a priority. Its total population is reportedly 16.8 million people – no census figures have been officially released – of which three million are foreign workers. The vast majority of Saudi Arabian citizens and many of the foreign workers are Sunni Muslims. Shia Muslims, largely based in the Eastern Province, constitute approximately 10 per cent of the population.

Political and legal structure

The Kingdom of Saudi Arabia was founded in 1932, when King Abdul-Aziz Al-Saud unified all the areas he ruled under one political system. Since King Abdul-Aziz's death in 1953, four of his sons have ruled successively: Saud, Faisal, Khaled and Fahd. King Fahd reigned from 1982 to early 1996 when he handed over the power to his half-brother, Crown Prince Abdullah. Saudi Arabia is an absolute monarchy, with no legislature or political parties. Royal decrees have been issued that provide for the formation of an advisory council and for a 'basic law of government'.

Constitutionally, the King rules in accordance with the *shariah* (Islamic law). The King appoints and leads a Council of Ministers, which serves as the instrument of royal authority in both legislative and executive matters. As result of growing pressure during the Gulf crisis from human rights groups, as well as from internal opposition, the King set up in August 1993, a Shura (Consultative) Council, composed of sixty appointed members. The Shura Council's role is limited to advising the King on issues he decides to submit to it.

Shariah is the fundamental law of the country as interpreted by the Hanbali school of thought. There are four sources of the *shariah*. The first is the Qur'an, the revealed word of God. The Qur'an is the ultimate authority on any legal issue. The second source is the Sunna, the deeds and sayings of the Prophet Mohammed. The third is Ijma, the consensus of Muslim scholars on any issue not addressed in the Qur'an or in the Sunna. The fourth is Qiyas or rule derived by juridical analogy.

The Board of Grievances was established in 1982 as a department of the executive, the Council of Ministers; its chairman and members are appointed by the head of state. It is the only body which has the power to review and annul government decisions, its role and function defined within the political context in which it was created; thus it has no power to examine sovereign acts. The Board has eroded the jurisdiction of the ordinary courts as the government has diverted non-administrative jurisdiction to the Board, thus undermining the rule of law. The Board's powers include jurisdiction over certain crimes, such as bribery, defined as *ta'zir* in the *shariah*, offences for which there is no prescribed punishment.

Everyday surveillance of religious practice is provided in Saudi society by the members of the Committee for the Propagation of Virtue and Prevention of Vice. Saudi courts apply the full force of the *hadd* punishments for crimes under *shariah hudud* law.

Religion and state

The Kingdom of Saudi Arabia's official creed is the Wahhabi doctrine of Islam. Wahhabism was propagated by Mohammed bin Abdul Wahhab, a Sunni Muslim religious scholar from Najd (1703–92). This doctrine is an interpretation of the Hanbali school of jurisprudence, one of the four schools of jurisprudence in Sunni Islam. The Wahhabi doctrine is said to interpret literally every passage of the Qur'an.

Wahhabism stresses the purity of the early Islamic community and recommends the emulation of early Muslims. It also calls for doing away with *bid'a* (novelty or innovation) in Islam after the second century of the Islamic (*Hijri*) calendar, the eighth century of the common era. Thus the public commemoration of the birth of the Prophet Mohammed, observed by all non-Wahhabi Muslims (Sunni and Shia alike) is banned in Saudi Arabia.

The central tenet of Wahhabism is considered to be the belief in the oneness of God (*tawhid*) and the strong condemnation of polytheism (*shirk*). In this context the definition of polytheism is quite broad, encompassing all non-Muslim worship and many non-Wahhabi Muslim religious beliefs and rites. For example, it is an act of polytheism to introduce the name of an angel or saint into prayer, as are supplicating for divine assistance, sacrificing, showing humility, fearing, hoping or expressing wishes to anyone but God.

Saudi authorities consider the practice of religious beliefs and rites other than the Wahhabi interpretation of Islam as an expression of political dissent. Consequently Shia Muslims and Christians have been arrested, detained and tortured for advocating freedom of religion and thought and equal rights for members of their communities.

In August 1993, the Special Rapporteur on Religious Intolerance forwarded a statement of allegations of discrimination and intolerance against Shia Muslims to the Saudi Arabian government. In reply, the government, far from cooperating with the Special Rapporteur, Mr Abdelfattah Amor, directed the argumentum *ad hominem* by impugning his status and knowledge of Islam, declaring that he was fulfilling his duties by 'bestowing on criminals the status of martyrs'.

It is clear, therefore, that there has been little change in the Saudi Arabian regime's deep intolerance towards non-Muslims over the years. In 1984, for instance, the Saudi representative had astounded all the participants in a United Nations seminar called to encourage understanding, tolerance and respect in matters relating to freedom of religion or belief, when he retold at length the medieval blood libel against the Jews in order to justify an argument that the Jewish people had drawn the Holocaust upon themselves. He knew, he said, that his quotation of the texts was accurate because his knowledge was based on ancient documents held in universities in the Islamic world.

The Shia Muslim minority

The Shia historically have been regarded by the Wahhabi religious leaders in Saudi Arabia as non-Muslim. In November 1927, in response to an inquiry by Ibn Saud about the

Shia, the *ulema* (experts in Islamic law) said that the Shia must be prohibited from performing their religious practices and must be deported from the land of Islam if they breach the prohibition.

Notwithstanding the pronouncement of the *ulema*, the government did not ban the Shia religious practices altogether and even permitted certain Shia practices in the Eastern Province as long as they were not directly contrary to Wahhabi sensibilities. The authorities allowed the Shia to celebrate their religious holidays, and have their own courts with limited jurisdiction over family law matters.

However, Shia Islam is seen by the Saudi authorities as incompatible with Wahhabi Islam and this official policy has led to systematic discrimination against Shia Muslims – men, women and children – in all fields of Saudi society. This discrimination in turn has resulted in Shia Muslims being seen as political dissidents. Shias have been convicted of apostasy – renouncing Islam – and sentenced, after unfair trials, to death. The Saudi press often contains distorted reports of Shia practices and beliefs and attacks Shias as non-Muslim heretics.

Shia practices are reduced to a minimum even in the Eastern Province. This community is not permitted to build mosques or expand their existing ones or to build *husseinat*, the places where Shias conduct funeral ceremonies, weddings and other religious services. Nor are they allowed to recite their own call to prayer.

During Friday prayers, there are certain topics the Saudi authorities forbid the Shia *imams* to discuss. The government also forbids Shia religious scholars from publishing their teachings and prohibits the importation of any Shia books into the country. Similarly there is a ban on religious cassettes. Those caught with Shia books, audio cassettes, or even pictures of Shia leaders are imprisoned and their possessions are confiscated and destroyed.

Many Shia religious shrines and schools are located in Iran, Iraq and Syria. Shias who desire to become religious leaders, for example, must study in Iran. In 1979, however, Saudi authorities imposed a ban on travelling to Iran, preventing Shias from visiting holy shrines and continuing their religious education. Some Saudi Shias still travel to Iran, often at great risk to themselves and their families.

Because it is virtually impossible to express an opinion freely in the domestic press, on radio or on television, the only location available for people are places of worship, charitable institutions, and sports clubs, where people try to exercise this right and carry out cultural activities. In recent years, however, the authorities have shown an increasing determination to limit and suppress cultural activities in such places.

Since January 1980, the Interior Ministry has forbidden foreign Shia clergy from visiting the country if they intend to deliver speeches or perform Shia religious rituals. Just before the start of each Islamic calendar year, Shia leaders must submit to police headquarters a written pledge that they will not invite any Shia clergy from abroad and that they will not allow any political debates nor criticise government religious policies during the traditional Shia ceremonies held during the first ten days of every Islamic year. This pledge is a precondition to receiving government permission to hold these ceremonies.

Saudi authorities have banned people from making a public speech in a mosque without an official permit and instructed all mosque *imams*, *muezzins* (those who give the call to prayer) and supervisors to inform the authorities if anyone has attempted to make a speech, deliver a sermon or hold a meeting in any mosque. Even with a permit to preach in mosques, many people were ordered by the Ministry of the Interior to avoid specific issues and topics. Such orders were frequently made to mosque *imams* during the Gulf War. Many Muslim scholars were forbidden to deliver their Friday sermons and weekly lectures because they criticised the government's policies during the Gulf crisis, especially the deployment of Western troops on Saudi soil, and the decision to allow them to commence military operations from Saudi Arabia.

During 1993, the government initiated a dialogue with Shia political figures in exile. In exchange for ceasing their political activity abroad and discontinuing their publications, the government released political prisoners and promised to consider Shia grievances seriously. In September 1993, exiles' groups suspended their publications and ceased political activities. Four Shia leaders returned to the Kingdom and met with the King. However, according to Saudi observers, there is no evident change in institutionalised discrimination against the Shia.

Opposition from the Salafi school of Sunni Islam

Since the Gulf War, a new political opposition has emerged in the Saudi Kingdom, inspired by the Sunni religious Salafi school of thought. This tendency, which has not been allowed to exist as a legal political party, chose the method of campaigning as a human rights organisation, the Committee for the Defence of Legitimate Rights in Saudi Arabia (CDLR). Many members of this group have been arrested, dismissed from their jobs or forced into exile. As they were pursued all over the world, exiled leaders made London their headquarters and the centre of their activism.

Their Islamist criticisms range from exposure of the extravagant and corrupt lifestyle of monarchy and the business world, to attacks on excessive religious strictures like the ban on women driving. Following the crackdown on the religious Sunni opposition, Saudi authorities took several measures. They ordered the closure of mosques outside the time of prayers to avoid their use for meetings and religious discussions. They banned all forms of religious sermons and preaching in the mosques, schools and universities without the prior consent of the Ministry of the Interior. They interfered in the writing of sermons for Friday prayers through ministerial directives. Clergy who refuse to implement the directives can be arrested or dismissed. They have also prohibited many religious scholars from giving seminars and talks in mosques or universities; these include Shaykh Suleiman al-Awdah, Shaykh Safar al-Hawali and Dr Mohammed al-Masa'ri. In addition, hundreds of Friday preachers have lost their post for speaking their minds, such as Shaykh Abdelwahab Triti, preacher at the King Abdelaziz Mosque in Riyadh, Shaykh Adel al-Kalbani, preacher at King Khaled Mosque in Riyadh, and Shaykh Hamdan-al-Hamdani, preacher at the University of King Saud Mosque.

The authorities have also banned any religious gatherings or meeting without prior authorisation, often using force to disperse and arrest those who infringe the ban. They have also banned private commercial recording and distribution of religious tapes. Tapes containing religious material are produced only by the Ministry of Information. A large quantity of privately produced tapes have been seized and destroyed by the authorities.

The Saudi authorities have also exercised stringent censorship on religious books. Only the official interpretation of religious matters may be published. They have prohibited the publication and distribution of all Shi'ite and many Sunni religious books.

The Christian minority

The Christian community in Saudi Arabia is predominantly formed of expatriate skilled workers with short-term residence. This community began to grow rapidly after the economic boom which came about as a result of the rise in the price of oil in the mid-1970s. This boom required the participation of a labour force that was larger and with more diverse skills than could be provided locally. Expatriate Christians are no longer only from North America, Europe, Egypt and Palestine, but include many from Asia and Africa. Many are manual, domestic or office workers, as opposed to management.

This wide, multi-ethnic community is represented mainly by the Roman Catholic Church, the Anglican Communion and the Greek Orthodox Church. The Roman Catholic Church has a Vicar Delegate for Saudi Arabia based in Abu Dhabi in the United Arab Emirate, and the Anglican Communion is part of the Episcopal Church in Jerusalem and the Middle East, where Saudi Arabia forms part of the diocese of Cyprus and the Gulf.

Public and private non-Muslim religious worship is banned in Saudi Arabia and there are no public places of worship for non-Muslims in the country. Numerous unsuccessful appeals have been made; for example, the Vatican has pressed for 'reciprocal' rights to build churches in Saudi Arabia, at a time when Saudi money is financing mosque construction in predominantly Christian societies. Although the Christian community tends to form private fellowships, for example in diplomatic compounds, hundreds of Christians have been arrested and ill-treated by the Saudi religious authorities and often deported for privately practising their religious beliefs. Amnesty International believes that:

> there appears to be discrimination in the pattern of arrest on the basis of nationality. Of the 329 Christian worshippers known to have been arrested in the kingdom since August 1990, 325 were nationals of developing countries while four were from Western Europe and North America.

Any foreign worker who attempts to bring religious mementoes and artefacts into Saudi Arabia is arrested and deported and the religious material confiscated. The artefacts confiscated include crosses, rosary beads and holy cards. It is alleged that foreign workers sent to the holy cities of Mecca and Medina are required to convert and practise Islam while in Saudi Arabia and that foreign workers in other Saudi cities are sometimes forced to attend Islamic religious services with their employer.

The media

The Saudi government controls all public channels of expression, including radio, television and the press, and imposes strict censorship on all newspapers, magazines and books imported from abroad. There are many religious newspapers and magazines published in Saudi Arabia, including the weekly *al-Muslimoon* (the Muslims) and the monthly *Rabitat al-Alam al-Islami* (The Journal of the Muslim World League) and two periodicals *Hajj* (Pilgrimage) and *at-Tadamoon al-Islami* (Islamic Solidarity), both published by the Ministry of Pilgrimage Affairs and Awqaf (endowment). All other newspapers and periodicals have a religious page which is strictly edited by a qualified religious censor. Saudi Arabia also financially supports hundreds of publications based abroad. The total control of media by the authorities has been significant in silencing many religious scholars whose beliefs differ from the official creed.

Women

Women are segregated in all fields of Saudi society affecting their freedom of movement, access to education and employment. Because employment is so restricted for women, over half the labour force is foreign. Saudi authorities claim that this discrimination is required by Islamic religious principles. A Saudi woman is not allowed to marry a non-

Saudi without government permission and she is prohibited from marrying a non-Muslim. *Shariah* laws make it extremely difficult for women to initiate divorce, the availability of contraception and abortion is limited and childbirth out of wedlock can be severely punished. In 1996, the president of the Shura Council explicitly ruled out the possibility of any woman sitting next to men and giving advice.

There is a large population of Bedouins in Saudi Arabia and many Bedouin women are traders in the women's marketplace. In more formal space, women are more constrained. Women students have very limited access to university libraries and until recently women professionals could not operate any private practice other than medicine. Women are not generally permitted to drive a car, although this is being challenged. They are required to wear veil and *abaya* (*hejab*) outside the home, although the veil is becoming a matter of choice. Women do not normally attend the mosque although permitted. They are usually in sole charge of a rich variety of domestic ritual and may visit shrines and go on pilgrimage, but teaching, preaching and other leadership positions are not available to them.

Despite all the restrictions, women's space is the locus of considerable material power. Women control up to 40 per cent of Saudi Arabia's wealth and women's bank branches, controlled and staffed by women, were established in the 1980s. Over the last decade women have emerged as a major social force and have increasingly moved into small business, at the same time demanding reform and social justice in relation to gender.

Select bibliography

BOOKS

Amnesty International (1993) *Greece, 5,000 Years of Prison: Conscientious Objectors in Greece*, London: Amnesty International Publications.

An Na'im, A. A. (ed.) (1992) *Human Rights in Cross-Cultural Perspectives: A Quest for Consensus*, Pennsylvania Series on Studies in Human Rights, Philadelphia: University of Pennsylvania Press.

Barker, Eileen (1989) *New Religious Movements: A Practical Introduction*, 4th edn, London: HMSO.

Beetham, D. and Boyle, K. (1995) *Introducing Democracy: Eighty Questions and Answers*, Oxford: Polity Press and UNESCO.

Boyle, K. (1992) 'Religious Intolerance and Incitement to Religious Hatred', in S. Coliver (ed.) *Striking A Balance: Freedom of Expression, Hate Speech and Non-Discrimination*, London: Article XIX, and University of Essex.

Cassese, A. (1990) *Human Rights in a Changing World*, Oxford: Polity Press.

Conference of European Churches (1966) *OSCE Human Dimension Seminar, Aspects of Freedom of Religion*, Warsaw, 16–19 April 1966, Hanover.

Cook, Rebecca J. (ed.) (1994) *Human Rights of Women: National and International Perspectives*, Philadelphia: University of Pennsylvania Press.

Council of Europe (1993) *Freedom of Conscience*, proceedings of the seminar organised by the Council of Europe in cooperation with the F. M. van Asbach Centre for Human Rights Studies, 12–13 November 1992, University of Leiden, Strasbourg: Council of Europe Press.

The Europa World Yearbook (1994) London: Europa Publishers.

Gee, S. (1994) *Human Rights and Religious Minorities in Europe*, London: Churches' Human Rights Forum.

Hamilton, C. (1995) *Family Law and Religion*, London: Sweet and Maxwell.

Lindholm, Tore and Vogt, Kari (eds) (1993) *Islamic Law Reform and Human Rights: Challenges and Rejoinders*, Copenhagen/Lund/Oslo/Abo/Turku: Nordic Human Rights Publications.

Little, D., Kelsay, J. and Sachedina, A. (1988) *Human Rights and the Conflict of Cultures: Western and Islamic Perspectives on Religious Liberty*, Columbia: University of South Carolina Press.

Marty, Martin E. and Appleby, R. Scott (eds) (1991) *Fundamentalisms Observed*, (The Fundamentalism Project, vol. 1) Chicago/London: University of Chicago Press.

Mernissi, Fatima (1991) *Women and Islam: An Historical and Theological Enquiry*, Oxford: Basil Blackwell.

Milne, A. J. (1986) *Human Rights and Human Diversity: An Essay in the Philosophy of Human Rights*, London: Macmillan.

Philip's Geographical Digest (1994–1995) Oxford: Heinemann Educational Books.

Sohn, L. B. (1995) *The Human Rights Movement: From Roosevelt's Four Freedoms to the Interdependence of Peace Development and Human Rights*, Cambridge, MA: Harvard Law School Human Rights Program.

459

Swidler, Leonard (ed.) (1986) *Religious Liberty and Human Rights in Nations and Religions*, Philadelphia/New York: Ecumenical Press/Hippocrene Books.

Swidler, Leonard and Mojzes, Paul (eds) (1990) *Attitudes of Religions and Ideologies Toward the Outsider: the Other*, (Religions in Dialogue, vol. 1) Lewiston/Queenston/Lampeter: Edwin Mellen Press.

Symonides, J. (1995) 'Prohibition of Advocacy of Hatred, Prejudice and Intolerance in the United Nations Instruments', in *Democracy and Tolerance Proceedings of the International Conference, Seoul, Republic of Korea*, Paris: UNESCO, pp. 79–100.

Tahzib, Bahiyyah G. (1996) *Freedom of Religion or Belief: Ensuring Effective International Legal Protection*, The Netherlands: Kluwer.

Traer, Robert (1991) *Faith in Human Rights: Support in Religious Traditions for a Global Struggle*, Washington, DC: Georgetown University Press.

UNESCO (1995) *Democracy and Tolerance*, proceedings of the International Conference, Seoul, Republic of Korea 1994, Paris: UNESCO.

United Nations Development Programme (1994) *Country Human Development Indicators*, Geneva: UN Human Development Report Office.

van Boven, T. (1989) *Elimination of All Forms of Intolerance and of Discrimination Based on Religion or Belief*, E/CN.4/Sub.2/1989/32.

van der Vyver, Johan D. and Witte, John Jnr. (eds) (1996) *Religious Human Rights in Global Perspective*, 2 vols, The Hague/Boston/London: Martinus Nijhoff.

World Fact Book (1995) Central Intelligence Agency, Washington, DC: Office of Public and Agency Information.

World University Service (1993) *Academic Freedom 2: A Human Rights Report*, London: Zed Books.

Wright, John W. (ed.) (1996) *The Universal Almanac*, Kansas City: Andrews and McMeel.

ARTICLES

Boyle, K. (1995) 'Stock-Taking on Human Rights. The Vienna World Conference on Human Rights, Vienna 1993', *Political Studies*, vol. 43, pp. 79–95.

Dickson, B. (1995) 'The United Nations and Freedom of Religion', *International and Comparative Law Quarterly*, vol. 44, p. 327.

Freeman, M. (1996) 'Human Rights, Democracy and Asian Values', *Pacific Review*, vol. 9, pp. 309–23.

Howard, R. E. (1993) 'Cultural Absolutism and the Nostalgia for Community', *Human Rights Quarterly*, vol. 15, pp. 315–38.

Jack, H. A. (1982) 'How the UN Religious Declaration Was Unanimously Adopted', New York, World Conference on Religion and Peace.

Neff, S. C. (1977) 'An Evolving International Legal Norm of Religious Freedom: Problems and Prospects', *California West International Law Journal*, vol. 7, pp. 543–86.

Sullivan, Donna J. (1988) 'Advancing the Freedom of Religion or Belief Through the UN Declaration on the Elimination of Religious Intolerance and Discrimination', *American Journal of International Law*, vol. 82, pp. 487–520.

Sullivan, Donna J. (1992) 'Gender Equality and Religious Freedom: Toward a Framework for Conflict Resolution', *New York University Journal of International Law and Politics*, vol. 24 (1992), pp. 795–856.

van Boven, Theo (1991) 'Advances and Obstacles in Building Understanding and Respect Between People of Diverse Religions and Beliefs', *Human Rights Quarterly*, vol. 13, pp. 437–52.

Walkate, J. A. (1989) 'The UN Declaration on the Elimination of All Forms of Intolerance and Discrimination Based on Religion or Belief (1981): An Historical Overview', *Conscience and Liberty*, vol. 2, Winter 1989.

HUMAN RIGHTS REPORTS

Academic Freedom reports, World University Service.

Amnesty International Report, annual publication, London: Amnesty International Publications.

Anti-Semitism World Report, annual publication, London: Institute of Jewish Affairs.

Human Rights Watch, various regional reports, New York: HRW.

Human Rights Watch World Report, Annual Publication, New York: HRW.

International Helsinki Federation, annual publication, Austria: IHF.

[United States] Department of State Reports, annual publication, Washington, DC.

United States Institute of Peace reports, various titles in the series Religion, Nationalism and Intolerance, Washington, DC: USIP Press.

UNITED NATIONS DOCUMENTS

Compilation of Standards

Reports of the Special Rapporteur on the Implementation of the Declaration on the Elimination of All Forms of Intolerance and of Discrimination Based on Religion or Belief.

Amor, Abdelfattah, E/CN.4/1994/79 (1994); E/CN.4/1995/91 and Add.1 (1994); E/CN.4/1996/95 (1995).

d'Almeida Ribeiro, A. Vidal, E/CN.4/1987/35 (1986); E/CN.4/1988/45 and Add.1 (1988) revised by E/CN.4/1988/45/Add.1/Corr.1 (1988); E/CN.4/1989/44 (1988); E/CN.4/1990/46 (1990); E/CN.4/1991/56 (1991); E/CN.4/1992/52 (1992); E/CN.4/1993/62 and Add.1 (1993), revised by E/CN.4/1993/62/Corr.1 (1993).

Other UN documents

Capotorti, Francesco (1979) *Study on the Rights of Persons Belonging to Ethnic, Religious and Linguistic Minorities*, E/CN.4/Sub.2/384/Rev.1, New York: United Nations.

Eide, A. and Mubanga-Chipoya (1983) *Question of Conscientious Objection to Military Service*, UN Commission on Human Rights, E/CN.4/Sub.2/1983/30.

General Comment No. 22 (48) (art. 18) (1993) *General Comment Adopted by the Human Rights Committee Under Article 40, Paragraph 4, of the International Covenant on Civil and Political Rights*, CCPR/C/21/Rev. 1/Add.4.

Krishnaswami, Arcot (1960) *Study of Discrimination in the Matter of Religious Rights and Practices*, E/CN.4/Sub.2/200/Rev.1, New York: United Nations.

Odio Benito, Elizabeth (1986) *Study of the Current Dimensions of the Problems of Intolerance and of Discrimination on Grounds of Religion or Belief*, E/CN.4/Sub.2/1987/26, New York: United Nations.

Seminar on the Encouragement of Understanding, Tolerance and Respect in Matters Relating to Freedom of Religion or Belief (1984), report, ST/HR/SER.A/16, Geneva: United Nations.

van Boven, T. (1989) 'Religious Freedom in International Perspectives: Existing and Future Standards', in *Des Menschen Recht Zwischen Freiheit Und Verantwortung*, Berlin: Ducker and Humbolt.

Index